Interpersonal
COMMUNICATION
Everyday
Encounters

Interpersonal COMMUNICATION Everyday Encounters

Second Edition

JULIA T. WOOD

The University of North Carolina, Chapel Hill

Ⓦ Wadsworth Publishing Company

I(T)P® An International Thomson Publishing Company

Belmont, CA • Albany, NY • Boston • Cincinnati • Johannesburg • London
Madrid • Melbourne • Mexico City • New York • Pacific Grove, CA • Scottsdale, AZ
Singapore • Tokyo • Toronto

Executive Editor:
　　Deirdre Cavanaugh
Assistant Editor:
　　Megan Gilbert
Editorial Assistant:
　　Matthew Lamm
Marketing Manager:
　　Mike Dew
Marketing Assistant:
　　Shannon Ryan
Advertising Project Manager:
　　Tami Strang
Project Editor:
　　Cathy Linberg
Print Buyer:
　　Barbara Britton
Permissions Editor:
　　Robert Kauser
Production:
　　Cecile Joyner,
　　The Cooper Company
Designer:
　　Norman Baugher Design
Copy Editor:
　　Jennifer Gordon
Illustrators:
　　Precision Graphics
Photo Researcher:
　　Judy Mason
Cover Design:
　　Norman Baugher Design
Cover Image:
　　Norman Baugher
Compositor: New England
　　Typographic Service
Printer: World Color Book
　　Services, Taunton
Cover Printer: Phoenix Color

For more information, contact Wadsworth Publishing Company, 10 Davis Drive, Belmont, CA 94002, or electronically at http://www.wadsworth.com

International Thomson Publishing Europe
Berkshire House
168–173 High Holborn
London, WC1V 7AA, United Kingdom

Nelson ITP, Australia
102 Dodds Street
South Melbourne
Victoria 3205 Australia

Nelson Canada
1120 Birchmount Road
Scarborough, Ontario
Canada M1K 5G5

International Thomson Editores
Seneca, 53
Colonia Polanco
11560 México D.F. México

International Thomson Publishing Asia
60 Albert Street
#15-01 Albert Complex
Singapore 189969

International Thomson Publishing Japan
Hirakawa-cho Kyowa Building, 3F
2-2-1 Hirakawa-cho, Chiyoda-ku
Tokyo 102 Japan

International Thomson Publishing Southern Africa
Building 18, Constantia Square
138 Sixteenth Road, P.O. Box 2459
Halfway House, 1685 South Africa

Chapter Opening Photograph Credits: p. 8, Jeff Greenberg/Photo Researchers, Inc. p. 46, Kopstein/Monkmeyer Press Photo. p. 79, Mike Yamashita/Woodfin Camp & Assoc. p. 112, Lien Nibauer/Gamma-Liaison. p. 146, Bernard Wolf/Monkmeyer Press Photo. p. 178, Sotographs/Gamma-Liaison. p. 212 and p. 244, Bruce Ayres/Tony Stone Images. p. 276, Kopstein/Monkmeyer Press Photo. p. 312, Charles Gupton/Tony Stone Images. p. 342, Joe Polillio/Gamma-Liaison.

Library of Congress Cataloging-in-Publication Data

Wood, Julia T.
　　Interpersonal communication : everyday encounters / Julia T. Wood.
　　　　p. cm.
　　Rev. ed. of: Everyday encounters. c1996.
　　Includes bibliographical references and index.
　　ISBN 0–534–54837–7
　　1. Interpersonal communication. 2. Interpersonal relations.
I. Wood, Julia T. Everyday encounters. II. Title.
BF637.C45W656　　　1999
153.6–dc21　　　　　　　　　　　　　　　　98–6766

 This book is printed on acid-free recycled paper.

Brief

CONTENTS

PART ONE
The Fabric of Interpersonal Communication   1

Introduction: Starting the Conversation   2

1   *A First Look at Interpersonal Communication*   8

2   *Communication and the Creation of Self*   46

3   *Perception and Communication*   79

4   *The World of Words*   112

5   *The World Beyond Words*   146

6   *Mindful Listening*   178

PART TWO
Weaving Communication into Relationships   211

7   *Emotions and Communication*   212

8   *Communication Climate:*

     The Foundation of Personal Relationships   244

9   *Managing Conflict in Relationships*   276

10   *Friendships in Our Lives*   312

11   *Committed Romantic Relationships*   342

Epilogue: Continuing the Conversation   382

Glossary   385

References   390

Index   404

CONTENTS

PART ONE

The Fabric of Interpersonal Communication   1

Introduction: Starting the Conversation   2

The Field of Communication   2

A Personal Introduction   3

Diversity in Interpersonal Life   4

Weaving the Book   7

CHAPTER 1   *A First Look at Interpersonal Communication   8*

The Interpersonal Imperative   10

Physical Needs   10

Safety Needs   11

Belonging Needs   11

Self-Esteem Needs   13

Self-Actualization Needs   14

Participating Effectively in a Diverse Society   15

Defining Interpersonal Communication   16

What Distinguishes Interpersonal Communication?   17

A Communication Continuum   17

Models of Interpersonal Communication   20

Linear Models   20

Interactive Models   21

Transactional Models   23

Definition of Interpersonal Communication   24

Principles of Interpersonal Communication   31

We Cannot Not Communicate   31

Communication Is Irreversible   32

Interpersonal Communication Involves Ethical Choices   32

Meanings Are Constructed in Interpersonal Communication   32

Metacommunication Affects Meanings   33

Interpersonal Communication Develops and Sustains Relationships   37

Interpersonal Communication Is Not a Panacea   38

Interpersonal Communication Effectiveness Can Be Learned   38

Guidelines for Interpersonal Communication Competence   38

Develop a Range of Skills   39

Adapt Communication Appropriately   39

Engage in Dual Perspective   41

Monitor Your Communication   42

Commit to Effective and Ethical Interpersonal Communication   43

Chapter Summary   44

Key Concepts   44

For Further Thought and Discussion   45

CHAPTER 2 *Communication and the Creation of Self   46*

What Is the Self?   47

The Self Arises in Communication with Others   47

The Self Is Multidimensional   57

The Self Is a Process   57

The Self Internalizes Social Perspectives   59

Social Perspectives on the Self Are Constructed and Variable   66

Guidelines for Improving Self-Concept   70

Make a Firm Commitment to Change   70

Gain Knowledge As a Basis for Personal Change   71

Set Goals That Are Realistic and Fair   72

Create a Context That Supports Personal Change   74

Chapter Summary   77

Key Concepts   78

For Further Thought and Discussion   78

CHAPTER 3 *Perception and Communication*   79

The Process of Human Perception   80

Selection   81

Organization   83

Interpretation   87

Influences on Perception   91

Physiology   91

Age   92

Culture   93

Social Roles   97

Cognitive Abilities   98

Guidelines for Improving Perception and Communication   101

Recognize That All Perceptions Are Partial and Subjective   101

Avoid Mindreading   103

Check Perceptions with Others   104

Distinguish Between Facts and Inferences   104

Guard Against the Self-Serving Bias   105

Guard Against the Fundamental Attribution Error   106

Monitor Labels   107

Chapter Summary   109

Key Concepts   110

For Further Thought and Discussion   110

CHAPTER 4 *The World of Words* 112

The Symbolic Nature of Language 113
Symbols Are Arbitrary 113
Symbols Are Ambiguous 114
Symbols Are Abstract 115

Principles of Verbal Communication 116
Language and Culture Reflect Each Other 116
Meanings of Language Are Subjective 119
Language Use Is Rule-Guided 119
Punctuation of Language Shapes Meaning 122

Symbolic Abilities 123
Symbols Define 124
Symbols Evaluate 126
Symbols Organize Perceptions 128
Symbols Allow Hypothetical Thought 129
Symbols Allow Self-Reflection 130

Speech Communities 132
Gender Speech Communities 132
Other Speech Communities 135

Guidelines for Improving Verbal Communication 137
Engage in Dual Perspective 137
Own Your Feelings and Thoughts 138
Respect What Others Say About Their Feelings and Thoughts 139
Strive for Accuracy and Clarity 141

Chapter Summary 144
Key Concepts 144
For Further Thought and Discussion 145

CHAPTER 5 *The World Beyond Words* 146

Defining Nonverbal Communication 147
Similarities Between Verbal and Nonverbal Communication 148
Differences Between Verbal and Nonverbal Communication 149

Principles of Nonverbal Communication 150
Nonverbal Communication May Supplement or
                 Replace Verbal Communication 151
Nonverbal Communication May Regulate Interaction 151
Nonverbal Communication Often Establishes
                 Relationship-Level Meanings 152
Nonverbal Communication Reflects and Expresses Cultural Values 155

Types of Nonverbal Communication 157
Kinesics 157
Haptics 160
Physical Appearance 160
Artifacts 162
Environmental Factors 165
Proxemics and Personal Space 167
Chronemics 169
Paralanguage 170
Silence 172

Guidelines for Improving Nonverbal Communication 173
Monitor Your Nonverbal Communication 173
Be Tentative When Interpreting Others' Nonverbal Communication 174

Chapter Summary 176
Key Concepts 177
For Further Thought and Discussion 177

CHAPTER 6 *Mindful Listening* 178

The Listening Process 180

Being Mindful 181

Physically Receiving Messages 182

Selecting and Organizing Material 183

Interpreting Communication 185

Responding 186

Remembering 187

Obstacles to Effective Listening 187

External Obstacles 188

Internal Obstacles 189

Forms of Nonlistening 193

Pseudolistening 193

Monopolizing 194

Selective Listening 196

Defensive Listening 196

Ambushing 197

Literal Listening 198

Adapting Listening to Communication Goals 199

Listening for Pleasure 199

Listening for Information 199

Listening to Support Others 202

Guidelines for Effective Listening 206

Be Mindful 206

Adapt Listening Appropriately 207

Listen Actively 208

Chapter Summary 208

Key Concepts 209

For Further Thought and Discussion 209

PART TWO

Weaving Communication into Relationships   211

CHAPTER 7   *Emotions and Communication*   212

Emotional Intelligence   214

The Nature of Emotions   217

Biological and Learned Emotions   217

Definition of Emotions   218

The Impact of Different Views of Emotions   228

Obstacles to Effective Communication of Emotions   229

Reasons We May Not Express Emotions   229

Ineffective Expression of Emotions   234

Guidelines for Communicating Emotions Effectively   237

Identify Your Emotions   237

Choose How to Communicate Your Emotions   237

Own Your Feelings   238

Monitor Your Self-Talk   239

Respond Sensitively When Others Communicate Emotions   242

Chapter Summary   243

Key Concepts   243

For Further Thought and Discussion   243

CHAPTER 8   *Communication Climate: The Foundation of Personal Relationships*   244

Elements of Satisfying Personal Relationships   245

Investment   247

Commitment   248

Trust   249

Comfort with Relational Dialectics   251

Confirming and Disconfirming Climates   256
Levels of Confirmation and Disconfirmation   256
Defensive and Supportive Climates   260

Guidelines for Creating and Sustaining Healthy Climates   266
Actively Use Communication to Shape Climates   266
Accept and Confirm Others   267
Affirm and Assert Yourself   268
Self-Disclose When Appropriate   270
Respect Diversity in Relationships   272
Respond to Others' Criticism Constructively   272

Chapter Summary   274
Key Concepts   275
For Further Thought and Discussion   275

CHAPTER 9   *Managing Conflict in Relationships*   276

Defining Conflict   279
Expressed Disagreement   279
Interdependence   279
Opposition   280

Principles of Conflict   280
Conflict Is a Natural Process in All Relationships   281
Conflict May Be Overt or Covert   282
Conflict May Be Managed Well or Poorly   284
Conflict May Be Good for Individuals and Relationships   285

Approaches to Conflict   287
Lose–Lose   287
Win–Lose   288
Win–Win   289

Responses to Conflict   291

Exit Response   292

Neglect Response   292

Loyalty Response   293

Voice Response   293

Social Influences on Conflict   294

Cultural Background   294

Gender   296

Sexual Orientation   297

Communication Patterns During Conflict   298

Unproductive Conflict Communication   299

Constructive Conflict Communication   302

Guidelines for Effective Communication During Conflict   305

Focus on the Overall Communication System   305

Time Conflict Effectively   306

Aim for Win–Win Conflict   307

Honor Yourself, Your Partner, and the Relationship   308

Show Grace When Appropriate   309

Chapter Summary   310

Key Concepts   311

For Further Thought and Discussion   311

CHAPTER 10   *Friendships in Our Lives*   312

The Nature of Friendship   314

Willingness to Invest   314

Emotional Closeness   315

Acceptance   318

Trust   320

Support   321

The Development and Rules of Friendship   324

The Developmental Course of Friendship   324

Rules of Friendship   327

Pressures on Friendships   329

Internal Tensions   329

External Constraints   322

Guidelines for Communication Between Friends   336

Engage in Dual Perspective   336

Communicate Honestly   338

Grow from Differences   339

Don't Sweat the Small Stuff   340

Chapter Summary   341

Key Concepts   341

For Further Thought and Discussion   341

CHAPTER 11   *Committed Romantic Relationships*   342

Committed Romantic Relationships   343

Cultural Shaping of Romantic Ties   344

Dimensions of Romantic Relationships   345

Styles of Loving   348

The Organization of Romantic Relationships   352

Growth Stages   353

Navigating   356

Deterioration Stages   358

Long-Term Commitments   360

Nonmarital Commitments   360

Marriage   362

The Family Life Cycle   366

Challenges to Sustaining Romantic Relationships   369

Ensuring Equity   370

Negotiating Safer Sex   372

Avoiding Violence and Abuse   373

Surviving Distance   375

Guidelines for Communication Between Romantic Partners   377

Show Respect and Consideration   378

Don't Sweat the Small Stuff   379

Make Daily Choices That Enhance Intimacy   379

Chapter Summary   380

Key Concepts   380

For Further Thought and Discussion   381

Epilogue: Continuing the Conversation   382

Communication Creates and Reflects Identity   382

Interpersonal Communication Is Central to Relationships   382

Interpersonal Communication Takes Place in a Diverse World   383

The Road Ahead   383

Glossary   385
References   390
Index   404

PREFACE

Interpersonal Communication: Everyday Encounters, Second Edition, offers a distinct alternative to existing textbooks for the introductory course in interpersonal communication. It is unique in its emphasis on theories, research, and skills that are anchored in the field of communication and in its attention to significant trends in social life as we prepare to enter the twenty-first century.

Focus on Communication Research and Theory

In the 1970s, when interpersonal communication was a very young intellectual area, research was limited. Because theoretical and research foundations for courses were not abundant, the content of most texts and courses either extended general principles of communication to interpersonal contexts or relied primarily on research in fields other than communication.

Although interpersonal communication continues to draw from other disciplines, by now it is a substantive field in its own right, complete with a base of knowledge, theories, and research founded in communication. The maturation of interpersonal communication as an intellectual area is evident in the substantial original research published in academic journals, as well as in the steady stream of scholarly books. It is clear that interpersonal communication is no longer a derivative field.

Textbooks for introductory communication courses no longer need to rely primarily on research and theories developed by scholars outside the communication field. *Interpersonal Communication: Everyday Encounters* reflects a strong focus on research in the communication discipline. For example, my discussions of personal relationships highlight Leslie Baxter's extensive research on relational dialectics. I also weave into all chapters emergent knowledge of differences in communication that are influenced by gender, economic class, sexual orientation, ethnicity, and race. Communication scholars' strong interest in ethics is also woven into this book. I identify ethical issues and choices in discussing the range of topics that are part of interpersonal communication. These and other topics in current communication inquiry are integrated into this book. As a result, students who read it will gain an appreciation of the scope and depth of scholarship in the field of communication.

Attention to Significant Social Trends

Social diversity is not merely a timely trend, a new buzz word, or a matter of political correctness. Instead, social diversity is a basic fact of life in the United States, a country (like many others) enriched by a cornucopia of people, heritages, customs, and ways of interacting. *Interpersonal*

Communication: Everyday Encounters reflects and addresses social diversity by weaving it into the basic fabric of interpersonal communication.

Addressing diversity adequately requires more than tacking paragraphs on gender or race to conventional approaches to topics. In writing this book, I have woven awareness of race, economic class, gender, age, and sexual orientation into discussions of communication theory and skills. For example, in exploring self-concept, I give detailed attention to race, gender, and sexual orientation as core facets of identity that shape how individuals communicate and interpret the communication of others. In examining patterns of interaction in families, I include research on families that are not White and middle class. Chapter 11 on romantic relationships discusses research on gay and lesbian relationships as well as studies of marriage and heterosexual families. Rather than highlighting the attention to diversity with diversity boxes or separate features, I have blended diverse social groups, customs, and lifestyles into the book as a whole.

Social diversity is not the only significant social trend that affects and is affected by interpersonal communication. *Interpersonal Communication: Everyday Encounters* addresses communication challenges, confusions, and issues that are part of personal and social life in our era. There is a full chapter on friendships, which have assumed enlarged importance in the face of increasing numbers of broken marriages and geographically dispersed families. The chapter on romantic relationships addresses abuse and violence between intimates, and it discusses using communication to negotiate safer sex in an era shadowed by HIV and AIDS. I also include a discussion of communication in long-distance relationships, which are part of many of our lives.

Special Features of Interpersonal Communication: Everyday Encounters

I've already mentioned two distinctive features of this book: emphasis on communication research and theories and attention to social diversity as integral to interpersonal communication. In addition to those features, there are other facets of the book that are designed to make it engaging and useful to students.

First, I adopt a conversational tone so that students realize there is a real person behind the words they're reading and studying. I share with students some of the communication challenges and encounters that surface in my life. The conversational writing style is also intended to invite students to interact with ideas on a personal level.

My voice is not the only one that students will encounter in this book. Every chapter is enhanced by commentaries written by students in interpersonal communication classes. The majority of the student commentaries were written by students in my courses. In addition, I've included a number of statements from students at universities around the nation. They read the first edition of this textbook and sent me some of their examples and reflections. The experiences, insights, and concerns expressed by these students broaden the conversation to include a large range of perspectives.

Interpersonal Communication: Everyday Encounters also includes three pedagogical features that promote development of interpersonal communication skills. Each chapter includes several Apply the Idea exercises, which encourage students to apply concepts and principles discussed in the text to their own lives. Each chapter also includes a number of Communication Notes features, which highlight interesting research and examples of interpersonal communication in everyday life. Following each chapter are several questions that invite students to engage in further reflection and discussion of ideas covered in the reading. For most chapters, at least one question focuses specifically on ethical issues in interpersonal communication, and at least one question suggests an activity using *InfoTrac College Edition*, which can be bundled with this text. For more information on this special offer, please contact your local Wadsworth/ITP sales representative or visit the Wadsworth Publishing Communications web site at http://www.wadsworth.com/communications

Additional Resources for Instructors

Accompanying *Interpersonal Communication: Everyday Encounters* are many instructional resources. An extensive *Instructor's Resource Manual* supplements the textbook. The manual discusses philosophical and pragmatic considerations involved in teaching the introductory course in interpersonal communication. It also includes suggestions for course emphases, sample syllabi, exercises and films appropriate for each chapter, masters for overheads of diagrams from the text, a correlation chart for the CNN Interpersonal Communication Video, a list of net resources, journal items, panel ideas, and a bank of test items.

I have also written a *Student Companion* that includes interactive content outlines, vocabulary terms for key concepts, activities, net addresses, and self-test questions for each chapter.

A third resource is a text-specific PowerPoint presentation that includes professionally created text and images to illustrate important concepts in this text—plus a built-in flexibility that lets you add your own materials. (Available in IBM and Macintosh formats.)

Wadsworth will also provide qualified instructors who adopt this book with a videotape produced by CNN that demonstrates everyday applications of principles and skills covered in this book. Check in with Wadsworth's *Communications Café*—a state-of-the-art, full-service web site featuring online material linked directly to this text: *http://www.wadsworth.com/communications*. Also available is *Thomson World Class Course*—the easy and effective way to create your own web site. You will be able to post your own course information, office hours, lesson information, assignments, and sample tests. Visit *http://www. worldclasslearning.com* for more information. If you choose to bundle *InfoTrac*

College Edition with this text, you and your students will get 24-hour access to a fully searchable online database containing complete articles—not simply abstracts—from more than 600 popular and scholarly periodicals. Finally, a computerized set of test items is available in various computer formats.

Acknowledgments

Although only my name appears as the author of this book, many people have contributed to it. I am especially indebted to Deirdre Cavanaugh, my editor at Wadsworth. From start to finish, she has been a full partner in this project and her interest and insights have greatly enhanced the book. Deirdre was also most generous in providing personal support, enthusiasm, and encouragement to me.

Also essential to the birth of this book were members of the publishing team who transformed an unembroidered manuscript into the final book that you are holding. Specifically, I thank Cathy Linberg, project editor; Barbara Britton, print buyer; Bob Krauser, permissions editor, whose detective skills were put to the test (they passed) in tracking down materials that required permissions; Megan Gilbert, assistant editor, who took charge of the ancillary materials for this book; and Matt Lamm, editorial assistant, who kept all of the team on track and in touch; Jennifer Gordon, who copyedited this book with unusual patience and skill; Cecile Joyner of The Cooper Company, who oversaw production of the book; Norman Baugher, who created the beautiful interior and cover designs; and Judy Mason, who was in charge of photo research.

In addition to the editorial and production team at Wadsworth, I am grateful to the many students and teachers who reviewed versions of the manuscript and whose comments and suggestions improved the final content of the book. For the first edition, I thank Patricia Amason, University of Arkansas; Lucinda Bauer, University of North Carolina at Chapel Hill; Betsy W. Bach, University of Montana; Cherie L. Bayer, Indiana University; Kathryn Carter, University of Nebraska, Lincoln; Joseph S. Coppolino, Nassau Community College; Laverne Curtis-Wilcox, Cuyahoga Community College; Michelle Miller, University of Memphis; John Olson, Everett Community College; William Foster Owen, California State University, Sacramento; Nan Peck, Northern Virginia Community College, Annandale Campus; Mary Jo Popovici, Monroe Community College; Sharon A. Ratliffe, Golden West College; Susan Richardson, Prince George's Community College; Cathey S. Ross, University of North Carolina, Greensboro; Kristi A. Schaller, Georgia State University; Michael Wallace, Indiana University/Purdue University at Indianapolis; and the students at North Virginia Community College, Annandale Campus, and University of Arkansas who class-tested the book.

For the second edition, thank you to reviewers Lynn Badertscher, Fresno City College; Diane Boynton, Monterey Peninsula College; Larry Nadler, Miami University of Ohio; John Olson, Everett Community College; Sally Planalp, University of Montana; Valerie Randhawa, Harrisburg Area

Community College; and Susan Richardson, Prince George's Community College.

Writing this book was not only a professional activity, it was also a personal engagement that benefited from the generous support of individuals who make up my family of choice. At the top of that list is Robbie Cox, my partner in love, life, and adventure for twenty-five years. He cheered me on when writing was going well and bolstered my confidence when it was not. He provided a critical ear when I wanted a sounding board and privacy when I was immersed in writing. Along with Robbie, I am fortunate to have the support of my sister Carolyn and my special friends Nancy and Linda Becker. And, of course, I must acknowledge the four-footed members of my family—Madhi, Sadie Ladie, and Wicca. Unlike my two-footed companions, these three willingly keep me company when I am writing at 2 or 3 in the morning.

The Fabric

of Interpersonal

Communication

When I was twenty years old, something happened that profoundly changed the rest of my life: I took an introductory course in interpersonal communication. A new world of meaning opened up for me as I learned about the power of communication to enhance or harm relationships. The more courses I took, the more fascinated I became, so I decided to make a career of studying and teaching interpersonal communication. I wrote *Interpersonal Communication: Everyday Encounters* because I wanted to awaken you to the wonder of interpersonal communication as my first course awakened me.

In these opening pages, I'll introduce you to the field of interpersonal communication, to myself, and to the special context of our interpersonal communication in this era.

The Field of Communication

The field of communication has a long and distinguished intellectual history. It dates back to ancient Greece where great philosophers such as Aristotle and Plato taught rhetoric, or public speaking, as a skill for participating in civic life. In the two thousand years since the field was founded, it has expanded to encompass many kinds of interaction including small-group discussion, family communication, oral traditions, and interpersonal communication.

In recent years, interest in interpersonal communication has mushroomed, making it one of the largest and most vibrant areas in the entire discipline. Student demand for courses in interpersonal communication is rising. Scholars have responded by conducting more and more research and offering a greater number of classes that help students learn to interact effectively in everyday encounters.

The impressive theory and research generated by scholars of communication over the past two thousand years are the fabric from which I wove this book. Reflecting the intellectual maturity of the field, communication theory and research offer rich insight into the importance of interpersonal communication to individual identity and personal relationships. In the chapters that follow, we'll learn what scholars have discovered about how communication affects our self-concepts and our relationships with others. We'll also discover how different kinds of communication create defensive or supportive climates and how they promote constructive or unproductive ways of managing conflict.

Because communication in its many forms is central to personal and social life, the concerns of people in the communication field intersect with the concerns of those in other disciplines studying human behavior. Thus, research in communication contributes to and draws from work in fields such as psychology, sociology, anthropology, and counseling. The interdisciplinary mingling of ideas enriches the overall perspective on human interaction that you will find in *Interpersonal Communication: Everyday Encounters*.

A Personal Introduction

When I was an undergraduate, most of the books I read seemed distant and impersonal. I never had the feeling a real human being had written them, and authors never introduced themselves except by stating their titles. Certainly that's no way to begin a book about interpersonal communication! Instead, I'd rather create a more personal basis for interaction between you and me.

So that you may know something about the person who has written your book, let me introduce myself. I'm in my late forties, and I'm more excited now about life and its possibilities than ever before. Particularly, teaching and talking with students enrich my life and fuel my energies. My students are never-failing sources of insight and vision. Because my students teach me so much, I've included many of their reflections in this book. The Student Voices that appear sprinkled throughout the chapters are taken from journals of students in my interpersonal communication classes. You'll encounter these in the chapters that follow. It's likely that you'll agree with some of my students' comments, disagree with others, and want to think further about still others. However you respond to their ideas, I suspect that you, like I, will find them interesting, insightful, and often challenging.

Now, more than twenty-five years since I took my first course in interpersonal communication, I am more fascinated by and committed to this field than ever. I love teaching principles and skills that enhance students' effectiveness in everyday encounters. I also find that what I teach enriches my own life by allowing me to be more effective in my interactions with others. In addition, I enjoy conducting research to learn more about communication. A number of my studies are reflected in this book.

Although teaching, research, and writing occupy a great deal of my time, I have other interests as well. I cherish close relationships and spend much time with Robbie Cox, who has been my partner for twenty-five years, and with special friends who grace my life: Nancy, Carolyn, and LindaBecker. My relationships with these people continuously enlarge my understandings of human nature and the vital role of interpersonal communication in our lives.

I am European American (White), Southern, middle class, heterosexual, married, and deeply committed to spiritual practice. Each facet of my identity shapes how I communicate and how I think about interaction, just as your race, class, gender, spirituality, and sexual orientation shape your communication. My race provides me with a greater understanding of Caucasian values and perspectives than of those held by women and men of color. However, being of one race doesn't mean that I, or you, can't develop understanding of and respect for the experiences of people of other races.

© Tom Levy/Photo 20-20

© Billy Barnes

Because I am middle class, I have been fortunate not to suffer economic deprivation. Yet I interact with many working-class people, and I've gained some insight into the views, values, concerns, and pleasures that make up the fabric of their lives. Although my heterosexuality implies that I don't have personal experience in gay and lesbian relationships, I have learned a good deal about them from gay and lesbian friends and students. All of us are limited by our own identities and the experiences and understandings they have given us. Yet, this doesn't mean we have to be ignorant of those who are different from us. In fact, the more I interact with a range of people, the more I discover we have important similarities as well as interesting differences.

Diversity in Interpersonal Life

In introducing myself, I've placed myself in the context of a highly diverse society. This social diversity is one of the distinguishing features of our era. Making up Western society are people of many races, ethnicities, physical abilities, socioeconomic classes, genders, ages, spiritual inclinations, and sexual orientations. "A Kaleidoscopic Culture" describes this diversity.

© David Young-Wolff/PhotoEdit

The social diversity of modern life fosters two types of insight. The more obvious one is increased understanding of and respect for perspectives and behaviors that differ from our own. Less obvious but equally important is the insight into ourselves that comes from learning about those who differ from us in certain ways. For instance, Western cultures define "normal" as being European American, heterosexual, middle class, and young. Gay and lesbian orientations are often seen as deviations from the culturally created norm of heterosexuality. This means that gay and lesbian individuals understand their sexual orientations in relation to the heterosexual standard the culture represents as natural. However, heterosexuals often do not understand their sexual orientation in relation to homosexuality. Similarly, African Americans, Asian Americans, and other people of color realize how they differ from European Americans more than European Americans perceive how they differ from people of color. We can also see our competitive attitude toward athletics in a new light when we consider the Japanese preference for ties in sporting events so that neither side loses face.

It is difficult to be aware of Whiteness, heterosexuality, middle-class status, or competitiveness because cultural practices make these appear natural and right in our lives. Thus, learning about people in other cultures and people who are outside of what the culture defines as mainstream inevitably teaches us about the mainstream as well.

The diversity of our society offers both opportunities and challenges. Differences in gender, race, class, cultural heritage, sexual preference, age, physical abilities, and spiritual beliefs present us with a rich array of perspectives on identity and interaction. Exploring variations among us enhances our appreciation of the range of human behavior and the options open to us. At the same time, diversity can complicate interaction, because people may communicate in dissimilar ways and misunderstand one another, as Yih-Tang Lin notes in her commentary.

COMMUNICATION NOTES

A Kaleidoscopic Culture

The city of Atlanta, Georgia, which didn't even have a pizza parlor until 1959, by 1990 had a Korean Chamber of Commerce, a Hmong church, Hispanic yellow pages, Baptist churches for Romanians and Haitians, and a Chinese community center.

Atlanta is home to 4,000 Vietnamese, 10,000 Indians, 25,000 Koreans, 30,000 Chinese, and 100,000 Hispanics. Currently, White citizens are in the minority in Atlanta and many major cities in the United States. Between 1980 and 1990, the Hispanic population in the United States grew by over 50 percent, while the Asian or Pacific Islander population grew by over 100 percent in the same decade.

Further evidence of the increasing diversity of the United States are these facts from the Census Bureau: In 1996 almost 10 percent of U.S. residents were born in countries outside the United States. That's double the number of citizens born outside the United States in 1970. If current immigration trends continue as predicted, by 2050 there will be no single majority group in the country.

SOURCES: Bates, E. (1994, fall). Beyond black and white. *Southern Exposure*, pp. 11–15; Dewar, H. (1997, May 11). Threads of a new nation. *Raleigh News and Observer*, pp. 23A–23B.

STUDENT VOICES

YIH-TANG LIN: *When I first came here to school I was amazed at how big the rooms in dormitories are, so I remarked on this. All of the Americans had a laugh at that and thought I was joking. In my country, individuals have very little space, and houses are tight together. The first time an American disagreed with me I felt angry that he would make me lose face. We don't ever contradict another person directly. I have had many miscommunications in this country.*

The process of socialization teaches us how to communicate and interpret what others say and do. This means that communication goals and styles vary according to the values and norms of particular social groups. Latinas and Eastern Europeans may have learned different ways of disclosing personal information, just as women and men may have been socialized into different styles of friendship. For this reason, we cannot simply tack discussions of diversity onto existing understandings of interaction. Instead, we must weave awareness of diversity into the basic fabric of interpersonal communication. Each identity and communication style contributes to the overall fabric of interpersonal communication in our everyday lives.

In this book, we will consider many ways in which diversity intersects with communication. We'll discover, for instance, that women and men, in general, listen differently and rely on distinct types of communication to create close-

© John Coletti/Stock, Boston

© Betty Press/Woodfin Camp & Associates, Inc.

© Craig Aurness/Woodfin Camp & Associates, Inc.

ness. We'll also learn that race and ethnicity influence personal styles of communication. To appreciate diversity in interpersonal communication, we will consider differences among people as natural and important dimensions of our everyday encounters.

Diversity is not something we add to communication but is a basic part of what communication means and how we engage in it. Rather than adding understandings of diversity onto conventional views of communication, we will weave differences among us into discussions of how we communicate and how we interpret others' communication. This means, for example, we can't discuss principles of listening and conflict and then tack on a few words about ethnicity or gender. Instead, we want to consider how gender integrally affects the way we listen and how ethnic identity influences orientations to conflict. Because many Eastern cultures view conflict as disruptive and offensive, some Asian Americans may be reluctant to be as assertive as many Westerners. It's important for us to understand that Westerners' assertiveness and Easterners' more yielding styles of communicating reflect the values and norms of different cultures. This highlights the fact that effective communication isn't the same everywhere. Instead, what is effective depends on cultural values and standards. Weaving diversity into how we think about interpersonal communication enlarges understandings of both communication and the range of people and perspectives it involves. Cherrie, a student in one of my courses, makes this point effectively in her commentary.

STUDENT VOICES

CHERRIE: *I am Hispanic, and I am tired of classes and books that ignore my people. Last year I took a course in family life, and all we talked about was Western middle-class families. Their ways are not my ways. A course on family should be about many kinds of families. I took a course in great literature, and there was only one author who was not Western and only three who were women. It's not true that only White men write great literature.*

Weaving the Book

I've written this book in a conversational tone, because I hope you and I will interact personally about ideas in the pages that follow. Another reason I chose to use a personal tone is that I want you to understand there is a real person behind the words you read. Like you, I am interested in interpersonal communication, and I am continuously trying to figure out how to be more effective in my everyday encounters with others. In this book, I share some of the ideas and skills that enhance my interactions, and I hope you will find them valuable in your life.

In addition to my voice, you'll encounter the voices of students like Cherrie and Yih-Tang Lin in this book. Woven throughout the pages that follow are reflections from my students' communication journals. In reading their commentaries, you'll discover that some of them are much like you and others are quite different. I believe we can learn from both those who are similar to us and those who differ from us. I think you will find, as I do, that it is enlarging to encounter a range of perspectives and issues relevant to interpersonal interaction.

Learning about interpersonal communication involves encounters with others, ourselves, and the world of ideas. I've woven these three kinds of encounters into the text as student commentaries and features titled Apply the Idea and Communication Notes. As noted above, the commentaries invite you to encounter others and to consider their perspectives on interpersonal communication. Apply the Idea features invite you to apply material discussed in the text to your own life. Some of the Apply the Idea features show you how to develop a particular communication skill; others ask you to reflect on ideas we've discussed to discover how those ideas surface in your everyday encounters. Finally, the Communication Notes spotlight interesting research and news items about interpersonal communication. Each of these features is woven into the text, just as encounters with ourselves, others, and ideas are woven into the fabric of our everyday lives.

Interpersonal Communication: Everyday Encounters is my effort to give back to all of the students who have taught me so much. It's also a way to contribute to the field that continues to enrich my life and to make teaching communication a continuous joy for me. I hope this book will enhance your appreciation of the power of interpersonal communication in our relationships. I also hope it will motivate you to apply the principles and skills presented here in your everyday life.

Julia T. Wood

Julia T. Wood
The University of North Carolina at Chapel Hill

A First Look

at Interpersonal

Communication

You've been interviewing for two months, and so far, you haven't gotten a single job offer. After another interview that didn't go well, you run into a close friend who asks what's wrong. Instead of just offering quick sympathy, your friend suggests the two of you go to lunch and talk. Over sandwiches, you disclose that you're starting to worry you won't find a job and you wonder what's wrong with you. Your friend listens closely and lets you know he cares about your concerns. Then he tells you about other people he knows who also haven't gotten job offers. All of a sudden you don't feel so alone. Your friend reminds you how worried you felt last term when you were struggling with that physics course and then you made a B on the final. Listening to him, your sagging confidence begins to recover. Before leaving, he helps you come up with new strategies for interviewing. You feel hopeful again by the time you leave.

This scenario reveals the importance of interpersonal communication in our everyday lives. We count on others who are special to us to care about what is happening in our lives and to help us sort through problems and concerns. We want them to share our worries, as well as our joys. In addition, we need others to encourage our growth. Friends and romantic partners who believe in us often enable us to overcome self-defeating patterns and to become more the selves we want to be. And sometimes we just want to hang out with people we like and trust. Interpersonal communication is common to the many ways close relationships contribute to our lives.

Interpersonal communication is the foundation of personal identity and growth, and it is a primary basis of building connections with others. Effective communication broadens us as individuals and enhances the quality of relationships, whereas ineffective communication diminishes us personally and can poison, or even destroy, our relationships. We engage in communication to develop identities, establish connections, deepen ties over time, and work out problems and possibilities. In short, interpersonal communication is central to our everyday lives and our happiness. It is the lifeblood of meaningful relationships.

In this chapter, we take a first look at interpersonal communication. We'll start by considering how communication meets important human needs. We will then distinguish interpersonal communication from communication in general. Next we will identify principles and skills of effective interpersonal communication. After reading this chapter, you should understand what inter-

SHOE Reprinted by permission of Tribune Media Services.

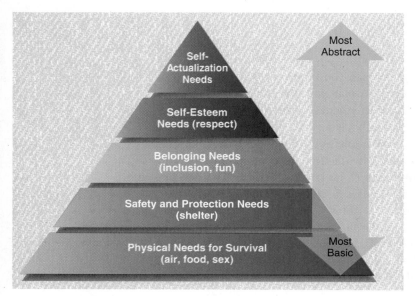

FIGURE 1.1
Maslow's Hierarchy of Needs

personal communication is (and is not), why it matters in our lives, and the skills and principles of competent interpersonal communication.

The Interpersonal Imperative

Have you ever thought about why we communicate with others? There are many reasons we seek interaction, and there are many human needs we meet by communicating. Abraham Maslow (1968), a psychologist, described a hierarchy of human needs; according to Maslow, basic needs must be satisfied before we can focus on those that are more abstract (Figure 1.1). As we will see, communication is a primary means of meeting our needs at each level in the hierarchy.

Physical Needs

At the most basic level, humans need to survive, and communication helps us meet this need. To survive, babies must alert others when they are hungry or in pain. And others must respond to these needs or babies will die. Beyond surviving, children need interaction to thrive. Linda Mayes, a physician at the Child Study Center at Yale University, reports that children can suffer lasting damage if they are traumatized early in their lives. Trauma increases the stress hormones that wash over infants' fragile brains. One result is inhibited growth of the limbic system, which controls emotions. Adults who suffered abuse as children often have reduced memory ability, anxiety, hyperactivity, and impulsiveness (Begley, 1997).

As we grow older, we continue to rely on communication to survive and thrive. We discuss medical problems with doctors in order to stay well, and our effectiveness in communicating affects what jobs we get and how much we earn to pay for basic needs such as medical care, food, and housing. Further, researchers have amassed impressive evidence to document the close link between physical health and relationships with others. At my university, researchers report that arthritis patients who have strong social support experience less severe symptoms and live longer (Whan, 1997).

At times we all rely on others. We might need assistance to understand difficult material in courses, fix a short in our stereo, learn a new computer program, or develop effective interviewing strategies. In each case, we communicate to gain assistance. Through communication we meet basic needs— whether those are gaining food and water or engaging in sex, which Maslow considered a basic human need. It may be easy to meet our needs or it may be difficult. Sometimes we may have to persuade or convince others to comply with our requests by explaining why they should. This too requires communication skill.

Safety Needs

We also meet safety needs through communication. If your roof is leaking or termites have invaded your apartment, you must talk with the property manager or owner to have the problem solved so that you have safe shelter. If someone is threatening you, you need to talk with law enforcement officers to gain protection. If your friend has been drinking and you take the car keys and say, "I'll drive you home," you may be saving a life. In an era under the shadow of AIDS, couples have to talk with each other about safer sex. Being able to discuss private and difficult issues surrounding sex is essential to our safety, although it may be embarrassing, as Navita comments.

© A. Seiveking/Petit/Photo Researchers, Inc.

S T U D E N T VOICES

NAVITA: *It's funny, but it's harder to talk about sex than to have it. I'm having to learn how to bring up the topic of safety and how to be assertive about protection. I used not to do that because it's embarrassing, but I'd rather be embarrassed than dead.*

Communication skills also allow us to protect ourselves from damaging, or even deadly, products. When foods are determined to be a health threat, news media inform the public of the danger. Car makers send owners recall messages when defects in a model are found. Communication is also required to protect ourselves from environmental toxins. Residents in communities with toxic waste dumps have to communicate with officials and media to call attention to environmental toxins that endanger their physical survival and safety. Later, the officials and media may communicate to compel corrective action from those responsible for dumping toxic wastes.

Belonging Needs

The third level in Maslow's hierarchy is belonging, or social, needs. All humans seek others to be happy, to enjoy life, and to enrich experiences. We want others' company, acceptance, and affirmation, and we want to give acceptance and affirmation to others. The alternative is loneliness, which can be very painful. Interaction with others provides us with a sense of social fit so that we feel we're part of various groups. Communication also allows us to structure time effectively—talking with others, watching films together, and working on projects are ways we interact to meet belonging needs. As well, interpersonal communication introduces us to perspectives that broaden our own views. Perhaps after talking with someone about an issue you've thought, "I never saw it that way before" or "Gee, that really changes my attitude." Chad notes how important this type of communication is in his commentary.

CHAD: *I never had a label for it before, but a lot of my communication is for belonging needs. When I feel down or bored, I find one of my friends and we hang out. It doesn't matter what we do, or whether we do anything really. Sometimes it's just important to have somebody to hang with.*

The connection between good relationships and well-being is demonstrated by a great deal of research. For instance, one study found that people who lack strong social ties are 200 to 300 percent more likely to die prematurely (Narem, 1980). Another report concluded that heart disease is far more prevalent in people lacking strong interpersonal relationships than in those who have healthy connections with others (Ruberman, 1992). Researchers have also found a significant link between having few friends and problems such as depression, anxiety, and fatigue (Hojat, 1982; Jones & Moore, 1989). Perhaps you've been through periods when all of your friends were unavailable, either because they were involved with their own priorities or because they moved away. Did you feel more lonely, less satisfied during those times? Most of us do feel less optimistic and less valued when we don't have good friends with whom we can interact and who let us know we matter to them.

A particularly dramatic finding is that people who are deprived of interaction often hallucinate, lose physiological coordination, and become depressed and disoriented (Wilson, Robick, & Michael, 1974). Two extreme cases demonstrate the effects of social isolation. Sociologist Kingsley Davis (1940, 1947) documented the cases of Anna and Isabelle, two girls, unrelated to one another, who received minimal human contact and care during the first six years of their lives. Both children were born out of wedlock, which may explain why they were rejected and removed from normal family life. Authorities who discovered the children reported that both girls lived in dark, dank attics. Anna and Isabelle were so undeveloped intellectually that they behaved like six-month-olds. Anna was startlingly apathetic and unresponsive to others. She did not progress well despite care, contact, and nutrition. She died four years after she was discovered. Isabelle fared better. When she was found, she communicated with grunts and gestures and was responsive to human interaction. After two years in systematic therapy, Isabelle approached normal intelligence levels for her age.

This research confirms that isolation is one of the cruelest forms of punishment and helps explain why isolation is considered an effective torture. Most people are better able to withstand hunger and physical pain than social isolation. How do we explain the difference between these two isolated children and what happened to them? There was one major difference. Anna was left alone all of the time and had no human contact. Food was periodically put in her room, but nobody talked to her or played with her. Isabelle, on the other hand, shared her space with her mother, who was deaf and mute. The family renounced both of them and sequestered them with each other. Although Isabelle didn't have the advantage of normal family interaction, she did have contact, apparently with a mother who loved her. Because the mother was deaf and mute, she couldn't teach Isabelle to speak, but she did teach Isabelle to interact with gestures and sounds that both of them understood. Thus, Isabelle suffered far less extreme deprivations than Anna.

LOW SELF-ESTEEM

The need for social contact continues throughout our lives. Even people who have been raised with normal social interaction can be affected if it is withdrawn later in life. British sociologist Peter Townsend (1962) reported that many institutionalized elderly people have few opportunities for social interaction. The result, according to Townsend, is progressive depression, resignation, and apathy.

Self-Esteem Needs

Moving up the hierarchy, we find self-esteem needs, which involve being valued by others and ourselves. We want others to respect us, and we want to respect ourselves. As we will see in Chapter 2, communication is the primary way we figure out who we are and who we can be. We gain our first sense of self from others who communicate how they see us. Parents and other family members tell children they are pretty or plain, smart or slow, good or bad, helpful or difficult. As family members communicate their perceptions, children begin to form images of themselves.

This process continues throughout life as we see ourselves reflected in others' eyes. In elementary school, how our teachers interact with us influences how we perceive ourselves. Our peers also express evaluations of us—how smart we are, how good we are at soccer, how attractive we are. Later, in professional life our co-workers and supervisors communicate in ways that suggest how much they respect us and our abilities. Through all the stages in our life, our self-esteem is shaped by how others communicate with us. People who lack strong interpersonal communication skills are unlikely to rise to the top in their fields, and many of them will suffer lowered self-esteem as a result.

The story of "Ghadya Ka Bacha," the "wolf boy," on page 14, demonstrates that communicating with others is essential to self-concept—and even to human identity (Shattuck, 1980). Ramu was a feral child, a child raised with little or no human contact. As a result, he did not have a high sense of his worth as a person, if indeed he had a sense of himself as a person at all. His self-concept and self-esteem were shaped by those with whom he interacted— presumably wolves.

Ghadya Ka Bacha

In 1954, a young naked boy who was starving found his way to the hospital at Balrampur, India. He showed no ability to interact with people and had heavy calluses as if he moved on all fours. In addition, there were scars on the boy's neck as if he had been dragged by animals. The boy, named Ramu by the hospital staff, spent most of his time playing with a stuffed animal as a wild animal might in its lair. He showed no interest in communicating; indeed, he seemed to feel no connection with other people. Only twice did Ramu seem excited: when he was taken to see wolves at a zoo and when he saw a dog.

Ramu would howl when he smelled raw meat in the hospital kitchen over 100 yards from his room—far too great a distance for the human sense of smell to detect a scent. Ramu also didn't eat like a human: He tore meat apart and lapped milk from a container. Most of the doctors and scientists who examined Ramu concluded he was a "wolf boy" who had grown up in the wild and been socialized by wolves. He had no concept of himself as a person. Instead, he saw himself as a wolf and was more interested in interacting with animals than humans, who were not "his kind." Thus, doctors referred to Ramu as "Ghadya Ka Bacha," Indian for "wolf boy."

SOURCE: Shattuck, T. (1980). *The forbidden experiment: The story of the wild boy of Aveyron.* New York: Farrar, Straus & Giroux.

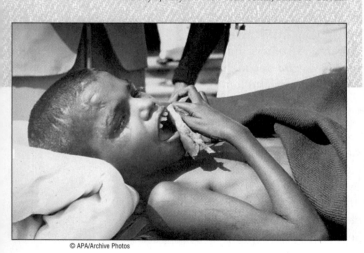

© APA/Archive Photos

Self-Actualization Needs

According to Maslow, the most abstract human need is self-actualization. By this he meant that each of us wants to have peak experiences that allow us to grow throughout life and to realize our unique potential. As humans, we seek more than survival, safety, belonging, and esteem. We also thrive on growth. Each of us wants to cultivate new dimensions, enlarge our perspectives, engage in challenging and different experiences, and learn new skills. We want to become our fullest selves by realizing our unique potential.

Communication fosters our growth as individuals. It is often in interaction with others that we first recognize possibilities for who we can be—possibilities that hadn't occurred to us. Perhaps you can recall someone who first noticed you had a talent and encouraged you to cultivate it. For me, one such person was my father, who told me I had some ability as a writer. He encouraged me to write, and he taught me how to edit and rewrite so that I progressed in my ability. Had he not nurtured my writing I doubt that writing would be a major part of my life today.

Others also help us grow by introducing us to new experiences and ways of thinking. Conversations can enrich our perspectives on ourselves, values, relationships, events, and situations. As a result, we are enlarged. Mother Teresa was well known for inspiring others to be generous, compassionate, and giving. She had the ability to see the best in others and to help them see it in themselves. Although she died in 1997, her influence on others lives on through the work she inspired them to do.

PEANUTS reprinted by permission of United Feature Syndicate, Inc. © 1970.

© Nita Winter

Another way that we seek personal growth is by experimenting with new versions of ourselves. For this too we rely on communication. Sometimes we talk with others about goals and challenges we are embracing. At other times we try out new styles of identity without calling explicit attention to what we're doing. We see how others respond and decide whether we like the effects of the new identity or whether we need to go back to the drafting board. We could not assess changes in ourselves in isolation. We need to interact with others to get feedback on our identities and actions. Lashelle's commentary stresses this point.

LASHELLE: *A person who changed my life was Mrs. Dickenson, my high school history teacher. She thought I was really smart, and she helped me see myself that way. I'd never considered myself all that intelligent, and I sure hadn't thought I would go to college, but Mrs. Dickenson helped me to see a whole new image of who I could be. She stayed after school a lot of days to talk to me about my future and to help me get ready for the SAT. If it weren't for her, I wouldn't be in college now.*

Others also help us self-actualize through inspiration and teaching. Gandhi, for instance, was a model of strength who didn't depend on aggression. Seeing him embody passive resistance with grace and impact inspired thousands of Indians to define themselves as passive resisters. Years later in the United States, the Reverend Martin Luther King, Jr., followed Gandhi's example with his non-violent resistance of racism. Religious leaders such as Lao-tzu, Confucius, Jesus, Muhammad, and Buddha also inspire people to grow personally. As we interact with teachers and leaders who inspire us, we may come to understand their visions of the world and of themselves and may weave those into our own self-concepts.

Participating Effectively in a Diverse Society

To the needs Maslow identified, I would add a sixth one. On the brink of a new millennium, we need to know how to live effectively in a richly diverse society. Our world includes people of different ethnicities, genders, social classes, sexual preferences, ages, and abilities. To function effectively in a world marked by diversity, we rely on communication. Through interaction with others, we learn about experiences and lifestyles that differ from our own; in addition, we share our experiences and values with people who seem unlike us in certain ways. Through interaction, diverse individuals come to understand their differences and similarities, and this recognition fosters personal growth.

Participating effectively in a diverse social world is critical to success in pro-

© Photo Researchers, Inc.

fessional life. According to a *Newsweek* survey, 85 percent of employers think it is very important for employees to be able to interact effectively with different kinds of people, but the majority of job applicants cannot do this (Eadie, 1997). In medicine, doctors need to realize that many Hispanic patients are reassured by eye contact, whereas Asian American patients may be uneasy when looked at directly. Social workers need to understand that many Hispanics and African Americans have extended families that are much larger than most Caucasian families. German-born individuals are more likely to leave work at the formal quitting time. Others would be mistaken if they interpreted this as a sign that workers of German origin are less committed professionals than those who work late.

Like the other needs in Maslow's hierarchy, living in a diverse world becomes salient to us when we meet more basic needs. As long as we need food, shelter, and a sense of belonging, engaging diversity may not be an issue to us. When more basic needs are met, however, we recognize the importance of appreciating diversity. It's also the case that learning to engage diversity may help us meet some of our more basic needs. For example, our safety may depend on communicating with someone from a different culture, and we may meet belonging needs by joining groups with people who represent a range of ethnicities, religions (see "Religions Around the World"), sexual orientations, and so forth. As we stand on the brink of the twenty-first century, one of the most vital functions of communication is helping us understand and participate in a diverse world.

APPLY THE IDEA
Communication and Your Needs

How do the needs we've discussed show up in your life? To find out, try this:

First, keep a diary of your communication for the next three days. Note the people you talk to, what is said, and how you feel about each interaction.

After you've completed a three-day diary, go back and classify each interaction according to one of the six needs we discussed. How much of your communication focuses on each need?

physical survival	self-esteem
safety	self-actualization
belonging	participating effectively in a diverse society

Defining Interpersonal Communication

So far we've seen that interpersonal communication is a primary way to meet a range of human needs. We now want to clarify what interpersonal communication is so that we have a shared understanding of what it includes and means.

What Distinguishes Interpersonal Communication?

When asked to distinguish interpersonal communication from communication in general, many people say that interpersonal communication involves fewer people, often just two. Although much interpersonal communication involves only two or three individuals, this isn't a precise way to define interpersonal communication. If it were, then an exchange between a shopper and a salesclerk would be interpersonal, but a family conversation wouldn't be. Clearly, the number of people involved is not a good criterion for defining interpersonal communication.

Some people suggest that intimate contexts define interpersonal communication. Using this standard, we would say that a couple on a first date in a romantic restaurant engages in more interpersonal communication than an established couple in a shopping mall. As this illustration shows, context doesn't tell us what is unique about interpersonal communication.

What distinguishes interpersonal communication is a special quality of interaction. This emphasizes what happens between people, not where they are or how many are present. For starters, then, we can say interpersonal communication is a special type of interaction between people.

A Communication Continuum

We can begin to understand the special character of interpersonal communication by tracing the meaning of the word *interpersonal*. It is derived from the prefix *inter* meaning "between" and the word *person*, so interpersonal communication literally occurs between persons. In one sense, all communication happens between persons, yet actually many interactions don't involve us personally. Communication exists on a continuum from impersonal to interpersonal (Figure 1.2).

A lot of our communication doesn't require that we or others interact personally.

COMMUNICATION NOTES

Religions Around the World

Christianity is the majority religion in the West, but around the world a number of religions are vital and growing.

Buddhism was founded by Prince Siddhartha Gautama (called the Buddha) in southern Nepal in the sixth century B.C.E. Buddhism emphasizes the interdependence of all living beings and seeks to reduce suffering in the world. By overcoming selfish desires, human beings attain the freedom of *nirvana*. There are more than 307 million Buddhists.

Confucianism, founded by Confucius, a Chinese philosopher, in the sixth century B.C.E., stresses the relationships among individuals, families, and society based on *li*, or proper behavior, and *jen*, or sympathetic attitudes. It is difficult to estimate the number of Confucians because many people in China follow the teachings of Buddhism, Confucianism, and Taoism at the same time. However, it is estimated that there are nearly 160 million Confucians.

Hinduism dates back to 1500 B.C.E. when indigenous religions of India combined with Aryan religions. Hindus believe in a strict caste system, which ranks people into different classes that one progresses through in a series of reincarnations. Today there are nearly 700 million Hindus.

Islam was founded early in the seventh century (C.E.) by the prophet Muhammad who received the holy scriptures of Islam (the Koran) from Allah. Islam teaches that Muhammad was the last in a long line of holy prophets including Abraham, Moses, and Jesus. *Islam* is an Arabic word that means "submission to God." Observant Muslims pray five times each day while facing Mecca, give money to the poor, follow dietary restrictions including not consuming pork and alcohol, and fast during the holy month of Ramadan, which is the ninth month in the Muslim year. At least once in their life, Muslims make a pilgrimage to Mecca (in Saudi Arabia). Today there are nearly 900 million followers of Islam.

Judaism, the oldest of the world's living religions, teaches that the human condition can be bettered by following the teachings of the Jewish, or Hebrew, Bible. The *Torah*, the first five books of the Bible, is especially revered. Today there are approximately 18 million followers of Judaism.

Taoism was founded in China by Lao-tzu, born about 604 B.C.E. Taoism encourages living simply, spontaneously, and in harmony with nature. The number of Taoists today is thought to be close to 30 million.

Shintoism is an ancient indigenous religion of Japan that has been traced to the sixth century B.C.E. Shintoists believe in veneration of multiple spiritual beings and ancestors, called *kami*. Shintoism is characterized by a lack of formal dogma. There are approximately 3.5 million Shintoists today.

SOURCE: *New York public library desk reference* (pp. 189–191). (1989). New York: Simon & Schuster/Songstone Press.

© Serge Attal/SYGMA

FIGURE 1.2
The Communication Continuum

Sometimes we don't acknowledge others as persons at all but treat them as objects. In other instances, we interact with others in stereotypical or role-bound ways but don't deal with them as distinct persons. And with a select few we communicate in deeply personal ways. These distinctions were captured in poetic terms by the philosopher Martin Buber (1970) who distinguished among three levels of communication: I–It, I–You, and I–Thou.

I–It Communication   In an I–It relationship, we treat others very impersonally, almost as objects. In **I–It communication*** we do not acknowledge the humanity of other persons; we may not even affirm their existence. Salespeople, servers in restaurants, and clerical staff are often treated not as people, but as instruments to take orders and produce what we want. We also tend not to have personal conversations with phone solicitors. In the extreme form of I–It relationships, others are not even acknowledged. When a homeless person asks for money for food, some people do not even respond, but look through and beyond the person as if she or he isn't there. In dysfunctional families, parents may ignore children, thereby treating the children as its, not as unique individuals. Students on large campuses may also feel they are treated as its, not as persons. Jason, a sophomore in one of my classes, makes this point.

STUDENT VOICES

JASON: *One thing that really bothers me about this school is that I get treated like a number a lot of the time. When I go to see my adviser, he asks what my Social Security number is—not what my name is. Most of my professors don't even know my name. We all knew each other in high school, and all the teachers called on us by name. It felt more human there. Sometimes I feel like an it on this campus.*

I–You Communication   The second level that Buber identified is **I–You communication,** which accounts for the majority of our interactions. I–You communication is midway between impersonal and interpersonal communication. People acknowledge one another as more than objects, but they don't fully engage each other as unique individuals. For example, suppose you go shopping and a salesclerk asks, "May I help you?" Chances are you won't have a deep conversation with the clerk, but you might treat him or her as more than

*Boldface terms are defined in the glossary at the end of the book.

© Mugshots/Gabe Palmer/The Stock Market

an it. Perhaps you say, "I'm just browsing today. You know how it is at the end of the month—no money." The clerk might laugh and commiserate about how money gets tight by the end of each month. In this interaction, you and the clerk treat each other as more than its: The clerk doesn't treat you as a face-less shopper, and you don't treat the clerk as just an agent of the store.

I–You relationships may also be more personal than interactions with sales-clerks. For instance, we talk with others in our classes and on our sports teams in ways that are somewhat personal. Interaction is still guided by our roles as peers, members of a class or team, and students. Yet we do affirm their exis-tence and recognize them as individuals within those roles. Teachers and stu-dents often talk personally yet stay within their social roles and don't reveal their private selves. In the workplace the majority of our relationships are I–You. We interact with peers, supervisors, and subordinates within our job roles. Most of our co-workers are not strangers, but neither are they intimates. We communicate in less depth with most people in our social circles than with those we love most. Casual friends, work associates, and distant family members typically engage in I–You communication.

I–Thou Communication   The rarest kind of relationship involves **I–Thou communication.** Buber regarded this as the highest form of human dialogue because each person affirms the other as cherished and unique. When we interact on an I–Thou level, we meet others in their wholeness and individu-ality. Instead of dealing with them as occupants of social roles, we see them as unique human beings whom we know and accept in their totality. Also, in I–Thou communication we don't mask ourselves; instead, we open ourselves fully, trusting others to accept us as we are with virtues and vices, hopes and fears, strengths and weaknesses.

Buber believed that only in I–Thou relationships do we become fully human, which for him meant we discard the guises we use most of the time and allow ourselves to be completely genuine in interaction (Stewart, 1986). Much of our communication involves what Buber called "seeming," in which we're preoccupied with our image and careful to manage how we present our-selves. In I–Thou relationships, however, we engage in "being," in which we reveal who we really are and how we really feel. For Buber, only I–Thou com-munication is fully interpersonal for only in I–Thou encounters do we meet each other as whole, existential persons.

I–Thou relationships are not commonplace, because we can't afford to reveal ourselves totally to everyone all of the time. We also don't want to be completely open or to form deeply personal ties with everyone. Thus, I–Thou relationships and the communication in them are rare and special. They repre-sent fully interpersonal relationships.

Communicating in Your Relationships

Consider how Buber's theory of communication applies to your life. Identify someone with whom you have each kind of communication: I–It, I–You, I–Thou. Describe what needs and values each relationship satisfies.

How does communication differ among the relationships? What don't you say in I–It and I–You relationships that you do say in I–Thou relationships? How do different levels of communication affect the closeness you feel with others?

Realizing that interpersonal communication is a matter of degree is a first step in understanding. Yet, we still don't have an appreciation of all that's involved in the process of interpersonal communication. To gain that, we'll now examine three models of interpersonal communication to see how it differs from public or social interaction.

Models of Interpersonal Communication

Models are attempts to represent what something is and how it works. Over the years scholars in communication have developed a number of models of interpersonal communication. Early models were simplistic, but later models offer sophisticated insight into the process of interpersonal communication.

Linear Models

In 1948 Harold Laswell developed an initial model of communication. According to Laswell's model, communication is a linear, or one-way, process in which one person acts on another person. Laswell didn't use a visual diagram to represent his view of communication. Instead, he provided a verbal model that consisted of five questions describing a sequence of acts that make up communication:

Who?
Says What?
In What Channel?
To Whom?
With What Effect?

A year later Claude Shannon and Warren Weaver (1949) revised Laswell's model. At the time, Shannon was a research scientist working for Bell Telephone and Weaver was a member of the Rockefeller Foundation and the Sloan-Kettering Institute on Cancer Research. In collaboration, they developed a model that portrays communication as the flow of information from a source to a destination. Their model extended Laswell's idea with the addition of noise. In their model, **noise** is anything that causes a loss of information as it flows from source to destination. Noise might be static in a phone line or activities going on that distract the sender or receiver of information.

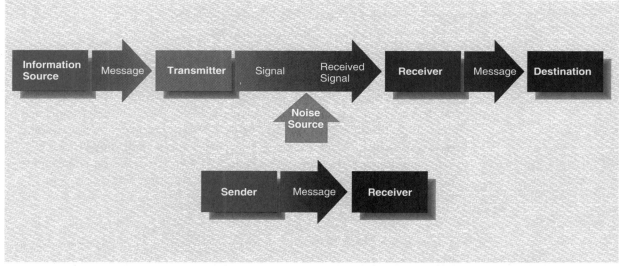

FIGURE 1.3
Linear Model of
Communication

(Adapted from Shannon & Weaver, 1949)

Figure 1.3 shows Shannon and Weaver's model. Although early models, such as those by Laswell and Shannon and Weaver, are useful starting points in thinking about what interpersonal communication is and how it works, these **linear models** have three serious shortcomings. First, they portray communication as flowing in only one direction—from a sender to a receiver. This suggests that listeners only listen; they never send messages. Also, it suggests that speakers only speak; they never listen or receive messages from listeners.

The second weakness of linear models is that they suggest that listeners passively absorb senders' messages and do not respond. Listeners aren't represented as active participants in interpersonal communication. Clearly, this isn't how communication occurs. Listeners affect what speakers do. Listeners nod, frown, smile, look bored or interested, and so forth. All of these types of nonverbal communication influence what speakers say and do. In other words, what others do affects how we communicate, and what we do and say affects their communication.

The third deficiency of linear models is that they represent communication as a sequential set of actions in which one step (listening) follows an earlier step (talking). In reality, communication is dynamic with interactions occurring simultaneously. As you talk to friends, you notice whether they seem engaged or bored. If they nod, you're likely to continue talking; if they yawn or turn away from you, you might stop. At any moment in the process of interpersonal communication, all participants are sending and receiving messages and adapting to one another.

Interactive Models

Awareness that listeners respond to speakers led to **interactive models,** which portray communication as a process in which listeners are involved in sending messages back to speakers. A key feature of interactive models is **feedback,** which is responses to a message (Weiner, 1967). Feedback may be verbal, nonverbal, or both, and it may be intentional or unintentional.

The best-known interactive model was advanced by Wilbur Schramm

(1955), who depicted feedback as a second kind of message in the communication process. In addition, Schramm pointed out that communicators create and interpret messages within personal fields of experience. The more communicators' fields of experience overlap, the better they can understand each other. With the additional factor of fields of experience added to the model, we can see why misunderstandings may occur. You jokingly put a friend down, and he takes it seriously and is hurt. You offer to help someone, and she feels patronized. Lori Ann's commentary gives an example of this type of misunderstanding.

LORI ANN: *I was born in Alabama, and all my life I've spoken to people whether I know them or not. I say hello or something to a person I pass on the street, just to be friendly. When I went to a junior college in Pennsylvania, I got in trouble for being so friendly. When I spoke to guys I didn't know, they thought I was coming on to them or something. And other girls would just look at me like I was odd. I'd never realized that friendliness could be misinterpreted.*

Adding fields of experience and feedback allowed Schramm to develop a model that portrays communication as an interactive process in which both senders and receivers participate actively (Figure 1.4).

Although interactive models are an improvement over linear ones, they don't fully capture the dynamism of human communication. A serious limitation of interactive models is that they portray communication as a sequential, linear process. One person communicates to another who then sends feedback to the first person. This view doesn't recognize that people may communicate simultaneously, instead of taking turns. Also, the interactive model designates one person as a sender and another as a receiver. In reality, everyone who is involved in communication both sends and receives messages. While making a press release, a speaker watches reporters to see if they express interest and if they understand the message—the speaker and the reporters are both "listening" and "speaking." When you are talking with someone you just met, you pay attention to how he or she responds to you. Does he look at you? Does he seem interested in you? Does he ask questions or make comments that invite further interaction?

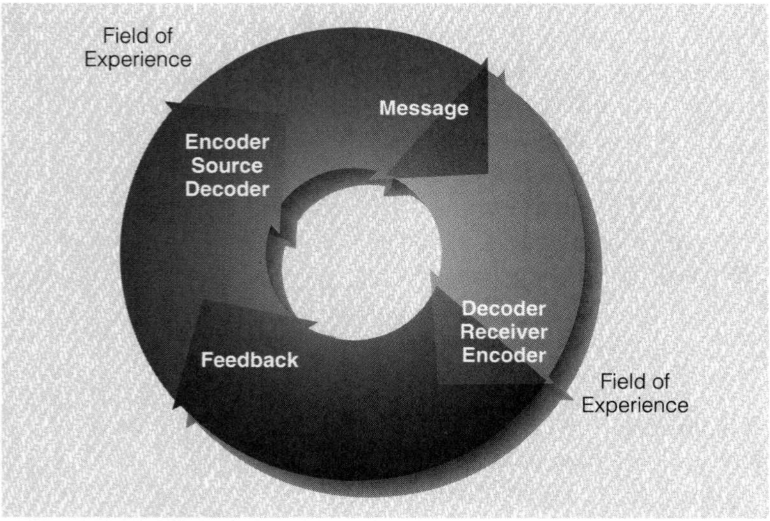

FIGURE 1.4
Interactive Model of Communication

(Adapted from Schramm, 1955)

Another shortcoming of the interactive model is that it doesn't capture the fact that interpersonal communication is a dynamic process. To do this, a model would need to show that communication changes over time as a result of what happens between people. For example, two people communicate more openly and casually after months of seeing each other than they do on their first date. What they talk about and how they talk have changed as a result of interacting.

Transactional Models

To overcome the weaknesses of interactive models, we need a model that emphasizes the dynamism of interpersonal communication and the multiple roles people assume during the process. An accurate model would include the factor of time and would depict other aspects of communication—such as messages, noise, and fields of experience—as varying over time, rather than as constant. Figure 1.5 is a **transactional model** of communication that highlights these features and others we have discussed.

The transactional model includes the strengths of earlier models and overcomes their weaknesses. The transactional model recognizes that noise is always present in interpersonal communication. Noise is anything that interferes with the intended communication. This includes sounds that are part of a communication situation. For instance, it's difficult to attend closely to a friend's disclosure if a lawn mower is roaring or if others around you are conversing loudly. Noise also includes personal obstacles, such as mental biases and preoccupations. In addition, this model emphasizes that interpersonal communication is a continuously changing process. The feature of time underlines this by reminding us that how people communicate varies over time.

The outer lines in the transactional model emphasize that communication occurs within systems that affect what and how people communicate and what meanings are created. Those systems, or contexts, include shared systems of both communicators (shared campus, town, and culture) as well as the personal systems of each person (family, religious association, friends).

Also notice that the transactional model, unlike previous ones, portrays each person's field of experience and the shared field of experience between communicators as changing over time. As we encounter new people and have new experiences that broaden us personally, we change how we interact with others. As we get to know others over time, I–It relationships may progress to I–You and sometimes to I–Thou relationships. Finally, our model doesn't label one person a "sender" and the other a "receiver." Instead, both individuals are defined as communicators who participate equally, and often simultaneously, in the communication process. This means that at a given moment in communication, you may be sending a message (speaking or nodding your head), receiving a message, or doing both at the same time (interpreting what someone says

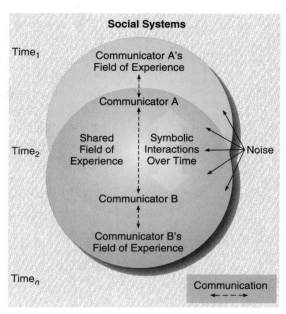

FIGURE 1.5
Transactional Model of Communication

while nodding to show you are interested). Because communicators continuously affect each other, there are strong ethical implications to interpersonal communication. Our verbal and nonverbal behaviors can enhance or diminish others, just as their communication can enhance or diminish us.

Now that we have examined models of interpersonal communication and learned what is involved in the process, we're ready to develop a precise definition.

Definition of Interpersonal Communication

Interpersonal communication is a selective, systemic, unique, and ongoing process of interaction between individuals who reflect and build personal knowledge of one another and create shared meanings. We'll discuss key terms in this definition so that we have a common understanding of interpersonal communication.

Selective   First, as we noted above, fully interpersonal communication is not something we engage in or desire with everyone. Instead, we invest the effort and take the risks of being genuinely open with only a few people. As Buber realized, the majority of our communication is relatively superficial and occurs on I–It or I–You levels. This is fine, because I–Thou relationships require more time, energy, and courage than we want to offer to everyone.

Systemic   Interpersonal communication is also **systemic,** which means it takes place within various systems. All communication occurs in contexts that influence what happens and the meanings we assign to communication. The communication between you and me right now is embedded in multiple systems including the interpersonal communication course, academic institutions, and U.S. society. Each of these systems influences what we expect of each other, what I write, and how you interpret what you read. The ways people communicate also vary across cultures. Whereas North Americans tend to communicate assertively and look at one another, in many Asian societies assertion and eye contact are considered rude. Native Americans are traditionally less verbal than Americans of European heritage.

Consider an example of the systemic character of communication. Suppose Ian gives Cheryl a solid gold pendant and says, "I wanted to show how much I care about you." What do his words mean? That depends in large part on the systems in which he and Cheryl interact. If Ian and Cheryl just started dating, an extravagant gift means something different than if they've been married for twenty years. On the other hand, if they don't have an established relationship and Cheryl is engaged to Manuel, Ian's gift may mean something else. What if Ian beat Cheryl the day before? Perhaps then the gift is to apologize, not to show love. If Ian is rich, a solid gold pendant may be less awesome than if he is short on cash. Systems that affect what this communication means include Cheryl and Ian's relationship, their socioeconomic classes, cultural norms for gift-giving, and Cheryl's and Ian's personal histories. All of these contexts affect their interaction and what it means.

Because interpersonal communication is systemic, situation, time, people, culture, personal histories, and so forth interact to affect meanings. We can't just add up the various parts of a system to understand their impact on communication. Instead, we have to recognize that all parts of a system interact, so that each part affects all others. In other words, elements of communication systems are interdependent; each is tied to all of the others.

Recall also that all systems include noise, which is anything that distorts communication or interferes with individuals' understandings of one another. Noise in communication systems, just like other kinds of noise, complicates understanding. Also, like other kinds of noise, noise in communication systems is both inevitable and unavoidable. We should simply be aware that it exists and try to compensate for the difficulties it causes (see "Anti-Noise").

There are three kinds of noise. Physical noise includes extreme temperatures, hunger that interferes with concentration, fatigue, or crowded conditions. Psychological noises occur in us and affect how we communicate and how we interpret others. For instance, if you are preoccupied with a problem, you may be inattentive. Likewise, prejudice, cultural differences, and defensive feelings can interfere with communication. Our needs may also affect how we interpret others. For example, if we really need affirmation or love, we may be predisposed to perceive others as communicating more commitment than they really do. Finally, semantic noise exists when words themselves are not mutually understood. Authors sometimes create semantic noise by using jargon or unnecessarily technical language. For instance, to discuss noise I could write that communication can be egregiously obstructed by phenomena extrinsic to an exchange that actuate misrepresentations and symbolic incongruities. Although that sentence may be accurate, it's not clear because it's filled with semantic noise.

STUDENT VOICES

CARMELLA: *I wish professors would learn about semantic noise. I really try to pay attention in class and to learn, but the way some faculty talk makes it impossible to understand what they mean, especially if English is a second language. I wish they would remember that we're not specialists like they are, so we don't know all the technical words.*

When we say that communication is systemic, then, we mean three things. First, all communication occurs within multiple systems that affect meanings.

Second, all parts and all systems of communication are interdependent, so they affect one another. Finally, all communication systems have noise that may be physical, psychological, or semantic.

Unique   Interpersonal communication is also unique. In relationships that go beyond social roles, every person is unique and, therefore, irreplaceable. We can substitute people in I–It and even I–You relationships (one clerk can ring up purchases as well as another; we can get another racquetball buddy), but we can't replace intimates. When we lose intimates, we find new friends and romantic partners, but they aren't interchangeable with the ones we lost.

Just as every person is unique, so is each friendship and romantic relationship. Each develops its own distinctive patterns and rhythms and even special vocabulary that are not part of other interpersonal relationships. In the process of becoming close, people work out personal roles and rules for interaction, and these may deviate from general social rules and roles. With one friend you might go roller blading and get together for athletic events and insult each other in jest. With a different, equally close friend you might talk openly about feelings. My sister Carolyn and I constantly play jokes on each other and engage in verbal duels in which we try to one-up each other. With my other sister these forms of communication create problems (as I discovered!). My communication with each sister reflects not only who we are as unique persons but also our particular relationships. In other words, interpersonal communication involves persons in relation to each other.

Ongoing Process   Interpersonal communication is an ongoing, continuous **process.** This means, first, that interpersonal communication evolves over time, becoming more interpersonal as individuals interact. Friendships and romantic relationships gain depth and significance over the course of time, and they may also decline in quality over time. Because relationships are dynamic, they don't stay the same, but continuously change just as we do.

An ongoing process also has no discrete beginnings and endings. Figure 1.5 highlights the processual character of interpersonal communication by including time as a dynamic feature that changes. Suppose a friend stops by and confides in you about a troubling personal problem. When did that communication begin? Although it may seem to have started when the friend came by, earlier interactions may have led the friend to feel it was safe to talk to you and that you would care about the problem. We can't be sure when this communication began. Similarly, we don't know where it will end. Perhaps it ends when the friend leaves, but perhaps it doesn't. Maybe your response to the problem helps your friend see new options. Maybe what you learn changes how you feel toward your friend. Because communication is ongoing, we can never be sure when it begins and ends, as Kate illustrates.

KATE: *It's really true about not knowing where communication stops. I'm a resident adviser for my dorm, and last year a freshman came in to talk. I started to ask her to come back later, because I was trying to finish a paper, but she looked so upset that I put it aside. She asked me what I planned to do when I got out of college and if things ever got so rough I just wanted to call it quits. I couldn't figure out what was bothering her, but I felt like I needed to keep talking. I told her about a counselor on campus who helped me through a bad time. After an hour or so, she thanked me for my time and left. A few months later, her best friend told me that she'd been considering killing herself and talking with me was what stopped her.*

Because interpersonal interaction is a process, what happens between people is linked to both past and future. In our earlier example, the meaning of Ian's gift reflects prior interactions between him and Cheryl, and their interaction about the gift will affect future interactions. All of our communication occurs in three temporal dimensions—past, which affects what happens now; present; and future, which is molded by what occurs in this moment (Dixson & Duck, 1993). How couples handle early arguments affects how they deal with later ones; what happened in a relationship last week shapes interaction today. Past, present, and future are always interwoven in communication.

The ongoing quality of interpersonal communication also suggests that we can't stop the process, nor can we edit or unsay what has been said. In this sense, communication is irreversible—we can't take it back. Interpersonal communication is always evolving, changing, moving ever onward.

Interaction   Interpersonal communication is a process of interaction between people. In interpersonal communication each person both sends and receives communication. As you speak to a friend, your friend smiles; while a teacher explains an idea, you nod to show you understand; as your parent scolds you, you wrinkle your brow resentfully. In interpersonal encounters, all parties communicate continuously and simultaneously.

The interactive nature of interpersonal communication implies that responsibility for effectiveness is shared among communicators. We often say, "You didn't express yourself clearly" or "You misunderstood me," as if understanding rests with a single person. In reality, responsibility for good communication is shared: The person speaking should use language carefully and be sensitive to others' responses both during and after speaking; at the same time, the person listening should try to understand and to give feedback to the speaker. Alone, neither person can make interaction successful. Because interpersonal communication is an ongoing, interactive process, all participants share responsibility for its effectiveness.

Individuals   From Buber we learned that fully interpersonal communication involves engaging others as individuals unlike any other persons. Interpersonal communication involves more than speaking from social roles (teacher–student, boss–employee, customer–salesclerk). Instead, to engage in interpersonal communication, we must treat others and be treated by them as individuals. This is possible only if we learn who they are and they come to understand us as distinct individuals, unlike anyone else. We can't automatically communicate with others as full, unique individuals because we don't know them personally when we first meet. Instead, we come to understand the unique fears and hopes, problems and joys, needs and abilities of persons as we interact with them meaningfully over a period of time. As trust builds, people disclose personal information that allows insight into their unique selves.

Personal Knowledge   Interpersonal communication creates personal knowledge of others. To connect as unique individuals, we have to get to know others personally. You can't interact with someone as a full person until you know something about that person. Over time, as we move toward more fully interpersonal relationships, our communication is based increasingly on personal knowledge (see "Pillow Talk"). My sisters feel differently about exchanging verbal insults and tricks because of experiences in their lives. As each of them revealed her history and feelings, I adapted my communication to reflect my personal knowledge of each of them.

Interpersonal communication also creates personal knowledge. As our relationships with others deepen, we build trust and learn how to communicate in ways that make each other feel comfortable and safe. In turn, the personal knowledge that allows us to do this encourages us to self-disclose further: We share secrets, fears, and experiences that we don't tell to just anyone. This is part of what Buber meant by "being" with others. Personal knowledge is a process—one that grows and builds on itself over time as people communicate interpersonally.

Sometimes we may even feel that our closest friends know us better than we know ourselves, as Lizelle explains.

S T U D E N T VOICES

LIZELLE: *What I like best about long-term relationships is all the layers that develop. I know the friends I've had since high school in so many ways. I know what they did and felt and dreamed in high school, and I know them as they are now. They have the same kind of in-depth knowledge of me. We tell each other everything, so it sometimes seems that my deepest friends know me better than I know myself.*

Sharing personal information and experiences highlights the ethical dimension of interpersonal communication. We confront ethical choices about what to do with personal information about others. We can use our inside knowledge to protect people we care about. We can also use it to hurt those people—for example, personal knowledge allows us to attack vulnerabilities others have revealed to us. Ethical communicators choose not to exploit personal information about others.

Meanings The heart of interpersonal communication is shared meanings between people (Duck, 1994a, 1994b). We don't just exchange words when we communicate. Instead, we create meanings as we figure out what each other's words and behaviors stand for, represent, or imply. Meanings grow out of histories of interaction between unique persons. For example, my partner Robbie and I are both continuously overcommitted in our professional obligations, and we worry about the pace of each other's life. Often one of us says to the other, "Bistari, bistari." That phrase means nothing to you unless you know Nepalese and can translate it as meaning "slow down, go gradually." When one of us says "bistari," we not only suggest slowing down but also remind ourselves of our special time living and trekking in Nepal. Most close friends and romantic partners develop vocabularies that have meaning only to them.

You might have noticed that I refer to meanings, not just one meaning. This is because all interpersonal communication has two levels of meaning (Watzlawick, Beavin, & Jackson, 1967). The first level, called the **content meaning,** deals with literal or denotative meaning. Content meanings concern information. If a parent says to a five-year-old child, "Clean your room now," the content meaning is that the room is to be cleaned.

The second level of meaning is the **relationship meaning.** This refers to what communication expresses about relationships between communicators. The relationship meaning of "Clean your room now" is that the parent has the right to order the child—they have an unequal power relationship. If the parent had said, "Would you mind cleaning your room?" the relationship meaning would have suggested a more equal relationship. Assume a friend says, "You're the only person I can talk to about this," and then discloses something that is worrying him. The content level includes the actual issue itself and the information that you're the only one with whom he will discuss this issue. But what has he told you on the relationship level? He has communicated that he trusts you, he considers you special, and he perhaps expects you to care about his troubles.

Pillow Talk

Counselors have discovered what couples have long known—that private codes of communication are part and parcel of intimacy. Recent studies indicate that most intimate partners develop private vocabularies to express themselves to each other in unique ways. Couples report having private nicknames for one another ("the redhead," "noodle brain"), special codes for indicating they want to make love ("want to read in bed tonight?"), and teasing routines and mock insults used to show affection.

What researchers also discovered is that closeness between partners seems linked to how extensive a private language they have developed. Thus, it may be that communication is not only the messenger of loving feelings but also the creator.

SOURCE: Public pillow talk. (1987, October). *Psychology Today*, p. 18.

S T U D E N T **VOICES**

ANI: *My father needs to learn about relationship meanings. Whenever I call home, he asks me if anything's wrong. Then he asks what the news is. If I don't have news to report, he can't understand why I'm calling. Then Mom gets on the phone, and we talk for a while about stuff—nothing important, just stuff. I don't call to tell them big news. I just want to touch base and feel connected.*

Scholars have identified three general dimensions of relationship-level meanings (Wood, 1994d). The first dimension is responsiveness, and it refers to how aware of others and involved with them we are. Perhaps you can remember a conversation you had with someone who shuffled papers and glanced at a clock. If so, you probably felt she wasn't interested in you or the conversation. Low responsiveness is communicated on the relationship level of meaning when people don't look at us or when they are preoccupied with something other than talking with us. Higher responsiveness is communicated by eye contact, nodding, and feedback that indicates involvement.

A second dimension of relationship meaning is liking, or affection. This concerns the degree of positive or negative feeling that is communicated. Although liking may seem synonymous with responsiveness, the two are actually distinct. We may be responsive to people we don't like but have to pay attention to, and we are sometimes preoccupied and unresponsive to people we care about. We communicate that we like or dislike others by what we actually say as well as by tone of voice, facial expressions, how close we sit to them, and so forth.

Power or control is the third dimension of relationship meaning. This refers to the power balance between communicators. A parent may say to a five-year-old, "Clean your room because I say so, that's why." This communicates that the parent has greater power than the child—the power to tell the child what to do. Friends and romantic partners sometimes engage in covert power struggles on the relationship level. One person suggests going to movie X and then to dinner at the pizza parlor. The other responds by saying she doesn't want to see that movie and isn't in the mood for pizza. They could be arguing on the content level about their different preferences for the evening. If arguments over what to do are recurrent and heated, however, chances are the couple is negotiating power. In interpersonal relationships, the relationship level of meaning is often the most important, for it sets the tone for interaction and for how people feel about each other.

APPLY THE IDEA
Levels of Meaning

For the next forty-eight hours, focus on relationship meanings in your communication. Record examples of the following:

- communicating responsiveness
- communicating lack of responsiveness
- expressing liking
- expressing dislike
- announcing superiority

© Esbin-Anderson/The Image Works

C O N T I N U E D

- showing subordination
- expressing equality

What does this tell you about the relationship issues being negotiated and expressed in your relationships?

In sum, we have seen that communication exists on a continuum, ranging from impersonal to interpersonal. We've also learned that it is best understood as a transactional process, not a linear exchange or an interaction. Based on the transactional model, we have also defined interpersonal communication as a selective, systemic, unique, and ongoing process of interaction between individuals who reflect and build personal knowledge of one another as they create meanings. Meanings, we have seen, reflect histories of interaction and involve both content and relationship levels. Building on this definition, we're now ready to identify basic principles of interpersonal communication.

Principles of Interpersonal Communication

The definition of interpersonal communication and our discussion of reasons we communicate suggest eight basic principles. Understanding these will help you communicate more effectively in a variety of contexts.

We Cannot Not Communicate

Whenever people are together, they communicate. We cannot avoid communicating when we are with others, because they interpret what we do and say as well as what we don't do and don't say. Even if we choose to be silent, we're communicating. What we mean by silence and how others interpret it will depend on cultural backgrounds. Because Westerners are more verbal than most cultural groups, they are likely to regard silence as a signal of uneasiness, anger, or disinterest. Native Americans and members of many Eastern societies might interpret silence as thoughtfulness or respect. Either way, silence communicates.

Although others sometimes misunderstand what we mean, they still respond to our presence and what we do and don't do and do and don't say. Even when we don't intend to communicate, we do so. We may be unaware of a grimace that gives away our disapproval or an eye roll that shows we dislike someone, but we are communicating nonetheless. Unconscious communication particularly occurs on the relationship level of meaning as we express feelings about others through subtle, often nonverbal communication. Regardless of whether we aim to communicate and whether others understand our intentions, we continuously, unavoidably communicate.

© Mark Antman/The Image Works

Communication Is Irreversible

Perhaps you have been in heated arguments in which you lost your temper and said something you later regretted. It could be that you hurt someone or revealed something about yourself you meant to keep private. Later you might have tried to repair the damage by apologizing, explaining what you said, or denying what you revealed. But you couldn't erase your communication; you couldn't unsay what you said. The fact that communication is irreversible means that what we say and do matters. It has impact. The irreversibility of interpersonal communication underlines our earlier discussion of communication as an ongoing process that reflects what has gone before and shapes what will follow. Once we say something to another person, that becomes part of the relationship. Remembering this principle keeps us aware of the importance of choosing when to speak and what to say—or not say!

Interpersonal Communication Involves Ethical Choices

Ethics is a branch of philosophy that focuses on moral principles and codes of conduct. Ethical issues concern what is right and what is wrong. Because interpersonal communication is irreversible and affects others, it always has ethical implications. What we say and do affects others—how they feel, how they perceive themselves, how they think about themselves, and how they think about others. Thus, responsible people think carefully about moral guidelines to direct their communication. They also recognize ethical choices that arise in interaction. For instance, in an argument with a friend, should you lie to defuse the anger? Whether or not to lie is an ethical choice. Should you not tell someone something that might make him less willing to do what you want? That is also an ethical choice. Do you judge others' communication from your own individual perspective and experience? Or do you try to understand their communication on their own terms and from their perspective? In these and many other instances, we face choices that have ethical implications.

Because interpersonal communication affects us and others, ethical considerations always underlie our interactions. Throughout this book we'll note ethical issues that arise when we interact with others. As you read, consider what kinds of choices you make and what moral principles guide your choices.

Meanings Are Constructed in Interpersonal Communication

Human beings construct the meanings of their communication. The significance of communication doesn't lie in words and nonverbal behaviors. Instead, meaning arises out of how we interpret one another. This calls our attention to the fact that humans use symbols, which sets us apart from other creatures (Mead, 1934; Wood, 1992a).

As we will see in Chapter 4, **symbols** such as words have no inherent or true

© Boiffin Vivier/Explorer/Photo Researchers, Inc.

meanings. Instead, we have to interpret symbols. What does it mean if someone says, "You're crazy"? To interpret the comment, you have to consider the context (a counseling session, a party, after a daredevil stunt), who said it (a psychiatrist, a friend, an enemy), and the words themselves, which may mean various things (a medical diagnosis, a compliment on your zaniness, disapproval).

In interpersonal communication, people continuously interpret each other. Although typically we're not aware that we assign meanings, inevitably we do so. Someone you have been dating suggests you need some time away from each other; a friend starts turning down invitations to get together; your supervisor at work seems less open to conversations with you than in the past. The meanings of such communications are neither self-evident nor inherent in the words. Instead, we construct their significance. In close relationships, partners gradually coordinate meanings so that they have shared understandings of issues and feelings important to their connection. When a relationship begins, one person may regard confrontation as healthy and the other may avoid arguments. Over time, partners come to share meanings for conflict—what it is, how to handle it, and whether it threatens the relationship or is a path to growth. The meaning of conflict, as well as other aspects of communication, is shaped by cultural backgrounds. North Americans, for example, value confrontation more than many Asians do, so conflict means different things to each group. Single words can take on different meanings depending on the speaker, as Byron notes.

S T U D E N T VOICES

BYRON: *Sometimes my buddies and I will call each other "boy" or even "Black boy," and we know we're just kidding around. But if a White calls me "boy," I get real mad. It doesn't mean the same thing when they call us "boy" that it does when we call ourselves "boy."*

Even one person's meanings vary over time and in response to experiences and moods. If you're in a good mood, a playful jibe might strike you as funny or as an invitation to banter, but the same remark might hurt or anger you if you're feeling down. The meaning of the jibe, like all communication, is not preset or absolute. Meanings are created by people as they communicate in specific contexts.

Metacommunication Affects Meanings

We use communication not only to discuss people, feelings, ideas, events, and objects. We also use communication to discuss our communication. The word **metacommunication** comes from two root terms: *meta*, which means "about," and *communication*. Thus, metacommunication is communication about communication. For example, during a conversation with your friend Pat, you notice Pat's body seems tight and her voice is sharp. You might say, "You sound really tense." The statement metacommunicates because it comments on Pat's verbal and nonverbal behaviors.

Metacommunication may be verbal or nonverbal. We can use words to talk about other words or nonverbal behaviors. If an argument between Joe and Marc gets out of hand, and Joe makes a nasty personal attack, Joe might say, "I didn't really mean what I just said. I was just so angry it came out." This metacommunication may soften the hurt caused by the attack. If Joe and Marc then have a productive conversation about their differences, one might conclude by saying, "This has really been a good talk. I think we understand each other a lot better now." This comment verbally metacommunicates about the conversation that preceded it.

We also metacommunicate nonverbally. Nonverbal metacommunication often reinforces verbal communication. For example, you might nod your head while saying, "I really know what you mean." Or you might move away from a person after you say, "I don't want to see you anymore." Yet, not all nonverbal metacommunication reinforces verbal messages. Sometimes our nonverbal expressions contradict our verbal messages. When teasing a friend, you might wink to signal you don't mean for the teasing to be taken seriously. Alternatively, you might smile when you say to a friend who drops by, "Oh, rats—you again!" The smile tells the friend you welcome the visit, despite the verbal comment to the contrary.

Metacommunication is important to effective interpersonal interaction. When you develop skill in communicating about your and others' messages, you can increase the chance of creating shared understanding. For instance, teachers sometimes say, "The next point is really important." This comment signals students to pay special attention to what follows. A parent might tell a child, "What I said may sound harsh, but I'm only telling you because I care about you." The comment tells the child how to interpret a critical message. A manager tells a subordinate to take a comment seriously by saying, "I really mean what I said. I'm not kidding." On the other hand, if we're not really sure what we think about an issue and we want to try out a stance, we might say, "I'm thinking this through as I go, and I'm not really wedded to this position, but what I tend to believe right now is . . ." This preface to your statement tells listeners not to assume what you say is set in stone.

We can also metacommunicate to check on understanding: "Was I clear?" "Do you see why I feel like I do?" "Is what I said logical?" "Can you see why I'm confused about the problem?" Questions such as these allow you to find out if another person understands what you intend to communicate. You may also metacommunicate to find out if you understand what another person expresses to you. "What I think you meant is that you are worried. Is that right?" "If I follow what you said, you feel trapped between what you want to do and what your parents want you to do. Is that what you were telling me?" You may even say, "I don't understand what you just told me. Can you say it another way?" This question metacommunicates by letting the other person know you did not grasp her message.

Improving Your Metacommunication

For each of the scenarios described below, write out one verbal or nonverbal metacommunication that would be appropriate to express your feelings about what has been said or to clarify understanding.

1. A friend tells you about a problem with his parents, and you aren't sure whether your friend wants advice or just a safe person with whom to vent feelings.

METACOMMUNICATION

_____

_____

_____

2. You are arguing with a person who seems more interested in winning the argument than in working things through so that both of you are satisfied. You want to change how the argument is proceeding.

METACOMMUNICATION

_____

_____

_____

3. Your manager at work routinely gives you orders instead of making requests. You resent it when she says to you, "Take over the front room," "Clean up the store-room now," and "I want you in early tomorrow." You want to change how your manager expresses expectations for your performance.

METACOMMUNICATION

_____

_____

_____

4. Lately, someone who used to be a close friend seems to be avoiding you. When you do see the friend, he seems eager to cut the conversation short. He doesn't meet your eyes and doesn't tell you anything about his life anymore. You want to know what is going on and how to interpret his communication.

METACOMMUNICATION

_____

_____

_____

5. You have just spent ten minutes telling your father why you want to study abroad next year. Earlier your father said that studying abroad was just an extravagance, but you've tried to explain why it will broaden your education and your marketability when you look for a job next year. You aren't sure your father has understood your points.

METACOMMUNICATION

_____

_____

_____

Effective metacommunication also helps friends and romantic partners express how they feel about their interactions. Linda Acitelli (1988, 1993) has studied what happens when partners in a relationship talk to each other about how they perceive and feel about their interaction. She reports that both women and men find metacommunication helpful when there is a conflict. Both sexes seem to appreciate knowing how the other feels about their differences; they are also eager to learn how to communicate to resolve those differences. During a conflict, one person might say, "I feel like we're both being really stubborn. Do you think we could each back off a little from our positions?" This expresses discontent with how communication is proceeding and offers an alternative. Following conflict, one partner might say, "This really cleared the air between us. I feel a lot better now." Tara explains this type of metacommunication in her commentary.

S T U D E N T VOICES

TARA: _I never feel like an argument is really over and settled until Andy and I have said that we feel better for having thrashed out whatever was the problem. It's like I want closure, and the fight isn't really behind us until we both say, "I'm glad we talked" or something to say what we went through led us to a better place._

Acitelli also found that women are more likely than men to appreciate metacommunication when there is no conflict or immediate problem to be resolved. While curled up on a sofa and watching TV, a woman might say to her male partner, "I really feel comfortable snuggling with you." This comments on the relationship and on the nonverbal communication between the couple. According to research by Acitelli and others (Wood, 1997, 1998), men in general may find talk about relationships unnecessary unless there is an immediate problem to be addressed. Understanding this gender difference in preferences for metacommunication may help you interpret your partner more accurately.

Interpersonal Communication Develops and Sustains Relationships

Interpersonal communication is the primary way we build, refine, and transform relationships. Communication is not merely a mechanism we use to convey preexisting meanings. Instead, it is a creative process of generating meanings. Partners talk to work out expectations, understandings of how to act with each other, which topics and styles of communicating are appropriate and which are off limits, and what the relationship itself is. Is it a friendship or a romantic relationship? How much and in what ways can we count on each other? How do we handle disagreements—confront them, ignore them, or use indirect strategies to restore harmony? What are the bottom lines—the "shalt not" rules for what counts as unforgivable betrayal? What counts as caring—words, deeds, both? What do certain responses, words, and strategies mean? Because communication has no intrinsic meanings, we must generate our own in the course of interaction. Steve Duck (1994a, 1994b), a relationship scholar, maintains that communication is relationships—that interaction is the crux of what a relationship is and what partners mean to each other.

Communication also allows us to construct, or reconstruct, individual and joint histories. For instance, when people fall in love, they often redefine former loves as "mere infatuations" or "puppy love," but definitely not the real thing. In the United States, marriage may be defined as a joining of two individuals. In many societies, however, marriage is regarded as a union of two families or communities. In some societies, marriage is not an individual choice, but a relationship arranged by parents. When something goes wrong in a relationship, partners may work together to define what happened in a way that allows them to continue. Marriage counselors report that couples routinely work out face-saving explanations for affairs so that they can stay together in the aftermath of infidelity (Scarf, 1987). As partners communicate thoughts and feelings, they generate shared meanings for themselves, their interaction, and their relationship.

Communication is also the primary means by which intimates construct a future for themselves, and a vision of shared future is one of the most powerful ties that link people (Dixson & Duck, 1993). Romantic couples often dream together by talking about the family they plan and how they'll be in twenty years. Likewise, friends discuss plans for the future and promise reunions if they must move apart. Communication allows us to express and share dreams, imaginings, and memories and to make all of these part of the joint world of relational partners. In her interpersonal communication journal, Karen explained how communication made the future of her relationship seem more real.

S T U D E N T VOICES

KAREN: *I love talking about the future with my fiancé. Sometimes we talk for hours about the kind of house we'll have and what our children will be like and how we'll juggle two careers and a family. I know everything won't work out exactly like we think now, but talking about it makes me feel so close to Dave and like our future is real.*

Interpersonal Communication Is Not a Panacea

As we have seen, we communicate to satisfy many of our needs and to create relationships with others. Yet it would be a mistake to think communication is a cure-all. Often it can help us work out problems and disagreements, but it isn't a panacea for everything that ails us and our relationships. Many problems can't be solved by talk alone. Communication by itself won't end hunger, abuses of human rights around the globe, racism, or physical diseases. Neither can words alone bridge irreconcilable differences between people or erase the hurt of betrayals. Although good communication may increase understanding and help us find solutions to problems, it is not a cure-all. We should also realize that the idea of "talking things through" is distinctly Western. Not all societies think it's wise or useful to communicate about relationships or to talk extensively about feelings. Just as interpersonal communication has many strengths and values, it also has limits, and its effectiveness is shaped by cultural contexts.

Interpersonal Communication Effectiveness Can Be Learned

One of the most important principles of interpersonal communication is that we can become more effective if we invest personal effort in learning and practicing good communication skills. It is erroneous to believe that effective communicators are born, that some people just have a natural talent and others don't. Although some people have extraordinary talent in athletics or music, all of us can become competent athletes and respectable musicians. Likewise, some people may seem naturally gifted at communicating, but all of us can become competent communicators. This book and the course that you are taking should sharpen your understandings of how interpersonal communication works and should help you learn skills that will enhance your effectiveness in relating to others.

The eight principles we have identified clarify what interpersonal communication is and is not and suggest ways to become more skillful in our own communicative endeavors. Building on all we have covered, we turn now to guidelines for becoming competent in interpersonal communication.

Guidelines for Interpersonal Communication Competence

Sometimes we handle interactions well, whereas in other cases we are ineffective. What are the differences between effective and ineffective communication? Scholars define **interpersonal communication competence** as the ability to communicate in ways that are effective and appropriate. Effectiveness involves achieving the goals we have for specific interactions. In different situations, your goals might be to explain an idea, comfort a friend, stand up for your position, negotiate a raise, or persuade someone to change behaviors. The more effectively you communicate, the more likely you'll be competent in achieving your goals.

Competence also emphasizes appropriateness. This means that competent communication is adapted to particular situations and individuals. Language that is appropriate at a party with friends may not be appropriate in a job interview. Somewhat reserved communication is appropriate with people with whom we have I–You relationships, whereas more open communication is appropriate in I–Thou relationships. Appropriateness also involves contexts. It may be appropriate to kiss an intimate in a private setting but not in a classroom. Similarly, many people choose not to argue in front of others, but prefer to engage in conflict when they are alone. Five skills are closely tied to competence in interpersonal communication: developing a range of communication skills, adapting communication appropriately, engaging in dual perspective, monitoring communication, and committing to interpersonal communication.

Develop a Range of Skills

No one style of communication is best in all circumstances, with all people, or for dealing with all issues. Because what is effective varies, we need to have a broad repertoire of communication behaviors. Consider the different skills required for interpersonal communication competence in several situations: To comfort someone, we need to be soothing and compassionate. To negotiate a good deal on a car, we need to be assertive and firm. To engage constructively in conflict, we need to listen and defuse defensive climates. To support a friend who is depressed, we need to affirm that individual, demonstrate we care, and encourage the friend to talk about problems. To grow closer to others, we need to know how and when to disclose personal information and how to express our caring in ways others appreciate. Sometimes it's effective to accommodate another person, yet in other cases we need to compromise or work out mutual solutions. Because no single set of skills composes interpersonal communication competence, we need to learn a range of communicative abilities.

Adapt Communication Appropriately

Being able to communicate in a range of ways doesn't make us competent unless we also know which kinds of communication are suitable at specific moments. For instance, knowing how to be both assertive and deferential isn't useful unless we can figure out when each style of communication is appropriate. Although there isn't a neat formula for adapting communication appropriately, it's generally important to consider personal goals, context, and the individuals with whom we communicate.

Your goals for communication are a primary guideline for selecting appropriate behaviors. If your purpose in a conversation is to give emotional support to someone, then it isn't effective to talk at length about your own experiences.

© Bonnie Kamin/PhotoEdit

On the other hand, if you are trying to let someone understand you better, talking in depth about your life is effective. If your goal is to win an argument and get your way, it may be competent to assert your point of view, point out flaws in your partner's ideas, and refuse to compromise. If you want to work through conflict in a way that doesn't harm a relationship, however, other communication choices might be more constructive. Mary Margaret is still learning how to select appropriate behaviors, as she notes here.

MARY MARGARET: *I think I need to work on figuring out when to be assertive and when not to be. For most of my life I wasn't at all assertive, even when I should have been. Last spring, though, I was so tired of having people walk all over me that I signed up for a workshop on assertiveness training. I learned how to assert myself, and I was really proud of how much more I would stand up for myself. The problem was that I did it all the time, regardless of whether something really mattered enough to be assertive. Just like I was always passive before, now I'm always assertive. I need to figure out a better way to balance my behaviors.*

Context is another influence on decisions of when, how, and about what to communicate. It is appropriate to ask your doctor about symptoms during an office exam, but it isn't appropriate to do so when you see the doctor in a social situation. Timing is an important aspect of context, because there are often better and worse times to bring up various topics. When a friend is feeling low, that's not a good time to criticize, although at another time criticism might be constructive. Children are geniuses at timing, knowing to wait until parents are in a good mood to ask for favors or new toys.

Remembering Buber's discussion of the I–Thou relationship, we know it is important to adapt what we say and how we say it to particular individuals. As we have seen, interpersonal communication increases our knowledge of others. Thus, the more interpersonal a relationship is, the more we can adapt our communication to unique partners. Abstract communicative goals such as supporting others call for quite distinct behaviors in regard to specific individuals. What feels supportive to one friend may not to another. One of my closest friends withdraws if I challenge her ideas, yet another of my friends relishes challenges and the discussions they prompt. What is effective in talking with them varies. We have to learn what our intimates need, what upsets and pleases them, and how they interpret various kinds of communication. Scholars use the term **person-centeredness** to refer to the ability to adapt messages effectively to particular individuals (Bernstein, 1974; Burleson, 1987; Zorn, 1995). Appropriately adapted communication, then, is sensitive to goals, contexts, and others.

Engage in Dual Perspective

Central to competent interpersonal communication is the ability to engage in **dual perspective,** which is understanding both our own and another person's perspective, beliefs, thoughts, or feelings (Phillips & Wood, 1983; Wood, 1992a). When we adopt dual perspective, we understand how someone else thinks and feels about issues. To meet another person in genuine dialogue, we must be able to realize how that person views himself or herself, the situation, and his or her thoughts and feelings. We may personally see things much differently, and we may want to express our perceptions. Yet we also need to understand and respect the other person's perspective.

People who cannot take the perspectives of others are egocentric. They impose their perceptions on others and interpret others' experiences through their own eyes. Consider an example. Roberto complains that he is having trouble writing a paper for his communication class. His friend Raymond responds, "All you have to do is outline the theory and then apply it. That's a snap." "But," says Roberto, "I've always had trouble writing. I just block when I sit down to write." Raymond says, "That's silly. Anyone can do this. It just took me an hour or so." Raymond has failed to understand how Roberto sees writing. If you have trouble writing, then composing a paper isn't a snap, but Raymond can't get beyond his own comfort with writing to understand Roberto's different perspective.

S T U D E N T   VOICES

ASHA: *Sometimes it's very difficult for me to understand my daughter. She likes music that sounds terrible to me, and I don't like the way she dresses sometimes. For a long time I judged her by my own values about music and dress, but that really pushed us apart. She kept saying, "I'm not you. Why can't you look at it from my point of view?" Finally, I heard her, and now we both try to understand each other's point of view. It isn't always easy, but you can't have a relationship on just one person's terms.*

As Asha says, engaging in dual perspective isn't necessarily easy, because all of us naturally see things from our own point of view and in terms of our own experiences. Yet, like other communication skills, we can learn how to do it. Three guidelines can help you increase your ability to take the perspective of others. First, be aware of the tendency to see things from your own perspective, and resist that inclination. Second, listen closely to how others express their thoughts and feelings so that you gain clues of what things mean to them and how they feel. Third, ask others to explain how they feel, what something means to them, or how they view a situation. Asking questions and probing for details communicates on the relationship level that you are interested and that you want to understand. Making a commitment to engage in dual perspective and practicing the three guidelines just discussed will enhance your ability to recognize and respond to others' perspectives.

Developing Dual Perspective

Practice the guidelines for improving dual perspective. During the next two days, do the following in conversations:

- Identify your own perspective on issues that others talk about. What do you think about the issues?
- Try not to impose your thoughts and feelings. Suspend them long enough to hear others.
- Pay close attention to what other people say. How do they describe feelings, thoughts, and views? Listen carefully to others without translating their communication into your own language.
- Ask questions. Ask, "What do you mean?" "How does that feel to you?" "How do you see the issue?" "What do you think about the situation?"
- Notice what you learn by suspending your own perspective and working to understand others.

Monitor Your Communication

The fourth ability that affects interpersonal communication competence is **monitoring,** which is the capacity to observe and regulate your own communication (Wood, 1992a, 1995c). Most of us do this much of the time. Before bringing up a touchy topic, you remind yourself not to get defensive and not to get pulled into counterproductive arguing. During the discussion, your partner says something that upsets you. You think of a really good zinger but stop yourself from saying it because you don't want to hurt the other person. Later, you're feeling defensive, so you prompt yourself to stay open. In each instance, you monitored your communication.

Monitoring occurs both before and during interaction. Often before conversations we indicate to ourselves how we feel and what we do and don't want to say. During communication we stay alert and edit our thoughts before expressing them. Our ability to monitor allows us to adapt communication in advance and gauge our effectiveness as we interact.

Of course, we don't monitor all of the time. When we are with people who understand us or when we are talking about unimportant topics, we don't necessarily need to monitor communication with great care. Sometimes, however, not monitoring can result in communication that hurts others or that leads us to regard ourselves negatively. In some cases, failure to monitor results from getting caught up in the dynamics of interaction. We simply forget to keep a watchful eye on ourselves, and so we say things we shouldn't. In addition, some people have poorly developed monitoring skills. They have limited awareness of how they come across to others. Communication competence involves learning to attend to feedback from others and to monitor the impact of our communication as we interact with others.

Commit to Effective and Ethical Interpersonal Communication

The final requirement for interpersonal competence is commitment to effective and ethical communication. Without a firm decision to try to meet another in honest, genuine dialogue, all of the other skills are insufficient. To commit to interpersonal communication means four things. First, it means you care about a relationship and are willing to invest energy in communicating ethically with your partner. This requires you to think about the moral implications of what you say and do and how that may affect others. Second, you must commit to the other as a unique and valuable individual. This implies you can't dismiss the other's feelings as wrong, inappropriate, or silly. Instead, you must honor the person and the feelings he or she expresses, even if you feel differently. Third, commitment involves caring about yourself and your ideas and feelings. Just as you must honor those of others, so too must you respect yourself and your own perspective. Finally, competent communicators are committed to the communication process itself. They realize that it is interactive and always evolving, and they are willing to deal with that complexity. In addition, they are sensitive to multiple levels of meaning and to the irreversibility of communication. Commitment, then, is vital to relationships, others, ourselves, and communication.

In sum, interpersonal communication competence is the ability to communicate in ways that are interpersonally effective and appropriate. Five requirements for competence are developing a range of communication skills; adapting them appropriately to goals, others, and situations; engaging in dual perspective; monitoring communication and its impact; and committing to interpersonal communication.

APPLY THE IDEA

Improving Communication Competence

Are you satisfied with your proficiency at each skill?

- How competent are you in various communication skills?
- Describe communication situations in which you don't feel you are as competent as you'd like to be.
- How well do you adapt your communication to different goals, situations, and people?
- How consistently and effectively do you engage in dual perspective when interacting with others? How can you tell when you really understand another's point of view?
- How well do you monitor your communication so that you gauge how you come across to others?
- Describe your commitments to others, relationships, yourself, and the interpersonal communication process.

Consider which aspects of communication competence you would most like to improve, and make a contract with yourself to work on those during this course.

CHAPTER
Summary

In this chapter, we launched our study of interpersonal communication. We began by noting that communication is essential to our survival and happiness. Communicating with others allows us to meet basic needs for survival and safety, as well as more abstract human needs for inclusion, esteem, self-actualization, and effective participation in a socially diverse world.

We learned that not all communication is interpersonal and that communication exists on a continuum that ranges from impersonal (I–It) to interpersonal (I–Thou). Fully interpersonal communication occurs when individuals engage each other as full, unique human beings who create meanings on both content and relationship levels.

To define interpersonal communication more precisely, we looked at three different models of the process. The best model is the transactional one because it emphasizes the dynamic nature and the systemic quality of interpersonal communication and because it recognizes that people simultaneously send and receive messages. This

model is the foundation for our definition of interpersonal communication as a selective, systemic, unique, and ongoing process of interaction between individuals who reflect and build personal knowledge and create meanings.

We discussed eight principles of interpersonal communication. First, it is impossible not to communicate. Whether or not we intend to send certain messages and whether or not others understand our meanings, communication always occurs when people are together. Second, communication is irreversible because we cannot unsay or undo what passes between us and others. Third, interpersonal communication always has ethical implications. The fourth principle maintains that meanings don't reside in words but rather in how we interpret them. Fifth, metacommunication affects meanings in interpersonal interaction. Sixth, we use communication to develop and sustain relationships. In fact, communication is essential to relationships because it is in the process of interacting with others that we develop expectations, understand-

ings, and rules to guide relationships. Seventh, although communication is powerful and important, it is not a cure-all. The final principle is that effectiveness in interpersonal communication can be learned through committed study and practice of principles and skills.

Competent interpersonal communicators interact in ways that are effective and appropriate. This means that we should adapt our ways of communicating to specific goals, situations, and others. Effectiveness and appropriateness require us to recognize and respect differences that reflect personal and cultural backgrounds. Guidelines for doing this include developing a range of communication skills, adapting communication sensitively, engaging in dual perspective, monitoring our own communication, and committing to effective and ethical interpersonal communication. In later chapters we will focus on developing the skills that enhance interpersonal communication competence.

KEY
Concepts

- content meaning
- dual perspective
- ethics
- feedback
- I–It communication
- interactive models
- interpersonal communication

- interpersonal communication competence
- I–Thou communication
- I–You communication
- linear models
- metacommunication
- models
- monitoring

- noise
- person-centeredness
- process
- relationship meaning
- symbols
- systemic
- transactional model

1. Use each of the three models presented in this chapter to describe an interpersonal communication encounter. What does each model highlight? What does each model neglect or ignore? Which model best explains the process of interpersonal communication?

2. Interview a professional in the field you plan to enter. Ask him or her to explain the communication skills necessary to succeed and advance in the field. Which of the skills do you now have? Which ones do you need to develop or improve? Write out a personal action plan for how you will use this book and the course

it accompanies to enhance your effectiveness in interpersonal communication.

3. Go to the placement office on your campus and read descriptions of job openings. Record the number of job descriptions that call for communication skills. Share your findings with others in your class.

4. Identify a relationship of yours that has become closer over time. Describe the earliest stage of the relationship. Was it an I–It or an I–You relationship at that time? During that early stage of the relationship, what did you talk about? Were there topics or kinds of talk you avoided? Now

describe the current relationship. What do you now talk about? Can you identify differences over time in shared fields of experience between you and the other person?

5. Use your *InfoTrac College Edition* to locate two articles that focus on ethical issues in communication. You might enter key words such as "ethics, communication" or "morality, interaction" or "impact on others." With classmates, identify basic ethical principles that you think could serve as good general guidelines for interpersonal communication.

Communication

and the Creation

of Self

© Richard T. Nowitz/Photo Researchers, Inc.

Who are you? Throughout our lives we ponder this question. We answer it one way at one time, then change our answer as we ourselves change. At the age of five, perhaps you defined yourself as your parents' daughter or son. That view of yourself implicitly recognized sex, race, and social class as parts of your identity. In high school, you may have described yourself in terms of academic strengths ("I'm good at math and science"), athletic endeavors ("I'm a forward on the team"), leadership positions ("I'm president of the La Rosa Club"), friends and romantic partners ("I'm going steady with Cam"), or future plans ("I'm starting college next year"; "I'm going to be an attorney"). Now that you're in college, it's likely you see yourself in terms of a major, a career path, and perhaps a relationship you hope will span the years ahead. You've probably also made some decisions about your sexual orientation, spiritual commitments, and political beliefs.

As you think about the different ways you've defined yourself over the years, you'll realize that the self is not a constant entity that is fixed early and then remains stable. Instead, the self is a process that evolves and changes continuously. The self emerges and is reborn throughout our lives. Among the influences that shape who we are are interactions with others and our reflections on them. In this chapter, we will explore how the self is formed and changed in the process of communicating with others.

What Is the Self?

The **self** arises in communication and is a multidimensional process that involves importing and acting from social perspectives. Although this is a complicated definition, as we will see, it directs our attention to some important propositions about what, in fact, *is* very complicated—the self.

The Self Arises in Communication with Others

Communication is essential to developing a self. Infants aren't born with clear understandings of who they are and what their value is. Instead, we develop selves in the process of communicating with others who tell us who we are. Just as countries sometimes import materials from other countries, individuals import ideas about themselves from the people and culture around them. As we import others' perspectives inside ourselves, we come to share their perceptions of the world and ourselves.

From the moment we enter the world, we interact with others. As we do, we learn how they see us, and we take their perspectives inside ourselves. Once we have internalized the views of particular others and the generalized other, we engage in internal dialogues in which we remind ourselves of social perspectives. Through the process of internal dialogues, or conversations with ourselves, we enforce the social values we have learned and the views of us that

A Positive Prophecy

For years, Georgia Tech ran a Challenge program, which was a bridge course designed to help disadvantaged students succeed academically. Yet when administrators reviewed the records, they found that students enrolled in Challenge did no better than disadvantaged students who didn't attend.

Norman Johnson, a special assistant to the president of Tech, explained the reason for the dismal results of Challenge: "We were starting off with the idea the kids were dumb. We didn't say that, of course, but the program was set up on a deficit model." Johnson suggested a new strategy: "Suppose we started with the idea that these youngsters were unusually bright, that we had very high expectations of them."

Challenge teachers were then trained to expect success from their students and to communicate their expectations through how they treated students. The results were impressive: In 1992, 10 percent of the first-year Challenge students had perfect 4.0 averages for the academic year. That 10 percent was more than all of the minority students who had achieved 4.0 averages in the entire 1980–1990 decade. By comparison, only 5 percent of the students who didn't participate in Challenge had perfect averages. When teachers expected Challenge students to do well and communicated those expectations, the students in fact did do well—a case of a positive self-fulfilling prophecy.

SOURCE: Raspberry, W. (1994, July 5). Major gains in minorities' grades at Tech. *Raleigh News and Observer*, p. 9A.

others communicate. How we perceive ourselves reflects the image of us that is reflected in others' eyes.

Self-Fulfilling Prophecy   One particularly powerful way in which communication shapes the self is **self-fulfilling prophecy,** which is acting in ways that bring about our expectations or judgments of ourselves. If you have done poorly in classes where teachers didn't seem to respect you, and done well with teachers who thought you were smart, then you know what self-fulfilling prophecy is. The prophecies that we act to fulfill are usually first communicated by others. However, because we import others' perspectives into ourselves, we may label ourselves as they do and then act to fulfill our own labels. We may try to live up or down to the ways others define us and the ways we define ourselves. The power of self-fulfilling prophecy is examined in "A Positive Prophecy."

A friend of mine constantly remarks that he is unattractive. As a child he was overweight, and his family called him "Fatty" and "Tubby." Later he had to wear braces and endure the nickname "Silvermouth." Now my friend is slender and has a great smile, but he can't see that. He still sees himself in terms of outdated labels. As a result, he avoids smiling and doesn't buy nice clothes, saying "What's the point?" He accepted others' judgments that he was unattractive and continues to fulfill the prophecy by considering himself to be less attractive than he is.

Like my friend, many of us believe things about ourselves that are inaccurate. Sometimes labels that were once true aren't any longer, but we continue to believe them. In other cases the labels were never valid, but we are trapped by them anyway. Unfortunately, children are often called "slow" or "stupid" when they have physiological difficulties such as impaired vision or hearing or they are from another culture and are struggling with a second language. Even when the true source of difficulty is discovered, it may be too late if the children have already adopted a destructive self-fulfilling prophecy. If we accept others' judgments, we may fulfill their prophecies.

STUDENT VOICES

RENEE: *I now see that I labeled myself because of others' perspectives. Since I was in first grade, my grandmother said I was fat and that I would never lose weight. Well, you can imagine what this did to my self-esteem. I felt* *there was nothing I could do about being fat. At one point I weighed 181 pounds—pretty heavy for a girl who's 5'5" tall. Then I got with some other people who were overweight and we convinced ourselves to shape up. I lost 50 pounds, but I still thought of myself as fat. That's only started to change lately as friends and my family comment on how slim I am. Guess I'm still seeing myself through others' eyes.*

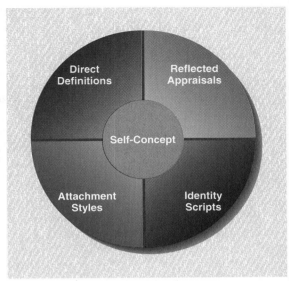

FIGURE 2.1
**Influences on
Self-Concept**

As Renee's comment shows, how others define us affects how we see ourselves. Yet not all others affect us equally. Communication with three kinds of others is especially influential in shaping self-concept.

Communication with Family Members   For most of us, family members are the first and most important influence on how we see ourselves. Because family interaction dominates our early years, it usually sculpts the foundations of our self-concepts. Parents and other family members communicate who we are and what we are worth through direct definitions, scripts, and attachment styles (Figure 2.1).

Direct definition, as the name implies, is communication that explicitly tells us who we are by labeling us and our behaviors. Parents and other family members define us by how they describe us. For instance, parents might say "You're my little girl" or "You're a big boy" and thus communicate to the child what sex it is. Having been labeled "boy" or "girl," the child then pays attention to other communication about boys and girls to figure out what it means to be a certain sex. Family members guide our understandings of gender by instructing us in what boys and girls do and don't do. Parents' own gender stereotypes are typically communicated to children, so daughters may be told "Good girls don't play rough," "Be nice to your friends," and "Don't mess up your clothes." Sons, on the other hand, are more likely to be told "Go out and get 'em," "Stick up for yourself," and "Don't cry." As we hear these messages, we pick up our parents' and society's gender expectations.

Family members provide direct communication about many aspects of who we are through statements they make. Positive labels enhance our self-esteem: "You're so smart," "You're sweet," "You're great at soccer." Negative labels can damage children's self-esteem: "You're a trouble maker," "You're stupid," and "You're impossible" are messages that demolish a child's sense of self-worth.

Family members also offer us direct definitions of our racial and ethnic identities. In cultures with a majority race, members of other races often make special efforts to impart racial identity to children. According to Susan Mosley-Howard and Cheryl Burgan Evans (1997), many African American parents and grandparents teach children to take pride in their ethnic heritage. They emphasize the strength and struggle that are part of African Americans' history. Yet many African American families also feel they must teach children that racism

Emotional Abuse

Andrew Vachss is an attorney and author who has devoted his life to helping children who have been abused. He has worked with children who have been sexually assaulted, physically maimed, abandoned, starved, and otherwise tortured. Yet, Vachss regards emotional abuse as the worst harm of all. He says,

> Of all the many forms of child abuse, emotional abuse may be the cruelest and longest-lasting of all. Emotional abuse is the systematic diminishment of another. It may be intentional or subconscious (or both), but it is always . . . designed to reduce a child's self-concept to the point where the victim considers himself unworthy—unworthy of respect, unworthy of friendship, unworthy of the natural birthright of all children: love and protection. . . . [T]here is no real difference between physical, sexual, and emotional abuse. All that distinguishes one from the other is the abuser's choice of weapons. (p. 4)

SOURCE: Vachss, A. (1994, August 28). You carry the cure in your own heart. *Parade*, pp. 4–6.

© David Young-Wolff/PhotoEdit

still exists in the United States (Mosley-Howard & Evans, 1997). Thus, the ethnic training stresses both positive identification with Black heritage and awareness of prejudice from non-Blacks.

Direct definition also takes place as family members respond to children's behaviors. If a child clowns around and parents respond by saying "What a cut-up; you really are funny," the child learns to see herself or himself as funny. If a child dusts furniture and receives praise ("You're great to help me clean the house"), being helpful to others is reinforced as part of the child's self-concept. From direct definition, children learn what parents value, and this shapes what they come to value. For instance, in my family, intelligence was a primary value: To be smart was good, and to be less than smart was unacceptable. I was great at outdoor activities such as building tree houses and leading "jungle expeditions" through the woods behind our home. Yet my parents were indifferent to my aptitudes for adventures and physical activity. What they stressed was learning and reading. I still have vivid memories of being shamed for a B in reading on my first-grade report card. Just as intensely I recall the excessive praise heaped on me when I won a reading contest in fourth grade. By then I had learned what I had to be to get approval from my family. Through explicit labels and responses to our behaviors, family members provide direct definitions of who we are and—just as important—who we are supposed to be.

T. Berry Brazelton is a renowned pediatrician and a professor emeritus of pediatrics at Harvard Medical School. According to Brazelton, parents and other family members boost or retard children's self-esteem by how they respond to children's behavior. Especially important is responding with enthusiasm to a child's accomplishments. When a baby masters walking, she or he will show a look of delighted accomplishment. For that feeling to be complete, however, the child needs positive responses from others. Family members need to smile and say, "Wow, you did it." Brazelton says that how a child is treated in the first eight months of life sets an expectation of success or failure. If the child's accomplishments are noticed and praised, the child gains progressive self-confidence and will undertake increasingly difficult challenges. If, on the

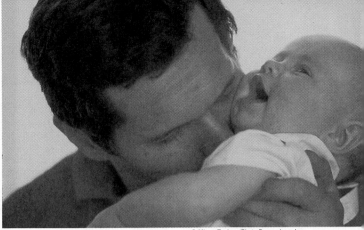

© Misser/Explorer/Photo Researchers, Inc.

other hand, the child's achievements are not noted and approved, the child is a candidate for low self-expectations and a defeating self-fulfilling prophecy (Brazelton, 1997). These negative messages are examined in "Emotional Abuse."

Identity scripts are another way family members communicate who we are. Psychologists define identity scripts as rules for living and identity (Berne, 1964; Harris, 1969). Like the scripts for plays, identity scripts define our roles, how we are to play them, and basic elements in the plots of our lives. Think back to your childhood to identify some of the principal scripts that operated in your family. Did you learn "We are responsible people," "Save your money for a rainy day," "Always help others," "Look out for yourself," "You have to work twice as hard to get ahead because you're female or Indian," or "Live by God's word"? These are examples of identity scripts people learn in families.

Most psychologists believe that the basic identity scripts for our lives are formed very early, probably by age five. This means that fundamental under-standings of who we are and how we are supposed to live are forged when we have virtually no control. We aren't allowed to co-author or even edit our initial identity scripts. Adults have the power, and children unconsciously internalize the scripts that others write. As adults, however, we are no longer passive tablets on which others can write out who we are. We have the capacity to review the identity scripts that were given to us and to challenge and change those that do not fit the selves we now choose to be.

APPLY THE IDEA

Reflecting on Your Identity Scripts

To take control of our own lives, we must first understand influences that shape it currently. Identify identity scripts your parents taught you.

1. First, recall explicit messages your parents gave you about "who we are" and "who you are." Can you hear their voices telling you codes you were expected to follow?
2. Next, write down the scripts. Try to capture the language your parents used in teaching the scripts.
3. Now review each script. Which ones make sense to you today? Are you still following any that are irrelevant to your present life? Do you disagree with any of them?
4. Finally, commit to changing scripts that aren't productive for you or that conflict with values you hold.

We *can* rewrite scripts once we are adults. To do so, we must become aware of what our families taught us and take responsibility for scripting our own lives.

Finally, parents communicate who we are through their **attachment styles,** which are patterns of parenting that teach us who we and others are and how to

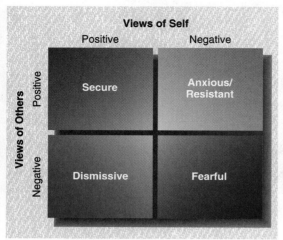

Views of Self

	Positive	Negative
Positive	Secure	Anxious/Resistant
Negative	Dismissive	Fearful

Views of Others

FIGURE 2.2
Styles of Attachment

approach relationships. From extensive studies of interaction between parents and children, John Bowlby (1973, 1988) developed a theory that we learn attachment styles in our earliest relationships. In these formative relationships, others communicate how they see us, others, and relationships.

Most children form their first human bond with a parent, usually the mother, because women do more of the caregiving in our society (Wood, 1994e). Clinicians who have studied attachment styles believe that the first bond is especially important because it forms expectations for later relationships (Ainsworth, Blehar, Waters, & Wall, 1978; Bartholomew & Horowitz, 1991; Miller, 1993). Four distinct attachment styles have been identified, as shown in Figure 2.2. A **secure attachment style** is the most positive. This style develops when the caregiver responds in a consistently attentive and loving way to the child. In response, the child develops a positive sense of self-worth ("I am lovable") and a positive view of others ("People are loving and can be trusted"). People with a secure attachment style tend to be outgoing, affectionate, and able to handle the challenges and disappointments of close relationships without losing self-esteem. Equally important, people who have secure attachment styles are comfortable with themselves when they are not involved in close relationships. Their security makes them able to engage in intimacy with others without depending on relationships for their self-worth.

A **fearful attachment style** is cultivated when the caregiver in the first bond communicates in negative, rejecting, or even abusive ways to the child. Children who are treated this way often infer that they are unworthy of love and that others are not loving. Thus, they learn to see themselves as unlovable and others as rejecting. Not surprisingly, people with a fearful attachment style are apprehensive about relationships. Although they often want close bonds with others, they fear others will not love them and that they are not lovable. Thus, as adults they may avoid others or feel insecure in relationships.

STUDENT VOICES

Z ONDI: *In South Africa where I was born, I learned that I was not important. Most daughters learn this. My name is Zondomini, which means between happiness and sadness. The happiness is because a child was born. The sadness is because I am a girl, not a boy. I am struggling now to see myself as worthy.*

A **dismissive attachment style** is also promoted by caregivers who are disinterested, rejecting, or abusive toward children. Yet, people who develop this style do not accept the caregiver's view of them as unlovable. Instead, they dismiss others as unworthy. Consequently, children develop a positive view of themselves and a low regard for others and relationships. Those with a dismissive attachment style often develop a defensive view of relationships and regard them as unnecessary and undesirable.

A final pattern is the **anxious/resistant attachment style,** which is the most complex of the four. Each of the other three styles results from some consistent pattern of treatment by a caregiver. The anxious/resistant style, however, is fostered by *inconsistent* treatment from the caregiver. Sometimes the adult is loving and attentive, yet at others she is indifferent or rejecting. The caregiver's communication is not only inconsistent but also unpredictable. He may respond positively to something a child does on Monday and react negatively to the same behavior on Tuesday. An accident that results in severe punishment one day may be greeted with indulgent laughter another day. Naturally, this unpredictability creates great anxiety for the child who depends on the caregiver (Miller, 1993). Because children tend to assume adults are always right, they believe they are the source of any problem—they are unlovable or deserve others' abuse. In her commentary, Noreen explains how inconsistent behaviors from her father confused and harmed her as a child.

S T U D E N T VOICES

NOREEN: *When I was little, my father was an alcoholic, but I didn't know that then. All I knew was that sometimes he loved me and played with me and sometimes he would shout at me for nothing. Once he told me I was his sunshine, but later that same night he told me he wished I'd never been born. Even though now I understand the alcohol made him act that way, it's still hard to feel I'm okay.*

In adult life, individuals who have an anxious/resistant attachment style tend to be preoccupied with relationships. On one hand, they know others can be loving and affirming. On the other hand, they realize that others can hurt them and be unloving. Reflecting the pattern displayed by the caregiver, people with an anxious/resistant attachment style are often inconsistent themselves. One day they invite affection; the next day they rebuff it and deny needing closeness.

Our probability for developing a particular attachment style is affected by socioeconomic class, as clinical psychiatrist Robert Karen reports (in Greenberg, 1997). Whereas nearly two-thirds of middle-class children in the United States are securely attached, the numbers are much lower for children from poor families. Karen thinks one major reason for the difference is that poor families face serious hardships brought on by poverty: lack of adequate and nutritious food, poor shelter or homelessness, and inadequate medical care. These hardships can preoccupy and depress parents, making it difficult for them to be as responsive and loving to children as parents who have more material resources (Greenberg, 1997).

The attachment styles we learned in our first close relationship tend to persist (Bartholomew & Horowitz, 1991; Belsky & Pensky, 1988; Bowlby, 1988).

Leigh M. Wilco

However, this is not inevitable. We can modify our attachment styles by challenging unconstructive self-perceptions communicated in our early years and by forming relationships that foster secure connections.

Communication with Peers A second major influence on our self-concepts is communication with peers. From childhood playmates to work associates, friends, and romantic partners, we interact with peers throughout our lives. As we do, we gain information about how others see us, and this affects how we see ourselves. The term **reflected appraisal** refers to the idea that we reflect the appraisals that others make of us. This concept is also called the looking-glass self, based on Charles Cooley's poetic comment, "Each to each a looking glass/Reflects the other that doth pass" (1961, p. 5). If others communicate that they think we are smart, we are likely to reflect that appraisal in how we act and think about ourselves. If others communicate that they see us as dumb or unlikable, we may reflect their appraisals by thinking of ourselves in those ways.

Peers also use reflected appraisals to let us know when our behaviors are not acceptable. This is one of the primary ways we learn social norms. The importance of peers' reflected appraisals is illustrated by an amusing example from Don Monkerud's (1990) research: Jeremy Bem was raised by parents who were committed to nonsexist child rearing. When Jeremy put barrettes in his hair, his parents expressed neither surprise nor disapproval. But a different response greeted Jeremy when he wore his barrettes to nursery school. His male peers repeatedly told him that "only girls wear barrettes." Jeremy tried to tell them that wearing barrettes had nothing to do with being a boy or a girl, but his peers were adamant that he couldn't be a boy if he wore barrettes. Finally, in frustration, Jeremy pulled down his pants and declared that because he had a penis, he was a boy. The other boys laughed at this and informed Jeremy, "Everybody has a penis; only girls wear barrettes" (1990, p. 83). We don't have a record of how Jeremy and his barrettes fared after this incident, but we do know that Jeremy, like all of us, was affected by the appraisals of him that his peers reflected. How others see us inevitably affects how we see ourselves. Reflected appraisals of peers join with those of family members and shape the images we have of ourselves.

S T U D E N T VOICES

RICKY: *For years I thought something was wrong with me because I didn't have ambitions like other guys. In high school I babysat a lot, because I really love kids. I thought I would like to become a kindergarten teacher, but the guys I hung out with really put me down for that. They wanted to become doctors and lawyers and accountants. They let me know that what I wanted to be was wrong or somehow not good enough. I would also like to be a* *stay-at-home dad, but I don't dare tell that to my guy friends. My girlfriend understands and that's cool with her because she wants kids but doesn't want to have to stay home with them. She makes me feel like I'm really special because I want to care for children. I like who I am in her eyes.*

A second way in which communication with peers affects self-concept is through **social comparison,** which involves comparing ourselves with others to form judgments of our own talents, abilities, qualities, and so forth. Whereas reflected appraisals are based on how others view us, social comparisons are our own use of others as measuring sticks for ourselves. We gauge ourselves in relation to others in two ways. First, we compare ourselves to others to decide whether we are like them or different from them. Are we the same age, color, religion? Do we hang out with the same people? Do we have similar backgrounds, political beliefs, and social commitments? Assessing similarity and difference allows us to decide with whom we fit. Research has shown that people generally are most comfortable with others who are like them, so we tend to gravitate toward those we regard as similar (Pettigrew, 1967; Whitbeck & Hoyt, 1994). This can, however, deprive us of perspectives of people whose experiences and beliefs differ from our own. When we limit ourselves to people like us, we impoverish the social perspectives that form our own understandings of the world.

We also use social comparison to gauge ourselves in relation to others. Because there are no absolute standards of beauty, intelligence, musical talent, athletic ability, and so forth, we measure ourselves in relation to others. Am I as good a batter as Hendrick? Do I play the guitar as well as Sam? Am I as smart as Serena? Am I as attractive as Jana? Through comparing ourselves to others, we crystallize a self-image based on how we measure up on various criteria. This is normal and necessary if we are to develop realistic self-concepts. However, we should be wary of using inappropriate standards of comparison. It isn't realistic to judge our attractiveness in relation to stars and models or our athletic ability in relation to professional players.

APPLY THE IDEA
Reviewing Your Social Comparisons

Find out if your social comparisons are realistic. First, write "I am" six times. Complete the first three sentences with words that reflect positive views of yourself. Complete the fourth through sixth sentences with words that express negative views of yourself. For example, you might write, "I am kind," "I am smart," "I am responsible," "I am clumsy," "I am selfish," and "I am impatient."

Next, beside each sentence write the names of two people you use to judge yourself for each quality. For "I am kind," you would list people you use to measure kindness. List your social comparisons for all self-descriptions.

Now, review the names and qualities. Are any of the people unrealistic comparison points for you? If so, whom might you select to make more realistic social comparisons?

Communication with Society   The third influence on our self-concepts is interaction with society in general. As members of a shared social community, we are influenced by its values, judgments, and perspectives. The perspectives of society (generalized other) are revealed to us in two ways. First, they surface in interactions with others who have internalized cultural values and pass them on to us. In the course of conversation we learn how society regards our sex, race, and class and what society values in personal identity. As we interact with others, we encounter not just their particular perspectives but also the perspective of the generalized other as they reflect it.

Broadly shared social perspectives are also communicated to us through media and institutions that reflect cultural values. For example, when we read popular magazines and go to movies, we are inundated with messages about how women and men are supposed to look and act. In the United States desirable women are invariably thin, beautiful, and deferential. Yet different ideals of femininity exist in non-Western cultures, as "Femininity—Muslim Style" shows. Attractive men are strong, in charge, and successful (Faludi, 1991). Mediated communication infuses our lives, telling us over and over again how we are supposed to be and providing us with a basis for assessing ourselves.

The institutions that organize our society further convey social perspectives by the values they uphold. For example, our judicial system reminds us that as a society we value laws and punish those who break them. The institution of Western marriage communicates society's view that when people marry they become a single unit, which is why joint ownership of property is assumed for married couples. In other societies, marriages are arranged by parents, and newlyweds become part of the husband's family. Our great numbers of schools and levels of education inform us that as a society we value learning. At the same time, institutional processes reflect prevailing social prejudices. For instance, we may be a lawful society, but wealthy defendants can often buy better "justice" than poor ones. Similarly, although we claim to offer equal educational opportunities to all, students from families with money and influence are often accepted into better schools than students from families without such resources. These and other values are woven into the fabric of our culture, and we learn them with little effort or awareness. Reflecting carefully on social values allows us to make conscious choices about which ones we will accept for ourselves.

APPLY THE IDEA
Identifying Social Values in Media

Select four popular magazines. Record the focus of their articles and advertisements. What do the articles and ads convey about what is valued in the United States? What themes and types of people are emphasized?

If you have a magazine aimed primarily at one sex, consider what cultural values it communicates about gender. What do articles in it convey about how women or men are regarded and what they are expected to be and do? Ask the same questions about advertisements. How many ads aimed at women focus on being beautiful, looking young, losing weight, taking care of others, and attracting men? How many ads aimed at men emphasize strength, virility, success, and independence?

To extend this exercise, scrutinize the cultural values that are conveyed by television, films, billboards, and news stories. Pay attention to who is highlighted and how different genders, races, and professions are represented.

We have seen that the self arises in communication. From interaction with family members, peers, and society as a whole, we are taught the prevailing values of our culture and of particular others who are significant in our lives. These perspectives become part of who we are. We'll now discuss more briefly other premises about the self.

The Self Is Multidimensional

There are many dimensions, or aspects, of the human self. You have an image of your physical self—how large, attractive, and athletic you are. In addition, you have perceptions of your cognitive self including your intelligence and aptitudes. You also have an emotional self-concept. Are you sensitive or not? Are you easily hurt? Are you generally upbeat or cynical? Then there is your social self, which involves how you are with others. Some of us are extroverted and joke around a lot or dominate interactions, whereas others prefer to be less prominent. Our social selves also include our social roles— daughter or son, student, worker, parent, or partner in a committed relationship. Finally, each of us has a moral self consisting of our ethical and spiritual beliefs, the principles we believe in, and our overall sense of morality. Although we use the word *self* as if it referred to a single entity, in reality the self is made up of many dimensions.

The Self Is a Process

Virtually all researchers and clinicians who have studied human identity conclude that we are not born with selves, but instead we acquire them. George

COMMUNICATION NOTES

Femininity—Muslim Style

The standards of feminine beauty aren't the same worldwide, so we shouldn't judge the appearance of women in one culture by the standards of femininity in another. U.S. citizens are quick to criticize Muslim women as oppressed because many prefer the *hijab* that covers them. However, Muslims may see their modest form of dressing as less oppressive than U.S. women's quest for beauty. This observation appeared in a 1984 issue of *Mahjubah: The Magazine for Moslem Women*:

> *If women living in western societies took an honest look at themselves, such a question [why Muslim women cover themselves] would not arise. They are the slaves of appearance and the puppets of a male chauvinistic society: Every magazine and news medium tells them how they should look and behave. They should wear glamorous clothes and make themselves beautiful for strange men to gaze and gloat over them. So the question is not why Muslim women wear hijab, but why the women in the West, who think they are so liberated, do not wear hijab.*

SOURCE: Cited in Ferrante, J. (1992). *Sociology: A global perspective.* Belmont, CA: Wadsworth.

© Christina Dameyer/Photo 20-20

The Unique Role of Fathers in Socializing Children

For years mothers have been regarded as essential in children's development. We've all heard about the maternal instinct and about mothers' intuition. Yet, mothers are only half of the picture. It turns out that fathers too play important roles in children's development, and the roles they play are distinct from those of mothers.

Fathers seem more likely than mothers to challenge and stretch children to achieve more. Fathers urge children to take initiative, tolerate risks, and experiment with unfamiliar activities and situations. Fathers also tend to focus on playing with their children, and fathers' play is generally physically stimulating. Roughhousing with fathers seems to develop courage and a willingness to take risks in children.

Mothers, in contrast, seem to specialize in giving children emotional reassurance and in protecting them. Mothers, more than fathers, accept children at their current levels and don't push them to go further. Mothers also spend more of their time with children in caretaking activities than in play.

Consider a typical family outing in a playground. A two-year-old girl is on the swings. The father pushes his daughter and cheers her on as she swings higher and higher. The mother watches apprehensively and says, "Careful, honey, don't go too high." Differences like this showed up in studies of how men and women parent. Again and again, researchers noted that mothers emphasized protection and reassurance, and fathers emphasized challenge and stimulation.

Researchers who have studied parents' interactions with children conclude that fathers and mothers typically contribute in unique and valuable ways to their children's development and self-esteem. Fathers seem especially prepared to help their sons and daughters develop confidence, autonomy, and high expectations for themselves. Mothers are more likely to provide children with a sense of self-acceptance and a sensitivity to others.

Researchers conclude that both mothers and fathers make substantial contributions to the full development of children. They emphasize, however, that fathers don't do mothering. They do fathering, and that's different.

SOURCES: Popenoe, D. (1996). *Life without father.* New York: Free Press; Stacey, J. (1996). *In the name of the father: Rethinking family values in a postmodern age.* Boston: Beacon.

Herbert Mead, a distinguished social psychologist, was among the first to argue that humans do not come into the world with a sense of themselves. Babies literally have no **ego boundaries,** which define where an individual stops and the rest of the world begins (Chodorow, 1989). To an infant, being held by a mother is a single sensation in which it and the mother are blurred. A baby perceives no boundaries between its mouth and a nipple or its foot and the tickle by a mother. As infants have a range of experiences and as others respond to them, they gradually begin to see themselves as distinct from the external environment. Both mothers and fathers help children define their identities. "The Unique Role of Fathers in Socializing Children" explains distinctions between how mothers and fathers typically contribute to children's self-development. This is the beginning of a self-concept—the realization that one is a separate entity.

Within the first year or two of life, as infants start to differentiate themselves from the rest of the world, the self begins to develop. Babies, then toddlers, then children devote enormous energy to understanding who they are. They actively seek to define themselves and to become competent in the identities they claim (Kohlberg, 1958; Piaget, 1932/1965). For instance, early on little girls and boys start working to be competent females and males, respectively. They scan the environment, find models of females and males, and imitate and refine their performances of gender. In like manner, children figure out what it takes to be smart, strong, attractive, and responsible, and they work to become competent in each. Throughout our lives, we continue the process of defining and presenting our identities. The ways we define ourselves vary as we mature. Struggling to be a swimmer at age four gives way to being popular in high school and being a successful professional and partner in adult life.

Some people feel uneasy with the idea that the self is a process, not a constant entity. We want to believe there is some stable, enduring core that is our essence—our true, unchanging identity. Of course, we all enter the world with certain biological abilities and limits, which constrain the possibilities of who we can be. Someone without the genes to be tall and coordinated, for instance, is probably not going to be a basketball superstar, and a person who is tone deaf is unlikely to perform in Carnegie Hall. Beyond genetic and biological limits, however, we have considerable freedom in sculpting who we will be. The fact that we change again and again during our lives is evidence of our capacity to be self-renewing and ever-growing beings.

The Self Internalizes Social Perspectives

In studying how infants acquire selves, Mead (1934) realized that we take social perspectives inside ourselves to form views of who we are. He spoke of this as "importing" social perspectives to indicate that we take into ourselves views that originally come from others. We rely on two kinds of social perspectives to define ourselves and to guide how we think, act, and feel.

© Spencer Grant/Stock, Boston

Particular Others   The first perspectives that affect us are those of **particular others**. As the term implies, these are specific individuals who are significant to us. Mothers, fathers, siblings, and often day-care providers are particular others who are significant to most infants. In addition, some families, particularly those of people of color, include aunts, uncles, grandparents, and others who live together. Hispanic and African American families, in general, have more extended families than do most European Americans, so children in these families often have a greater number of particular others who affect how they come to see themselves (Gaines, 1995).

S   T   U   D   E   N   T   VOICES

CLARK: *My brother Alan was really significant in my life. He was four years older than me, and I thought he was perfect. I wanted to be just like him, and I remember imitating what he did and how he talked so that I could be manly. When he said I did something well, I was so proud, and when Alan made fun of me I worked harder to get it right. I think I still see myself through his eyes a lot.*

As babies interact with particular others in their world, they learn how others see them. This is the beginning of a self-concept. Notice that the self starts from outside—from others' views of who we are. Recognizing this, Mead said that we must first get outside ourselves to get into ourselves. By this he meant that the only way we can see ourselves is from the perspectives of others. We first see ourselves in terms of how particular others see us. If parents communicate to children that they are special and cherished, the children will come to see themselves as worthy of love. On the other hand, children whose parents communicate that they are not wanted or loved may come to think of themselves as unlovable.

Earlier in this chapter, we discussed this process as reflected appraisal and the "looking-glass self." Reflected appraisals are not confined to childhood but continue throughout our lives. Sometimes a teacher first sees potential that students have not recognized in themselves. When the teacher communicates that students are talented in a particular area, the students may come to see themselves that way. Later, as you enter professional life, you will encounter co-workers and bosses who reflect their appraisals of you—you're on the fast track, average, or not suited to your position. The appraisals of us that others communicate shape our sense of who we are. Thus, reflected appraisals can lead to self-fulfilling prophecies—with positive or negative effects on our self-esteem.

S T U D E N T   VOICES

MARTA: *I can still hear my mother's voice saying, "If you eat that you're going to be fat." That's what she said all the time. She said it if I was eating cookies after school or if I had second helpings at dinner or if I wanted ice cream on hot summer days. Now when I reach for a cookie, her voice echoes in my head—I can't get that voice, that message, out of my mind.*

APPLY THE IDEA
Reflecting on Reflected Appraisals

To understand how reflected appraisals have influenced your self-concept, try this exercise.

1. First, list five words that describe ways you see yourself. Examples are *responsible, ambitious, unattractive, clumsy, funny, intelligent, shy,* and *athletic.*
2. Next, identify the particular individuals who have been and are especially significant in your life. Try to list at least five individuals who matter to you.
3. Now, think about how these special people communicated to you about the traits you listed in step 1. How did they express their appraisals of what you defined as important parts of yourself?

Can you trace how you see yourself to the appraisals reflected by particular others in your life?

Generalized Other   The second social perspective that influences how we see ourselves is called the **perspective of the generalized other.** The generalized other is the collection of rules, roles, and attitudes endorsed by the whole social community in which we live (Mead, 1934). In other words, the generalized other represents the views of society. The process of socialization is one in which individuals internalize the perspective of the generalized other and thus come to share that perspective. In U.S. culture, the perspective of the generalized other views murder, rape, robbery, and embezzlement as wrong, and each of us learns that as we participate in the society. In addition, we learn which aspects of identity society considers important, how society views various social groups, and, by extension, how it views us as members of specific groups. Modern Western culture emphasizes gender, race, affectional preference, and socioeconomic class as central to personal identity (Andersen & Collins, 1992; Wood, 1995b, 1996).

In Western society, race is considered a primary aspect of personal identity, as "The Construction of Race in America" explores. The race that has been historically favored and privileged in the United States is Caucasian. In the early years of this country's life, it was considered normal and right for White men to own Black women, men, and children and to require them to work for no wages and in poor conditions. Later, it was considered natural that White men could vote but Black men could not. White men had rights to education, professional jobs, ownership of property, and other basic freedoms that were denied Blacks. Even today, Caucasian privilege continues: White children often have access to better schools with more resources than do people of color. The upper levels of government, education, and businesses are dominated by Caucasian men, whereas people of color and women continue to fight overt and covert discrimination in admission, hiring, and advancement. The color of one's skin makes a difference in how society treats us, our material lives, and who we are told we are. "Buying into Racial Stereotypes" on page 62 examines the dangers of internalizing racial prejudices.

"Buying into Racial Stereotypes" on page 62

COMMUNICATION NOTES

The Construction of Race in America

The term *White* wasn't used to describe race or identity until Europeans colonized the United States. They invented the label "White" as a way to increase solidarity among European settlers who actually had diverse ethnic backgrounds. By calling themselves "White," these diverse groups could gloss over differences among them and use their common skin hue to distinguish themselves from people of color. *White*, in other words, is a term that was created to legitimize slavery.

During the time when slavery was an institution in the United States, Southern plantation owners invented a system of racial classification known as "the one drop rule." According to this system, a person with as little as one drop of African blood was classified as Black. Thus, racial divisions were established, though arbitrarily.

Social demographer William Petersen says that ethnicity is incredibly difficult to measure reliably. One problem is that increasing numbers of people have multiple racial and ethnic identities. For example, if a man is one-fourth Black, one-fourth Chinese, one-fourth Thai, one-eighth White, and one-eighth American Indian, what race is he?

SOURCES: Bates, E. (1994, fall). Beyond black and white. *Southern Exposure*, pp. 11–15; Petersen, W. (1997) *Ethnicity counts*. New York: Transaction.

Reprinted by permission of Steve Kelley, *The San Diego Union-Tribune*.

STUDENT VOICES

DERRICK: *If my mama told me once, she told me a million times: "You got to work twice as hard to get half as far because you're Black." I knew that my skin was a strike against me in this society since I can remember knowing anything. When I asked why Blacks had to work harder, Mama said, "Because that's just how it is." I guess she was telling me that's how this society looks on African Americans.*

Buying into Racial Stereotypes

Stereotypes are general views that people apply to others, right? Well, not always. According to Stanford University researcher Claude Steele, groups that are negatively stereotyped by others may *internalize* those negative stereotypes in themselves, thereby creating a self-fulfilling prophecy. Steele says that groups that are victims of widely held negative perceptions often fear that the stereotypes about them are true.

To test his idea, Steele designed an experiment. He told undergraduate students that they would be taking a test that measured their verbal reasoning. Half of the students were asked to identify their race before taking the test. The other half were not asked to identify their race. Steele's results were dramatic. When Blacks were required to state their race, they tested signicantly lower than Whites. When students weren't asked to identify their race, scores for Blacks and Whites were equivalent.

SOURCE: Woo, E. (1995, December 18). Stereotypes may psych out students. *Raleigh News and Observer*, pp. 1A, 10A.

Gender is another important category in Western culture. Historically, men have been more valued and considered more rational, competent, and entitled to privilege than women. In the 1800s, women were not allowed to own property, gain professional training, or vote. It was considered appropriate for a husband to beat his wife; the phrase "rule of thumb" comes from the law that stated a man could beat his wife as long as he used a stick no larger than the size of his thumb. Even on the verge of the twenty-first century, women and men are not considered equal in many societies. Some scholars argue that gender is the most important aspect of personal identity in Western culture (Fox-Genovese, 1991). From the pink and blue blankets hospitals wrap around newborns to differential salaries earned by women and men, gender is a major facet of identity. Given the importance our society places on gender, it is no wonder that one of the first ways children learn to identify themselves is by their sex (Wood, 1996). When my niece Michelle was four years old, I asked her who she was. Her immediate response was "I'm a girl." Only after naming her sex did she describe her family, her likes and dislikes, and other parts of herself.

Western cultures have strong gender prescriptions. Girls and women are expected to be caring, deferential, and cooperative, whereas boys and men are supposed to be independent, assertive, and competitive (Wood, 1994d). Consequently, women who assert themselves or compete are likely to receive social disapproval, be called "bitches," and otherwise reprimanded for violating gender prescriptions. Men who refuse to conform to social views of masculinity and who are gentle and caring risk being labeled "wimps." Our gender, then, makes a great deal of difference in how others view us and how we come to see ourselves.

S T U D E N T VOICES

ALLISON: *When I was real young, I was outside playing in a little swimming pool one day. It was hot and my brothers had their shirts off, so I took mine off too. When my mother looked up and saw me, she went berserk. She told me to get my shirt back on and act like a lady. That's when I knew that girls have to hide and protect their bodies, but boys don't.*

A third aspect of identity that is salient in our culture is sexual orientation. Historically and today, heterosexuality is viewed as the normal sexual orientation, and lesbians, bisexuals, and gays are regarded as abnormal. Society communicates this viewpoint not only directly but also through privileges given to heterosexuuals but denied to gays, lesbians, and bisexuals. For example, a woman and man who love each other can be married and have their commitment recognized religiously and legally. Two men or two women who love each other and want to be life partners are denied social and legal recognition (Wood, 1995c). Heterosexuals can cover partners on insurance policies and inherit from them without paying taxes, but people with other sexual preferences cannot. To be homosexual or bisexual in modern Western culture is to be socially devalued. However, many gays and lesbians reject negative social views of their identity; instead they form communities that support positive self-images.

A fourth important aspect of identity in our society is socioeconomic class. Even though the United States is relatively open with regard to class, as examined in "Creating Class," the class we belong to affects everything from how much money we make, to the kinds of schools, jobs, and lifestyle choices we see as possibilities for ourselves. Class is difficult to point to because, unlike sex and race, it is not visible. Class isn't just the amount of money a person has. It's a basic part of how we understand the world and how we think, feel, and act. Class affects which stores, restaurants, and schools are part of our life. It influences who our friends are, where we live and work, and even the kind of car we drive (Langston, 1992).

Creating Class

Societies around the world have created systems of classifying people. Relatively open systems, such as the system in the United States, allow interaction among different classes and assume individuals can move from one class to another. In contrast, caste classifications are closed systems that assume individuals are locked into the social status ascribed to them at birth. These strongly discourage interaction among members of different castes.

Apartheid, an Afrikaans word that means "apartness," has prevailed in South Africa for hundreds of years and was made the official policy of the country in 1948. Once the Nationalists, a conservative White political party, seized power, they legislated hundreds of laws to enforce rigid racial separation in virtually every area of life and to support domination of the country by the White minority.

In 1990, South Africa abolished the Separate Amenities Act, which had mandated separate and unequal cemeteries, parks, trains, hotels, hospitals, and so forth for Whites and Blacks. Other discriminatory practices and laws are gradually being dismantled in South Africa.

SOURCES: Ferrante, J. (1992). *Sociology: A global perspective.* Belmont, CA: Wadsworth; Wren, C. S. (1990, October 16). A South Africa color bar falls quietly. *The New York Times,* pp. Y1, Y10.

S T U D E N T **VOICES**

DEL: *I'm gay and many people think that gay is all I am. Once they find out I'm gay, nothing else about me seems relevant to them. They can't see all the ways in which we are alike and that we have more similarities than differences. They don't see that once they find out I'm gay. They don't see that I am a student (just like them), that I am working my way through school (just like them), that I am Christian (just like them), that I worry about tests and papers (just like them), that I love basketball (just like them). All they see is that I am gay, and that is not like them.*

In 1995 Barney Dews and Carolyn Law edited a book titled *This Fine Place So Far From Home: Voices of Academics from the Working Class.* Although the

Language and Class

For years Herbert Gans has studied urban poverty in the United States. After all of his research, he advances this conclusion: The real war is not the war against poverty, but the war of words. Gans's point is that the language widely used to talk about the poor creates negative labels and stereotypes that harm the very people being discussed. Gans particularly objects to two terms: *the culture of poverty* and *underclass*. He thinks both terms suggest that poor people are morally inferior to those who aren't poor.

Another respected scholar, Jonathan Kozol, joins Gans in criticizing language that creates a false sense of enormous differences between the character of poor and non-poor people. Kozol rejects terms such as *underclass* and *the culture of poverty* because they suggest that the differences between poor and non-poor individuals are so great that nothing would change the lives of the poor. After all, you can't change a "culture," whereas you could change poorness by providing material resources.

Both Gans and Kozol believe that it is misguided to divide people into categories that imply different degrees of moral worth or fundamental character that are not amenable to change. According to Gans and Kozol, it's time for all of us to mind and mend how we talk about those who are poor.

SOURCES: Gans, H. (1995). *The war against the poor: The underclass and antipoverty policy.* New York: Basic; Kozol, J. (1995). *Amazing grace: The lives of children and the conscience of a nation.* New York: Crown.

academics who contributed to this book have entered a middle-class world, they say that they don't feel at ease or fully accepted. Many report wrenching identity conflicts as they interact with their working-class families and their middle-class colleagues. "Torn between two worlds and two identities" is how they describe themselves. The values and self-concepts that they grew up endorsing are at odds with the values and identities regarded as appropriate where they now live and work.

Class influences which needs we focus on in Maslow's hierarchy. For example, people with economic security have the resources and leisure time to contemplate higher-level needs such as self-actualization. They can afford therapy, yoga, spiritual development, and elite spas to condition their bodies. These are not feasible for people who are a step away from poverty. Members of the middle and upper classes assume they will attend college and enter good professions, yet these are often not realistic options for working-class people (Langston, 1992). Guidance counselors may encourage academically gifted working-class students to go to work or pursue vocational education after high school, whereas middle-class students of average ability are routinely steered toward good colleges and status careers. In patterns such as this, we see how the perspective of the generalized other shapes our identities and our concrete lives. In "Language and Class" we see how pervasive and potentially devastating our choice of words can be in pepetuating classism.

S   T   U   D   E   N   T

GENEVA: *I may be in a first-class university, but I don't fit with most of the folks here. That hits me in the face every day. I walk across campus and see girls wearing shoes that cost more than all four pairs I own. I hear students talking about restaurants and trips that I can't afford. Last week I heard a guy complaining about being too broke to get a CD player for his car. I don't own a car. I don't know how to relate to these people who have so much money. I do know they see the world differently than I do.*

Race, gender, sexual preference, and class dominate our society's views of individuals and their worth. In thinking about these four social constructions of identity, it's important to realize they intersect with one another. Race interacts with gender, so that women of color experience double oppression and devaluation in our culture (Higginbotham, 1992; Lorde, 1992). Class and sexual preference also interact: Homophobia, or fear of homosexuals, is particularly pronounced in the working class, so a lesbian or gay person in a poor community may be socially ostracized (Langston, 1992). Class and gender are also interlinked, with women being far more likely to exist at the poverty level than men (Stone, 1992). Gender and race intersect, so that Black men have burdens and barriers not faced by White men (Gibbs, 1992). All facets of our identity interact.

© Esbin-Anderson/The Image Works

Although race, gender, sexual preference, and socioeconomic class are especially salient in social views of identity and worth, there are many other views of the general society that we learn and often internalize. For instance, Western societies clearly value intelligence, ambition, rugged individualism, and competitiveness. People who do not conform to these social values receive less respect than those who do. Another value our society endorses is slimness, particularly in Caucasian women. Being slim (and beautiful) is considered very important, and those who don't measure up are often shunned and regarded as less worthy than those who do. Because society places such emphasis on slenderness in women, eating disorders are epidemic; as many as 80 out of 100 fourth-grade girls diet—and most of them are well within normal weight limits (Wolf, 1991). Because preoccupation with self is a luxury of class, the quest for thinness is more pronounced among Caucasian women than among women of color and more in middle and upper classes than in working classes (Wood, 1994d). Society imposes physical requirements on men as well. Strength and sexual prowess are two expectations of "real men," which may explain why increasing numbers of men are having pectoral implants and penis enlargement surgery. People not born with bodies society favors may feel compelled to construct them!

APPLY THE IDEA

Internalizing the Generalized Other

Which views of the generalized other have you internalized?

- How do you evaluate women? How important is physical appearance to your judgments?
- How do you evaluate men? To what extent do strength and ambitiousness affect your judgments?

A Cross-Cultural Look at Sexual Identity

The Navajo and Mohave Indian tribes gave special respect to *nadles,* who were considered neither male nor female but a combination of the two sexes. The identity of *nadle* was sometimes conferred at birth on babies born with ambiguous genitals. Individuals could also adopt the *nadle* identity later in life. When working on weaving or other tasks assigned to women, the *nadle* dressed and acted as a woman. When engaged in activities assigned to men, the *nadle* dressed and acted as a man. *Nadles* could marry either women or men. Within their tribes, *nadles* were regarded as very wise and were given special privileges and deference.

SOURCE: Olien, M. (1978). *The human myth.* New York: Harper & Row.

- What were you taught about African Americans, Hispanics, and members of Asian cultures? Which of the views you were taught have you imported into yourself?
- How do you see heterosexuals, bisexuals, gays, and lesbians? How did you develop these views?

Are there social perspectives and attitudes that you hold but don't really respect or like? If so, consider challenging them and reforming those parts of yourself.

As we interact with particular others and participate in general social life (the generalized other), we learn what and whom our society values. Social perspectives, however, do not remain outside of us. In most cases, we import them into ourselves, and we thus come to share the views and values generally endorsed in our society. In many ways this is useful, even essential, for collective life. If we all made up our own rules about when to stop and go at traffic intersections, car accidents would skyrocket. If each of us operated by our own code for lawful conduct, there would be no shared standards regarding rape, murder, robbery, and so forth. Life would be chaotic.

Yet not all social views are as constructive as traffic rules and criminal law. The generalized other's unequal valuing of different races, genders, and sexual preferences fosters discrimination against whole groups of people whose only fault is not being what society defines as normal or good. Each of us has a responsibility to exercise critical judgment about which social views we personally accept and use as guides for our own behaviors, attitudes, and values. This leads to a third proposition about the self.

Social Perspectives on the Self Are Constructed and Variable

We have seen that we gain a sense of personal identity and an understanding of social life by encountering and internalizing social perspectives of particular others and the generalized other. This could lead you to think that our self-concepts are determined by fixed social values. As we will see, however, this isn't the case. Social views are constructed and variable, so they can be changed. An example of the variability of social values is examined in "A Cross-Cultural Look at Sexual Identity."

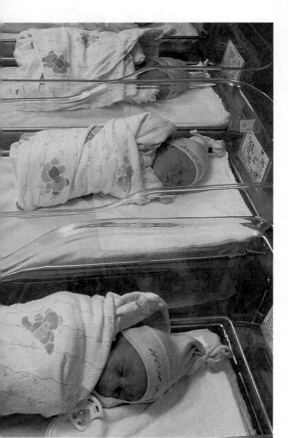

© Lori Adamski Peek/Tony Stone Images, Inc.

© Bill Aron/Photo Edit

Constructed Social Views   Social perspectives are constructed in particular cultures at specific times. What a society values does not reflect divine law, absolute truth, or the natural order of things. The values that are endorsed in any society are arbitrary and designed to support dominant ideologies, or the beliefs of those in power. For example, it was to White plantation owners' advantage to define Africans as slaves and as inferior human beings. Doing so supported the privileges that White landowners enjoyed. Similarly, it was to men's advantage to deny women the right to vote, because doing so preserved men's power to control the laws of the land. By approving of heterosexuality and not homosexuality, the culture supports a particular, arbitrary family ideal. When we reflect on widely endorsed social values, we realize that they tend to serve the interests of those who are privileged by the status quo.

Differing Social Views   The constructed and arbitrary nature of social values becomes especially obvious when we consider how widely values differ from culture to culture. For example, in Sweden, Denmark, and Norway, same-sex marriages are allowed and are given full legal recognition. Prescriptions for femininity and masculinity also vary substantially across cultures. In some places, men are emotional and dependent, and women are assertive and emotionally controlled. In many countries south of the United States, race is less prominent than in North America, and mixed-race marriages are common and accepted.

S T U D E N T   VOICES

HANNAH: *Because I'm an older student, I have a good understanding of how much views change in society. Twenty years ago when I first started college, women were not taken very seriously. I had no female professors, and there wasn't a women's studies department at my school. Our professors and all of us just expected that most women at the school would become wives and mothers who either worked little part-time jobs or didn't work outside the home. Any woman who said she wanted to pursue a full-time career was considered kind of strange. Attitudes on campus are so different today. There are a number of female professors, who are role models to young women—they are living proof that women can have careers and families. And this generation of students doesn't assume women are going to school to get their "Mrs. degrees." A majority of the female students I know have serious career ambitions, and most of the male students seem to assume their female classmates and girlfriends will work full time for most of their lives. What a difference twenty years has made in how women are viewed.*

The individualistic ethic so prominent in the United States is not valued or considered normal in many other countries, particularly Asian and African ones

Hulton Getty Picture Collection

(Gaines, 1995). There are also countries in which heterosexuality is not the only sexual preference regarded as normal. Some cultures even recognize more than two genders!

Social meanings also vary across time within single cultures. For example, in the 1700s and 1800s, women in the United States were defined as too delicate to engage in hard labor. During the World Wars, however, women were expected to do "men's work" while men were at war. When the men returned home, society once again decreed that women were too weak to perform in the labor market, and they were reassigned to home and hearth. The frail, pale appearance considered feminine in the 1800s gave way to robust, fleshy ideals in the mid-1900s as embodied by Marilyn Monroe. Today a more athletic body is one of the ideals prescribed for women. Magazines such as *Women's Sports and Fitness* reflect and encourage the current view that strength and athletic ability are feminine.

Social prescriptions for men have also varied. The rugged he-man who was the ideal in the 1800s disposed of unsavory rustlers and relied on his physical strength to farm wild lands. After the Industrial Revolution, physical strength and bravado gave way to business acumen, and money replaced muscle as a sign of manliness. Today, as our society struggles with changes in women, men, and families, the ideals of manhood are being revised yet again. Increasingly, men are expected to be involved in caring for children and to be sensitive as well as independent and strong.

APPLY THE IDEA
Social Definitions of Masculinity and Femininity

To find out how society in general (the generalized other) defines ideals for women and men today, review five current popular magazines. You may review them in the library or on-line, using your *InfoTrac College Edition.* Select magazines that aim at college-age readers. Ideally, your sample should include ones that aim primarily at White (*Cosmopolitan, Sports Illustrated*) and non-White audiences (*Essence, Ebony*). In reviewing the magazines, answer the following questions:

- How many females are shown actively involved in pursuits such as sports or manual labor?
- How many females are shown in passive roles such as relaxing, eating, or waiting for others?
- How many females are shown in domestic settings or engaged in domestic activities such as preparing meals and caring for children?
- How many males are shown actively involved in pursuits such as sports or manual labor?
- How many males are shown in passive roles such as relaxing, eating, or waiting for others?

CONTINUED

- How many males are shown in domestic settings and/or engaged in domestic activities such as preparing meals and caring for children?
- How many females are slender and thin?
- How many males are muscular and strong?
- How many members of minorities are shown?
- How many members of minorities have features that are more typical of Caucasians than their racial or ethnic groups?

COMMUNICATION NOTES

The Reality of Race

For centuries race has been used as a primary way of classifying people. Yet, most scientists now reject the concept of race as a valid means of defining individual and group identities. According to Jonathan Marks, a biologist at Yale University, "race has no biological reality."

Increasingly scientists assert that race is only a socially constructed category. DNA research reveals that there is no scientific basis for the racial categories widely used in society. According to DNA studies, there is actually far more genetic variation within a single African population than in all non-African populations together. Loring Brace, an anthropologist at the University of Michigan, reports that intelligence is one human trait that doesn't vary from population to population. According to Brace, the differences among people grouped into different races that show up on intelligence tests reflect environmental and cultural factors, including differing levels of nutrition and quality of education. The differences on the IQ tests don't reflect innate intellectual capacity, says Brace.

SOURCE: Boyd, R. (1996, October 9). Notion of separate races rejected. *Raleigh News and Observer*, pp. 1A, 15A.

The meaning of homosexuality has also been revised over time in Western culture. Until fairly recently, our society strongly disapproved of gays, lesbians, and bisexuals, so most nonheterosexuals did not publicly acknowledge their affectional preference. Although much prejudice still exists, it is gradually diminishing. As we noted earlier, homosexual marriages are recognized in some places around the world. Laws protecting lesbians and gays against housing and job discrimination are also being enacted. As social views of homosexuality change, more and more gays and lesbians are openly acknowledging their sexuality.

The meaning our society assigns to different races has also varied markedly over our history as a nation. African Americans who once had no basic rights now have the same legal rights as Caucasians. Hispanics, Latinas and Latinos, Asian Americans, and other peoples of color are increasingly recognized and valued in the United States. Although racial ignorance and prejudice still haunt our nation, they are lessening. Today many teachers recognize and celebrate the strengths of students of various races: As the generalized other's perspective on diverse ethnicities enlarges, people of color gain more positive reflected appraisals of their identity than was the case years ago. "The Reality of Race" discusses the issue of race as a social, not biological, reality.

Other socially constructed views are also variable. In the 1950s and 1960s, people with disabilities were often kept in their homes or put in institutions. Today, many schools endorse mainstreaming, which places students who have physical or mental handicaps in regular classrooms. Sensitivity to people who have special problems grows as nonhandicapped students become familiar with people with disabilities.

The meaning of age has also varied throughout U.S. history. In the 1800s, the average lifespan was less than sixty years, and it was not uncommon for people to die in their forties or fifties. Then, fifty was considered old, but few people today would regard fifty as old. The average lifespan today is nearly seventy, making fifty seem considerably less old. In the 1800s, people typically married in their teens, and they often had five or more children before reaching thirty.

Today many people wait until their thirties to begin having children, and parents in their forties aren't considered "too old."

Changing Social Views   Our discussion suggests that social perspectives are changeable. As we have seen, they have, in fact, changed significantly over time. Social perspectives are fluid and respond to individual and collective efforts to weave new meanings into the fabric of social life. From 1848 until 1920, many women fought to change social views of women, and they succeeded in gaining rights for women to vote, attend universities, and so forth. In the 1960s, civil rights activism launched nationwide rethinking of actions and attitudes toward non-Whites. The battle to recognize and value gays and lesbians is more recent, yet already it has altered social perspectives. Each of us has the responsibility to speak out against social perspectives that we perceive as wrong or harmful. By doing so we participate in the ongoing process of refining who we are as a society.

STUDENT VOICES

JENNIFER: *My parents are pretty straight-laced and conservative. They brought me up to think homosexuals are sinners and Whites are better than any other race. But I don't think like that now, and I've been speaking my mind when I'm home to visit my folks. At first they got angry and said they didn't send me to college to get a bunch of crazy liberal ideas, but gradually they are coming around a little. I think I am changing how they think by voicing my views.*

In sum, meanings for facets of identity are socially created. Because they are arbitrary constructions, they vary over time and across cultures. This highlights the power of individuals and groups to shape social understandings that make up the generalized other. Just as our culture shapes who we are, we too shape our culture. In the final section of this chapter, we consider guidelines for improving self-concept.

Guidelines for Improving Self-Concept

So far we have explored how we form our self-concepts through interaction with others and participation in society. Although this information helps us understand how we developed our current views of ourselves, it doesn't tell us a great deal about how we might transform aspects of our self-concepts that are unconstructive and hold us back. As we will see, there are ways to strengthen our identities.

Make a Firm Commitment to Change

The first principle for changing self-concept is the most difficult and most important. You must make a firm commitment to cultivating personal growth.

This isn't as easy as it might sound. A firm commitment involves more than saying "I want to be better" or "I want to like myself more." Saying these sentences is simple. What is more difficult is actually investing energy and effort to bring about change. A firm commitment requires that we keep trying. From the start, you need to realize that changing how you think of yourself is a major project.

It is difficult to change self-concept for two reasons. First, doing so requires continuous effort. Because the self is a process, it is not formed in one fell swoop, and it cannot be changed in a moment of decision. We have to be willing to invest effort in an ongoing way. In addition, we must realize at the outset that there will be setbacks, and we can't let them derail our resolution to change. Last year a student said she wanted to be more assertive, so she began speaking up more often in class. When a professor criticized one of her contributions, her resolution folded. Changing how we see ourselves is a long-term process.

A second reason it is difficult to change self-concept is that the self resists change. Morris Rosenberg (1979), a psychologist who has studied self-concept extensively, says that most humans tend to resist change and that we also seek esteem or a positive view of ourselves. The good news is that we want esteem or a positive self-image; the bad news is that we find it difficult to change, even in positive directions. Interestingly, Rosenberg and others have found that we are as likely to hold on to negative self-images as we are positive ones. Apparently, consistency itself is comforting. If you realize in advance that you may struggle against change, you'll be prepared for the tension that accompanies personal growth. Because change is a process and the self resists change, a firm commitment to improving your self-concept is essential.

Gain Knowledge As a Basis for Personal Change

Commitment alone is insufficient to bring about constructive changes in who you are. In addition, you need several types of knowledge. First, you need to understand how your self-concept was formed. In this chapter, we've seen that much of how we see ourselves results from socially constructed values. Based on what you've learned, you can exercise critical judgment about which social perspectives to accept and which to reject. For instance, you may not wish to go along with our society's evaluations of race, gender, sexual preference, and class.

STUDENT VOICES

TINA: One social value I do not accept is that it's good to be as thin as a rail if you're female. A lot of my girlfriends are always dieting. Even when they get weak from not eating enough, they won't eat because they'll gain weight. I know several girls who are bulimic, which is really dangerous, but they are more scared of gaining a pound than of dying. I just flat refuse to buy into this social value. I'm not fat, but I'm not skinny either. I'm not as thin as models, and I'm not aiming to be. It's just stupid to go around hungry all the time because society has sick views of beauty for women.

Second, you need to know what changes are desirable and how to bring them about. Often our ideas about changing ourselves are too vague and abstract to be useful. For instance, "I want to be more skillful at intimate communication" or "I want to be a better friend" are very abstract objectives. You can't move toward such fuzzy goals until you know something about the talk that enhances and impedes intimacy and what people value in friends. Books such as this one will help you pinpoint concrete skills that facilitate your own goals for personal change. Someone who wants to be a better friend might focus on developing empathic listening skills and creating supportive communication climates. The goal of being adept at intimate communication requires learning how to self-disclose appropriately, manage conflict constructively, and engage in dual perspective. In later chapters, we will discuss these and other specific skills that advance interpersonal communication competence in particular relationships and settings.

In addition to reading this book and learning from your class, there are other ways to gain knowledge to help you set and achieve goals of personal improvement. One very important source of knowledge is other people. Talking with others is a way to learn about relationships and what people want in them. Others can also provide useful feedback on your interpersonal skills and your progress in the process of change. Finally, others can provide models. If you know someone you think is particularly skillful in supporting others, observe her or him carefully to identify particular communication skills. You may not want to imitate this person exactly, but observing will make you more aware of concrete skills involved in supporting others. You may choose to tailor some of the skills others display to suit your personal style.

Set Goals That Are Realistic and Fair

Although it is true that willpower can do marvelous things, it does have limits. We need to recognize that trying to change how we see ourselves works only when our goals are realistic. If you are shy and want to be more extroverted, it is reasonable to try to speak up more and socialize more often. On the other hand, it may not be reasonable to aim at being the life of the party you're going to next week.

Realistic goals require realistic standards. Often dissatisfaction with ourselves stems from unrealistic expectations. In a culture that emphasizes perfectionism, it's easy to be trapped into expecting more than is humanly possible. If you define a goal of being a totally perfect communicator in all situations, you are setting yourself up for failure. It's more reasonable and constructive to establish a series of realistic small goals that can be met. You might focus on improving one of the skills of communication competence we discussed in Chapter 1. When you are satisfied with your ability at that skill, you can move on to a second one. Remembering our discussion of social comparison, it's also important to select reasonable measuring sticks for ourselves. It isn't realistic to compare your academic work to that of a certified genius. It *is* reasonable to measure your academic performance against others who have intellectual abilities similar to your own. Setting realistic goals and selecting appropriate standards of comparison are important in bringing about change in yourself.

KENDRICK: *I really got bummed out my freshman year. I had been the star on my high school basketball team, so I came to college expecting to be a star here too. The first day of practice, I saw a lot of guys who were better than I was. They were incredible. I felt like nothing. When I got back to my room, I called my mom and told her I was no good at basketball here. She told me I couldn't expect to compete with guys who had been on the team for a while and who had gotten coaching. She asked how I stacked up against just the other first-year players, and I said pretty good. She told me they were the ones to compare myself to.*

Being realistic also involves making fair assessments of ourselves. This requires us to place judgments in context and to see ourselves as in process. To assess ourselves effectively, we need to understand not just our discrete qualities and abilities, but also how all of our parts fit together to form the whole self. One of the ways we treat ourselves unfairly is to judge particular abilities out of context. For example, my friend Meg is a very accomplished writer, but she faults herself constantly for not spending as much time as her neighbor in volunteer activities. Meg's neighbor doesn't work outside of the home, so she has more time to volunteer for social causes. The lesson here is that we have to appreciate our particular skills and weaknesses in the overall context of who we are. It might be reasonable for my friend to acknowledge she doesn't volunteer a great deal of time if she also recognizes her impressive achievements in writing. However, when judging her writing she compares herself to Marilyn French, Pat Conroy, Marge Piercy, and other writers of national stature. Meg's self-assessment is unrealistic because she compares herself to people who are extremely successful in particular spheres of life, yet she doesn't notice that her models are not especially impressive in other areas. As a result, she mistakenly feels she is inadequate in most ways. In our efforts to improve self-concept, then, we should acknowledge our strengths and virtues as well as parts of ourselves we wish to change.

SALLY FORTH © 1997. Reprinted with special permission of King Features Syndicate.

TIMOTEO: *I've really struggled with my academic goals. It's very important to me and my whole family that I do well in school. I am the first in my family to go to college, so I must succeed. I've felt bad when I make Bs and Cs and others in my classes make As. For a long time, I said to myself, "I am not as smart as they are if they make better grades." But I work 35 hours a week to pay for school. Most of the others in my classes either don't have to work or work fewer hours than I do. They have more time to spend writing papers and studying for tests. I think better of my academic abilities when I compare myself to other students who work as much as I do. That is a more fair comparison than comparing myself to students who don't work.*

A key foundation for improving self-concept is accepting yourself as *in process*. Earlier in this chapter, we saw that one characteristic of the human self is that it is continuously in process, always becoming. This implies several things. First, it means you need to accept who you are now as a starting point. You don't have to like or admire everything about yourself, but it is important to accept who you are today as a basis for going forward (Wood, 1992a). The self that you are results from all of the interactions, reflected appraisals, and social comparisons you have made during your life. You cannot change your past, but neither do you have to be bound by it forever. Only by realizing and accepting who you now are can you move ahead.

Accepting yourself as in process also implies that you realize you can change. Who you are is not who you will be in five or ten years. Because you are in process, you are always changing and growing. Don't let yourself be hindered by defeating self-fulfilling prophecies or the mindtrap that you cannot change (Rusk & Rusk, 1988). You can change if you set realistic goals, make a genuine commitment, and then work for the changes you want. Remember that you are not fixed as you are; you are always in the process of becoming.

Create a Context That Supports Personal Change

Just as it is easier to swim with the tide than against it, it is easier to change our views of ourselves when we have some support for our efforts. You can do a lot to create an environment that supports your growth by choosing contexts and people who help you realize your goals.

First think about settings. If you want to improve your physical condition, it makes more sense to go to intramural courts than to hang out in bars. If you want to lose weight, it's better to go to restaurants that serve healthy foods and offer light choices than to go to cholesterol castles. If you want to become more extroverted, you need to put yourself in social situations, rather than in libraries. But libraries are a better context than parties if your goal is to improve academic performance.

BOB: *I never drank much until I got into this one group at school. All of them drank all the time. It was easy to join them. In fact, it was pretty hard not to drink and still be one of the guys. This year I decided I was drinking too much, and I wanted to stop. It was hard enough not to keep drinking, because the guys were always doing it, but what really made it hard was the ways the guys got on me for abstaining. They let me know I was being uncool and made me feel like a jerk. Finally, to stop drinking, I had to get a different apartment.*

Who we are with has a great deal to do with how we see ourselves and how worthy we feel we are. This means we can create a supportive context by consciously choosing to be around people who believe in us and encourage our personal growth. It's equally important to steer clear of people who pull us down or say we can't change. In other words, people who reflect positive appraisals of us enhance our ability to improve who we are.

One way to think about how others' communication affects how we feel about ourselves is to realize that others can be uppers, downers, and vultures. **Uppers** are people who communicate positively about us and who reflect positive appraisals of our self-worth. They notice our strengths, see our progress, and accept our weaknesses and problems without discounting us. When we're around uppers, we feel more upbeat and positive about ourselves. Uppers aren't necessarily unconditionally positive in their communication. A true friend can be an upper by recognizing our weaknesses and helping us work on them. Instead of putting us down, an upper believes in us and helps us believe in ourselves and our capacity to change. Identify two uppers in your life.

Downers are people who communicate negatively about us and our self-worth. They call attention to our flaws, emphasize our problems, and put down our dreams and goals. When we're around downers, we tend to feel down about ourselves. Reflecting their perspectives, we're more aware of our weaknesses

FoxTrot

and less confident of what we can accomplish when we're around downers. Identify two downers in your life.

Vultures are an extreme form of downers. They not only communicate negative images of us, but attack our self-concepts just as actual vultures prey on their victims (Simon, 1977). Sometimes vultures initiate harsh criticism. They say, "That outfit looks dreadful on you" or "You really blew that one." In other cases, vultures pick up on our own self-doubts and magnify them. They find our weak spots and exploit them; they pick us apart by focusing on sensitive areas in our self-concept. For example, a friend of mine is inefficient in managing his time and is very sensitive about this. I once observed a co-worker pick him apart just as a vulture picks apart its prey. The co-worker said, "I can't believe this is all you've done. You're the most unproductive person I've ever known. What a waste! Your output doesn't justify your salary." That harangue typifies the attack on self-worth that vultures enjoy. By telling us we are inadequate, vultures demolish our self-esteem. Can you identify vultures in your life?

Reflect on how you feel about yourself when you're with uppers, downers, and vultures. Can you see how powerfully others' communication affects your self-concept? You might also think about the people for whom you are an upper, downer, or vulture.

Others aren't the only ones whose communication affects our self-concepts. We also communicate with ourselves, and our own messages influence our esteem. One of the most crippling kinds of self-talk we can engage in is **self-sabotage.** This involves telling ourselves we are no good, we can't do something, there's no point in trying to change, and so forth. We may be repeating judgments others made of us or may be inventing negative self-fulfilling prophecies ourselves. Either way, self-sabotage defeats us because it undermines belief in ourselves. Self-sabotage is poisonous; it destroys our motivation to change and grow. We can be downers or even vultures, just as others can be. In fact, we can probably do more damage to our self-concepts than others can because we are most aware of our vulnerabilities and fears. This may explain why vultures were originally described as people who put themselves down.

We can also be uppers for ourselves. We can affirm our strengths, encourage our growth, and fortify our sense of self-worth. Positive self-talk builds motivation and belief in yourself. It is also a useful strategy to interrupt and challenge negative messages from yourself and others. The next time you hear yourself saying "I can't do . . ." or someone else says "You'll never change," challenge the self-defeating message with self-talk. Say out loud to yourself, "I can do it. I will change." Use positive self-talk to resist counterproductive communication about yourself.

Before leaving this discussion, we should make it clear that improving your self-concept is not facilitated by uncritical positive communication. None of us grows and improves when we listen only to praise, particularly if it is less than honest. The true uppers in our lives offer constructive criticism as a way to encourage us to reach for better versions of ourselves.

Improving Your Self-Concept

1. Define one change you would like to make in yourself. It might be a behavior or a self-fulfilling prophecy or anything about yourself you would like to alter.

2. Write down the change you desire to make. Use strong, affirmative language to motivate yourself. For example, "I will listen more carefully to friends," or "I will start speaking up in classes."

3. Refine your general goal by making sure it is realistic and fair. Write out your refined goal using specific language. For example, "I want to show my two best friends that I am paying attention when they talk to me," or "I want to make one comment in each meeting of one class this week."

4. Place the card or paper where you will see it often. Each time you see the card, repeat the message aloud to yourself. This should help sustain your commitment to making the change.

5. Observe others who are models for what you want to be. Write down what they do. Use specific language to describe how they communicate. For example, "Tracy nods a lot and repeats back what others say so they know she is listening," or "James provides examples of concepts in class so that the ideas are more concrete."

6. Select contexts that assist you in reaching your goal. For example, "I will talk with my friends in private settings where there aren't distractions that interfere with listening well," or "I will begin speaking up in class in my Communication 100 course because it is the most discussion-oriented and because other students make a lot of comments there. Later I will speak up in my sociology course, which is more lecture-oriented."

In sum, improving your self-concept requires being in contexts that support growth and change. Seek out experiences and settings that foster belief in yourself and the changes you desire. Also, recognize uppers, downers, and vultures in yourself and others, and learn which people and which kinds of communication assist you in achieving your own goals for self-improvement.

C H A P T E R
Summary

In this chapter, we explored the self as a process that evolves over the course of our lives. We saw that the self is not present at birth, but develops as we interact with others. Through communication we learn and import social perspectives, both those of particular others and those of the generalized other, or society as a whole. Reflected appraisals, direct definitions, and social comparisons are communication processes that shape how we see ourselves and how we change over time. The perspective of the generalized other includes social views of aspects of identity, including race, gender, sexual preference, and class. These, however, are arbitrary social constructions that we may challenge once we are adults. When we resist counterproductive social views, we promote change in society.

The final section of the chapter focused on ways to improve self-concept. Guidelines for doing this are to make a firm commitment to personal growth, acquire knowledge about desired changes and concrete skills, set realistic goals, assess yourself fairly, and create contexts that support the changes you seek. Transforming how we see ourselves is not easy, but it is possible. We can make amazing changes in who we are and how we feel about ourselves when we embrace our human capacity to make choices.

Concepts

- anxious/resistant attachment style
- attachment styles
- direct definition
- dismissive attachment style
- downers
- ego boundaries
- fearful attachment style

- identity scripts
- particular others
- perspective of the generalized other
- reflected appraisal
- secure attachment style
- self

- self-fulfilling prophecy
- self-sabotage
- social comparison
- uppers
- vultures

F O R   F U R T H E R

Thought & Discussion

1. Complete the last Apply the Idea exercise in this chapter. Set a specific, fair, realistic goal for improving your interpersonal communication. For the next two weeks focus on making progress toward that goal, following the guidelines in this chapter. Share the results of your work with others in your class.

2. Talk with one man and one woman who are twenty years older than you. Talk with one man and one woman who are forty years older than you. In each conversation, ask them to explain how men and women were expected to be when they were twenty years old. Ask them to describe how women and men were expected to act and dress. Ask them to explain what behaviors, goals, and attitudes were considered inappropriate for women and men when they were twenty years old. Compare their responses to views held by twenty-year-olds today.

3. Discuss the idea of race with members of your class. You may want to reread "The Construction of Race in America" and "The Reality of Race" in this chapter. What is race? Is it a useful way of classifying people? Why or why not? Do you think the Census Bureau should allow individuals to check off multiple races to define themselves?

4. Think about a time when you tried to create some change in yourself and were not successful. Review what happened by applying the four principles for improving self-concept presented in the last section of this chapter. Now that you understand these principles, how might you be more effective if today you wanted to create that same change in yourself?

5. Use your *InfoTrac College Edition* to locate one article in a journal that discusses the concept of race. What did you learn from reading this article about the relationship between race and personal identity?

Perception

and

Communication

• • •

• • •

• • •

This chapter focuses on meaning, which is the heart of communication. To understand how humans create meanings for themselves and their activities, we need to explore relationships between perception and communication. As we will see, these two processes interact so that each affects the other in an ongoing cycle of influence. In other words, perception shapes how we understand others' communication and how we ourselves communicate. At the same time, communication influences our perceptions of people and situations. The two processes are intricately intertwined in the overall quilt of perception. Before reading further, try to connect the nine dots at left. You may use no more than four lines, the lines must be straight, and the lines must be connected to one another.

To understand how perception and communication interact, we will first discuss the three-part process of perception. Next, we'll consider factors that affect our perceptions. Finally, we will explore ways to improve our abilities to perceive and communicate effectively.

Before we get into those topics, let's return to the nine dots problem. Could you solve it? Most people who have trouble solving the problem are stymied because they label the nine dots a "square," and they try to connect the dots staying within the boundaries of a square. However, it's impossible to connect the dots with four straight lines if you define them as a closed square. One solution appears at the end of the chapter, on page 111.

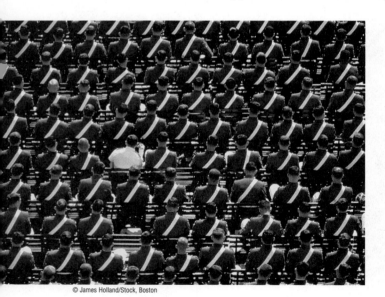
© James Holland/Stock, Boston

This exercise makes an important point about the topics we'll consider in this chapter. The label "square" affects how you perceive the nine dots. In the same fashion, our words affect how we perceive others, situations, and ourselves. At the same time, our perceptions, which are always incomplete and subjective, shape what things mean to us and the labels we use to describe them. As long as we perceive the nine dots as a square, we won't be able to solve the problem. Similarly, we communicate with others according to how we perceive and define them, and we may miss opportunities when our labels limit what we perceive. In the pages that follow, we want to unravel the complex relationships between perception and communication.

The Process of Human Perception

When we talk about perception, we're concerned with how we make sense of the world and what happens in it. **Perception** is an active process of creating meaning by selecting, organizing, and interpreting people, objects, events, situations, and activities. The first thing to notice about this definition is that perception is an active process. We are not passive receivers of what is "out there" in the external world. Instead, we actively work to make sense of ourselves, others, and our interactions. To do so, we select only certain things to notice, and then we organize and interpret what we have selectively noticed. What anything means to us depends on which aspects of it we attend to and how we organize and interpret what we notice. Thus, perception is not a simple matter of recording external reality. Instead, we actively interact with the world to construct what it means to us (see Figure 3.1).

Perception consists of three processes—selecting, organizing, and interpreting. These processes are continuous, so they blend into one another. They are also interactive, so each of them affects the other two. For example, what we select to perceive in a particular situation affects how we organize and interpret the situation. At the same time, how we organize and interpret a situation affects our subsequent selections of what to perceive in the situation.

Selection

Organization
Cognitive schemata

Interpretation
Attributions

FIGURE 3.1
The Process of Human Perception

Selection

Stop for a moment and notice what is going on around you right now. Is there music in the background or perhaps several different kinds of music from different places? Is the room warm or cold, messy or clean, large or small, light or dark? Is there laundry in the corner waiting to be washed? Can you smell anything—food being cooked, the stale odor of cigarette smoke, traces of cologne? Who else is in the room and nearby? Do you hear other conversations? Is the window open? Can you hear muted sounds of activities outside? Now think about what's happening inside you: Are you alert or sleepy, hungry, comfortable? Do you have a headache or an itch anywhere? On what kind of paper is your book printed? Is the type large, small, easy to read? How do you like the size of the book, the colors used, the design for inserts in the text?

Chances are that you weren't conscious of most of these phenomena when you began reading the chapter. Instead, you focused on reading and understanding the material in the book. You narrowed your attention to what you defined as important in this moment, and you were unaware of many other things going on around you. This is typical of how we live our lives. We can't attend to everything in our environment, because there is simply far too much there, and most of it isn't relevant to us at a particular time.

We select the stimuli we attend to based on a number of factors. First, some qualities of external phenomena draw attention. For instance, we notice things that **STAND OUT** because they are larger, more intense, or more unusual than other phenomena. So we're more likely to hear a loud voice than a soft one and to notice someone in a bright shirt than someone in a drab one. Change also compels attention, which is why we may take for granted all of the

FIGURE 3.2
Perception

pleasant interactions with a friend and notice only the tense moments.

Sometimes we deliberately influence what we notice by indicating things to ourselves (Mead, 1934). In fact, in many ways education is a process of learning to indicate to ourselves things we hadn't seen. Right now you're learning to be more conscious of the selectiveness of your perceptions, so in the future you will notice this more on your own. In English courses, you learn to notice how authors craft characters and use words to create images. Women's studies classes heighten awareness of the consistent absence of women in conventional accounts of history. In every case, we learn to perceive things we previously didn't recognize. Take a look at Figure 3.2. What do you see?

Suzanne illustrates how we can use selective perception to our advantage.

S T U D E N T **VOICES**

SUZANNE: *I decided to use the information about selective attention to stop smoking. Usually when I smoked, I noticed how relaxing it was to puff a cigarette and how much I liked the flavor. But this week when I lit up, I would focus on the burning smell of the match. Then I would notice how the smoke hurt my eyes when it rose from the cigarette. I also noticed how nasty ashtrays look with butts in them and how bad a room smells when I've been smoking in it. Once I really paid attention to everything I disliked about cigarettes, I was able to stop. I haven't had one in six days!*

What we select to notice is also influenced by who we are and what is going on in us. Our motives and needs affect what we see and don't see. If you've just broken up with a partner, you're more likely to notice attractive people at a party than if you are in an established relationship. Motives also explain the oasis phenomenon in which thirsty people stranded in a desert see an oasis although none really exists. Our expectations further affect what we notice. We are more likely to perceive what we expect to perceive and what others have led us to anticipate, as discussed in "Expectations and Perception." This explains the self-fulfilling prophecy that we discussed in Chapter 2. A child who is told she is unlovable may perceive herself that way and may notice rejecting but not affirming communication from others. We selectively tune in to only some stimuli, so that we simplify the complexities of the total reality in which we live.

Cultures also influence what we selectively perceive. In countries such as Sweden, homosexuality is socially and legally accepted. In the United States there is less acceptance of gays and lesbians. Because homosexuality isn't defined as normal in this country, we notice gays and lesbians more than heterosexuals. They stand out because our culture has led us to perceive them as unusual. Assertiveness and competitiveness are encouraged and considered good in the United States, so we don't find it odd when people compete and try to beat each other. By contrast, traditional Asian cultures emphasize group loyalty, cooperation, and not causing others to lose face. Thus, in many Asian societies competitive individuality is noticed and considered negatively. In Korea, age is a very important aspect of individuals—the older a person is, the more he or she is to be respected. Koreans also place a priority on family relations. Consequently, Koreans learn to selectively perceive the age and family role of people to whom they are speaking. Korean

COMMUNICATION NOTES

Expectations and Perception

In a class experiment, racially prejudiced and unprejudiced Caucasians were asked to describe African Americans pictured in photographs. The prejudiced viewers "saw" stereotypical racial characteristics such as broadness of noses and fullness of lips, even when those features were not objectively present. The unprejudiced viewers did not notice stereotypical racial qualities. This study demonstrates how powerfully our expectations can mold what we see.

SOURCE: Secord, P. F., Bevan, W., & Katz, B. (1956). The Negro stereotype and perceptual accentuation. *Journal of Abnormal and Social Psychology, 54,* 78–83.

language reflects the cultural value placed on age and family tie by including distinct words to refer to people of different ages and different family status: *gahndah* is used to refer to a teenage peer; *gah*, to a parent; and *gahneh*, to a grandparent (Ferrante, 1995; Park, 1979).

Organization

Once we have selected what to notice, we must make sense of it. We don't simply collect perceptions and string them together randomly; instead, we organize them in meaningful ways. The most developed and useful theory for explaining how we organize experience is **constructivism,** which states that we organize and interpret experience by applying cognitive structures called schemata. Originally developed by George Kelly in 1955, constructivism has been elaborated by scholars in communication and psychology. We rely on four schemata to make sense of interpersonal phenomena: prototypes, personal constructs, stereotypes, and scripts (Figure 3.3).

Prototypes   **Prototypes** are knowledge structures that define the clearest or most representative examples of some category (Fehr, 1993). For example, you probably have a prototype of great teachers, boring teachers, true friends, and perfect romantic partners. Each of these categories is exemplified by a person who is the ideal case—that's the prototype. We use prototypes to place others in categories: Jane is a confidante, Burt is someone to hang out with, Corina is a romantic interest, Elvira is an enemy. Each category of people is exemplified by one person who best represents the whole group.

S T U D E N T   VOICES

DAMION: *The person who is my ideal of a friend is my buddy Jackson. He stood by me when I got into a lot of trouble a couple of years ago. I got mixed up with some guys who used drugs, and I started using them too. Pretty soon the coach figured out what was going on, and he suspended me from the team. I felt like I was finished when he did that, and then I really got into drugs. But Jackson wouldn't give up on me, and he wouldn't let me give up either.*

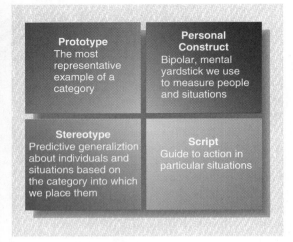

| **Prototype** The most representative example of a category | **Personal Construct** Bipolar, mental yardstick we use to measure people and situations |
| **Stereotype** Predictive generaliztion about individuals and situations based on the category into which we place them | **Script** Guide to action in particular situations |

FIGURE 3.3
Cognitive Schemata

HMMM ... COLD HEARTED, SERVES NO APPARENT FUNCTION, AND CAN'T MAKE A MOVE WITHOUT ASSISTANCE... GOOD LORD, HE'S *PERFECT!*

THE DISCOVERY OF THE EXECUTIVE PROTOTYPE

1-3

©1997 Washington Post Writers Group

E-mail: Wileytoon@aol.com
www.washingtonpost.com/wiley

NON SEQUITUR © 1997 Washington Post Writers Group.

He took me to a drug center and went there with me every day for three weeks. He never turned away when I was sick or even when I cried most of one night when I was getting off the drugs. He just stood by me. Once I was straight, Jackson went with me to see the coach about getting back on the team.

We also have prototypes for relationships. We have models for the ideal friendship, family, business group, or romantic relationship. Communication scholar Beverly Fehr and her colleagues (Fehr, 1993; Fehr & Russell, 1991) report that in the United States the prototype of romantic relationships is made up of five qualities: trust, caring, honesty, friendship, and respect. Although passion may come to mind when we think of love, it seems less central to our prototype of love than companionship and caring.

Prototypes define categories by identifying ideal cases. We classify people by asking which of our prototypes they most closely resemble. Prototypes organize our perceptions by allowing us to place people and other phenomena in broad categories. We then consider how close they are to the prototype, or exemplar, of that category.

Personal Constructs **Personal constructs** are "mental yardsticks" we use to measure people and situations along bipolar dimensions of judgment (Kelly, 1955). Examples of personal constructs are intelligent–unintelligent, kind–unkind, interesting–boring, arrogant–modest, assertive–passive, and attractive–unattractive. To size up an individual, we measure her or him by personal constructs that we use to distinguish among people. How intelligent, kind, or attractive is this person? Whereas prototypes help decide into which broad category a person or event fits, personal constructs let us make more detailed assessments of particular qualities of phenomena we perceive.

S   T   U   D   E   N   T   VOICES

NAI LEE: *One of the ways I look at people is by whether they are indepen-dent or related to others. That is one of the first judgments I make of others. In Korea we are not so individualistic or independent as people in the United States. We think of ourselves more as members of families and communities than as individuals. The emphasis on independent identity was the first thing I noticed when I came to this country, and it is still an important way I look at people.*

The personal constructs we rely on fundamentally shape our perceptions, because we define something only in the terms of the constructs we use. Notice that we structure what we perceive and what it means by the constructs we choose to use. Thus, we may not notice qualities of people that aren't covered by the constructs we apply.

Changing Constructs — Changing Perceptions

Use the left-hand column below to list five constructs that are important in how you perceive potential romantic partners.

1. _____   1. _____
2. _____   2. _____
3. _____   3. _____
4. _____   4. _____
5. _____   5. _____

Now use the right-hand column to list five other constructs that you could use when you are perceiving potential romantic partners.

How would using the constructs on the right alter or enlarge your perceptions of people you are considering as romantic partners?

Stereotypes **Stereotypes** are predictive generalizations about people and situations. Based on the category in which we place someone or something and how it measures up against personal constructs we apply, we predict what it will do. For instance, if you define someone as a liberal, you might stereotype her or him as likely to vote Democratic, support social legislation, be pro-environment, and so forth. You may have stereotypes of fraternity and sorority members, athletes, and people from other cultures. The stereotypes you have don't necessarily reflect actual similarities among people. Instead, stereotypes are based on our perceptions of similarities among people or on widely held stereotypes we've internalized. We may perceive similarities that others don't, and we may fail to perceive commonalities that are obvious to others.

STUDENT VOICES

PHYLLIS: *I'll tell you what stereotype really gets to me: the older student. I'm thirty-eight and working on my degree, and everyone at this college treats me like a housewife who's dabbling in courses. The students treat me like their mother, not a peer. And the faculty are even worse sometimes. I've had several professors who don't take my questions or my work seriously. One even said to me that I shouldn't worry about grades, since I didn't have to plan a career like the younger students. Well, I am planning a career, I am a student, and I am serious about my work.*

Social critic Eric Bates (1994) worries that grouping people into racial categories and basing expectations on race may perpetuate racist stereotypes. Bates also believes that racial categories are no longer accurate for describing people with increasingly multiracial heritages, as discussed in "I'm Cablinasian!" and in "Life in the Missing Boxes" on page 88. Even the U.S. Census Bureau is struggling with how to create categories that can provide useful and accurate information on social groups. Is the term *Asian*, for instance, useful for describing people from varied cultures including Japan, Malaysia, Nepal, and China? A student of mine, Winowa, asks a similar question about the term *Native American*.

S T U D E N T VOICES

WINOWA: *People have a stereotype of Native Americans. People who are not Native American think we are all alike—how we look, how we act, what we believe, what our traditions are. But that isn't true. The Crow and Apache are as different as people from Kenya and New York. Some tribes have a history of aggression and violence; others have traditions of peace and harmony. We worship different spirits and have different tribal rituals and customs. All of these differences are lost when people stereotype us all into one group.*

Stereotypes may be accurate or inaccurate. In some cases we have incorrect understandings of a group, and in other cases individual members of a group don't conform to the behaviors typical of a group as a whole. Although we need stereotypes in order to predict what will happen around us, they can be harmful if we forget that they are based on our perceptions, not objective reality.

Scripts   The final cognitive schemata we use to organize perceptions is **scripts**, which are guides to action based on our experiences and observations of interaction. Scripts consist of a sequence of activities that define what we and others are expected to do in specific situations. Many of our daily activities are governed by scripts, although we're often unaware of them. You have a script for greeting casual acquaintances as you walk around campus ("Hey, how ya doing?" "Fine—can't complain," "See ya"). You also have scripts for dating, managing conflict, talking with professors, dealing with clerks, and hanging out with friends. Scripts organize perceptions into lines of action. ("A Script for Romance" on page 89 describes the commonly held ideas of romance in our culture.)

Prototypes, personal constructs, stereotypes, and scripts are cognitive schemata that organize our thinking about people and situations. We use them to make sense of what we notice and to figure out how we and others will act in particular situations. All four cognitive schemata reflect the perspectives of particular others and the generalized other. As we interact with people, we internalize our culture's ways of classifying, measuring, and predicting phenomena and its norms for acting in various situations.

Social perspectives are not always accurate or constructive, so we shouldn't accept them blindly. For instance, if your parents engaged in bitter, destructive quarreling, you may have learned a script for conflict that will undermine your relationships. Similarly, cultural views of groups that are not mainstream are often negative and inaccurate, so we should assess them critically before using them to organize our own perceptions and direct our own activities.

APPLY THE IDEA

Sizing Up Others

Pay attention to the cognitive schemata you use the next time you meet a new person. First notice how you classify the person. Do you categorize her or him as a potential friend, date, bureaucrat, neighbor? Next, identify the constructs you use to assess the person. Do you focus on physical characteristics (attractive–unattractive), mental qualities (intelligent–unintelligent), psychological features (secure–insecure), and/or interpersonal qualities (eligible–committed)? Would different constructs be prominent if you used a different prototype to classify the person? Now, note how you stereotype the person. What do you expect him or her to do based on the prototype and constructs you've applied? Finally, identify your script—how you expect interaction to unfold between you.

Interpretation

Even after we have selectively perceived people, interactions, and situations, and we have organized our perceptions, what they mean is not clear. There are no intrinsic meanings in phenomena. Instead, we assign meaning by interpreting what we have noticed and organized. **Interpretation** is the subjective process of explaining perceptions in ways that let us make sense of them. To interpret the meaning of another's actions, we construct explanations for what she or he does.

Attributions   **Attributions** are explanations of why things happen and why people act as they do (Heider, 1958; Kelley, 1967). Attributions have four dimensions, as shown in Figure 3.4. The first is internal/external locus, which attributes what a person does to either internal factors (he's got a mean personality) or external factors (the traffic jam frustrated him). The second dimension is stable/unstable, which explains actions as the result of

I'm Cablinasian!

Tiger Woods firmly, but politely, rejects it when others label him "African American" or "Asian." I'm both and more, he says. As a young boy he made up the term *Cablinasian* to symbolize his ethnic heritage. He is part Caucasian (Ca), part Black (bl), part Indian (in), and part Asian (asian).

Tiger's not alone in embracing his multiracial identity. Keanu Reeves defines his ethnicity as Hawaiian, Chinese, and White. Mariah Carey identifies herself as Black, Venezuelan, and White. Johnny Depp is Cherokee and White.

We can expect to see more and more people who have multiple ethnic heritages. According to the 1994 U.S. Census Bureau, interracial marriages are rising. In the 1990s over 400,000 marriages in the United States are between Asians or Pacific Islanders and Whites, over 300,000 are between Native Americans and Whites, and nearly 100,000 are between Blacks and Whites. As more and more people reflect multiple ethnic heritages, stereotypes of ethnic groups will prove to be very unreliable bases for perceptions of individuals.

SOURCES: Leland, J., & Beals, G. (1997, May 5). In living color. *Newsweek*, pp. 58–60; Strege, J. (1997). *Tiger: A biography of Tiger Woods.* New York: Bantam Doubleday; U.S. Bureau of the Census. (1994). Current population reports, geographic mobility. Washington, DC: U.S. Government Printing Office.

© Ponopresse/Gamma-Liaison

Life in the Missing Boxes

Check the box that describes your race:

_____ Black
_____ White
_____ Native American
_____ Aleutian

If you can't figure out which box to check for yourself, join the crowd. Many people of mixed race feel boxed in—literally—by conventional demographic categories. Until very recently, the U.S. Census Bureau included only the four racial categories shown at the start of this Communication Notes.

In an interview for *Hues* magazine, Stefanie Liang talked with women who don't fit the standard categories. Melanie defines herself as Black, White, and Latina. Hayley says she is part Black and part White, but identifies as Black. Allison says she is half Filipino and half White. Deana is half Arab and half White. And Stefanie is half German and half Chinese. Echoing the thoughts of these five women is Melanie's feeling that she should check multiple boxes because one alone does not describe her.

SOURCE: Liang, S. (1997, Summer). Mix. A multiethnic women's dialogue. *Hues*, pp. 22–23.

FIGURE 3.4
Dimensions of Attributions

stable factors that won't change (she's a Type A personality) or temporary occurrences (she acted that way because she just had a fight with the boss). Global/specific is the third dimension, and it defines behavior as the result of a general pattern (he's an angry person) or a specific instance (he gets angry about sloppy work). Finally, there is the dimension of responsibility, which attributes behaviors to either factors people can control (she doesn't try to overcome her depression) or to those they cannot (she is depressed because of a chemical imbalance). In judging whether others can control their actions, we decide whether to hold them responsible for what they do. How we account for others' actions affects our feelings about them and our relationships with them. We can be more or less positive toward others depending on how we explain what they do. "Attributional Patterns and Relationship Satisfaction" on page 90 discusses the connection between attributions couples make and how they feel about their partner.

Our attributions critically influence the meanings we attach to others and their behaviors. For example, how do you account for the fact that a 5'2" woman weighs 200 pounds? Is she an undisciplined glutton (internal, stable attribution for which the person has control)? Or does she have a hormonal imbalance (internal, not necessarily stable attribution over which the person doesn't have control)? Or is she in a period of severe stress (external, unstable attribution for which control may be arguable)? Each of the three attributions invites a distinct overall view of the individual who weighs 200 pounds.

Attributional Errors Researchers who have studied the ways that humans explain behaviors have identified two common attributional errors. The first is the **self-serving bias.** As the name implies, this is a bias to favor ourselves and our interests. Research indicates that we tend to construct attributions that serve our personal interests (Hamachek, 1992; Sypher, 1984). Thus, we are inclined to make internal, stable, and global attributions for our positive actions and our successes. We're also likely to claim good results come about because of personal control we exerted. For example, you might say that you did well on a test because you are a smart (internal and stable) person who is always responsible (global) and studies hard (personal control).

The self-serving bias also works in a second way. We tend to avoid taking responsibility for negative actions and failures by attributing them to external, unstable, and specific factors that are beyond personal control. To explain a failing grade on a test, you might say that you did poorly because the professor (external) put a lot of tricky questions on that test (unstable, specific factor) so that all of your studying didn't help (outside of personal control). In other words, our misconduct results from outside forces that we can't help, but all the good we do reflects our personal qualities and efforts. This self-serving bias can distort our perceptions, leading us to take excessive personal credit for what we do well and to abdicate responsibility for what we do poorly. When we make faulty attributions for our behaviors, we form an unrealistic image of ourselves and our abilities.

In a 1996 interview with *Newsweek*'s John McCormick and Sharon Begley, Tiger Woods described how his father taught him to accept responsibility for his bad shots in golf. When he was a preschooler and hit a bad shot, he slammed his club on the ground. His father would ask him, "Who's responsible for that bad shot? The crow that made the noise during your backswing? The bag somebody dropped? Whose responsiblity was that?" (p. 55). Tiger learned to say it was his responsibility. As he took responsibility for his bad shots, Tiger Woods learned that he could control his skill.

COMMUNICATION NOTES

A Script for Romance

Researchers Christine Bachen and Eva Illouz wanted to know how much mass media influence young people's ideas about romance. To find out, they asked students in the fourth, seventh, and tenth–eleventh grades to pick three out of six photos shown to them that represented a man and a woman who were in love. They then asked the students to select the single photo that best exemplified a man and a woman in love. Next, the researchers asked the students to use their own words to describe a romantic dinner and to describe what happens on a typical first date. Finally, the researchers asked the students to tell an ideal love story.

There was high consensus among students. For the first task, they overwhelmingly chose pictures of couples in exotic locales who were looking directly at each other and touching or kissing. For the second task, the majority of students selected a photo showing a couple on a boat—the most exotic of the pictures they were shown. Descriptions of romantic dinners emphasized atmosphere and visual features of settings—soft lighting, music, exquisite food. Students also agreed on the script for a first date: going out to dinner, although not necessarily a romantic dinner, and/or a movie. Most interesting to the researchers was what students offered as ideal love stories: The stories involved falling in love and getting married, but that wasn't the end. The final focus of students stories was having children and acquiring material goods to give them comfortable lives.

After analyzing the data, Bachen and Illouz concluded that students' perceptions of love and romance reflect media ideals. Advertising and broadcast media link romance to leisure, consumption, and exotic places and activities—the very things that students associate with love and romance.

SOURCE: Bachen, C., & Illouz, E. (1996). Imagining romance: Young people's culture models of romance and love. *Critical Studies of Mass Communication, 13,* 279–308.

S T U D E N T   VOICES

CHICO: *When I do badly on a test or paper, I usually say either the professor was unfair or I had too much to do that week and couldn't study like I wanted to. But when my friends do badly on a test, I tend to think they're not good in that subject or they aren't disciplined or whatever.*

Attributional Patterns and Relationship Satisfaction

Investigations have shown that happy and unhappy couples have distinct attributional styles. Happy couples make relationship-enhancing attributions. Individuals attribute nice things a partner does to internal, stable, and global reasons. "He got the film for us because he is a good person who always does sweet things for us." Unpleasant things a partner does are attributed to external, unstable, and specific factors. "She yelled at me because all of the stress of the past few days made her not herself."

Unhappy couples employ reverse attributional patterns. They explain nice actions as results of external, unstable, and specific factors. "She got the tape because she had some extra time this particular day." Negative actions are seen as stemming from internal, stable, and global factors. "He yelled at me because he is a nasty person who never shows any consideration to anybody else."

Negative attributions fix pessimistic views and undermine motivation to improve a relationship. Whether positive or negative, attributions may be self-fulfilling prophecies.

SOURCES: Bradbury, T. N., & Fincham, F. D. (1990). Attributions in marriage: Review and critique. *Psychological Bulletin, 107,* 3–33. Fletcher, G. J., & Fincham, F. D. (1991). Attribution in close relationships. In G. J. Fletcher & F. D. Fincham (Eds.), *Cognition in close relationships* (pp. 7–35). Hillsdale, NJ: Erlbaum.

The second kind of attributional error is so common it is called the **fundamental attribution error.** This involves overestimating the internal causes of others' undesirable behaviors and underestimating the external causes. Conversely, we are likely to underestimate the internal causes of our own misdeeds and failures and overestimate the external causes. The fundamental attributional error was obvious in a legal case on which I consulted in 1997. A woman sued her employer for transferring her. She alleged that he did so because her boss was biased against women. Her boss denied being biased against women. He claimed that he transferred her because he needed someone at another office location, and her poor performance made her the most expendable person in his department. Written records, such as yearly performance reviews, and the woman's own testimony revealed that she had not met all of her job responsibilities and had been told this repeatedly. Further, her boss's record of hiring and promotions proved that nearly 50 percent of his hires and promotions over the past decade had gone to women and minorities. At the trial, the plaintiff was asked if she had considered her performance or the need for new staff at another location to have influenced her boss's decision to transfer her. "No, he did it because he doesn't want to work with women," she replied. Thus, she totally discounted external factors that could explain his decision and placed full responsibility on internal qualities—his alleged sex bias. When asked if she thought her performance might have made her more expendable than others who worked in her former department, she said, "No, the only problems with my performance were due to interruptions and lack of cooperation from others." Thus, she discounted any personal responsibility for errors in her work and laid full responsibility on circumstances beyond her control. In court, I explained the fundamental attribution error to the jury and showed how it surfaced in the woman's testimony. The jury came back with a judgment against the woman who had sued.

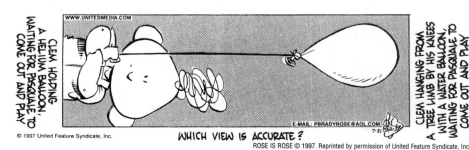

WHICH VIEW IS ACCURATE?

© 1997 United Feature Syndicate, Inc.

ROSE IS ROSE © 1997. Reprinted by permission of United Feature Syndicate, Inc.

We've seen that perception involves three interrelated processes. The first of these, selection, involves noticing certain things and ignoring others out of the total complexity of what is going on. The second process is organization, whereby we use prototypes, personal constructs, stereotypes, and scripts to order what we have selectively perceived. Finally, we engage in interpretation to make sense of the perceptions we have gathered and organized. Attributions are a primary way we explain what we and others do.

Although we discussed selection, organization, and interpretation separately, in reality they may occur in a different order or simultaneously. Thus, our interpretations shape the knowledge schemata we use to organize experiences, and the ways we organize perceptions affect what we notice and interpret. For instance, in her commentary earlier in this chap-ter, Nai Lee's interpretations of Westerners' individualism were shaped by the schemata she learned in her homeland of Korea. Also, reliance on the construct of individualistic–communal shaped what she noticed about Americans. Now that we understand the complex processes involved in perception, we're ready to consider a range of factors that influence what and how we perceive.

Influences on Perception

Recently I attended the first meeting of a student–faculty group that was founded to bring a new leadership development program to campus. At the end of the session, the facilitator said, "This has been a great first meeting. Participation was so high!" Beside me, a young African American woman grumbled, "Yeah—White participation." I then noticed there were only three African American students, one Asian American student, and no faculty of color. Thinking back, I realized none of the minority students had spoken during the meeting. As a member of the majority group, I hadn't realized how few people of color were in the room, and I hadn't noticed that none of them spoke. The African American student beside me had perceived the meeting differently than I initially did, because her ethnicity and personal experiences on a campus dominated by Whites made her attentive to racial dynamics I didn't notice.

As this example illustrates, everyone doesn't perceive situations and people in the same way. In this section, we consider some of the influences on our perceptions.

Physiology

One reason perceptions vary among people is that we differ in our sensory abilities and physiologies. The five senses are not the same for all of us. Music that one person finds deafening is barely audible to another. Salsa that is painfully hot to one diner may seem mild to someone else. On a given day on my campus, students wear everything from shorts and sandals to jackets, indicating they have different sensitivities to cold. Some people have better vision than others,

© Grant LeDuc/Monkmeyer Press Photo

and some are color-blind. These differences in sensory abilities affect our perceptions.

Our physiological states also influence perception. If you are tired or stressed, you're likely to perceive things more negatively than you normally would. For instance, a playful insult from a friend might anger you if you're feeling down, but wouldn't bother you if you felt good. Also, you might attribute a stressed friend's behaviors to unstable and specific causes rather than to enduring personality. Each of us has our own biorhythm, which influences the times of day when we tend to be alert and fuzzy. I'm a morning person, so that's when I prefer to teach classes and write. I am less alert and creative late in the day. Thus, I perceive things in the morning that I simply don't notice when my energy level declines.

Medical conditions are another physiological influence on perceptions. If you've ever taken drugs that affected your thinking, you know how dramatically they can alter perceptions of time and experiences. Doctors who prescribe drugs to treat various conditions report that they can alter patients' perceptions radically. People may become severely depressed, paranoid, or uncharacteristically happy under the influence of hormones and other drugs. Changes in our bodies due to medical conditions may also affect what we selectively perceive. I have a serious back disorder that periodically renders me immobile or dependent on canes. When my back is out of order, I am far more aware of stairs, uneven ground, and any activities that require me to bend. When my back is working well, I don't notice any of these things any more than someone without back problems.

Age

Age is another factor that influences our perceptions. The older we get, the richer our perspective for perceiving life and people. Thus, compared to a person of twenty, a sixty-year-old has a more complex fund of experiences to draw on in perceiving situations and people. When I was twenty-two years old and in graduate school, I mentioned to my father that it was hard to get by on the salary from my teaching assistantship. He said that during the early 1930s he would have been deliriously happy to have had enough money just to eat.

HI AND LOIS Reprinted with special permission of King Features Syndicate.

Because my father had lived through the Great Depression, he had a broader persective than I did on deprivation. You probably think nothing of paying 75 cents for a soft drink, but I recall buying it for a quarter when I was younger. To me, the current prices seem high because I have a comparison point that you lack.

Age also influences our perceptions of time. My seven-year-old niece perceives a year as lasting much longer than I do at age forty-seven. A year is a full one-seventh of her life, but only one-forty-seventh of mine; a year really is longer in her perspective than in mine. As we grow older and have more experiences, our perspective on many things changes. For example, I used to feel down if my teaching didn't go well on a given day or if I had an unexpected expense. But when I was 36 my father died, and that radically changed my perceptions of which things merit feeling low. The experience of losing him gave me a different perspective on what is bad and hard to endure.

Age and the wealth of experiences it brings can also change our perceptions of social life and its problems. The extent of discrimination still experienced by women and minorities understandably discourages many college students. I am more hopeful than some of them because I have seen many changes in my life-

© Keren Su/Stock, Boston

© Bob Daemmrich/The Image Works

time. When I attended college, women were not admitted on an equal basis with men, and almost all students of color attended minority colleges. When I entered the job market, few laws protected women and minorities against discrimination in hiring, pay, and advancement. The substantial progress made during my life leads me to perceive current inequities as changeable.

Culture

A **culture** consists of beliefs, values, understandings, practices, and ways of interpreting experience that are shared by a number of people. It is a set of assumptions that form the pattern of our lives and that guide how we think, feel, and act. The influence of culture is so pervasive that it's hard to realize how powerfully it shapes our perceptions. Perhaps the best way to recognize the assumptions of our own culture is to travel to places where values, understandings, and codes of behavior differ.

Consider a few aspects of modern Western culture that influence our perceptions. One characteristic of our culture is the emphasis on technology and its offspring: speed. We expect things to happen fast—almost instantly. Whether it's instant photos, 5-minute copying, or 1-hour martinizing, we live at an accelerated pace (Wood, 1995c). We send letters by express mail, jet across the country, and microwave meals. Social commentators suggest that the cultural emphasis on speed may diminish patience and thus our willingness to invest in long-term projects, such as relationships (Toffler, 1970, 1980). In countries such as Nepal and Mexico, life proceeds at a more leisurely pace, and people spend more time talking, relaxing, and engaging in low-key activity. And in Germany, citizens spend little time on small talk because they tend to regard it as boring and useless.

The United States is also a fiercely individualistic culture in which personal initiative is expected and rewarded. Other cultures, particularly many Asian ones, are more communal, and identity is defined in terms of one's family, rather than as an individual quality. Because families are more valued in communal cultures, elders are given greater respect and care than they often receive in the United States. The difference between communal and individualistic cultures is also evident in child-care practices. More communal countries have policies that reflect the value they place on families. In every developed country except the United States, new parents, including adoptive parents, are given at least six weeks of paid parental leave, and some countries provide nearly a year's paid leave (Wood, 1994d).

APPLY THE IDEA

Cultural Values

How do values in Western culture affect your everyday perceptions and activities? See if you can trace concrete implications of these cultural values:

EXAMPLE: Competition. This value is evident in concrete practices such as competitive sports, grading policies, and attempts to get the last word in casual conversations.

- productivity
- individualism
- speed
- youth
- wealth

Discuss with classmates the impact of cultural values on your day-to-day perceptions and activities.

In the *Wall Street Journal*, George Anders (1997) recently reported that many doctors in the United States are being encouraged to attend workshops that teach them about the cultural practices and folk beliefs of nonnative citizens. One doctor, Jeffrey Syme, found immediate application for what he learned in the workshop. He had a number of patients who had immigrated from Cape Verde, islands off West Africa. Many of these patients asked him for

Valium but refused to discuss their problems with him. Syme's training and U.S. drug policies define Valium as a medication for serious depression that should only be prescribed for good reason. In the workshop Syme learned that in Cape Verde Valium is an over-the-counter treatment people routinely take for everyday blues. Thus, they perceived Valium as a mild medication, which they could take as casually as aspirin. Anders also reported on another case in which ignorance of folk beliefs led a doctor to faulty perceptions of a patient. During a workshop in Massachusetts a folk belief among many Guatemalans was discussed. This belief is that giant worms in the stomach govern well-being. One doctor attending the workshop said, "I just had a patient like that." What had the doctor done when her patient complained that giant worms in his stomach were making him feel bad? She referred him to mental health specialists because she perceived his statement to indicate that he was mentally imbalanced. In both cases, the doctors' perceptions were based on customs and practices in U.S. culture and did not take into account the customs and beliefs of their patients' native lands. Another example of how ignorance of a particular culture can cause offense is presented in "Keep Religion out of the Bathroom."

Standpoint In recent years, scholars have realized that we are affected not only by the culture as a whole, but by our particular location within the culture (Haraway, 1988; Harding, 1991). *Standpoint* refers to your point of view as it is influenced by your social circumstances. **Standpoint theory** claims that a culture includes a number of social groups that distinctively shape perceptions, identities, and opportunities of members. As we saw in Chapter 2, race, gender, class, and sexual preference are primary ways that Western culture groups people. Our society attaches differential value to different social groups. The way we perceive the world and ourselves is shaped by our experiences as members of the particular groups to which we belong. This is why the African American woman at the student–faculty meeting noticed the absence of participation by people of color and I didn't.

In an early discussion of standpoint, the philosopher Georg Hegel (1807) pointed out that standpoints reflect power positions in social hierarchies. To illustrate, he noted that the institution of slavery is perceived very differently by masters and slaves. Extending Hegel's point, we can see that those in positions of power have a vested interest in preserving the system that gives them privileges. Thus, they are unlikely to perceive its flaws and inequities. On the other hand, those who are disempowered by a system are able to see inequities and discrimination (Harding, 1991).

Women and men, as social groups, have different standpoints, although not every individual man and woman shares the standpoint typical for his or her sex. For instance, the caregiving we generally associate with women is not due to maternal instinct but rather to the social role of mother, which teaches women to care for others, notice who needs what, and defer their own needs (Ruddick, 1989). Other researchers have discovered that men who are in caregiving roles become nurturing, accommodative, and sensitive to others' needs as a consequence of being in the social role of caregiver (Kaye & Applegate, 1990).

S T U D E N T **VOICES**

JANICE: *I'll vouch for the idea of standpoint affecting how we communicate. I was always a pretty independent person. Some people even thought I was kind of selfish, because I really would prioritize myself. Then I had my first baby, and I stayed home with him for a year. I really changed—and I mean in basic ways. I believed that my most important job was to be there for Timmy, and so my whole day focused on him. He was the person I thought about first, not myself. I learned to hear the slightest difference in his cries, so I could tell when he was hungry or needed his diapers changed or wanted company. When I went back to work after a year, a lot of my former colleagues said I was different—much more attentive and sensitive to what they said and more generous with my time than I had been. I guess I developed new patterns of communication as a result of mothering.*

Gendered standpoints are also evident in marital conflict. Researchers have found that conflict lessens wives' love for husbands more than it lessens husbands' love for wives (Huston, McHale, & Crouter, 1985; Kelly, Huston, & Cate, 1985). This makes sense when we realize that husbands generally exercise more power over decision making, so they usually prevail in conflict. Naturally, the winners of conflicts are more satisfied with relationships than the losers!

Gendered standpoints are also obvious in the effort that women and men in general invest in maintaining relationships. Socialized into the role of relationship expert, women are expected by others and themselves to take care of relationships (Tavris, 1992; Wood, 1993, 1994d, 1998). They are supposed to know when something is wrong and to resolve the tension. This may explain why women tend to be more aware than men of problems in relationships (Brehm, 1992; Wood, 1998).

Other standpoints also influence our perceptions. Ethnicity, for example, affects how we perceive ourselves and our families. As we noted previously, many cultures are less individualistic than mainstream U.S. culture. Yet, even within this country, there are differences among distinct social groups. Stan

Gaines (1995), who studies minority groups in the United States, reports that African Americans and Latinos and Latinas tend to perceive family and extended community as more central to their identities than most European Americans. Perceiving self as a part of larger social groups is also characteristic of families in many Asian cultures.

APPLY THE IDEA

Exploring Standpoints

To become more aware of diverse perspectives on social life, talk with someone whose standpoint differs from your own. Discuss how you and the other person think about families, careers, and attending college. Explore how the individual perceives college life and activities on campus. How do these perceptions differ from your own? Does interaction with this person give you new perspectives on familiar things in your life?

Both our membership in an overall culture and our standpoint as members of particular social groups shape how we perceive people, situations, events, and ourselves.

Social Roles

Our perceptions are also shaped by our social roles. Both the training that we receive to fulfill a role and the actual demands of the role affect what we notice and how we interpret and evaluate it. My perceptions of my classes focus on how interested students seem, whether they appear to have read the material, and whether what they're learning is useful in their lives. Students have told me that they think about classes in terms of number and difficulty of tests, whether papers are required, and whether the professor is interesting. We have different perspectives on what classes are. In working on this book, I've focused on ideas, whereas Deirdre, my editor, thinks about layout, design features, and marketing issues that don't occur to me.

The professions people enter influence what they notice and how they think and act. Prior to her professional training, my sister Carolyn did not have highly developed analytic thinking skills. However, after law school she was extremely analytical, and her conversational style shifted to be more argumentative, logical, and probing. Physicians are trained to be highly observant of physical symptoms. Once at a social gathering, a friend of mine who is a physician asked me how long I had had a herniated disk. Shocked, I told him I didn't have one. "You do," he insisted, and, sure enough, a few weeks later a disk ruptured. His medical training enabled him to perceive subtle changes in my posture and walk that I hadn't noticed.

Social roles can also influence how we perceive communicating about our feelings. Professions that call for detachment and objectivity may encourage members to withhold expressing emotions and to be uncomfortable if others do. We'll discuss the relationship between social roles and communication about emotions more fully in Chapter 7.

© Frank Siteman/ The Picture Cube

Cognitive Abilities

In addition to physiological, cultural, and social influences, perception is also shaped by our cognitive abilities. How elaborately we think about situations and people, and our personal knowledge of others, affect how we select, organize, and interpret experiences.

Cognitive Complexity   People differ in the number and type of knowledge schemata they use to organize and interpret people and situations. **Cognitive complexity** refers to the number of constructs (remember, these are bipolar dimensions of judgment) used, how abstract they are, and how elaborately they interact to shape perceptions. Most children have fairly simple cognitive systems: They rely on few schemata, focus more on concrete categories than abstract and psychological ones, and often are not aware of relationships among different perceptions. For instance, toddlers often call any and every adult male "Daddy," because they haven't learned more complex ways to distinguish among men.

Adults also differ in cognitive complexity, and this affects the accuracy of our perceptions. If you can think of people only as nice or mean, you have a limited range for perceiving the motives of others. Similarly, people who focus on concrete data tend to have less sophisticated understandings than people who also perceive psychological data. For example, you might notice that a person is attractive, tells jokes, and talks to others easily. These are concrete perceptions. At a more abstract, psychological level, you might reason that the concrete behaviors you observe reflect a secure, self-confident personality. This is a sophisticated explanation because it provides a rich perception of why the individual acts as she or he does.

What if you later find out that the person is very quiet in classes? Someone with low cognitive complexity would have difficulty integrating the new information into prior observations. Either the new information would be dismissed because it doesn't fit or the most recent data would replace the former perception and the person would be redefined as shy. A more cognitively complex person would integrate all of the information into a coherent account. Perhaps a cognitively complex individual would conclude that the person is very confident in social situations but less secure in academic ones.

Research has shown that cognitively complex individuals are flexible in interpreting complicated phenomena and are able to integrate new information into how they think about people and situations. Individuals who are less cognitively complex are likely to ignore discrepant information that doesn't fit with their impressions or to throw out old ideas and replace them with new impressions (Crockett, 1965; Delia, Clark, & Switzer, 1974). Either way they fail to recognize the nuances and inconsistencies that are human nature. The complexity of our cognitive systems affects how intricately we perceive people and interpersonal situations.

Person-Centeredness   Person-centeredness is related to cognitive complexity because it requires abstract thinking and a breadth of schemata. As discussed in Chapter 1, person-centeredness is the ability to perceive another as a unique and distinct individual apart from social roles and generalizations based on the person's membership in groups. Our ability to perceive others as unique depends, first, on how well we make cognitive distinctions. People who are cognitively complex rely on more numerous and more abstract schemata to interpret others. Second, person-centered communicators base their interactions on knowledge of particular others. Thus, they use vocabulary and nonverbal behaviors that suit those with whom they interact, and they tailor the content of what they say to the experiences, values, and interests of others. The result is communication that is centered on a specific person.

Recalling the discussion of I–Thou relationships in Chapter 1, you may remember that these are relationships in which people know and value each other as unique individuals. To do so, we must learn about another, and this requires considerable time and interaction. As we get to know another better, we gain insight into how she or he differs from others in a group ("Rob's not obsessive like other political activists I've known," "Ellen's more interested in people than most computer science majors"). The more we interact with another and the greater the variety of experiences we have together, the more insight we gain into her or his motives, feelings, and behaviors. As we come to understand others as individuals, we fine-tune our perceptions of them. Consequently, we're less likely to rely on stereotypes to perceive them. This is why we often communicate more effectively with people we know well than with strangers or casual acquaintances.

S   T   U   D   E   N   T   VOICES

STEVE: *You really have to know somebody on an individual basis to know what she or he likes and wants. When I first started dating Sherry, I sent her red roses to let her know I thought she was special. That's the "lovers' flower," right? It turns out that was the only flower her father liked, and they had a million red roses at his funeral. Now they make Sherry sad because they remind her he's dead. I also took her chocolates once, then later found out she's allergic to chocolate. By now I know what flowers and things she likes, but my experience shows that the general rules don't always apply to individuals.*

Person-centeredness is not the same as empathy. **Empathy** is the ability to feel with another person—to feel what she or he feels in a situation. Feeling with another is an emotional response that some scholars believe we cannot fully achieve. Our feelings tend to be guided by our own emotional tendencies and experiences, so it may be impossible to feel exactly what another person feels. What we can do is realize that another is feeling something and connect as well as we can based on our own, different experiences. A more realistic goal is to learn to adopt dual perspective so that we adapt our communication to other people's frames of reference (Phillips & Wood, 1983; Wood, 1982, 1995a, 1995c). With commitment and effort, we can learn a lot about how others see the world, even if that differs from how we see it. This knowledge, along with cognitive complexity, allows us to be person-centered communicators.

When we take the perspective of others, we try to grasp what something means to them and how they perceive things. This requires suspending judgment at least temporarily. We can't appreciate someone else's perspective when we're imposing our evaluations of whether it is right or wrong, sensible or crazy. Instead, we have to let go of our own perspective and perceptions long enough to enter the world of another person. Doing this allows us to understand issues from another person's point of view, so that we can communicate more effectively with her or him. At a later point in interaction we may choose to express our own perspective or to disagree with another's views. This is appropriate and important in honest communication, but voicing our own views is not a substitute for the equally important skill of recognizing another's perspective.

Self A final influence on our perceptions is ourselves. What we selectively perceive and how we organize and interpret phenomena are shaped by many aspects of our selves. Attachment style, which we discussed in Chapter 2, is one obvious influence on interpersonal perceptions. Consider how differently people with the four attachment styles would perceive and approach close relationships. People with secure attachment styles assume that they are lovable and that others are trustworthy. Thus they tend to perceive others and relationships in positive ways. In contrast, people with fearful attachment styles perceive themselves as unlovable and others as not loving. Consequently, they may perceive relationships as dangerous and potentially harmful. The dismissive attachment style inclines individuals to perceive themselves positively, others negatively, and close relationships as undesirable. Individuals who have anxious/resistant attachment styles are often preoccupied with relationships and perceive others in unpredictable ways.

Implicit personality theory also helps explain how the self influences interpersonal perceptions. Implicit personality theory is unspoken and sometimes unconscious assumptions about how various qualities fit together in human personalities (Schneider, 1973). Most of us think certain qualities go together in people. For instance, you might think that a person whom you have observed being outgoing and friendly is also confident and fun. The assumptions that the person is confident and fun are not based on direct knowledge of the person; instead, they are inferences based on your observation that she or he is outgoing and friendly, coupled with your implicit personality theory of what qualities usually accompany outgoingness and friendliness.

Discovering Your Implicit Personality Theories

Below are three descriptions of people. After reading each one, list other qualities that you would expect to find in the person described.

- Jane is highly intelligent and analytical, and she is planning for a career as a trial attorney. She loves to argue issues and enjoys being with others who have sharp reasoning and verbal skills.
- Andrew is a loner. He spends a lot of his time in his room reading or surfing the Net. At first, others in the dorm invited him to parties, but he never went, so they quit asking him. He is always polite and pleasant to others, but he doesn't seek out company.
- Pat loves jokes, including pranks. Those around Pat have learned to expect practical jokes and, also, that Pat enjoys being the recipient of pranks. Pat studies enough to get decent grades, but academics aren't a priority. Seldom seen alone, Pat is a sociable person who likes to have a good time.

In the Apply the Idea exercise above you made inferences about Jane, Andrew, and Pat based on what you already knew about them. What is the basis of your inferences? If you're like most people, the basis is others you have known or observed. Thus, how you perceive Jane, Andrew, and Pat reflects as much about you and your experiences as about those individuals. This underlines the fact that how we perceive others and relationships is not simply based on what is external to us but also on what is internal.

In sum, we've seen that many factors influence perception and account for differences among people in perceptions. Differences based on physiology, culture and standpoint, social roles, cognitive abilities, and ourselves affect what we perceive and how we interpret others and experiences. In the final section of the chapter, we consider ways to improve the accuracy of our perceptions.

Guidelines for Improving Perception and Communication

Perception is a foundation of interpersonal communication. Yet, as we have seen, many factors influence how we perceive others and situations. To be a competent communicator, it's important to form perceptions carefully and check their accuracy. We'll discuss seven guidelines for improving the accuracy of perceptions and, ultimately, the quality of interpersonal communication.

Recognize That All Perceptions Are Partial and Subjective

What you've read so far makes it clear that our perceptions are inevitably partial and subjective. Each of us perceives from a particular perspective that is shaped by our physiology, culture, standpoint, social roles, cognitive abilities, and aspects of ourselves and our personal experiences. This means that what we

"May I suggest that in today's group-therapy session we all work on our contact with reality."

Reprinted courtesy *Omni* Magazine © 1979.

perceive is always partial and subjective. It is partial because we cannot perceive everything but instead select only certain aspects of phenomena to notice. We then organize and interpret those selected stimuli in personal ways that are necessarily incomplete. Perception is also subjective because it is influenced by individual background and physiology and our personal modes of interpretation.

Objective features of reality have no meaning until we notice, organize, and interpret them. It is our perceptions that construct meanings for the people and experiences in our lives. An outfit perceived as elegant by one person may appear cheap to another. A teacher one student regards as fascinating may put another student to sleep. A weekend camping trip may be a joy to a person who loves the outdoors and an ordeal to an individual not accustomed to roughing it. It is difficult, if not impossible, to determine the truth or falsity of perceptions, because they are not objective descriptions. Instead, perceptions represent what things mean to individuals.

S T U D E N T VOICES

THALENA: *So this girl I met a few weeks ago said she was having a party, and it would be lots of fun with some cool people. She asked if I wanted to come, so I said, "Sure—why not?" When I got there everybody was drinking—I mean seriously drinking. They were playing this weird music—sort of morbid—and they had the tape of* Rocky Horror Picture Show *going nonstop. They got so loud that the neighbors came over and told us to hold it down. In a couple of hours most of the people there were totally wasted. That's not my idea of fun. That's not my idea of cool people.*

The subjective and partial nature of perceptions has implications for interpersonal communication. One implication is that when you and another person disagree about something, neither of you is necessarily wrong or crazy. It's more likely that you have attended to different things and that there are differences in your personal, social, cultural, and physiological resources for perceiving. A second implication is that it's wise to remind ourselves that we profoundly influence how we perceive others. As we have seen, our perceptions are based at least as much on ourselves as on anything external to us. If you perceive another person as domineering, there's a chance that you are feeling insecure in your ability to interact. If you perceive others as unfriendly toward you, it may be that you think of yourself as unworthy of friends. Remembering that perceptions are partial and subjective curbs the tendency to think our perceptions are the only valid ones or that they are based exclusively on what lies outside of us.

Avoid Mindreading

Because perception is subjective, people differ in what they notice and in what it means to them. One of the most common problems in interpersonal communication is **mindreading,** which is assuming we understand what another person thinks or perceives. When we mindread, we don't check with another person to see what he or she is thinking. Instead, we act as if we know what's on another's mind, and this can get us into considerable trouble. John Gottman and his colleagues identify mindreading as one of the behaviors that contributes to interpersonal tension (Gottman, 1993; Gottman, Notarius, Gonso, & Markman, 1976). The danger of mindreading is that we may misinterpret others and have no way of checking on the accuracy of our perceptions. Sometimes we do understand one another but sometimes we don't.

© Mangino/The Image Works

Consequently, for the most part mindreading is more likely to harm than help interpersonal communication. Consider a few examples. One person might say to her partner, "I know you didn't plan anything for our anniversary because it doesn't matter to you." Whether or not the partner made plans, it's impossible to guess motives or to know why the partner forgot if indeed he did. A supervisor might notice an employee is late for work several days in a row and say, "Obviously, you're no longer committed to your job." One friend might say to another, "You were late coming over because you're still mad about what happened yesterday." The speaker is guessing reasons for the friend's tardiness and could well be wrong. Mindreading also occurs when we say things such as "I know why you're upset" (Has the person said she or he is upset?) or "You don't care about me anymore" (maybe the other person is too preoccupied or worried to be as attentive as usual). We also mindread when we tell ourselves we know how somebody else will feel or react, or what he or she will do. The truth is we don't really know—we're only guessing. When we mindread, we impose our perspectives on others instead of allowing them to say what they think. This can cause misunderstandings as well as resentment, because most of us prefer to speak for ourselves.

S T U D E N T VOICES

CONSUELA: *Mindreading drives me crazy. My boyfriend does it all the time, and he's wrong as often as he's right. Last week he got tickets to a concert because he "knew" I'd want to go. Maybe I would have if I hadn't already planned a trip that weekend, but he never checked on my schedule. A lot of times when we're talking, he'll say something, then before I can answer he says, "I know what you're thinking." Then he proceeds to run through his ideas about what I'm thinking. Usually he's off base, and then we get into a sideline argument about why he keeps assuming what I think instead of asking me. I really wish he would ask me what I think.*

Check Perceptions with Others

The third guideline follows directly from the first two. Because perceptions are subjective and partial, and because mindreading is an ineffective way to figure out what others think, we need to check our perceptions with others. In the first example above, it would be wise to ask, "Did you forget our anniversary?" If the partner did forget, then the speaker might ask, "Why do you think you forgot?" The person may not know why or the reasons may not be satisfactory, but asking is a better way to open a productive dialogue than attributing bad motives to another.

Perception checking is an important communication skill because it helps people arrive at mutual understandings of each other and their relationships. To check perceptions, you should first state what it is that you have noticed. For example, a person might say, "Lately you've seemed less attentive to me." Then the person should check to see whether the other perceives the same thing: "Do you feel you've been less attentive?" Finally, it's appropriate to ask the other person to explain her or his behavior. In the example, the person might ask, "Why do you think you're less attentive?" (If the partner doesn't perceive that she or he is less attentive, the question would be "Why have you wanted to be together less often and seemed distracted when we talk?") When checking perceptions, it's important to use a tentative tone, rather than a dogmatic or accusatory one. This minimizes defensiveness and encourages good discussion. Just let the other person know you've noticed something and would like him or her to clarify his or her perceptions of what is happening and what it means.

APPLY THE IDEA

Checking Perceptions

To gain skill in perception checking (and all communication behaviors), you need to practice. Try these exercises:

- Monitor your tendencies to mindread, especially in established relationships in which you feel you know your partner well.
- The next time you catch yourself mindreading, stop. Instead, tell the other person what you are noticing and invite her or him to explain how she or he perceives what's happening. First, find out whether your partner agrees with you about what you noticed. Second, if the two of you agree, find out how your partner interprets and evaluates the issue.
- Engage in perception checking for two or three days so that you have lots of chances to see what happens. When you're done, reflect on the number of times your mindreading was inaccurate.
- How did perception checking affect interaction with your friends and romantic partners? Did you find out things you wouldn't have known if you'd engaged in mindreading?

Distinguish Between Facts and Inferences

Competent interpersonal communication also depends on distinguishing facts from inferences. A fact is an objective statement based on observation. An inference involves an interpretation that goes beyond the facts. For example, a student consistently comes to class late and sits at the back of the room, sometimes dozing off during discussions. The teacher might think, "That student is rude and unmotivated." The facts are that the student comes late, sits toward the rear of the classroom, and sometimes falls asleep. Defining the student as rude and unmotivated is an inference that goes beyond the facts. The fact might be that the student is tired because he or she has a job that ends right before the class.

It's easy to confuse facts and inferences because we sometimes treat the latter as the former. When we say, "The student is rude," we've made a statement that sounds factual, and we may then regard it that way ourselves. To avoid this tendency, substitute more tentative words for *is*. For instance, "The student seems rude" or "This student may be being rude" are more tentative statements that keep the speaker from treating an inference as a fact. "The Truth, the Whole Truth, and Nothing but the Truth" explores the influence of language on our perceptions. Our implicit personality theories consist of inferences—assumptions beyond what we have observed about others. Inferences aren't necessarily bad. In fact, we must make inferences to function in the world. Yet, we risk misperceptions and misunderstandings if we don't distinguish our inferences from facts. Learning to make the distinction is an important interpersonal communication skill.

COMMUNICATION NOTES

The Truth, the Whole Truth, and Nothing but the Truth

Research indicates that eyewitness testimony may not be as accurate as we often assume. Studies show that witnesses' perceptions are shaped by the language attorneys use.

In one experiment, viewers were shown a film of a traffic accident and then were asked, "How fast were the cars going when they *smashed* into each other?" Other viewers were asked how fast the cars were going when they *bumped* or *collided*. Viewers testified to significantly different speeds depending on which word was used in the question.

In a separate experiment, viewers were shown a film of a traffic accident and then filled out a questionnaire that included questions about things that had not actually been on the film. Viewers who were asked, "Did you see *the* broken headlight?" more frequently testified they saw it than did viewers who were asked, "Did you see *a* broken headlight?"

The accidents that viewers "saw" were shaped by the words used to describe them.

SOURCE: Trotter, R. J. (1975, October 25). "The truth, the whole truth, and nothing but ..." *Science News, 108*, 269.

APPLY THE IDEA
Using Tentative Language

To become more sensitive to our tendencies to confuse facts and inferences, pay attention to the language you use for the next 24 hours when you describe people and interactions. Listen for words like *is* and *are* that imply factual information. Do you find there are instances in which more tentative language would be more accurate?

Now extend your observations to other people and the language they use. When you hear others say, "she is," "they are," or "he is," are they really making factual statements or are they making inferences?

Guard Against the Self-Serving Bias

Earlier in this chapter, we discussed the self-serving bias, which involves attributing our successes and positive behaviors to internal and stable qualities in us that we control and attributing our failures and negative behaviors to external, unstable factors beyond our control. Because this bias can distort perceptions, we need to monitor it carefully. Try to catch yourself in the act of explaining away your failures or adverse behaviors as not your fault and taking personal credit for accomplishments that were helped along by luck or situational factors. The self-serving bias also inclines us to notice what we do and to be less aware of what others do. Obviously, this can affect how we feel about others, as Janet illustrates in her comments.

JANET: *For years my husband and I have argued about housework. I am always criticizing him for not doing enough, and I have felt resentful about how much I do. He always says to me that he does a lot, but I just don't notice. After studying the self-serving bias in class, I did an "experiment" at home. I watched him for a week and kept a list of all the things he did. Sure enough, he was—is—doing a lot more than I had thought. I never noticed that he sorted laundry or walked the dog four times a day or wiped the kitchen counters after we'd finished fixing dinner. I noticed everything I did but only the big things he did like vacuuming. I simply wasn't seeing a lot of his contributions to keep our home in order.*

Monitoring the self-serving bias also has implications for how we perceive others. Just as we tend to judge ourselves generously, we may also be inclined to judge others too harshly. Monitor your perceptions to see whether you attribute others' successes and admirable actions to external factors beyond their control and their shortcomings and blunders to internal factors they can (should) control. If you do this, substitute more generous explanations for others' behaviors and notice how that affects your perceptions of them.

Guard Against the Fundamental Attribution Error

A second error in interpretation that we discussed is the fundamental attribution error. As you recall, this occurs when we overestimate the internal causes and underestimate external causes for undesirable behavior from others and when we underestimate the internal causes and overestimate the external causes for our own failings or bad behaviors. Engaging in the fundamental attribution error distorts perceptions—both of ourselves and others. Thus, we want to guard against it in our interpersonal interactions.

To reduce your chances of falling victim to the fundamental attribution error, you can prompt yourself to look for external causes of behaviors from others that you don't appreciate. Instead of assuming the unwanted behavior reflects the other's motives or personality, ask yourself, "What factors in the person's situation might lead to this behavior?" You can ask the converse question to avoid underestimating internal influences on your own undesirable actions. Instead of letting yourself off the hook by explaining a misdeed as due to circumstances you couldn't control, ask yourself "What inside of me that is my responsibility influenced what I did?" Looking for external factors that influence others' communication and internal factors that influence your communication checks our tendency to engage in the fundamental attribution error.

Guarding Against the Fundamental Attribution Error

For each scenario described below, write out an alternate explanation based on *external* factors that might account for the other person's behavior.

- The person you've been dating for a while is late to meet you. It is the third time this month you've had to wait, and you are angry that your date is so inconsiderate.
- You're talking with a friend about your serious concerns about what you will do after you graduate. You notice that your friend seems uninterested and keeps looking at her watch. You think to yourself, "If you are so self-centered you can't make time for me, I don't need you for a friend."

For each scenario described below, write out an alternate explanation based on *internal* factors that could influence your behavior.

- You are running late, so when a friend stops by to chat, you don't invite him in and don't encourage conversation. Your friend says, "You're being a real jerk." You think to yourself, "This has nothing to do with me. It has to do with all of the pressures I'm facing."
- During an argument with your roommate about who is going to do grocery shopping, you get really angry. Without thinking, you blurt out, "With all of the weight you've gained, you should stop thinking about groceries." Your roommate looks hurt and leaves the room. Afterward, you think, "Well, I wouldn't have said that if she hadn't been so belligerent."

Monitor Labels

Words crystallize perceptions. Until we label an experience, it remains nebulous and less than fully formed in our thinking. Only when we name our feelings and thoughts do we have a clear way to describe and think about them. But just as words crystallize experiences, they can also freeze thought. Once we label our perceptions, we may respond to our own labels rather than to actual phenomena. If this happens, we may communicate in ways that are insensitive and inappropriate.

Consider this situation. Suppose you get together with five others in a study group, and a student named Andrea monopolizes the whole meeting with her questions and concerns. Leaving the meeting, one person says, "Gee, Andrea is so selfish and immature! I'll never work with her again." Another person responds, "She's not really selfish. She's just insecure about her grades in this course, so she was hyper in the meeting." Chances are these two people will perceive and treat Andrea differently depending on whether they label her "selfish" or "insecure." The point is that once the two people have labeled Andrea's behavior based on their subjective and partial perceptions, they may not respond to Andrea herself, but to the words they use to label their perceptions of her.

Effective communicators realize that the words they use influence their perceptions. In Chapter 4, we consider in depth how language affects perception. For now, remember that when we engage in interpersonal communication, we abstract only certain aspects of the total reality around us. Our perceptions are one step away from reality, because they are always partial and subjective. We move a second step from reality when we label a perception. We move even further from the actual reality when we respond not to behaviors or our perceptions of them but instead to the label we impose. This process can be illustrated as a ladder of abstraction (Figure 3.5), a concept emphasized by one of the first scholars of interpersonal communication (Hayakawa, 1962, 1964).

We should also monitor our labels to adapt our communication to particular individuals. Competent interpersonal communicators choose words that are sensitive to others and their preferences. This is especially important when we are talking with or about identities. Many adult females resent being called "girls," so it is better to address and refer to them as "women." Most gays and lesbians reject the label "homosexual," and they may resent hearing themselves described by that label. A great many people who have disabilities do not want to be called "disabled persons." Many feel this label suggests they are disabled *as persons* simply because they have some physical or mental condition. Most of them refer to themselves as "persons with disabilities," and that is how they prefer others to refer to them (Braithwaite, 1996).

In 1995 the U.S. Department of Labor surveyed 60,000 households to learn what identity labels different ethnic groups prefer. Not surprisingly, the survey revealed that members of various racial groups do not have uniform preferences. Among Blacks, 44 percent want to be called "Black," 28 percent want to be called "African American," 12 percent prefer the label "Afro-American," and 16 percent prefer other labels or have no preference. Nearly half of American Indians prefer to be called "American Indian," yet 37 percent want to be called "Native American." A majority of Hispanics want to be called "Hispanic," not "Latino." Among Whites, the overwhelmingly preferred identity label is "White"; only 3 percent want to be called "European-American" ("Politically Correct," 1995).

Is effective, sensitive communication possible when there are no universal guidelines for what to call people? Yes, if we are willing to invest thought and effort in our interactions. We begin by assuming we may not know how others want to be labeled and that not all members of a group have the same preferences. Just because my friend Marsha wants to be called "Black," I shouldn't assume others share that preference. It's appropriate to ask others how they identify themselves. Asking shows that we care about their preferences and want to respect them. This is the heart of person-centered communication.

Perceiving accurately is neither magic nor an ability that some people just naturally have. Instead, it is a communication skill that can be developed and practiced. Following the seven guidelines we have discussed will allow you to make more careful and accurate perceptions in interpersonal communication situations.

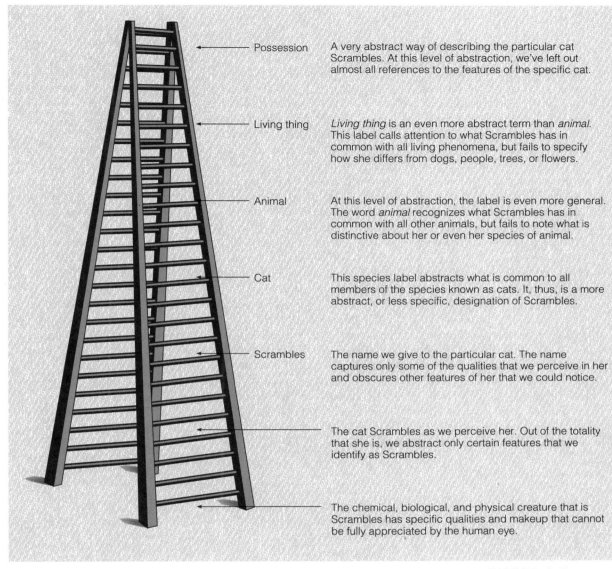

Possession — A very abstract way of describing the particular cat Scrambles. At this level of abstraction, we've left out almost all references to the features of the specific cat.

Living thing — *Living thing* is an even more abstract term than *animal*. This label calls attention to what Scrambles has in common with all living phenomena, but fails to specify how she differs from dogs, people, trees, or flowers.

Animal — At this level of abstraction, the label is even more general. The word *animal* recognizes what Scrambles has in common with all other animals, but fails to note what is distinctive about her or even her species of animal.

Cat — This species label abstracts what is common to all members of the species known as cats. It, thus, is a more abstract, or less specific, designation of Scrambles.

Scrambles — The name we give to the particular cat. The name captures only some of the qualities that we perceive in her and obscures other features of her that we could notice.

The cat Scrambles as we perceive her. Out of the totality that she is, we abstract only certain features that we identify as Scrambles.

The chemical, biological, and physical creature that is Scrambles has specific qualities and makeup that cannot be fully appreciated by the human eye.

FIGURE 3.5
Perception,
Communication,
and Action

CHAPTER
Summary

In this chapter, we've explored human perception, a process that involves selecting, organizing, and interpreting experiences. These three processes are not separate in practice; instead, they interact so that each one affects the others. What we selectively notice affects what it is that we interpret and eval-uate. At the same time, our interpre-tations become a lens that influ-ences what we notice in the world around us. Selection, interpretation, and evaluation interact continuously in the process of perception.

We have seen that perception is influenced by many factors. Our sensory capacities and our physio-logical condition affect what we notice and how astutely we recog-nize stimuli around us. In addition, our cultural backgrounds and stand-points in society shape how we see and interact with the world. Social roles are another influence on per-ception. Thus, our professional training and our roles in families affect what we notice and how we organize and interpret it. Interpersonal perception is also influenced by cognitive abilities including cognitive complexity, person-centeredness, and perspective taking. Finally, our perceptions are shaped by who we are and what experiences we have had. Thus, interpersonal perceptions reflect both what is inside of us and what is outside of us.

Understanding how perception works provides a foundation for improving our perceptual capacities. We discussed seven guidelines for improving the accuracy of perceptions. First, realize that all perceptions are subjective and partial, so there is no absolutely correct or best understanding of a situation or a person. Second, because people perceive differently, we should avoid mindreading or assuming we know what others are perceiving and what their actions mean. Third, it's a good idea to check perceptions, which involves stating how you perceive something and asking how another person does. A fourth guideline is to distinguish facts from inferences. Avoiding the self-serving bias is also important, because it can lead us to perceive ourselves too charitably and to perceive others too harshly. We should also guard against the fundamental attribution error, which can undermine the accuracy of our explanations for how we and others communicate. Finally, it's important to monitor the labels we use. This requires us to be aware that our labels reflect our perceptions of phenomena and to be sensitive to the language others prefer, especially in describing their identities. Just as we can't see how to solve the nine dots problem if we label the dots "a square," so we cannot see aspects of ourselves and others when our labels limit our perceptions. Realizing this encourages us to be more sensitive to the power of language and to make more considered word choices.

Perception is a process of abstracting in which we move further and further away from the concrete reality as we select, organize, interpret, evaluate, and label phenomena. We need to know when we are making factual descriptions and when we are making inferences that require checking.

What we have covered in this chapter allows us to understand how we perceive others and situations and how we might improve our perceptual skills. In the next chapter, we explore the power of language in greater depth, and we will see how what we say affects our interpersonal relationships.

KEY
Concepts

- attributions
- cognitive complexity
- constructivism
- culture
- empathy
- fundamental attribution error

- implicit personality theory
- interpretation
- mindreading
- perception
- personal constructs
- prototypes

- scripts
- self-serving bias
- standpoint theory
- stereotypes

FOR FURTHER
Thought & Discussion

1. To understand how your standpoint influences your perceptions, try visiting a social group that is different from your own. If you are White, you might attend services at a Black church or go to a public meeting of Native Americans on your campus. If you are Christian, you could go to a Jewish synagogue or a Buddhist temple. While in the unfamiliar setting, what stands out to you? What verbal and nonverbal communications do you notice? Do these stand out because they are not present in your usual settings? What does your standpoint highlight and obscure?

2. Think of two situations: one in which you perceive that the majority of people are like you (same sex, race, sexual orientation, age) and one in which you perceive that you are a minority. How does your sense of being a majority or minority in each setting influence your perceptions of others who are present?

3. Identify an example of the self-serving bias in your interpersonal perceptions. Describe how you explained your and others'

behaviors. Then, revise your explanation so that the self-serving bias is eliminated.

4. Identify an example of the fundamental attribution error in your interpersonal perceptions. Describe how you explained your and others' behaviors. Then, revise your explanation so that it doesn't reflect the fundamental attribution error.

5. Use your *InfoTrac College Edition* to check the table of contents of the last four issues of *Cultural Studies* and *Journal of American Ethnic History*. Can you find articles dealing with how race is defined? Describe the controversy among scholars regarding how races are perceived. Based on the articles you read, do you agree or disagree that race is socially constructed?

6. Conduct a survey to find out how students on your campus prefer to define their identities. Ask Blacks whether they prefer to be called "Black," "African American," "Afro-American," or another label. Ask Whites how they identify their race. Ask Hispanic students what term they use to describe their ethnicity. Compare your findings to those of the U.S. Department of Labor that were discussed on page 108. Do students on your campus reflect national preferences?

7. Use the ladder of abstraction to describe the relationships among perception, communication, and action in one interpersonal encounter in your life. First, describe the total situation as fully as you can (your descriptions won't be absolutely complete—that's impossible). Next, describe what behaviors and environmental cues you noticed. Then, identify the way you labeled what was happening and others who were present. Finally, describe how you acted in the situation. Now, consider alternative selective perceptions you might have made and how those might have influenced your labels and actions.

Solution to the problem on p. 80:

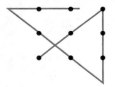

The World

of Words

Many children in the United States have heard the nursery rhyme, "Sticks and stones can break my bones, but words can never hurt me." By now, most of us have figured out that isn't true. Words can hurt us, sometimes very deeply. Words can also enchant, comfort, teach, amuse, and inspire us. We use language to plan, dream, remember, evaluate, and reflect on ourselves and the world around us. Words, in short, are powerful aspects of everyday life. "How Words Hurt Us" provides some examples of the power of words.

The human world is a world of words and meanings. Just as weavers weave individual threads together to create fabric, so do we weave words together to create meaning in our lives. We use words to express ourselves and to give meaning to our lives and activities. In this chapter, we take a close look at the verbal dimension of communication and how it affects personal identity and interpersonal interaction. We begin by defining symbols and symbolic abilities. Next we explore different communication cultures to appreciate how various social groups communicate. We close the chapter by discussing guidelines for effective verbal communication.

The Symbolic Nature of Language

As we discovered in our discussion of perception, we do not deal with raw reality most of the time. Instead, we abstract only certain parts of reality to notice and label. After we label experiences, we often respond to our labels, not to the experiences themselves. This means that our perceptions and experiences are filtered through symbols. To appreciate the importance of symbols in our lives, we'll discuss what they are and how they affect us personally and interpersonally.

Symbols are arbitrary, ambiguous, abstract representations of other phenomena. For instance, your name is a symbol that represents you. House is a symbol that stands for a particular kind of building. Love is a symbol that represents intense feelings. All language and much nonverbal behavior is symbolic, but not all symbols are language. Art, music, and objects also are symbols that stand for feelings, thoughts, and experiences. We'll consider three key qualities of symbols: they are arbitrary, ambiguous, and abstract (see Figure 4.1).

Symbols Are Arbitrary

Symbols are **arbitrary,** which means they are not intrinsically connected to what they represent. For instance, the word *Julia* has no necessary or natural connection to me. All of our symbols are arbitrary because we could easily use

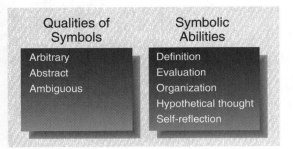

Qualities of Symbols	Symbolic Abilities
Arbitrary	Definition
Abstract	Evaluation
Ambiguous	Organization
	Hypothetical thought
	Self-reflection

FIGURE 4.1
Symbols

other symbols as long as we all agreed on their meanings. Certain words seem right because as a society we agree to use them in particular ways, but they have no natural correspondence with their referents. Further, meanings change over time. In the 1950s, *gay* meant lighthearted and merry; today it is generally understood to refer to homosexuals. The majority of publishers and dictionaries no longer allow male-generic language, which uses male terms (*chairman, postman, mankind*) to represent both women and men. Our language also changes as we invent new words. African Americans began using *disrespect* as a verb to describe behaviors that demean someone. Now the term *disrespect* and its abbreviated form, *dis,* are in the general language and are included in the newest dictionaries: In April 1996 Random House, which sets the standard on dictionaries of the English language, published its latest *College Dictionary*; *dis* appears, along with the definition "to show disrespect for; affront; disparage; belittle" (Kilpatrick, 1996).

Symbols Are Ambiguous

Symbols are also **ambiguous,** which means their meanings aren't clear-cut or fixed. There are variations in what words mean. A *good friend* means someone to hang out with to one person and someone to confide in to another. The term *nice clothes* means different things to people in the working class and to people who are very affluent. *Christmas, Hanukkah,* and *Thanksgiving* carry distinct connotations for people who have families and for those who don't. *Affirmative action* has different meanings for people who have experienced discrimination and for those who have not. Although the words are the same, what they mean varies as a result of individuals' unique experiences.

Although words don't mean exactly the same thing to everyone, within a culture many symbols have an agreed-on range of meanings (Mead, 1934). In learning language, we learn not only words but the meanings and values of our society. Thus, all of us know that dogs are four-footed creatures, but each of us also has personal meanings based on dogs we have known and our experiences with them.

The ambiguity of symbols explains why misunderstandings so often arise in interpersonal communication. We tend to assume that words mean the same thing to others as they do to us. But the ambiguity of symbols implies that people don't always agree on meanings. Recently, a friend of mine told her three-year-old daughter she needed to be more responsible about putting away her toys. Later we discovered the little girl had tucked all of her stuffed animals into beds around the house. That's what being more responsible meant to her.

S T U D E N T VOICES

RON: *A while ago I told my girlfriend I needed more independence. She got all upset because she thought I didn't love her anymore and was pulling away. All I meant was that I need some time with the guys and some for just myself. She said that the last time a guy said he wanted more independence, she found out he was dating others.*

Reprinted by permission of John Grimes. © John Grimes.

Ambiguity frequently surfaces in friendships and romantic relationships. Martina tells her boyfriend that he's not being attentive, meaning that she wants him to listen more closely to what she says. However, he infers she wants him to call more often and open doors for her. The word *love* means different things to people brought up in abusive and nonabusive families. Similarly, spouses often have different meanings for "doing their share" of home chores. To most women, it means doing half of the work, but to men it tends to mean doing more than their fathers, which is still less than many wives do (Hochschild with Manchung, 1989).

According to a relationship counselor, a common problem between intimates is language that creates ambiguity (Beck, 1988). A wife asks her husband to be more loving, but she and he have different understandings of what being more loving means. Suggesting that a friend should be more sensitive doesn't provide a very clear idea of what you want. To minimize the problems of ambiguity, it's important to be as clear as possible when communicating. Thus, it's more effective to say "I would like for you to look at me and give feedback when I'm talking" than to say "I wish you'd be more attentive."

APPLY THE IDEA
Communicating Clearly

To express yourself clearly, it's important that you learn to translate ambiguous words into concrete language. Practice translating with the statements below.

EXAMPLE: Ambiguous language: You are rude.
                     Clear language: I don't like it when you interrupt me.

AMBIGUOUS LANGUAGE

You're conceited.
I want more freedom.
Let's have a low-key evening.
We need to be closer.

Symbols Are Abstract

Finally, symbols are **abstract,** which means they are not concrete or tangible. They stand for ideas, people, events, objects, feelings, and so forth, but they are not the things they represent. In Chapter 3, we discussed the process of abstraction whereby we move further and further away from concrete reality. The sym-

Julia T. Wood

bols we use vary in abstractness. "Scrambles" is the name of the particular cat who lounges on the back of my chair while I'm writing. "Cat" is a more abstract label for her. "Animal" is even more abstract.

As our symbols become increasingly abstract, the potential for confusion mushrooms. One of the ways this happens is overgeneralization. Couple counselor Aaron Beck (1988) reports that overly general language distorts how partners think about a relationship. They may make broad, negative statements such as "You never go along with my preferences" or "You always interrupt me." In most cases, such statements are overgeneralizations that are not entirely accurate. Yet by symbolizing experience this way, partners frame how they think about it. Researchers have shown that we are more likely to recall behaviors that are consistent with how we've labeled people than those that are inconsistent (Fincham & Bradbury, 1987). When we say a friend is always insensitive, we'll probably remember all of the occasions in which she or he was insensitive, and we'll overlook times when she or he was sensitive.

Bobby Patton and Kurt Ritter (1976), two communication scholars, suggest that misunderstandings can be minimized by using specific language. It's clearer to say "I wish you wouldn't interrupt when I'm talking" than "Don't be so dominating."

Principles of Verbal Communication

We've seen that language is symbolic, which means it consists of arbitrary, ambiguous, and abstract representations of other phenomena. Building on this understanding, we can now explore how verbal symbols work. We'll discuss four principles of verbal communication.

Language and Culture Reflect Each Other

Language and cultural life are intricately interconnected. Each reflects the other in an ongoing process. Intercultural communication scholars Larry Samovar and Richard Porter (1995) claim that communication and culture cannot be separated, because each influences the other. "Our Multicultural Language" demonstrates the various cultures reflected in the United States.

Communication reflects cultural values and perspectives. The words in a language reflect what the mainstream in a particular culture regards as worth naming. We do not name what we consider unimportant. Cultures also don't give symbolic reality to practices of which the majority of members disapprove. In 1996 and 1997 there was a great uproar in the United States because Hawaii was considering recognizing gay and lesbian commitments as legal marriages. Legislators from other states fought fiercely (and successfully) against allowing the word *marriage* to apply to enduring relationships between members of the same sex.

The mainstream values of a culture are also reflected in calendars by which social groups' important days are and are not named. Look at a calendar. Do you find the following holidays recognized: Christmas, Thanksgiving, New Year's Day, Easter? Do you find these holidays on the calendar: Hanukkah, Kwanzaa, Passover, Yom Kippur, Elderly Day, Ramadan? Standard Western calendars reflect the Christian heritage of the mainstream members of the culture. In the United States we are given time off from work or school to celebrate Christmas (but not Hanukkah or Kwanzaa), Thanksgiving (which is not a celebratory day to many Native Americans), and Easter (but not Passover).

To understand further how cultural values are woven into language, consider the adages of a culture and what they express about social values. What is meant by the common U.S. saying "Every man for himself"? Does it reflect the idea that men, and not women, are the standard? Does it reflect individualism as a value? What is meant by the phrase "The early bird gets the worm"? Compare the values in common adages in the United States with those from other cultures. In Africa, two popular adages are "The child has no owner" and "It takes a whole village to raise a child," and in China a common saying is "No need to know the person, only the family" (Samovar & Porter, 1994). What values are expressed by these sayings? How are they different from mainstream Western values and the language that embodies them?

To recognize the values woven into cultures and their languages, it's useful to compare different cultures and the ways in which they use language. For example, many Asian languages include specific words to describe numerous particular relationships, such as my grandfather's sister, my mother's uncle, my youngest son. These words reflect traditional Asian cultures' emphasis on family relationships (Ferrante, 1995). The English language has far fewer words to represent specific kinship bonds, which suggests that Western culture places less priority on ties beyond those in the immediate family.

Scholars of language and culture maintain that the language we learn shapes how we categorize the world and even how we perceive and think about our world (Fantini, 1991; Hakuta, 1986). For example, Hopi Indians have one word for water in open space and a separate word for water in a container. The English language has only the one noun, *water*. In the United States we perceive saying good-bye to guests as a single event. In contrast, in Japan, saying good-bye is a process. Hosts and guests say good-bye in the living room and again at the front door. Guests walk a distance from the house, then turn and wave good-bye to the hosts who are waiting at their gate or door to wave the third good-bye. "The Whorf-Sapir View of Language" on page 118

"The Whorf-Sapir View of Language" on page 118

COMMUNICATION NOTES

Our Multicultural Language

Although the term *multicultural* has only recently come into popular usage, our society and our language have always been multicultural. See if you recognize the cultural origins of the following everyday words.

1. brocade
2. chocolate
3. cotton
4. klutz
5. khaki
6. silk
7. skunk
8. gingham
9. noodle
10. zombie

Answers: 1. Spanish; 2. Nahuatl (Native American); 3. Arabic; 4. Yiddish; 5. Hindi; 6. Greek; 7. Algonquian (Native American); 8. Malay; 9. German; 10. Congo.

SOURCE: Carnes, J. (1994, Spring). An uncommon language. *Teaching Tolerance*, 56–63.

The Whorf-Sapir View of Language

Studies by anthropologists reveal that our perceptions are guided by language. The language of the Hopi Indians makes no distinction between stationary objects and moving processes, whereas English uses nouns and verbs respectively. The English word *snow* is the only word we have to define frozen, white precipitation that falls in the winter. In Arctic cultures where snow is a major aspect of life, there are many words to define snow that is powdery, icy, dry, wet, and so forth. The distinctions are important to designate which snows allow safe travel, hunting, and other activities.

SOURCE: Whorf, B. (1956). *Language, thought, and reality.* New York: MIT Press/Wiley.

argues that how we perceive our world is guided by language.

Communication also changes cultures. A primary way that communication changes cultural values and perspectives is by naming things in ways that alter understandings. For example, the term *date rape* was coined in the late 1980s. Although probably many women had been forced to have sex with dates before that time, until the term was born there was no way to describe what happened as a violent and criminal act (Wood, 1992b). Cultural understandings of other sexual activities have been similarly reformed by the coining of terms such as *sexual harassment* and *marital rape*, both of which characterize negatively activities that previously had been perceived as acceptable.

STUDENT VOICES

MARY: *It was fifteen years ago when I was just starting college that a professor sexually harassed me, only I didn't know what to call it then. I felt guilty, like maybe I'd done something to encourage him, or I felt maybe I was overreacting to his kissing and touching me. But after the Clarence Thomas–Anita Hill hearings in 1991, I had a name for what happened—a name that said he was wrong, not me.*

Language is a primary tool of social movements that change cultural life and meanings. In the 1960s the civil rights movement in the United States relied on communication to transform public laws and, more gradually, public views of Blacks. Powerful speakers such as the Reverend Martin Luther King, Jr., and Malcolm X raised Black Americans' pride in their heritage and identity. The phrase "Black is beautiful," which came out of that movement, marked a turning point in Blacks' definition of themselves. In the 1990s Black leaders organized the Million Man March, which relied on powerful rhetoric to redefine the role and responsibilities of Black men. Language has also been influential in altering social views of persons with disabilities. Whereas "disabled person" was a common phrase for many years, many people are now aware that this label can offend, and they know the preferred phrase is "person with disability" (Braithwaite, 1996). Social views of deaf people have also been altered in recent times. People with limited hearing have challenged the idea that deafness is related to intelligence. In addition, deaf, as a medical condition, has been distinguished from Deaf, as a culture with rich linguistic resources (Carl, 1998).

Language and culture are closely related. As we learn language, we also learn the values, perspectives, and beliefs of our culture. In turn, as we use language we often reflect and reinforce the cultural values it entails. In other cases, we use language to challenge and change taken-for-granted ideas and values in our culture.

© Bruce Ayres/Tony Stone Images

Meanings of Language Are Subjective

Because symbols are abstract, ambiguous, and arbitrary, their meanings are never self-evident or absolute. Instead, we have to interpret symbols to figure out what they mean. We construct meanings in the process of interacting with others and through dialogues we carry on in our own head (Duck, 1994a, 1994b; Shotter, 1993). The process of constructing meaning is itself symbolic, because we rely on words to think about what things mean.

Interpretation is an active, creative process we use to make sense of words. If we say "dinner" to a dog, the dog will respond in a predictable manner because "dinner" has a fixed, exact meaning to the dog. To us, however, the word *dinner* may mean many things—time for family talk, a romantic experience, a struggle to stick to a diet, or tension among those present at the meal. For humans, words are ambiguous and layered with multiple meanings. Although we're usually not conscious of the effort we invest to interpret words, we continuously engage in the process of constructing meanings.

When somebody says "Blow off," you have to think about the comment and the person who made it to decide whether it's insulting, friendly needling, or colloquially saying you are out of line. What the words mean also depends on the self-esteem and previous experiences of the individual who is told to blow off. Individuals who are secure and have high self-esteem are not as likely to be hurt as individuals who have less self-confidence. Relationship-level meanings rely especially on understandings of the person speaking and the context of communication. Because symbols require interpretation, communication is an ongoing process of creating meanings.

S T U D E N T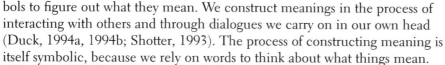

DONIKA: *It took me a long time to understand certain words in my fiancé's family. When I first met them, I heard them talk about the wife's career, but I knew she did not work. In the family, they say her career is keeping track of all the children. They also talked about the husband's hobby of being broke. I thought this meant he spent a lot of money on collecting stamps or something, but what they mean is he likes to give to causes and this takes a lot of money. It took several visits for me to understand the family vocabulary.*

Language Use Is Rule-Guided

Verbal communication is patterned by unspoken but broadly understood rules (Argyle & Henderson, 1985; Schiminoff, 1980). **Communication rules** are shared understandings of what communication means and what behaviors are

© David Young-Wolff/PhotoEdit

appropriate in various situations. For example, we understand that people take turns speaking and that we should speak softly in libraries. In the course of interacting with our families and others, we unconsciously absorb rules that guide how we communicate and how we interpret others' communication. According to Judi Miller (1993), children begin to understand and follow communication rules by the time they are one to two years old.

There are two kinds of rules that govern communication (Cronen, Pearce, & Snavely, 1979; Pearce, Cronen, & Conklin, 1979). **Regulative rules** regulate interaction by specifying when, how, where, and with whom to talk about certain things. For instance, Westerners know not to interrupt when someone else is speaking in a formal setting, but in more casual situations, interruptions may be appropriate. In other cultures, there are strong rules against interrupting in any context. Some families have a rule that people cannot argue at the dinner table. Families also teach us rules about how to communicate in conflict situations (Honeycutt, Woods, & Fontenot, 1993; Jones & Gallois, 1989; Yerby, Buerkel-Rothfuss, & Bochner, 1990). Regulative rules also define when, where, and with whom it's appropriate to show affection and disclose private information. Regulative rules vary across cultures so that what is considered appropriate in one society may be regarded as impolite or offensive elsewhere.

YUMIKO: *I try to teach my children to follow the customs of my native Japan, but they are learning to be American. I scold my daughter, who is seven this year, for talking loudly and speaking when she has not been addressed, but she tells me all the other kids talk loudly and talk when they wish to talk. I tell her it is not polite to look directly at others, but she says everyone looks at others here. She communicates as an American, not a Japanese.*

Constitutive rules define what communication means by specifying how certain communicative acts are to be counted. We learn what counts as respect (paying attention), affection (kisses, hugs), and rudeness (interrupting). We also learn what communication is expected if we want to be perceived as a good friend (showing support, being loyal), a responsible employee (meeting deadlines, developing strong reports), and a desirable romantic partner (showing respect and trust, being faithful, sharing confidences). We learn constitutive and regulative rules from both particular others and the generalized other. Like regulative rules, constitutive ones are shaped by cultures. Boasting outrageously about personal abilities is considered egotistical and offensive by most Caucasians. Among African Americans, however, this form of communication, called braggadocio or "woofing," is viewed as a way of showing verbal wit.

Communication Rules

Think about the regulative and constitutive rules you follow in your communication. For each item below identify two rules you learned.

REGULATIVE RULES

List rules that regulate how you:

- talk with elders
- interact at dinner time
- have first exchanges in the morning
- greet casual friends on campus
- talk with professors

CONSTITUTIVE RULES

How do you communicate to show:

- respect
- love
- disrespect
- support

After you've identified your rules, talk with others in your class about the rules they follow. Are there commonalities among your rules that reflect broad cultural norms? What explains differences in individuals' rules?

Everyday interaction is guided by rules that tell us when to speak, what to say, and how to interpret others' communication. Our social interactions, which involve I–It and I–You relationships, tend to adhere to rules that are widely shared in our society. Interaction between intimates also follows rules, but these may not be broadly shared by members of the culture. Intimate partners negotiate private rules to guide how they communicate and what certain things mean (Wood, 1982, 1995c). Couples craft personal rules for whether and how to argue, express love, make decisions, and spend time together (Beck, 1988; Fitzpatrick, 1988).

It's important to understand that we don't have to be aware of communication rules in order to follow them. For the most part, we're not conscious of the rules that guide how, when, where, and with whom we communicate about various things. We may not realize we have rules until one is broken and we become aware that we had an expectation. A study by Victoria DeFrancisco (1991) revealed that between spouses there was a clear pattern in which husbands interrupted wives and were unresponsive to topics wives initiated. Both husbands and wives were unaware of the rules, but their communication nonetheless sustained the pattern. Becoming aware of communication rules empowers you to change ones that don't promote good interaction, as Emily's commentary illustrates.

EMILY: *My boyfriend and I had this really frustrating pattern about planning what to do. He'd say, "What do you want to do this weekend?" And I'd say, "I don't know. What do you want to do?" Then he'd suggest two or three things and ask me which of them sounded good. I would say they were all fine with me, even if they weren't. And this would keep on forever. Both of us had a rule not to impose on the other, and it kept us from stating our preferences, so we just went in circles about any decision. Well, two weekends ago, I talked to him about rules, and he agreed we had one that was frustrating. So we invented a new rule that says each of us has to state what we want to do, but the other has to say if that is not okay. It's a lot less frustrating to figure out what we want to do since we agreed on this rule.*

Punctuation of Language Shapes Meaning

We punctuate communication to decide what it means. This isn't the kind of punctuation you study in grammar classes, although punctuation of communication is also a way of marking a flow of activity into meaningful units. In writing we use commas, periods, and semicolons to define where ideas stop and start and where pauses are needed. Similarly, in interpersonal communication, **punctuation** defines beginnings and endings of interaction episodes (Watzlawick, Beavin, & Jackson, 1967).

To decide what communication means, we must establish its boundaries. Usually this involves deciding who started the interaction. When we don't agree on punctuation, problems may arise. If you've ever heard children arguing about who started a fight, you understand the importance of punctuation. A common instance of conflicting punctuation is the demand–withdraw pattern (Bergner & Bergner, 1990; Christensen & Heavey, 1990; James, 1989). In this pattern, one person tries to create closeness with personal talk, and the other strives to maintain autonomy by avoiding intimate discussion (Figure 4.2). The more the first person pushes for personal talk ("Tell me what's going on in your life," "Let's talk about our future"), the further the second withdraws ("There's nothing to tell," "I don't want to talk about the future," silence). Each

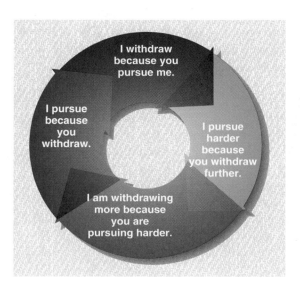

FIGURE 4.2
The Demand–Withdraw Pattern

> I withdraw because you pursue me.
>
> I pursue because you withdraw.
>
> I pursue harder because you withdraw further.
>
> I am withdrawing more because you are pursuing harder.

partner punctuates interaction as starting with the other's behavior. Thus, the demander thinks "I pursue because you withdraw" and the withdrawer thinks "I withdraw because you pursue."

There is no objectively correct punctuation because it depends on subjective perceptions. When partners don't agree on punctuation, they don't share meanings for what is happening between them. To break out of unconstructive cycles, such as demand–withdraw, partners need, first, to realize they may punctuate differently and, second, to discuss how each of them experiences the pattern. This reminds us of a guideline discussed in Chapter 1: Dual perspective is essential to effective communication.

STUDENT VOICES

HAL: *Punctuation helps me understand what happens with me and my girlfriend a lot of times. Sometimes when we first get together she's all steamed and I can't figure out why. I'm like, what's going on? How can you be mad at me when we haven't even started talking? But she's steamed about something that happened the night before or even longer ago. For me, whatever argument we might have had is over—it ended when we separated the last time. But for her, it may not be over—we're still in that episode.*

APPLY THE IDEA
Punctuating Interaction

The next time you and another person get in an unproductive cycle, stop and discuss how each of you punctuates interaction.

1. What do you define as the start of interaction?
2. What does the other person define as the beginning?
3. What happens when you learn about each other's punctuation? How does this affect understanding between you?

The meaning of verbal communication arises out of cultural teachings, subjective interpretations, communication rules, and punctuation. These four principles highlight the creativity involved in constructing meaning. We're now ready to probe how verbal communication affects us and our relationships.

Symbolic Abilities

The ability to use symbols allows humans to live in a world of ideas and meanings. Instead of just reacting to our concrete environments, we think about them and sometimes transform them. Philosophers of language have identified five ways symbolic capacities affect our lives (Cassirer, 1944; Langer, 1953,

It's Only Skin Deep

The gifted filmmaker Spike Lee resents the fact that he is often totalized as a *Black* filmmaker. Lee says, "I want to be known as a talented young filmmaker. That should be first. But the reality today is that no matter how successful you are, you're black first" (McDowell, 1989, p. 92).

John Hope Franklin is a distinguished historian who has gained national stature for his books on the South. He is sometimes introduced as a man who has written twelve books on Black history. Franklin says that because he is Black many people assume he only knows and writes about Blacks. Actually, he notes, his books—like the region they describe—are about both Whites and Blacks.

Pro basketball player Isiah Thomas is offended by the different ways Black and White players are described. He points out, "When Bird [Larry Bird—a White player] makes a great play, it's due to his thinking, and his work habits." But Thomas says when Black players—for instance Thomas, Michael Jordan and Magic Johnson—make equally good plays, they are described as "playing on God-given talent" and "wild in the jungle." Says Thomas, the media represent Black players as if "all we do is run and jump. We never practice or give a thought to how to play. It's like I came dribbling out of my mother's womb" (Berko, 1987, p. D27).

SOURCES: Berko, I. (1987, June 2). The coloring of Bird. *The New York Times*, p. D27; McDowell, D. (1989, July 17). He's got to have his way. *Time*, pp. 92–94; McGurl, M. (1990, June 3). That's history, not black history. *The New York Times Book Review*, p. 13.

1979). As we discuss each, we'll consider how to realize the constructive power of symbols and minimize the problems they can prompt.

Symbols Define

The most basic symbolic ability is definition. We use symbols to define experiences, people, relationships, feelings, and thoughts. As we saw in Chapter 3, the definitions we impose shape what things mean to us.

Labels Shape Perceptions   When we label someone, we focus attention on particular aspects of that person and her or his activities, and we necessarily obscure other aspects of who she or he is. We might define a person as an environmentalist, a teacher, a gourmet cook, or a father. Each definition directs our attention to certain aspects of the person. We might talk with the environmentalist about wilderness legislation, discuss class assignments with the teacher, swap recipes with the chef, and exchange stories about children with the father. If we define someone as an Asian American or a Latina, then that may be all we notice about the person, although there are many other aspects of her or him. We tend to perceive and interact with people according to how we define them.

Our language reflects our subjective perceptions and, at the same time, it shapes and fixes our perceptions. If you saw a person eat a very large meal, how would you describe what you saw? If the person was a teenage boy, you might describe him as being a growing boy. If the person was a slender woman, you might describe her as having a healthy appetite. If the person was overweight, you may describe him as a glutton. Notice that the amount of food and the act of eating don't change, but our perceptions and labels do.

The labels that we apply to people and things shape how we evaluate and respond to them. According to Joel Best (1989), the impact of labels is especially evident in language about AIDS. Calling it a "moral problem" defines people with the disease as having behaved badly and suggests the solution is to change behavior. By contrast, calling AIDS a "medical problem" defines people with the disease as having certain biological processes that are not the fault or responsibility of individuals. Consequently, the solution to AIDS as a "medical problem" lies in medical treatment.

PART ONE
The Fabric of
Interpersonal
Communication

124

Labels Can Totalize   **Totalizing** occurs when we respond to a person as if one label (one we have chosen or accepted from others) totally represents who he or she is. We fix on one symbol to define someone and fail to recognize many other aspects of who he or she is (Wood, 1998). "It's Only Skin Deep" illustrates how people are sometimes totalized by their race. Some individuals totalize gay men and lesbians as if sexual orientation is their only important facet. Interestingly, we don't totalize heterosexuals on the basis of their sexuality. Totalizing also occurs when we dismiss people by saying, "He's a Republican," "She's old," "She's preppy," or "He's just a jock." Totalizing is not the same as stereotyping. When we stereotype someone, we define him or her in terms of characteristics of a group. When we totalize others, we negate most of who they are by spotlighting a single aspect of their identity.

S   T   U   D   E   N   T

JAMAL: *I know all about totalizing. A lot of people relate to me as Black, like that's all I am. Sometimes in classes, teachers ask me to explain the "African American perspective" on something, but they don't ask me to explain my perspective as a premed major or a working student. I am an African American, but that's not all I am.*

Labels Affect Relationships   The symbols we use to define experiences in our relationships affect how we think and feel about those relationships. In a study, my colleagues and I asked romantic couples how they defined differences between them (Wood, Dendy, Dordek, Germany, & Varallo, 1994). We found that some individuals define differences as positive forces that energize a relationship and keep it interesting. Others define differences as problems or barriers to closeness. There was a direct connection between how partners defined differences and how they acted. Partners who viewed differences as constructive approached disagreements with curiosity, interest, and a hope for growth through discussion. On the other hand, partners who labeled differences as "problems" tended to deny differences and to avoid talking about them.

A number of communication scholars have shown that the language we use to think about relationships affects what happens in them (Duck, 1985, 1994a, 1994b; Honeycutt, 1993; Spencer, 1994). People who consistently use negative labels to describe their relationships heighten awareness of what they don't like and diminish perceptions of what they do like (Cloven & Roloff, 1991). It's also been shown that partners who focus on good facets of their relationships are more conscious of virtues in partners and relationships and less bothered by imperfections (Bradbury & Fincham, 1990; Fletcher & Fincham, 1991).

These studies show us that our definitions of relationships can create self-fulfilling prophecies. Because verbal language is ambiguous, arbitrary, and abstract, there are multiple ways we can define any experience. Once we select a label, we tend to see the experience in line with our label. This suggests we

Nondiscrimination in Housing

Whoops! Real estate ads may lead to lawsuits if they contain language that offends certain groups. "Great view" excludes persons with visual impairments; "walking distance to shops" offends people in wheelchairs; "master bedroom" suggests sexism; "family room" discriminates against child-free couples and singles; and "newlyweds" excludes gay and lesbian couples who cannot be legally wed.

In 1994, Pennsylvania's Association of Realtors, Newspaper Association, and Human Relations Commission issued a list of about seventy-five unacceptable words and phrases for real estate ads. Among the forbidden terms:

bachelor pad	couples	mature
children	traditional	senior citizens
private	newlyweds	exclusive

should reconsider definitions that undermine healthy self-concepts and interpersonal relationships.

Symbols Evaluate

Symbols are not neutral or objective descriptions. They are laden with values. This is an intrinsic quality of symbols. In fact, it's impossible to find words that are completely neutral or objective.

Values in Language Reflect and Shape Perceptions We describe people we like with language that accents their good qualities and downplays their flaws. Just the reverse is true of our descriptions for people we don't like. Restaurants use positive words to heighten the attractiveness of menu entrees. A dish described as tender London broil gently sautéed in natural juices and topped with succulent mushrooms sounds more appetizing than one described as cow carcass cooked in blood and topped with fungus grown in compost and manure.

Perhaps you've seen humorous illustrations of how differently we describe the same behaviors enacted by ourselves, people we like, and people we don't like. I am casual; you are messy; she's a slob. I am organized; you are methodical; he is obsessive-compulsive. I am assertive; you are aggressive; she's a bully. Although these are funny, they also reflect our tendencies to use labels with different evaluations to describe behavior.

Of course, there are degrees of evaluation in language. We might describe people who speak their minds as assertive, outspoken, courageous, or authoritarian. Each word has a distinct connotation. In recent years, we have become more sensitive to how symbols can hurt people. Most individuals with disabilities prefer not to be called disabled, because that totalizes them in terms of a disability. ("Nondiscrimination in Housing" discusses some forbidden terms in real estate.) The term *African American* emphasizes cultural heritage, whereas *Black* focuses on skin color. Designations for homosexuals are currently in transition. The term *homosexual* has negative connotations and even more so do words like *fairy*, *dyke*, and *faggot*. Some gays and lesbians use the term *sexual orientation* to suggest they didn't choose their sexuality. Others use the term *sexual preference* to indicate their sexuality is a matter of choice, not genetics. Still others speak of *affectional preference* to signal that their commitment concerns the entire realm of affection, not just sexual activity.

Language Can Be Loaded **Loaded language** is words that strongly slant perceptions and thus meanings. For example, radio personality Rush Limbaugh refers to feminists as Feminazis, which implies feminists are also Nazis. Loaded language also encourages negative views of older people. Terms such as *geezers* and *old fogies* incline us to regard older people with contempt or pity. Alternatives such as *senior citizen* and *mature person* reflect more respectful attitudes.

Probably many of us have sympathy with Maynard, who was fifty-four years old when he took a course with me. It is hard to keep up with changes in language, and it's inevitable that we will occasionally offend someone unintentionally. Nonetheless, we should try to learn what terms hurt or insult others and avoid using those. It's also advisable for us to tell others when they've referred to us with a term that we dislike. As long as we speak assertively but not confrontationally, it's likely that others will respect our ideas. "Reappropriating Language" examines a trend toward defusing some loaded language.

Reappropriating Language

An interesting communicative phenomenon is the reappropriation of language. This happens when a group reclaims terms others use to degrade it and treats those terms as positive self-descriptions. Reappropriation intends to take the sting out of a term that others use pejoratively.

Some feminists and women musicians have reappropriated the term *girl* to define themselves and to resist the general connotations of childishness.

Some gays have reappropriated the term *queer* and are using it as a positive statement about their identity.

The writer Reynolds Price developed cancer of the spine that left him paraplegic. He scoffs at terms such as *differently abled* and *physically challenged* and refers to himself as a "cripple" and others as "temporarily able-bodied."

S T U D E N T VOICES

MAYNARD: *I'm as sensitive as the next guy, but I just can't keep up with what language offends what people anymore. When I was younger, "Negro" was an accepted term, then it was Black, and now it's African American. Sometimes I forget and say "Black" or even "Negro," and I get accused of being racist. It used to be polite to call females "girls," but now that offends a lot of the women I work with. Just this year I heard that we aren't supposed to say "blind" or "disabled" anymore; we're supposed to say "visually impaired" and "differently abled." I just can't keep up.*

Language Can Degrade Others   Haig Bosmajian is a scholar of communication and ethics. Throughout his career, he has been concerned with the ways in which language is used to degrade and dehumanize others. Bosmajian notes that how we see ourselves is profoundly influenced by the names we are called (1974). One form of degrading language is **hate speech,** which is language that radically dehumanizes others. Recently Brown University student Dennis Hann made national news because of how he chose to celebrate turning twenty-one. After drinking heavily, Hann went to a central quad on campus and spewed out a string of curse words and epithets, including *nigger, jew,* and *faggots*. Hann was promptly and permanently expelled from Brown.

Unfortunately, Hann's actions are not an isolated incident. Around the nation hate speech erupts both on and off campus. Malicious and abusive messages are scrawled on the cars and homes of minority citizens. Graffiti in bathrooms and on public buildings insults gays, lesbians, and other social groups. Hate speech has become so prevalent that nine of ten Americans in a 1996 poll said they thought incivility was a serious problem in the United States (Morris, 1997).

Language is powerful. The values inherent in the words we use shape our perceptions and those of others. This implies that each of us has an ethical responsibility to recognize the impact of language and to guard against engaging in incivil speech ourselves, as well as not tolerating it from others.

Symbols Organize Perceptions

We use symbols to organize our perceptions. As we saw in Chapter 3, we rely on cognitive schemata to classify and evaluate experiences. How we organize experiences affects what they mean to us. For example, your prototype of a good friend affects how you judge particular friends. When we place someone in the category of friend, the category influences how we interpret the friend and his or her communication. An insult is likely to be viewed as teasing if made by a friend, but a call to battle if made by an enemy. The words don't change, but their meaning varies depending on how we organize them.

Symbols Allow Abstract Thought   The organizational quality of symbols also allows us to think about abstract concepts, such as justice, integrity, and good family life. We use broad concepts to transcend specific, concrete activities and to enter the world of conceptual thought and ideals. Because we think abstractly, we don't have to consider every specific object and experience individually. Instead, we can think in general terms.

Symbols Can Stereotype   Our capacity to abstract can also distort thinking. A primary way this occurs is through stereotyping, which is thinking in broad generalizations about a whole class of people or experiences. Examples of stereotypes are "sorority women are preppy," "teachers are smart," "jocks are dumb," "feminists hate men," "religious people are good," and "conflict is bad." Notice that stereotypes can be positive or negative generalizations.

Common to all stereotypes is classifying an experience or person into a category based on general knowledge of that category. When we use stereotypical terms such as *African Americans, lesbians, White males,* and *working class,* we may see only what members of each group have in common and not perceive differences among individuals. We may not perceive the uniqueness of the individual person if we label them only as members of one group. Stereotyping is related to totalizing, because when we stereotype someone, we may not perceive other aspects of them—ones not represented in the stereotype. For example, if we stereotype someone as a fraternity man, we may see only what he has in common with other members of fraternities. We may not notice his other aspects such as his political stands, individual values, ethnic background, and so forth.

Clearly, we have to generalize. We simply cannot think about each and every thing in our lives as a specific instance. However, stereotypes can blind us to important differences among phenomena we lump together. Thus, it's important to reflect on stereotypes and to stay alert to differences among people and things we place in any category. We should also remind ourselves that *we* place others in categories—the categories are our tools. They are not objective descriptions.

Symbols Allow Hypothetical Thought

Where do you hope to be five years from now? What is your fondest childhood memory? To answer these questions, you must think hypothetically, which means thinking about experiences and ideas that are not part of your concrete, present situation. Because we can think hypothetically, we can plan, dream, remember, set goals, consider alternative courses of action, and imagine possibilities.

We Can Think Beyond Immediate, Concrete Situations

Hypothetical thought is possible because we use symbols. When we symbolize, we name ideas so that we can hold them in our minds and reflect on them. We can contemplate things that currently have no real existence, and we can remember ourselves in the past and project ourselves into the future. Our ability to live simultaneously in all three dimensions of time explains why we can set goals and work toward them even though there is nothing tangible about them in the moment (Dixson & Duck, 1993).

"Well, then, if 'commandments' seems too harsh to me, and 'guidelines' seems too wishy-washy to you, how about 'The 10 Policy Statements'?"

Reprinted from The Chronicle of Higher Education. By permission of Mischa Richter and Harald Bakken.

For example, you've invested many hours studying and writing papers because you have the idea of yourself as someone with a college degree. The degree is not real now, nor is the self that you will become once you have the degree. Yet the idea is sufficiently real to motivate you to work hard for many years.

We Live in Three Dimensions of Time

Hypothetical thought also allows us to live in more than just the present moment. We infuse our present lives with knowledge of our histories and plans for our futures. Both past and future affect our experience in the present. Close relationships rely on ideas of past and future. One of the strongest glues for intimacy is a history of shared experiences (Bellah, Madsen, Sullivan, Swindler, & Tipton, 1985; Wood, 1995c). Just knowing that they have weathered rough times in the past helps partners get through trials in the present. Belief in a future also sustains intimacy. We interact differently with people we don't expect to see again than with ones who are continuing parts of our lives. Talking about the future also knits intimates together because it makes real the idea that more lies ahead (Acitelli, 1993; Duck, 1990).

We Can Foster Personal Growth

Thinking hypothetically helps us improve who we are. In Chapter 2 we noted that one guideline for improving self-concept is accepting yourself as in process. This requires you to remember how you were at an earlier time, to appreciate progress you've made, and to keep an ideal image of how you want to be in the future to fuel continued self-improvement. Personal growth also requires that we symbolize a vision of ourselves that is different from how we perceive ourselves currently. If you want to become more outgoing, you imagine yourself talking easily to others, going to parties, and so forth. You rely on symbols to represent the idea of yourself as sociable, and this spurs you forward in your quest for growth.

Julia T. Wood

Symbols Allow Self-Reflection

Just as we use symbols to reflect on what goes on outside of us, we also use them to reflect on ourselves. Humans don't simply exist and act. Instead, we think about our existence and reflect on our actions. Mead (1934) considered self-reflection to be the basis for human selfhood. He believed that our capacity to look at ourselves and our activities was responsible for civilized society.

STUDENT VOICES

DUK-KYONG: *Sometimes I get very discouraged that I do not yet know English perfectly and that there is much I still do not understand about customs in this country. It helps me to remember that when I came here two years ago I did not speak English at all, and I knew nothing about how people act here. Seeing how much progress I have made helps me not to be discouraged with what I do not know yet.*

The ME Reflects on the I's Activities According to Mead, there are two aspects to the self. First, there is the I, which is the spontaneous, creative self. The I acts impulsively in response to inner needs and desires, regardless of social norms. The ME is the socially conscious part of the self that monitors and moderates the I's impulses. The ME reflects on the I from the social perspectives of others. The I is impervious to social conventions and expectations, but the ME is keenly aware of them. In an argument, your I may want to hurl a biting insult at someone you don't like, but your ME censors that impulse and reminds you that it's impolite to put others down.

Mead regarded the ME as the reflective part of the self. The ME reflects on the I, so we simultaneously author our lives as the I acts and reflect on them as the ME analyzes the I's actions. This means we can think about who we want to be and set goals for becoming the self we desire. We can feel shame, pride, and regret for our actions—emotions that are possible because we self-reflect. We can control what we do in the present by casting ourselves forward in time to consider how we might later feel about our actions.

STUDENT VOICES

RACHAEL: *During the first week of my freshman year, I went to a mixer and got plowed. I'd never drunk in high school, so I didn't know what alcohol could do to me. I was a mess—throwing up, passing out. The next morning I hated myself for how I'd been. But in the long run, I think it was good that it happened. Whenever I feel like having more to drink than I should, I just* *remember what I was like that night and how much I hated myself that way, and that stops me from having anything more to drink.*

Self-Reflection Allows Us to Monitor Communication   Self-reflection also empowers us to monitor ourselves, a skill we discussed in Chapter 1. When we monitor ourselves, we (the ME) notice and evaluate our (the I's) actions and may modify them based on our judgments (Phillips & Wood, 1983; Wood, 1992a). For instance, during a discussion with a friend you might say to yourself, "Gee, I've been talking nonstop about me and my worries and I haven't even asked how she's doing." Based on your monitoring, you might inquire about your friend's life. When interacting with people from different cultures, we monitor by reminding ourselves they may not operate by the same values and communication rules that we do. Self-reflection allows us to monitor our communication and adjust it to be effective.

APPLY THE IDEA
I–ME Dialogues

To see how the I and the ME work together, monitor your internal dialogues. These are conversations in your head as you consider different things you might say and do.

Monitor your I–ME dialogues as you talk with a professor, a close friend, and a romantic partner. What creative ideas and desires does your I initiate? What social controls does your ME impose? What urges and whims occur to your I? What social norms does your ME remind you of?

How do the I and the ME work together? Does one sometimes muffle the other? What would be lost if your I became silent? What would be missing if your ME disappeared?

Self-Reflection Allows Us to Manage Our Image   This is the identity we present to others. Because we reflect on ourselves from social perspectives, we are able to consider how we appear in others' eyes. When talking with teachers, you may consciously present yourself as respectful, attentive, and studious. When interacting with parents, you may repress some of the language and topics that surface in discussions with your friends. When communicating with someone you'd like to date, you may choose to be more attentive and social than you are in other circumstances. Continuously, we adjust how we present ourselves so that we sculpt our image to fit particular situations and people.

STUDENT VOICES

M YRELLA: *I have a really bad temper that can get me into serious trouble if I'm not careful. Sometimes I feel like telling someone off or exploding or whatever, but I stop myself by thinking about how bad I'll look if I do it. I remind myself that others might see me as hysterical or crazy or something, and that helps me to check my temper.*

Julia T. Wood

Summing up, we use symbols to define, classify, and evaluate experiences; to think hypothetically; and to self-reflect. Each of these abilities helps us create meaning in our personal and interpersonal lives. Each of them also carries with it ethical responsibilities for how we use communication and the impact it has on ourselves and others.

Speech Communities

Although all humans use symbols, we don't all use them in the same way. As we have seen, symbols are social conventions whose meanings we learn in the process of interacting with others. For this reason, people from different social groups use communication in different ways and attach different meanings to particular communicative acts.

A **speech community** exists when people share norms about how to use talk and what purposes it serves (Labov, 1972). Members of speech communities share perspectives on communication that outsiders do not have. Conversely, members of particular speech communities may not understand the ways communication is used in other speech communities. This explains why cross-cultural communication is sometimes difficult.

Speech communities are not defined by countries or geographic locations, but by shared understandings of how to communicate. In Western society there are numerous speech communities, including Native Americans, gay men, lesbian women, Deaf individuals, and people with disabilities. Each of these groups has distinct understandings of communication and ways of using it— ways that are not familiar to people outside of the group. For example, in general, African Americans engage in more dramatic and elaborate verbal play than European Americans. Signifying, playing the dozens, and woofing are positive verbal activities in African American culture, yet most Whites don't understand, much less appreciate, these forms of communication.

Gender Speech Communities

Of the many speech communities that exist, gender has received particularly intense study. Because we know more about it than other speech communities, we'll explore gender as a specific example of speech communities and the misunderstandings that surface between members of different speech communities. Researchers have investigated both the way in which women and men are socialized into different understandings of how communication functions and the way their communication differs in practice.

Socialization into Gender Speech Communities One of the earliest studies showed that children's games are a primary agent of gender socialization (Maltz

© Dagmar Fabricius/Stock, Boston

& Borker, 1982). Typically, children's play is sex-segregated, and there are notable differences between the games the sexes tend to play. These differences seem to teach boys and girls some distinct rules for using communication and interpreting the communication of others.

Games girls favor, such as house and school, involve few players, require talk to negotiate how to play (because there aren't clear-cut guidelines), and depend on cooperation and sensitivity between players. Baseball, soccer, and war, which are typical boys' games, require more players and have clear goals and rules, so less talk is needed to play. Most boys' games are highly competitive both between teams and for individual status within teams. Interaction in games teaches boys and girls distinct understandings of why, when, and how to use talk. Table 4.1 summarizes rules of feminine and masculine speech communities.

T A B L E 4 . 1

RULES OF GENDER SPEECH COMMUNITIES

Feminine Communication Rules	Masculine Communication Rules
1. Include others. Use talk to show interest in others, and respond to their needs.	1. Assert yourself. Use talk to establish your identity, expertise, knowledge, and so on.
2. Use talk cooperatively. Communication is a joint activity, so people have to work together. It's important to invite others into conversation, wait your turn to speak, and respond to what others say.	2. Use talk competitively. Communication is an arena for proving yourself. Use talk to gain and hold attention, to wrest the talk stage from others; interrupt and reroute topics to keep you and your ideas spotlighted.
3. Use talk expressively. Talk should deal with feelings, personal ideas, and problems and should build relationships with others.	3. Use talk instrumentally. Talk should accomplish something such as solving a problem, giving advice, or taking a stand on issues.

Gendered Communication in Practice   Research on women's and men's communication reveals that the rules taught through childhood play remain with us. For instance, women's talk is generally more expressive and focused on feelings and personal issues, whereas men's talk tends to be more instrumental and competitive (Aries, 1987; Beck, 1988; Coates & Cameron, 1989; Johnson, 1989; Treichler & Kramarae, 1993; Wood, 1994c, 1994d, 1998). Notice that differences between men and women are matters of degree. They are not absolute dichotomies (Wood, 1997). Your everyday experiences will show you that men sometimes do use talk expressively and women sometimes do use talk instrumentally.

THE EMERGENCE OF LANGUAGE

WE NEED TO TALK.

UH-OH.

Drawing by Leo Cullum. © 1995 The New Yorker Magazine, Inc.

Another general difference between the sexes is what members of each sex tend to perceive as the primary foundation of close relationships. For most men, activities tend to be the primary foundation of close friendships and romantic relationships (Swain, 1989; Wood & Inman, 1993). Thus, men typically cement friendships through doing things together and for one another. For women, communication is the primary foundation of relationships. Talk is not only a means to instrumental ends, but also an end in itself. Women also do things with and for people they care about, yet most women see talk as an essential foundation for intimacy. For many women, communicating is the essence of building and sustaining closeness (Aries, 1987; Becker, 1987; Riessman, 1990).

Misunderstandings Between Gender Speech Communities   Given the differences between how women and men, in general, use communication, it's hardly surprising that the sexes often misunderstand each other. One clash between gender speech communities occurs when women and men discuss problems. Typically, if a woman tells a man about something that is troubling her, his response is to offer advice or a solution (Tannen, 1990; Wood, 1994d, 1996). His view of communication as primarily instrumental leads him to show support by doing something. Because feminine communities see communication as a way to build connections with others, however, women often want empathy and discussion of feelings before advice is useful. Thus, women sometimes feel men's responses to their concerns are uncaring and insensitive. On the other hand, men may feel frustrated when women offer empathy and support instead of advice for solving problems. In general, men are also less comfortable making personal disclosures, which women regard as an important way to enhance closeness (Aries, 1987; Wood & Inman, 1993).

Another conundrum in interaction between men and women concerns different styles of listening. Socialized to be responsive and expressive, women tend to make listening noises such as "um hm," "yeah," and "I know what you mean" when others are talking (Tannen, 1990; Wood, 1996, 1998). This is how they show they are attentive and interested. Yet masculine communities don't emphasize using communication responsively, so men tend to make fewer listening noises when another is talking. Thus, women sometimes feel men aren't listening to them because men don't symbolize their attention in the ways women have learned and expect. Notice that this does *not* mean that men don't listen well. Rather, the ways that many men listen aren't perceived as listening carefully by some women because women and men tend to have different regulative and constitutive rules for listening. Recall from Chapter 3 that perception shapes meaning.

Perhaps the most common complication in gender communication occurs when a woman says "Let's talk about us." To men this often means trouble, because they interpret the request as implying there is a problem in a relationship. For women, however, this is not the only—or even the main—reason to talk about a relationship. Feminine speech communities regard talking as the primary way to create relationships and build closeness (Riessman, 1990). In general, women regard talking about a relationship as a way to celebrate and increase intimacy. Socialized to use communication instrumentally, however, men tend to think talking about a relationship is useful only if there is some problem to be resolved (Acitelli, 1988, 1993). For men, the preferred mode of enhancing closeness is to do things together. Suzie's commentary illustrates this gender difference.

S T U D E N T   VOICES

SUZIE: *Gender speech communities explain a big fight my boyfriend and I had. We've been dating for three years, and we're pretty serious, so I wanted our anniversary to be really special. I suggested going out for a romantic dinner where we could talk about the relationship. Andy said that sounded dull, and he wanted to go to a concert where there would be zillions of people. At the time, I thought that meant he didn't care about us like I do, but maybe he feels close when we do things together instead of when we just are together.*

Other Speech Communities

Gender, of course, is not the only basis of speech communities, and communication between men and women is not the only kind of interaction that may be plagued by misunderstandings. Research indicates that communication patterns vary among social classes. For example, working-class people tend to use shorter, simpler sentences, less elaborate explanations, and more conventional grammar than members of the middle class (Bernstein, 1973).

Speech communities are also shaped by race and ethnicity so that different groups engage in distinct communication patterns. Imagine this scenario: An American businessman goes to Japan to negotiate a deal. When the American makes his proposal, the Japanese businessman responds, "I see you have put much thought into this idea." Assuming this indicates the Japanese executive is pleased with the proposal, the American says, "Then, shall we sign the contract and be on our way?" The Japanese executive replies, "I think we have much to talk about on your good proposal." What's happening here? If you are unfamiliar with Japanese communication styles, you might assume that the Japanese businessman is being evasive or not putting his cards on the table. However, Japanese culture prioritizes cooperation, politeness, and not causing others to lose face. The Japanese businessman's communication reflects the rules of his speech community that require him not to say no directly to another person (Cathcart & Cathcart, 1997; Dolan & Worden, 1992).

A recent report on African American speech indicates that it is typically more assertive than that of European Americans (Ribeau, Baldwin, & Hecht, 1994). What African Americans consider authentic, powerful exchanges may be perceived as antagonistic by individuals from different speech communities. The

Black Talk

Geneva Smitherman is a linguist who studies distinctive features of African American oral traditions. In her 1994 book, *Black Talk: Words and Phrases from the Hood to the Amen Corner,* Smitherman documents the richness and uniqueness of African American language. The following is a sampling from *Black Talk:*

TERM	DEFINITION
chill	relax
sweet	outstanding
all that	excellent, great, all that something seems to be. *Example:* That woman is bad. She is definitely all that.
amen corner	place in Black churches where traditionally elders, especially women, sit
drop a dime	tell on someone who is doing something wrong or illegal; reporting the person
git ovah	refers to making it over to a spiritually good life after struggling to overcome sin
jump salty	become angry
mojo	originally, a magical charm. In modern usage it refers to [a] source of personal magic that an individual may draw upon to put others under a spell
scared of you	a compliment that acknowledges another person's achievements. *Example:* I'm scared of you now that you've been promoted.
that how you living?	a criticism that asks why someone is acting a particular way

SOURCE: Smitherman, G. (1994). *Black talk: Words and phrases from the hood to the amen corner.* Boston: Houghton Mifflin.

rappin' and stylin' of African Americans is not practiced (or understood) by most European Americans (see "Black Talk"). Another feature of African American speech is extensive verbal play in which members play the dozens (a game of exchanging insults), speak indirectly, and use highly dramatic language. These forms of verbal play are thought to be valves for aggression and creativity that oppressed groups cannot safely express explicitly (Garner, 1994). As a group, African Americans are more oriented toward collective interests such as family or race than are European Americans, who tend to be more individualistic (Gaines, 1995). As a rule, African Americans also communicate more interactively than European Americans (Weber, 1994). This explains why African Americans call out responses such as "Tell it," "All right," and "Keep talking" during speeches, church sermons, and classes. What Whites regard as interruptions many African Americans perceive as positive participation in communication.

Appreciating Speech Communities

Were you socialized into a gender speech community? Are the gender communication rules we've discussed evident in how you communicate and interpret others? What about your ethnic and racial speech communities? Identify rules you learned for being polite, showing interest, and indicating disapproval.

After thinking about your own speech communities, talk with people from different speech communities. Identify differences in the rules you follow for public and private interaction. Do you recognize communication rules that explain differences between how you and others talk?

Although people may use the same language, they don't all use it in the same way. Within our country, diverse speech communities exist and operate by some distinct rules about how, when, why, and with whom to talk. Recognizing and respecting different speech communities increases our ability to participate competently in a diverse culture.

Guidelines for Improving Verbal Communication

© Goldberg/Monkmeyer Press Photo

We've explored what symbols are and how they may be used differently in distinct speech communities. Building on these understandings, we can now consider guidelines for improving effectiveness in verbal communication.

Engage in Dual Perspective

A critical guideline for effective verbal communication is to engage in dual perspective. This involves recognizing another person's perspective and taking that into account as you communicate. Effective interpersonal communication is not a solo performance, but a relationship between people. Awareness of others and their viewpoints should be reflected in how we speak. For instance, it's advisable to refrain from using a lot of idioms when talking with someone for whom English is a second language (see "Missing the Boat" on page 138). Similarly, instead of giving advice when a woman tells him about a problem, a man who uses dual perspective might realize empathy and supportive listening are likely to be more appreciated. The point is that competent communicators acknowledge and respect the perspectives of those with whom they interact.

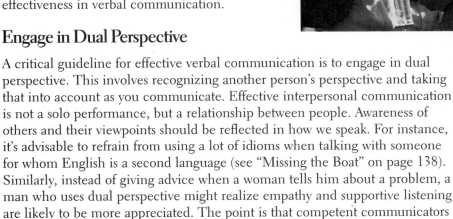

STUDENT VOICES

SPANKY: *For so long my mother and I have argued with each other. I have always felt she was overly protective of me and tried to intrude in my life with all the questions she asked about what I'm doing, who I'm seeing, and everything. For years almost any discussion between us wound up in an argument. I would just resist and challenge her. But for the last month I've been trying to understand where she's coming from. When she asks who I'm seeing, I don't just say "None of your business" or "Get off my case" like I used to. Now I ask her why she wants to know. What she says is she's interested in who I hang with and why I like them. That's kind of cool, I think—that my mom is really interested in my life. That's a lot different than seeing her questions as coming from a mother hen who wants to run my life. Trying to understand her perspective has been really really tough, but it has made an incredible difference in our relationship.*

We don't need to abandon our own perspectives to accommodate those of others. In fact, it would be as unconstructive to stifle your own views as to ignore those of others. Dual perspective, as the term implies, consists of two perspectives. It requires understanding both our own and another's point of view and giving voice to each when we communicate. Most of us can accept and grow from differences, but we seldom feel affirmed if we are unheard or

Missing the Boat

Communication scholar Wen Shu Lee (1994) reports that one of the greatest barriers to cross-cultural communication is idioms. Although people from other cultures learn formal English, they often aren't taught slang and jargon. Examples of idioms that confuse nonnative speakers are *kick the bucket, hang a right, flip the bird, miss the boat,* and *get up to speed.*

SOURCE: Lee, W. S. (1994). On not missing the boat: A processual method for intercultural understanding of idioms and lifeworld. *Journal of Applied Communication Research, 22,* 141–161.

disregarded. Understanding and heeding others' viewpoints in how you communicate paves the way for affirming relationships.

Own Your Feelings and Thoughts

We often use verbal language in ways that obscure our responsibility for how we feel and what we think. For instance, people say "You made me mad" or "You hurt me," as if what they feel is caused by someone else. On a more subtle level, we sometimes blame others for our responses to what they say. "You're so demanding" really means that you feel put upon by what someone else wants or expects. The sense of feeling pressured by another's expectations is in *you*, not the other person. Even though others' behaviors can influence us, they can't really determine how we feel.

Our feelings and thoughts result from how we interpret others' communication. Although how we interpret what others say may lead us to feel certain ways, others do not directly cause our responses. In certain contexts, such as abusive relationships, others may powerfully shape how we think and feel. Yet even in these extreme situations, we need to remember that we, not others, are responsible for our feelings. Telling others they make you feel some way is likely to arouse defensiveness, which doesn't facilitate healthy interpersonal relationships.

Effective communicators take responsibility for themselves by using language that owns their thoughts and feelings. They claim their feelings and do not blame others for what happens in themselves. To take responsibility for your own feelings, rely on **I-language,** rather than **you-language.** I-language owns thoughts and feelings and does not blame them on others. Table 4.2 gives examples of the difference.

TABLE 4.2

YOU-LANGUAGE AND I-LANGUAGE

You-Language	I-Language
You hurt me.	I feel hurt when you ignore what I say.
You make me feel small.	I feel small when you tell me that I'm selfish.
You're so domineering.	When you shout, I feel dominated.
You humiliated me.	I felt humiliated when you mentioned my problems in front of our friends.

There are two differences between I-language and you-language. First, I-language owns responsibility, whereas you-language projects it onto another person. Second, I-language offers considerably more description than you-language. You-language tends to be accusations that are very abstract. This is one of the reasons they're ineffective in promoting change. I-language, on the other hand, provides concrete descriptions of behaviors that we dislike without directly blaming the other person for how we feel.

© Bryce Flynn/Stock, Boston

Some people feel awkward when they first start using I-language. This is natural because most of us have learned to rely on you-language. With commitment and practice, however, you can learn to communicate with I-language. Once you feel comfortable using it, you will find that I-language has many advantages. It is less likely than you-language to make others defensive, so I-language opens the doors for dialogue. I-language is also more honest. We deceive ourselves when we say "You made me feel . . ." because others don't control how we feel. Finally, I-language is more empowering than you-language. When we say you did this or you made me feel that, we give control of our emotions to others. This reduces our personal power and, by extension, our motivation to change what is happening. Using I-language allows you to own your own feelings while also explaining to others how you interpret their behaviors.

APPLY THE IDEA
Using I-Language

For the next three days, whenever you use you-language, try to rephrase what you said or thought in I-language. How does this change how you think and feel about what's happening? How does using I-language affect interaction with others? Are others less defensive when you own your feelings and describe, but don't evaluate, their behaviors? Does I-language facilitate working out constructive changes?

Now that you're tuned into I- and you-language, monitor how you feel when others use you-language about you. When a friend or romantic partner says "You make me feel . . . ," do you feel defensive or guilty? Try teaching others to use I-language so that your relationships can be more honest and open.

STUDENT VOICES

NEELY: *I thought that the idea of I-language was kind of silly, but I did the exercise assigned in class anyway. Surprise. I found out I was using a lot of you-language, and it had the effect of letting me off the hook for what I felt and did. Like, I would say, "You pushed me to say that" when really I had control over whether to say it or not. But when I said "You pushed me," I could dismiss what I said as not my fault. I've continued to focus on not using you-language even though the assignment is over.*

Respect What Others Say About Their Feelings and Thoughts

Has anyone ever said to you, "You shouldn't feel that way"? If so, you know how infuriating it can be to be told that your feelings aren't valid, appropriate, or acceptable. It's equally destructive to be told our thoughts are wrong. When someone says, "How can you think something so stupid?" we feel disconfirmed. Effective communicators don't disparage what others say about what they feel and think. Even if you don't feel or think the same way, you can still respect another person as the expert on her or his own perspective.

THALASHA: *I go crazy when someone tells me I shouldn't feel what I'm feeling. I can't help what I feel. Feelings aren't something we control. They just are. When someone tells me I should feel a certain way, I get so angry and I just shut up. I feel like they're not even trying to understand me. They are just evaluating how I feel as wrong. That is totally toxic to me! There's no point in talking to someone who says (and thinks) that.*

One of the most disconfirming forms of communication is speaking for others when they are able to speak for themselves. Recently, I had a conversation with a couple at a party in which one person spoke for another. The man in the couple said, "She's having trouble balancing career and family," "She's really proud of sticking with her exercise program," and "She's worried about how to take care of her parents now that their health is declining." His wife, who was with us, wasn't allowed to say where she had trouble, felt pride, or experienced worry. His automatic tendency to answer questions I addressed to her left her voiceless. The same pattern occurs when parents speak for children by responding to questions the children could answer. Generally, it's arrogant and disempowering to speak for others.

Just as we should not speak for others, we also should not assume we understand how they feel or think. As we have seen, our distinct experiences and ways of interpreting life make each of us unique. We seldom, if ever, completely grasp what another person feels or thinks. Although it is supportive to engage in dual perspective, it isn't supportive to presume we fully grasp what's happening in someone else, especially when he or she differs from us in important ways.

It's particularly important not to assume we understand people from other cultures, including ones within our society. Recently, an Asian woman in one of my classes commented on discrimination she faces, and a White man in the class said, "I know what you mean. Prejudice really hurts." Although he meant to be supportive, his response angered the woman, who retorted, "You have no idea how I feel, and you have no right to act like you do until you've been female and non-white." When we claim to share what we haven't experienced, we take away from others' lives and identities, as is explained in "Respecting Others' Experiences."

Respecting what others say about what they feel and think is a cornerstone of effective interpersonal communication. We also grow when we open ourselves to perspectives, feelings, and thoughts that differ from our own. If you don't understand what others say, ask them to elaborate. This shows you are interested and respect their expertise or experience. Inviting others to clarify, extend, or explain their communication enlarges understanding between people.

Strive for Accuracy and Clarity

Because symbols are arbitrary, abstract, and ambiguous, the potential for misunderstanding always exists. In addition, individual and cultural differences foster varying interpretations of words. Although we can't completely eliminate misunderstandings, we can minimize them.

Be Aware of Levels of Abstraction

Misunderstanding is less likely when we are conscious of levels of abstraction. Much confusion results from language that is excessively abstract. For instance, assume a professor says, "Your papers should demonstrate a sophisticated conceptual grasp of material and its pragmatic implications." Would you know how to write a paper to satisfy the professor?

Probably not, because the language is very abstract and unclear. Here's a more concrete description: "Your papers should include definitions of the concepts and specific examples that show how they apply in real life." With this more concrete statement, you would have a clear idea of what the professor expected.

COMMUNICATION NOTES

Respecting Others' Experiences

Marsha Houston, an accomplished communication scholar, explains how claiming understanding can diminish a person. She writes that White women should never tell African American women that they understand Black women's experiences. Here's Houston's explanation:

I have heard this sentence completed in numerous, sometimes bizarre, ways, from "because sexism is just as bad as racism," to "because I watch the 'Cosby Show,'" to "because I'm also a member of a minority group. I'm Jewish . . . Italian . . . overweight.". . .

Similar experiences should not be confused with the same experience; my experience of prejudice is erased when you identify it as "the same" as yours (p. 138).

SOURCE: Houston, M. (1994). When black women talk with white women: Why dialogues are difficult. In A. González, M. Houston, & V. Chen (Eds.), *Our voices: Essays in culture, ethnicity, and communication* (pp. 133–139). Los Angeles: Roxbury.

APPLY THE IDEA
Using Concrete Language

Rewrite each statement below so that you replace abstract terms with ones that are more concrete.

EXAMPLE: I want to be more responsible.
(*Rewrite*: I want to be on time for work and classes, and I want to live within my budget each month and not run up charges on my credit card.)

1. I get really angry when people are rude.

_____

_____

2. I like teachers who are flexible and open-minded.

_____

_____

3. My roommate is such a slob.

_____

_____

4. I believe intimate relationships are based on unconditional love and acceptance.

_____

_____

5. I think the media in this country are irresponsible.

_____

_____

_____

Sometimes, however, abstract language is inadvisable. As we have seen, abstract language allows us to generalize, which is necessary and useful. The goal is to use a level of abstraction that suits particular communication objectives and situations. Abstract words are appropriate when speakers and listeners have similar concrete knowledge about what is being discussed. For example, a couple who have been dating might talk about "lighthearted comedies" and "heavy movies" as shorthand ways to refer to two film genres. Because they have seen many movies together, they have shared referents for the abstract terms *lighthearted* and *heavy*, so confusion is unlikely. Similarly, long-term friends can say "Let's just hang out" and understand the activities implied by the abstract term *hang out*. More concrete language is useful when communicators don't have shared experiences and interpretations. For example, early in a friendship the suggestion to "hang out" would be more effective if it included specifics: "Let's hang out today—maybe watch the game and go out for pizza." In a new dating relationship, it would be clearer to say, "Let's get a lighthearted movie like *Men in Black*. I don't want anything heavy like *The Piano* or *Schindler's List*." Providing examples of general terms clarifies meanings.

Abstract language is particularly likely to lead to misunderstandings when people talk about changes they want in one another. Concrete language and specific examples help individuals have similar understandings of which behaviors are unwelcome and which ones are wanted. For example, "I want you to be more helpful around the house" does not explain what would count as being more helpful. Is it vacuuming and doing laundry? Shopping for groceries? Fixing half of the meals? It isn't clear what the speaker wants unless more concrete descriptions are supplied. Likewise, "I want to be closer" could mean the speaker wants to spend more time together, talk about the relationship, do things together, have a more adventurous sex life, or any number of other things. Vague abstractions promote misunderstanding if individuals don't share concrete referents.

Qualify Language   Another strategy for increasing the clarity of communication is to qualify language. Two types of language require qualification. First, we should qualify generalizations so that we don't mislead ourselves or others into mistaking a general statement for an absolute one. "Politicians are crooked" is a false statement because it overgeneralizes. A more accurate statement would be "A number of politicians have been shown to be dishonest." Qualifying reminds us of limitations on what we say.

Using Qualified Language

Study the unqualified and qualified statements below.

UNQUALIFIED

Foreign cars are better than American ones.

Science courses are harder than humanities courses.

Television is violent.

QUALIFIED

Hondas and Mazdas generally require less maintenance than Fords and Chevys.

Most students find chemistry tougher than music.

Many commercial programs include a lot of violence.

Practice your skill in qualifying language by providing appropriate restrictions for the overgeneralizations below.

UNQUALIFIED

Teaching assistants aren't as good as professors.

Affirmative action gives jobs to unqualified people.

Men are more competitive than women.

Textbooks are boring.

We should also qualify language when describing and evaluating people. The term **static evaluation** refers to assessments that suggest something is unchanging or static. These are particularly troublesome when applied to people: Ann is selfish; Don is irresponsible; Bob is generous; Vy is dependent. Whenever we use the word *is,* we suggest something is inherent and fixed. In reality, we aren't static but continuously changing. A person who is selfish at one time may not be at another. An individual who is irresponsible on one occasion may be responsible in other situations.

STUDENT VOICES

KEN: *Parents are the worst for static evaluations. When I first got my license seven years ago, I had a fender bender and then got a speeding ticket. Since then I've had a perfect record, but you'd never know it from what they say. Dad's always calling me "hot-rodder," and Mom goes through this safety spiel every time I get ready to drive somewhere. You'd think I was the same now as when I was sixteen.*

Indexing is a technique developed by early communication scholars to remind us that our evaluations apply only to specific times and circumstances (Korzybski, 1958). To index, we would say Ann$_{\text{June 6, 1997}}$ acted selfishly,

Don_{on the task committee} was irresponsible, Bob_{in college} was generous, and Vy_{in her relationships with men in high school} was dependent. See how indexing ties description to a specific time and circumstance? Mental indexing reminds us that we and others are able to change in remarkable ways.

Effective interpersonal communication is accurate and clear. We've considered four principles for improving the effectiveness of verbal communication. Engaging in dual perspective is the first principle and a foundation for all others. A second guideline is to take responsibility for our own feelings and thoughts by using I-language. Third, we should respect others as the experts on what they feel and think and not presume we know what they mean or share their experiences. The fourth principle is to strive for clarity by choosing appropriate degrees of abstraction, qualifying generalizations, and indexing evaluations, particularly ones applied to people.

CHAPTER Summary

In this chapter, we discussed the world of words and meaning—the uniquely human universe that we inhabit because we are symbol users. Because symbols are arbitrary, ambiguous, and abstract, they have no inherent meanings. Instead, we actively construct meaning by interpreting symbols based on perspectives and values that are endorsed in our culture and social groups and based on interaction with others and our personal experiences. We also punctuate to create meaning in communication.

Instead of existing only in the physical world of the here and now, we use symbols to define, evaluate, and classify ourselves, others, and our experiences in the world. In addition, we use symbols to think hypothetically, so we can consider alternatives and simultaneously inhabit all three dimensions of time. Finally, symbols allow us to self-reflect so that we can monitor our own behaviors.

Although members of a society share a common language, we don't all use it the same way. Speech communities, which exist both within and between countries, teach us rules for talking and interpreting others. Because communication rules vary among social groups based on gender, race, class, and so forth, we shouldn't assume others use words just as we do. Likewise, we shouldn't assume that others share our meanings for how we communicate.

The final section of this chapter discussed principles for improving effectiveness in verbal communication. Because words can mean different things to various people and because different social groups instill some distinct rules for interacting, misunderstandings are always possible. To minimize them, we should engage in dual perspective, own our thoughts and feelings, respect what others say about how they think and feel, and monitor abstractness, generalizations, and static evaluations.

In the next chapter, we continue our discussion of the world of human communication by exploring the fascinating realm of nonverbal behavior.

KEY Concepts

- abstract
- ambiguous
- arbitrary
- communication rules
- constitutive rules
- hate speech
- I-language
- indexing
- loaded language
- punctuation
- regulative rules
- speech community
- static evaluation
- totalizing
- you-language

1. Think about different metaphors for U.S. society. For many years, the country was described as a "melting pot," which suggests that differences among citizens are supposed to melt down and blend into one unified character. Recently, some have criticized this melting pot metaphor because it emphasizes wiping out differences, not respecting them. The Reverend Jesse Jackson refers to the United States as both a "rainbow" and a "family quilt." Both of Jackson's metaphors emphasize recognizing and appreciating differences. What metaphor would you propose?

2. Use your *InfoTrac College Edition* to read two articles in journals that focus on experiences and perspectives of minority groups in the United States. You might find articles in journals such as *Black Collegian, American Indian Quarterly,* and *Asian Survey.* What does reading these articles teach you about the perspectives of minority groups on mainstream U.S. culture? Focus on the language used in the articles to describe minority and majority culture. What definitions and evaluations are in the language?

3. To appreciate the importance of hypothetical thought, enabled by symbols, try to imagine the following: living only in the present with no memories and no anticipations of the future; having no goals for yourself; knowing only the concrete, immediate reality. How would not having hypothetical thought affect your life?

4. In this chapter we learned that language changes. We coin new words when we feel the need to represent something that is not currently named in our language. Can you think of experiences, situations, or relationships that are not currently named? What names would you give them?

5. Check out the graffiti on your campus. Do you see examples of loaded language, stereotyping, and hate speech? Share your findings with your classmates.

6. What should be done about hate speech? Should we censor it? Would doing so violate our constitutional right to freedom of speech? Are there other, perhaps less formal, ways to reduce hate speech?

7. What labels that you dislike have been applied to you or to groups to which you belong? Explain how the labels affect you.

8. Does your school have a code or policy on hate speech? If so, what limits does the policy impose on freedom of speech?

9. Notice how media describe Black and White people in the news. Do television programs, newspapers, and other media spotlight race when the person is not White? How often are minorities described in terms of their races (Black, Asian, Hispanic, and so on)? Are people ever described as White?

CHAPTER 5

The World

Beyond Words

Jay and Emma gaze into each other's eyes as they nibble their salads, beautifully prepared and topped with marinated mushrooms and herb croutons. They can hear only muffled sounds from people at other tables, spread sparsely throughout the dining area. The comfortable upholstered chairs, gracious subtle lighting, and soft music add to the leisurely, intimate mood of the evening. Twenty minutes after bringing the salads, the server returns with their entrees and asks if there is anything else they would like.

Amy and Ted's eyes meet across the Formica table in the diner. They speak loudly to be heard above the clamor of rock music, conversations at other tables crowded around them, and order announcements from the grill. Within 5 minutes of placing their orders, the server plops loaded plates in front of them and leaves the check. Ted and Amy eat their burritos quickly and leave, spending less than 20 minutes total time for the meal.

© Grant LeDuc/Monkmeyer Press Photo

Emma and Jay had a very different dining experience from Ted and Amy. Much of the reason for the difference lies in nonverbal factors. The restaurant where Jay and Emma dined featured lighting, spatial arrangements, music, and a gracious pace of service that encouraged lingering and intimate conversation. In contrast, Ted and Amy's restaurant was crowded and loud, and the service was fast and functional, all of which discouraged lingering or intimate conversation.

In the previous chapter we explored verbal communication. To complement that focus, this chapter examines **nonverbal communication,** which is a major dimension of human interaction. We will discuss the fascinating world beyond words that is central to interpersonal communication. To launch our discussion, we'll examine the nature of nonverbal communication and how it differs from verbal communication. Next we will identify four principles of nonverbal communication. The third section of the chapter discusses different types of nonverbal behavior. We complete the chapter with guidelines for improving personal effectiveness in nonverbal communication.

Defining Nonverbal Communication

© Will & Deni McIntyre/Photo Researchers, Inc.

The world beyond words is an important dimension of interpersonal communication. Scholars estimate that nonverbal behaviors account for between 65 and 93 percent of the total meaning of communication (Birdwhistell, 1970; Mehrabian, 1981). Even if we accept the lesser figure, clearly nonverbal communication is a major influence on what happens between people.

Similarities	Differences
Both are symbolic.	Nonverbal communication
Both are rule-guided.	is usually perceived
Both can be intentional	as more believable.
or unintentional.	Nonverbal can be multichanneled.
Both are culture-bound.	Nonverbal is continuous.

FIGURE 5.1
Comparing Verbal and Nonverbal Communication

Nonverbal communication is all aspects of communication other than words themselves. It includes not only gestures and body language, but also *how* we utter words—inflection, pauses, tone, volume, and accent. These nonverbal features affect the meanings of our words. Nonverbal communication also includes features of environments that affect interaction, personal objects such as jewelry and clothes, physical appearance, and facial expressions.

Verbal and nonverbal dimensions of interpersonal communication typically work together to create meaning in human interaction. To understand how each dimension of communication operates, we'll identify both similarities and differences between verbal and nonverbal communication, as shown in Figure 5.1.

Similarities Between Verbal and Nonverbal Communication

Nonverbal communication is similar to verbal communication in many respects. We'll consider four similarities.

Nonverbal Communication Is Symbolic   Like verbal communication, nonverbal communication is symbolic. It consists of nonverbal representations of other things. To represent different moods, we shrug our shoulders, lower our eyes, and move away from or toward others. We smile to symbolize pleasure in seeing a friend, frown to show anger or irritation, and widen our eyes to indicate we are surprised.

Because nonverbal communication is symbolic, it, like verbal communication, is arbitrary, ambiguous, and abstract. Thus, we cannot be sure what a wink or hand movement means. Depending on the context and the people involved, a wink might express romantic interest, signal that the person winking is joking, or mean that the person winking has something in her or his eye. Also, we can't guarantee that others will perceive the meanings we intend to communicate with our nonverbal actions. You might move closer to someone to indicate you like the person, but he or she may feel you are crowding and imposing.

Nonverbal Communication Is Rule-Guided   Another similarity between the two kinds of communication is that both are rule-guided. Within particular societies we share general understandings of what specific nonverbal behaviors are appropriate in various situations and what they mean. For example, in the United States, as well as many other countries, handshakes are the conventional method of beginning and ending business meetings. Smiles are generally understood to express friendliness, and scowls are generally perceived as indicating displeasure of some type.

We follow rules (often unconsciously) to arrange settings to create particular moods. For a formal speech, a room might be set up with a podium that is at a distance from listeners' chairs. The chairs would probably be arranged in neat rows. Flags, banners, or other ceremonial symbols might be displayed near the

© B. Seitz/Photo Researchers, Inc.

podium. To symbolize a less formal speaking occasion, a podium might be omitted, chairs might be arranged in a circle, and the person speaking might be seated. The different spatial arrangements symbolize different moods and set the stage for distinct kinds of interaction.

Nonverbal Communication May Be Intentional or Unintentional   Both verbal and nonverbal communication may be deliberately controlled or unintentional. For example, you may carefully select clothes to create a professional impression when you are going to a job interview. You may also deliberately control your verbal language in the interview to present yourself as assertive, articulate, and respectful. We exert conscious control over much of our nonverbal communication.

Sometimes, however, both verbal and nonverbal communication are unconscious and unplanned. Without awareness you may wince when asked a tough question by the interviewer. Without knowing it, you may use incorrect grammar when speaking. Thus, both verbal and nonverbal communication are sometimes controlled and sometimes inadvertent.

Nonverbal Communication Is Culture-Bound   Like verbal communication, nonverbal behavior is shaped by cultural ideas, values, customs, and history. Just as we learn the language of a culture, we also learn its nonverbal codes. In learning both language and nonverbal codes, we also learn cultural values that are embedded in communication. Many aspects of nonverbal behavior vary across cultures. For example, in the United States most people use knives, forks, and spoons to eat. In Korea, Japan, China, Nepal, and other Asian cultures, chopsticks are the primary implement for eating. Most Westerners wear slacks, shirts, dresses, and suits, whereas saris are traditional dress in India. In the United States, it is common for friends and romantic partners to sample food from each other's plate, but Germans consider this extremely rude. Later in this chapter we'll look more closely at cultural influences on nonverbal behavior as one of the principles of the nonverbal communication system.

Differences Between Verbal and Nonverbal Communication

There are also differences between the two dimensions of communication and between the meanings we attach to each. We'll consider three distinctions between the two kinds of communication.

Nonverbal Communication Is Perceived to Be More Believable   One major difference is that most people perceive nonverbal communication as more trustworthy than verbal communication, especially when verbal and nonverbal messages are inconsistent. If someone glares and says "I'm glad to see you," you are likely to believe the nonverbal message, which communicates dislike. People are particularly likely to think that nonverbal communication accurately reflects true feelings. If you are slumping and the corners of your mouth are turned down, others will probably perceive you as unhappy or depressed.

The fact that people tend to believe nonverbal behaviors doesn't mean that nonverbal behaviors are always accurate. Although people generally trust nonverbal behaviors more than verbal ones, we shouldn't necessarily share that tendency. It's possible that someone whose mouth is down-turned and who is slumped over is deeply engaged in reflection or is working out a problem and isn't unhappy or depressed. It's also possible for individuals to manipulate their nonverbal communication, just as we manipulate our verbal communication.

Nonverbal Communication Is Multichanneled   A second difference between the two communication systems is that nonverbal communication often occurs simultaneously in two or more channels, whereas verbal communication tends to take place in a single channel. Nonverbal communication may be seen, felt, heard, smelled, and tasted, and we may receive nonverbal communication through several of these channels at the same time. You might touch a person while smiling and whispering an endearment—nonverbal communication occurring in three channels at once. In contrast, vocal verbal communication is received through hearing while written verbal communication and American Sign Language are received through sight—one channel at a time.

One implication of the multichanneled nature of nonverbal communication is that selective perception is likely to operate. If you are visually oriented, you may tune in more to visual cues than to smell or touch. On the other hand, if you are touch-oriented, you may pay more attention to tactile cues than to visual ones.

Nonverbal Communication Is Continuous   Finally, nonverbal communication is more continuous than verbal communication. Verbal symbols start and stop. We say something or write something and then we stop talking or writing. Yet, it is difficult, if not impossible, to stop nonverbal communication. As long as two people are together, they are engaging in nonverbal behaviors, deliberately or unintentionally. How we enter and leave rooms, how we move, even how we tilt our head may affect others' interpretations of us. Further, nonverbal features of environment, such as lighting or temperature, are ongoing influences on interaction and meaning. Understanding similarities and differences between verbal and nonverbal behavior gives us insight into each form of communication and helps us appreciate how they work together in the totality of interpersonal interaction.

Principles of Nonverbal Communication

Now that we have defined nonverbal communication and compared and contrasted it with verbal communication, let's explore how nonverbal communication actually works. Four principles of nonverbal communication enhance understanding of how it affects meaning in human interaction.

Nonverbal Communication May Supplement or Replace Verbal Communication

Communication researchers have identified five ways in which nonverbal behaviors interact with verbal communication (Malandro & Barker, 1983). First, nonverbal behaviors may repeat verbal messages. For example, you might say "yes" while nodding your head. Second, nonverbal behaviors may highlight verbal communication. For instance, you can emphasize particular words by speaking more loudly, and you can indicate you mean something sarcastically by tone of voice. Third, we use nonverbal behavior to complement or add to words. When you see a friend, you might say "I'm glad to see you" and underline the verbal message with a warm embrace. Fourth, nonverbal behaviors may contradict verbal messages, as when someone says "Nothing's wrong" in a frosty, hostile tone of voice. Finally, we sometimes substitute nonverbal behaviors for verbal ones. For instance, you might roll your eyes to indicate you disapprove of something. In all of these ways, nonverbal behaviors augment or replace verbal communication. "The Case of Clever Hans" illustrates the impact of nonverbal communication.

COMMUNICATION NOTES

The Case of Clever Hans

In the 1900s, Herr von Osten trained his horse Hans to count by tapping his front hoof. Hans learned quickly and was soon able to multiply, add, divide, subtract, and perform complex mathematical calculations. He could even count the number of people in a room or the number of people wearing eyeglasses. Herr von Osten took Hans on a promotional tour. At shows he would ask Hans to add 5 and 8, divide 100 by 10, and do other computations. In every case, Hans performed flawlessly, leading others to call him "Clever Hans." Because some doubters thought Clever Hans's feats involved deceit, proof of his mathematical abilities was demanded.

The first test involved computing numbers that were stated on stage by people other than von Osten. Using his hoof, Hans pounded out the correct answers. However, he didn't fare so well on the second test in which one person whispered a number into Hans's left ear and a different person whispered a number into his right ear. Hans was told to add the two numbers and pound out the sum, an answer not known by anyone present. Hans couldn't solve the problem. On further investigation, it was deduced that Hans could solve problems only if someone he could see knew the answer. When Hans was given numbers and asked to compute them, viewers leaned forward and tensed their bodies as Hans began tapping his hoof. When Hans tapped the correct number, onlookers relaxed their body postures and nodded their heads, which Hans took as a signal to stop tapping.

Hans was clever, not because he could calculate but because he could read people's nonverbal communication.

SOURCE: Sebeok, T. A., & Rosenthal, R. (Eds.). (1981). *The Clever Hans phenomenon: Communication with horses, whales, apes and people*. New York: New York Academy of Sciences.

Nonverbal Communication May Regulate Interaction

We also use nonverbal behaviors to regulate interpersonal interaction. More than verbal cues, we rely on nonverbal behaviors to know when to speak and when to let others speak, as well as how long to talk. Intricate and often unconscious nonverbal behaviors regulate the flow of communication between people.

In conversations, we generally know when someone else is through speaking and when it is our turn to talk. We also sense when a professor welcomes discussion from students and when the professor is in a lecture mode. We can even perceive when a professor or friend expects or wants us specifically to enter conversation. Seldom do explicit, verbal cues tell us when to speak and when to keep silent. When talking, friends typically don't say "Your turn to talk" or hold up signs saying "I am through now." Instead, turn-taking in conversation usually is regulated nonverbally (Malandro & Barker, 1983). We sig-

© Cynthia Johnson/Gamma-Liaison

nal we don't want to be interrupted by averting our eyes or by maintaining a speaking volume and rate to thwart interruption. When we're through talking, we look back to others to signal "Okay, now somebody else can speak." We invite specific individuals to speak by looking directly at them, often after asking a question.

Although we aren't usually aware of nonverbal actions that regulate interaction, we rely on them to know when to speak and when to remain silent. Without conscious realization, we signal others they should enter a conversation or wait until we're through speaking. We send and respond to subtle nonverbal cues whenever we communicate with others.

Nonverbal Communication Often Establishes Relationship-Level Meanings

You'll recall that in Chapter 1, we discussed two levels of meaning that are always present in communication. To review, the content level of meaning concerns actual information or literal meaning. The relationship level of meaning defines individuals' identities and relationships between people. More than verbal language, nonverbal communication conveys relationship-level meanings (Keeley & Hart, 1994). In fact, communication scholars refer to nonverbal communication as the "relationship language" and note that it, more than verbal messages, expresses the overall feeling of relationships (Burgoon, Buller, Hale, & deTurck, 1984; Sallinen-Kuparinen, 1992). There are three dimensions of relationship-level meanings that are conveyed primarily through nonverbal communication (Mehrabian, 1981). As we will see, how we express and interpret each of these dimensions varies among different speech communities.

Responsiveness   One facet of relationship-level meaning is responsiveness. Through eye contact, facial expressions, and body posture, we indicate our interest in others' communication. Westerners signal interest by holding eye contact and assuming an attentive posture. To express lack of interest or boredom, we decrease visual contact and adopt a passive body position. Also, synchronicity, or harmony, between people's postures and facial expressions reflects how comfortable they are with each other (Berg, 1987; Capella, 1991). We're more likely to feel that others are involved with us if they look at us, nod, and lean forward than if they gaze around the room, look bored, and fiddle with papers as we speak (Miller & Parks, 1982).

S T U D E N T   VOICES

ALLAN: *The most useful professional development seminar I've ever had was on listening. Our instructor showed us how to sit and look at people to show we were interested. We learned that most men don't show their interest*

with head nods and eye contact. That explained to me why some of the women I supervise complained that I never seemed interested when they came to talk to me. It wasn't that I wasn't interested. I just didn't show it with my nonverbal behavior.

Different speech communities teach members distinct rules for showing responsiveness. Because feminine speech communities tend to emphasize building relationships by expressing interest in others, women generally display greater emotional responsiveness than men (Montgomery, 1988; Ueland, 1992). In addition to communicating their own feelings nonverbally, women are generally more skilled than men in interpreting others' emotions (Hall, 1978; Noller, 1986). African Americans also tend to be more skilled than Whites in reading emotions, which suggests decoding is a survival strategy for those who have historically had subordinate standpoints (women and minorities). Prisoners, another subordinate group, also show strong decoding capacity (Wood, 1994e). The well-being and sometimes physical safety of those with low power depend on being able to decipher the feelings and intentions of those with more power.

Liking   A second dimension of relationship meaning is liking. Nonverbal behaviors are often keen indicators of how positively or negatively we feel toward others. Smiles and friendly touching tend to indicate positive feelings, whereas frowns and belligerent postures express antagonism (Keeley & Hart, 1994). Opening your arms to someone signals affection and welcome, whereas turning your back on someone indicates dislike.

In addition to these general rules shared in Western society, more specific rules are instilled by particular speech communities. Masculine speech communities tend to emphasize emotional control and independence, so men are less likely than women to use nonverbal behavior that reveals how they feel. Reflecting the values of feminine socialization, women, in general, sit closer to others and engage in greater eye contact than men (Montgomery, 1988; Reis, Senchak, & Solomon, 1985). They are also more openly expressive of their inner feelings, because that is encouraged in feminine speech communities. Women are also more likely than men to initiate hand-holding and touch others to show affection.

Nonverbal behaviors reflect liking between marriage partners. Happy couples sit closer together and engage in more eye contact than unhappy couples. Further, couples who like each other tend to touch more often and to orient their body postures toward each other than do couples who are less fond of each other (Miller & Parks, 1982; Noller, 1986).

C ARLA: *I swear, it's so hard to figure out what guys think of you. When you're around a guy, he's like Mr. Stone Face, so he doesn't give away anything about how he feels. I can't tell by how he acts if a guy likes me or is interested. My girlfriends say the same thing—guys are just inscrutable. Girls aren't like that at all. If we like someone, we smile and let him or her know instead of acting distant and aloof.*

Power   The third dimension of relationship-level meaning is power. We rely greatly on nonverbal behaviors to assert dominance and to negotiate for status and influence (Henley, 1977). Given what we have learned about gender socialization, it is not surprising that men typically exceed women in efforts to exert control. In general, men assume greater amounts of space and use greater volume and more forceful gestures to assert their ideas than women (Hall, 1987; Major, Schmidlin, & Williams, 1990). Men are also more likely than women to use gestures and touch to symbolize control (Henley, 1977; Leathers, 1986).

Gender, however, is not the only influence on the power dimension of relationship meaning. Individuals' status is tied to how they communicate power on nonverbal levels. The prerogative to touch another reflects power, so individuals with power touch those with lesser power. For instance, bosses touch secretaries far more often than secretaries touch bosses (Spain, 1992). Time is also linked to individuals' status. People who are considered important can keep others waiting—how often have you waited for your appointment at a doctor's office? People with high status can also be late to appointments and events without risking serious repercussions. Yet, if someone with lower power is late, she or he may suffer undesirable consequences such as disapproval, penalties, or having an appointment canceled.

J ERRY: *Last summer I had an internship with a big accounting firm in Washington, and space really told the story on status. Interns like me worked in two large rooms on the first floor with partitions to separate our desks. New employees worked on the second floor in little cubicles. The higher up you were in the hierarchy of the firm, the higher up your office was—literally. I mean, the president and vice presidents—six of them—had the whole top floor, while there were forty or more interns crowded onto my floor.*

As Jerry's observations indicate, space also expresses power relations. Individuals who have power usually command more space than individuals with less power. The connection between power and space is evident in the fact that most bosses have large, spacious offices whereas their secretaries have smaller offices or workstations, even though they have to handle far more paperwork than bosses. Office size and decor may also be tied to an individual's status in the workplace hierarchy. As people move up the organizational ladder, they tend to have larger offices with more and larger windows and more luxurious carpeting and art. Homes also reflect power differences among family members. Adults usually have more space than children, and men more often than women have their own rooms and sit at the head of the table.

Power may also be exerted through silence, a forceful form of nonverbal communication. By not responding, we can discourage others from speaking and clear the way to talk about our own preferred topics. Victoria DeFrancisco (1991) found that some husbands respond with silence to their wives' communication, a behavior that discourages wives from further interaction. In extreme form, power is nonverbally enacted through violence and abuse, both of which reflect and sustain dominance (Wood, 1994d).

Responsiveness, liking, and power are dimensions of relationship-level meanings that are often expressed through nonverbal communication.

COMMUNICATION NOTES

"I'll Move When I'm Ready and Not Before!"

Have you ever felt that a driver was really slow in pulling out of a parking space for which you were waiting? It turns out that your imagination may not be playing tricks on you. A recent study of 400 drivers in a shopping mall found that drivers took longer to pull out of a space if someone was waiting than if nobody was there to claim the space. On average, if nobody was waiting for the space, drivers took 32.2 seconds to pull out of a spot after opening a car door. If someone was waiting, drivers took about 39 seconds. And woe to the person who honks to hurry a driver: Drivers took 43 seconds to pull out of a space when the waiting driver honked!

SOURCE: Raphael, M. (1997, May 13). It's true: Drivers move slowly if you want their space. *Raleigh News and Observer*, p. 1A.

Nonverbal Communication Reflects and Expresses Cultural Values

Earlier in this chapter, we noted that nonverbal communication is similar to verbal communication in expressing cultural values. Like verbal communication, nonverbal patterns reflect the values, perspectives, and heritage of specific cultures. This implies that the majority of nonverbal actions are not instinctive but are learned as we are socialized in particular cultures. We've already noted a number of differences between nonverbal behaviors encouraged in feminine and masculine speech communities. In addition to diversity among groups within our country, nonverbal behaviors vary from one country to another. As you might expect, dissimilarities reflect distinct cultural values.

Have you ever seen the bumper sticker "If you can read this, you're too close"? That slogan proclaims North Americans' fierce territoriality. We prize private space, and we resent, and sometimes fight, anyone who trespasses on what we consider our turf. "I'll Move When I'm Ready and Not Before!" shows our territoriality when driving. The German culture also emphasizes private space. Germans routinely build walls and hedges to insulate themselves from neighbors. In cultures where individuality is not such a pronounced value, people are less territorial. For instance, Brazilians stand close in shops, buses, and elevators, and when they bump into one another they don't apologize or draw back (Wiemann & Harrison, 1983). In many middle Eastern countries, men often walk with their arms around other men, but in the United States touch between male friends is uncommon.

SANDY: *I was so uncomfortable when I traveled to Mexico last year. People just crammed into buses even when all the seats were taken. They pushed up together and pressed against each other. I felt they were really being rude, and I was uptight about having people on top of me like that. I guess it was a learned cultural difference, but it sure made me uneasy at the time. I never knew how territorial I was until I felt my space was being invaded.*

Norms for touching also reflect cultural values. In one study, North Americans, who are relatively reserved, were observed engaging in an average of only two touches an hour. The emotionally restrained British averaged zero touches per hour. Parisians, long known for their emotional expressiveness, touched 110 times per hour. Puerto Ricans touched most, averaging 180 touches an hour (Knapp, 1972).

Patterns of eye contact also reflect cultural values. In North America, frankness and assertion are valued, so meeting another's eyes is considered appropriate and a demonstration of personal honesty. Eye contact is also valued among most Hispanics. Yet in many Asian and northern European countries, direct eye contact is considered abrasive and disrespectful (Hall, 1968). In Brazil, eye contact is often so intense that people from the United States consider it rude. Imagine the confusion this causes in intercultural business negotiations.

Cultural training also influences how we express emotions and which emotions we express. In some ethnic groups dramatic emotional displays are typical. For example, many people raised in Italian and Jewish communities are more emotionally expressive than people raised in English or German communities. In Japan and many other Asian cultures, it is considered rude to express negative feelings toward others. Thus, the Japanese may not show dislike, disrespect, or irritation, even if they feel those emotions. In the United States there is less constraint on displaying negative feelings.

Cultures also differ in their orientations toward time. Anthropologist Edward Hall (1976) distinguished between cultures that have monochronic and polychronic orientations toward time. *Monochronic* (one time) cultures, such as the United States, view time as a valuable commodity to be saved, scheduled, and carefully guarded. Within monochronic cultures punctuality and efficiency are valued. Thus, people are expected to be on time for appointments and classes, and they are expected to complete work quickly. In contrast, *polychronic* (many times) cultures take a more holistic, systemic view of time. Members of these cultures assume that many things are happening simultaneously. Thus, punctuality is seldom stressed. Meetings may start late, with people joining in after discussions begin. Tangential discussions and social conversations are part of normal meetings in polychronic cultures. People may even cancel meetings without the dramatic reasons required for politeness in monochronic cultures. The belief that time is holistic leads members of polychronic cultures to assume that the rhythms of life—working, socializing, attending to personal matters—are interrelated.

The influence of culture on nonverbal communication will become clearer as you read the rest of this chapter. As we discuss different types of nonverbal communication we'll highlight examples that reflect the values, traditions, and heritages of particular cultures.

We've discussed four principles that provide a foundation for understanding nonverbal communication. First, nonverbal behavior may supplement or replace verbal communication. Second, nonverbal behaviors may regulate interaction. Third, nonverbal behavior is more powerful than verbal behavior in expressing relationship-level meanings. Finally, nonverbal communication reflects and expresses cultural values. Thus, much of our nonverbal communication is learned rather than instinctive. We're now ready to explore types of nonverbal behavior that make up this intricate communication system.

Types of Nonverbal Communication

Because so much of our interaction is nonverbal, this system includes many types of communication. In this section, we will consider nine forms of nonverbal behavior, and we will point out how we use each to establish relationships and to express personal identity and cultural values.

Kinesics

Kinesics is a technical term that refers to body position and body motions, including those of the face. Clearly, we signal a great deal about how we see ourselves by how we hold our bodies. Someone who stands erectly and walks confidently announces self-assurance, whereas someone who slouches and shuffles seems to be saying "I'm not very sure of myself." "How to Discourage Assault" discusses how thieves read nonverbal behavior to choose their victims. We also communicate moods with body posture and motion. For example, someone who walks quickly with a resolute facial expression appears more determined than someone who saunters along with an unfocused gaze. We sit more rigidly when we are nervous or angry and adopt a relaxed posture when we feel at ease.

An interesting example of using body motions to sculpt others' perceptions comes from Ted Conover's book, *Coyotes: A Journey Through the Secret World of America's Illegal Aliens* (1987). Conover helped many Mexican workers illegally enter the United States. Critical to the workers' success in not getting caught was learning how to not call attention to themselves. Conover taught the workers how to blend in by controlling their nonverbal behaviors, especially kinesics. According to Conover, his biggest challenge was teaching Mexicans how to look at home in airports, where they were most likely to be detected and

deported. He taught them how to walk nonchalantly, control furtive eye movements, and sit with a relaxed posture. All these behaviors communicate "I've done this hundreds of time. No need to pay any special attention to me."

Body postures may signal whether we are open to interaction. Someone who sits with arms crossed and looks downward seems to say "Don't bother me." That's also a nonverbal strategy students sometimes use to dissuade teachers from calling on them in classes. To invite interaction, Westerners look at others and smile, signaling that conversation is welcome. Yet in many Asian societies, direct eye contact and smiling at nonintimates might be considered disrespectful. We also use gestures to signal what we think of others. We use a hand gesture to indicate okay and a different gesture to communicate contempt. The gestures are arbitrary—ones that our culture has decided stand for particular things. This explains why gestures often don't translate into other cultures. For example, the hand gesture that stands for okay in the United States is the gesture for worthlessness in France.

Our faces are intricate communication messengers. The face alone is capable of over a thousand distinct expressions that result from variations in tilt of the head and movements of the eyebrows, eyes, and mouth (Eckman, Friesen, & Ellsworth, 1971). Our eyes can shoot daggers of anger, issue challenges, or radiate feelings of love. With our faces we can indicate disapproval (scowls), doubt (raised eyebrows), admiration (warm eye gazes), and resistance (stares). The face is particularly powerful in conveying responsiveness and liking (Keeley & Hart, 1994; Patterson, 1992).

One of the most important interpersonal aspects of kinesics concerns how we position ourselves relative to others and what our positions say about our feelings toward them. Couples communicate dissatisfaction by increasing distance between them and by smiling less and looking away from each other (Miller & Parks, 1982). We also use nonverbal behaviors—such as smiles, close seating, and warm gazes—to signal we like others and are happy with them (Walker & Trimboli, 1989).

APPLY THE IDEA
Communicating Closeness

To become more aware of subtle nonverbal behaviors that reflect intimacy, try this. Watch a television show and keep a careful record of characters' kinesic communication.

CONTINUED

- How close to each other do characters who are intimate stand or sit? How close do characters who are antagonistic stand or sit? What is the distance between characters who are just meeting or who have casual relationships?
- Watch patterns of eye contact between characters who are intimates, enemies, and casual acquaintances. How often do they look at each other? How long is eye gaze maintained in each type of relationship?
- Notice facial expressions for characters who do and don't like each other. How often do they smile or stare?

As a class, discuss what your observations reveal about kinesic communication and relationship-level meanings.

Freedom of (Nonverbal) Speech

Nonverbal communication has been costly for some sports stars. When German midfielder Stefan Effenberg made an obscene gesture to fans during a World Cup match in the summer of 1994, his coach promptly kicked him off the squad. In 1993, Bryan Cox, linebacker for the Miami Dolphins, flipped an obscene gesture in Buffalo. The NFL slapped him with a $10,000 fine that was later reduced to $3,000.

Private companies such as athletic teams can make their own rules. However, in the United States, nonverbal behavior is protected by freedom of speech laws. Thus, Louis Sirkin, a First Amendment attorney, successfully defended a motorist who insulted a traffic officer with an obscene hand gesture.

SOURCE: Be civil. (1994, July 5). *Wall Street Journal*, p. A1.

For good reason, poets call the eyes "the mirrors of the soul." Our eyes communicate some of the most important and complex messages about how we feel about others. If you watch infants, you'll notice that they focus on others' eyes. Babies become terrified if they can't see their mothers' eyes, but they aren't bothered when other parts of their mothers' faces are hidden (Spitz, 1965). Even as adults, we tend to look at eyes to judge emotions, honesty, interest, and self-confidence.

For years, many attorneys have used body language to sway jurors' feelings and impressions of cases. For example, to suggest that a witness is lying, attorneys sometimes roll their eyes in full sight of jurors. Standing further away from witnesses during questioning enhances the witnesses' credibility with jurors. Some attorneys look conspicuously at their watches to signal jurors that the opposition's arguments are boring or ridiculous. Recently, some judges have tried to set limits on allowable nonverbal behavior by attorneys. A growing number of judges now require attorneys' to stand at lecterns, which restricts face and body motions that might influence jurors. Perhaps the most stringent restriction of attorneys' nonverbal behavior comes from Samuel Kent, a U.S. District Court judge in Galveston, Texas. In his courtroom Judge Kent says, "Facial gestures, nods of the head, audible signs, anything along those lines is strictly prohibited" (Schmitt, 1997, p. B7).

Gestures are the special interest of David McNeill, a professor of linguistics and psychology at the University of Chicago. According to McNeill, much of what we want to communicate involves imagery, and imagery is not well conveyed by words. Thus, to communicate the images we have, we rely heavily on gestures, especially hand movements. McNeill says that as much as 75 percent of the meaning of communication is conveyed by motions (McNeill, 1992). In an interview with Barbara Mahany (1997), McNeill offered the interesting observation that the gesture of an extended middle finger, which is used to convey contempt, was used for the same message over two thousand years ago by ancient Romans. "Freedom of (Nonverbal) Speech" on page 159 explains how this gesture can be costly.

Haptics

Haptics, the sense of touch, is the first of our five senses to develop (Leathers, 1976), and many communication scholars believe touching and being touched are essential to a healthy life. Research on dysfunctional families reveals that mothers touch babies less often and less affectionately than mothers in healthy families. In disturbed families, mothers tend to push children away, nonverbally signaling rejection (Birdwhistell, 1970). In contrast, babies who are held closely and tenderly tend to develop into self-confident adults who have secure attachment styles (Main, 1981).

Touching also communicates power and status. People with high status touch others and invade others' spaces more than people with less status (Henley, 1977). Cultural views of women as more touchable than men are reflected in gendered patterns of contact. Parents touch sons less often and more roughly than they touch daughters (Condry, Condry, & Pogatshnik, 1983). These patterns early in life teach the sexes different rules for using touch and interpreting touches from others. As adults, women tend to engage in touch to show liking and intimacy (Montgomery, 1988), whereas men rely on it to assert power and control (Henley, 1977; Leathers, 1986). For example, women frequently hug others and touch the hands and arms of friends during conversation. Men are more likely than women to use touch aggressively to exert power over others or to repel physical aggression. Feminine training to be nice to others and preserve relationships explains why women may be reluctant to object to touching, even if it is unwanted. These gendered patterns contribute to sexual harassment where women are often the targets of unwelcome touch (LePoire, Burgoon, & Parrott, 1992), as Claire's commentary illustrates.

S T U D E N T **VOICES**

CLAIRE: *There's a guy where I work who really bothers me. He doesn't really cross a clear line, but it seems like he's always brushing against me. Like when he comes to my desk, he leans over just enough that his chest presses against me. Sometimes he touches my arm or hand when he's showing me a paper, and the other day he stood behind me to show me how to run a new spreadsheet program. He had both arms around me when it would have been easier to work the mouse if he'd sat on the side. I've never said anything because I don't want to hurt his feelings or seem hysterical or something, but it really bothers me.*

Physical Appearance

Western culture places an extremely high value on physical appearance. For this reason, most of us notice how others look, and we form initial evaluations of others based on their appearance, over which they have limited control. We first notice obvious physical qualities such as sex and race. After interpreting these, we then form judgments of how attractive others are and make inferences about their personalities. In one study, researchers found that people associate plump, rounded bodies with laziness and weakness. Thin, angular physiques were thought to reflect youthful, hard-driven, nervous, stubborn personalities, and athletic body types were seen as indicating strong, adventurous, self-reliant personalities (Wells & Siegel, 1961).

Does physical appearance affect what people earn? It may. According to a recent *Wall Street Journal* report, a study of 2,500 male and female lawyers revealed a relationship between physical attractiveness and earning power. The attorneys who were judged more attractive earned as much as 14 percent more than attorneys who were judged less attractive ("Good-Looking Lawyers," 1996). This report is consistent with other research showing that people who are considered attractive make more money than their less attractive peers.

Cultures stipulate ideals for physical form. Currently in the West, the cultural ideals emphasize thinness and youth in women and muscularity and height in men. Women and gay men seem particularly vulnerable to cultural pressures to be thin because they are judged so keenly by their attractiveness, whereas heterosexual men are judged primarily by their accomplishments (Spitzack, 1990, 1993). The cultural emphasis on thinness is so great that many people consider being seriously overweight a greater social stigma than a criminal record, cancer, facial scar, or missing hand (Harris, Walters, & Waschall, 1991). These cultural pressures lead to serious problems, as "Help with Eating Disorders" explains.

STUDENT VOICES

ANDREA: *Nearly all of the girls I know have eating problems. Some constantly diet, and a lot of others binge and purge. We're all afraid to gain any weight—afraid that guys won't want to date us if we weigh even a little extra. Usually I stick to dieting, but if I eat too much I do throw it up. I hate that, but it's better than being fat.*

This culture's value on thinness is qualified by ethnic identity. In traditional African societies, full-figured bodies are perceived as symbolizing health, prosperity, and wealth, which are all desirable (Villarosa, 1994). African Americans who embrace this value accept or prefer women who weigh more than the current ideal for Caucasians (Root, 1990; Thomas, 1989).

SHUPHORA: *I hear White girls talking all the time about their weight—*
wanting to lose weight, thinking they're too fat, working out for
hours to drop some pounds. I almost never hear this kind of talk when I'm with
Black girls. We've got to worry about keeping our grades up, doing our jobs to pay
for school, and just surviving in a mainly White school. Weight just isn't impor-
tant relative to the real issues in our lives.

Class membership further modifies ethnic values concerning weight. In 1994, *Essence* magazine reported that African American women who were either affluent or poor were likely to have strong Black identities that allowed them to resist White preoccupations with thinness. On the other hand, middle-class African American women who were upwardly mobile were more inclined to deemphasize their ethnic identities to get ahead, and they were more suscep-tible to obsessions with weight and eating disorders (Villarosa, 1994).

Artifacts

Artifacts are personal objects we use to announce our identities and heritage and to personalize our environments. We craft our image by how we dress and what objects, if any, we carry and use. Nurses and physicians wear white and frequently drape stethoscopes around their neck; professors travel with brief-cases, whereas students more often tote backpacks. White-collar professionals tend to wear tailored outfits and dress shoes, whereas blue-collar workers more often dress in jeans or uniforms and boots. The military requires uniforms that define individuals in terms of the group. In addition, stripes and medals signify rank and accomplishments.

The importance of artifacts was dramatically illustrated in 1996. On May 16 Admiral Jeremy M. Boorda, the Navy's most senior officer, shot a .38-caliber bullet into his chest, causing his death. Why did he commit suicide? A widely-read magazine had disclosed that Admiral Boorda had never earned two of the war decorations that he wore. Bernard Trainor, a retired Marine Corps lieu-tenant general, explains that "when service people meet for the first time they immediately look at the ribbons each wears. In a way, it establishes a hierarchy of respect . . . for a soldier, sailor, airman or Marine a decoration is the symbol of status within the military fraternity" (Trainor, 1996, p. A8).

Artifacts may also define territories. To claim our spaces, we fill them with objects that matter to us and that reflect our experiences and values. Lovers of art adorn their homes with paintings and sculptures that announce their inter-ests and personalize their private space. Religious families often express their commitments by displaying pictures of holy scenes and the Bible, the Koran, or other sacred texts. We exhibit artifacts that symbolize important relationships and experiences in our lives. For example, many people have pictures of family members in their offices and homes. On my writing desk, I have a photograph of my sister Carolyn; an item that belonged to my father; the first card my partner Robbie ever gave me; and a jar of rocks from a beach where I retreat whenever possible. These artifacts personalize my desk and remind me of people and experiences I cherish.

S   T   U   D   E   N   T

JENETTA: *Whenever I move, the first thing I have to do is get out the quilt that my grandmother made. Even if it is summer and I won't use the quilt, I have to unpack it first and put it out where I can see it. She brought me up, and seeing that quilt is my way of keeping her in my life.*

In her book *Composing a Life*, Mary Catherine Bateson (1990) comments that we turn houses into homes by filling them with what matters to us. We make impersonal spaces familiar and comfortable by imprinting them with our artifacts. We use mugs given to us by special people, nurture plants to enliven indoor spaces, surround ourselves with books and magazines that announce our interests, and sprinkle our world with objects that reflect what we care about.

Artifacts communicate important relationship meanings. We use them to announce our identities (see "Piercing Punishment" on page 164) and to express how we perceive and feel about others. Although clothing has become more unisex in recent years, once you venture off campus, gendered styles are evident. To declare gender, we dress to meet cultural expectations of men and women. Thus, women sometimes wear makeup, dresses that may have lace or other softening touches, skirts, high-heeled shoes, jewelry, and hose, all of which conform to the cultural ideal of women as decorative objects. Typically, men wear little, if any, jewelry, and their clothes and shoes are functional. Flat shoes allow a person to walk comfortably or run if necessary; high heels don't. Men's clothing is looser and less binding, and it includes pockets for wallets, change, keys, and so forth. In contrast, women's clothing tends to be more tailored and often doesn't include pockets, making a purse necessary.

We also use artifacts to establish racial identity. In recent years, marketers have offered more ethnic clothing and jewelry, so people of color can more easily acquire artifacts that express their distinctive cultural heritages. In addition, African Americans often dress more stylishly and dramatically than Caucasians and may even engage in stylin', which is dressing to appear as if you are well-off, especially if you aren't (Ribeau, Baldwin, & Hecht, 1994; Wood, 1998). Stan explained to Caucasians in my class what stylin' means within the African American culture.

S   T   U   D   E   N   T

STAN: *We have to do stylin' if we want any respect in this society. It's not like we're putting on airs or trying to be something we're not. What it is is a way to challenge stereotypes about our race. Whites think Blacks are lazy, ugly, and uncultivated, and they've tried to make us see ourselves that way too. But we*

Piercing Punishment

It seems not everyone appreciates the rage for body piercing. Restaurants seem most sensitive to piercing. At the Woodward Cafe in Detroit, manager Svetlana Bogdonavoich spent 20 minutes soothing a customer who was upset over a clerk's pierced lip. Some employers set limits on which body parts can be pierced or how many piercings an employee may have. Starbucks draws the line at two piercings per ear and those are okay only if the earrings match. At Chili's restaurant chain only earrings are allowed. But other restaurants leave piercing up to employees. At Zingerman's Deli in Ann Arbor, Michigan, some employees have up to ten piercings.

SOURCE: Business bulletin. (1996, July 18). *Wall Street Journal*, p. A1.

© A. Ramey/Stock Boston

defy their stereotypes when we dress fine. We say to ourselves and to Whites that we look good. That's why brothers and sisters do stylin'.

Artifacts communicate our identity from an early age. Many hospitals still swaddle newborns in blue and pink blankets to designate sex, and even though many parents today try to be nonsexist, many still send gender messages through the toys they give their children. In general, parents, and especially fathers, give sons toys that encourage rough and active play (balls, trains) and competitiveness (baseball gloves, toy weapons), whereas they give daughters toys that cultivate nurturing (dolls, toy kitchens) and attention to appearance (makeup kits, frilly clothes) (Caldera, Huston, & O'Brien, 1989; Lytton & Romney, 1991; Pomerleau, Bolduc, Malcuit, & Cossette, 1990).

APPLY THE IDEA
Artifacts and Identity

How did artifacts in your childhood contribute to your gender identity? What kinds of toys did your parents give you? Did they ever discourage you from playing with particular kinds of toys? Did you ask for toys that aren't ones society prescribes for your gender—boys asking for dolls, girls for train sets? Did your parents let you have the toys?

Now think about the clothing your parents gave you. If you're a woman, did your parents expect you to wear frilly dresses and stay clean? If you're a man, did your parents give you clothes meant for rough play and getting dirty?

Do you have artifacts that reflect your ethnic identity? What objects are part of your celebrations and spiritual observances? Do you have any jewelry or clothes that reflect your ethnic heritage?

Gifts are conventional ways to say "you matter to me." Some objects are invested with cultural meanings as well: Engagement rings and wedding bands signify commitment in ways broadly understood within Western culture. We also symbolize that we're connected to others by wearing their clothes, as when women wear male partners' shirts or partners exchange sweatshirts.

Cultures, as well as social groups within a single culture, have artifacts that are especially important reflections of heritage and values. For example, Jewish people light candles in a menorah to symbolize sacred values. Christians rely on crosses and manger replicas to symbolize reverence for Jesus. In 1966 Kwanzaa was designated a time for African Americans to remember their African heritage and the values it entails. Kwanzaa is observed from December 26 through January 1. A kinara holds seven candles that symbolize seven distinct principles rooted in African culture. On the sixth day of Kwanzaa a magnificent feast, the karamu, draws together whole communities who celebrate their heritage and their connections (see "Kwanzaa").

Environmental Factors

Environmental factors are another nonverbal influence on interpersonal interaction. Environmental factors are elements of settings that affect how we feel and act. For instance, we respond to architecture, colors (see "How Colors Affect Mood" on page 166), room design, temperature, sounds, smells, and lighting. Rooms with comfortable chairs invite relaxation, whereas rooms with stiff chairs prompt formality. Dimly lit rooms can enhance romantic feelings, although dark rooms can be depressing. We feel solemn in churches and synagogues with their somber colors and sacred symbols.

We tend to feel more lethargic on sultry summer days and more alert on crisp fall ones. Delicious smells can make us feel hungry, even if we weren't previously interested in food. Our bodies synchronize themselves to patterns of light, so that we feel more alert during daylight than during the evening. In settings where people work during the night, extra lighting and even artificial skylights are used to simulate daylight so that workers stay alert. "Let the Sun Shine In" on page 167 shows how light affects productivity.

Think about restaurants in which you've eaten. As the examples that opened this chapter illustrate, the environment of most fast-food restaurants encourages customers to eat

COMMUNICATION NOTES

Kwanzaa

Kwanzaa blends a time of special celebration with friends and family with the everyday activities of keeping a home. In this way, Kwanzaa symbolizes the centrality of home and family to African Americans, historically and today.

The kinara is a branched candleholder that holds seven candles, one to be lit on each day of the Kwanzaa observance. Three red candles, which symbolize struggles, are placed on the left for days two, four and six of the celebration. The day two candle symbolizes the principle of *kujichagulia*, or self-determination. The day four candle symbolizes *ujamma*, cooperative economics within communities. The day six candle represents *kuumba*, or creativity. On the right side of the kinara are placed three green candles to symbolize the future. The day three candle on the far right represents *ujima*, collective work and responsibility. The day five candle symbolizes *nio*, or purpose. The day seven candle represents *imani*, or faith. The middle candle is black to stand for *umoja*, unity among black people.

On the sixth day of Kwanzaa there is a feast called Karamu. During the feast traditional African foods and family favorites are featured. Thus, Kwanzaa celebrates foods that have been passed down through generations of Africans and African Americans.

SOURCES: Bellamy, L. (1996, December 18). Kwanza cultivates cultural and culinary connections. *Raleigh News and Observer*, pp. 1F, 9F; George, L. (1995, December 26). Holiday's traditions are being formed. *Raleigh News and Observer*, pp. C1, C3.

© Paul Barton/The Stock Market

How Colors Affect Mood

How much is mood influenced by color? Research reports these relations between colors and moods:

red	exciting, stimulating
blue	secure, comfortable, soothing
orange	distressed, upset, disturbed
brown	dejected, unhappy, melancholy
green	calm, serene, peaceful
black	powerful, strong, defiant
yellow	cheerful, joyful, jovial
purple	dignified, stately

The effects of color are not limited to their visual impact. Rebecca Ewing, a color consultant in Atlanta, reports that she learned about the power of color from three women—all of whom were blind. The blind women could identify different colors, a phenomenon that has been documented, by sensing distinct vibrations from different colors; these vibrations affect feeling and moods. Ewing compared the blind women's responses to colors with those of sighted people, and she found the same reactions to colors. So, how does color affect our feelings? Says Ewing, red stimulates the appetite, blue stifles conversation, black evokes reverence, and green is calming.

SOURCE: Varkonyi, C. (1996, June 22). Colorcode. *Raleigh News and Observer*, pp. 1E–2E.; Wexner, L. B. (1954). The degree to which colors (hues) are associated with mood-tones. *Journal of Applied Psychology*, 38, 432–435.

"I suggest you get yourself a real briefcase, Miller. A tote bag just doesn't say vice president."

PEPPER AND SALT © Mike Shapiro. Wall Street Journal, 8/21/97. Reprinted by permission of Cartoon Features Syndicate.

quickly and move on, whereas more expensive restaurants are designed to promote longer stays and extra money on wines and desserts. For the same reason, fast-food restaurants are brightly lit and have fast music, if any. Finer restaurants tend to have dim lighting and soft, slow music, which encourages diners to linger.

The effect of restaurant atmosphere on diners was verified by an experiment. Over a sixteen-day period, researchers played music in a cafeteria. On the first day, the researchers played music with 122 beats per minute. The next day, they played slow instrumentals with only 56 beats per minute. On day three they played no music. The researchers repeated the sequence for sixteen days while they observed diners. The results confirmed the relationship between the pace of the music and the pace of eating. When no music was played, people averaged 3.23 bites per minute. When slow music was played, customers ate slightly more quickly: 3.83 bites per minute. But when the fast music with 122 beats per minute was played, diners sped up their eating to 4.4 bites per minutes (Bozzi, 1986).

An interesting illustration of cultural influences on environment is feng shui (pronounced "fung shway"). Feng shui, which stands for wind and water, is the ancient Chinese art of placement. Have you ever walked into a room and felt uncomfortable or unhappy? Have you ever entered a place and felt immediately warm and at ease? If so, you may have experienced feng shui in action. Dating back over three thousand years, feng shui is rooted in Taoism and aims to balance life energy, or *chi* (Spear, 1995). Feng shui consultants help homeowners and business-people arrange spaces to promote a smooth flow of energy and a harmony with nature. Some of the feng shui principles are consistent with Western research on nonverbal communication: Don't put large furniture in the path to the front door; you should never see a stairway from the front door; use green to increase good fortune; use mirrors where you want to stimulate creativity (Cozart, 1996; O'Neill, 1997).

Proxemics and Personal Space

Proxemics refers to space and how we use it (Hall, 1968). Every culture has norms for using space and for how close people should be to one another. In the United States, we interact with social acquaintances from a distance of 4 to 12 feet but are comfortable with 18 inches or less between us and close friends and romantic partners (Hall, 1966). When we are angry with someone, we tend to move away and to resent it if she or he approaches us. People who want to even out power in business negotiations often seek neutral territories for interaction. Gary makes this point in his commentary.

STUDENT VOICES

GARY: *Part of our training for management was to learn how to manage turf. We were taught we should always try to get competitors into our offices—not to go to theirs. This gives us the advantage, just like playing on the home court gives a team an advantage. We also learned that we should go to subordinates' offices if we needed to criticize them so that they would feel less threatened and more willing to improve performance. The trainers also stressed the importance of meeting on neutral ground when we had to negotiate a deal with another company. They warned us never to meet on the other guys' turf because that would give them the advantage.*

The amount of space we think we need to be comfortable is not strictly individual. There are notable cultural differences in the amount of space with which people feel comfortable (see "Room Enough to Grow . . . and Grow" on page 168). In China, for example, the average person has about 36 square feet, which amounts to a 6-foot by 6-foot room. Further, members of Chinese families often sleep in the same room and share bathrooms and kitchens with other families (Butterfield, 1982).

Space also announces status, with greater space being assumed by those with higher status (Henley, 1977). Substantial research shows that women and minorities generally have less space than White men in our society (Spain, 1992). The prerogative to invade someone else's personal space is also linked to power, with those having greater power also being most likely to trespass into others' territory (Henley, 1977). Responses to invasions of space also reflect power, with men likely to respond aggressively when their space is invaded

Room Enough to Grow . . . and Grow

Americans' love of space and lots of it is obvious in changing housing patterns. Consider this: Lori and Ron Simek spent over $650,000 to build a four-bedroom, six-bathroom, 5,700-square-foot "cabin" near Yellowstone Park. They will be the only occupants.

In 1994, nearly half of the homes constructed in the United States exceeded 3,000 square feet and were lived in by couples who had no children at home. This reflects a dramatic change in the housing patterns in the United States. Since 1969, the average size of a new single-family home has jumped by 33 percent—from 1,400 square feet to 2,100 square feet. During this time period, the size of the average U.S. family has decreased by the same 33 percent—from 3.6 people in 1969 to 2.7 people in 1994.

SOURCE: Templin, N. (1994, October 17). Wanted: Six bedrooms, seven baths for empty nesters. *Wall Street Journal*, pp. B1, B7.

"Sorry, Ridgely, but this area is my personal space."

© 1994 by Sidney Harris. The Wall Street Journal.

(Fisher & Byrne, 1975). This reflects gendered socialization, which encourages women to defer and accommodate and men to vie for status. "Environmental Racism" on page 169 reveals another connection between space and power.

How people arrange space reflects how close they are and whether they want interaction. Couples who are very interdependent tend to have greater amounts of common space and less individual space in their homes than do couples who are more independent (Fitzpatrick, 1988; Fitzpatrick & Best, 1979; Werner, Altman, & Oxley, 1985; Werner & Haggard, 1985). Similarly, families that value interaction arrange furniture to invite conversation and eye contact. Less interactive families arrange furniture to discourage conversation. Chairs may be far apart and may face televisions instead of one another (Burgoon, Buller, & Woodhall, 1989; Keeley & Hart, 1994). People also invite or discourage interaction by how they arrange office spaces. Some of your professors may have desks that face the door and a chair beside the desk for open communication with students; other professors may have desks turned away from the door and may position chairs across from their desks to preserve status and distance.

The effects of proxemics on behavior have not gone unnoticed by companies that make money by moving people quickly. At McDonald's around the world, seats tilt forward at a 10-degree angle to discourage customers from lingering. The fast-food giant further fosters quick eating by making seats at the two person tables only 2'2" apart when it has been established that the distance most people find comfortable for interaction is about 3½ feet (Eaves & Leathers, 1991).

A P P L Y   T H E   I D E A

What Does Your Space Say?

Survey your room or apartment. Is furniture arranged to promote or discourage interaction? How much space is common and how much is reserved for individuals? Is space divided evenly among you and your roommate(s), or do some people have more space than others?

Now think about your home. How is the space arranged there? Is there a living room or family room? If so, is furniture set up to invite interaction? Is there a lot, a little, or a moderate amount of common space?

How do spatial arrangements in your home and your room or apartment regulate interaction and reflect the styles and status of people who live there?

Chronemics

Chronemics refers to how we perceive and use time to define identities and interaction. Nonverbal scholar Nancy Henley (1977) reports that we use time to negotiate and convey status. She has identified a cultural rule that stipulates important people with high status can keep others waiting. Conversely, people with low status are expected to be punctual in Western society. It is standard practice to have to wait, sometimes a good while, to see a physician, even if you have an appointment. This carries the message that the physician's time is more valuable than yours. Professors can be late to class and students are expected to wait, but students may be reprimanded if they appear after a class begins. Subordinates are expected to report punctually to meetings, but bosses are allowed to be tardy.

Chronemics express cultural attitudes toward time, as illustrated in "Cultural Views of Time" on page 170. In Western societies, time is valuable, so speed is highly valued (Keyes, 1992; Schwartz, 1989). Linguists (Lakoff & Johnson, 1980) have noted many everyday U.S. phrases that reflect the cultural view that time is very valuable: Don't waste time; save time; spend time; can't spare time; invest time; run out of time; budget time; borrowed time; lose time; use time profitably.

The U.S. emphasis on speed is reflected in how we go about daily activities. We want computers, not typewriters, and we replace hardware and software as soon as faster models and programs hit the market. We often try to do several things at once to get more done, rely on the microwave to cook faster, and take for granted speed systems such as instant copying, photos, and so forth. Many other cultures have far more relaxed attitudes toward time and punctuality. It's not impolite in many South American countries to come late to meetings or classes, and it's not assumed people will leave at the scheduled time for ending. Whether time is savored or compulsively counted and hoarded reflects larger cultural attitudes toward living.

Environmental Racism

The term *environmental racism* arose to describe a pattern whereby toxic waste dumps and hazardous plants are disproportionately located in low-income neighborhoods and communities of color. Whether this is deliberately planned or not, many industries expose our most vulnerable communities to pollutants and carcinogens that seldom affect middle- and upper-class neighborhoods. The pattern is very clear: The space of minorities and poor people can be invaded and contaminated, but the territory of more affluent citizens cannot.

SOURCE: Cox, R. (1995). President of the national Sierra Club, 1994–1996. Personal communication.

© Don Smetzer/Tony Stone Images, Inc.

Cultural Views of Time

North Americans and Germans differ in the time they invest in work. The typical job in Germany requires 37 hours a week, and a minimum of five weeks' paid leave annually is guaranteed by law. Stores close on weekends and four of five weeknights so that workers can have leisure time. In the United States, jobs typically require 44 to 80 hours a week, and many workers can't take more than a week's leave at a time. Further, many North Americans take second jobs even when their first jobs allow a comfortable standard of living. Germans can't understand this, remarking that "free time can't be paid for" (p. B1). Personal time is considered so precious in Germany that it is illegal to work more than one job during holidays, which are meant to allow people to restore themselves.

SOURCE: Benjamin, D., & Horwitz, T. (1994, July 14). German view: "You Americans work too hard—and for what?" *Wall Street Journal*, pp. B1, B6.

The duration of time we spend with different individuals reflects our interpersonal priorities. When possible, we spend more time with people we like than with those we don't like or who bore us. Researchers report that increasing contact is one of the most important ways college students intensify relationships, and reduced time together signals decreasing interest (Baxter, 1985; Dindia, 1994; Tolhuizen, 1989). Time is also related to status in work settings. Bankers spend more time with important clients who have major accounts; brokers spend more time with clients who have a lot of money than with clients who have less; architects meet more often and for longer periods with companies that are building a series of large structures than with individuals who want to build a single home; and fundraisers invest greater amounts of time in well-off donors than in moderate contributors.

Chronemics also involve expectations of time, which are established by cultural norms. For example, you expect a class to last 50 to 75 minutes. Several minutes before the end of a class period, students often close notebooks and start gathering their belongings, signaling the teacher that time is up. Similarly, we expect weekly religious services to last approximately an hour, and we might be upset if a rabbi or minister talked beyond the time we've allowed. These expectations reflect our culture's general orientation toward time, which is that it is a precious commodity that we should not give away easily.

Paralanguage

Paralanguage refers to communication that is vocal but that does not use words themselves. It includes sounds, such as murmurs and gasps, and vocal qualities, such as volume, rhythm, pitch, and inflection. Paralanguage also includes how we pronounce words, the accents we use, and the complexity of our sentences. Our voices are versatile instruments that tell others how to interpret us and what we say. Vocal cues signal others to interpret what we say as a joke, threat, statement of fact, question, and so forth.

APPLY THE IDEA
Paralinguistic Cues

Say "Oh, really" to express the following meanings:

- I don't believe what you just said.
- Wow! That's interesting.
- I find your comment boring.

- That's juicy gossip!
- What a contemptible thing to say.

Now say "You love me" to convey these meanings:

- You really do? I hadn't realized that.
- That ploy won't work. I told you we're through.
- You couldn't possibly love me after what you did!
- Me? I'm the one you love?
- You? I didn't think you loved anyone.

COMMUNICATION NOTES

To Tell the Truth

Dektor Counterintelligence and Security, Inc., believes our voices reveal whether we are lying or telling the truth. Dektor invented the PSE (Psychological Stress Evaluator), a machine that measures vocal stress. Dektor claims the PSE has a 94.7 percent success rate in detecting lies, and this machine has been used several times in trials.

We use our voices to communicate feelings to friends and romantic partners. Whispering, for instance, signals secrecy and intimacy, whereas shouting conveys anger. Depending on the context, sighing may communicate empathy, boredom, or contentment. Research indicates that tone of voice is a powerful clue to feelings between marital partners. Negative paralanguage, such as sneering and ridiculing by tone of voice, are closely associated with marital dissatisfaction (Gottman, Markman, & Notarius, 1977; Noller, 1987). A derisive or sarcastic tone communicates scorn or dislike more emphatically than words. The reverse is also true: A warm voice underlines feelings of love, and a playful lilt invites frolic and fun. Tone of voice and inflection are also primary gauges for interpreting honesty, as illustrated in "To Tell the Truth."

Our voices affect how others perceive us. To some extent, we control vocal cues that influence image. For instance, we can deliberately sound firm and sure of ourselves in job interviews when we want to project self-confidence. Similarly, we can consciously make ourselves sound self-righteous, seductive, and unapproachable when those images suit our purposes. In addition to the ways we intentionally use our voices to project an image, vocal qualities we don't deliberately manipulate affect how others perceive us. For instance, individuals with accents are often stereotyped: Someone with a pronounced Bronx accent may be perceived as brash and someone with a Southern drawl may be stereotyped as lazy. People with foreign accents are often falsely perceived as less intelligent than native speakers.

STUDENT VOICES

MELISSA: *I got so much grief for my accent when I went to a junior college in New England. I never thought of myself as having an accent because everyone in Alabama talks like I do, but I guess I really stood out in Connecticut. People not only made fun of my accent, but they had all these other stereotypes about Southerners being slow and unassertive. It was really hard to get anyone to judge me on my merits.*

We modulate our voices to reflect our cultural heritage and to announce we are members of specific cultures. For example, African American speech has more vocal range, inflection, and tonal quality than Caucasian speech (Garner, 1994). In addition, among themselves African Americans often engage in highly rhythmical rappin' and "high talk" to craft desired identities (Ribeau, Baldwin, & Hecht, 1994).

We also use paralanguage to declare gender by behaving in a masculine or feminine manner. To appear masculine, men use strong volume, low pitch, and limited inflection, all of which conform to cultural prescriptions for men to be assertive and emotionally controlled. To enact femininity, women tend to use higher pitch, less volume, and more inflection, vocal features that reflect cultural views of women as deferential and polite.

We also enact class by how we pronounce words, the accents we use, and the complexity of our sentences. Class is expressed by vocabulary (greater vocabulary is generally associated with higher education) and by grammar. In addition to paralinguistic cues, other nonverbal behaviors communicate class. For example, artifacts generally differ in the homes of working-class and upper-class people. Affluent individuals possess more books, expensive art, and valuable jewelry than do less affluent individuals.

Silence

A final type of nonverbal behavior is silence, which can communicate powerful messages. "I'm not speaking to you" actually speaks volumes. We use silence to communicate different meanings. For instance, it can symbolize contentment when intimates are so comfortable they don't need to talk. Silence can also communicate awkwardness, as you know if you've ever had trouble keeping conversation going with a new acquaintance. We feel pressured to fill the void. In some cultures, including many Native American ones, silence indicates respect and thoughtfulness.

The positive value of silence has been proved in the case of seriously ill babies. Hospital intensive care nurseries have found that special headphones that block noise reduce the stress caused by the sounds of respirators, ventilators, and other hospital machinery. Within the headphones is a mini-microphone that detects irritating low-frequency noises and eliminates them by generating anti-noise waves. In trials of the headphones, babies who wore them had fewer sleep disturbances and less abnormal changes in blood pressure (Cyberscope, 1996).

Yet silence isn't always comforting. It is sometimes used to disconfirm others. In some families, children are disciplined by being ignored. No matter what the child says or does, parents refuse to acknowledge his or her existence. In later life, the silencing strategy may also surface. You know how disconfirming silence can be if you've ever said hello to someone and gotten no reply. Even if the other person didn't deliberately ignore you, you feel slighted. We sometimes deliberately freeze out intimates when we're angry with them. In some military academies, such as West Point, silencing is a recognized method of stripping a cadet of personhood if he or she is perceived as having broken the academy code. Similarly, the Catholic Church excommunicates people who violate its canons.

GINDER: *Silencing is the cruelest thing you can do to a person. That was how my parents disciplined all of us. They told us we were bad and then refused to speak to us—sometimes for several hours. I can't describe how awful it felt to get no response from them, to be a nonperson. I would have preferred physical punishment. I'll never use silencing with my kids.*

In this section, we've discussed nine types of nonverbal behavior. The complex system of nonverbal communication includes face and body motions, touch, physical appearance, artifacts, environmental features, space, chronemics, paralanguage, and silence. We use these nonverbal behaviors to announce our identities and to communicate how we feel about relationships with others. In the final section of this chapter, we consider guidelines for improving the effectiveness of our nonverbal communication.

Guidelines for Improving Nonverbal Communication

© Peter Cade/Tony Stone Images, Inc.

Nonverbal communication, like language, is symbolic and open to misinterpretation. Following two guidelines should help you avoid misunderstanding others' nonverbal behaviors and having others misperceive your actions.

Monitor Your Nonverbal Communication

The monitoring skills we have stressed in other chapters are also important for competent nonverbal communication. Self-reflection allows you to take responsibility for how you present yourself and your nonverbal messages. Think about the foregoing discussion of ways we use nonverbal behaviors to announce our identities. Are you projecting the image you desire? Do your facial and body movements represent how you see yourself and how you want others to perceive you? Do friends ever tell you that you seem uninterested or far away when they are talking to you? If so, you can monitor your nonverbal actions so that you convey greater involvement and interest in conversations.

Have you set up your spaces so that they invite the kind of interaction you prefer, or are they arranged to interfere with good communication? Paying attention to nonverbal dimensions of your world can empower you to use them more effectively to achieve your interpersonal goals.

Be Tentative When Interpreting Others' Nonverbal Communication

Although stores are filled with popular advice books that promise to show you how to read nonverbal communication, there really aren't any sure-fire formulas. It's naive to think we can precisely decode something as complex and ambiguous as nonverbal communication. When we believe that we can, we risk misjudging others.

In this chapter, we've discussed findings about the meanings people attach to nonverbal behaviors. It's important to realize these are only generalizations about conclusions people draw. We have not and cannot state what any particular behavior ever means to specific individuals in a given context. For instance, we've said that satisfied couples tend to sit closer together than unhappy couples. As a general rule, this is true, at least in Western societies. However, sometimes very contented couples prefer autonomy and like to keep distance between them some of the time. In addition, someone may maintain distance because she or he has a cold and doesn't want a partner to catch it. In work settings, people who don't look at us and who discourage conversation may be preoccupied with solving a problem and not mean to ignore us. Also, people socialized in non-Western cultures use space in different ways and have different meanings for physical closeness and distance. Because nonverbal communication is ambiguous and personal, we should not assume we can interpret it with absolute precision. You will be more effective if you qualify interpretations of nonverbal communication with awareness of personal and contextual considerations.

S T U D E N T   V O I C E S

KINCAID: *One of the most unsettling experiences of my life was trying to negotiate a deal between my company and a Japanese one. I traveled to Japan and met with a representative of the Japanese company. He wouldn't look at me when I spoke, and that made me wonder if he was being evasive. Also, he would never say "no" point blank, even if he totally disagreed with something I said or if there was no way he was going to agree to terms I proposed. His style was to say, "We will have to think about that very important idea." After two days of frustrating negotiations, I met with another American businessman who explained to me that Japanese think direct eye contact is rude and that they never refuse or disagree because that would make the other person lose face. I had to learn how to read Mr. Watanabe.*

Personal Qualifications   Generalizations about nonverbal behavior tell us only what is generally the case. They don't tell us about the exceptions to the rule. Nonverbal patterns that accurately describe most people may not apply to particular individuals. Although eye contact generally indicates responsiveness in Western culture, some individuals close their eyes to concentrate when listening. In such cases, it would be inaccurate to conclude a person who doesn't look at us isn't listening. Similarly, people who cross their arms and have a rigid posture are often expressing hostility or lack of interest in interaction. However, the same behaviors might mean a person is cold and trying to conserve body heat. Most people use less inflection, fewer gestures, and a slack posture when they're not really interested in what they're talking about. However, we all exhibit these same behaviors when we are tired.

Because nonverbal behaviors are ambiguous and vary among people, we need to be cautious about how we interpret others. A key principle to keep in mind is that nonverbal behaviors, like other symbols, have no intrinsic meaning. Meaning is something we construct and assign to behaviors. A good way to keep this distinction in mind is to rely on I-language, not you-language, which we discussed in Chapter 4. You-language might lead us to inaccurately say of someone who doesn't look at us, "You're communicating lack of interest." A more responsible statement would use I-language to say, "When you don't look at me, I feel you're not interested in what I'm saying." Using I-language reminds us to take responsibility for our judgments and feelings. In addition, it reduces the likelihood we will make others defensive by inaccurately interpreting their nonverbal behavior.

APPLY THE IDEA

Using I-Language About Nonverbal Behaviors

I-language makes communication about nonverbal behaviors more responsible and clear. Practice the skill of translating you-language into I-language to describe nonverbal behavior.

EXAMPLE: You-language: You're staring at me.
I-language: When you look at me so intensely, I feel uneasy.

YOU-LANGUAGE

You make me angry when you don't clean your side of the room.
I can tell you don't believe me by your expression.
Don't crowd me.
Your T-shirt is offensive.

Contextual Qualifications   Like the meaning of verbal communication, the significance of nonverbal behaviors depends on the contexts in which they occur. How we act doesn't reflect only how we see ourselves and how we feel. In addition, our actions reflect the various settings we inhabit. We are more or less formal, relaxed, and open depending on context. Most people are more at ease on their own turf than someone else's, so we tend to be friendlier and more outgoing in our homes than in business meetings and public places. We also dress according to context. Students who see me in professional clothing on campus are often surprised to find me in jeans or running clothes when they come by my home or see me in town. Like all of us, I costume myself differently for various occasions and contexts.

Immediate physical setting is not the only context that affects nonverbal communication. As we have seen, all communication, including the nonverbal dimension, reflects the values and understandings of particular cultures. We are

© E. Williamson/The Picture Cube

likely to misinterpret people from other cultures when we impose the norms and rules of our own. An Arabic man who stands very close to others to talk with them is not being rude according to the standards in his culture, although he might be interpreted as pushy by Westerners. A Tibetan woman who makes little eye contact is showing respect by the norms in her country, although she might be interpreted as evasive if judged by North American rules of interaction.

STUDENT VOICES

MEI-LING: *I often have been misinterpreted in this country. My first semester here a professor told me he wanted me to be more assertive and to speak up in class. I could not do that, I told him. He said I should put myself forward, but I have been brought up not to do that. In Taiwan, that is very rude and ugly, and all of us are taught not to speak up to teachers. Now that I have been here for three years, I sometimes speak in classes, but I am still more quiet than Americans. I know my professors think I am not so smart because I am quiet, but that is the teaching of my country.*

Even within our own country we have diverse speech communities, and each has its own rules for nonverbal behavior. We run the risk of misinterpreting men if we judge them by the norms of feminine speech communities. A man who doesn't make "listening noises" may well be listening intently according to the rules of masculine speech communities. Similarly, men often misperceive women as agreeing when they nod and make listening noises while another is talking. According to feminine speech communities, ongoing feedback is a way of signaling interest, not necessarily approval. Within the understandings of many African American communities, stylin' is not arrogant egotism as the same behaviors might be according to Caucasian norms. We have to adopt dual perspective when interpreting others, especially when different social groups are involved.

We can become more effective nonverbal communicators if we monitor our own nonverbal behaviors and qualify our interpretation of others by keeping personal and contextual considerations in mind. Using I-language is one way to help us avoid the danger of misreading others.

CHAPTER Summary

In this chapter, we've explored many facets of the fascinating world beyond words. We began by noting both similarities and differences between verbal and nonverbal communication. Next, we discussed how that nonverbal communication functions to supplement or replace verbal messages, to regulate interaction, to reflect and establish relationship-level meanings, and to express cultural membership. These four principles of nonverbal behavior help us understand the complex ways in which nonverbal communication operates and what it may mean.

We discussed nine types of nonverbal communication. These are kinesics (face and body motion), proxemics (use of space), physical appearance, artifacts, environmental features, haptics, chronemics (use of and orientations to time), paralanguage, and silence. Each of these forms of nonverbal communication reflects cultural understandings and values and also expresses our personal identities and feelings toward others. We use nonverbal behaviors to announce and perform identities, using actions, artifacts, and contextual features to embody the rules we associate with gender, race, class, sexuality, and ethnicity. In this sense, nonverbal communication has a theatrical dimension, because it is a primary way we create and present images of ourselves.

Because nonverbal communication, like its verbal cousin, is symbolic, it has no inherent meaning that is fixed for all time. Instead, its meaning is something we construct as we notice, organize, and interpret nonverbal behaviors that we and others enact. Effectiveness requires that we learn to monitor our own nonverbal communication and to exercise caution in interpreting that of others.

KEY Concepts

- artifacts
- chronemics
- haptics
- kinesics
- nonverbal communication
- proxemics

FOR FURTHER Thought & Discussion

1. Think about the information on lawyers' nonverbal communication (see page 159). What ethical issues are involved in lawyers' use of nonverbal behaviors in an effort to influence jurors? What ethical issues are involved in judges' restrictions of lawyers' nonverbal communication? Is this a violation of the right to free speech?

2. Visit six restaurants near your campus. Describe the seats, lighting, music (if any), distance between tables, and colors of decor. Do you find any relationship between nonverbal communication patterns and expensiveness of restaurants?

3. Describe the spatial arrangements in the family in which you grew up. How large was your home or apartment? How many people lived there? Did each member of the family have her or his own bedroom? Did anyone in the family have a separate work or hobby room or a special chair in which others did not sit? Do the proxemic patterns in your family reflect status differences among members?

4. Is it ethical to interpet others' nonverbal communication without recognizing their cultural perspective? If so, how does doing this reflect unethical behavior and/or attitudes?

5. What does silence mean to you? Does its meaning differ in various contexts? What do you mean when you are silent? Do you ever use silence strategically?

6. What ethical issues are involved in dumping toxic wastes in poor communities? Is it fair for all citizens to enjoy the benefits of petrochemical products but for only some of them to absorb the risks of producing these products?

7. Use your *Infotrac College Edition* to skim articles and advertisements in *Better Homes and Gardens*, which has a predominantly White readership, and *Essence*, which has a predominantly Black readership. How many articles and advertisements that focus on weight (losing, controlling) do you find in each of these magazines? What can you conclude about the salience of weight for women in White and Black speech communities?

8. Use your *InfoTrac College Edition* to review the table of contents for the last four issues of *Environmental Action Magazine*. Is the topic of environmental justice (also called environmental racism) discussed in any of the issues? Do you find any recent reports on patterns in location of toxic waste dumps and other environmental dangers?

Mindful

Listening

BEN: Mom just called to tell me she and Dad are divorcing. I can't believe it. My folks have been together for twenty-three years.

MIKE: Well, half of marriages end in divorce so it's not so unusual.

BEN: Maybe half of other people's marriages, but not *my* parents.

MIKE: Why not your parents? Divorce is pretty common. It just isn't a big deal anymore.

BEN: It's a big deal to me. Mom and Dad have always been there for me. It feels so strange to think I won't have my family anymore.

MIKE: Okay, so you weren't expecting this news, but still, it's not like the end of the world. Just get on with your life.

BEN: How can I when everything my life is based on has suddenly blown up in my face?

MIKE: They'll still pay for your last year of college, won't they?

BEN: I guess, but that's not the issue. The problem is that I don't have a home or family anymore.

MIKE: Get a grip, man. It's not like you're a ten-year-old living at home. You left home when you came to college. Their divorce doesn't affect you or your life—not unless you let it.

How would you describe Mike's communication in the conversation? Is he being a good communicator? Does he let Ben know he understands how Ben feels? Does Mike respond sensitively to Ben's concerns?

Usually when we think about communication, we think about talking. Yet, talking is not the only or even the greatest part of communication. For people to interact and share meaning, they must also listen to one another. As obvious as this is, few of us devote as much energy to effective listening as we do to effective talking. In the example, Mike doesn't listen very well. He isn't sensitive to Ben's feelings, and he doesn't communicate support to his friend. Although most of us are probably better listeners than Mike was in this instance, few of us listen as well as we could or should.

If you think about your normal day, you'll realize that listening—or trying to—takes up about half of your waking time. Listening is the single greatest communication activity in which we engage. We spend more time listening than talking, reading, or writing. This point is well made by Marilyn Buckley, who says "students listen to the equivalent of a book a day; talk the equivalent of a book a week; read the equivalent of a book a month; and write the equivalent of a book a year" (1992, p. 622).

Studies of people, ranging from college students to professionals, indicate that the average person spends between 45 and 53 percent of waking time listening to others (Barker, Edwards, Gaines, Gladney, & Holley, 1981; Weaver, 1972). You listen in classes, listen to acquaintances in casual conversation, listen to your parents during phone calls, listen to clerks in stores, listen to your supervisor and customers when you're at work, and listen to friends when they talk to you about important concerns or issues in their lives. If we don't listen effectively, we're communicating poorly about half of the time! And if we don't listen well, we are diminished emotionally, intellectually, and spiritually. This

Signing As a Foreign Language

About half of the colleges and universities in the United States currently recognize American Sign Language (ASL) as a language that fulfills the academic requirements for a foreign language. Among the Ivy League universities that give foreign language credit for ASL are Harvard, Brown, Georgetown, and MIT.

The first lesson students learn is that ASL is not just a visual form of English. Rather, it is a complex linguistic system with its own syntactical and grammatical structure. ASL is also more conceptual than spoken English. There are signs for distinct concepts such as walking quickly and walking slowly and being smart and being very smart. Spoken English relies on modifiers to make these distinctions: The word *walking* gets modified by *quickly* or *slowly*; the word *smart* gets modified by *very*.

As with learning any language, learning ASL introduces students not just to words but to the values of the Deaf culture. For example, students learn that in ASL there is only one word for music—a sweeping gesture with the right hand under the left arm. Because deaf individuals cannot hear, they don't need the many terms hearing individuals use to describe different kinds of music.

SOURCES: Carl, W. (1998). A sign of the times. In J. T. Wood, *But I thought you meant . . . : Misunderstandings in human communication* (pp. 95–208). Mountain View, CA: Mayfield; Manning, A. (1996, March 6). Signing catches on as a foreign language. *USA Today*, p. 4D.

point was well made in an advertisement sponsored by the Unisys Corporation: "How can we expect him to learn when we haven't taught him how to listen?" (cited in Berko, Wolvin, & Wolvin, 1995, p. 81). If we can't listen, we can't learn.

Although listening—or trying to—takes up a great deal of our time, we don't always do it as effectively as we could and should. Because listening is a vital and major form of communication, in this chapter we will explore what it is and how to listen effectively. First, we'll consider what's involved in listening, which is more than most of us realize. Next we'll discuss obstacles to effective listening and how we can minimize these. We'll also consider some common forms of nonlistening. The third section of the chapter explains different types of listening and the distinct skills required for each. To wrap up the chapter, we'll identify guidelines for improving listening effectiveness.

The Listening Process

Listening is a complex process that involves far more than our ears. To listen well, we rely on our ears, minds, and hearts. Although we often use the words *listening* and *hearing* as if they were synonyms, actually they are distinct. **Hearing** is a physiological activity that occurs when sound waves hit our eardrums. People who are deaf or hearing impaired receive messages visually either through lip reading or ASL (American Sign Language; see "Signing As a Foreign Language"). Listening has psychological and cognitive dimensions that mere hearing, or physically receiving messages, does not. The multifaceted aspects of listening are reflected in the Chinese character in Figure 6.1, which includes the symbols for eyes, ears, and heart.

Listening is an active, complex process that consists of being mindful, hearing, selecting and organizing information, interpreting communication, responding, and remembering. Listening is not just hearing but also includes interpreting and responding to what others communicate. The International Listening Association (1995) emphasizes that listening is an active process, which means we have to exert effort to listen well. We have to be involved with our ears and hearts and minds, if we want to listen effectively. Figure 6.2 shows the listening process.

Being Mindful

The first step in listening is making a decision to be mindful. **Mindfulness** is a concept from Zen Buddhism that refers to being fully present in the moment. The Reverend Jisho Perry says that "to pay attention is to stop putting our own ideas and opinions on the situation" (1996, p. 22). To be mindful is to keep your mind on what is happening in the here and now. When we are mindful, we don't let our thoughts wander from the present situation. We don't think about what we did yesterday or plan to do this weekend, nor do we focus on our own feelings and responses. Instead, when we listen mindfully we tune in fully to another person and try to hear that person without imposing our own ideas, judgments, or feelings on him or her. Mindfulness is symbolized by paying attention, adopting an involved posture, keeping eye contact, and indicating interest in what another person says (Bolton, 1986). Mindfulness is the first step in effective listening, and it is the foundation for all other parts of the process.

Ears

Eyes

Heart

Listening

FIGURE 6.1
The Chinese Character for the Word *Listening*

Mindfulness enhances communication in two ways. First, attending fully to others allows us to understand them better than if we pay only superficial attention. Listening mindfully enables us to grasp the relational meanings of messages so that we have an idea of how another person feels about what she or he is saying. In other words, mindfulness fosters dual perspective, which is a cornerstone of effective communication. In addition, mindfulness enhances the effectiveness of another's communication. When people sense we are really listening, they tend to engage us more fully, elaborate their ideas, and express themselves in more depth.

Being mindful is a choice we make. It is not a talent that some people have and others don't, nor is it something that results from what others do. Instead, it is a matter of making a personal commitment to attend fully and without diversion to another person. No amount of skill will make you a good listener if you don't choose to attend mindfully to others. Thus, it is your choice whether or not to be mindful and thus a good listener.

> Mindfulness
>
> Physical Reception of Communication
>
> Selective Perception of Communication
>
> Organizing Perceived Communication
>
> Interpreting Communication
>
> Responding to Others
>
> Remembering Communication

FIGURE 6.2
The Listening Process

A P P L Y   T H E   I D E A
Being Mindful

To develop your ability to be mindful, follow these guidelines in a situation that calls on you to listen:

- Empty your mind of thoughts, ideas, plans, and concerns so that you are open to the other person.
- Concentrate on the person with whom you are interacting. Say to yourself, "I want to focus on this person and what she or he is feeling and thinking."

© Photo Researchers, Inc.

CONTINUED

- If you find yourself framing responses to the other person, try to push those aside—they interfere with your concentration on what the other person is saying.
- If your mind wanders, don't criticize yourself—that's distracting. Instead, gently refocus on the person you are with and what that person is communicating to you. It's natural for other thoughts to intrude, so just push them away and stay focused on the other person.
- Let the other person know you are attending mindfully by giving nonverbal responses (nods, facial expressions), asking questions to encourage elaboration, and keeping eye contact.
- Evaluate how mindfully you listened. Did you understand the other person's thoughts and feelings? Did you feel more focused on that person than you usually do when listening to others?

STUDENT VOICES

MARISA: *I always thought I was a good listener, until I spent two years living in Japan. In that culture there is a much deeper meaning to listening. I realized that most of the time I was only hearing others. Often I was thinking of my responses while they were still talking. I had not been listening with my mind and heart.*

Physically Receiving Messages

The second process involved in listening is hearing, or physically receiving messages. As we noted earlier, hearing is a physiological process in which sound waves hit our eardrums so that we become aware of noises, such as music, traffic sounds, or human voices. For individuals who have hearing impairments, messages are received in other ways—through writing, lip reading, or ASL. Whether we hear messages or receive them in other ways, the mere reception of messages is not listening. Instead, it is a passive process: If we are present when vibrations are in the air, we will hear them. If someone signs to us, we can see the signs and decode them. Hearing, or otherwise receiving messages, requires no real effort on our part.

Although receiving messages is not the same as listening, we have to receive messages in order to listen. For most of us, hearing is automatic and unhindered. However, individuals with hearing impairments may have difficulty actually receiving oral messages. When we speak with someone who has a hearing disability, we should face the person and check to make sure we are coming across clearly. In addition to physiological problems, hearing ability may decline when we are fatigued from concentrating on communication. You may have noticed that it's harder to pay attention in classes that run 75 minutes or 2 hours than 50-minute sessions. Background noise can also interfere with good hearing. If loud music is playing, a television is blaring, or others are talking in our vicinity, it's difficult to hear well. Even though this is evident, as Betsy points out, we often don't control noises that interfere with effective hearing and listening.

BETSY: *My parents are so strange! To watch them, you'd think they were deliberately trying to make it impossible to hear each other. Here's what happens: Dad will turn on the radio, and then Mom will start talking. He won't hear part of what she says, and then she'll get in a huff that he ignored her. Or sometimes Mom will have the television on, and Dad will say something from the other room. When she doesn't hear him, he'll get on her case about caring more about whatever program is on than about him. They do this all the time— no wonder they can't hear each other!*

Even among people who have normal hearing, there may be physiological differences in how we hear. Women and men seem to differ in their listening styles. As a rule, women are more attentive than men to the many things that are happening around them. Thus, men tend to focus their hearing on specific content aspects of communication, whereas women are more likely to attend to the whole of communication, noticing details, tangents, and major themes (Weaver, 1972). Judy Pearson (1985), a prominent communication scholar, suggests this could be due to the brain's hemispheric specializations. Women usually have more developed right lobes, which govern creative and holistic thinking, whereas men typically have more developed left lobes, which control analytic and linear information processing.

MARK: *My girlfriend amazes me. We'll have a conversation, and then later one of us will bring it up again. What I remember is what we decided in the talk. She remembers that too, but she also remembers all the details about where we were and what was going on in the background and particular things one of us said in the conversation. I never notice all of that stuff, and I sure don't remember it later.*

Selecting and Organizing Material

The third element of listening is selecting and organizing material. As we noted in Chapter 3, we don't perceive everything around us. Instead, we selectively attend to some messages and elements of our environments, and we disregard others. What we attend to depends on many factors, including our interests, cognitive structures, and expectations. If we realize that our own preoccupations can hamper listening, we can curb interferences. Once again, mindfulness comes into play. Choosing to be mindful doesn't necessarily mean our minds won't stray when we try to listen, but it does mean that we will bring ourselves back to the present moment. We have to remind ourselves to focus attention and concentrate on what another is saying.

We can monitor our tendencies to attend selectively by remembering that we are more likely to notice stimuli that are intense, loud, or unusual, or that otherwise stand out from the flow of communication. This implies that we may overlook communicators who speak quietly and don't call attention to themselves. Intan, an Asian American student, once told me that Caucasians often ignore what she says because she speaks softly and unassertively. Westerners who are accustomed to outspoken, individualistic speaking styles may not attend to speaking styles that are less bold. If we're aware of the tendency not to notice people who speak quietly, we can guard against it so that we don't miss out on people and messages that may be important. "Hard Times for Listening" explores the effect of our rushed lifestyles on listening.

Once we've selected what to notice, we then organize the stimuli to which we've attended. As you'll recall from Chapter 3, we organize our perceptions by relying on cognitive schemata, which include prototypes, personal constructs, stereotypes, and scripts. As we listen to others, we decide how to categorize them by asking which of our prototypes they most closely resemble—good friend, person in trouble, student, teacher, and so forth. We then apply personal constructs to define in more detail others and their messages. We evaluate whether they are smart or not smart, upset or calm, reasonable or unreasonable, open or closed to advice, and so on. Based on how we construct others, we then apply stereotypes that predict what they will do. When friends are clearly distraught, as Ben was at the beginning of this chapter, we can reasonably predict they will want to ventilate and may not want advice until after they have a chance to express their feelings. Finally, we apply scripts, which specify how interaction should proceed, including how we should act.

The schemata we use to organize our perceptions help us figure out how to respond to others and what they say. When we decide someone is angry and needs to spout off, we're likely to rely on a script that tells us to back off and let the person air his or her feelings. If, on the other hand, we perceive someone as confused, we might follow a script that says we should help the person clarify her or his feelings and options. It's important to remember that *we construct others and their communication* when we use our schemata to organize perceptions. In other words, we create meaning by how we select and organize communication. This reminds us to keep perceptions tentative and open to revision. In the course of interaction, we may want to modify initial perceptions.

S T U D E N T **VOICES**

TONYA: *I work as a volunteer counselor at the women's center, and the other day something happened that shows how wrong a script we can have. This woman came in, a student about my age, and she told me she was pregnant. She was very upset and having trouble talking, so I tried to help out by going into the discussion most pregnant women who come to the center want. I told her a lot of people have untimely pregnancies and that it doesn't have to interfere with her life. Then I said that I could recommend several doctors who could perform abortions. By then she was crying even harder, and I started trying to tell her that abortions weren't a serious medical procedure. Finally, she managed to get out that she wanted to have the baby and needed help working out that decision. Well, that's a whole different script than abortion counseling. I had misperceived her, and that led me to adopt an inappropriate script.*

Interpreting Communication

The fourth part of listening is interpreting others' communication. When we interpret, we put together all that we have selected and organized in a manner that makes sense of the overall situation. The most important principle for effective interpretation is to engage in dual perspective so that you interpret others in their terms. Certainly, you won't always agree with other people and how they see themselves, others, or situations. Engaging in dual perspective doesn't require you to share another's perspective; it does, however, require you to make an earnest effort to understand others.

To interpret someone on her or his own terms is one of the greatest gifts we can give another. What we give is personal regard so deep that we open our minds to how another sees the world. A genuine effort to understand others and what things mean to them is rare and very precious. Too often we impose our meanings on others, or we try to correct or argue with them about what they feel, or we crowd out their words with our own. As listening expert Robert Bolton (1986, p. 167) has observed, good listeners "stay out of the other's way," so they can learn how the speaker views his or her situation. Because fully interpersonal communication involves recognizing others as unique individuals, we must try to grasp what their experiences mean to them. Effective listening involves trying to understand others on their terms.

COMMUNICATION NOTES

Hard Times for Listening

Have you noticed that there's a lot more talk than listening going on these days? Television talk shows, call-in radio programs, and hot lines encourage people to talk, talk, talk. But is anyone listening?

Scholars of communication point to several factors that have reduced Americans' listening skills. First, there is the fast pace of everyday life. Hurrying is a national pastime. Even when we don't need to hurry, we seem habituated to do so. In conversations, we're thinking, "Get to the point."

Another contributor to poor listening is media. Television and radio encourage passive attention, not active listening. Further, says communication consultant Sheila Bentley, the constant interruption of commercials decreases our skills in sustaining attention for periods of time.

Poor listening causes mistakes and problems, which explains why many companies now require employees to attend listening workshops. Starbucks, for instance, requires employees to learn to listen to orders and rearrange customers' requests in the sequence of size, flavoring, milk, and caffeine. That's helpful when customers often spurt out "double-shot decaf grande" or "iced, skim, cappucino, small."

SOURCE: Crossen, C. (1997, July 10). Blah, blah, blah. *Wall Street Journal*, pp. 1A, 6A.

S T U D E N T   V O I C E S

BART: *I'd been married and working for years when I decided I wanted to come back to school and finish my degree. When I mentioned it to the guys I worked with, they all came down hard on me. They said I was looking for*

© Peter L. Chapman

an easy life as a college Joe and trying to get above them. My dad said it would be irresponsible to quit work when I had a wife and child, and he said no self-respecting man would do that. It seemed like everyone had a view of what I was doing and why, and their views had nothing to do with mine. The only person who really listened to me was Elaine, my wife. When I told her I was thinking about going back to school, the first thing out of her mouth was "What would that mean to you?" She didn't presume she knew my reasons, and she didn't start off arguing with me. She just asked what it meant to me, then listened for a long long time while I talked about how I felt. She focused completely on understanding me, and that made it easy to talk. Maybe that's why we're married.

Responding

Effective listening also involves **responding,** which is communicating attention and interest. As we noted in Chapter 1, interpersonal communication is not a linear process in which one person speaks at another. Rather, it is a transactive process in which we simultaneously listen and speak. Skillful listeners give outward signs that they are following and interested. In the United States, signs of responsive listening include eye contact, nodding, attentive posture, and questions and comments that invite others to elaborate. These behaviors signal that we are involved in what is happening in the moment. All of us tend to communicate more clearly and interestingly when we feel others are committed to us and our communication. "The Impact of Responsive Listening" describes an experiment that shows the power of this type of listening skill.

We don't respond only when others finish speaking; rather, we respond throughout interaction. This is what makes listening such an active process. As we saw earlier, we cannot avoid communication, so the issue is *what* we communicate when we are listening. Nonverbal behaviors, such as looking out a window, making notes to ourselves, and slouching, signal that we aren't involved. Disinterest is also signaled by passivity. In a book titled *Who's Listening?* psychiatrist Franklin Ernst (1973, p. 113) remarked that "to listen is to move. To listen is to be moved. . . . The non-moving, unblinking person can reliably be estimated to be a non-listener."

Good listeners let others know they are interested during conversation. They adopt a posture of involvement, nod their heads, make eye contact, and give vocal responses such as "um hmm," "okay," and "go on." All of these nonverbal behaviors show we are attentive, interested, and ready to hear more. On the relationship level of meaning, responsiveness communicates that we care about the other person and what she or he says.

APPLY THE IDEA
Responsive Listening

The next time a friend starts talking with you, express disinterest by slouching, avoiding eye contact, and giving no vocal feedback. You might want to look at something else—a paper or book—while your friend is talking. Note what happens as you communicate a lack of interest. How does your friend act? What happens to her or his communication? Does she or he criticize you for not listening?

Now reverse the experiment. When somebody starts talking to you, show interest. Put aside what you were doing, incline your body slightly forward, make eye contact, and give vocal feedback to indicate you are following. Note what happens as you listen responsively. Does your friend continue talking? Does she or he become more engaging?

Finally, try varying your listening style during a single conversation. Begin by listening responsively, then lapse into a passive mode that expresses disinterest. What happens when you vary your listening style?

The Impact of Responsive Listening

Two researchers decided to test the impact of responsive listening on a speaker. They taught students in a college psychology course to respond with nonverbal communication cues. The professor in the class was a boring lecturer who read his notes in a monotone voice, seldom gestured, and did little to engage students. After the first few minutes of class, the students who had been trained in responsiveness began to show interest in the lecturer. They changed their postures, kept greater eye contact, nodded their interest, and so forth. Within half a minute after the students began to respond, the lecturer started to use gestures, his speaking rate and inflection increased, and he began to interact with students visually and verbally. Then, at a prearranged signal, the students stopped responding and communicated disinterest. For a few awkward minutes the lecturer sought responses, but then he lapsed back into his monotone lecture, not engaging the students. Simply by demonstrating interest in the teacher's communication, the students were able to make him more effective and the class more exciting for everyone.

SOURCE: Bolton, R. (1986). Listening is more than merely hearing. In J. Stewart (Ed.), *Bridges, not walls* (4th ed., pp. 159–179). New York: Random House.

Remembering

The final part of listening is **remembering,** which is the process of retaining what you have heard. According to communication scholars Ron Adler and Neil Towne (1993), we remember less than half a message immediately after we hear it. As time goes by, retention decreases further so that we recall only about 35 percent of a message 8 hours after hearing it. Because we forget about two-thirds of what we hear, it's important to make sure we hang on to the most important third. Effective listeners let go of a lot of details in order to retain basic ideas and general impressions (Fisher, 1987). By being selective about what to remember, we enhance our listening competence. Later in this chapter, we'll discuss more detailed strategies for retaining material.

Effective listening is a complex process that involves being mindful, hearing, interpreting, responding, and remembering. Next we'll consider hindrances to our ability to enact the five processes that make up effective listening.

Obstacles to Effective Listening

Now that we've seen how much is involved in listening, it's easier to understand why we don't listen effectively to all the communication in our lives. There are two broad types of obstacles to good listening—obstacles related to the communication situation and obstacles that are inside of us. (Did you notice that a

series of ideas to be discussed were organized into two broad classes to aid your retention of the basic idea?)

External Obstacles

Much of what interferes with effective listening has to do with communication situations themselves. Although we can't always control external obstacles, knowing what situational factors hinder effective listening can help us guard against them or compensate for the noise they create.

Message Overload   The sheer amount of communication we engage in makes it difficult to listen fully all of the time. We simply aren't able to be mindful and totally involved in all of the listening we do, because it consumes up to 53 percent of our total communication activity. Think about your typical day. Perhaps you go to class for 3 hours. How much you learn and how well you do on examinations depends on your ability to listen mindfully to material that is often difficult. After listening for 50 minutes in a history class, you listen for 50 minutes in a communication class, and 50 more minutes in a business class. A great deal of information came your way in those three lectures. Then you go to work and your supervisor tells you there will be some new procedures you are expected to follow. The supervisor, feeling a need to get on to other matters, describes the changes quickly, and you are expected to understand and remember them immediately.

Obviously, we can and do experience message overload at times. We may feel overwhelmed by the amount of information we are supposed to understand and retain. Clearly, we can't give equal attention to all that information. Instead, we screen the talk around us, much as we screen calls on our answering machines, to decide when to listen carefully.

STUDENT VOICES

RAYMOND: *I've been married nearly thirty years, so I've figured out when I have to listen sharply to Edna and when I can just let her talk flow in one ear and out the other. She's a talker, but most of what she talks about isn't important. But if I hear code words, I know to listen up. If Edna says, "I'm really upset about such and such," or if she says, "We have a problem," my ears perk up and I listen carefully.*

Message Complexity   Listening is also impeded by messages that are complex. The more detailed and complicated ideas are, the more difficult it is to follow and retain them. People for whom English is a second language often find it hard to understand English speakers who use complex sentences that have multiple clauses or that include slang expressions. Even native speakers of English often feel overwhelmed by the complexity of some communication. It's tempting to tune out people who use technical vocabularies, focus on specifics, and use complex sentences. Yet we might miss interesting or important messages if we disregard complex ones.

There are ways to manage complex messages in ways that maximize how much we understand and retain. When we have to listen to messages that are dense with information, we should summon up extra energy. In addition, taking notes may help us understand and retain difficult information. A third strategy is to group material as you listen—organize the ideas in ways that will be easy for you to recall later.

"He's not a very good listener."

MARMADUKE Reprinted by permission of United Feature Syndicate, Inc.

Noise   A third impediment to effective listening is noise. Sounds around us can divert our attention or even make it difficult to hear clearly. Perhaps you've been part of a crowd at a rally or a game. If so, you probably had to shout to the person next to you just to be heard. Although most noise is not as overwhelming as the roar of crowds, there is always some noise in communication situations. It might be music or television in the background, other conversations nearby, or muffled traffic sounds from outside.

S T U D E N T   VOICES

G REGORY: *I've been a salesman for a long time, and I know when clients are really interested and when they're not. When someone answers a phone when I'm in his or her office, I know he or she is not really focused on what I'm saying. Taking calls or leaving the door open for people to drop in communicates that they're not interested in me or the service I represent.*

Gregory makes an important point by reminding us that allowing distractions communicates the relationship-level meaning that we're not interested. Good listeners do what they can to create nondistracting environments. It's considerate to turn off a television or lower the volume on music if someone wants to talk with you. Professionals often instruct secretaries to hold their calls when they want to give undivided attention to a conversation with a client or business associate. It's also appropriate to suggest moving from a noisy area in order to cut down on distractions. Even if we can't always eliminate noise, we can usually reduce it or change our location to one that is more conducive to good communication.

Internal Obstacles

In addition to external interference, listening is hindered by things we do or don't do. In other words, some of the obstacles to effective listening are ones we can control. We'll discuss four psychological obstacles to effective listening.

Preoccupation   A common hindrance to listening is preoccupation. When we are absorbed in our own thoughts and concerns, we can't focus on what someone else is saying. Perhaps you've attended a lecture right before you had a test in another class and later realized you got virtually nothing out of the lecture. That's because you were distracted by thoughts and anxieties about the upcoming test, which was of more immediate concern to you than what was being discussed in the lecture. Or maybe you've been in conversations with friends and realized after a few minutes that you weren't listening at all because you were thinking about your own concerns.

DAWN: *I think my biggest problem as a listener is preoccupation. Like my friend Marta came to me the other day and said she wanted to talk about her relationship with her boyfriend. I followed her for a few minutes, but then I started thinking about my relationship with Ted. After a while—I don't know how long—Marta said to me, "You're not listening at all. Where is your head?" She was right. My head was in a totally different place.*

When we are preoccupied with our own thoughts, we can't be present for others. In other words, we're not being mindful. One method of enhancing mindfulness is to call our minds back to the present situation and the listening we want to do. It's natural for our thoughts to wander occasionally, especially if something is worrying us. However, we don't have to be passive when our thoughts roam. Instead, we may actively call our minds back by reminding ourselves to focus on the person who is speaking and the meaning of his or her message.

Prejudgment   Another reason we don't always listen effectively is that we prejudge others or their communication. Sometimes we think we already know what is being said and don't need to listen carefully. In other cases, we decide in advance that others have nothing to offer us, so we tune them out. When you are talking to people with whom you disagree, do you listen mindfully to them? Do you assume you might learn something or do you prejudge their communication as not worth your attention?

A third kind of prejudgment occurs when we impose our preconceptions about a message on the person who is communicating. When this happens, we assume we know what another feels, thinks, and is going to say, and we then assimilate her or his message into our preconceptions. In the workplace, we may not pay close attention to what a co-worker says because we think we already know what is being expressed. Recalling our earlier discussion of mindreading, you'll realize that it's not wise to assume we know what others think and feel. When we mindread, misunderstandings are likely. We may misinterpret what the person means because we haven't really listened on her or his terms.

ABBIE: *My boyfriend drives me crazy. He never listens, I mean really listens, to what I am saying. He always listens through his own version of what I think and mean. Yesterday I said to him that I was having trouble with my parents about wanting to come to summer school. Before I could even explain what the trouble was, he said, "Yeah, they get real tight when you want them to pay for summer session. I've been through that one. Just keep at them and they'll come around." Well, as it so happens, money wasn't the issue at all. My parents wanted me to do an internship to get some practical experience in my field, so Jake's advice is totally irrelevant to why they are opposing me.*

Prejudgments disconfirm others, because we deny them their own voices. Instead of listening openly to them, we force their words into our own preconceived mind-set. This devalues others and their messages. When we impose our prejudgments on others' words at the relational level of meaning, we express a disregard for them and what they say.

Prejudgments also reduce what we can learn in communication with others. If we decide in advance that another person has nothing to say that interests us, we foreclose the possibility of learning something from that person. This diminishes the richness of our own perspective.

Lack of Effort It takes considerable effort to listen carefully, and sometimes we don't invest the necessary energy. It is hard work to be mindful—to focus closely on what others are saying, to grasp their meanings, to ask questions, and to give responses so that they know we are interested and involved. In addition to these activities, we also have to control distractions inside ourselves, monitor external noise, and perhaps fight against fatigue, hunger, or other physiological conditions that can impede listening.

Because active listening requires so much effort, we're not always able or willing to do it well. Sometimes we make a decision not to listen fully, perhaps because the person or topic is not important to us. In other cases, we really want to listen, but have trouble marshaling the energy required. When this happens, an effective strategy is to ask the other person to postpone interaction until a time when you will have the energy and mindfulness to listen with care. If you explain to the other that you want to defer communication because you really are interested and want to be able to listen well, she or he is likely to appreciate your honesty and commitment to listening.

Failing to invest the necessary effort in listening also occurs in classrooms. You may feel tired when you go to a class. As a result, you may sit passively and not work to understand what your instructor is teaching. If you don't involve yourself actively in listening, you cannot get much out of the class.

Not Recognizing Diverse Listening Styles A final way in which we sometimes hinder our listening effectiveness is by not realizing and adjusting to different listening styles. How we listen differs for two reasons. First, different skills are

© Bob Daemmrich/The Image Works

required when we listen for information, to support others, and for pleasure. We'll discuss these kinds of listening later in the chapter.

A second basis for diverse listening styles is differences in what we learn about listening in our speech communities. The more we understand about different people's rules for listening, the more effectively we can signal our attention in ways others understand. For example, Nepalese citizens give little vocal feedback when another is speaking. In that culture it would be considered rude and disrespectful to make sounds while someone else is talking. Cultures also vary in what they teach members about eye contact. In the United States, it is considered polite to make frequent, but not constant, eye contact with someone who is speaking. In other cultures, continuous eye contact is normative, and still others frown on virtually any eye contact.

Even within the United States, there are differences in listening rules based on membership in gender, racial, and other speech communities. Because feminine socialization emphasizes talking as a way to form and develop relationships, responsive listening is emphasized. Thus, women, in general, make more eye contact, give more vocal and verbal feedback, and use nodding and facial expressions to signal interest (Tannen, 1990; Wood, 1994d, 1998). Masculine culture, with its more instrumental orientation and focus on emotional control, deemphasizes obvious responsiveness. For this reason, men typically provide fewer verbal and nonverbal clues about their interest and attentiveness. If you understand these general differences between the genders, you can adapt your listening style to provide appropriate responses to both women and men.

S T U D E N T   VOICES

JENIFER: *I used to get irritated at my boyfriend because I thought he wasn't listening to me. I'd tell him stuff, and he'd just sit there and not say anything. He didn't react to what I was saying by showing emotions in his face or anything. Several times, I accused him of not listening, and he said back to me exactly what I'd said. He was listening, just not my way. I've learned not to expect him to show a lot of emotions or respond to what I say as I'm talking. That's just not his way, but he is listening.*

Race also shapes differences in listening. Most Whites follow the communication rule that one person shouldn't speak while another is talking, especially in formal speaking situations. Among African Americans, however, talking when another is also talking is a form of showing interest and active participation (Houston & Wood, 1996). Thus, African Americans may signal they are listening intently by interjecting comments such as "Tell me more" or "I like what I'm hearing." Verbal responses during another's talk also occur in formal speaking situations within the African American community. Black churches are much more participatory than White ones, with members of the congregation routinely calling out responses to what a preacher is saying. When the Reverend Martin Luther King, Jr., delivered his "I Have a Dream" speech to a crowd of thousands, his words were echoed and reinforced by the listeners.

Listening competence includes being sensitive to differences in listening and speaking styles. Because others may speak and listen differently than we do, we shouldn't automatically impose our rules and interpretations on them. Instead, we should try to understand and respect their styles. By exercising dual perspective, we are more likely to listen effectively to others on their terms.

"BOY, MARGARET HAS MORE WORDS THAN TWO EARS CAN HANDLE!"

DENNIS THE MENACE Reprinted by permission of Hank Ketcham and © by North America Syndicate.

Forms of Nonlistening

Now that we've discussed obstacles to effective listening, let's consider forms of nonlistening. We refer to these patterns as nonlistening because they don't involve real listening. We will discuss six kinds of nonlistening that may seem familiar to you, because we all engage in these at times.

Pseudolistening

Pseudolistening is pretending to listen. When we pseudolisten, we appear to be attentive, but really our minds are elsewhere. We engage in pseudolistening when we want to appear conscientious, although we really aren't interested. Sometimes we pseudolisten because we don't want to hurt someone who is sharing experiences, even though we are preoccupied with other things.

S T U D E N T **VOICES**

RENEE: *Pseudolistening should be in the training manual for flight attendants. I had that job for six years, and you wouldn't believe the kinds of things passengers told me about—everything from love affairs to family problems. At first I tried to listen, because I wanted to be a good attendant. After a year, though, I learned just to appear to be listening and to let my mind be elsewhere.*

We also pseudolisten when communication bores us, but we have to appear interested. Superficial talk in social situations and dull lectures are two communication situations in which we may consciously choose to pseudolisten so that we seem polite even though we really aren't involved. Although it may be appropriate to decide consciously to pseudolisten in some situations, there is a cost: We run the risk of missing information because we really aren't attending.

BELLINO: *I get in a lot of trouble because I pseudolisten. Often I slip into pretending to listen in classes. I'll start off paying attention and then just drift off and not even realize I've stopped listening until the teacher asks me a question and I don't even know what we're discussing. That's humiliating!*

Pseudolisteners often give themselves away by revealing that they haven't been attending to communication. Common indicators of pseudolistening are responses that are tangential, irrelevant, or impervious to what was said. For example, if Martin talks to Charlotte about his interviews for a new job, she might respond tangentially by asking about the cities he visits: "Did you like New York or Atlanta better?" Although this is related to the topic of Martin's job interviews, it is tangential to the main issue. An irrelevant response would be "Where do you want to go for dinner tonight?" An impervious response such as "You're lucky to have a job that suits you" indicates that Charlotte didn't listen to what Martin said.

Monopolizing

Monopolizing is continuously focusing communication on ourselves instead of the person who is talking. Two tactics are typical of monopolizing. One is conversational rerouting in which a person shifts the topic back to him- or herself. For example, if Ellen tells her friend Marla that she's having trouble with her roommate, Marla should respond by showing interest in Ellen's problem and feelings. Instead, however, Marla might reroute the conversation by saying, "I know what you mean. My roommate is a real slob." Then Marla would go off on an extended description of her own roommate problems. Rerouting takes the conversation away from the person who is talking and focuses it on the self.

Another monopolizing tactic is interrupting to divert attention to ourselves or to topics that interest us. Interrupting can occur in combination with rerouting, so that a person interrupts and then directs the conversation to a new topic. In other cases, diversionary interrupting involves questions and challenges that are not intended to support the person who is speaking (see "Doctor, Are You Listening?"). Monopolizers may fire questions that express doubt about what a speaker says ("What makes you think that?" "How can you be sure?" "Did anyone else see what you did?") or prematurely offer advice to establish their own command of the situation and possibly to put down the other person ("What you should do is . . . ," "You really blew that," "What I would have done is . . ."). Both rerouting and diversionary interrupting are techniques to monopolize a conversation. They are the antithesis of good listening.

The following transcript illustrates monopolizing in action and also shows how disconfirming of others it can be:

CHUCK: I'm really bummed about my econ class. I just can't seem to get the stuff.

SALLY: Well, I know what you mean. Econ was a real struggle for me too, but it's nothing compared to the stat course I'm taking now. I mean this one is going to destroy me totally.

CHUCK: I remember how frustrated you got in econ, but you finally did get it. I just can't seem to, and I need the course for my major. I've tried going to review sessions, but

SALLY: I didn't find the review sessions helpful. Why don't you focus on your other classes and use them to pull up your average?

CHUCK: That's not the point. I want to get this stuff.

SALLY: You're blowing this all out of proportion. Do you know that right now I have three papers and one exam hanging over my head?

CHUCK: I wonder if I should hire a tutor.

SALLY: I don't want you to take any of our time away. This weekend we are getting together with Sam and Lucy, remember? I've really been looking forward to that.

COMMUNICATION NOTES

Doctor, Are You Listening?

If you've ever been frustrated by doctors who didn't listen well, you're not alone. Communication researcher Michael Nyquist studied doctor–patient interaction. He found that, on average, patients had only 18 seconds to describe their problems before doctors interrupted them. Once the doctor interrupted, she or he tended to ask specific, closed questions that discouraged patients from explaining symptoms, life situations, and so forth that might affect diagnosis and treatment. Once interrupted, only one of fifty-two patients asserted themselves to complete what they had originally wanted to tell the doctor.

Sheila Bentley presents communication workshops to medical practitioners. Listening is a primary focus in her training because she has found that many of the mistakes doctors make—ones that often lead to expensive malpractice suits—result from poor listening on the part of doctors.

SOURCES: Crossen, C. (1997, July 10). Blah, blah, blah. *Wall Street Journal*, pp. 1A, 6A; Nyquist, M. (1992, Fall). Learning to listen. *Ward Rounds*. Evanston, IL: Northwestern University Medical School, pp. 11–15.

In this transcript, Sally shows she is not interested in Chuck's concerns, and she pushes her conversational agenda. Chances are good that she doesn't even understand what he is feeling because she is not focusing on what he says.

Monopolizing is costly not only to those who are neglected but also to the monopolizers. A person who dominates communication has much less opportunity to learn from others than a person who listens to what others think and feel. We already know what we think and feel so there's little we can learn from hearing ourselves!

It's important to realize that not all interruptions are attempts to monopolize communication. We also interrupt the flow of others' talk to show interest, voice support, and ask for elaboration. Interrupting for these reasons doesn't divert attention from the person speaking; instead, it affirms that person and keeps the focus on her or him. Research indicates that women tend to interrupt to show interest and support, whereas men tend to interrupt to control conversations and capture the talk stage (Aries, 1987; Beck, 1988; Mulac, Wiemann, Widenmann, & Gibson, 1988; Stewart, Stewart, Friedley, & Cooper, 1990). Because masculine communication cultures emphasize using talk to compete for attention, men more than women engage in diversionary interrupting. Consistent with the rules of feminine communication cultures, women tend to interrupt to support and affirm others and what they are saying. Thus, women may make supportive interruptions such as "I know what you mean," "I really feel for you," or "I've had the same problem."

© Ariel Skelley/The Stock Market

Selective Listening

A third form of nonlistening is **selective listening,** which involves focusing on only particular parts of communication. We listen selectively when we screen out parts of a message that don't interest us or with which we disagree; conversely, we listen selectively when we rivet attention on topics that do interest us or with which we do agree. For example, if you are worried about a storm, you will selectively listen to weather reports while disregarding news, talk, and music on the radio. Students often become highly attentive in classes when teachers say "This will show up on the test," because they regard information about testing as particularly important. We also listen selectively when we give only half an ear to a friend until the friend mentions spring break, and then we zero in because that topic interests us.

Selective listening also occurs when we reject communication that bores us or makes us uncomfortable. Many smokers, for instance, selectively block out reports on the dangers of smoking and of second-hand smoke. Taking in that information would be upsetting. We may also choose not to hear certain requests. For instance, my partner Robbie is skillful at not hearing my requests for him to clean out the attic, and I'm equally adept at not hearing his appeals for me to increase my aerobics program. Neither of us wants to do what the other asks, so we screen out communication on those topics.

Many people listen selectively to criticism. We may screen out communication from others that calls attention to our weaknesses or pushes us to change in ways we find uncomfortable. For months I tried to suggest financial strategies to one of my friends who has no retirement savings or investments. Finally, I realized that she wasn't listening to me because the topic made her feel uncomfortable and like a failure. We all have subjects that bore us or disturb us, and we may selectively avoid listening to communication about them. What is important is to avoid listening selectively when doing so could deprive us of information or insights that could be valuable to us.

Defensive Listening

Defensive listening involves perceiving personal attacks, criticisms, or hostile undertones where none are intended. When we listen defensively, we assume others don't like, trust, or respect us, and we read these motives into whatever they say, no matter how innocent their communication actually is. Some individuals are generally defensive, expecting insults and criticism from all quarters. They hear threats and negative judgments in almost anything said to them. Thus, an innocent remark such as "Isn't that a new shirt?" may be perceived as a veiled suggestion that the shirt is ugly or that all the other shirts in the person's wardrobe are tacky.

In other instances, defensive listening is confined to specific topics or vulnerable times when we judge ourselves to be inadequate. A man who is defensive about money may perceive phone solicitations as reproaches for his lack of earning power; a woman who fears she is selfish may interpret offers of help as proof others don't think of her as helpful; a woman who feels unattractive may hear genuine compliments as false; a student who has just failed a test may hear questioning of his intelligence in benign comments. Defensive listening can deprive us of information and insights that might be valuable, even if not pleasant. Defensive listening also tends to discourage others from giving us honest feedback. If stating genuine thoughts and feelings leads to quarrels and anger, others may learn not to be honest with us.

S T U D E N T   VOICES

DAN: *I remember a time when I was a defensive listener. I had just gotten laid off from work—the recession, you know—and I felt like nothing. I couldn't support my family, and I couldn't stand the idea of going on unemployment. Nobody in my family ever did that. Once when my son asked me for a few bucks for a school outing, I just lit in to him about how irresponsible he was about money. My wife mentioned the car needed some repair work, and I shouted at her that I wasn't a money machine. I'd never been like that before, but I was just so sensitive to being out of work that I had a chip on my shoulder. You couldn't talk to me about money without my taking it as a personal attack.*

Ambushing

Ambushing is listening carefully for the purpose of attacking a speaker. Unlike the other kinds of nonlistening we've discussed, ambushing involves very careful listening, but it isn't motivated by openness and interest in another. Instead, ambushers listen intently to gather ammunition they can use to attack a speaker. They don't mind bending or even distorting what you say in order to advance their combative goals. One of the most common instances of ambushing is public debates between political candidates. Each person listens carefully to the other for the sole purpose of later undercutting the opponent. There is no openness, no effort to understand the other's meaning, and no interest in genuine dialogue.

S T U D E N T   VOICES

KRALYN: *My first husband was a real ambusher. If I tried to talk to him about a dress I'd bought, he'd listen just long enough to find out what it cost and then attack me for spending money. Once I told him about a problem I was having with one of my co-workers, and he came back at me with all of the things I'd done wrong and didn't mention any of the things the other person had done. Talking to him was like setting myself up to be assaulted.*

Not surprisingly, people who engage in ambushing tend to arouse defensiveness in others. Few of us want to speak up when we feel we are going to be attacked. In Chapter 8 we'll look more closely at communication that fosters defensiveness in others.

Literal Listening

The final form of nonlistening is **literal listening,** which involves listening only to the content level and ignoring the relationship level of meaning. As we have seen, all communication includes both content or literal meaning and relationship meaning, which pertains to the power, responsiveness, and liking between individuals. When we listen literally, we attend to only the content meaning and overlook what's being communicated about the other person or our relationship with that person. When we listen only literally, we are insensitive to others' feelings and to our connections with them.

Perhaps the greatest danger of literal listening is that it may disconfirm others. When we listen literally, we don't make the effort to understand how others feel about what they say and how it affects their self-concepts. As a result, any responses we make are unlikely to confirm their identities and worth.

S T U D E N T   VOICES

CAMMY: *My sister is a literal listener. I swear, she just doesn't get all of the meaning that is between words. The last time we were home together, Mom was talking about how bad she felt that she didn't seem to have the interest in cleaning the house as it should be and making elaborate meals. Lannie heard that, and her response to Mom was that the house wasn't clean and Mom needed to either devote more time to it or hire someone. Then Lannie told her she ought to plan the week's dinners on Sunday so that she could shop and set aside time to make nice meals. Give me a break! Mom just had a double radical mastectomy a month ago, and she's really depressed. She feels bad about losing her breasts, and she's worried that they didn't get all of the cancer. Who would feel like scrubbing floors and fixing gourmet food after going through that? What Mom needed was for us to hear that she was worried and unhappy and for us to tell her the house and fancy meals didn't matter. Anybody with an ounce of sensitivity could figure that out.*

We have seen that there are many obstacles to effective listening. Ones in messages and situations include message overload, difficulty of messages, and external noise. In addition to these, there are four potential interferences inside of us: preoccupation, prejudgment, lack of effort, and failure to recognize and adapt to diverse expectations of listening. The obstacles to effective listening combine to create six types of nonlistening. These are pseudolistening, monopolizing, listening selectively, listening defensively, ambushing, and listening literally. Learning about hindrances to mindful listening and learning to recognize forms of nonlistening enable you to exercise greater control over your listening and, thus, your relationships with others.

APPLY THE IDEA
Identifying Your Ineffective Listening

Apply the material we've just discussed by identifying times when you listen ineffectively.

- Describe a situation in which you pseudolistened.
- Describe an instance in which you monopolized communication.
- Report on a time when you listened defensively.
- Discuss an example of ambushing someone else.
- Describe an instance when you listened selectively.
- Identify a time when you listened literally.

Now repeat this exercise, but this time focus on examples of others who engage in each of the six types of ineffective listening.

Adapting Listening to Communication Goals

Now that you recognize some of the common pitfalls to effective listening, let's focus on how to listen well. The first requirement is to determine your reason for listening. We listen differently when we listen for pleasure, to gain information, and to support others. We'll discuss the specific attitudes and skills that contribute to effective listening of each type.

Listening for Pleasure

Often the goal is **listening for pleasure** or enjoyment. Rather than trying to learn something or to support someone else, we're listening for sheer enjoyment. Often we listen to music for entertainment. We may also listen to television shows and nightclub routines for enjoyment. Because listening for pleasure doesn't require us to remember or respond to communication, there are few guidelines for effective listening for enjoyment. The only suggestions are to be mindful and control distractions. Being mindful is important for all types of listening. Just as being mindful in lectures allows us to gain information, being mindful when listening for pleasure allows us to derive the full enjoyment from what we hear. Controlling interferences is also important when we are listening for pleasure. A beautifully rendered Mozart concerto can be wonderfully satisfying, but not if a television is on in the background.

Listening for Information

Much of the time we are **listening for information,** to gain and evaluate information. We listen informationally in classes, at political debates, when important news stories are reported, and when we need guidance on everything from

© Chromosohm/Sohm/Stock, Boston

© Robert Rathe/Stock, Boston

medical treatments to directions to a new place. In all of these cases, the primary purpose of listening is to gain and understand information in order to act appropriately or be successful. To do this, we need to use skills for critical thinking and for organizing and retaining information.

Be Mindful   Our discussion of obstacles to listening suggests some important clues for how we can listen critically to information. First, it's important to make a decision to be mindful, choosing to attend carefully even if material is complex and difficult. Don't let your mind wander if information gets complicated or confusing. Instead, stay focused on your goal and take in as much as you can. Later you may want to ask questions about material that isn't clear even when you listen mindfully.

Control Obstacles   You can also minimize noise in communication situations. You might shut a window to block out traffic noises or adjust a thermostat so that room temperature is comfortable. In addition, you should try to minimize psychological distractions by emptying your mind of the many concerns and ideas that can divert your attention from the communication at hand. This means you should try to let go of preoccupations as well as prejudgments that can interfere with effective listening.

Ask Questions   Also important is posing questions to speakers. Asking speakers to clarify or elaborate their message allows you to gain understanding of information you didn't grasp at first and enhances insight into content that you did comprehend. "Could you explain what you meant by . . . ?" "I didn't follow your explanation of . . ." and "Can you clarify the distinction between . . . ?" are questions that allow listeners to gain further information to clarify content. Questions compliment a speaker because they indicate you are interested and want to know more.

Use Aids to Recall   To understand and remember important information, we can apply the principles of perception we discussed in Chapter 3. For instance, we learned that we tend to notice and recall stimuli that are repeated. To use this principle in everyday communication, repeat important ideas to yourself immediately after hearing them. This moves the ideas from short-term to long-term memory (Estes, 1989). Repetition can save you the embarrassment of having to ask people you just met to repeat their names.

Another way to increase retention is to use mnemonic (pronounced "new-monic") devices, which are memory aids that create patterns for what you've heard. You probably already do this in studying. For instance, you could create the mnemonic MASIRR, which is made up of the first letter of each of the six parts of listening (Mindfulness, Attending, Selecting and organizing, Interpreting, Responding, Remembering). You can also invent mnemonics to help you recall personal information in communication. For example, KIM is a mnemonic to remember that Kelly from Iowa is going into Medicine.

Organize Information   A third technique to increase retention is to organize what you hear. When communicating informally, most people don't order their ideas carefully. The result is a flow of information that isn't coherently organized and so is hard to retain. We can impose order by regrouping what we hear. For example, suppose a friend tells you he's confused about long-range goals, then says he doesn't know what he can do with a math major, wants to locate in the Midwest, wonders if graduate school is necessary, likes small towns, needs some internships to try out different options, and wants a family eventually. You could regroup this stream of concerns into two categories: academic information (careers for math majors, graduate school, internship opportunities) and lifestyle preferences (Midwest, small town, family). Remembering those two categories allows you to retain the essence of your friend's concerns, even if you forget many of the specifics. Repetition, mnemonics to create patterns, and regrouping are ways to enhance what we remember.

APPLY THE IDEA
Improving Recall

Apply the principles we've discussed to enhance memory.

- The next time you meet someone, repeat his or her name to yourself three times in a row after you are introduced. Do you find you remember the name better when you do this?
- After your next interpersonal communication class, take 15 minutes to review your notes. Try reading them aloud so that you hear as well as see the main ideas. Does this increase your retention of material covered in class?
- Invent mnemonics to help you remember basic information in communication.
- Organize complex ideas by grouping them into categories. Try this first in relation to material in classes. To remember the main ideas of this chapter, you might use major subheadings to form categories: the listening process, obstacles to listening, forms of nonlistening, listening goals, and guidelines. The mnemonic PONGG (Process, Obstacles, Nonlistening, Goals, Guidelines) could help you remember those categories. You can also group ideas in interpersonal interactions.

By choosing to be mindful, minimizing distractions, asking questions, repeating and organizing ideas, and using mnemonic devices, we can increase our abilities to understand and remember informational communication.

Listening Totally

Gerald Egan has studied listening extensively. In his view of mindful relationship listening, we don't just listen with our ears; we also listen with our eyes and sense of touch, with our minds, hearts, and imaginations. Total listening is more than attending to another person's words. According to Egan, total listening entails listening to the meanings that are buried in the words and between the words and in the silences in communication.

SOURCE: Egan, G. (1973). Listening as empathic support. In J. Stewart (Ed.), *Bridges, not walls.* Reading, MA: Addison-Wesley.

Listening to Support Others

Listening for information focuses on the content level of meaning in communication. Yet, often we're more concerned with the relationship level of meaning, which involve another's feelings and perceptions. We engage in relationship listening, **listening to support others,** when we listen to a friend's worries, hear a romantic partner discuss our relationship, or help someone work out a problem. Our primary interest is the other person and our relationship, rather than information. Specific attitudes and skills enhance relationship listening.

Be Mindful The first requirement for effective relationship listening is to be mindful. You'll recall this was also the first step in listening for information and pleasure. When we're interested in relationship-level meanings, however, a different kind of mindfulness is needed. Instead of focusing our minds on informational content, we need to concentrate on understanding feelings that may not be communicated explicitly. Thus, mindful relationship listening calls on us to pay attention to what lies between the words, the subtle clues to feelings and perceptions. The essence of mindfulness is to listen to the other and focus on what he or she is feeling, thinking, and wanting in the conversation. Mindful listening is described in "Listening Totally."

Suspend Judgment When listening to help another person, it's important to avoid judgmental responses, at least initially. Although Western culture emphasizes evaluation, often we don't need to judge others or what they feel or do. Making judgments clutters communication by adding our evaluations to the others' experiences. When we do this, we are one step removed from them and their feelings. We've inserted something between us. To curb evaluative tendencies, we can ask whether we really need to pass judgment.

Yet there are times when it is appropriate and supportive to offer opinions and to make evaluative statements. Sometimes people we care about genuinely want our judgments, and in those cases we should be honest about how we feel. Particularly when others are confronting ethical dilemmas, they may seek the judgments of people they trust. Once my friend Cordelia was asked to work for a presidential candidate, but she had agreed to take a job at a large law firm. She talked to me about her quandary and asked me what I thought she should do. Although it was clear to me that Cordelia wanted to renege on the job and join the campaign, I couldn't honestly approve of that. I told her that I thought it would be dishonorable to go back on her word. After a long talk, Cordelia told me that I was the only friend who cared enough about her to have been so honest. Part of being a real friend in this instance was making a judgment. Yet that's appropriate only if someone invites our evaluation or if we believe

© Peter L. Chapman

another person is in danger of making a serious mistake.

Even positive evaluations ("That's a good way to approach the problem") may seem to indicate we think we have the right to pass judgment on others and their feelings. If someone asks our opinion, we should try to present it in a way that doesn't disconfirm the other person. Many times people excuse critical comments by saying, "Well you asked me to be honest" or "I mean this as constructive criticism." Too often, however, the judgments are not constructive and are more harsh than candor requires. If we are committed to helping others, we respond in ways that support them rather than tear them down.

S T U D E N T VOICES

LOGAN: *I hate the term* constructive criticism. *Every time my dad says it, what follows is a put-down. By now I've learned not to go to him when I have problems or when I'm worried about something in my life. He always judges what I'm feeling and tells me what I ought to feel and do. All that does is make me feel worse than I did before.*

Understand the Other Person's Perspective   One of the most important principles for effective relationship listening is to concentrate on grasping the other person's perspective. This means we have to step outside of our own point of view, at least long enough to understand another's perceptions. We can't respond feelingly to others until we understand their perspective and meanings. To do this, we must put aside preconceptions about issues and how others feel and try to focus on their words and nonverbal behaviors for clues about how they feel and think.

Paraphrasing is a method of clarifying others' meaning or needs by reflecting our interpretations of their communication back to them. For example, a friend might confide, "I think my kid brother is messing around with drugs." We could paraphrase this way: "So you're really worried that your brother's experimenting with drugs." This paraphrase allows us to clarify whether the friend has any evidence of the brother's drug involvement. The response might be, "No, I don't have any real reason to suspect him, but I just worry, because drugs are so pervasive in high schools now." This clarifies by telling us the friend's worries are more the issue than any evidence that the brother is experimenting with drugs. Paraphrasing also helps us figure out what others feel. If a friend screams, "This situation is making me crazy," it's not clear whether your friend is angry, hurt, upset, or going insane. We could find out which emotion prevails by saying, "You seem really angry." If anger is the emotion, your friend would agree; if not, she would clarify what she is feeling.

Learning to Paraphrase

Practice effective listening by paraphrasing the following statements.

- I've got so many pressures closing in on me right now.
- I'm worried about all of the money I've borrowed to get through school.
- I'm nervous about telling my parents I'm gay when I see them next weekend.
- I don't know if Kim and I can keep the relationship together once she moves away for her job.

Another strategy for increasing understanding of another's thoughts and feelings is to use **minimal encouragers.** These communications gently invite another person to elaborate by expressing interest in hearing more. Examples of minimal encouragers are "Tell me more," "Really?" "Go on," "I'm with you," "Then what happened?" "Yeah?" and "I see." We can also use nonverbal minimal encouragers such as a raised eyebrow to show involvement, a head motion to indicate we understand, or widened eyes to indicate we're fascinated. Minimal encouragers indicate we are listening, following, and interested. They encourage others to keep talking so that we can more fully understand what they mean. Keep in mind that these are *minimal* encouragers. They should not interrupt or take the talk stage away from another. Instead, effective minimal encouragers are very brief interjections that prompt, rather than interfere with, the flow of another's talk.

Using Minimal Encouragers

Practice encouraging others to elaborate their thoughts and feelings by developing minimal encouragers in response to each of these comments:

- I'm feeling really worried about getting into grad school.
- I just learned that I'm a finalist for a scholarship next year.
- I think my girlfriend is cheating on me.
- I haven't gotten any job offers yet and I've been interviewing for four months. I'm beginning to wonder if I'll get a job at all.
- I'm so excited about how this relationship is going. I've never been with someone as attentive and thoughtful as Pat.

A third way to enhance understanding of what another feels or needs is to ask questions. Sometimes it's helpful to ask questions that yield insight into what a speaker thinks or feels. For instance, we might ask "How do you feel about that?" "What do you plan to do?" or "How are you working this through?" Another reason we ask questions is to find out what a person wants from us. Sometimes it isn't clear whether someone wants advice, a shoulder to cry on, or a safe place to vent feelings. If we can't figure out what's wanted, we

© Mark Antman/The Image Works

can ask the other person: "Are you looking for advice or a sounding board?" "Do you want to talk about how to handle the situation or just air the issues?" Asking direct questions signals that we want to help and allows others to tell us how we can best do that.

Express Support   Once understanding of another's meanings and perspective is shown, relationship-level listeners should focus on communicating support. This doesn't neces-sarily require us to agree with the other person's perspective or feelings, but it does require that we communicate support for the person. To illustrate how we can support a person even if we don't agree with his or her position, consider the following dialogue:

JANICE: I just don't see how I can have a baby right now.

ELAINE: Tell me more about what you're feeling.

JANICE: I feel trapped. I mean, I've still got two years of school, and we're not ready to get married.

ELAINE: So?

JANICE: (silence, then) I hate the thought, but I guess I'll have to get an abor-tion.

ELAINE: Sounds as if you don't feel very comfortable with that choice.

JANICE: I'm not, but it seems like the only answer.

ELAINE: What other options have you considered?

JANICE: Well, I guess I really don't know of any other answers. Do you?

ELAINE: You could have the baby and place it for adoption or maybe even work out an arrangement with a couple that can't have a baby of their own.

JANICE: No, I really can't afford to give up nine months of my life right now. Besides, I don't think I could give away a baby after carrying it all that time. Don't you think I should have an abortion?

ELAINE: Gee, I don't want to tell you what to do. I'm not comfortable endors-ing abortion for myself, but you may not feel the same way.

JANICE: I don't endorse abortion either, but I don't feel like I have a realistic choice.

ELAINE: I respect you for the way you're going about making this choice. It's a good idea to talk with people like we're doing now.

JANICE: I just hate the idea of having an abortion.

ELAINE: It sounds like you're not very sure that's the right answer for you, either. Let's talk a little more. How do you think you'd feel if you did have an abortion?

This dialogue illustrates several principles of effective relationship listening. First, notice that Elaine's first two comments are minimal encouragers, designed to nudge Janice to elaborate her perspective. Elaine's third response is a paraphrase to make sure she understands what Janice is feeling. Elaine then tries suggesting alternatives to abortion, but when Janice rejects those Elaine doesn't push her. Elaine makes her own position on abortion clear—she doesn't condone it—but she separates her personal stance from her respect for Janice and the way Janice is thinking through the decision.

Particularly important in this conversation is Elaine's effort to collaborate with Janice in problem solving. By showing that she's willing to talk further and that she wants to help Janice work out the problem, Elaine behaves as an active listener and a committed friend. Elaine's listening style allows Janice to talk through a very tough issue without Elaine imposing her own judgments. Sometimes it's difficult to listen openly and nonjudgmentally, particularly if we don't agree with the person speaking. However, if your goal is to support another person, then sensitive, responsive involvement including collaboration, if appropriate, is an ideal listening style.

S T U D E N T VOICES

SHERYL: *I think the greatest gift my mother ever gave me was when I told her I was going to marry Bruce. He isn't Jewish, and nobody in my family has ever married out of the faith before. I could tell my mother was disappointed, and she didn't try to hide that. She asked me if I understood how that would complicate things like family relations and rearing kids. We talked for a while, and she realized I had thought through what it means to marry out of the faith. Then she sighed and said she had hoped I would find a nice Jewish man. But then she said she supported me whatever I did, and Bruce was welcome in our family. She told me she'd raised me to think for myself and that's what I was doing. I just felt so loved and accepted by how she acted.*

Guidelines for Effective Listening

To develop pragmatic strategies for effectiveness, let's summarize what we've learned about listening. Three guidelines integrate and extend information already covered.

Be Mindful

By now you've read this suggestion many times. Because it is so central to effective listening, however, it bears repeating. Mindfulness is a choice to be wholly present in an experience. It requires that we put aside preoccupations and preconceptions in order to attend fully to what is happening in the moment. Mindful listening is a process of being totally with another person in communication. It is one of the highest compliments we can pay to others because it conveys the relationship-level meaning that they matter to us. Being mindful is a choice, not a knack or a natural aptitude. It is a matter of discipline and commitment. We have to discipline our tendencies to judge others, dominate the talk stage, and let our minds wander away from what another is saying.

Mindfulness also requires commitment to another person and the integrity of the interpersonal communication process. Being mindful is the first and most important principle of effective listening.

Adapt Listening Appropriately

Like all communication activities, listening varies according to goals, situations, and individuals. What we've discussed in this chapter makes it clear that there is no one best way to listen. What's effective depends on our purpose for listening, the context in which we are listening, and the needs and circumstances of the other person.

The purpose for listening is a primary influence on what skills are appropriate. When we listen for pleasure, we simply need to be mindful and minimize distractions so that we derive as much enjoyment as possible from listening. When we listen for information, a critical attitude, evaluation of material, and a focus on the content level of meaning are desirable listening behaviors. Yet, when we engage in relationship listening, very different skills are needed. We want to communicate openness and caring, and the relationship-level meaning is more important than the content-level meaning. Thus, we need to adapt our listening styles and attitudes to different goals.

Effective listening is also adapted to individuals. Some people need considerable prompting and encouraging to express themselves, whereas others need only for us to be silent and attentive. Paraphrasing helps some individuals clarify what they think or feel, whereas others don't need that kind of assistance. Because people respond to different kinds of listening, we need to be skillful in using a variety of listening behaviors and to know when each is appropriate. Recall from Chapter 1 that the ability to employ a range of skills and knowledge of when each is called for are two of the foundations of effective interpersonal communication.

Although fully interpersonal communication requires us to interact with others as unique individuals, there are some generalizations that can guide our choices for how to listen. We've noted, for instance, that men and women have generally different listening styles. As a rule, women provide a good deal of vocal and visual response to speakers to indicate that they are interested and following. Men generally make fewer listening noises, providing less overt feedback on their involvement and their feelings about what is being said. Because our listening styles reflect the rules we learned in our communication cultures, they also reflect our expectations of how others should listen to us. Knowing this, we might remind ourselves to give more overt responses when listening to women than when listening to men. Conversely, if we have feminine listening inclinations, we might want to curb some of our responsiveness. In masculine speech communities, nodding and saying "yes" or "um hmm" are interpreted to mean agreement, not just involvement, so a feminine listening style can be misinterpreted by a masculine speaker. Of course, there are exceptions to these generalizations. Some women don't provide a great deal of feedback, and some men do. Thus, our best bet is to treat generalizations as hypotheses, not truths.

This allows us to act on the basis of what is generally appropriate, but at the same time to stay open to the possibility that we may need to revise our behaviors in particular cases.

Listen Actively

We've seen that effective listening is an active process that requires substantial effort. When we realize all that's involved in listening, we appreciate how active an effort it is. Hearing is a physiological process that is passive; we don't have to do anything but be in the vicinity of sound waves to hear. Listening, however, is a highly active process. To do it effectively, we have to be willing to focus our minds, organize and interpret others' ideas and feelings, generate responses that signal our interest and that enhance both content and relationship levels of meaning, and retain what we have learned in the process of listening. In some situations, we also become active partners by listening collaboratively and engaging in problem solving. Doing all of this is hard work! Recognizing that genuine listening is an active process prepares us to invest the amount of effort required to do it effectively.

CHAPTER
Summary

Zeno of Citium was an ancient philosopher who once remarked that "we have been given two ears and but a single mouth, in order that we may hear more and talk less." Thousands of years later, the wisdom of that comment is still relevant. Listening is a major and vital part of communication, yet too often we don't consider it as important as talking. In this chapter, we've explored the complex and demanding process of listening. We began by distinguishing hearing and listening. Hearing is a straightforward physiological process that doesn't require effort on our part. Listening, in contrast, is a complicated process involving hearing, attending, selecting and organizing, interpreting, responding, and remembering. Doing it well requires commitment and skill.

To understand what interferes with effective listening, we discussed obstacles that are in situations and messages and obstacles that are in ourselves. Listening is complicated by message overload, complexity of material, and external noise in communication contexts. In addition, listening can be hampered by our preoccupations and prejudgments, by a lack of effort, and by our not recognizing differences in listening styles. These obstacles to careful listening give rise to various types of ineffective listening, including pseudolistening, monopolizing, selective listening, defensive listening, ambushing, and literal listening. Each form of nonlistening signals that we aren't fully present in the interaction.

We also discussed different purposes for listening and identified the skills and attitudes that advance each. Listening for pleasure is supported by mindfulness and efforts to minimize distractions and noise.

Informational listening requires us to adopt a mindful attitude and to think critically, organize and evaluate information, clarify understanding through asking questions, and develop aids for retention of complex material. Relationship listening also requires mindfulness, but it calls for different listening skills: Suspending judgment, paraphrasing, giving minimal encouragers, and expressing support enhance the effectiveness of relationship listening.

The ideas we've discussed yield three guidelines for improving listening effectiveness. First, we need to be mindful—to be fully present in communication and focused on what is happening between us and others. Second, we should adapt our listening skills and style to accommodate differences in listening purpose and individuals. Finally, a summary suggestion is to remember that listening is an active process and to be prepared to invest energy and effort in doing it skillfully. Because

listening is important in all speech communities, we will revisit some of the ideas covered here as we discuss

dynamics in relationships in the following chapters.

KEY Concepts

- ambushing
- defensive listening
- hearing
- listening
- listening for information
- listening for pleasure

- listening to support others
- literal listening
- mindfulness
- minimal encouragers
- monopolizing
- paraphrasing

- pseudolistening
- remembering
- responding
- selective listening

FOR FURTHER Thought & Discussion

1. Review the six types of nonlistening discussed in this chapter. Are any of them common in your communication? Select one of your nonlistening practices and work to reduce its occurrence.

2. What ethical principles can you identify to guide the three kinds of listening? Are different ethical principles appropriate when listening for information and listening to support others?

3. Keep a record of your listening for the next two days. How much time do you spend listening for information, listening to support others, and listening for pleasure?

4. Use your *InfoTrac College Edition* to read pamphlets published by professional associations such as the American Academy of Family Physicians. Also skim articles in recent issues of *Quarterly Journal of Business and Economics* and *Quarterly Review of Economics and Business*. Is the importance of listening mentioned in these publications? Discuss your findings with others in your class.

5. Apply the strategies for remembering that we discussed in this chapter. Create mnemonics, organize material as you listen, and review material immediately after listening. Do you find that using these strategies increases your listening effectiveness?

6. Who is your prototype, or model, for an effective listener? Describe what the person does that makes him or her effective. How do the person's behaviors fit with guidelines for effective listening discussed in this chapter?

Part TWO

Weaving

Communication

into Relationships

Emotions

and

Communication

My sister, Carolyn, and I had been very close for years when her daughter Michelle was born in 1990. I shared Carolyn's delight in the new baby, yet I also felt pushed out of her life. Carolyn was so entranced with her daughter that she had little interest in other people. Phone calls from her, which had been frequent, virtually ceased. When I called Carolyn, she often was preoccupied with Michelle or would abbreviate our conversation because it was time to feed Michelle or get her up or take her for a walk.

Over lunch with my friend Nancy, I mentioned the changes in my relationship with Carolyn. "She never has time for me anymore," I complained. "I am so angry with her!"

"Sounds to me more like you're hurt than angry," Nancy observed. "Is that right?"

What was I feeling? Was it anger or hurt or a mixture of the two? **Emotions,** or feelings, are part of our lives. We feel happiness, sadness, shame, pride, embarrassment, envy, disappointment, and a host of other emotions. And we express our emotions in interpersonal communication. We may express emotions nonverbally (smiling, trembling, blushing) or verbally ("I'm scared," "I feel anxious about the interview"). Sometimes we express emotions through complex verbal messages such as metaphors and similes (Kovecses, 1990). For instance, you might say, "I feel like a plane that's soaring" or "I am a bomb, just waiting to explode." And of course, in many situations, we communicate emotions both verbally and nonverbally, for example, saying "I'm so happy right now" while smiling.

Although we experience and express feelings, we don't always do so effectively. Sometimes we aren't able to identify exactly what we feel, as I wasn't in the conversation with Nancy. Even if we can recognize our emotions, we aren't always sure how to express them clearly and constructively. We may not realize what goal we have for expressing emotions. Do we just want to get feelings out, or do we want another person to comfort us, reassure us, or behave differently toward us? In order to communicate well, we need to develop skill in identifying and expressing our feelings in ways that support particular communication goals.

This part of the book focuses on communication within interpersonal relationships. In this chapter and the four that follow it, we examine the ways in which communication shapes the character and quality of interpersonal relationships. To launch Part Two, Chapter 7 discusses emotions that are a constant dimension of interpersonal communication. Chapter 8 builds on what we cover here by looking closely at the relationship between communication and interpersonal climate. We'll extend our discussion of climate with Chapter 9, which focuses on conflict as a natural process in close relationships. In that chapter, we learn that a healthy relationship climate and good communication skills can help us realize the constructive potential of conflict. The final two chapters explore links between ideas and skills discussed in the first nine chapters and communication between friends and romantic partners.

In this chapter we'll examine how to identify and communicate emotions in healthy, effective ways. We'll begin by considering the idea that there is *emo-*

tional intelligence, analagous to cognitive intelligence. Next, we will define emotions and examine the sources of emotions and expression of them. Third, we'll explore the difference between experiencing emotions and expressing them. Finally, we'll discuss guidelines for communicating emotions in ways that foster our individual growth and the quality of our relationships with others.

Emotional Intelligence

Emotions are intricately woven into the fabric of interpersonal communication and close relationships. By extension, how effectively and constructively we communicate emotions profoundly influences the depth and quality of our relationships. According to Daniel Goleman, emotional development and skill are critical to personal, social, and professional success. In his 1995 book *Emotional Intelligence*, Goleman claims that there is a kind of intelligence distinct from the type measured by standard IQ tests.

Goleman's book popularized an idea that Carol Saarni (1990) originated. In Saarni's early work she emphasized a quality she called emotional competence, which includes the awareness of our own emotions, the ability to recognize and empathize with others' emotions, the realization of the impact of our expression of emotions on others, and the sensitivity to cultural rules for expressing emotions. Saarni also emphasized that we often experience several emotions simultaneously. Being aware that we sometimes feel multiple emotions at the same time is another aspect of emotional competence.

Emotional intelligence is the ability to recognize which feelings are appropriate in which situations and the skill to communicate those feelings effectively. According to Goleman (1995a,1995b), people who have high EQs (emotional intelligence quotients) are more likely than people with lower EQs to create satisfying relationships, to be comfortable with themselves, and to succeed in careers that require skills in reading people and responding sensitively to others and situations.

Emotional intelligence includes a number of qualities that aren't assessed by conventional intelligence tests:

- being in touch with your feelings
- managing your emotions without being overcome by them (for example, not letting anger consume you)
- not letting setbacks and disappointments derail you
- channeling your feelings to assist you in achieving your goals
- having a strong sense of empathy—being able to understand how others feel without their spelling it out
- listening to your and others' feelings so you can learn from them
- having a strong yet realistic sense of optimism

Goleman notes that "so far, there's no single, well-validated paper-and-pencil test for emotional intelligence" (1995b, p. 74). However, Goleman has developed some questions (1995b, pp. 74, 75) that allow you to get an approximate measure of your EQ, which I've adapted in Apply the Idea so that you can test your EQ.

What's Your EQ?

1. Imagine you're on an airplane and it suddenly begins rolling dramatically from side to side. What would you do?
   a. Keep reading your book and ignore the turbulence.
   b. Become vigilant in case there is an emergency. Notice the flight attendants and review the card with instructions for emergencies.
   c. A little of a and b.
   d. Not sure—I never noticed an airplane's motion.

2. Imagine that you expect to earn an A in a course you are taking, but you get a C− on your midterm exam. What would you do?
   a. Develop a specific plan to improve your grade and resolve to implement the plan.
   b. Resolve to do better in the future.
   c. Nurture your self-concept by telling yourself the grade doesn't really matter and focus on doing well in your other courses.
   d. Go to see the professor and try to talk him or her into raising your midterm grade.

3. While riding in a friend's car, your friend becomes enraged at another driver who just cut in front of him. What would you do?
   a. Tell your friend to let it slide—that it's no big deal.
   b. Put in your friend's favorite CD and cut up the volume to distract him.
   c. Agree with him and show rapport by talking about what a jerk the other driver is.
   d. Tell him about a time when someone cut in front of you and how mad you felt, but explain you then found out the other driver was on her way to the hospital.

4. You and your girlfriend/boyfriend have just engaged in an argument that has become a heated shouting contest. By now you're both very upset, and each of you has started making nasty personal attacks on the other. What do you do?
   a. Suggest the two of you take a 20-minute break to cool down and then continue the discussion.
   b. Decide to put an end to the argument by not talking anymore. Just be silent and don't speak no matter what the other person says.
   c. Apologize to your partner and ask him or her to say "I'm sorry" too.
   d. Pause to collect your thoughts, then explain your views and your side of the issue clearly.

Scoring your EQ: Award yourself the following points for each response:

1. a = 20, b = 20, c = 20, d = 0
2. a = 20, b = 0, c = 0, d = 0
3. a = 0, b = 5, c = 5, d = 20
4. a = 20, b = 0, c = 0, d = 0

Higher scores indicate greater emotional intelligence.

Chelsey's Smile

At five years old, Chelsey Thomas was used to being ridiculed by her schoolmates. "She's ugly," they taunted. "Her face is funny." The problem was that Chelsey had a rare congenital condition called Moebius syndrome. This condition causes incomplete or absent development of muscles that control facial expressions. As a result, the corners of Chelsey's mouth perpetually sagged. She couldn't move her mouth to express the range of emotions she felt. Most important to Chelsey, she couldn't smile. Her peers thought she was unfriendly or bored because she never smiled at them. Consequently, Chelsey had few friends.

There's a happy ending to Chelsey's story. She had surgery in which muscles from her thigh were transplanted to her fifth cranial nerve. After the surgery, she could pronounce words more clearly, prevent her lower lip from drooping, and chew normally. And she could smile. People no longer perceived her as unfriendly because she had the physical ability to communicate feelings with facial expressions.

SOURCES: Dimmitt, B. (1997, July). Chelsey's missing smile. *Reader's Digest*, pp. 87–93; Little girl has smile surgery. (1995, December 16). *Raleigh News and Observer*, p. 14A.

© Nick Ut/AP

© Michael Tweed/AP

Goleman insightfully notes that being aware of our emotions and being able to express them appropriately enhance our personal health and the quality of our relationships with others. Yet we are not always as effective as we might be in recognizing and expressing our emotions. Thus, developing skill in understanding and expressing your emotions will enable you to be more effective in your interpersonal communication. Understanding between people depends on their being able to know what they feel and to be able to express their feelings clearly. "Chelsey's Smile" demonstrates how important it is to be able to express emotions.

Emotional intelligence is not just understanding your feelings. It also requires skill in knowing how to express your feelings constructively. To illustrate this point, let's return to my conversation with Nancy. After we had talked a while, I said, "I think I'll call Carolyn and tell her I resent being pushed out of her life."

"Well, when my friend Penny had a child and was totally preoccupied with him, I felt what I think you're feeling," she disclosed to me.

"And what did you do?" I asked.

"I told her I missed her."

"Missed her?" I thought it over. I did miss Carolyn. Telling her that would be an honest and affirming way to express my feelings to her. Telling Carolyn I missed her would be likely to advance my goal of reviving our closeness. Telling her I was angry probably wouldn't serve that goal.

Through the conversation with Nancy, I realized that anger wasn't the only emotion I felt. I was hurt that someone I loved seemed to have no room for me in her life. Anger was a defensive reaction I was using to avoid admitting that I was vulnerable to Carolyn. Later that day I called Carolyn and told her I missed her. Her response was immediate and warm: "I miss you too. I'll be so glad when we get adjusted enough to Michelle for you and me to have time for us again."

I was effective in communicating my feelings to Carolyn, thanks to Nancy's insight into emotions and her skill in helping me figure out what I was feeling.

Identifying Your Emotions

Not everyone experiences the full range of emotions, and most of us don't experience all emotions with equal frequency. Check the emotions listed below that are most familiar to you.

_____ anger	_____ passion
_____ anxiety	_____ peacefulness
_____ apathy	_____ pleasure
_____ depression	_____ pressure
_____ disappointment	_____ sadness
_____ embarrassment	_____ security
_____ envy	_____ shame
_____ fear	_____ surprise
_____ gratitude	_____ suspicion
_____ guilt	_____ sympathy
_____ happiness	_____ tenderness
_____ hope	_____ uncertainty
_____ hopelessness	_____ vindictiveness
_____ insecurity	_____ weariness
_____ jealousy	_____ weepiness
_____ joy	_____ woe
_____ loneliness	_____ yearning

Compare your list of familiar emotions with the lists of classmates. What can you conclude about yourself and others?

The concept of emotional intelligence highlights the importance of emotions to our everyday communication and our relationships. All aspects of our lives are affected by what we feel, how skillfully we identify our feelings, and how effectively we communicate them to others.

So far we've discussed emotions without defining exactly what they are. In the next section, we will pin down the nature of emotions by defining them and identifying their diverse components.

The Nature of Emotions

Although emotions are basic to human beings and communication, they are difficult to define precisely. Yet a clear definition is necessary so that we share an understanding of what we are discussing. In this section, we'll clarify what emotions are and explore different views of how we experience emotions in our lives.

Biological and Learned Emotions

Some researchers assert that humans experience two types, or levels, of emotions: ones that are based in biology and, thus, instinctual and universal and others that we learn in social interaction. Theodore Kemper (1987) claims that

© Chuck Savage/The Stock Market

there are only four emotions that are grounded in human physiology: fear, anger, depression, and satisfaction. He believes we experience these four emotions because we are biologically wired to do so.

Yet, scholars don't agree on *which* emotions are basic (Izard, 1991; Shaver, Schwartz, Kirson, & O'Connor, 1987; Shaver, Wu, & Schwartz, 1992). Also, many scholars don't believe it's useful to think of some emotions as basic and others as learned (Ekman & Davidson, 1994). In her 1989 book *Anger: The Misunderstood Emotion*, Carol Tavris argues that anger is not entirely basic or instinctual. Tavris shows that our ability to experience anger is influenced by social interaction through which we learn whether and when we are supposed to feel angry.

A majority of scholars believe that most or all emotions are socially constructed to a substantial degree. For example, we learn when and for what to feel guilty or proud. We learn from significant others and the generalized other when to feel gratitude, embarrassment, indignation, and so forth. The current consensus is that it is simplistic and not useful to draw a firm line between basic and learned emotions.

Emotions are very complex, and we experience them holistically, not individually. In many instances, we don't feel a single emotion but experience several mingled together as I did when Carolyn was preoccupied with her new daughter. Paul Ekman and Richard Davidson (1994) surveyed research on emotions and concluded that blends of emotion are common. For instance, you might feel both sad and happy at your graduation or both grateful and frustrated when someone helps you.

S T U D E N T VOICES

KENNETH: *Last year my daughter got married, and I've never felt so many things in one moment. As I walked her down the aisle and took her arm from mine and placed it on the arm of her future husband, I felt sadness and happiness, hope and anxiety about her future, pride in the woman she'd become and her confidence in starting a new life, and loss because we would no longer be her primary family.*

Definition of Emotions

Most researchers who have studied emotions agree on a definition: Emotions are processes that are shaped by physiology, perceptions, and social experiences. In addition, some scholars think that language influences the emotions we assume we are experiencing. Notice that emotions are defined as processes rather than as distinct events. Physiological, perceptual, and social influences are not independent. Instead, they blend and interact with one another in an ongoing process that shapes our experience of emotions. Although researchers vary in how much they emphasize each of these influences, most people who have studied emotions agree that physiology, perceptions, and social experience all play parts in our emotional lives.

We'll explore each of these dimensions of emotions and the different ways they have been viewed by scholars. Our discussion should give you a foundation for understanding feelings and how you and others communicate them.

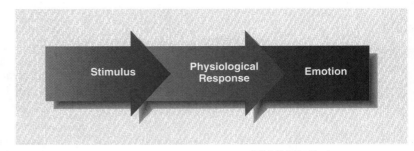

FIGURE 7.1
The Organismic View of Emotions

Physiological Influences on Emotions   Have you ever felt a knot in your stomach when you were anxious? Have you ever blushed when you were embarrassed? Have you ever felt a surge of physical energy when you were angry or frightened? In each case, you experienced a physiological reaction to something. Some early theorists of emotion believed that physiological changes are caused by external phenomenon. This theory is called the **organismic view of emotions,** and it is shown in Figure 7.1. For example, early theorists of emotions believed that the knot in your stomach is a direct response to a low score on an exam and blushing is a direct response to a comment someone made that called attention to you.

This view of emotions was originally advanced by philosopher William James (1890) and James and his colleague Carl Lange (1922). The organismic view, also called the James–Lange view, proposes that when some event occurs, we respond physiologically, and only after that do we experience emotions. This perspective assumes emotions are reflexes that follow from physiological arousal. In other words, in this view emotions are both the product and the expression of what happens in our bodies.

James wrote that emotional expression begins with a perception of something—perhaps seeing a gift with your name on it or noticing that someone with a weapon is running toward you. Following the perception, James believed we experience changes in our bodies: We smile on seeing the gift; adrenaline surges when we are approached by someone with a weapon. Finally, said James, we experience emotion: We feel joy at the present, fear at the aggressor.

The organismic view of emotions regards emotions as instinctual. They are impulses that arise reflexively in response to physiological arousal caused by some external stimulus. James specifically claimed that there is none of what he called "intellectual mind stuff" (Finkelstein, 1980) that shapes our perceptions of stimuli and, by extension, our emotions. For James and others who shared his view, emotions result from physiological factors that are instinctual and beyond our conscious analysis or control. Since the time of James, the organismic view of emotions has been shown to be seriously flawed. More recent research demonstrates that physiological reactions are neither as instinctual nor as subject to conscious control as James assumed (Ekman & Davidson, 1994; Frijda, 1986).

Perceptual Influences on Emotions   Clearly, physiological experiences can be related to emotions, but James's view of the relationship between bodily states and feelings is not widely accepted by current scholars of emotions (Ekman &

Davidson, 1994; Frijda, 1986; Reisenzaum, 1983). Today most researchers think the physiological factors are less important than perceptual and social factors in shaping emotions. For these scholars, perception involves a lot more than James's idea of becoming aware of objective stimuli.

The **perceptual view of emotions,** which is also called appraisal theory, asserts that subjective perceptions shape what external phenomena mean to us. External objects and events, as well as physiological reactions, have no intrinsic meaning. Instead, they gain meaning only as we attribute significance to them. We might interpret a cake as a symbol of celebration, a raised fist as a threat, and a knot in the stomach as anxiety. We act on the basis of our interpretation, not the actual cake, raised fist, or knot in our stomach.

As we learned in Chapter 4, however, symbols are arbitrary, ambiguous, and abstract so their meanings are not fixed or clear-cut. A cake might be a symbol of freedom to a prisoner who knows there's a file hidden in it; a raised fist might be a symbol of power and racial pride as it was during the civil rights movement of the 1960s and 1970s; and a knot in the stomach might represent excitement about receiving a major award.

The ancient Greek philosopher Epictetus observed that people are not disturbed by things, but by the views we take of them. Our view of things leads us to feel disturbed, pleased, sad, joyous, afraid, and so forth. In other words, our perceptions filter our experiences, and it is the filtered experiences that influence what we feel.

S   T   U   D   E   N   T   VOICES

HARIHAR: *Buddhism teaches us that our feelings arise not from things themselves, but from what we attach to them. In my life, this is true. If I find myself upset about how a conversation is going, I ask myself, "Harihar, what is it that you were expecting to happen? Can you let go of that and enter into what is actually happening here?" That helps me realize and let go of my attachment to certain outcomes of the conversation.*

We respond differently to the same phenomenon, depending on the meaning we attribute to it. For example, if you receive a low score on a test, you might interpret it as evidence that you are not smart. This interpretation could lead you to feel shame or disappointment or other unpleasant emotions. The emotion of shame might lead you to lower your head or act in other ways that physically express your emotion. On the other hand, you might interpret the low score as the result of a tricky or overly rigorous exam, an interpretation that might lead you to feel anger at the teacher or resentment at the situation. Anger might lead you to stomp out of the room or ball up the test and throw it in a trash can.

Anger is a very different feeling than shame. Which one you feel depends on how you perceive the score and the meaning you attribute to it. In turn, the emotion you feel shapes your physiological response—slouching away in mortifiction or stomping belligerently out of the room. The perceptual view of emotions is represented in Figure 7.2.

A third view of emotions is the **cognitive labeling view of emotions** (Schachter, 1964; Schachter & Singer, 1962). This perspective claims that how we label our physiological responses influences how we interpret and respond to events. Phrased another way, what we feel may be shaped by the labels we attach to physiological responses. For example, if you feel a knot in your stomach when you see that you received a low grade on an exam, you might label the knot as evidence of anxiety. Thus, what you felt would not result from either the event itself (the grade) or your perceptions of the event. Instead, it would be shaped by how you labeled your physiological response to the event. This view of emotions is represented in Figure 7.3.

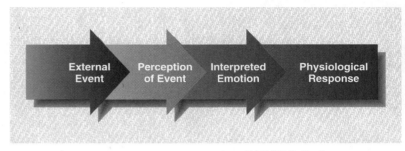

FIGURE 7.2
The Perceptual View of Emotions

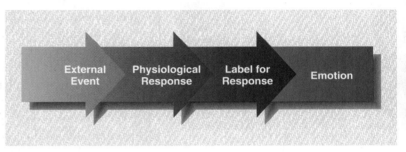

FIGURE 7.3
The Cognitive Labeling View of Emotions

S T U D E N T VOICES

ARMANO: *The most important lesson I learned when my family first moved to the United States was that a bad grade on a test is not a judgment that I am stupid. It is a challenge for me to do better. My English teacher taught me that. He said if I saw a bad grade as saying I am dumb or a failure that I would never learn English. He taught me to see grades as challenges that I could meet. That attitude made it possible for me not to give up and to keep learning.*

I witnessed how labels for events and our responses to them influence what we feel. When my niece Michelle was two years old and weighed less than 30 pounds, she visited me in my home. Shortly after she came in the house, my 65-pound dog Madhi ran out to greet her and started licking her. Michelle started crying, "Mommy, Mommy, I'm scared." Carolyn held Michelle who said, "My heart is going so fast because she came after me and made me scared." Carolyn cuddled Michelle and said, "Your heart isn't going fast because you're scared, sweetheart. It's because Madhi surprised you and you were startled. Madhi was trying to show you how glad she is to see you. Dogs are our friends." Carolyn and I then petted Madhi and let her lick us and said repeatedly, "Oh, Madhi jumped on me because she loves me. She startled me."

Michelle quickly picked up our language and began to laugh, not cry, when Madhi bowled her over. By the end of the day Michelle and Madhi were fast

© Network Pro/The Image Works

friends. Before she went to bed that night, Michelle told us, "Madhi makes my heart beat faster because I love her." What happened here? Madhi's exuberance didn't diminish, nor did Michelle's physiological response of increased heart rate. What did change was how Michelle interpreted the event: She defined Madhi's behavior as friendly and exciting instead of threatening. Michelle's interpretation of her bodily response also changed: scared became startled.

As a consequence of reinterpreting Madhi's behavior and her physiological responses, Michelle changed how she labeled her emotion. Carolyn offered Michelle a different interpretation for what Madhi was doing and for what was happening in her body when Madhi enthusiastically greeted her. In turn, this led Michelle to define her emotion not as fright but as surprise or being startled.

How we label events (a dog's greeting) and our physiological responses (fear, surprise) affects how we think and act. In Michelle's case, we taught her not to feel fearful of dogs. In other cases, however, we would be wise to label our feelings as fear and to heed them. Sometimes it's difficult to know whether to trust our emotions (feeling fearful, for example) or to redefine them. Although there is no sure-fire rule for knowing when to trust emotions, one guideline is to analyze the basis for what you feel. Is there a sound basis for your emotions? Are there subtle environmental cues that alert you to be fearful? "The Gift of Fear" explains why it is sometimes smart to trust feelings of fear.

Probably there is some validity to each view of emotions that we've explored. The organismic view calls our attention to the physiological aspects of emotions—we do have bodily responses to what happens around us. The perceptual view reminds us that how we perceive external events and our own physiological reactions influences the meanings we attach to experiences and the emotions that we think are appropriate. Finally, the cognitive labeling view emphasizes the role of language in shaping our interpretation of events and our emotions in response to them. Language may shape our feelings by providing interpretations of events, our physiological responses, appropriate emotions, or all three.

Each of the models we've considered so far helps us understand the role of particular aspects of emotions. Yet, none of these models is complete because none adequately accounts for the critical influence of culture in shaping emotions and how we communicate them.

Social Influences on Emotions As we learned in Chapter 3, perception is influenced by the social groups to which we belong, as well as by the overall culture (generalized other). The society and communities in which we live affect what we perceive (and don't perceive) and how we interpret, organize, and respond to what we perceive. Our social circumstances also influence our beliefs about which emotions are good or bad, which emotions we should express or repress, and with whom we can appropriately communicate which emotions. Thus, a full understanding of emotions requires us to explore what our culture teaches us about emotions and how they should be expressed.

Insight into social influences on emotions and how we express them is fairly recent. Beginning in the 1970s, some scholars began advancing an **interactive view of emotions** (Hochschild, 1979), which proposes that social rules and understandings shape what individuals feel and how they do or don't express their feelings. Arlie Hochschild (1979, 1983, 1990) has pioneered in this area by conducting in-depth studies of how individuals experience and communicate feelings, as well as how they control feelings. The interactive view of emotions rests on three key concepts: framing rules, feeling rules, and emotion work. Each of these concepts helps us understand how strongly social factors influence what we feel and how we express our emotions.

COMMUNICATION NOTES

The Gift of Fear

Don't ignore your fear. That's the message of Gavin de Becker's book, *The Gift of Fear*. For years, de Becker has worked as a security consultant to celebrities. He notes that many people tend to dismiss feelings of fear by labeling them "silly" or "stupid." If you're waiting for an elevator and when the door opens you have a strong, fearful reaction to a person in the elevator, what do you do? De Becker says many people try to talk themselves out of the fear with thoughts such as "There's nothing to be afraid of. This is a public building." Wrong, says de Becker. He advises us to wait for the next elevator. If you have a feeling that someone is lurking in a parking lot, don't dismiss it as paranoia, says de Becker. Heed it and find someone to walk with you.

SOURCE: de Becker, G. (1997). *The gift of fear: Survival signs that protect us from violence.* New York: Little, Brown.

Framing Rules **Framing rules** are guidelines for defining the emotional meaning of situations. For example, Western culture defines funerals as sad and respectful occasions and weddings as joyful events. Within any single culture, however, there are multiple social groups and resulting standpoints.

Different social groups may teach members distinct framing rules for the same situations. For example, many Irish Americans hold wakes when a person dies. The wake is defined as a festive occasion during which people tell stories about the departed person and celebrate his or her life. Within Western culture other groups define funerals and receptions following them as somber occasions at which any mirth or festivity would be perceived as disrespectful and inappropriate. "The Social Shaping of Grief" on page 224 explores cultural differences in framing rules for death.

STUDENT VOICES

BECKER: *I remember the nasty things mother would say about women whose houses weren't clean. It was a mark against their character. When I first came to college, if I saw my boyfriend's apartment was dirty, I thought I was supposed to clean it up, and I did. I remember once when a boyfriend complained that I hadn't cleaned the dishes, and I felt ashamed. How I saw things started to change when I took some women's studies classes and began to think differently about women and men and what we're supposed to do. Now if I see my boyfriend's apartment is dirty, I don't think I should clean it up. If he fusses at me, I don't feel shame; now I feel angry that he would think I should do it.*

Feeling Rules **Feeling rules** tell us what we have a right to feel or what we are expected to feel in particular situations. Feeling rules reflect and perpetuate the

The Social Shaping of Grief

What people feel about death and how they express their feelings is not universal. Different cultures have distinct framing rules for death. In some African tribes death is regarded as a cause to celebrate a person's passage to a higher and better form of living. Among Buddhists, the death of a body is not regarded as the end of what a person is because the person is assumed to continue in other forms. In some cultures people are expected to feel deep grief over the loss of cousins to whom they have deep and lasting attachments. In contrast, there are other cultures that define cousins as distant relations whose death seldom provokes deep sadness.

Framing rules for death also vary over time in a single culture. Modern Western cultures enjoy a low infant mortality rate (approximately 9 deaths per 1,000 infants) and a long life expectancy. Today the average life expectancy for people living in the United States is 73 years, although Caucasian women have higher life expectancy than Caucasian men and African Americans have lower life expectancies than Caucasians.

In earlier times the infant mortality rate in Western societies ranged from 50 to 400 deaths per 1,000 infants, and the life expectancy was decades shorter than today. Scholars who have studied historical and diary research from earlier times report that death was viewed as a normal, routine part of life that did not call for intense and prolonged mourning.

SOURCE: Lofland, L. (1985). The social shaping of emotion: The case of grief. *Symbolic Interaction, 8,* 171–190.

© FSP/Gamma-Liaison

values of a specific society. For example, societies that emphasize individuality promote the feeling rule that it is appropriate to feel pride about personal accomplishments. Among many Asians and Asian Americans, however, individuality is less esteemed than group identity, and what an individual achieves is regarded as the result of and a reflection on the larger family and community. Thus, a feeling rule might be that it is appropriate for an individual to feel gratitude to family and community for personal accomplishments. All social communities have feeling rules that specify acceptable and unacceptable ways to express feelings. "Wild Pigs Run Amok" describes a unique cultural expression of aggression.

Hochschild (1979) points out that we often talk about feelings in terms of rights and duties. This tendency reveals our awareness of social expectations and responsibilities that accompany and shape our emotions and how we express them. The following phrases—all ones we commonly hear and use—highlight the language of duty and rights that infuses feeling rules:

I'm entitled to feel sad.
You have no right to feel unhappy. Look at all you have!
She should be grateful to me for what I did.
You shouldn't feel bad.
I ought to feel happy my friend got a job.
I shouldn't feel angry at my father.
Men shouldn't cry.
Women should feel nurturing toward children.

Hochschild (1979) perceives a strong connection between feeling rules and social order. She claims that one way a society attempts to control individuals is through feeling rules that uphold broad social values and structures. For example, teaching people they should feel pride in their personal accomplishments reinforces the value Western culture places on individualism. Teaching people to regard accomplishments as communal, not individual, upholds the value accorded to groups that is esteemed in many non-Western cultures.

APPLY THE IDEA
Religions and Feeling Rules

Religions urge individuals to follow particular feeling rules. For example, Judeo-Christian commandments direct individuals to "honor thy father and thy mother" and to "not covet thy neighbor's house, nor his wife." Buddhism commands individuals to feel compassion for all living beings and to do what one can do to alleviate suffering. Hinduism commands followers to accept their place (caste) in this life.

Make a list of all the feeling rules you can identify that are proposed by your spiritual or religious affiliation. Be sure to list both what you are supposed to feel and what you are not supposed to feel.

1. _____

2. _____

3. _____

4. _____

5. _____

6. _____

Compare your responses with those from students who have different religious or spiritual beliefs. What similarities and differences among feeling rules can you identify?

COMMUNICATION NOTES
Wild Pigs Run Amok

Imagine you felt extremely aggressive and needed to release your tension. How would you do it? Would you go for a long, hard run? Would you work out in the gym? Would you kick a wall or closet door? Would you go on a shooting rampage?

Anthropologist Philip Newman and sociologist Susan Shott report a very different way of expressing extreme aggression. They observed that certain societies in the New Guinea highlands have a well-established custom for venting aggression. A person who feels aggressive is defined as a wild pig, or wild man, who is out of control. Because he is out of control, the individual is allowed to behave in bizarre ways that would never be condoned in a normal person.

The wild man is said to "run amok." He is able to vent aggression without being judged as deviant. After all, he's not himself—he's a wild pig. By running amok, the individual expresses aggressive feelings and can then return to normal identity. Thus, these New Guinea communities have created a safety valve for individuals who feel overcome by unruly impulses.

But the safety valve for the troubled individual may not be very safe for those who are attacked by the wild pig running amok. Sometimes people are killed by the untamed aggression. The negative effects of this custom have led some observers to regard it as a syndrome that provides an excuse for unacceptable behavior that is not socially approved.

SOURCES: Newman, P. (1964, February). "Wild man" behavior in New Guinea highlands community. *American Anthropologist, 66,* 1–19; Shott, S. (1979). Emotion and social life: A symbolic interactionist analysis. *American Journal of Sociology, 84,* 1317–1334; Winzeler, R. (1990). Amok: Historical, psychological, and cultural perspectives. In W. J. Karim (Ed.), *Emotions of culture: A Malay perspective* (pp. 97–122). Oxford: Oxford University Press.

A second way in which feeling rules uphold social structure is by condoning the expression of more negative feelings toward people with limited power. Hochschild's studies of people in service industries reveal that the less power employees have, the more they tend to be targets of negative emotional expressions from others. People who have greater power may learn they have a right to express anger, offense, frustration, and so forth, whereas people who have less power may learn it isn't acceptable for them to express such emotions. To test the validity of this idea, ask yourself who is the target of greater complaints and hostility: servers or restaurant managers, flight attendants or pilots, receptionists or CEOs?

Finally, Hochschild notes there are differences in the feeling rules that are taught to children in middle- and working-class families. Middle-class parents generally encourage children to control their inner feelings by **deep acting,** which is management of inner feelings. In bringing up children, the parents

© Michael Kagan/Monkmeyer Press Photo

emphasize what they should and should not feel. Children may be taught, for instance, that they should feel grateful for gifts and should not feel angry when a sibling takes a toy.

According to Hochschild, working-class parents place greater emphasis on **surface acting,** which involves controlling the outward expression of emotions, not controlling what is felt. Parents who emphasize surface acting teach children to control their outward behaviors, not necessarily their inner feelings. Children learn, for example, that they should say thank you when they receive a gift and they should not hit a sibling who takes a toy. Expressing gratitude is emphasized more than feeling grateful, and refraining from hitting someone who takes a toy is stressed more than being willing to share toys.

Emotion Work   The final concept that Hochschild advanced is **emotion work,** which she defines as the effort we invest to generate what we think are appropriate feelings in particular situations. Notice emotion work concerns our effort to fashion how we feel, not necessarily the outcome of that effort. Our success at squelching feelings we think are inappropriate or at generating the feelings we think we should experience varies from occasion to occasion.

Although we do emotion work much of the time, we tend to be most aware of engaging in it when we think what we are feeling is inappropriate in a specific situation. For example, you might think it is wrong to feel gleeful when someone you dislike is hurt. Hochschild refers to this as "the pinch," which is a discrepancy between what we *do* feel and what we think we *should* feel. Typically, what we think we should feel is based on what we've learned from our social groups and the larger culture. If you feel sad at a wedding, you might engage in emotion work to make yourself feel happy.

S   T   U   D   E   N   T   VOICES

H UANG: *In my native country students are supposed to be respectful of teachers and never speak out in class. It has been hard for me to learn to feel I have a right to ask questions of a professor here. Sometimes I have a question or I do not agree with a professor, but I have to work to tell myself it is okay to assert myself. To me, it still feels disrespectful to speak up.*

Emotion work involves more than outward expression of feelings—for example, smiling even though you really feel sad. It also involves efforts at deep acting by striving to generate the feeling we think we should have. We do emotion work to suppress or extinguish feelings we think are wrong (for example, feeling jealous over a friend's good fortune or happy over the misfortune of someone we dislike). We also engage in emotion work to cultivate feelings we think we should have—for example, propelling ourselves to feel joy for our friend's good fortune.

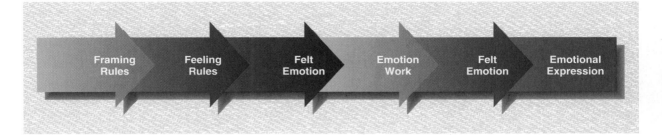

FIGURE 7.4
Interactive View of Emotions

Framing rules, feeling rules, and emotion work are interrelated. Framing rules that define the emotional meaning of situations lead to feeling rules that tell us what we should feel or have a right to feel given the meaning of the situation. If we don't feel what our feeling rules designate as appropriate, we may engage in emotion work to squelch inappropriate feelings or to bring about feelings that we perceive are proper in the circumstances. We can then express our feelings by following rules for what is accepted as suitable expression of particular emotions.

The interactive view of emotions assumes that what we feel involves thinking, perceiving, and imagining while being influenced by social rules for framing situations and specifying what we should and can feel. This view of emotions emphasizes the extent to which social factors affect how we perceive, label, and respond emotionally to experiences in our lives. A noteworthy feature of this model is that it calls attention to cultural differences in feelings and how we express them. This model of emotions is represented in Figure 7.4.

A P P L Y   T H E   I D E A

Identifying Feeling Rules

To become more aware of the feeling rules that influence you, write out what you think you should feel or have a right to feel in each of the following situations.

1. You find out that the person you have been dating exclusively for two years has been dating someone from another school for the last six months.

I SHOULD FEEL

_____

_____

I HAVE A RIGHT TO FEEL

_____

_____

2. You and a close friend have both been interviewing for jobs. Your friend gets a great job offer, and you still haven't received one.

I SHOULD FEEL

_____

_____

I HAVE A RIGHT TO FEEL

_____

_____

3. Your roommate criticizes you for not doing your share of the cleaning, and you know you haven't been pitching in fairly.

I SHOULD FEEL

_____

_____

I HAVE A RIGHT TO FEEL

_____

_____

4. Your parents tell you that they are separating.

I SHOULD FEEL

_____

_____

I HAVE A RIGHT TO FEEL

_____

_____

The Impact of Different Views of Emotions

Does it make a difference which view of emotions you believe? Yes, because how we view feelings affects our belief in whether we can control what we experience and express in everyday life. If you agree with William James that feelings are instinctual, then you will probably assume that feelings cannot be analyzed or controlled. Whatever you feel, you feel. That's it.

On the other hand, if you accept the interactive view of emotions, you are more likely to think you can analyze your feelings and perhaps change them and how you express them through your own emotion work. The interactive view assumes we are agents who can affect what happens to us and how we feel and act. If you agree with this perspective, you are more likely to monitor your feelings and to make choices about how to communicate them.

This isn't an all or nothing issue. The most reasonable perspective is probably that we have some control if we choose to exercise it. We may not be able to totally control what we feel, but usually we can exert some control. Further, we can exercise considerable control over how we do or don't express our feelings and to whom we express them.

Reprinted by permisson of Creators Syndicate.

There isn't a clear dividing line between what we feel and how we express feelings. The two interact in the process of emotions. What we feel influences how we express (or don't express) our emotions. It's equally true that how we express our feelings echoes back into us to affect how we interpret our feelings (Fridlund, 1994). Taking personal responsibility for when, how, and to whom you express feelings is a cornerstone of ethical interpersonal communication.

Obstacles to Effective Communication of Emotions

We've seen that emotions are not strictly personal, individual phenomena. Emotions are profoundly social. We learn what to feel based on the values, norms, and traditions of the social groups to which we belong. We also learn from our social groups how we are expected to express or not express what we feel. How we communicate or don't communicate feelings can hurt or enrich relationships and can foster or impede understanding between people. In addition, our expression or lack of expression of our feelings can encourage or stunt personal growth.

Because many people repress emotions or express them ineffectively, it's important for us to explore obstacles to effective emotional communication. In this section we'll consider two topics related to ineffective communication of emotions. We'll first examine common reasons that we may not express emotions. Then we'll identify some common, yet ineffective, ways of communicating feelings. Following this section, we'll conclude the chapter by focusing on ways to communicate emotions clearly and effectively.

Reasons We May Not Express Emotions

We don't always express our emotions to others. This is not necessarily bad. Sometimes we make an ethical choice not to express emotions that would hurt another person. At other times we decide not to burden another person with our feelings. There are ways to express feelings without sharing them with specific others. We might write the feelings in a personal journal or talk about them with a counselor or friend who would not be disturbed by them. Choosing not to express emotions in some situations or to some people can be constructive and generous.

TARA: *My best friend Fran is a marriage saver. When I'm really angry with my husband, I vent to her. If there's a really serious problem between me and Al, I talk with him. But a lot of times I'm upset over little stuff. I know what I'm feeling isn't going to last and isn't any serious problem in our marriage, but I may be seething anyway. Letting those feelings out to Fran gets them off my chest without hurting Al or our marriage.*

Sometimes it *is* appropriate to express feelings to a particular person. When we feel something strongly, finding appropriate ways to express our emotions is important. The cost of repressing emotions or not communicating them can be high (Pennebaker, 1997). Relationships suffer when emotional connections are weak or when feelings are not understood and addressed. Individuals also experience a range of negative consequences when they deny themselves emotional outlets. They may suffer from headaches, ulcers, high blood pressure, eating disorders, and other serious problems.

CHUCK: *I guess I fell prey to the idea that real men don't whine or give in to problems. It took a nervous breakdown to teach me otherwise. Two years ago I was going to school part time and working full time. My company downsized, which meant that those of us who weren't fired had to pick up the work of those who were. I began putting in more hours at the job. Then I gave up my daily workout to create more time for studying and working. I just kept stuffing down all I felt—the resentment, the stress, the anxiety about getting everything done. I didn't talk to my girlfriend or brother or co-workers or anyone. I didn't want anyone to think I couldn't take the heat. One day I couldn't get up. I just couldn't get out of bed. I stayed there all day and the next day and the next. Finally, my brother hauled me to a hospital where I was diagnosed with acute stress. By that time, I also had an ulcer and my blood pressure was really elevated. My doctor said I needed counseling. I said no. He asked whether I'd rather learn how to deal with my emotions or die in the next year. Given that choice, I went into counseling. What I discovered was that I've spent my whole life stuffing emotions down. I had to learn what I should have learned as a child—that it's okay to feel things and that it really helps to talk about what I'm feeling.*

Chuck's commentary is forceful testimony to the dangers of not expressing feelings. The impact of denying or repressing our emotions can be devastating to us personally and to our relationships (Schmanoff, 1985, 1987). Thus, we should understand and critically evaluate why people sometimes don't express what they feel. In this section we'll consider four common reasons why people don't communicate emotions.

Social Expectations   As we have noted, social factors shape feelings and expression of them. In the United States emotional expression is generally discouraged, especially in men. Although the strong, silent model of manhood exemplified by John Wayne is no longer prominent, in the United States men are still expected to be more restrained than women in expressing emotions—or most emotions. Men are allowed to express anger, which is often disapproved of in women. Anger and other emotions regarded as powerful are allowed and often admired in men.

In other ways, however, men who live in the United States are expected to be emotionally restrained. Expressing hurt, fear, depression, or other soft emotions is not encouraged or admired in men. This social expectation is not universal. For example, Italian men routinely express a range of emotions dramatically and openly. In Western society, however, most men are taught the feeling rule that they are not entitled to feel or express many emotions. This can lead some men to deny certain feelings or avoid expressing how they feel. Over time, men who do this may become alienated from their feelings—unable to recognize what they do feel because society has taught them they aren't allowed to experience a great many feelings.

Women face different restrictions on the feelings society allows them. Anger is an emotion that women are generally taught they should not feel or express. Our culture considers anger unattractive and undesirable in women—unfeminine (Tavris, 1989). Thus, many women are constrained by the feeling rule that they should not feel anger and, if they do, they should definitely not communicate it. This discourages many women from acknowledging legitimate anger and from expressing it assertively.

There are other feeling rules learned by many Western women. Most women in our society are encouraged from childhood to be caring toward others. Luise Eichenbaum and Suzie Orbach (1987) and Lillian Rubin (1985) point out that feeling rules for women make it difficult for them not to feel caring all the time, because not being empathic and supportive of others would be inconsistent with cultural definitions of femininity. Thus, many women engage in emotion work to make themselves feel caring when they don't naturally feel that way.

Even more often, report researchers, women squelch feelings of jealousy toward friends and feelings of competitiveness in personal and professional relationships. Because most Western women are taught they should support others, they learn it is inappropriate to experience or express envy or competitiveness. Not being able to express or even acknowledge such feelings can interfere with honest communication in interpersonal relationships.

S T U D E N T   **VOICES**

SADIE: *The other night I got home after working the dinner shift at my restaurant. I was dead tired. The phone rang and I almost didn't answer. Now I wish I hadn't. It was my friend Chelsey, and she was upset about a fight with her boyfriend. I tried to cut the call short, but she said, "I'm really hurt-*

ing and I need to talk." And so I reminded myself that I do care about Chelsey. I told myself that my fatigue wasn't as important as Chelsey's problem. So we stayed on the phone for over an hour and we talked through what was happening. Sometimes I wish I could just say, "I'm not available for you now," but I'd feel like a real jerk if I did that.

When women squash these taboo feelings, there can be undesirable personal and relationship effects. Denying or refusing to act on competitive feelings can limit women's career advancement. Not dealing openly with feelings of jealousy or envy in friendships can create barriers and distance. And demanding of themselves that they always be emotionally available and caring to anyone who wants their help can be overwhelming.

It's important for men and women to review critically the feeling rules they have been taught. This enables us to decide which ones we think are appropriate and desirable and to follow those in our communication. Equally important, critical review of social feeling rules may help us identify ones that are dysfunctional and choose not to adhere to them in our personal lives.

Vulnerability A second reason we may not express our feelings is that we don't want to expose ourselves to others. Telling others how we feel or expressing feelings nonverbally may give others inside information that could affect how they perceive us. We may fear that someone will like us less if we disclose that we feel angry with them. We may worry that someone will lose respect for us if our nonverbal behaviors show we feel weak or scared. We may be afraid that if we disclose how deeply we feel about another person, she or he will reject us. Further, we may be concerned that others could use intimate knowledge against us. To protect ourselves from being vulnerable to others, we may not express feelings verbally or nonverbally.

Protecting Others Another reason we often choose not to express feelings is that we fear we could hurt or upset others. If you tell a friend that you feel disappointed in her, she may be hurt. If your facial expressions and body posture show that you feel depressed, those who care about you may share your pain and worry about your well-being. We may also choose not to express feelings to protect our relationships from conflicts. If a friend of yours behaves in ways you consider irresponsible, you may refrain from verbally or nonverbally expressing your disapproval because doing so might cause tension between you.

Totally open and unrestrained expression of feeling isn't necessarily a good idea. Sometimes it is both wise and kind not to express feelings. It's often not productive to vent minor frustrations and annoyances. Romantic partners may want to deal with some issues privately—at least for a while. And if someone we care about is already overburdened with anxiety or emotional problems, we may choose to monitor our nonverbal communication so that the other person doesn't have to respond to our feelings at the moment. Thus, there can be good reasons not to show or discuss feelings, or not to show or discuss them at a specific time.

ISHMAEL: *Last week I got rejected by the law school that was my top choice. Normally, I would have gone over to Jason's apartment to hang out with him and let him boost me up. Ever since we met freshman year, we've been tight friends and we talk about everything in our lives. But right now Jason's struggling with his own stuff. His mother just got diagnosed with cancer and his father is out of work. I know we'll talk about my disappointment some time, but I figured it could wait until he gets into a better place.*

Ishmael's commentary provides a good example of instances in which it is caring not to express feelings. Yet, we would be mistaken to think it's always a good idea to keep feelings to ourselves. Avoiding expression of negative or upsetting feelings can be harmful if they directly affect relationships with others or if doing so may threaten our own health. Susan Schmanoff (1987) found that intimacy wanes when couples' communication consistently lacks emotional disclosures, even unpleasant ones. If not expressing feelings is likely to create barriers in relationships or to cause us serious personal distress, then we should try to find a context and mode of expression that allows us to communicate our emotions.

Social and Professional Roles   A final reason why we may not express some feelings is that our roles make it inappropriate. An attorney who cried when hearing a sad story from a witness might be perceived as unprofessional. A doctor or nurse who talked about personal feelings about a patient might be regarded as too personally involved with the case. Police officers and social workers would probably be judged out of line if they expressed anger instead of objective detachment when investigating a crime.

When I testify as an expert witness in trials, the attorneys questioning me often try to ruffle me with personal attacks, tricky questions, or deliberate misstatements of my testimony. This is a routine and normal tactic in cross examinations. If I were to respond emotionally—perhaps with an angry outburst—I would lose credibility with the jury. To be effective in the role of an expert witness, I have to control expression of my feelings.

We've identified five common reasons that we may not express emotions. Although we can understand all of them, they are not equally constructive in their consequences. There is no simple rule for when to express feelings. Instead, we have to exercise judgment. We have an ethical obligation to make thoughtful choices about whether, when, and how to express our feelings. As a responsible communicator, you should strive to decide when it is necessary, appropriate, and constructive to express your feelings, keeping in mind that you, others, and relationships will be affected by your decision.

© Chip Henderson/Tony Stone Images

Ineffective Expression of Emotions

We don't always deny or repress our emotions. Sometimes we realize we have feelings and we try to express them, but we don't communicate effectively. We'll consider three of the most common forms of ineffective expression of emotions.

Speaking in Generalities "I feel bad." "I'm happy." "I'm sad." Statements such as these do express emotional states, but they do so ineffectively. Why? Because they are so general and abstract that they don't clearly communicate what it is the speaker feels. Does "I feel bad" mean the person feels depressed or angry or guilty or ashamed or anxious? Does "I'm happy" mean the speaker is in love, pleased with a grade, satisfied at having achieved a personal goal, delighted to be eating chocolate, or excited about an upcoming vacation? When we use highly general, abstract emotional language, we aren't communicating effectively about what we feel.

Also, our nonverbal repertoire for expressing emotions may be limited. Withdrawing from interaction may be an expression of sadness, anger, depression, or fear. Lowering our head and eyes may express a range of emotions including reverence, shame, and thoughtfulness.

There are many many emotions that we are capable of experiencing. Yet, most of us only recognize or express the most limited number. In *Anger: The Struggle for Emotional Control in America's History* (1986), Carol Stearns and Peter Stearns report that people in the United States actually express very few emotions; in other words, many people recognize only a few of the many possible emotions humans can experience, and they express those emotions whenever they feel something. This limits insight into ourselves and restricts our ability to communicate feelings.

Some people routinely describe what they feel by relying on one or a few emotions. An acquaintance of mine says "I'm frustrated" when he is angry, confused, anxious, hurt, disappointed, and so forth. In the example that opened this chapter, I said I felt angry when hurt would have more accurately described my feeling. Michelle described her feeling as scared when Madhi bounded toward her—the same word she used to describe how she felt when going to see a doctor or when her parents swung her in a circle. Until she enlarged her emotional vocabulary, she couldn't distinguish between feeling startled and feeling scared.

APPLY THE IDEA
Enlarging Your Emotional Vocabulary

Reflect on your emotional vocabulary and how and when you use words to describe emotions. Listed below are some of the more common emotion words people use. For each one, write out four other emotion words that describe subtle distinctions in feeling.

EXAMPLE: anger: *resentment, outrage, offense, vindictiveness*

sadness	_____	_____	_____	_____
happiness	_____	_____	_____	_____
fear	_____	_____	_____	_____
anxiety	_____	_____	_____	_____
love	_____	_____	_____	_____

Extend this exercise by trying to be more precise in how you describe your feelings for the next week. Does expanding your emotional vocabulary give you and others more understanding of what you feel?

Not Owning Feelings   A second ineffective way of expressing emotions is to state feelings in a way that disowns personal responsibility for the feeling. You'll recall our discussion of I-language and you-language in Chapter 4. The ideas we covered there also apply to our present concern with expressing emotions.

"You make me angry" states a feeling (although the word *angry* may be overly general). Yet this statement relies on you-language to suggest that somebody other than the speaker is the source or cause of the angry feeling. As we noted in Chapter 4, nobody else can *make* us feel anything. We define and interpret what people say and do. We attach meaning to their actions. Thus, it's not accurate to say "You make me angry." True, others certainly say and do things that affect us; they may even do things *to* us. But we—not anyone else—decide what their actions mean, and we—not anyone else—decide how we feel.

Russell Proctor (1991) studied the effects of owning and not owning feelings in emotional communication. Proctor's research indicates that failing to own feelings may be the most common obstacle to effective communication about feelings. Let's return to the example of "You make me angry." The statement would be a more effective emotional expression if the speaker said "I feel angry when you don't call when you say you will." The statement would be even more effective—more precise and clearer—if the speaker said, "I feel hurt and unimportant to you when you don't call when you say you will." And the statement would be still more effective if it included information about what the speaker wants from the other person: "I feel hurt and unimportant to you when you don't call when you say you will. Would you be willing to work on calling if we agreed that it's okay for calls to be short sometimes?" This last statement accepts responsibility for a feeling, communicates clearly what is felt, and offers a solution that could help the relationship.

Counterfeit Emotional Language   A third ineffective form of emotional communication is relying on **counterfeit emotional language.** This is language that seems to express emotions but does not actually describe what a person is feeling. For example, shouting "Why can't you leave me alone!" certainly reveals that the speaker is feeling something, but it doesn't describe what she or he is feeling. Is it anger at the particular person, frustration at being interrupted, stress at having to meet a deadline, or the need for time alone? We can't tell which of these—or another—feelings the speaker is experiencing.

To foster understanding between people, it's important to provide clear descriptions of our feelings and the connection between what we feel and others' behaviors. "I feel frustrated because when I'm working and you walk in, I lose my train of thought" is a more constructive statement than "Why can't you leave me alone!" The first statement communicates what is troubling you and states that it is situation-specific. The second comment could be interpreted to mean that you don't want the other person around at all.

It's also counterfeit and unproductive not to explain feelings. "That's just how I feel" doesn't tell a person how her or his behavior is related to your feelings or what you would like her or him to do. Sometimes we say "That's just how I feel" because we haven't really figured out why we feel as we do or what we want from another person. In such cases, we should try to identify situations and our emotional reactions to them so that we can communicate clearly to others (Planalp, 1997).

Another form of counterfeit emotional language uses feeling words but really expresses thoughts, for example, "I feel this discussion is getting sidetracked." The perception that a discussion is going off on tangents is a thought, not a feeling. Maybe the speaker feels frustrated that the discussion seems to be wandering, but that feeling is not communicated by the statement. "This has been a terrible day" suggests that the speaker isn't feeling too great about the day, but what the speaker feels is entirely unclear because she or he offered no description of feelings.

APPLY THE IDEA
Avoiding Counterfeit Emotional Language

Listed below are five statements that include counterfeit emotional language. Rewrite each statement so that it describes a feeling or an emotional state. Make sure you also rely on I-language, not you-language, and you offer precise, clear descriptions, not vague ones.

1. Shut up! I don't want to hear anything else from you.
2. You're a wonderful person.
3. I feel like we should get started on our group project.
4. I can't believe you were here all day and didn't ever clean up the mess.
5. Can't you see I'm working now? Leave me alone.

It's not surprising that many people engage in ineffective emotional communication. As we've seen in this chapter, there are many hindrances to expressing emotions authentically. The three specific forms of ineffective emotional communication we've considered give us insight into some of the more common ways we may evade—consciously or not—clear and genuine communication about our feelings. In the final section of this chapter, we consider alternatives to ineffective methods of communicating emotions. We'll see that there are specific ways to improve communicating our feelings effectively and constructively and to respond sensitively to others' communication about their emotions.

Guidelines for Communicating Emotions Effectively

In the previous section we examined reasons people don't express emotions and ineffective ways we may express them. What we've explored so far in this chapter suggests several guidelines for becoming skilled at communicating our feelings. In this section we'll extend what we've already discussed to identify five guidelines for effective communication of emotions.

Identify Your Emotions

You cannot communicate your feelings if you don't understand them. Thus, the first step in communicating emotions effectively is to identify what you feel. As we have seen, this isn't always easy. For reasons we've discussed, people may be alienated from their emotions—unable to recognize what they feel. Overcoming this requires giving mindful attention to your inner self. Just as some people learn to ignore their feelings, we can teach ourselves to notice and heed them.

Another challenge to identifying emotions is sorting out complex mixtures of feeling. For example, we sometimes feel both anxious and hopeful. To recognize only that you feel hopeful is to overlook anxiety. To realize only that you feel anxious is to ignore your feeling of hopefulness. Recognizing the existence of both feelings allows you to tune in to yourself and to communicate accurately to others what you are experiencing.

When sorting out intermingled feelings it's useful to identify the primary or main feeling—the one or ones that are dominant in the moment. Doing this allows you to communicate clearly to others what is most important in your emotional state. Think back to the example that opened this chapter. I said I felt angry that Carolyn didn't seem to have time for me. I did feel anger, but that wasn't my primary emotion. Hurt was the dominant feeling, and it was the one I communicated to Carolyn. This gave her an understanding of what I felt that was different and more accurate than if I'd told her I felt angry.

Choose How to Communicate Your Emotions

Once you know what you feel, you are ready to decide how to express your emotions. The first choice facing you is whether you wish to communicate your emotions to particular people. As we noted in the previous section, sometimes it is both wise and compassionate to choose not to tell someone what you feel. You may decide that expressing particular emotions would hurt others and would not lead to a constructive outcome. This is not the same thing as not expressing emotions just to avoid tension because tension between people can be healthy, leading to growth for individuals and relationships.

We may also decide not to communicate emotions because we prefer to keep some of our feelings private. This is a reasonable choice if the feelings we keep to ourselves are not ones that others need to know in order to understand

"I know this probably isn't the best time to tell you this—but, Alma, I'd like a trial separation."

I NEED HELP Reprinted with special permission of King Features Syndicate.

us and be in healthy relationships with us. We don't have a responsibility to bare our souls to everyone, nor are we required to tell all of our feelings even to our intimates.

If you decide you do want to communicate your emotions, then you should assess the different ways you might do that and select the one that seems likely to be most effective. Three criteria can help guide our choice of how to express emotions. First, you should evaluate your current state. If you are agitated or enraged, you may not be able to express yourself clearly and fairly. In moments of extreme emotionality, our perceptions may be distorted, and we may say things we don't mean. Remember that communication is irreversible—we cannot unsay what we have once said. According to Daniel Goleman (1995b), it takes about 20 minutes for us to cleanse our minds and bodies of anger. Thus, if you are really angry or feeling other negative emotions, you may wish to wait until you've cooled down so that you can discuss your feelings more fruitfully.

A second criterion is to select appropriate times to discuss feelings. Timing can be very important because most of us are more able to listen and respond when we are not preoccupied, stressed, rushed, or tired. Generally, it's not productive to launch a discussion of feelings when we or others don't have the ability to focus on the conversation. It may be better to defer discussion of a feeling until a time when you and the other person have the psychological and physical resources to engage mindfully in discussion.

A third criterion is to select a setting that is appropriate for discussing feelings. Many feelings can be expressed well in a variety of settings. It would be appropriate, for instance, to tell a friend you felt happy while strolling with him through a shopping mall, walking on campus, or in a conversation in a private setting. However, it might not be appropriate or constructive to tell a friend you felt angry or disappointed in her in a public setting. Doing so could make the other person feel on display, which is likely to arouse defensiveness. Thus, there's less likelihood that the two of you can have a constructive, open discussion of feelings.

Own Your Feelings

We noted the importance of owning your emotions in Chapter 4 and again in this chapter's discussion of ineffective ways of communicating feelings. Owning your feelings is so important to effective communication that the guideline bears repeating. Using I-language to express feelings has two noteworthy benefits. First, it reminds you that you—not anyone else—have responsibility for your feelings. When we rely on you-language ("You hurt me"), we risk misleading ourselves about our accountability for our emotions.

A second reason to avoid you-language is that it tends to make others feel defensive. When others feel on guard, they are less likely to listen thoughtfully and respond sensitively to our expression of emotion. We expand the possibility for healthy, rich interpersonal relationships when we take responsibility for our own feelings by using I-language.

Monitor Your Self-Talk

A fourth guideline for communicating feelings effectively is to monitor your self-talk. You'll recall from Chapter 2 that the ways we communicate with ourselves affect how we feel and act. **Self-talk** is intrapersonal communication, or communication we have with ourselves. We engage in self-talk to do the emotion work we discussed earlier in this chapter. We might say, "I shouldn't feel angry" or "I don't want to come across as a wimp by letting on how much that hurt." Thus, we may talk ourselves out of or into feelings and out of or into ways of expressing our feelings.

Self-talk can work for us or against us, depending on whether we manage it or it manages us. This point is stressed by Tom Rusk and Natalie Rusk in their book *Mind Traps* (1988); they assert that many people have self-defeating ideas that get in the way of their effectiveness and happiness. According to the Rusks, "feelings are the key to personal change" (p. xix). Unless we learn to manage our feelings effectively, we cannot change patterns of behavior that leave us stuck in ruts.

Psychologist Martin Seligman (1990) agrees with this point. According to Seligman, "our thoughts are not merely reactions to events; they change what ensues" (p. 7). In other words, the thoughts we communicate to ourselves affect what happens in our lives. Given this, it is worthwhile to develop skill in monitoring our self-talk so that we can *choose* how to think and feel.

Much of what we say to ourselves reflects social perspectives that we have internalized. The ME part of self monitors what the I part of self experiences. So I feels embarrassed, and ME instructs I not to express that feeling. Sometimes the ME does a good job of helping us control emotional communication that could reflect badly on us or hurt others. Yet at other times, the ME encourages us to stuff feelings in unhealthy ways. By tuning in to your self-talk about emotions, you can make careful, informed choices about what to express and what not to express.

APPLY THE IDEA

Tuning in to Your Self-Talk

What kinds of self-talk do you engage in when you feel emotions? To find out, describe what you think when you feel the following emotions.

PERCEIVED EMOTION	SELF-TALK
EXAMPLE: Helplessness	"There's nothing I can do to change things."
	"I'm just a little fish in this pond."
self-pity	_____
jealousy	_____

impatience _____

sadness, verging on tears _____

FIGURE 7.5
The Rational-Emotive Approach to Feelings

Step 1	Monitor emotional reactions.
Step 2	Identify commonalities in events and experiences to which you respond emotionally.
Step 3	Tune into your self-talk; notice irrational beliefs and fallacies.
Step 4	Use self-talk to dispute fallacies.

Fallacy	Typical Effects
Perfectionism	Unrealistically low self-concept Stress Chronic dissatisfaction with self Jealousy and envy of others
Obsession with shoulds	Saps energy for constructive work Can make others defensive Can alienate self from feelings Unrealistic standards set the self up for failure
Overgeneralization	Perceive one failure as typical of self Generalize inadequacies in some domains to total self
Taking responsibility for others	Thinking you are responsible for others' feelings Guilt for how others feel Deprives others of taking responsibility for selves
Helplessness	Believing that there is nothing you can do to change how you feel Resignation; depression
Fear of catastrophic failure	Extreme negative fantasies and scenarios of what could happen Inability to do things because of what might happen

FIGURE 7.6
Common Fallacies About Emotions

Monitoring self-talk about feelings also allows us to gain more accurate and constructive understandings of ourselves. This happens when we learn to identify and challenge irrational beliefs about ourselves and how we should feel and act. **Irrational beliefs** are debilitating ways of evaluating our emotions and ourselves. These irrational beliefs hinder our ability to manage and express emotions effectively.

Albert Ellis (1962) is a therapist who developed the **rational-emotive approach to feelings.** This approach emphasizes using rational thinking to challenge debilitating emotions and beliefs that undermine healthy self-concepts and relationships. The rational-emotive approach to feelings proceeds through four steps, as shown in Figure 7.5. (Ellis's original ideas are discussed further in "Albert Ellis in Action.")

The first step is to monitor your emotional reactions to events and experiences that distress you. Notice what's happening in your body; notice your nonverbal behavior. Does your stomach tighten? Do you feel light-headed? Are you clenching your teeth? Is your heart racing? Do you feel nauseous?

The second step in Ellis's approach is to identify the events and situations to which you have unpleasant responses. Look for commonalities among situations. For example, perhaps you notice that your heartbeat races and your palms get clammy when you talk with professors, supervisors, and academic advisers, but you don't have any of these physiological responses when you interact with friends, co-workers, or people whom you supervise. You label your emotions as insecurity in the former cases and security in the latter ones. One commonality among the situations in which you feel insecure is the power differential between you and the other person. This could suggest that you feel insecure when talking with someone who has more power than you.

The third step is to tune in to your self-talk. Listen to what's happening in your head. What is your ME saying? Is it telling you that you shouldn't feel certain emotions ("It's stupid to feel anxious," "Don't be a wimp")? Is it telling you to stuff your feelings ("Don't let on that you're insecure")? Is it telling you that you should feel something you don't ("You're supposed to feel confident and in command")?

Ellis places special emphasis on identifying fallacies in our self-talk about emotions. These fallacies encourage us to evaluate ourselves negatively, and the negativity is not based on logic but on invalid, unrealistic thought. Figure 7.6 lists some of the most common fallacies that sabotage realistic appraisals of ourselves, our feelings, and our actions.

Therapists who teach their clients to use the rational-emotive approach to feelings emphasize learning to dispute irrational fallacies. Following this advice, we can use our self-talk to challenge the debilitating fallacies. For example, assume that Tyronne has been working well at his job and thinks his boss should give him a raise. He tunes in to his self-talk (step 3) and hears himself saying, "Well, maybe I shouldn't ask for a raise because after all, I have made some mistakes. I could do better." This self-talk reflects the fallacy of perfectionism. Tyronne listens further to himself and hears this message: "If I ask him for a raise and he gets angry, he might fire me, and then I wouldn't have a job and couldn't stay in school. Without a degree I have no future." This self-talk exemplifies the fear of catastrophic failure.

How might Tyronne dispute these fallacies? To challenge the perfectionism fallacy, he could say, "True, I'm not perfect, but I'm doing more and better work than the other employees hired at the same time I was." To dispute the fallacy of catastrophic failure, Tyronne might say to himself, "Well, he's not likely to fire me because I do my job well and training someone new would be a headache and an expense he doesn't need. And what if he does fire me? It's not like this is the only job in the world. With my good work record I could get

COMMUNICATION NOTES

Albert Ellis in Action

Albert Ellis was not a mild-mannered, detached sort of therapist—nor did he want to be. He was known for his dramatic style and for pushing, pushing, pushing his clients. He firmly believed that people whom many clinicians diagnosed as neurotics were really not neurotic but only suffering from irrational thinking. He often described this as stupid thinking on the part of non-stupid people. And Ellis was convinced that we can un-learn stupid behaviors in order to function more effectively.

In dealing with clients, Ellis would berate them for stupid thinking, all the while insisting that they were not stupid people. He wanted his clients to learn new and better ways of thinking. "You're living under a tyranny of shoulds. Stop shoulding yourself to death," he would demand. "Quit thinking wrong and start thinking right," he urged. And his clients responded to Ellis's unorthodox style and therapy. Many learned to think differently, and this led them to feel and act differently and more effectively in their lives.

SOURCES: Ellis, A. (1962). *Reason and emotion in psychotherapy.* New York: Lyle Stuart; Ellis, A., & Harper, R. (1975). *A new guide to rational living.* Englewood Cliffs, NJ: Prentice-Hall; Seligman, M.E.P. (1990). *Learned optimism: How to change your mind and your life.* New York: Simon & Schuster/Pocket Books.

another job pretty fast." Instead of letting our self-talk defeat us with irrational beliefs and debilitating fallacies, we can use our self-talk to question and challenge the irrational thinking that undermines us.

Respond Sensitively When Others Communicate Emotions

A final guideline is to respond sensitively when others express their feelings to you. Learning to communicate your emotions effectively is only half the process of communicating about emotions. You also want to become skilled in listening and responding to others when they share their feelings with you.

Many people feel inadequate when others express feelings. Often they respond with highly general statements such as "Things will look better after you get a good night's sleep," "Time heals all wounds," "You'll be fine," "Your anger is only hurting you," "You'll feel better if you get this in perspective."

Although such statements may be intended to reassure others, they can devalue others' feelings. In effect, they tell others that they aren't allowed to feel what they feel or that they will be okay (right, normal) once they stop feeling what they are feeling. This denies others the right to feel.

Another mistake many people make when responding to others' expression of feelings is to try to solve the other person's problem or to make the feeling go away. Scholars who have studied gender (Tannen, 1990; Wood, 1997) observe that the tendency to try to solve others' problems is more common in men than women. Helping another solve a problem may be appreciated, but usually it's not the first support a person needs when she or he is feeling strong emotions. What most of us need first is the freedom to feel what we are feeling and to have others accept that.

A more effective approach is to let others talk about their feelings and offer support. You don't have to try to feel as another person does to accept what she or he is feeling as legitimate. While listening, it's helpful to interject a few minimal encouragers, which we discussed in Chapter 6. Saying "I understand" and "Go on," state that you accept the other person's feelings and invite him or her to continue talking. It is appropriate to mention your own experiences briefly to show you empathize. However, it's not advisable to refocus the conversation on you and your experiences. You may briefly offer personal information and then return to focus on the other.

Paraphrasing, which we discussed in Chapter 6, is another way to show that you understand what another feels. When you mirror back not just the content, but the feeling of what another says, it confirms the other and what he or she feels. "So, it sounds as if you were really surprised by what happened. Is that right?" "What I'm hearing is that you are more hurt than angry. Does that sound right to you?" These examples of paraphrasing mirror the speaker's feelings and also show that you are listening actively.

The guidelines we've identified may not make emotional communication easy or comfortable in all situations. Following them, however, will give you a firm foundation for understanding and expressing your feelings and responding effectively when others discuss their feelings with you.

Summary

In this chapter we explored the complex world of emotions and our communication about them. We considered different views of what's involved in experiencing and expressing emotions. From our review of theories we learned that emotions have physiological, perceptual, linguistic, and social dimensions. We also examined some of the reasons people don't express feelings or express them ineffectively. The final focus of our attention was guidelines for effective communication about emotions. We identified five guidelines that can help us be effective when expressing our feelings or responding to the feelings of others. Because these guidelines are critical to interpersonal communication, we'll close the chapter by restating them:

1. Identify your emotions.
2. Choose how to communicate your emotions.
3. Own your feelings.
4. Monitor your self-talk.
5. Respond sensitively when others communicate emotions.

Concepts

- cognitive labeling view of emotions
- counterfeit emotional language
- deep acting
- emotional intelligence
- emotions
- emotion work
- feeling rules
- framing rules
- interactive view of emotions
- irrational beliefs
- organismic view of emotions
- perceptual view of emotions
- rational-emotive approach to feelings
- self-talk
- surface acting

Thought & Discussion

1. Do you rely on only a few emotional words to express your feelings? If so, monitor your emotional language and work to enlarge your emotional vocabulary. Can you generate more precise words to describe your feelings?

2. Use your *InfoTrac College Edition* to survey advice about communicating emotions that is published in popular magazines. Survey articles in magazines such as *Essence* and *Working Woman*. How does advice in popular magazines compare with what you read in this chapter?

3. Review the fallacies discussed in the last section of this chapter. Do any of those fallacies show up in your intrapersonal communication? After reading about the fallacies and ways to challenge them, can you monitor and revise your intrapersonal communication?

4. We discussed different perspectives on emotions. Which of the perspectives makes most sense to you? Why? Explain how the perspective you favor gives you insight into emotions that you don't get from other perspectives.

5. Reread "Wild Pigs Run Amok." Can you identify analogous rituals for expressing emotions in Western culture? What socially accepted ways exist for expressing grief, anger, and other emotions?

6. As we noted in this chapter, repression of many emotions is encouraged in the United States. Do you think this is healthy for individuals and society? What are the advantages of repressing emotions? What are the disadvantages?

7. How did you learn which emotions it was acceptable for you to express? Do you think what you were taught reflects gender expectations?

8. What ethical principles can you identify to guide when and how people express emotions to others? Is honesty always the best policy? Is it ethical for one person to decide what another should know or can handle?

Communication Climate:

The Foundation of Personal Relationships

© Catherine Karnow/Woodfin Camp & Associates, Inc.

Do you feel foggy-headed or down when the sky is overcast and upbeat when it's sunny? Does your mood ever shift as the weather changes? Most of us do respond to the climate. We feel more or less positive depending on the conditions around us. In much the same way that we react to physical weather, we also respond to **interpersonal climates.**

Sunshine or clouds, warmth and cold, fog or clear skies contribute to the climate in outdoor contexts. In the same way, how we communicate with others establishes the climate in personal relationships. Interpersonal climate is the overall feeling, or emotional mood between people. Interpersonal climate is not something we can see or measure objectively, and it's not made up of things people do together. Instead, climate is the dominant feeling between people who are involved with each other. Two couples might live in the same apartment complex, have similar jobs, and distribute responsibilities for cleaning, cooking, and shopping in the same way. Yet in one of the relationships there is constant tension, marked by short and sometimes cutting remarks and frequent flares of temper. In the other relationship the pervasive feeling is comfortable and friendly. Although the two couples do similar things, the climates of their relationships differ dramatically. In the workplace, interpersonal climates make some of our relationships easy and comfortable and others difficult and defensive.

Because interpersonal climate concerns the overall feeling between people, it is the foundation of personal relationships. Both friendships and romantic relationships develop climates that reflect and establish emotional moods. In this chapter, we focus on climate as a cornerstone of satisfying interpersonal relationships. We'll begin by discussing the elements of healthy interpersonal relationships. Next, we'll examine confirming and disconfirming climates and identify kinds of communication that foster each. The third section of the chapter identifies guidelines for creating and sustaining healthy interpersonal climates. In the next chapter, we'll see how building confirming climates assists us in managing conflict effectively.

Elements of Satisfying Personal Relationships

Personal relationships are basic to our lives. As we saw in Chapter 1, we relate to others to fulfill human needs for survival, safety, belonging, esteem, self-actualization, and participation in a diverse social world. People who lack friends are more depressed and have lower self-esteem than people who have satisfying friendships (Hojat, 1982; Jones & Moore, 1989). Just having relationships, however, doesn't necessarily enhance us. To feel good about ourselves and our connections with others, we need to build relationships that are confirming and satisfying.

Building good relationships depends not only on others, but on ourselves— especially our perceptions and attributions that shape how we feel about others and relationships. Communication scholars report that some lonely people are locked into a "negativity cycle" in which they focus on negative aspects of interaction and discount positive aspects. This leads them to feel more pessimistic about their relationships and themselves, which, in turn, heightens their awareness of negative features (Duck, Pond, & Leatham, 1994). The converse is also true: When we are involved in satisfying relationships, we feel more positive about ourselves and life. Researchers have shown that people who fall in love see the world through "rose-colored glasses" (Hendrick & Hendrick, 1988).

S T U D E N T VOICES

FIONA: *The worst time in my whole life was my first semester here. I felt so lonely being away from my family and all my friends at home. Back there we were really close, and there was always somebody to be with and talk to, but I didn't know anybody on this campus. I felt all alone and like nobody cared about me. I became depressed and almost left school, but then I started seeing a guy and I made a couple of friends. Everything got better once I had some people to talk to and be with.*

Many people feel as Fiona does. Research indicates that loneliness during the first year of college depends more on whether a person has friends than on good family ties and romantic relationships (Cutrona, 1982). It seems that we look primarily to friends to satisfy our needs for belonging and acceptance, especially after we have moved away from home.

Because personal relationships make such a difference in our lives, we need to understand what makes relationships healthy and gratifying. In a book on personal relationships, I reviewed over 700 articles and books on intimacy (Wood, 1995c). I concluded that four features characterize satisfying close relationships: investment, commitment, trust, and comfort with relational dialectics. We'll discuss each of these. As we do, realize that members of different speech communities may have distinct rules for what each feature is and how it is communicated. For example, in general, Westerners rely heavily on verbal disclosures to build trust, whereas most Asians are less verbally revealing and depend on actions to build trust. Caucasians tend to regard commitment as a tie between two people whereas Asians, Hispanics, and African Americans often perceive commitment more as a broad tie that links families and communities (Gaines, 1995). Although people may experience and express these four features in diverse ways, they appear to be cornerstones of closeness for most of us. Taken together, these four features create a strong nucleus for a relationship and confirm the value of each partner.

Investment

© Bachmann/Photo Researchers, Inc.

Good relationships grow out of **investment**, which is what we put into relationships that we could not retrieve if the relationship were to end. When we care about another person, we invest time, energy, thought, and feelings into interaction. In doing this, we invest *ourselves* in others. Investment is powerful because it consists of personal choices. Further, investment cannot be recovered, so the only way to make good on it is to stick with a relationship (Brehm, 1992). We can't get back the time, feelings, and energy we invest in a relationship. We cannot recover the history we have shared with another person. Thus, to leave is to lose the investment we've made.

APPLY THE IDEA
Your Investment in Relationships

What have you invested in your closest friendship and romantic relationship?

- How much time have you spent?
- How many decisions have you made to accommodate your friend? Your romantic partner?
- How much money have you spent?
- How much is your history entwined with that of your friend? Your romantic partner?
- How much trust have you given each intimate?
- How much support have you given each intimate?
- Do your partners' investments roughly equal yours?

Finally, explain what would be lost if these relationships ended. Could you recover your investment?

Perceived equality of partners' investment affects satisfaction with relationships. Researchers report that in the happiest dating and married couples, partners feel they invest equally (Fletcher, Fincham, Cramer, & Heron, 1987; Hecht, Marston, & Larkey, 1994). When we feel we are investing more than a partner, we tend to be dissatisfied and resentful. When it seems our partner is investing more than we are, we may feel guilty. Because imbalance of either sort is disconfirming, perceived inequity erodes satisfaction (Brehm, 1992). Not surprisingly, communication is affected by perceived inequity. Partners who feel they are investing unequally tend to communicate limited support to each other and to minimize major disclosures (Brehm, 1992).

STUDENT VOICES

SIBBY: *I dated this one guy for a long time before I finally had to cut my losses. He said he loved me, but he wouldn't put anything in the relationship. I gave so much—always accommodating him, doing things for*

Love and Commitment: Different Matters

To find out what holds a relationship together, Mary Lund studied 129 heterosexual college seniors. She measured their commitment and love for partners in February and in the summer following graduation. She found that the continuation of relationships depended more on commitment than love. Couples who had high levels of love but low commitment to a shared future were less likely to remain together than couples who were highly committed to a joint future. Thus, the *intention* to stay together is a more powerful glue than positive feelings between partners.

Lund's study also showed that commitment is more strongly linked to making investments than to perceptions that a relationship is rewarding or that love exists. Investments increase commitment because they are personal choices, whereas loving and being loved are not acts of will.

Summarizing her findings, Lund said that although love usually accompanies commitment, commitment and investment have more to do with whether a relationship lasts than do love and rewards.

SOURCE: Lund, M. (1985). The development of investment and commitment scales for predicting continuity of personal relationships. *Journal of Social and Personal Relationships, 2,* 3–23.

him, loving him, but there just wasn't any reciprocity. It was a one-way street with him, and I felt like he didn't value me very much at all.

Commitment

Closely related to investment is **commitment,** which is a decision to remain with a relationship. Notice that commitment is defined as a decision, not a feeling. The hallmark of commitment is the assumption of a future. In committed relationships, partners assume they will continue together. Unlike passion or attraction, which exist in the present, commitment links partners together in the future. Because partners in committed relationships view their connection as continuing, they are unlikely to bail out during the inevitable rough times. Instead, they weather those, confident that they will stay together. Communication between committed partners reflects the assumed continuity of the relationship. Problems and tensions that inevitably arise aren't seen as reasons to end a relationship. Instead, partners try to work through their conflicts. We'll discuss ways to manage conflicts in detail in Chapter 9.

STUDENT VOICES

ERIN: *I've been married for six years, and it has been a very difficult relationship. We were married right out of high school because I was pregnant. This set our marriage off to a rocky start. We separated twice, which tells you that we weren't totally committed. The last time we separated and got back together we agreed this would be our last try at making the marriage work. We decided that if it was going to have a chance of working, both of us had to put everything we have into it. We also decided to get the words separation and divorce out of our vocabulary. I can't believe the change that we have had in our relationship since we decided to put everything into it and not to talk about breaking up. We now have a true commitment.*

Whereas love is a feeling we can't necessarily control, commitment is a decision, as explained in "Love and Commitment: Different Matters." It is a personal choice to maintain a relationship. Partners who make this choice strive for dual perspective and commit to listening and speaking

effectively to each other. Aaron Beck (1988), a counselor, believes that the decision to commit injects responsibility into
relationships. When partners make a commitment, they take
responsibility for continuing to invest in and care for their bond.
Without responsibility, relationships are subject to the whims
of feeling and fortune, which are hardly a stable basis for
enduring intimacy.

Trust

A third cornerstone of healthy personal relationships is a high
degree of **trust** between partners. Trust involves believing in
another's reliability (he or she will do what is promised) and
emotionally relying on another to care about and protect our
welfare (Brehm, 1992). Trust doesn't come automatically in relationships. Instead, it is earned. Individuals earn each other's trust
by communicating honestly and by honoring each other's perspective. They show that they care about each other and are willing to make
the investments necessary to understand how each other thinks and feels.
When we trust someone, we count on her or him to be loving and respectful.
These feelings allow us to feel psychologically safe.

This is such a dumb time, Jack, to start talking about whether or not something is written in stone.

KEEPING UP by William Hamilton is reprinted by permission of William Hamilton.

S T U D E N T   VOICES

JAMIE: *I was really crazy about this girl my sophomore year, but I just didn't
trust that she really cared about me. I was always doing little things to
show her I cared, like taking her a flower or changing the oil in her
car. But she never did little things for me. As long as I was taking care of her, she
was great. But when I needed to feel she was there for me, things didn't work very
well. I just didn't trust her to look out for me.*

One reason that trust is so important to close friendships and romantic
relationships is that it allows us to take risks with others. For intimacy to grow,
we have to risk ourselves. We have to be willing to let another into our hearts
and heads, and that requires trust. We only open ourselves to others if they
have earned our trust and if we feel we can count on them to protect our
confidences and to care about us and our feelings. Trust develops as people
do what they say they will and as they provide support and safety to each
other.

Self-Disclosure   One clear influence on trust is self-disclosure, which can both
build and reflect trust between people. **Self-disclosure** is revealing personal
information about ourselves that others are unlikely to discover in other ways.
According to researchers who have studied communication between intimates,
self-disclosure is a key gauge of closeness, at least among Westerners (Derlega &

Berg, 1987; Hansen & Schuldt, 1984). Self-disclosure should take place gradually and with appropriate caution. It's unwise to tell anyone too much about ourselves too quickly, especially if revelations could be used against us. We begin by disclosing relatively superficial information ("I'm from a small town," "I love Mexican food," "I'm afraid of heights"). If a person responds with empathy to early and limited disclosures, we're likely to reveal progressively more intimate information ("My father served time in prison," "I am lesbian," "I go through periods of real depression"). If these disclosures are also met with understanding and confidentiality, trust continues to grow.

In the early stages of relationship development, it is important that there be reciprocity of disclosures. We're willing to make disclosures of our private feelings only so long as the other person is also revealing personal information (Cunningham, Strassberg, & Haan, 1986). The need for reciprocity exists because trust is still developing and being earned. When a relationship is just beginning, we feel vulnerable—the other could betray a confidence or reject us because we disclose something negative. Our feeling of vulnerability is reduced if the other person is also trusting us with self-disclosures.

The need to match disclosures recedes in importance once trust is established. Partners in stable relationships don't feel the need to reciprocate disclosures immediately. Unlike beginning acquaintances, they have the time to reciprocate on a more leisurely schedule. Thus, disclosure between established intimates is more likely to be greeted with a response to what has been revealed than with an equivalent disclosure. Of course, there are exceptions to these general patterns. People vary in how much they want to self-disclose, so an absolute amount of disclosure is not a sure-fire measure of closeness. Also, people vary in their perceptions of the link between disclosure and intimacy, so we need to respect individual differences.

Although all of us disclose some personal information in close relationships, not everyone discloses equally or in the same ways. Cultural differences shape our tendencies to self-disclose. People raised in traditional Chinese society disclose less personal information than most Westerners. Among Pakistanis disclosures between parents and children are much more rare than among native-born U.S. residents. Gender also seems to affect how and how much people disclose, as discussed in "Different Modes of Closeness." In general, women make more verbal disclosures both to other women and to men. Women also tend to place greater value on verbal disclosures than most men (Floyd & Parks, 1995). Men are generally less inclined to talk about personal feelings, even to intimates. Many men disclose feelings through their actions rather than through words. Russell's comments make this point.

S T U D E N T   VOICES

RUSSELL: *When I really need some support from my girlfriend, I don't just come out and say "I need you." What I do is go over to her place or call her to see if she wants to come to my place. Sometimes we just sit together watching TV or something. And that helps. I know she knows that I am down and need her, but I don't have to say it. I do the same thing when I think she is feeling low. It's hard for me to say "I love you and am sorry you feel bad." But I can be with her and I can hug her and let her know through my actions that I care.*

Although self-disclosing is important early in relationships, it is not a primary communication dynamic over the long haul. When we're first getting to know another, we have to reveal ourselves and learn about the other, so disclosures are necessary and desirable. In relationships that endure, however, disclosures make up very little of the total communication between partners. Although disclosure wanes over time, partners continue to reap the benefits of the trust and depth of personal knowledge created by early disclosures. Also, partners do continue to disclose new experiences and insights to each other; however, there is less disclosure as a relationship matures. Radical decreases in disclosures, other than explosions of negative feelings, are key signals of trouble in a relationship (Baxter, 1987). We are reluctant to entrust others with our secrets and personal emotions when intimacy is fading or gone.

COMMUNICATION NOTES

Different Modes of Closeness

Research indicates that women generally disclose more frequently and more deeply than men. This difference was interpreted to mean that men are less interested in or comfortable with intimacy. However, recent work suggests instead that the sexes do not differ in how much they value closeness; they merely create it in different ways.

Feminine speech communities emphasize using personal talk to create and sustain closeness. Thus, in general, women learn to disclose personal thoughts and feelings as a primary way of enhancing intimacy. This is called *closeness in dialogue.*

Because masculine speech communities place less emphasis on personal talk, men typically don't regard intimate conversation and self-disclosure as a path to closeness. Instead, they usually learn to bond with others through doing things together. Their mode is called *closeness in the doing.*

These two modes of closeness, although related to gender, aren't dichotomized by sex. Recent studies indicate that both women and men do things for people they care about. Instrumental shows of affection, or closeness in the doing, seems less gender-bound than closeness in dialogue. Research also indicates that men sometimes express closeness through dialogue, just not as frequently as most women.

Both modes of closeness are ways for people to connect. The two ways of expressing and experiencing closeness are equally valid, and both should be respected.

SOURCES: Canary, D., & Dindia, K. (Eds.). (1998). *Sex Differences and Similarities in Communication,* Mahwah, NJ: Erlbaum; Floyd, K., & Parks, M. (1995). Manifesting closeness in the interactions of peers: A look at siblings and friends. *Communication Reports,* 8, 69–76; Wood, J. T., & Inman, C. C. (1993). In a different mode: Masculine styles of communicating closeness. *Journal of Applied Communication Research,* 21, 279–295.

STUDENT VOICES

CRAIG: *I think what first clued me in that Shelby was losing interest was that she stopped telling me private stuff about herself. For the first couple of months we dated, she shared so much about her dreams, plans, and fears. The more she told me about herself and the more I told her, the closer I felt. But then she seemed to withdraw and not want to share her private thoughts. That was really the start of the end.*

Comfort with Relational Dialectics

A final quality of healthy relationships is understanding and being comfortable with **relational dialectics.** These are opposing forces, or tensions, that are normal parts of all relationships. Leslie Baxter, a scholar of interpersonal communication, has identified three dialectics of relationships (Baxter, 1988, 1990, 1993; Baxter & Simon, 1993). We'll discuss the three, shown in Table 8.1, to clarify how they operate as normal, productive processes in relational life.

TABLE 8.1
RELATIONAL DIALECTICS

Autonomy/Connection	I want to be close.
	I need my own space.
Novelty/Predictability	I like the familiar rhythms we have.
	We need to do something new and different.
Openness/Closedness	I like sharing so much with you.
	There are some things I don't want to talk about with you.

Autonomy/Connection   All close friends and romantic partners experience tension between wanting to be autonomous, or individual, and wanting to be close, or connected. Because we want to be deeply linked to others, we seek intimacy and sharing. Friends and lovers want to spend time with each other, have joint interests, and talk personally. At the same time, each of us needs a sense of independent identity. We want to know that our individuality is not swallowed up by relationships. We need our own space, so we seek distance even from our intimates.

Relationship counselors agree that the most central and continuous friction in most close relationships arises from the contradictory impulses for autonomy and connection (Beck, 1988; Scarf, 1987). When Robbie and I take vacations, we are intensely together for a week or more. We travel together, eat all meals together, and sleep and interact in confined spaces where privacy is limited. Typically, when we return home after a vacation, we interact very little for several days. Having been immersed in togetherness, we both seek distance to reestablish our autonomous identities. Both autonomy and closeness are natural human needs. The challenge is to preserve individuality while also creating unity in a relationship.

STUDENT VOICES

KEN: *Dialectics explains something that has really confused me. I've never understood how I could want so much to be with Ashley for a while and then feel suffocated and need to get away. I've worried that it means I don't love her anymore or there is something wrong between us. But now I see how both needs are normal and okay.*

Novelty/Predictability   The second dialectic is the tension between wanting routine, or familiarity, and wanting novelty in a relationship. All of us like a certain amount of routine to provide security and predictability to our lives. For example, my friend Nancy and I long ago agreed to get together every Sunday for brunch and visiting. We count on that as a steady, habitual time to see each other. Yet too much routine becomes boring, so it's also natural to seek novel experiences. Every so often Nancy and I decide to explore a new restaurant or make a day trip just to introduce variety into our customary routine.

KIRA: *Most of the time I like how Michael and I are. We've worked out some nice, comfortable routines for time together, so we don't have to figure out what we're going to do all the time. But every now and then I get bored, and I want to break out of the routines. I want something that stimulates me—something new and different in our relationship. I think that's healthy.*

Openness/Closedness   The third dialectic is a tension between wanting open communication and needing a degree of privacy, even with intimates. With our closest partners, we want to share our inner selves and be open with no holds barred. Even so, we also desire a zone of privacy, and we want our partners to respect that. Some partners agree not to talk about certain topics, such as money or religion. Although they are open about other matters, these topics are respected as off limits. It's also normal to be temporarily closed after we have revealed something highly personal.

ANDY: *My girlfriend has trouble accepting the fact that I won't talk to her about my brother Jacob. He died when I was eight, and I still can't deal with all my feelings, especially with feeling guilty that he died and I'm alive. I just can't talk about that to anybody. With my girlfriend, I talk about lots of personal stuff, but Jacob is just too private and too hard.*

Although intimate relationships are sometimes idealized as totally open and honest, in reality completely unbridled expressiveness would be intolerable (Baxter, 1993; Petronio, 1991). There is nothing wrong when we seek privacy; it doesn't mean a relationship is in trouble. It means only that we need both openness and closedness in our lives.

The three dialectics create ongoing tensions in healthy relationships. This is a problem only if partners don't understand that dialectics and the tension they generate are natural parts of relational life. If we think it's wrong to be closed at times or not to want togetherness always, then we'll misinterpret our feelings and what they mean. Once we realize that dialectics are normal in all relationships, we can accept and grow from the tensions they generate.

Dialectics do not operate in isolation. Instead, they interact and affect one another within the overall system of a relationship. Thus, friends who are

© Gale Palmer/Mugshots/The Stock Market

highly open are also likely to be very connected, whereas a more closed couple tends to favor greater autonomy (Aries, 1987). Relational dialectics also interact with other facets of interpersonal communication. For instance, partners who prefer a high amount of individuality tend to create more individual spaces and fewer common ones in their homes than do partners who favor greater connection (Fitzpatrick, 1988; Fitzpatrick & Best, 1979). Frequent and in-depth disclosures are most likely in relationships that are highly open and connected. Like all aspects of interpersonal communication, relational dialectics operate systemically.

Responding to Dialectics   There is no single correct method of responding to relational dialectics. Baxter (1990) has identified four ways partners deal with the tension generated by opposing needs. One response, called neutralization, is to negotiate a balance between the two poles of a dialectic. This involves striking a compromise in which each need is met to an extent, but neither is fully satisfied. A couple that does this might have a fairly consistent equilibrium between the amount of novelty and the amount of routine in their relationship.

A second response is selection in which we give priority to one of the needs in a dialectic and neglect the other. For example, friends might focus on novelty and suppress their needs for ritual and routine. Some partners cycle between competing poles of dialectics, so that they favor each one alternately. A couple could be open and continuously together for a period and then be autonomous and closed for a time.

S T U D E N T   VOICES

BEVERLY: *My folks are so funny. They plod along in the same old rut for ages and ages, and my sister and I can't get them to do anything different. Mom won't try a new recipe for chicken because "we like ours like I always fix it." Dad won't try a new style of shirt because "that's not the kind of shirt I wear." Dynamite wouldn't blow them out of their ruts. But then all of a sudden they'll do a whole bunch of unusual things. Like once they went out to three movies in a day, and the next day they went for a picnic at the zoo. This kind of zaniness goes on for a while, then it's back to hum-drum for months and months. I guess they get all of their novelty in occasional bursts.*

A third way to manage dialectics is called separation. When we separate dialectics, we assign one dialectical need to certain spheres of interaction and the opposing dialectical need to other aspects of interaction. For instance, friends might be open about many topics but respect each other's privacy in one or two areas. A couple might have rigid daily schedules and patterns of socializing but be very spontaneous on vacations. Many dual-career couples are autonomous about their work, relying little on each other for advice, although they are very connected about family, collaborating, and being close in that area.

The final method of dealing with dialectics is called reframing. This is a complex and transformative strategy in which partners redefine contradictory needs as not in opposition. In other words, they reframe their perceptions by redefining what is happening. My colleagues and I found an example of this when we studied differences between intimate partners (Wood et al., 1994). Some partners transcended the opposition between autonomy and connection by defining differences and disagreements as enhancing intimacy. Another example of reframing is deciding that novelty and predictability are not opposites, but allies. A couple I know regards routine and spontaneity as supporting each other. Their routines make novelty interesting, and novelty makes routines comforting.

APPLY THE IDEA
Applying Relational Dialectics

How do relational dialectics operate in your life? To find out, select three of your relationships: a very close friendship, a current or past romantic relationship, and a friendly but not really intimate relationship. For each relationship answer these questions:

- How are needs for autonomy expressed and satisfied?
- How are needs for connection expressed and met?
- How are needs for novelty expressed and met?
- How are needs for predictability expressed and met?
- How are needs for openness expressed and satisfied?
- How are needs for closedness expressed and met?

Now think about how you manage the tension between opposing needs in each dialectic. When do you rely on neutralization, selection, separation, and reframing? How satisfied are you with your responses? Experiment with new ways of managing dialectical tensions.

Dialectics can be effectively managed in a variety of ways. However, research indicates that, in general, the least effective and least satisfying response is to honor one need and repress the opposing one (Baxter, 1990). Squelching any natural human impulse diminishes us. The challenge is to find ways to accommodate all of our needs, even when they seem contradictory.

Healthy relationships exist when partners create a climate in which each feels valued and comfortable with the other. This tends to happen when partners make commitments and investments, build trust, and effectively manage dialectical tensions. Underlying all the elements we've discussed is confirmation, which is at the heart of fulfilling interpersonal relationships. Because confirmation is so important to relationships, the next section of the chapter explores how communication influences confirming climates.

FIGURE 8.1
Continuum of
Interpersonal Climates

Confirming and Disconfirming Climates

The philosopher Martin Buber (1957) believed that each of us needs confirmation to be healthy and to grow. Buber also emphasized that full humanness can develop only when people confirm others and are confirmed by them. The essence of confirmation is valuing. We all want to feel we are valued, especially by our intimates. When others confirm us, we feel cherished and respected. When they disconfirm us, we feel discounted and less contented with ourselves.

Interpersonal climates exist on a continuum from confirming to disconfirming (Figure 8.1). Of course, few relationships are purely confirming or disconfirming. In reality, most fall in between the two extremes of the continuum. In these, some messages are confirming whereas other messages are disconfirming, or communication cycles between being basically confirming and basically disconfirming.

Relationships also don't usually move abruptly and completely from being at one spot on the continuum to being in a different spot. Usually, one level of confirmation flows into the next in a gradual way. You might feel less than confirmed by a person you are just getting to know. As the two of you talk and interact more, the other person may communicate that he or she values you and your ideas, so you begin to feel more confirmed. Over time, you move to feeling that the relationship is basically confirming.

Levels of Confirmation and Disconfirmation

Building on Buber's ideas, as well as those of psychiatrist R. D. Laing (1961), communication scholars have extended insight into confirming and disconfirming climates (Cissna & Sieburg, 1986). They have identified specific kinds of communication that confirm or disconfirm others on three levels. The most basic form of confirmation is recognizing that another person exists. We do this with nonverbal behaviors (a smile, hug, or touch) and verbal communication ("Hello," "Good to meet you," "I see you're home").

We disconfirm others at a fundamental level when we don't acknowledge their existence. For example, you might not speak to or look at a person when you enter a room. Not responding to someone's question also disconfirms their presence. Parents who punish a child by refusing to speak to her or him disconfirm the child's existence. A person who uses the silent treatment disconfirms another's existence.

S T U D E N T   V O I C E S

REGGIE: *Any African American knows what it means to have your existence denied. The law may forbid segregation now, but it still exists. When I go to an upscale restaurant, sometimes people just look away. They ignore me, like I'm not there. I've even been ignored by waiters in restaurants.*

© Peter L. Chapman

This is especially true in the South where a lot of Whites still don't want us in their clubs and schools.

A second and more positive level of confirmation is acknowledgment of what another feels, thinks, or says. Nonverbally we acknowledge others by nodding our heads or by making strong eye contact to indicate we are listening. Verbal acknowledgments are direct responses to others' communication. If a friend says, "I'm really worried that I blew the LSAT exam," you could acknowledge that by responding, "So you're scared that you didn't test well on it, huh?" This paraphrasing response acknowledges both the thoughts and the feelings of the other person.

We disconfirm others when we don't acknowledge their feelings or thoughts. For instance, if you respond to your friend's statement about blowing the LSAT by saying, "Want to go out and shoot some darts tonight?" that would be an irrelevant response that ignores the friend's comment. It is also disconfirming when we deny our friend's feelings and communication: "You did fine on the LSAT."

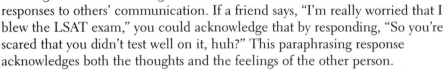

STUDENT VOICES

LORI: *You'd be amazed by how often people refuse to acknowledge what differently abled people say. A hundred times I've been walking across campus and someone has come up and offered to guide me. I tell them I know the way and don't need help, and they still put an arm under my elbow to guide me. I may be blind, but there's nothing wrong with my mind. I know if I need help. Why won't others acknowledge that?*

Lori makes an important point. We shouldn't assume we know what others will perceive as confirming. You may recall that in Chapter 4 we emphasized that we shouldn't presume to speak for others. It is fundamentally disconfirming to be made voiceless when others ignore what we say and think. Especially when we deal with people who differ from us in important ways, we should take time to learn what they perceive as confirming and disconfirming. This idea is illustrated in "Guidelines for Communicating with Persons with Disabilities," which appears on the next page.

The final level of confirmation is endorsement. Endorsement involves accepting another's feelings or thoughts as valid. In the foregoing example, you could endorse by saying, "It's natural to be worried about the LSAT when you have so much riding on it." We disconfirm others when we don't accept their thoughts and feelings. If you respond to the friend by saying, "That's crazy" or "How can you worry about the LSAT when people are starving in Rwanda?" you reject the validity of the expressed feelings.

Guidelines for Communicating with Persons with Disabilities

- When talking with someone who has a disability, speak directly to the person, not to a companion or interpreter.
- When introduced to a person with a disability, offer to shake hands. People who have limited hand use or who have artificial limbs can usually shake.
- When meeting a person with a visual impairment, identify yourself and anyone who is with you. If a person with a visual impairment is part of a group, preface comments to him or her with a name.
- You may offer assistance, but don't provide it unless your offer is accepted. Then ask the person how you can best assist (ask for instructions).
- Treat adults as adults. Don't patronize people in wheelchairs by patting them on the shoulder or head; don't use childish language when speaking to individuals who have no mental disability.
- Respect the personal space of persons with disabilities. It is rude to lean on a wheelchair because that is part of an individual's personal territory.
- Listen mindfully when talking with someone who has difficulty speaking. Don't interrupt or supply words to others. Just be patient and let them finish. Don't pretend to understand if you don't. Instead, explain what you didn't understand and ask the person to respond.
- When you talk with persons who use a wheelchair or crutches, try to position yourself at their eye level and in front of them to allow good eye contact.
- It is appropriate to wave your hand or tap the shoulder of persons with hearing impairments as a way to get their attention. Look directly at the person and speak clearly, slowly, and expressively. Face those who lip-read, place yourself in a good light source, and keep hands, cigarettes, and gum away from your mouth.
- Relax. Don't be afraid to use common expressions such as "See you later" to someone with a visual impairment or "Did you hear the news?" to someone with a hearing difficulty. They're unlikely to be offended and may turn the irony into a joke.

SOURCE: Adapted from AXIS Center for Public Awareness of People with Disabilities, 4550 Indianola Avenue, Columbus, OH 43214.

Endorsement isn't always possible if we are trying to be honest with others. Sometimes we cannot accept what another feels or thinks, so we can't make an endorsing response. Last year, I spent a lot of time with a fifteen-year-old who had a troubling family situation. Bobby and I found many things to do and talk about, and I continuously looked for ways to confirm his worth and his ideas. Gradually, the trust between us grew, and Bobby and I shared more and more personal information. One day he told me that he had tried acid because all of his friends were using it. He also told me he was looking forward to doing acid more in the future. Because I know about the dangers of mind-altering drugs, I couldn't endorse what Bobby had done, and I couldn't support his desire to continue using acid. What I told Bobby was I cared about him, but couldn't approve of this behavior. I informed him of some of the consequences acid can have, of which Bobby was unaware. In this situation, I found it was possible to confirm him as a person without endorsing a particular behavior.

Table 8.2 illustrates the different levels on which confirmation and disconfirmation occur. The most essential confirmation we can give is to recognize another exists. Conversely, the most basic kind of disconfirmation is to deny someone exists. When we don't speak to others or when we look away when they approach us, we disconfirm their existence. We say, "You aren't there." On the second level, we confirm others by acknowledging their ideas and feelings, which carries the relationship-level meaning that they matter to us. In essence, we say "I am paying attention because your feelings and ideas matter to me." We disconfirm others on this level when we communicate that they don't matter to us, that we don't care what they feel or think. The highest form of confirmation is acceptance of others and what they communicate. We feel validated when others accept us as we are and accept what we think and feel. Disconfirmation is not mere disagreement. Disagreements, after all, can be productive and healthy, and they imply that people matter enough to each other to argue.

What is disconfirming is to be told that we or our ideas are crazy, wrong, stupid, or deviant.

WAYNE: *I've gotten a lot of disconfirmation since I came out. When I told my parents I was gay, Mom said, "No, you're not." I told her I was, and she and Dad both said I was just confused, but I wasn't gay. They refuse to acknowledge I'm gay, which means they reject who I am. My older brother isn't any better. His view is that I'm sinful and headed for hell. Now what could be more disconfirming than that?*

When we understand that confirmation is basic for all of us and that it is given or withheld on different levels, we gain insight into relationships. If you think about what we've discussed, you'll probably find that the relationships in which you feel most valued and comfortable are those with a high degree of confirmation.

TABLE 8.2
CONFIRMING AND DISCONFIRMING MESSAGES

	Confirming Messages	**Disconfirming Messages**
Recognition	You exist.	You don't exist.
	"Hello."	Silence
Acknowledgment	You matter to me.	You don't matter.
	We have a relationship.	We are not a team.
	"I'm sorry you're hurt."	"You'll get over it."
Endorsement	What you think is true.	You are wrong.
	What you feel is okay.	You shouldn't feel what you do.
	"I feel the same way."	"Your feeling doesn't make sense."

APPLY THE IDEA
Analyzing Your Relationships

Think about two relationships in your life. One should be a relationship in which you feel good about yourself and safe in the connection. The second relationship should be one in which you feel disregarded or not valued. Identify instances of each level of confirmation in the satisfying relationship and instances of each level of disconfirmation in the unpleasant one. Recognizing confirming and disconfirming communication should give you insight into why these relationships are so different.

Confirming and disconfirming messages are important influences on the climate of personal relationships. In addition, other kinds of communication contribute to the overall feeling of a relationship. We'll now consider specific forms of communication that shape the interpersonal atmosphere between friends and romantic partners.

RELATIONSHIP TIP # 42: TRY TO SEE THE BEAUTY IN LIFE'S LITTLE IRONIES.

SELF-CENTERED? MOI? HOW DO YOU THINK THAT MAKES ME FEEL?

Reprinted by permission of Jennifer Berman.

Defensive and Supportive Climates

Communication researcher Jack Gibb (1961, 1964, 1970) studied the relationship between communication and interpersonal climates. He began by noting that with some people we feel defensive and on guard, so we are unlikely to communicate openly with them. Gibb called these defensive climates. Gibb also noted that with other people we feel supported and comfortable, so we are likely to communicate freely with them. Gibb referred to these as supportive climates. The two kinds of feelings, and the interpersonal climates that foster them, are not typically pure in form. Even in the most healthy and supportive relationships there are usually some defensive moments and some situations in which we don't feel comfortable. Yet, most established relationships have a fairly stable climate.

Gibb believed that the different feelings we have around various people are due largely to communication that promotes feeling defensive or feeling supported. Gibb identified six types of communication that promote defensive climates and six opposite types of communication that foster supportive climates, as shown in Table 8.3.

TABLE 8.3
COMMUNICATION AND CLIMATE

Defensive Communication	Supportive Communication
Evaluation	Description
Certainty	Provisionalism
Strategy	Spontaneity
Control	Problem orientation
Neutrality	Empathy
Superiority	Equality

Evaluation Versus Description　We tend to become defensive when we feel that others are evaluating us. Few of us feel what Gibb called "psychologically safe" when we are the targets of judgments. Other communication researchers report that evaluative communication evokes defensiveness (Eadie, 1982; Stephenson & D'Angelo, 1973). It's not surprising that Wayne in the last commentary felt judged by his family when he told them he was gay. His parents and brother made evaluations—very negative ones of him and of being gay. As we noted in Chapter 6, even positive evaluations can sometimes make us defensive because they carry the relationship meaning that another person feels entitled to judge us. Here are several examples of evaluative statements: "You have no discipline," "It's dumb to feel that way," "You shouldn't have done that," "You did the right thing," "That's a stupid idea."

Descriptive communication doesn't evaluate others or what they think and feel. Instead, it describes behaviors without passing judgment. I-language, which we learned about in Chapter 4, describes what the person speaking feels or thinks, but it doesn't evaluate another (you-language does evaluate). For example, "I wish you hadn't done that" describes your feelings, whereas "You shouldn't have done that" evaluates another's behavior. Descriptive language may also refer to another, but it does so by describing, not evaluating, the other's behavior: "You seem to be sleeping more lately" versus "You're sleeping too much"; "You've lost your temper three times today" versus "Quit flying off the handle"; "You are running late" versus "You shouldn't have kept me waiting."

APPLY THE IDEA
Using Descriptive Language

To develop skill in supportive communication, translate the following evaluative statements into descriptive ones.

EXAMPLE:
Evaluative: This report is poorly done. Descriptive: This report doesn't include background information.

EVALUATIVE

You're lazy. _____

I hate the way you dominate conversations with me. _____

Stop obsessing about the problem. _____

You're too involved. _____

Certainty Versus Provisionalism   Certainty language is absolute and often dogmatic. It suggests there is one and only one answer, valid point of view, or reasonable course of action. Because communication laced with certainty proclaims an absolutely correct position, it slams the door on further discussion. There's no point in talking with people whose minds are made up and who demean any point of view other than theirs. Sometimes certainty is expressed by restating a position over and over, instead of responding to alternate ideas from others (Alexander, 1979).

Perhaps you've been in a conversation with someone who says "I don't want to hear it" or "You can't change my mind" or "I've already figured out what I'm going to do, so just save your breath." These comments reflect certainty and an unwillingness to engage in interaction with others. When confronted with such statements, we're likely to follow the advice and "save our breath." We're also likely to be uninterested in communicating with people who imply that our ideas are wrong because they don't agree with their ideas. "I know what I'm talking about; you don't" is a disconfirming comment that squelches motivation to continue interacting.

One form of certainty communication is **ethnocentrism,** which is the assumption that our culture and its norms are the only right ones. For instance, someone who says "It is just plain rude to call out during a sermon" doesn't understand the meaning of the call–response pattern in African culture. The speaker instead assumes that Western Anglo communication styles are the only correct ones. Dogmatically asserting "It's disrespectful to be late" reveals a lack of awareness of cultures that are less obsessed with speed and efficiency than the United States. Additional examples of certainty statements are "This is the only idea that makes sense," "My mind can't be changed because I'm right," and "Only a fool would vote for that person."

S T U D E N T VOICES

MONIKA: *My father is a classic case of closed-mindedness. He has his ideas and everything else is crazy. I told him I was majoring in communication studies, and he hit the roof. He said there was no future in learning to write speeches, and he told me I should go into business so that I could get a good job. He never even asked me what communication studies is. If he had, I would have told him it's a lot more than speech writing. He starts off sure that he knows everything about whatever is being discussed. He has no interest in other points of view or learning something new. He just locks his mind and throws away the key. We've all learned just to keep our ideas to ourselves around him — there's no communication.*

An alternative to certainty is provisionalism, which communicates openness to other points of view. When we speak provisionally, or tentatively, we suggest we have a point of view, yet our minds aren't sealed. We signal we're willing to consider alternative positions, and this encourages others to voice their ideas. Provisional communication includes statements such as "The way I tend to see the issue is . . . ," "One way to look at this is . . . ," and "Probably what I would do in that situation is . . ." Notice how each of these comments signals that the speaker realizes there could be other positions that are also reasonable. Tentativeness signals an open mind, which is why it invites continued communication.

Strategy Versus Spontaneity   Most of us feel on guard when we think others are manipulating us or being less than upfront about what's on their minds. Defensiveness is a natural response to feeling that others are using strategies in an effort to control us. Strategic communication doesn't allow openness between people, because one person is keeping something from another (Eadie, 1982). An example of strategic communication is this: "Would you do something for me if I told you it really matters?" If the speaker doesn't tell us what we're expected to do, it feels like a setup.

We're also likely to feel that another is trying to manipulate us with a comment such as "Remember when I helped you with your math last term and when I did your chores last week because you were busy?" With a preamble like that, we can smell a trap. We also get defensive when we suspect others of using openness to manipulate how we feel about them. For instance, people who disclose intimate personal information early in a relationship may be trying to win our trust and to trick us into revealing details of our own personal life. Nonverbal behaviors may also convey strategy, as when a person pauses a long time before answering or refuses to look at us when he or she speaks. A sense of deception pollutes the communication climate.

S T U D E N T VOICES

MAJA: *A guy I dated last year was a real con artist, but it took me a while to figure that out. He would look me straight in the eye and tell me he really felt he could trust me. Then he'd say he was going to tell me something he'd never told anyone else in his life, and he'd tell me about fights with his father or how he didn't make the soccer team in high school. The stuff wasn't really that personal, but the way he said it made it seem that way. So I found myself telling him a lot more than I usually disclose and a lot more than I should have. He started using some of the information against me, which was when I started getting wise to him. Later on, I found out he ran through the same song and dance with every girl he dated. It was quite an act!*

Spontaneity is the counterpoint to strategy. Spontaneous communication feels open, honest, and unpremeditated. "I really need your help with this computer glitch" is a more spontaneous comment than "Would you do something for me if I told you it really matters?" Likewise, it is more spontaneous to ask for a favor in a straightforward way ("Would you help me?") than to preface a request with a recitation of all we've done for someone else. Whereas strategic communication comes across as contrived and devious, spontaneous interaction feels authentic and natural.

Control Versus Problem Orientation   Controlling communication is also likely to trigger defensiveness. Similar to strategies, controlling communication more overtly attempts to manipulate others. A common instance of controlling communication is when a person insists her or his solution or preference should prevail. Whether the issue is trivial (what movie to see) or serious (where to locate after college), controllers try to impose their point of view on others. This disconfirms and disrepects others. Defensiveness arises because the relational meaning is that the person exerting control thinks she or he has greater power, rights, or intelligence than others. It's disconfirming to be told our opinions are wrong, our preferences don't matter, or we aren't smart enough to have good ideas. Controlling communication is particularly objectionable when it combines with strategies. For example, a wife who earns a higher salary might say to her husband, "Well, I like the Honda more than the Ford you want, and it's my money that's going to pay for it." The speaker not only pushes her preference, but also tells her husband that she has more power than he does because she makes more money.

PAT: *My roommate freshman year was a real jerk. Her goal in life was to control me and everyone else around her. Sometimes she'd say she felt like going out for dinner and I'd agree and then she'd ask me where I wanted to go. Even if I picked her favorite place, she would insist on going somewhere else. She just had to be in charge. Once I moved things around in the room, and she fussed a lot and moved them back. Later, she moved things the way I had, but then it was her choice. She didn't care about issues or working things through. All she cared about was being in control.*

Problem-oriented communication is less likely than control to generate defensiveness. Rather than imposing a preference, problem-oriented communication focuses on finding answers that satisfy everyone. The goal is to come up with a solution that all parties find acceptable. Here's an example of problem-oriented communication: "It seems that we have really different ideas about how to spend our vacation. Let's talk through what each of us wants and see if there's a way for both of us to have a good vacation." Notice how this statement invites collaboration and emphasizes the goal of meeting both people's needs. According to communication researchers, problem-oriented behaviors tend to reduce conflict and keep lines of communication open (Alexander, 1979; Civickly, Pace, & Krause, 1977).

One of the benefits of problem-oriented communication is that the relationship level of meaning emphasizes the importance of the relationship between communicators. When we convey that we want to collaborate with another person to resolve some mutual problem, we let the other know that we care more about the relationship than getting our own way. In contrast, controlling behaviors aim for one person to triumph over the other, an outcome that undercuts interpersonal harmony.

Neutrality Versus Empathy   Gibb's (1961, 1964, 1970) observations of group interaction revealed that people tend to become defensive when others act in a neutral, or detached, manner. It's easy to understand why we might feel uneasy with people who seem distant and removed, especially if we are talking about personal matters. Research on interview climates indicates that defensiveness arises when an interviewer appears withdrawn and distant (Civickly, Pace, & Krause, 1977). Neutral communication implies a lack of regard and caring for others. Consequently, it disconfirms their worth.

NEL: *My brother never responds to what I say. He listens, but he just gives me nothing back. Sometimes I push him and ask "What do you think?" or "Does what I'm saying make sense to you?" All he does is shrug or say "Whatever." He simply won't show any involvement. So I say, why bother talking to him?*

In contrast to neutrality, expressed empathy confirms the worth of others and our concern for their thoughts and feelings. Empathic communication is illustrated by these examples: "I can understand why you feel that way," "It sounds like you really feel uncomfortable with your job," "You seem to feel very secure in the relationship." Gibb stressed that empathy doesn't necessarily mean agreement; instead, it conveys acceptance of other people and recognition of their perspectives. Especially when we don't agree with others, it's important to communicate that we respect them as persons. Doing so fosters a supportive communication climate, even if differences exist.

Superiority Versus Equality   Like many of the other communication behaviors we've discussed, the final pair of behaviors affecting climate is most pertinent to the relationship level of meaning. Communication that conveys superiority says "I'm better" or "You are inadequate." We feel understandably on guard when talking with people who act as if they are better than we are. When others act as if they are superior to us, it disconfirms our worth by making us feel inadequate in their eyes.

© Steven Peters/Tony Stone Images, Inc.

Consider several messages that convey superiority: "I know a lot more about this than you," "You just don't have my experience," "Is this the best you could do?" "I can't believe you did that," "You really should go to my hairdresser." Each of these messages clearly says "You aren't as good (smart, savvy, competent, attractive) as I am." Predictably, the result is that we protect our self-esteem by defensively shutting out the people and messages that belittle us.

Communication that conveys equality is confirming and fosters a supportive interpersonal climate. We feel more relaxed and comfortable when communicating with people who treat us as equals. At the relationship level of meaning, expressed equality communicates respect and equivalent status between people. This promotes an open, unguarded climate in which interaction flows freely. Communicating equality has less to do with actual skills and abilities, which may differ between people, than with interpersonal attitudes. We can have outstanding experience or ability in certain areas and still show regard for others and what they have to contribute to interaction. Creating a climate of equality allows everyone to be involved without fear of being judged inadequate.

APPLY THE IDEA
Assessing Communication Climate

Use the behaviors we've discussed as a checklist for assessing communication climates. The next time you feel defensive, ask whether others are communicating superiority, control, strategy, certainty, neutrality, or evaluation. Chances are one or more of these are present in communication.

For a communication climate you find supportive and open, check to see whether

FIRST, THE GOOD NEWS: FUTURE DOWNSIZING WILL ONLY BE DONE THROUGH ATTRITION...

1-1
©1997 Washington Post
Writers Group

E-mail: Wileytoon@aol.com
www.washingtonpost.com/wiley
NON SEQUITUR © 1997 Washington Post Writers Group.

CONTINUED

the following behaviors are present: spontaneity, equality, provisionalism, problem orientation, empathy, and description.

To improve defensive climates, try modeling supportive communication. Resist the normal tendencies to respond defensively when a climate feels disconfirming. Instead, focus on being empathic, descriptive, and spontaneous; showing equality and tentativeness; and solving problems.

We've seen that confirmation, which may include recognizing, acknowledging, and endorsing others, is the basis of healthy communication climates. Our discussion of defensive and supportive forms of communication enlightens us about the specific behaviors that tend to make us feel confirmed or disconfirmed. Now that we understand how communication creates interpersonal climates, we're ready to consider guidelines for communicating to create healthy, positive climates for your relationships.

Guidelines for Creating and Sustaining Healthy Climates

We've seen that communication plays a vital role in creating the climate of relationships. To translate what we've learned into pragmatic information, we'll discuss six guidelines for building and sustaining healthy climates.

Actively Use Communication to Shape Climates

The first principle is to use what you've learned in this chapter to enhance climates in your relationships. Now that you know what generates defensive and supportive climates, you can monitor your communication to make sure it contributes to open, positive interaction. You can identify and stifle disconfirming patterns of talk such as evaluation and superiority. In addition, you can actively work to use supportive communication such as problem orientation and tentativeness.

Active management of communication climate also involves accepting and growing from the tension generated by relational dialectics. Although friction between contradictory needs can naturally make us uncomfortable, we should recognize its constructive potential. Communication scholars who have studied dialectics point out that such tension can generate growth and change in relationships (Baxter, 1990, 1993; Wood et al., 1994).

The discomfort of tension pushes us to transform our relationships by changing the dynamics in them. When a couple feels bored, they are motivated to inject novelty into their relationship; when there is too much innovation, they

© Rhoda Sidney/PhotoEdit

crave rituals and find ways to increase predictability. Our growth as individuals and as
partners in relationships depends on honoring
our needs for both autonomy and connection,
both novelty and routine, and both openness
and closedness. When any of these needs is
not met, we experience tension that leads to
change. Thus, the friction of dialectics keeps
us aware of our multiple needs and the importance of fulfilling each of them.

Accept and Confirm Others

Throughout this chapter, we've seen that confirmation is an ethical cornerstone of healthy climates and fulfilling relationships. Although we can understand how important it is, it isn't always easy to give confirmation. Sometimes
we disagree with others or don't like certain things they do. Being honest
with others is important because it enhances trust between people. Communication research indicates that, in fact, people expect real friends to be
sources of honest feedback, even if it isn't always pleasant to hear (Rawlins,
1994). This implies we should express honest misgivings about our friends'
behaviors or other aspects of their identity. False friends tell us only what we
want to hear. Deceit, no matter how well intentioned, diminishes personal
growth and trust between people. We can offer honest feedback within a
context that assures others we value and respect them, as Houston's commentary explains.

S T U D E N T   VOICES

HOUSTON: *The best thing my friend Jack ever did for me was to light into
me about experimenting with drugs. He told me it was stupid to
play with my mind and to risk my health just for kicks, and he kept at me until I
tapered off. What made it work was that Jack was clear that he thought too much
of me to stand by when I was hurting myself. A lot of my other so-called friends
just stood by and said nothing. Jack is the only one who was a real friend.*

It can be difficult to accept and affirm others when we find their needs tax-
ing or discover conflicts between our preferences and those of others. It's not
unusual for one partner to desire more closeness than another or for partners to
differ in the paths they travel to achieve closeness. These are common problems, and partners need to discuss them in order to work out mutually agree-
able solutions.

For a relationship to work, both partners must be confirmed. Confirmation
begins with accepting others and the validity of their needs and preferences.
This doesn't mean that you feel the same way or that you defer your own

I HAVE TROUBLE ASSERTING MYSELF.

BE QUIET, I'M TRYING TO SLEEP.

PIRARO ©DAN PIRARO 1996. DIST. BY UNIVERSAL PRESS SYND. WWW.VPGI.COM/BIZARRO 10-23

BIZARRO © 1996 by Dan Piraro 1996. Reprinted with permission of Universal Press Syndicates.

needs. Instead, the point is to recognize and respect others' needs just as you wish them to respect yours. Dual perspective is a primary tool for accepting others because it calls on us to consider them on their own terms. Although intimate talk may be what makes you feel closest to your partner, your partner may experience greater closeness by doing things together. To meet both of your needs, you could take turns honoring each other's preferred paths to closeness. Alternatively, you might combine the two styles of intimacy by doing things together that invite conversation. For example, backpacking is an activity in which talking naturally occurs.

Affirm and Assert Yourself

It is just as important to affirm and accept yourself as to do that for others. You are no less valuable; your needs are no less important; your preferences are no less valid. It is a misunderstanding to think interpersonal communication principles we've discussed concern only how we behave toward others. Equally, they pertain to how we should treat ourselves. Thus, the principle of confirming people's worth applies just as much to yourself. Likewise, we should respect and honor both our own and others' needs, preferences, and ways of creating intimacy.

Although we can't always meet the needs of all parties in relationships, it is possible to give voice to everyone, including yourself. If your partner favors greater autonomy than you do, you need to recognize that preference and also assert your own. If you don't express your feelings, there's no way others can confirm you. Thus, you should assert your feelings and preferences while simultaneously honoring different ones in others.

STUDENT VOICES

LAQUANDA: *It took me a long time to learn to look out for myself as well as I look out for others. I was always taught to put others first, probably because I'm a girl. I mean neither of my brothers had that drilled into them. But I did, and for years I would just muffle my needs and whatever I wanted. I concentrated on pleasing others. I thought I was taking care of relationships, but really I was hurting them, because I felt neglected and I resented that. What I'm working on now is learning to take care of myself and others at the same time.*

Unlike aggression, assertion doesn't involve putting your needs above those of others. At the same time, assertion doesn't subordinate your needs to those of others, as does deference. **Assertion** is a matter of clearly and nonjudgmentally stating what you feel, need, or want (see Table 8.4). This should be done without disparaging others and what they want. You should simply make your feelings known in an open, descriptive manner.

TABLE 8.4

AGGRESSION, ASSERTION, AND DEFERENCE

Aggressive	Assertive	Deference
We're going to spend time together.	I'd like to create more time for us.	It's okay with me not to spend time with each other.
Tell me what you're feeling; I insist.	I would like to understand more of how you feel.	If you don't want to talk about how you feel, okay.
I don't care what you want; I'm not going to a movie.	I'm really not up for a movie tonight.	It's fine with me to go to a movie if you want to.

Because relationships include more than one person, they must involve acceptance and affirmation of more than one. Good relationships develop when partners understand and respect each other. The first requirement for this to happen is for each person to communicate honestly how she or he thinks and feels and what she or he wants and needs. A second requirement is for each person to communicate respect for the other's feelings and needs.

APPLY THE IDEA

Communicating Assertively

The statements below are deferential or aggressive. Revise each one so that it is assertive.

1. I guess your preference for going to the party is more important than my studying.
2. I don't need your permission to go out. I'll do what I please.
3. I suppose I could work extra next week if you really need a loan.
4. I don't like it when you spend time with Tim. Either stop seeing him or we're through.

We should remember that the meaning of assertion varies among different cultures. For instance, openly asserting your own ideas is considered disrespectful in Korea and parts of China. Even if Koreans or Chinese don't want to do something, they seldom directly turn down another's request. Thus, people with diverse cultural backgrounds may have different ways of affirming and asserting themselves. To communicate effectively with others, we need to learn how they affirm themselves and how they express their feelings directly or indirectly.

We can tolerate sometimes not getting what we want without feeling personally devalued. However, it is far more disconfirming to have our needs go unacknowledged. Even when partners disagree or have conflicting needs, each person can state his or her feelings and express awareness of the other's perspective. Usually there are ways to acknowledge both viewpoints, as Eleanor illustrates.

ELEANOR: *About a year after George and I married, he was offered a promotion if he'd move to Virginia. We were living in Pennsylvania at the time, and that's where our families and friends were. I didn't want to move, because I was rooted with my people, but we could both see how important the move was to George's career. The week before we moved, George gave me the greatest present of our lives. He handed me two tickets—one for a round-trip flight from Virginia to Pennsylvania so that I could visit my family, and a second ticket he'd gotten for my best friend so that she could visit me after we moved. I felt he really understood me and had found a way to take care of my needs. I still have the ticket stubs in my box of special memories.*

Self-Disclose When Appropriate

As we noted earlier, self-disclosure allows people to know each other in greater depth. For this reason, it's an important communication skill, especially in the early stages of relationships. Research indicates that appropriate self-disclosure tends to increase trust and feelings of closeness (Cosby, 1973). In addition, self-disclosure can enhance self-esteem and security in relationships because we feel that others accept the most private parts of us. Finally, self-disclosure is an important way to learn about ourselves. As we reveal our hopes, fears, dreams, and feelings, we get responses from others that give us new perspectives on who we are. In addition, we gain insight into ourselves by seeing how we interact with others in new situations.

Although self-disclosure has many potential values, it is not always advisable. As we have seen, self-disclosure necessarily involves risks—the risk that others will not accept what we reveal or that they might use it against us. Appropriate self-disclosure minimizes these risks by proceeding slowly and in climates where sufficient trust has been proved. It's wise to test the waters gradually before plunging into major self-disclosures. Begin by revealing information that is personal but not highly intimate or able to damage you if exploited. Before disclosing further, observe how the other person responds to your communication and what she or he does with it. You might also pay attention to whether the other person reciprocates by disclosing personal information to you. Because self-disclosures involve risk, we need to be cautious about when and to whom we reveal ourselves. When trust exists and we want to intensify a relationship, self-disclosure is one of many communication practices that can be healthy. Table 8.5 lists key benefits and risks of self-disclosing communication.

TABLE 8.5
BENEFITS AND RISKS OF SELF-DISCLOSING COMMUNICATION

Benefits	Risks
May increase trust	Others may reject us
May increase closeness	Others may think less of us
May enhance self-esteem	Others may violate our confidences
May increase security	
May enhance self-growth	

A number of years ago, Joseph Luft and Harry Ingham created a model of different sorts of knowledge that affect self-development. They called the model the Johari Window (Figure 8.2), which is a combination of their first names, Joe and Harry.

Four types of information are relevant to the self. Open, or public, information is known to both us and others. Your name, height, major, and tastes in music are probably free information that you share easily with others. The blind area contains information that others know about us, but we don't know about ourselves. For example, others may see that we are insecure even though we think we've hidden that well. Others may also recognize needs or feelings that we've not acknowledged to ourselves. The third area includes hidden information, which we know about ourselves but choose not to reveal to most others. You might not tell many people about your vulnerabilities or about traumas in your past because you consider this private information. The unknown area is made up of information about ourselves that neither we nor others know. This consists of your untapped resources, your untried talents, and your reactions to experiences you've never had. You don't know how you will manage a crisis until you've been in one, and you can't tell what kind of parent you would be unless you've had a child.

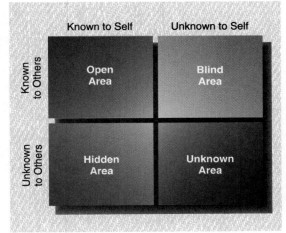

FIGURE 8.2
The Johari Window

Because a healthy self-concept requires knowledge of ourselves, it's important to gain access to information in our blind and unknown areas. One way to do this is to expand our experiences by entering unfamiliar situations, trying novel things, and experimenting with new kinds of communication. Another way to increase self-knowledge is to interact with others to learn how they see us. We can gain insight into ourselves by reflecting on their perceptions. Others are likely to offer us insights into ourselves only if we make it safe for them to do so. If a friend states a perception of you that you dislike and you become defensive, the friend may not risk sharing other perceptions in the future. If we learn to respond nondefensively to others' perceptions of us, including criticism, then we pave the way for honest appraisals from them.

Respect Diversity in Relationships

Just as individuals differ, so do relationships. There is tremendous variety in what people find comfortable, affirming, and satisfying in interpersonal interaction. It's counterproductive to try to force all people and relationships to fit into a single mode. For example, you might have one friend who enjoys a lot of verbal disclosure and another who prefers less. There's no reason to try to persuade the first friend to disclose less or the second one to be more revealing. Similarly, you may be comfortable with greater closeness in some of your relationships and more autonomy in others. The differences between people create a rich diversity of relationships we can experience.

S T U D E N T   VOICES

DORZIUS: *Communication has a lot to do with climate in work relationships too. When I first came here from Haiti, I had many job interviews. People would say to me, "We've never hired one of you," like Haitians are not normal people. They also would say I would have to work hard and was I ready to do that, which told me they assumed I was lazy. When I did get a job, my supervisor watched me much more closely than he watched nonforeign workers. He was always judging.*

Even a single relationship varies over time, and we should accept this as normal. Because dialectics generate constant tension, partners continuously shift their patterns and ways of honoring contradictory needs. It's natural to want more closeness at some times and more distance at others in the life of a relationship. It's also advisable to experiment with different responses to dialectical tensions. You may find it's effective to compromise between closeness and autonomy and to satisfy your desire for openness by sharing certain topics while meeting your need for privacy by not discussing other topics.

Because people and relationships are diverse, we should strive to respect a range of communicative choices and relationship patterns. In addition, we should be cautious about imposing our meaning on others' communication. People from various cultures, including ones within the United States, have learned different communication styles. What Westerners consider openness and healthy self-disclosure may feel offensively intrusive to people from some Asian societies. The dramatic, assertive speaking style of many African Americans can be misinterpreted as abrasive from a Western Caucasian perspective. The best way to understand what others' behavior means is to ask. This conveys the relational message that they matter to you, and it allows you to gain insight into the interesting diversity around us.

Respond to Others' Criticism Constructively

A sixth guideline is to learn to respond effectively when others offer constructive criticism. Sometimes others communicate criticism in language that fosters defensiveness: "You are so inconsiderate!" "You're selfish." We tend to react defensively to such judgmental language, and we may dismiss the criticism—think that it isn't true—or just think the other person is being mean. These are natural and understandable responses, but they aren't necessarily constructive ways to deal with criticism. The problem with denying or dismissing criticism is that it deprives us of a chance to learn more about how others see us and to reevaluate our own actions. Refusing to acknowledge others' criticism is also likely to erect barriers in relationships.

© Gary A. Conner/PhotoEdit

A better response to criticism is to begin by seeking more information: "What do you mean I'm inconsiderate?" "What do I do that you see as selfish?" Asking these questions allows you to get concrete information. Remember that others may not have your understanding of how to communicate effectively. Thus, they may use abstract terms that you can help them translate into specifics to be addressed. They may also use you-language ("You hurt me") that you can explore to determine if there is something that you do to which they respond by feeling hurt.

A second step in responding constructively to criticism is to consider it thoughtfully. Is the criticism valid? Are you inconsiderate in some ways? Are you selfish in some respects? If after reflection you don't think the criticism is accurate, offer your interpretation of the behaviors the other perceived as inconsiderate or selfish. You might say, "I can see how you might feel it's selfish of me to go out with my friends so often, but to me it's because I care about them, just like I spend time with you because I care about you." Or you might say, "I can see where it would seem inconsiderate that I didn't call, but the battery on my cell phone was dead and I didn't want to delay getting here by stopping to call. I wanted to be with you as soon as possible." Notice that both of these responses not only offer an alternative interpretation of particular behavior but also affirm the other person and his or her worth to you.

If you decide that the criticism is valid, then consider whether you want to change how you act. Do you want to be perceived by others as inconsiderate or selfish? If not, you can choose to change how you act. For suggestions on how to bring about changes in yourself, you may want to review the guidelines offered at the end of Chapter 2.

PEANUTS Reprinted by permission of United Feature Syndicate, Inc.

BETSY: *I didn't appreciate it when my roommate called me a slob. But because of what I've learned in this course, I didn't just ignore what Marie said or fire back an insult to her. Instead, I asked her what she meant. She told me she hated coming home to our apartment and finding my clothes on the bathroom floor and dishes in the sink. Well, I could deal with that. So I resolved to pick my clothes up and wash my dishes before I left each day. Before if this had happened, I would have felt hurt and probably wouldn't have done anything different. But I felt less hurt and more in control because of how I responded to Marie's criticism, and I know she's a lot happier living with me now!*

A final suggestion is to thank the person who offered the criticism. At first, this may seem absurd. After all, criticism doesn't feel good, so it's hard to be grateful. But on second thought, you may realize that criticism is a gift. It offers us opportunities to see ourselves through others' eyes. In addition, it gives us insight into how others feel about us and what we do. Both of these effects of criticism can foster personal growth and healthy relationships that allow honest expression of feelings. Even if we disagree with a criticism, we should let others know we are glad they shared their perceptions of us. This keeps the door open for communication in the future.

The guidelines we've discussed combine respect for self, others, and relationships with communication that fosters healthy, affirming climates for connections with others. We can transform our relationships when we take responsibility for shaping interpersonal climates and when we develop the knowledge and communication skills to do so.

CHAPTER
Summary

In this chapter, we've explored personal relationships and the communication climates that make them more or less satisfying. Four elements of healthy interpersonal connections are investment, commitment, trust, and comfort with relational dialectics. Even though love is important for intimacy, it alone is insufficient. To it we must add personal choices to invest ourselves, make enduring commitments to remain with others even in hard times, develop trust, and learn to manage the ongoing dialectical tensions that promote change and growth.

Perhaps the most basic requirement for healthy communication climates is confirmation. Each of us wants to feel valued, especially by those for whom we care most deeply. When partners recognize, acknowledge, and endorse each other, they give the important gift of confirmation. They communicate "You matter to me." We discussed particular kinds of communication that foster supportive and defensive climates in relationships. Defensiveness is bred by evaluation, certainty, superiority, strategies, control, and neutrality. More supportive climates arise from communication that is

descriptive, provisional, equal, spontaneous, empathic, and problem-oriented.

To close the chapter, we considered six guidelines for building healthy communication climates. The first one is to assume responsibility for communicating in ways that actively enhance the mood of a relationship. Second, we should accept and confirm our friends and romantic partners, communicating that we respect them, even though we may not always agree with them or feel the same as they do. The third guideline is a companion to the second one: We should accept and confirm ourselves just as fully as we do others. Each of us is entitled to assert our own thoughts, feelings, and needs. Doing so allows us to honor ourselves and to help our partners understand us. A fourth guideline is to self-disclose when appropriate so that we increase our security in relationships and add to the information we have about ourselves. Fifth, we should realize that diversity in relationships is a source of personal and interpersonal growth. People vary widely, as do the relationship patterns and forms they prefer. By respecting differences among us, we all expand our insights into the fascinating array of ways that humans form and sustain intimate relations. Finally, personal growth and healthy relationships are fostered by dealing constructively with criticism.

In the next three chapters, we'll look in greater detail at personal relationships. Chapter 9 extends our discussion of climate by examining how we can create constructive relationship contexts for dealing effectively with conflict. Chapter 10 discusses friendships, and Chapter 11 considers romantic relationships. In each chapter, we consider what these relationships are, how communication affects them, and how we might cope with some of the inevitable problems and challenges of sustaining close relationships over time. What we have learned about climate, as well as what we've learned about other facets of interpersonal communication in earlier chapters, will serve as a foundation for a more in-depth look at the dynamics of close relationships.

K E Y
Concepts

- assertion
- commitment
- ethnocentrism

- interpersonal climate
- investment
- relational dialectics

- self-disclosure
- trust

F O R   F U R T H E R
Thought & Discussion

1. Have you found it difficult to confirm others when you disagree with them? If so, does reading this chapter help you distinguish among recognition, acknowledgement, and endorsement? Can you distinguish between confirming others as persons and endorsing particular ideas or behaviors?

2. What ethical principles are implied in communication that confirm and disconfirm others? Is it wrong to disconfirm others? All others? Intimates?

3. To what extent do you honor yourself and others in communication situations? Do you give equal attention to both your needs and those of others? If not, focus on balancing your efforts to confirm yourself and others in future interactions.

4. Think of an interaction in which you felt disconfirmed and defensive. Describe how others in the situation communicated toward you. How many of Gibb's defensive-producing communication behaviors can you identify as present in the situation?

5. How often are you deferential, assertive, and aggressive in your communication? What are the situations and relationships in which each kind of behavior is most likely for you? Do the behaviors you select advance your own goals and your relationships?

6. Use your *InfoTrac College Edition* to locate recent reports on assertion. How do researchers define assertion? Do they advocate any guidelines for when assertiveness is appropriate and inappropriate?

7. Practice following the guidelines in this chapter for responding to criticism. What happens when you listen to criticism without becoming angry and when you let others know you appreciate their perceptions of you and your behavior?

Managing

Conflict

in Relationships

DAVE: You really made me angry when you flirted with other guys at the party last night.

PAM: Yeah, well you made me angry that you didn't know when to stop drinking.

DAVE: Well, maybe I was drinking a lot because my girlfriend was too busy dancing with other guys to pay any attention to me.

PAM: Well, maybe I'd pay more attention to you if you'd clean up your act. Why don't you get serious about graduate school and start acting responsible?

DAVE: I'll do that right after you quit smoking and spend some time with me instead of always burying yourself in readings for your classes.

PAM: You just say that because you're jealous that I'm in a graduate program and you're not.

DAVE: I wouldn't exactly call social work much of a graduate program.

PAM: At least it's *a* graduate program. That's more than you have.

DAVE: You never do anything but complain, complain, complain. You really are a drag.

PAM: It takes one to know one.

Clearly Dave and Pam are having trouble. The real problem isn't the issues they're discussing, but how they manage conflict. Dave and Pam are not communicating constructively. What we've learned in previous chapters helps us understand how negative communication fuels discord between them. For example, Dave launched the conversation with you-language. Instead of owning his anger, he blamed Pam for it. In turn, she didn't own her anger. Dave may also have misidentified what he was feeling. Is he really feeling angry at Pam, or is he hurt that she spent more time with others than him? Both Dave and Pam disconfirmed the other with personal attacks. Further, neither of them really recognized and acknowledged the other's point of view. Each of them listened defensively and engaged in ambushing the other. Pam and Dave pursued their individual agendas and failed to connect with each other. The result is that Pam and Dave clash. Their argument did nothing for either of them or the relationship.

Let's start the conversation over and see how more positive communication might improve what happens.

DAVE: I felt hurt when you flirted with other guys at the party last night, and then I felt angry. [*Dave identifies hurt as the more basic feeling. He also owns his feelings.*]

PAM: I can understand that. I know you don't like for me to pay attention to other men. [*She acknowledges Dave's feelings.*] I got upset when you drank too much, and I want you to understand how I feel about that. [*Pam owns her feelings and asserts her needs in the situation.*]

DAVE: You're right. I know you hate it when I drink a lot. [*He acknowledges and endorses her concern.*]

PAM: Well, I guess neither of us was at our best last night. [*She shares responsibility for what happened.*] I was really tired, so I probably got more irritated than I usually would.

© Bob Daemmrich/The Image Works

DAVE: And I've been feeling kind of down because you're so focused on your graduate program, and I can't seem to get started. *[Because an affirming climate has been created, Dave can disclose his deeper worries to Pam.]*

PAM: I know you feel discouraged right now. *[She again acknowledges his feelings.]* I would too. *[She shows empathy.]* But you're so smart, and you'll do great once you settle on a course of action. *[She confirms him by showing that she believes in him.]* Why don't we put our heads together to sort through some of the options and try to figure out how you can proceed. *[She offers support and shows commitment to his welfare.]*

DAVE: That would really help me. I just need to talk through a lot of possibilities. *[He acknowledges her offer of help.]* I'd really like to get your perspective on some ideas I've got. *[He shows he values her viewpoint.]*

PAM: I've got all the time you want. *[She confirms his value and her commitment to the relationship. Her comment also addresses Dave's relationship-level concern that she may not want to spend time with him.]*

DAVE: (smile) Okay, and I promise I won't drink while we're talking. *[He uses humor to restore good climate. On the relationship-level of meaning, he is asking "Are we okay now?"]*

PAM: (smile) And I promise I won't flirt with other guys while we're talking. *[She responds to his relationship-level message by signaling that she too feels friendly again.]*

The conflict proceeded very differently in the second instance. Both Pam and Dave owned their feelings and confirmed each other by acknowledging expressed concerns. The supportive climate they established enabled Dave to reveal deeper worries that lay below his opening complaint about flirting, and Pam responded supportively to his disclosure. They also came up with a plan to address Dave's worries. Especially important, they communicated effectively at the relationship level of meaning. The relationship probably will be strengthened by how they managed their conflict in the second scenario.

Not all conflicts can be turned around as effectively as this one. There is no magic bullet for handling conflict constructively. Even skillful communication is not a remedy for all of the tensions that come up in relationships. However, communication is one of the most important influences on how conflict affects relationships. Skillful speaking and listening help us manage conflict, regardless of the difficulties we face. Research shows that communication problems contribute to dissatisfaction with relationships and breakups (Dindia & Fitzpatrick, 1985). We also know that positive communication is one of the strongest influences on long-term satisfaction (Markman, 1981). Communication powerfully sculpts conflict and its consequences.

In this chapter, we'll explore how communication and conflict weave together in interpersonal relationships. We'll begin by defining conflict. Next, we'll consider principles of conflict so that we understand what it is and the roles it plays in our relationships. Third, we'll consider basic orientations to conflict and the ways in which individuals' approaches to conflict are shaped by their membership in various social groups. The fourth section of the chapter focuses on specific communication patterns that enhance or impede constructive management of conflict. We'll conclude by identifying guidelines for communicating effectively when engaging in conflict.

Defining Conflict

We've all experienced conflict in our relationships, so we have a general idea of what it is. Yet, our general ideas may not help us zero in on what conflict involves and how it operates in relationships. A clear definition of **conflict** is that it exists when individuals who depend on each other express different views, interests, or goals and perceive their views as incompatible or oppositional. We'll look more closely at each part of this definition.

Expressed Disagreement

Conflict is expressed disagreement, struggle, or discord. Thus, it is not conflict if we don't recognize disagreement or anger or if we repress it completely so that it is not expressed at all. Conflict involves some means of expressing disagreements or tensions.

We express disagreement both verbally and nonverbally. Shooting daggers with your eyes communicates anger and discord every bit as clearly as saying "I'm angry with you." Walking out on a conversation and slamming a door express hostility, as does refusing to talk to someone. Often we express conflict with both verbal and nonverbal communication. For instance, you might shout, "I'm so angry with you" while slamming your fist on a desk. The verbal communication—the words themselves—states the anger, while the nonverbal communication—volume and kinesics—emphasize the extent of the anger.

Although all conflict is expressed, *how* it is expressed varies. Some means of expressing disagreement are overt, such as saying "I'm furious with you." Other modes of communicating conflict are more covert, such as deliberately not answering the phone because you don't want to talk to someone. In both cases, the individuals realize they have differences and they both express their disagreeements, although in distinct ways.

Interdependence

Conflict can occur only between people who depend on each other. Differences don't have to be resolved between people who don't affect each other. I have no stake in my neighbors' yard, and they don't need my approval to landscape as they wish. My in-laws and I have differing preferences about dogs, but those preferences don't interfere with our relationship as long as we each leave our dog home when we visit. Because I am not dependent on my in-laws or my neighbors on matters of dogs and landscaping, we don't have conflicts over these issues.

Conflict occurs because people depend on each other and need each other's agreement or approval. If Robbie and I disagreed on pets, then there might be conflict because we live together and our pets affect both of us. Two friends who have agreed to spend the evening together could have conflict if they disagreed on what to do or which film to see. Couples often experience disagreements about money. If one person wants to save money or pay off bills and the other wants to splurge on a vacation, conflict is likely to arise.

We may disagree with others and even make negative judgments of them, but that alone doesn't mean conflict will occur. Conflict exists only when it is expressed by individuals who affect one another. Lenore, a twenty-year-old student, explains that conflict assumes connection.

S   T   U   D   E   N   T   VOICES

LENORE: *It's kind of strange, but you really don't fight with people who don't matter. With a lot of guys I dated, if I didn't like something they did, I'd just let it go because they weren't important enough for the hassle. But Rod and I argue a lot, because we do affect each other. Maybe fighting is a sign that people care about each other.*

Opposition

Conflict is more than just having differences. We disagree with many people about many things, but this doesn't invariably lead to conflict. For example, I don't like the way my neighbors landscaped their yard, my in-laws don't like large dogs like our Labrador, and Robbie and I don't see eye to eye on art and furniture for our home. None of these disagreements, however, sparks conflict: I realize that my neighbors have a right to fix their yard as they please; my in-laws tolerate our Labrador, and we accept their Boston bulldog; and Robbie and I long ago decided that each of us could be in charge of decorating certain rooms in the house, and we take turns on decisions for the remaining rooms. In these cases, the disagreements don't result in opposition.

Conflict involves opposition, which is a tension between goals, preferences, or decisions that are perceived as incompatible. In other words, conflict involves two perceptions: (1) the perception that our concerns are at odds with those of another and (2) the perception that we and another must reconcile our differences. When those two perceptions exist, so does conflict.

Principles of Conflict

Many people fear conflict and view it as negative. That is a misunderstanding of what conflict is and how it operates. To address that and other misunderstandings, we'll discuss four principles of conflict.

Conflict Is a Natural Process in All Relationships

Conflict is a normal, inevitable part of all interpersonal relationships. When people matter to each other and affect each other, disagreements are unavoidable. You like meat, and your friend is a strict vegetarian. You prefer to rent a condo and avoid the hassles of home ownership, but your mate's fondest dream is to own a home. You like to work alone, and your co-worker likes to interact on teams. You believe money should be enjoyed, and your partner lives by the philosophy of saving for a rainy day. You want to move where there's a great job for you, but the location has no career prospects for your partner. You prefer to bring work home rather than staying late at the office, but your partner resents it when you work at home. Again and again, we find ourselves seemingly at odds with people who matter to us. When this happens, we have to resolve the differences, preferably in a way that doesn't harm the relationship.

The presence of conflict does not indicate a relationship is unhealthy or in trouble, although how partners manage conflict does influence relational health. Actually, conflict indicates that individuals are involved with each other. If they weren't, there would be no need to resolve differences. This is a good point to keep in mind when conflicts arise because it reminds us that a strong connection underlies even disagreement.

S T U D E N T   VOICES

RON: *It sounds funny, but the biggest thing my fiancée and I fight about is whether it's okay to fight. I was brought up not to argue and to think that conflict is bad. In her family, people did argue a lot, and she thinks it is healthy. What I'm coming to realize is that there is a lot of conflict in my family but it's hidden, so it never gets dealt with very well. I've seen her and her parents really go at it, but, I have to admit, they work through their differences and people in my family don't.*

Ron's insight is important. He has realized that conflict is an undercurrent in his family, but it remains unresolved because people won't discuss tensions. Most of us have attitudes about conflict that reflect scripts we learned in our families. Like Ron, some of us were taught that conflict is bad and should be avoided whereas others learned that airing differences is healthy.

APPLY THE IDEA
Understanding Your Conflict Script

What conflict script did you learn in your family? Think back to your childhood and adolescence and try to remember what implicit rules for conflict your family modeled and perhaps taught.

- Did people disagree openly with each other?
- What was said when disagreements surfaced? Did your parents suggest it was rude or bad manners to argue? Did they encourage open discussion of differences?

- How do you currently reflect your family's conflict script? Now that you can edit family scripts and author your own, how would you like to deal with conflict?

Read on in this chapter to consider ways you might write a conflict script that is constructive and reflects your values.

Although conflict itself is inevitable, how we manage it is not. We can deal with differences more or less effectively, and our choices have personal and relational impact.

Conflict May Be Overt or Covert

When we defined conflict, we noted that disagreement could be expressed either overtly or covertly. We'll now elaborate that point. Overt conflict is out in the open and explicit. It exists when individuals deal with their differences in a straightforward manner. They might calmly discuss their disagreement, intensely argue about ideas, or engage in a shouting match. Overt conflict may also involve physical attacks, although of course that's not recommended!

Yet, much conflict isn't overt. Covert conflict is hidden and often unacknowledged. It exists when partners camouflage disagreements and express their feelings indirectly. When angry, a person may deliberately do something to hurt or upset a partner. For instance, Janet is annoyed because her roommate Myra has cleaned up Janet's half of the apartment, so when Myra is studying, Janet turns the stereo on at high volume. Knowing that Elliott hates to be kept waiting, his wife intentionally arrives 20 minutes late for a dinner date. These individuals expressed their anger indirectly and conflict was covert.

One common form of covert conflict is **passive aggression,** which is aggression that is denied or disguised by the aggressor. This allows someone who is angry to vent the anger while also denying that she or he is doing so. If Dedra doesn't call her mother every week, her mother forgets to send Dedra a check for spending money. When Eloise has obnoxious customers at the restaurant where she waits tables, she accidentally spills something on them. When Arlene won't forgo studying to go out, Clem coincidentally decides to call friends and talk to them in the room adjacent to Arlene. Passive aggressive behaviors are efforts to punish another person without accepting responsibility for the punishment. They undercut the possibility of honest, healthy relationships.

S   T   U   D   E   N   T   VOICES

STACI: *I was recently in a relationship that I thought was the greatest ever strictly because we never fought. I've had relationships with lots of arguments, so I thought it was fabulous that Steve and I never fought. I grew up with a twice-divorced mom, and I've seen her and my father and stepfather really go at it. All I ever wanted was a conflict-free relationship because I thought that would be a good relationship. One time Steve called me to say he had to break our date to cover at work for another guy. All I did was sigh and say, "Fine, if* *that is what you need to do." But it wasn't fine with me; I resented his putting the other guy ahead of me. A little later he called me back to say he'd changed his mind and would join me and two friends of ours. So, what happened? He sat at the table all night and barely said two words. I was so mad, but I didn't say a word about the evening and neither did he. Just a month later we broke up. Even then, there was no overt conflict.*

Much covert conflict takes place in **games,** which Eric Berne (1964) catalogued in a fascinating book titled *Games People Play.* Games often involve passive aggression, but they can be much more complicated than that. According to Berne, games are highly patterned interactions in which the real conflicts are hidden or denied and a counterfeit excuse is created for arguing or criticizing. In addition to being highly patterned, games also require two players if they are to continue. In contrast, passive aggression doesn't require significant cooperation from the target of aggression.

The nature of games will become clear if we analyze a few. In a game called "Blemish," one person pretends to be complimentary but actually puts another down. If Ann asks her friend if she looks okay for an important interview, the friend could respond, "Gee, you look really great with the new suit and hair style. There's just this one little thing. You seem to be kind of overweight lately. Your stomach and hips look big, and that suit doesn't hide the extra pounds." The friend is playing "Blemish" because she focuses on one thing that is wrong and downplays all that is right. Her unexpressed anger or resentment surfaces covertly.

Another game is "NIGYYSOB" ("Now I've Got You, You Son of a Bitch"). In this one, an individual deliberately sets another person up for a fall. Knowing that her husband has poor taste in furniture, Nina asks him to pick out a new chair for their home. When it arrives and predictably is ugly, Nina criticizes her husband. She worked to find a way to make him fail and then pounced on him when he did. Another game is "Mine Is Worse than Yours." Suppose you tell a friend that you are overloaded with two tests and a paper due next week, and your friend says, "You think that's bad? Listen to this: I have two tests, three papers, and an oral report all due in the next two weeks." Your friend expressed no concern for your plight; rather, he told you that his situation is worse. In this game, people try to monopolize rather than listening and responding to each other.

S T U D E N T   V O I C E S

CHUCK: *My parents specialize in games. Dad likes to set Mom up by asking her to take care of some financial business or get the car fixed. Then he explodes about what she does. I think he is just trying to find excuses for blessing her out. Mom also plays games. Her favorite is Blemish. She always finds something wrong with an idea or a paper I've written or a vacation or whatever. Then she just harps and harps on the defect. Sometimes being around them is like being in a mine field.*

"Yes, but" is a game in which a person pretends to be asking for help but then refuses all help that's offered. Doing this allows the player to make the other person feel inadequate for being unable to help. Lorna asks her boyfriend to help her figure out how to better manage her money. When he suggests she should spend less, Lorna says, "Yes, but I don't buy anything I don't need." When he suggests she might work extra hours at her job, she responds, "Yes, but that would cut into my free time." When he mentions she could get a job that pays more per hour, Lorna says, "Yes, but I really like the people where I work now." When he points out that she could save a lot by packing lunches instead of buying them, she replies, "Yes, but I'd have to get up earlier." "Yes, but" continues until the person trying to help finally gives up in defeat. Then the initiator of the game can complain "You didn't help me."

Games and passive aggression are ineffective ways to manage conflict. Both approaches are dishonest, because they camouflage the real issues behind counterfeit communication. As long as conflict remains hidden or disguised, it's virtually impossible for friends and romantic partners to resolve the real problems.

APPLY THE IDEA
Identifying Games in Your Communication

Apply what you've read about covert conflict to your own life. Describe an example of when you or someone you have a relationship with played each of these games:

Blemish _____

NIGYYSOB _____

Mine Is Worse than Yours _____

Yes, but _____

What was accomplished by playing the game? Were the real conflicts addressed?

Conflict May Be Managed Well or Poorly

The third principle is that conflict may be managed more or less constructively. Because conflict is natural and inevitable, we need to learn to deal with it in ways that benefit us as individuals and our relationships. People respond to conflict in a variety of ways, ranging from physical attack to verbal aggression to

CATHY © 1994 Cathy Guisewite. Reprinted by permission of Universal Press Syndicate. All rights reserved.

reflective problem solving. Although each method may resolve differences, some are clearly preferable to others. Depending on how we handle disagreements, conflict can either promote continuing attachment or split a relationship apart.

One of the main reasons that conflict is handled poorly is because it often involves intense feelings that many people do not know how to identify or express. We may feel deep disappointment, resentment, or anger toward someone we care about, and this is difficult to manage. Our discussion in Chapter 7 should help you recognize what you are feeling and choose effective means of communicating your emotions in conflict situations. Other skills we've discussed—such as using I-language and monitoring the self-serving bias—will also help you manage the feelings that often accompany conflict.

Communication skills are especially important when dealing with differences. We need to know how particular behaviors affect interpersonal conflict so that we can make intelligent decisions about how to act. Without a base of good information about communication and conflict, we can only follow scripts that we have learned from previous interactions and observations. Unfortunately, not all of us have learned constructive scripts for managing conflict. Later in this chapter, we'll identify specific kinds of communication that foster healthy and unhealthy conflict.

Some forms of communication can actually enhance relationships as well as resolving disagreements effectively. Other kinds of communication can erode trust, climate, and the self-esteem of partners. Learning how different kinds of communication affect relationships, individuals, and resolution of conflict empowers you to make informed choices about how to deal with conflict in your relationships. The ideas and skills we cover in this chapter should give you a better understanding of how to manage conflict effectively so that it cultivates personal growth and relationship maturity.

Conflict May Be Good for Individuals and Relationships

Although we tend to think of conflict negatively, actually it can be beneficial in a number of ways. When managed constructively, conflict can help us grow as individuals and strengthen our relationships. We can enlarge our perspectives when we engage in conflicts that propel personal growth and learning (see Figure 9.1). We deepen insight into our ideas and feelings when we have to express them and consider critical responses. Sometimes this supports our own identity by clarifying how we differ from others. In a study I co-authored, romantic partners indicated that one value of differences was strengthening awareness of partners' individuality (Wood et al., 1994).

Differences can also prompt personal growth by helping us see when it's appropriate to change our minds. Conflict allows us to consider points of view different from our own. Based on what we learn, we may change our opinions, behaviors, or goals. As Jaleh points out, conflict can enhance understanding and spur positive personal growth.

Danger   Opportunity

FIGURE 9.1
Chinese Character for Crisis

JALEH: *A while back I was arguing with a buddy of mine about quotas. I've always supported them because I think that's the only way minorities have a chance of getting the education and jobs they deserve. Without quotas, people of color will still be shut out no matter how skilled or smart or achieving they are. But the guy I was debating is against quotas because he thinks they hurt us. He said that as long as quotas are used, any minority person in a good school or with a status job will be regarded as there because of quota not merit. What really made me think was when he said that quotas can be used against minorities—like if a school has a quota for 10 percent minorities, it can refuse to admit more than 10 percent minorities even if more are qualified. Arguing with him has pushed me to rethink my position.*

Conflict can also benefit relationships. In fact, a book titled *The Intimate Enemy: How to Fight Fair in Love and Marriage* states that verbal conflict between intimates is highly constructive and desirable if it is managed constructively (Bach & Wyden, 1973). One potential benefit of conflict is its ability to expand partners' understandings of each other. What begins as a discussion of some particular issue usually winds up providing broader information about why partners feel as they do and what meanings they attach to the issue. In the example that opened this chapter, the original complaint about Pam's flirting led to the discovery that Dave felt insecure about his identity and Pam's respect for him, because she was succeeding in graduate work and he wasn't. Once his concern emerged, the couple could address the *real* issue.

Ron Arnett (1986), a scholar of communication ethics, points out that lack of conflict isn't necessarily a symptom of a healthy relationship. It's at least as likely that low levels of conflict reflect lack of emotional depth between partners or repression of disagreements. Researchers report that there is no association between the number of arguments spouses have and marital happiness (Howard & Dawes, 1976). Some of the respondents in the study I mentioned previously (Wood et al., 1994) said differences energized their relationships by providing zest and excitement. This may explain the interesting finding that sexual activity and arguments are positively related. It seems that partners who argue more also have livelier sex lives (Howard & Dawes, 1976). One group of researchers refers to this as "keeping a positive balance in the marital bank account" (Gottman, Notarius, Markman, Banks, Yoppi, & Rubin, 1976b). When conflict is managed well, it can be constructive for both individuals and relationships.

JANA: *Geoff and I have a pretty intense relationship. We fight a lot and we fight hard. Some of my friends think this is bad, but we don't. Nothing is brushed under the carpet in our relationship. If either of us is angry or*

© Audrey Gottlieb/Monkmeyer Press Photo

upset about something, we hash it out then and there. But we are just as intense in positive ways. Geoff lets me know all the time that he loves me, and I am always hugging and kissing him. I guess you could just say our relationship is passionate—in bad moments and good ones.

To review, we've discussed four basic principles of conflict. First, we noted that conflict is both natural and inevitable in interpersonal relationships. Second, we discovered that conflict may be overtly communicated or covertly expressed through indirect communication or games that camouflage real issues. The third principle is that how we manage conflict influences its resolution and its impact on interpersonal climates. Finally, we saw that conflict can be constructive for both individuals and relationships. We can now build on these principles by discussing diverse ways people think about and respond to conflict.

Approaches to Conflict

We've noted that conflict can be managed in various ways, some more effective than others. We now want to look at three distinct orientations toward conflict. Each orientation has fairly predictable consequences on how interaction proceeds.

Our orientations toward conflict affect how we approach conflict situations. Based on what we've learned from social groups and personal experiences, we approach conflict from one of three basic orientations. Each is appropriate in some relationships and situations; the challenge is to know when a particular approach is constructive.

Lose–Lose

A **lose–lose** orientation assumes that conflict results in losses for everyone. Behind this approach to conflict is the belief that expressing disagreement is unhealthy and destructive for everyone. A wife might feel that conflicts over money hurt her, her husband, and the marriage. Similarly, a person may not argue with a friend, believing the result would be wounded pride for both of them. The lose–lose view presumes that conflict cannot produce winners or benefits.

S T U D E N T —

THEO: *I hate to fight with friends. I do just about anything to avoid an argument. But sometimes what I have to do is sacrifice my preferences or even my rights just to avoid conflict. And sometimes I have to go along*

COMMUNICATION NOTES

Japanese and American Styles of Negotiation

The differences between Japanese and American views of conflict shape specific communication patterns during business negotiations. Consider how each of the following negotiation strategies reflects values typical of Japanese or U.S. society.

JAPANESE STYLE	AMERICAN STYLE
Understate your own initial position or state it vaguely to allow the other room to state his or her position.	Overstate initial position to establish a strong image.
Find informal ways to let the other person know your bottom line in order to move agreement forward without directly confronting the other with your bottom line.	Keep your bottom line secret from the other person to preserve your power and gain the most.
Look for areas of agreement and focus talk on them.	Where there are differences, assert your position and attempt to win the other's assent.
Avoid confrontation.	Be adversarial.
Work to make sure that neither you nor the other person fails.	Work to win all you can.

SOURCE: Weiss, S. E. (1987). The changing logic of a former minor power. In H. Binnendijk (Ed.), *National negotiating styles* (pp. 44–74). Washington, DC: Department of State.

with something I don't believe in or think is right. I'm starting to think that maybe conflict would be better than avoiding it—at least in some cases.

Theo's insight is worth our attention. When we seek to avoid conflict at all costs, the costs may be high indeed. We may have to defer our own needs or rights, and we may feel unable to give honest feedback to others. Avoiding conflict doesn't necessarily avoid undesirable consequences as Theo has discovered.

Although the lose–lose orientation is not usually beneficial in dealing with conflicts in close relationships, it has merit in some circumstances. One obvious value of this approach is that it prompts us to ask whether we want or need to engage in conflict. Some issues aren't worth the energy and the discomfort that conflict arouses. For instance, Robbie and I have very different ideas about the appropriate timetable for airline travel. He prefers to get to the airport at least 90 minutes before a flight, whereas I prefer to arrive just a few minutes in advance. For the first years of our marriage this was a source of discord that yielded no benefits for either of us. Finally, I decided that the schedule was a dumb thing to argue about, and I simply planned to leave when Robbie preferred. We also disagree on cars, but Robbie defers to my preference, because cars matter more to me than to him. Neither cars nor flight schedules are worth conflict. We might also have a more peaceful planet if national leaders believed that war only produces losers, regardless of whether one side officially wins.

Win–Lose

Win–lose orientations assume one person wins at the expense of the other. A person who sees conflict as a win–lose matter thinks disagreements are battles that can have only one victor. What one person gains is at the other's loss; what one person loses benefits the other. Disagreements are seen as zero-sum games in which there is no possibility for everyone to benefit.

The win–lose orientation is cultivated in cultures that place value on individualism, self-assertion, and competition. If you guessed the United States emphasizes those values, you're right. Other cultures, such as Japan, place priority on quite different values: cooperation, keeping others from failing, and finding areas of agreement. Not surprisingly, the win–lose orientation to conflict is more common in the United States than in Japan. "Japanese and American Styles of Negotiation" explains how these differences may create problems in business dealings.

Partners who disagree about whether to move to a new location might adopt a win–lose orientation. In turn, this would lock them into a yes–no view in which only two alternatives are seen: move or stay put. The win–lose orientation virtually guarantees that the individuals won't make a strong effort to find or create a mutually acceptable solution, such as moving to a third place that meets both partners' needs or having a long-distance relationship so that each person can have the best individual location. The more person A argues for moving, the more person B argues for not moving. Eventually one of them "wins" but at the cost of the other and the relationship. A win–lose orientation toward conflict tends to undermine relationships, because someone has to lose. There is no possibility that both can win, much less that the relationship can.

Before you dismiss win–lose as a totally unconstructive view of conflict, let's consider when it might be effective. Win–lose can be appropriate when we have low commitment to a relationship and little desire to take care of the person with whom we disagree. When you're buying a car, for instance, you want the best deal you can get, and you have little concern for the dealer's profit. I adopted a win–lose approach to conflict with doctors when my father was dying. The doctors weren't doing all they could to help him, because they saw little value in investing time in someone who was dying. On the other hand, I had a very different view of what should be done. I wanted the doctors to do everything possible to help my father. The doctors and I had opposing views, and I cared less about whether the doctors were happy and liked me than about winning the best medical care for my father.

Win–Win

Win–win orientations assume there are usually ways to resolve differences so that everyone gains. For people who view conflict as win–win, the goal is to come up with a resolution that everyone involved can accept. Ideally, the solution might be that everyone felt was the best possible one. When both people are committed to finding a solution that pleases both, a win–win resolution to conflict is possible.

Recently I watched two close friends work through a conflict using the win–win orientation. After three years of renting a house, Becker and Shelly wanted to build their own home. The conflict arose because Shelly was willing to borrow heavily to pay for construction of the home, and Becker was not willing to take on a serious debt. Becker wanted to save money before they built their home; Shelly wanted to borrow and not wait. For several months they talked and talked, neither willing to defer to the other and neither willing to force a position. One day Becker jokingly reminded Shelly that Shelly had done some construction work in the past. Becker suggested that maybe Shelly

could build their house herself. After initially laughing, Shelly took the idea seriously and realized she could do some of the building and be the general contractor for the rest of the construction. With Shelly in charge, the couple would have to borrow far less money to build. Becker volunteered to take a second job so that Shelly could take off from work during the building. Shelly was able to keep daily check on the construction and to incorporate special touches that reflect her and Becker's lifestyle. When the house was finished, both Becker and Shelly loved it and agreed it was more their kind of house than one that strangers would have built. Because they kept talking and kept looking for a solution both could celebrate, they were able to create a plan that was better than either of their original ideas.

STUDENT VOICES

TESS: *One of the roughest issues for Jerry and me was when he started working most nights. The time after dinner had always been "our time." When Jerry took the new job, he had to stay in constant contact with the California office. Jerry and I used to do something together at 6 P.M., but because of the time difference, it's only 3 P.M. on the West Coast and the business day is still going. I was hurt that he no longer had time for us, and he was angry that I wanted time he needed for business. We kept talking and came up with the idea of spending a day together each weekend, which we'd never done. Although my ideal would still be to share evenings, this solution keeps us in touch with each other.*

As Tess's story illustrates, not all win–win solutions maximize each person's preferences. Sometimes people can't find or create a solution that is each person's ideal. In those cases, each person may be able to redefine his or her priorities. Each individual may make some accommodations in order to build a solution that lets the other win also. When partners adopt win–win views of conflict, they often discover solutions that neither had thought of previously. This happens because they are committed to their own and the other's satisfaction. Sometimes win–win attitudes result in compromises that satisfy enough of each person's needs to provide confirmation and to protect the health of the relationship.

APPLY THE IDEA
Identifying Orientations Toward Conflict

For each statement below, decide which of the three orientations to conflict it reflects.

_____ 1. We can't both be satisfied on this issue.

_____ 2. Since we disagree about which movie to see, let's just not go out tonight.

_____ 3. We're never going to see eye to eye on this, so I'll just defer to you.

_____ 4. If we keep talking, I think we'll figure out something that will work for both of us.

_____ 5. I can't stand fighting. Nobody ever wins.

_____ 6. No matter what you say, I'm not giving any ground on this issue. I feel very strongly about it, so you'll just have to go along with me.

_____ 7. We may not have a solution yet, but I think we're finding some areas of agreement. Let's try to build on those.

Key: 1 = win–lose; 2 = lose–lose; 3 = win–lose; 4 = win–win; 5 = lose–lose; 6 = win–lose; 7 = win–win

Lose–lose, win–lose, and win–win are basic ways individuals think about conflict. What we learned in Chapter 3 reminds us that how we perceive something has a powerful impact on what it means to us and on the possibilities of resolution that we imagine. Remember how you couldn't solve the nine dots problem in Chapter 3 if you perceived it as a square? In a similar way, we're unlikely to find a win–win solution if we perceive conflict as win–lose or lose–lose.

APPLY THE IDEA
Identifying Your Conflict Tendencies

Could you identify your orientation to conflict from this discussion? To check, answer these questions:

1. When conflict seems about to occur, do you
   a.   marshal arguments for your solution
   b.   feel everyone is going to get hurt
   c.   feel there's probably a way to satisfy everyone
2. When involved in conflict, do you
   a.   feel competitive urges
   b.   feel resigned that everyone will lose
   c.   feel committed to finding a mutual solution
3. When you disagree with another person, do you
   a.   assume the other person is wrong
   b.   assume neither of you is right
   c.   assume there are good reasons for what each of you thinks and feels

Key: (a) answers indicate a win–lose orientation; (b) answers suggest a lose–lose orientation; (c) answers reflect a win–win orientation.

Responses to Conflict

In addition to orientations toward conflict, most individuals have fairly consistent patterns for responding to conflict. A series of studies identified four distinct ways North Americans respond to relational distress (Rusbult, 1987;

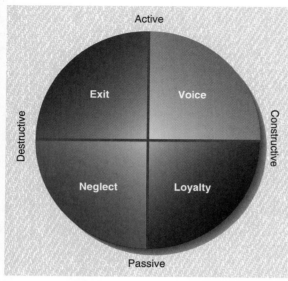

FIGURE 9.2
Responses to Relational Distress

Rusbult, Johnson, & Morrow, 1986; Rusbult & Zembrodt, 1983; Rusbult, Zembrodt, & Iwaniszek, 1986). These are represented in Figure 9.2. According to this model, responses to conflict can be either active or passive, depending on how emphatically they address problems. Responses can also be constructive or destructive in their capacity to resolve tension and to preserve relationships.

As we discuss four common responses to conflict, you'll notice their connection to the orientations toward conflict we discussed in the prior section. This reminds us of the systemic character of interpersonal communication: Each part of communication is connected to all other parts.

Exit Response

The **exit response** involves leaving a relationship either by physically walking out or by psychologically withdrawing. Refusing to talk about a problem is an example of psychological exit. Ending a relationship rather than deal with a conflict is an example of literal exit. Because exit doesn't address problems, it is destructive. Because it is a forceful way to avoid conflict, it is active.

Exit responses are associated with lose–lose and win–lose orientations toward conflict. Individuals who have a lose–lose orientation assume that nobody can benefit if conflict takes place, so they see no point in engaging in conflict and prefer to avoid it. For different reasons, the win–lose orientation may promote the exit response. A person who sees conflicts as win–lose situations may exit physically or psychologically if she or he perceives she or he will lose if the conflict is allowed to take place.

Neglect Response

The **neglect response** occurs when an individual denies or minimizes problems, disagreements, anger, tension, or other matters that could lead to overt conflict. Individuals communicate that they prefer to neglect conflicts by making statements such as "There isn't a disagreement here," "You're creating a problem where none exists," or "You're making a mountain out of a molehill." These statements either deny a problem exists or deny that a problem is important. Neglect is generally destructive, because it doesn't promote any resolution of tension. It is passive because it avoids discussion. In some specific situations, however, neglect may be an effective response to conflict. For instance, if an issue can't be resolved, discussing it may further harm a relationship. Also, if a conflict isn't important to you, it may be appropriate not to deal with it.

Which orientations toward conflict would you think foster a neglect response? Either lose–lose or win–lose may prompt the neglect response for the same reasons each of those orientations is associated with the exit response. That's not surprising because both exit and neglect are destructive responses to conflict. Either the person thinks escalating disagreement will harm everyone or the person perceives she or he will lose if conflict is allowed to progress.

Loyalty Response

The **loyalty response** is staying committed to a relationship despite differences. In other words, the person who adopts loyalty as a response to conflict decides to stay committed to the relationship and tolerate the differences. Loyalty often involves deferring to another in order to preserve a relationship. This may be desirable if the deference doesn't cost too much, but deferring your own needs and goals may be too high a price for harmony. In other cases, loyalty is enacted by focusing on what is good and desirable about the relationship and by deemphasizing problems in it. Loyalty is silent allegiance that doesn't actively address conflict, so it is a passive response. Because it doesn't end a relationship and it preserves the option of addressing tension later, loyalty is constructive.

Loyalty is most likely to spring from a lose–lose orientation toward conflict. Believing that engaging in overt disagreement only hurts everyone, individuals may choose to remain loyal to the relationship and not express anger, resentment, disappointment, and disagreement.

S T U D E N T   VOICES

ZONDOMONI: *In South Africa, the tradition is for women not to speak out against their husbands. Women are supposed to support whatever the husband says or does. A woman who speaks out or who disagrees with her husband or any male relative is considered bad; she is behaving inappropriately.*

But some of us are now challenging this custom. I disagreed with my father about my marriage, and he did not speak to me for many months after. Now he speaks to me again. I also sometimes disagree with my husband. Life is changing in South Africa.

Voice Response

Finally, the **voice response** is an active, constructive strategy for dealing with conflict by talking about problems and trying to resolve them. Individuals who respond with voice identify problems or tensions and assert a desire to deal with them. Voice implies that people care enough about a relationship to notice when something is wrong and to want to do something to improve the situation. Thus, voice is often the most constructive strategy for enduring intimate relationships.

The voice response is most likely to be fostered by a win–win orientation toward conflict. It requires belief in yourself and the other person to give voice to problems and disagreements. Voicing concerns also expresses belief in the relationship. We're unlikely to give voice to disagreements unless we believe a relationship can withstand conflict and that the partners will work to resolve the tension in ways that both people find acceptable.

Although each of us has developed a preferred response, we can become skillful in other responses if we choose. Constructive strategies (voice and loyalty) are advisable for relationships that matter to you and that you want to maintain. Of those two, voice is stronger, because it actively intervenes to resolve conflict. Exit may be useful as an interim strategy when partners need time to reflect or cool off before dealing with conflict directly. Loyalty may be appropriate in situations where conflict is temporary and provoked by external pressures. For example, if you want more time with a friend who is under a lot of pressure at work, it may be wise not to assert your preferences and to quietly accept the short-term disappointment. Developing skill in using a range of responses to conflict increases your ability to communicate sensitively and effectively.

A P P L Y   T H E   I D E A

Enlarging Your Responses to Conflict

Identify two responses to conflict that you do not presently use much. For each one, specify two strategies for increasing your skill in using that response.

EXAMPLE: **RESPONSE TO CONFLICT**	**STRATEGIES FOR ACHIEVING COMPETENCE**
Voice response: I have trouble talking about conflict	1. When I feel like avoiding conflict, I will remind myself that avoiding has never made problems go away. 2. When friends ask what's wrong, I will stop saying "nothing's wrong."

Social Influences on Conflict

Our orientations toward conflict and our typical ways of responding to conflict aren't random. They reflect many social influences. We've already noted that our views of conflict reflect personal experiences, especially ones in our families. Along with personal experiences, our membership in social groups affects how we view and respond to conflict. In this section, we'll examine the relationship between conflict and membership in social groups defined by culture, gender, and sexual orientation.

Cultural Background

As we have seen throughout this book, cultures vary in the attitudes, values, and communication practices they approve and disapprove. This is especially true concerning conflict. Different cultures have distinct attitudes toward conflict and what it means (constitutive rules). The majority of Mediterranean cultures regard conflict as a normal and valuable part of everyday life. Within these cultures, people routinely argue and wrangle and nobody gets upset or angry. Customers haggle with merchants over prices; neighbors argue, sometimes quite dramatically, over community issues; people bargain with one another for favors. In France and Arabic countries, men routinely debate one another for the sheer fun of it. It doesn't matter who wins the argument—the process of arguing is itself enjoyable (Copeland & Griggs, 1985).

Many Hispanic cultures also regard conflict as both normal and interesting. Because Hispanic cultures tend to value emotionalism, they perceive conflict as an opportunity to be emotionally expressive and dramatic. The calm, reserved, rational style of discussion prized in many Western societies is perceived as boring and unimaginative.

COMMUNICATION NOTES

Win–Win Athletics

North Americans view sports as competitions in which one person or team wins and the other loses. This perspective is in dramatic contrast to the Japanese attitude toward athletics. In baseball, for instance, the goal is not for one team to win, but for a tie to be achieved. The Japanese play for ties because that way nobody loses face. Everyone plays hard and competitively, yet nobody loses—no face is lost. That's a perfect game! When the Japanese win a championship, they try to win by only slim margins. One team may be ahead by many games at a point in the season, but by the end of the season that team will have trimmed its lead to one or two games. This preserves the face of the other teams, because they don't lose by an embarrassing degree.

SOURCE: American games, Japanese rules. (1988). Frontline documentary. National Public Television. Cited in Ferrante, J. (1992). *Sociology: A global perspective* (p. 102). Belmont, CA: Wadsworth.

In the United States, assertiveness and individuality are emphasized, so native citizens tend to be more active and competitive in responding to conflict. More than many peoples, Westerners adopt an exchange view of relationships in which each person expects (and sometimes demands) to get their fair share. As a people, we are reluctant to give in, defer, or be passive.

In more communal societies such as the Netherlands, people have less individualistic perspectives and are less likely to focus on winning at conflict (Vanyperen & Buunk, 1991). Similarly, in Japan and many other Asian cultures, open disagreement is strongly condemned. Japanese society teaches people to accommodate or appear to do so and not to express disagreement openly. In line with this cultural norm, Japanese persons tend to favor the exit approach to conflict (Ting-Toomey, 1991).

The attitude toward conflict that prevails in Japan and China, as well as many other Asian cultures, places high value on interpersonal harmony and cooperation. Any overt conflict is considered in very bad taste and is regarded as disrespectful of others. Rather than trying to win at another's expense, the goal is to find points of agreement and build from those to a solution that benefits everyone and that sustains harmony. Great effort is made to avoid disagreement and to avoid winning at the cost of causing another person to lose face (Rowland, 1985; Weiss, 1987). Avoiding embarrassment or causing another to lose face is also found in sports, as "Win–Win Athletics" explains.

STUDENT VOICES

VALAYA: *One of the hardest adjustments for me has been how Americans assert themselves. I was very surprised that students argue with their teachers. We would never do that in Taiwan. It would be extremely disrespectful. I also see friends argue, sometimes very much. I understand this is a cultural differ-*

© Anne Dowie

ence, but I have trouble accepting it. I learned that disagreements hurt relationships.

Gender

There are some general differences in how women and men respond to conflict. In general, women are more likely to enact loyalty and voice, both of which have constructive implications for relationships. Men, on the other hand, respond more often with exit and neglect. These differences in response tendencies make sense in light of what we know about gendered socialization. As we noted in Chapter 4, women are taught to place a priority on relationships and to use talk to create and sustain closeness. Thus, it's natural for women to want to talk about problems. Women are also more likely than men to defer and compromise, which reflects gendered prescriptions for women to accommodate others (Wood 1986, 1992b).

The different response tendencies of women and men pave the way for misunderstandings in relationships (Wood, 1998). Men sometimes feel overwhelmed by the number of issues women want to discuss and resolve. Women sometimes feel that men are unwilling to discuss anything about relationships. Of course, neither perception is likely to be accurate. Both are very broad generalizations that probably overstate how men and women act. Nonetheless, women and men often find themselves responding very differently to relationship tensions and not understanding each other's perspective.

S T U D E N T **VOICES**

NICK: *My girlfriend drives me crazy. She thinks anytime the slightest thing is wrong in our relationship, we have to have a long, drawn-out analysis of it. I just don't want to spend all that time dissecting the relationship.*

S T U D E N T **VOICES**

GINA: *My boyfriend is a world-class avoider. When something is wrong between us, I naturally want to talk about it and get things right again. But he will evade, tell me everything's fine when it's not, say the problem is too minor to talk about, and use any other tactic he can come up with to avoid facing the problem. He seems to think if you don't deal with problems they somehow solve themselves.*

Masculine socialization places less emphasis on talk as a means to intimacy, so as a group, men are less likely than women to see discussion as a good way to handle conflict in personal relationships. In professional situations and athletics, however, men may be very vocal in dealing with conflict. Yet in their personal lives, men often deny or minimize problems rather than deal openly with them. However, research indicates that in Western relationships, avoiding discussion seldom helps matters, and it often compounds tension between partners in a relationship. Long-term studies of marriage indicate that husbands are more inclined than wives to withdraw from conflict and that stonewalling by husbands is a strong predictor of divorce (Bass, 1993). The other response preferred by men, exit, is a unilateral show of power, which is part of masculine socialization. Men, more than women, use coercive tactics, both verbal and physical, to avoid discussing problems and to force their resolutions on others (Snell, Hawkins, & Belk, 1988; White, 1989).

© Thelma Shumsky/The Image Works

Before leaving our discussion of gender, we should note one other important finding. Psychologist John Gottman (1993) reports that men experience greater and longer-lasting physical responses to interpersonal conflict. Compared to women, during conflict men's heart rate rises more quickly and to higher levels and it stays elevated for a longer period of time. Thus, engaging in conflict generally may be more physically and psychologically painful to men than to women. This may offer a partial explanation of why men are more likely than women to deny or minimize issues that could cause conflict.

APPLY THE IDEA
Gendered Styles of Conflict

Reflect on responses to conflict used by you and two women and two men you know well. Do your observations indicate that women are more likely than men to defer and accommodate and to want to talk about problems? Do the men you observe tend to avoid problems or exit when they arise?

Sexual Orientation

Do gays and lesbians respond to conflict differently than heterosexuals? Actually, sexual preference doesn't seem to be a major influence on how individuals see and deal with conflict. Caryl Rusbult and her colleagues (1986) found that gay men were much like heterosexual men, and lesbians were similar to heterosexual women, in their responses to conflict. Similarly, a major national study reported that gender explains far more of the differences between partners than does affectional preference (Blumstein & Schwartz,

1983). I drew the same conclusion from my research on how gay, lesbian, and heterosexual couples manage relationship crises (Wood, 1986, 1994b).

At first this finding seems surprising, because sexual orientation is such a core part of identity. On closer examination, however, it makes sense that gays and lesbians don't approach conflict differently than heterosexuals. The majority of children, regardless of sexual orientation, are socialized on the basis of their sex. Thus, boys, both gay and straight, tend to learn masculine orientations toward interaction, whereas lesbian and straight girls are socialized toward feminine styles of interaction.

Although gays, lesbians, and heterosexuals seem similar in how they think about and respond to conflict, sexual orientation is linked to some differences in relationship tensions. First, gays and lesbians appear to have fewer sexual conflicts and to talk more openly about sexual issues than heterosexuals (Masters & Johnson, 1979). This can be significant, because sexual tensions can poison overall satisfaction with a relationship (Cupach & Comstock, 1990).

On the whole, gay and lesbian couples may have less overall conflict than heterosexuals. It's possible that gay and lesbian partners have an intragender empathy that heterosexual couples lack (Masters & Johnson, 1979). Because most homosexual partners were socialized in the same gender culture, they often share views of the importance of talk and activities in relationships. Of all couples, lesbians most often rely on voice to talk through tensions. Because both partners usually view communication as the primary path to intimacy, they are similarly inclined to engage in process talk. Gay male couples, in contrast, talk less about relationship issues than other couples and are more likely than other partners to exit when problems arise (Wood, 1994b). Heterosexual couples talk more than gays and less than lesbians about their relationship, reflecting a combination of gendered socialization.

In this section, we've seen that people differ in how they view and respond to conflict. Although lose–lose and win–lose perceptions of conflict are appropriate in situations where there is low commitment to relationships and others, the win–win view is generally ideal when partners care about each other and want to stay together.

People respond to conflict either actively (voice, exit) or passively (neglect, loyalty) and in ways that either help (voice, loyalty) or harm (exit, neglect) relationships. How we think about and respond to conflict is learned, not innate. It reflects our cultural background, gender, and affectional preference. The fact that conflict orientations are learned suggests that we can develop skills for managing tension constructively. In the next section, we discuss specific communication behaviors that affect the process of conflict and its impact on relationships.

Communication Patterns During Conflict

Marriage counselors have particularly keen insight into how conflict dynamics affect relationships. Communication scholar Anita Vangelisti (1993) reports that counselors stress communication training for couples who manage conflict

© Peter L. Chapman

unproductively. Therapeutic training teaches partners to recognize destructive and constructive patterns of communication and to use constructive patterns in their relationships. In this section, we discuss specific kinds of communication that foster or impede effective conflict (Gottman, 1979, 1993; Gottman et al., 1976a, 1976b).

Unproductive Conflict Communication

Ineffective communication can have serious consequences. It damages efforts to resolve problems, harms individuals, and jeopardizes relational health. The communication that creates unproductive patterns in conflict reflects a preoccupation with self and a disregard for the other. This is not genuine interpersonal communication, because partners don't recognize and engage each other as unique individuals.

Specific communication behaviors make up the syndrome of destructive conflict communication. Table 9.1 identifies behaviors that foster constructive or unproductive conflict communication (Gottman, 1993; Gottman et al., 1976a).

TABLE 9.1
SUMMARY OF CONSTRUCTIVE AND UNPRODUCTIVE COMMUNICATION

Constructive	Unproductive
Validations of each other	Disconfirmation of each other
Sensitive listening	Poor listening
Dual perspective	Preoccupation with self
Recognize other's concerns	Cross-complaining
Asking for clarification	Hostile mindreading
Infrequent interruptions	Frequent interruptions
Focus on specific issues	Kitchensinking
Compromises and contracts	Counterproposals
Useful metacommunication	Excessive metacommunication
Summarizing the concerns of both partners	Self-summarizing

Early Stages   The foundation for destructive conflict is established by communication that fails to confirm individuals. If John says "I want us to spend more time together," Shannon may reply, "That's unreasonable." This disconfirms John's feeling and request. Shannon could also disconfirm him by not replying at all, which would be a refusal to acknowledge him. During early stages, partners tend not to listen well. They may listen selectively, taking in only what they expect or want to believe. In addition, partners display little mindfulness.

They don't show that they are interested in what the other is saying. Instead, they may give feedback that disconfirms the other. For instance, Shannon could roll her eyes to tell John his request is outrageous, or she might shrug and turn away to signal she doesn't care what he wants. Poor listening is also demonstrated when partners don't respond to each other.

Cross-complaining occurs when one person's complaint is met by a counter-complaint. Shannon could respond to John's request for more time by saying, "Yeah, well what I want is a little more respect for what I do." That response doesn't address John's concern; it is an attempt to divert the conversation and to switch the fault from Shannon to John. Poor listening and disconfirmation establish a climate in which dual perspective is low and defensiveness is high.

Negative climates tend to build on themselves. As partners continue to talk, mindreading is likely. Instead of asking John to clarify or explain his feelings, Shannon assumes she knows his motives. Perhaps she thinks he wants to divert her from her work so that she doesn't succeed. If Shannon makes this assumption, she discounts what John wants. Mindreading in distressed relationships has a distinctively negative tone. Partners assume the worst motives and feelings of each other. The negative assumptions they make fuel hostility and mistrust.

Middle Stages   Once a negative climate has been set, it is stoked by other unconstructive communication. Focusing on specific issues is one of the clearest differences between partners who resolve conflicts constructively and those who don't. In unproductive conflict interaction, partners engage in **kitchensinking,** in which everything except the kitchen sink is thrown into the argument. John may add to his original complaint by recalling all sorts of other real and imagined slights from Shannon. In turn, she may reciprocate by hauling out her own laundry list of gripes. The result is such a mass of grievances that partners are overwhelmed. They can't solve all of the problems they've dragged into the discussion, and they may well forget what the original issue was. Kitchensinking is particularly likely to occur when partners have a host of concerns they've repressed for some time. Once a conflict begins, everything that has been stored up is thrown in.

The middle stages of unproductive conflict are also marked by frequent interruptions that disrupt the flow of talk. These interruptions aren't efforts to clarify ideas or feelings. Instead, they are objections to what a partner says: "How dare you say I don't know how to manage money?" Interruptions may also be attempts to derail a partner's issues and reroute discussion: "I have no interest in talking about time together. What I'd like to discuss is your responsibility for this house." Cross-complaining frequently continues in this middle stage of the syndrome. Because neither partner is allowed to develop thoughts fully (or even to finish a sentence), discussion never focuses on any topic long enough to make headway in resolving it.

Later Stages   Even if partners make little progress in solving their problems, limited time and energy guarantee an end to an episode of conflict. Solutions become the focus in the final stage of unproductive conflict. Unfortunately, preceding stages didn't lay the groundwork for effective discussion of solutions. As a result, each person's proposals are met with counterproposals. The self-preoccupation that first surfaced in the early phase persists now so that each person is more interested in pushing his or her solution than in considering that of the other. John proposes, "Maybe we could spend two nights together each week." Shannon counterproposes, "Maybe you could assume responsibility for half of the chores around here." Her counterproposal fails to recognize and acknowledge his suggestion, so her communication does not confirm him. Compounding self-preoccupation is self-summarizing, which is when a person keeps repeating what she or he has said. This is egocentric communication. It is not genuine interpersonal communication, because it ignores the other person and simply restates the speaker's feelings and perspective.

A final form of negative communication in the middle and later phases of unproductive conflict is excessive metacommunication. Metacommunication is communication about communication. For example, John might say, "I think maybe we're getting sidetracked in this discussion," or Shannon might say, "I think we're avoiding talking about the real issue here." Both of these are comments about the communication that is happening. Gottman and his associates (1976a,1976b, 1977) have found that both distressed and satisfied couples engage in metacommunication. However, they do so in very different ways.

Couples who manage conflict effectively use metacommunication to keep discussion on track, and then they return to the topics at hand. For instance, during a disagreement, Aaron might comment that Norma doesn't seem to be expressing her feelings and invite her to do so. Then he and Norma would return to their discussion. In contrast, couples who manage conflict ineffectively often become embroiled in metacommunication and can't get back to the issues. For example, Norma and Aaron might get into an extended argument about whether she's expressing feelings and not return to the original topic of conflict. Excessive metacommunication is more likely to block partners than to resolve tensions cooperatively.

These forms of communication that make up the unproductive conflict syndrome reflect and promote egocentrism and dogmatism because negative communication tends to be self-perpetuating. Unproductive conflict doesn't involve dual perspective, and it seals off awareness of common grounds as well as potential avenues of compromise.

You may recall that in Chapter 1 we described interpersonal communication as systemic, because all aspects of communication interact and affect one another. This is clearly the case in the unproductive conflict syndrome. Egocentrism leads to poor listening, which promotes disconfirmation, which fuels defensiveness, which stokes dogmatism, which leads to hostile mindreading and kitchensinking, which pave the way for self-summarizing. Each negative form of communication feeds into the overall negative system. Unproductive communication fosters a defensive, negative climate, which makes it virtually impossible to resolve conflicts. When egocentrism prevails, each partner is more interested in getting his or her own way than in creating a solution that both can accept. In addition, unconstructive communication is so disconfirm-

How to Fight

RULES FOR FIGHTING DIRTY

1. Apologize prematurely.
2. Refuse to take the fight seriously.
3. Chain-react by piling on all the issues and gripes (kitchensinking).
4. Hit below the belt. Use intimate knowledge to humiliate the other person.
5. Withdraw and avoid confrontation: walk out, be silent.
6. Withhold affection, approval, recognition, or material things.
7. Encourage others to side with you against your partner.
8. Play demolition derby with your partner's character—tell her or him what's wrong with her or him, what she or he thinks, feels, means, and so on (mindreading).
9. Demand more—nothing is ever enough. Push to have everything your way.
10. Attack a person, activity, value, or idea that your partner holds dear.

RULES FOR FIGHTING CLEAN

1. Fully express your positive and negative feelings.
2. Define your out-of-bounds areas of vulnerability.
3. Paraphrase the other's arguments in your own words and allow the other to do likewise.
4. Think *before* fighting, not after fighting. Try not to let your feelings undermine reason and fair play.
5. Consider the merit of the other person's opinions of you before rejecting or accepting them.
6. Focus on the other person's behavior and ideas.
7. Define what the fight is about and stay within limits.
8. Look for where you and your partner agree, as well as where you disagree
9. Decide how each of you can help the other resolve the issue in a way that satisfies her or him.
10. Avoid discussing a problem or conflict when you are emotionally raw.

SOURCE: Adapted from Bach, G. R., & Wyden, P. (1973). *The intimate enemy: How to fight fair in love and marriage.* New York: Avon.

ing that it damages individual partners and the long-term health of the relationship. "How to Fight" compares fair and unfair conflict tactics.

Constructive Conflict Communication

According to relationship counselors, healthy, constructive communication during conflict is open, nonjudgmental, confirming, and non-strategic. In addition, it reflects dual perspective by focusing on both partners and the relationship even when tension is high. Constructive communication creates a supportive, positive climate that increases the possibility of resolving conflict without harming the relationship. Let's look at how constructive communication plays out in the three phases of the conflict syndrome.

Early Stages   The foundation for constructive management of conflict is established long before a specific disagreement is aired. Climate, which is the foundation for both the overall relationship and conflict, sets the tone for communication during conflict. To establish a good climate, partners confirm each other by recognizing and acknowledging each other's concerns and feelings. Returning to our example, when John says "I want us to spend more time together," Shannon could confirm him by replying, "I wish we could too. It's nice that you want us to have more time together." That simple act on Shannon's part communicates to John that she is listening and that she cares about his concerns and about him. After she says that, a different conversation unfolds. It might go like this:

JOHN: Yeah, it just seems that we used to spend a lot more time together, and we felt closer then. I miss that.

SHANNON: I do too. It sounds as if what's really on your mind is how close we are, not specifically the amount of time we spend together. Is that right?

JOHN: Yeah, I guess that is more what's bothering me, but I kind of think they're connected, don't you?

SHANNON: I see what you mean. But we won't feel closer just by spending more time together. I think we also need some shared interests like we used to have.

JOHN: I'd like that. Do you have any ideas?

© Peter L. Chapman

Let's highlight several things in this conversation. First, notice that when Shannon began by reflecting John's opening statement, he elaborated and clarified what was troubling him. Instead of time per se, the issue is closeness. Listening sensitively, Shannon picks up on this and refocuses their conversation on closeness. We should also notice that Shannon doesn't mindread; instead, she asks John whether she understood what he meant. When he asks Shannon whether she thinks time and closeness are related, John shows openness to her perceptions; thus, he confirms her and doesn't mindread. The openness they create clears the way for effective discussion of how to increase closeness. Once a supportive climate is established, the couple can proceed to the middle stages of conflict knowing they are not fighting each other but working together to solve a problem.

Middle Stages   The positive groundwork laid in the early phase of conflict supports what happens as partners dig into issues. The middle stages of constructive conflict are marked by what Gottman (1993) calls "agenda building," which involves staying focused on the main issues. Kitchensinking is unlikely to derail discussion, because partners keep communication on target. It's not that other issues might not come up as they do in unproductive conflict. However, partners who have learned to communicate effectively control digressions. One useful technique is **bracketing,** which is noting that an issue that comes up in the course of conflict is important and needs to be discussed at a later time. Bracketing allows partners to stay effectively focused on a specific issue at one time, but to agree to deal with other issues later. Bracketing confirms partners' feelings that issues brought up are important by promising to deal with them later. Yet by bracketing topics that are peripheral to the current discussion, partners are able to stay on track and make progress in resolving the immediate issue.

During the middle stage of constructive conflict, partners continue to show respect for each other by interrupting infrequently. Any interruptions that occur are to clarify meanings ("Before you go on, could you explain what you mean by closeness?") or to check perceptions ("So you think time together leads to closeness?"). Unlike disruptive interruptions, ones that clarify ideas and check perceptions confirm the person speaking by showing that the listener wants to understand the meaning. In this stage, partners continue to recognize and acknowledge each other's points of view. Rather than the cross-complaining that characterizes unproductive conflict, partners acknowledge each other's feelings, thoughts, and concerns. This doesn't mean they don't put their own concerns on the table. Constructive conflict requires that we assert our own feelings and needs as part of engaging in honest dialogue. There is no conflict between honoring ourselves and others; doing both is the essence of good interpersonal communication.

Final Stages The opening phase of constructive conflict establishes a supportive climate for discussion. The focus of the middle stages is to elaborate issues
and feelings so that partners understand all that is involved. In the culminating
phase, attention shifts to resolving the tension between partners. Whereas in
unproductive conflict this involves meeting proposals with counterproposals, in
constructive conflict partners continue to operate cooperatively. Keeping in
mind that they share a relationship, they continue using dual perspective to
remain aware of both individuals' perspectives. Instead of countering each
other's proposals, partners engage in **contracting,** which is building a solution
through negotiation and acceptance of parts of proposals. The difference
between counterproposals and contracting is illustrated in this example:

COUNTERPROPOSALS

JOHN: I want us to spend three nights a week doing things together.
SHANNON: I can't do that right now, because we're short-handed at work and I
    am filling in nights. Get a hobby so you aren't bored nights.
JOHN: Not being bored isn't the same as our being close. I want us to spend
    time together again.
SHANNON: I told you, I can't do that. Don't be so selfish.
JOHN: Aren't we as important as your job?
SHANNON: That's a stupid question. I can't take three nights off. Let's take
    more vacations.

CONTRACTING

JOHN: I want us to spend three nights a week doing things together.
SHANNON: I'm all for that, but right now we're short-handed at work. How
    about if we use your idea but adjust it to my job. Maybe we could start with
    one night each week and expand that later.
JOHN: Okay, that's a start, but could we also reserve some weekend time for us?
SHANNON: That's a good idea. Let's plan on that. I just can't be sure how much
    I'll have to work on weekends until we hire some new people. What if we
    promise to give ourselves an extra week's vacation to spend together when we
    have full staff?
JOHN: Okay, that's a good back-up plan, but can we take weekend time when
    you don't work?
SHANNON: Absolutely. How about a picnic this Sunday? We've haven't gone on
    a picnic in so long.

In the counterproposal scenario, John and Shannon were competing to get
their own ways. Neither tried to identify workable parts of the other's proposals
or to find common ground. Because each adopts a win–lose view of the conflict, it's likely that both of them and the relationship will be losers. A very different tone shows up in the contracting scenario. In it, both partners look for
ways to agree with each other, while also asserting their own concerns. Neither
partner represses personal needs, but each is committed to finding what might
be workable in the other's proposals.

BETTINA: *My son and I used to argue all the time, and we never got anywhere because we were each trying to get our own way and we weren't paying attention to the other. Then we went into family counseling, and we learned how to make our arguments more productive. The most important thing I learned was to be looking for ways to respond to what my son says and wants. Once I started focusing on him and trying to satisfy him, he was more willing to listen to my point of view and to think about solutions that would satisfy me. We still argue a lot—I guess we always will—but now it's more like we're working things through together instead of trying to tear each other down.*

Specific differences between unproductive and productive conflict can be summarized as the difference between confirming and disconfirming communication. The particular kinds of communication that generate unproductive conflict share the quality of disconfirming the partner, the relationship, or both. On the other hand, the communication in constructive conflict consistently confirms both partners and the relationship. This reminds us of the importance of supportive, confirming climates, which we explored in Chapter 7. The climate, or emotional mood, of interpersonal relationships is created by communication. Our discussion of specific skills highlights communication that fosters affirming climates in which conflicts can be productively resolved without damage to relationships.

Guidelines for Effective Communication During Conflict

Our study of conflict, along with many of the ideas we've considered in previous chapters, suggests five guidelines for dealing with conflict. Following these should increase your ability to handle conflicts effectively.

Focus on the Overall Communication System

Conflict does not occur in a vacuum. Instead, it takes place in the context of relationships and the overall communication climate established over time. As we noted in Chapter 1, communication is systemic, which means it occurs in contexts, and it is composed of many interacting parts. Applying the principle of systems to conflict, we can see that how we deal with conflict is shaped by factors beyond an immediate disagreement. This means that we must attend to the overall systems of relationships and communication if we wish to make conflict constructive.

Couples who have developed negative interpersonal climates cannot argue constructively simply by practicing "good conflict techniques" such as focusing talk and not interrupting. Those techniques occur within larger contexts that affect how they are interpreted. Partners who have learned to be generally

defensive and distrustful are unlikely to respond openly to even the best conflict methods. By the same reasoning, in climates that are generally supportive and confirming, even unconstructive conflict communication is unlikely to derail relationships. Conflict, like all interaction, is affected by its contexts.

To make conflict more constructive in your relationships you should apply the information and guidelines discussed throughout this book. These will allow you to create positive, affirming interpersonal climates in which conflict can be managed most constructively. Engaging in mindful listening, which we discussed in Chapter 6, is essential to effective management of conflict. Also important is creating confirming climates, which we examined in Chapter 8. In addition, it's a good idea to apply the guidelines for effective verbal and nonverbal communication that we considered in Chapters 4 and 5. What you've learned about self-concept and perception should also help you control the multiple factors that influence how you deal with conflict in your relationships. In other words, conflict is part of a larger whole, and we must make that whole healthy in order to create a context in which conflict can be resolved without jeopardizing partners or relationships. Keep in mind that conflict always has three parties: you, another person, and the relationship between the two of you. Healthy conflict communication honors all three.

Time Conflict Effectively

Timing affects how we communicate about conflicts. There are three ways to use chronemics so that conflicts are most likely to be effective. First, try not to engage in serious conflict discussions at times when one or both people will not be fully present psychologically. Most of us are more irritable when we are sick or stressed. We're also less attentive and less mindful listeners when we are tired. It's generally more productive to discuss problems in private rather than in public settings. If time is limited or we are rushing, we're less likely to take the time to deal constructively with differences. It's impossible to listen well, develop ideas, and respond thoughtfully when a stopwatch is ticking in our minds. One guideline to keep in mind, then, is to time when you have conflicts.

A second guideline for timing is to be flexible about when you deal with differences. Constructive conflict is most likely when everyone's needs are accommodated. If one partner feels ready to talk about a problem but the other doesn't, it's probably wise to delay discussion. This only works, of course, if the person who isn't ready agrees to talk about the issue at a later time. Because research indicates that men are more likely than women to avoid discussing relationship conflicts, they may be especially reluctant to talk about disagreements without first gaining some distance (Beck, 1988; Rusbult, 1987). Some individuals prefer to tackle problems as soon as they arise, whereas others need time to percolate privately before interacting. It's generally a good idea not to discuss conflict in the heat of anger. The danger is that anger may provoke us to hurl cruel words and insults which we cannot take back later. Constructive, healthy conflict communication is more likely when tempers aren't flaring.

STEPHANIE: *I have a really hot temper, so I can cut someone to pieces if I argue when I'm mad. I have hurt a lot of friends by attacking them before I cooled off, and I hate myself when I act like that. I have finally figured out that I can handle fights constructively if I cool down. Now when I'm hot, I tell my friends or my boyfriend that I can't discuss it right then. Later, when I'm calm, I can talk without saying things that hurt them and that I feel bad about.*

A third way to use chronemics to promote positive conflict is bracketing, which we discussed earlier in this chapter. It is natural that a variety of issues needing attention come up in the course of conflict. If we try to deal with all the sideline problems that arise, however, we can't focus on the immediate problem. For example, during an argument about cleaning their apartment Eddy may say to Brian, "I know I sometimes dump my clothes on the floor, but I don't keep you awake talking to people at all hours of the night." Eddy's comment is a countercomplaint that could sidetrack the conversation from a focus on cleaning. Brian might respond, "Fair enough. We do need to talk about my telephone calls, but let's resolve the issue of cleaning first. Then we can talk about late-night phone calls." Bracketing other concerns for later discussion lets us keep conflict focused productively. Keep in mind, however, that bracketing works only if partners return to the issues they set aside.

Aim for Win–Win Conflict

How you approach conflict shapes what will happen in communication. As we have seen in this chapter, each orientation to conflict can be appropriate in certain circumstances. When conflict exists between two people who care about each other and want to sustain a good relationship, however, the win–win style is most desirable. Thus, we should aim to manage conflict so that both we and the other person come out ahead. If you enter conflict with the assumption that you, the other person, and the relationship can all benefit from conflict, it's likely that you will bring about a resolution that benefits everyone. Adopting a win–win orientation to conflict reflects a commitment to honoring yourself and your needs, the other person and her or his needs, and the integrity of your shared relationship.

To maximize the chance of a win–win resolution of conflict, begin by identifying your feelings and your needs or desires in the situation. You may want to review Chapter 7 to remind yourself of ways to clarify your emotions. Understanding what you feel and want is essential to productive conflict communication. Once you figure out what you feel and need, express yourself in clear language. It's not effective to make vague or judgmental statements such as, "I

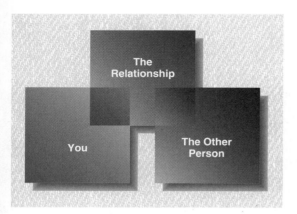

FIGURE 9.3
The Parties Involved in Conflict

don't like the way you ignore me, and I want you to be more sensitive." It would be more effective to say, "I feel hurt when you don't call, and I want us to find some way that I can be assured of your feelings about me without making you feel handcuffed."

The second step is to identify what the other person feels, needs, or wants. If you don't already know what the other person wants and feels, don't mindread. Instead, ask the other person what she or he is feeling and what she needs or wants in terms of a resolution to the conflict. When the other person expresses his or her feelings and preferences, listen mindfully. Resist the temptation to countercomplain or argue. Just listen and try to understand the other person's perspective as fully as you can. Minimal encouragers and paraphrasing are valuable because they let the other person know you are listening closely and are committed to understanding her or his perspective.

Third, focus on language that promotes cooperation and mutual respect. To do this, rely on supportive communication and monitor any communication that might foster a defensive climate. You should also use I-language to own your thoughts and feelings. Throughout conflict communication, mindful listening is critical. Being fully present in the discussion and focusing on the other achieve two important goals: First, those skills allow you to gain the maximum understanding of the other person's perspective and feelings; second, by modeling mindfulness in your own communication you foster mindfulness in the other's.

Throughout conflict communication, keep reminding yourself that win–win solutions are usually possible when both people balance concerns for themselves and each other. On the relationship level of meaning you want to communicate this message: "I care about you and your feelings and desires, and I know you care about me and how I feel and what I want." If that message underlies your conflict communication, chances are good that you will attain a win–win resolution.

Honor Yourself, Your Partner, and the Relationship

The guidelines we've discussed so far share a key principle: Effective interpersonal communication attends to each person and the relationship between them (see Figure 9.3). Throughout this book we've emphasized the importance of honoring yourself, others, and relationships. It's important to keep all three in balance, especially when conflicts arise.

Healthy, constructive conflict communication is impossible if we disregard the other person's needs and feelings. Doing so disconfirms the other and sets a win–lose tone for conversation. Being sensitive to others, however, is not enough. Just as it is ineffective to disregard others' concerns, it is also unwise to muffle your own. In fairness to yourself and the other person, you should express your feelings and needs clearly. For conflicts to be resolved in truly satisfying ways, each person must put her or his ideas, feelings, and needs on the table. Only then can partners engage in informed, open efforts to generate workable solutions to their problems.

In addition to attending to ourselves and our friends and romantic partners, we must remember that relationships are affected by how we handle conflict. For this reason, win–lose orientations toward conflict should really be called win–lose–lose, because when one person wins, both the other person and the relationship lose. Win–win orientations and constructive forms of communication make it possible for both individuals and the relationship to be winners.

© David Bitters/The Picture Cube, Inc.

Show Grace When Appropriate

Finally, an important principle to keep in mind during conflict is that grace is sometimes appropriate. Although the idea of grace has not traditionally been discussed in communication texts, it is very much a part of spiritual and philosophical thinking, which should influence how we interact with others. You don't have to be religious to show grace, nor do you have to have a knowledge of philosophy. All that's required is a willingness to sometimes excuse someone who has no formal right to expect your compassion.

By definition, **grace** is granting forgiveness or putting aside our own needs when there is no standard that says we should or must do so. Rather than being prompted by rules or expectations, grace springs from a generosity of personal spirit. Grace is not forgiving when we *should*—for instance, excusing people who aren't responsible for their actions. Also, grace isn't allowing others to have their way when we have no choice. Instead, grace is unearned and unnecessary kindness. For instance, two roommates agree to split chores and one doesn't do her share because she has three tests in a week. Her roommate might do all the chores even though there is no agreement or expectation of this generosity. This is an act of grace. It's also an act of grace to defer to another person's preference when you could hold out for your own. Similarly, when someone hurts us and has no right to expect forgiveness, we may choose to forgive anyway. We do so not because we *have* to, but because we want to. Grace is a matter of choice.

Grace involves the Zen concept of **letting go,** which is to free ourselves of anger, blame, and judgments about another and what she or he did. When we let go of these feelings, we release both ourselves and others from their consequences. Sometimes we tell a friend we forgive him for some offense, but then later we remind him of it. We might say we'll forget a transgression by our romantic partner, but later hold it against her. When we continue to hang on to blame and judgment, we haven't really let go, so we have not really shown grace. There's no grace when we blackmail others for kindness or hang on to hostile feelings. An act of grace must also be done gracefully. It is not grace if we yield to a friend and snap, "Okay, have it your own darned way." Grace doesn't create feelings of debt in others. Grace involves letting go of hostile feelings and blame with a style that is as graceful as what we actually do.

"Look, instead of constantly grading one another, let's make this a simple pass/fail relationship."

Reprinted from The Chronicle of Higher Education with the permission of Carole Cable.

Grace is given without strings. Arthur Osborne (1996), who believes grace is essential in loving relationships, makes this point clearly when he says, "the person who asks for a reward is a merchant, not a lover" (p. 6). We show kindness, defer our needs, or forgive a wrong *without any expectation of reward.* Grace isn't doing something nice to make a friend feel grateful or indebted to us. It's also not acting in grace when we do something with the expectation of a payback. To do a favor for your partner because you want a reciprocal favor is a matter of bargaining, not grace. For an act to be one of grace, it must be done without conditions or expectations of return.

Grace is not always appropriate, and it can be exploited by individuals who take advantage of kindness. Some people repeatedly abuse and hurt others, confident that pardons will be granted. When grace is extended and then exploited, it may be unwise to extend it again. However, if you show grace in good faith and another takes advantage, you should not fault yourself. Kindness and a willingness to forgive are worthy moral precepts. Those who abuse grace, not those who offer it, are blameworthy.

Because Western culture emphasizes assertion and protection of self-interests, grace is not widely practiced or esteemed. We are told to stand up for ourselves, not let others walk all over us, not put up with being hurt, and not tolerate transgressions. It is important to honor and assert ourselves, as we've emphasized throughout this book. However, self-interest and self-assertion alone are insufficient principles for creating rich interpersonal relationships.

None of us is perfect. We all make mistakes, hurt others with thoughtless acts, and occasionally do things we know are wrong. Sometimes there is no *reason* others should forgive us when we wrong them; we have no right to expect exoneration. Yet, in human relations there has to be some room for redemption, for the extension of grace when it is not required or earned. Clearly we should not always forgive others if they betray or hurt us, and certainly we should be cautious of granting grace repeatedly to someone who exploits it. At the same time, the richest relationships allow room for grace occasionally.

C H A P T E R
Summary

This chapter focused on conflict as a natural, inevitable, and potentially constructive aspect of interpersonal life. Because conflicts are normal and unavoidable in any relationship of real depth, the challenge is to learn to manage conflicts effectively. Patterns of conflict are shaped by how individuals view conflict. We discussed lose–lose, win–lose, and win–win approaches to conflict, and explored how each affects interaction. In addition, conflict patterns are influenced by how individuals respond to tension. Inclinations to exit, neglect, show loyalty, or voice conflict vary in how actively they deal with tension and how constructive they are for relationships. In most cases, voice is the preferred response because only voice allows partners to intervene actively and constructively when conflicts arise.

Communication is particularly important in influencing the process of interpersonal conflict. Research by communication scholars as well as clinicians indicates that patterns of interaction that promote constructive management of conflict include being mindful, confirming others, showing dual perspective, listening sensitively, focusing discussion, contracting solutions, and avoiding mindreading, interrupting, self-summarizing, and cross-complaining.

Finally, we considered five guidelines for increasing the constructiveness of interpersonal conflict. First, we need to remember that conflicts occur within overall systems of communication and relationships. To be constructive, conflict must take place within supportive, confirming climates in which good interpersonal communication is practiced. Second, it's important to time conflicts so that all individuals have the time they need for private reflection and for productive discussion. A third principle is to aim for win–win solutions to conflict. Consistent with these three guidelines is working to balance commitments to yourself, others, and relationships when conflict arises. It is unwise to squelch any of these three, because all are affected by how we manage disagreements. Finally, we saw that it is sometimes appropriate to show grace in our personal relationships.

Although grace can be exploited, it can also infuse relationships with kindness and make room for inevitable human errors. It's important to balance the tensions inherent in the notion of grace so that we recognize both its potential values and its dangers.

In the next two chapters, we'll explore the worlds of friendship and romance. As we do so, we'll carry forward the information and guidelines we've considered in this chapter, because how we manage conflicts affects the health of our friendships and romantic relationships.

KEY Concepts

- bracketing
- conflict
- contracting
- exit response
- games

- grace
- kitchensinking
- letting go
- lose–lose
- loyalty response

- neglect response
- passive aggression
- voice response
- win–lose
- win–win

FOR FURTHER Thought & Discussion

1. What ethical principles are implicit in lose–lose, win–lose, and win–win orientations toward conflict? Some styles of conflict emphasize fairness, whereas other styles place greater value on cooperation. Do you identify more strongly with either of these value orientations?

2. Think about the ways that you typically respond to conflict. Do you tend to rely on one or two of the four responses we discussed (exit, voice, loyalty, neglect)? Are your response tendencies consistent with research findings about women and men, in general?

3. Have you ever been in a relationship in which conflict was stifled? Using the concepts you learned in this chapter, can you now describe how the conflict was repressed? Can you now think of ways you might have engaged in more effective conflict communication in that relationship?

4. Identify one situation in your life in which each orientation to conflict was, or would have been, appropriate. When would lose–lose have been appropriate? When would win–lose have been a reasonable approach? When would win–win have been the best approach?

5. Use your *InfoTrac College Edition* to review the table of contents for the five most recent issues of *Journal of Family Practice* and *Journal of Comparative Family Studies.* Do you find articles that discuss how conflicts affect families or how families can handle conflicts productively?

6. This chapter emphasizes aiming for a win–win approach to conflict in personal relationships. Do you believe that in most cases both people can benefit (or win) if each is committed to honoring self and other?

7. Have you been in relationships in which you felt there was grace? How was grace communicated? What was the impact of grace? Have you extended grace to others?

Friendships

in Our

Lives

For most of us, friends are important. Friends help us pass time, grow person-ally, celebrate moments of joy, and get through the trials and tribulations of everyday life. The intricate design of our lives is made richer by the friendships that thread through them. Each new friend we weave into our lives enriches us and our interpersonal world.

What Is Friendship?

Think about your close friends, and respond to the six questions below.

	VERY	SOMEWHAT	NOT VERY
1. How important are friends in your life?	_____	_____	_____
2. How important is it for friends to accept each other?	_____	_____	_____
3. How important is it for friends to trust each other?	_____	_____	_____
4. How important is it for friends to feel emotionally close to each other?	_____	_____	_____
5. How important is it for friends to provide companion-ship in doing activities?	_____	_____	_____
6. How important is it for friends to help each other with practical assistance?	_____	_____	_____

The six questions you just answered focus on primary expectations of friend-ship. If you are like most people, you responded that friendship is very impor-tant in your life and that most or all of items 2 through 6 are very important to you. Across differences in race, gender, class, and sexual preference, most of us expect friends to provide intimacy, acceptance, trust, practical assistance, and support. These are common threads in diverse friendships. However, people dif-fer in how they express trust, intimacy, acceptance, and support in friendship.

In this chapter, we will explore what friendships are, how they work, and how they differ among us. To launch our discussion, we'll identify common fea-tures of friendship as well as variations that result from diverse cultural back-grounds. Second, we'll explore the development and rules of friendships. Next, we'll consider pressures on friendship and how we can deal with these. Guidelines for effective communication between friends conclude the chapter.

© Roy Morsch/The Stock Market

The Nature of Friendship

Friendship is a unique relationship. In contrast to most relationships, friendship is voluntary. Biology or legal procedures establish relationships among family members, and proximity defines neighbors and co-workers. Friends, however, come together voluntarily. Friendships are also unique in lacking institutionalized structure or guidelines. There are legal and religious ceremonies for marriage and social and legal rules for governing marital relationships. We have no parallel ceremonies to recognize friendships and no formal standards to guide interaction among friends. The lack of social standards and recognition makes friendship a particularly challenging and exciting relationship.

S T U D E N T VOICES

WILL: *It's funny. Kids have ways to symbolize friendship, but adults don't. I remember when Jimmy down the block and I became blood brothers. It was a big, big deal for me at eight. My sister and her best friend bought matching friendship rings and wore them until their fingers turned green. But what do we have to symbolize friendships when we grow up? Nothing.*

Even though there are no formal standards for friendship, we have generated some fairly consistent ideas about what a friend is and what happens between friends. Regardless of race, sexual orientation, gender, age, and class, Westerners share some basic expectations of what friends do and what friendship is.

Willingness to Invest

Most people assume friendships require personal investments (Duck & Wright, 1993; Monsour, 1992). We expect to invest time, effort, energy, thought, and feeling in our friendships. Women and men of both homosexual and heterosexual orientations report that having friends is important for a fulfilling life (Mazur, 1989; Nardi & Sherrod, 1994; Sherrod, 1989). Although people differ in how they build and experience friendship, most of us agree it's important.

S T U D E N T VOICES

LAKISHA: *I don't know what I'd do without my friends. More than once they've held me together when I had a fight with my mom or broke up with a guy. When something good happens, it's not quite real until I share it with my friends. I don't think I could be happy without friends.*

DENNIS: *I really count on my buddies to be there for me. Sometimes we talk or do stuff, but a lot of times we just hang out together. That might not sound important, but it is. Hanging out with friends is a big part of my life.*

Emotional Closeness

We also expect emotional closeness with friends. We want our friends to know our inner selves and to let us know theirs. In addition, intimacy implies that friends like or love each other and care about each other's happiness. Yet the shared view that friendship includes intimacy isn't paralleled by shared ideas about what intimacy is. Research on friendship suggests that how we experience and express intimacy with friends depends on our backgrounds.

APPLY THE IDEA
Your Style of Friendship

Before reading further, answer the following questions about how you experience and express closeness with friends.

With your closest or best friends, how often do you:
1. talk about family problems
2. exchange favors (provide transportation, lend money)
3. engage in sports (shoot hoops, play tennis, and so forth)
4. try to take their minds off problems with diversions
5. disclose your personal anxieties and fears
6. talk about your romantic relationships and family relationships
7. do things together (camp, go to a game, shop)
8. confide secrets you wouldn't want others to know
9. just hang out without a lot of conversation
10. talk about small events in your day-to-day life
11. provide practical assistance to help friends
12. talk explicitly about your feelings for each other
13. discuss and work through tensions in your friendship
14. physically embrace or touch to show affection
15. ignore or work around problems in the friendship

   Items 1, 5, 6, 8, 10, 12, 13, and 14 have been found to be more prominent in women's friendships; items 2, 3, 4, 7, 9, 11, and 15 tend to be more pronounced in men's friendships.

Closeness Through Dialogue   One way to build and express intimacy is through communication. For many people, communication is the centerpiece of intimate friendship. This is especially true for people socialized in feminine speech communities, which emphasize talk as a primary path to intimacy. In general, women see talking and listening as the main activities that create and

© Mark Antman/The Image Works

sustain feelings of closeness (Aries, 1987; Becker, 1987; Rubin, 1985). Talk between women friends tends to be disclosive and emotionally expressive. Women discuss not only major events and issues but also day-to-day activities. This small talk isn't really small at all, because it allows friends to understand the rhythms of each other's life. Intimacy is created as friends talk about themselves and their relationships and as they reveal personal feelings and information. Out of intimate conversation friends weave their separate worlds into a shared mosaic. This builds a strong and deep sense of connection.

A majority of women expect to know and be known by close friends. This is also true of androgynous men, who incorporate both feminine and masculine values into their identities (Jones & Dembo, 1989; Williams, 1985). Communication is a primary path to rich, personal knowledge, so women friends talk in depth about personal feelings and information. They want friends to know and understand their deepest selves and they want to know their friends in emotional depth. Because it is disclosive and personal, communication between women friends is highly expressive (Brehm, 1992).

Reflecting feminine socialization, communication between women friends is typically responsive and supportive (Wright & Scanlon, 1991). Friends use facial expressions and head movements to show involvement. In addition, they ask questions and give feedback that signals they are following and want to know more. Women friends also offer generous emotional support to one another. They do this by accepting one another's feelings and staying involved in the other's dreams, problems, and lives.

Closeness Through Doing   A second way to create and express closeness is by sharing activities. Friends enjoy doing things together and doing things for one another. Activities and companionship are the center of friendship for some individuals. Closeness through doing is often the primary, although not the only, emphasis in men's friendships (Swain, 1989; Wood & Inman, 1993). As we have seen in previous chapters, masculine speech communities pivot on activities such as sports. This may be why men, in general, find it more natural to build intimacy through doing things than through talking. Sharing activities and working toward common goals (winning the game or battle) build a sense of camaraderie (Sherrod, 1989).

S T U D E N T

JOSH: *The thing I like about my buddies is that we can just do stuff together without a lot of talk. Our wives expect us to talk about every feeling we have as if that's required to be real. I'm tight with my buddies, but we don't have to talk about feelings all the time. You learn a lot about someone when you hunt together or coach the Little League.*

Josh has a good insight. We do reveal ourselves and learn about others in the process of doing things together. In the course of playing football or soccer, teammates learn a lot about one another's courage, reliability, willingness to take risks, and security. Soldiers who fight together also discover one another's strengths and weaknesses. Strong emotional bonds and personal knowledge can develop without verbal interaction (Rubin, 1985).

Intimacy through doing also involves expressing care by doing things for friends. Scott Swain (1989) says men's friendships typically involve a give and take of favors. Jake helps Matt move into his new apartment, and Matt later assists Jake with a glitch in his computer. As a rule, men perceive giving and receiving practical help as expressions of caring and closeness. Perhaps because masculine socialization emphasizes instrumental activities, men are more likely than women to see doing things for others as a primary way to say they care. Notice that the gender difference is a matter of degree, not absolute dichotomy. Although men tend to place more emphasis on instrumental expressions of care than women, most men also value and engage in expressive communication with close friends. Similarly, although women tend to place more emphasis on expressive shows of care than men, most women value and engage in instrumental expressions of caring.

Sometimes the different emphases men and women place on instrumental and expressive behaviors leads to misunderstandings. If Myra sees intimate talk as the crux of closeness, she may not interpret Ed's practical help in fixing her computer as indicating that he cares about her.

S T U D E N T

KAYA: *My husband's life centers on doing things for me and our kids. He looks for things to do for us. Like when our son came home over break, he tuned up his car and replaced a tire. I hadn't even noticed the tire was bad. When I wanted to return to school, he took a second job to make more money. One day he came home with a microwave to make cooking easier for me. All the things he does for us are his way of expressing love.*

Let's repeat a key point that is often overlooked: It would be a mistake to conclude that women and men differ entirely in how they create intimacy; they are actually more alike than we often think (Canary & Dindia, 1998). Recent studies reveal that the sexes are not as different as they are sometimes stereo-

© Mark Antman/The Image Works

typed to be (Duck & Wright, 1993). Although women generally place a special priority on communication, men obviously talk with their friends. Like women, men disclose personal feelings and vulnerabilities. They simply do it less, as a rule, than women. Similarly, although men's friendships may be more instrumental, women friends also do things with and for one another and count these as important in friendship (Duck & Wright, 1993). Many of the differences between how women and men create and express intimacy are matters of degree, not absolute contrasts. It's also wise to keep in mind that both talking and doing are legitimate ways to show you care about others.

APPLY THE IDEA

Appreciating Talking and Doing in Friendships

For each scenario described below, write out one thing you might *say* and one thing you might *do* to show you cared about the person described.

1. Your best friend has just broken up with his/her long-term boyfriend/girlfriend. Your friend calls you and says, "I feel so lonely."

You say _____

You do _____

2. A good friend of yours tells you he/she has been cut from the team and won't get to play this year.

You say _____

You do _____

3. Your best friend from high school calls and says she/he thinks about you often even though the two of you no longer maintain much contact.

You say _____

You do _____

4. A close friend stops you on campus and excitedly says, "I just found out I've been accepted into the law school here. Can you believe it?"

You say _____

You do _____

Acceptance

A third common expectation of friends is that they will accept us. We expect friends to like us for who we are and to accept us, warts and all. Each of us has shortcomings and vices, but we count on friends to accept us in spite of these. With people we don't know well, we often feel we need to put on our best face to impress them. With friends, however, we don't want to put up false fronts. If we feel low, we can act that way instead of faking cheerfulness. If we are unhappy, we can express our feelings openly without fear of being rejected. If we are upset, we don't have to hide it. We expect friends to accept us as we are and as we change over time.

The essence of acceptance is feeling that we are okay as human beings. As we saw with Maslow's hierarchy of human needs in Chapter 1, being accepted by others is important to our sense of self-worth. Most of us are fortunate enough to gain acceptance from family as well as friends. However, this is not always true for lesbians and gays. Sadly, some parents reject sons and daughters who are homosexual. They refuse to validate the basic worth of a child who isn't heterosexual. Parental rejection echoes Western culture's general hostility to homosexuality. Because social and familial acceptance is sometimes lacking for them, gays and lesbians may count on friends for acceptance even more than heterosexuals do (Nardi & Sherrod, 1994). Friendships may have heightened importance because they often substitute for families, as reflected in the book title *Families We Choose* (Weston, 1991).

S T U D E N T **VOICES**

DOUG: *About a year ago, I came out to my parents, and they acted like I was from another planet. It was like once I said I was gay, nothing else about me mattered. Just being gay made me less than human. They shouted and cried and threatened and begged me to get therapy. The only thing they didn't do was consider that maybe I didn't need therapy—maybe it's okay to be gay. The gay community became my family. They are the people who accept me and support who I am. I still hope Mom and Dad will come around one day, but in the meantime I've made another family for myself.*

Notice in Doug's commentary that he felt judged by his parents, which probably made him feel defensive. Doug's experience also illustrates the damage done by totalizing—focusing on a single aspect of a person's identity and ignoring many others. Doug is still a student, a loving son, a person who has dreams, ambitions, hopes, and fears. Yet, he feels that his parents see only his sexual orientation and disregard everything else about him.

Although lesbians and gays may depend more heavily than heterosexuals on friends for acceptance, there are few other differences in how their friendships

HAGAR THE HORRIBLE Reprinted with special permission of King Features Syndicate.

operate. Like heterosexuals, gays and lesbians value friendship and distinguish among casual, close, and best friends. Also like heterosexuals, gays and lesbians rely on both communication and activities as paths to intimacy.

Trust

A key component of close friendships is trust, which has two dimensions. First, trust involves confidence in others to be dependable. We count on them to do what they say and not to do what they promise they won't. Second, trust assumes emotional reliability, which is the belief that a friend cares about us and our welfare. When we feel both dimensions of trust, we don't need to preface private information with warnings not to tell anyone, and we don't have to have detailed knowledge about what our friends do and who they talk with to believe that they will not hurt us.

STUDENT VOICES

SARINI: *Trust is the bottom line for friends. It's the single most important thing. It takes me a long time to really trust someone, but when I do, it's complete. I was so hurt when a friend told another person something I told her in confidence. We still get together, but the trust is gone. I don't tell her private things, so there's no depth.*

Like most qualities of friendship, trust is something that develops gradually and in degrees. We learn to trust people over time as we interact with them and discover they do what they say they will and they don't betray us. As trust develops, friends increasingly reveal themselves to one another. If each new disclosure is accepted and kept confidential, trust continues to grow. When a high level of trust develops, friends feel less of the uncertainty and insecurity that are natural in early stages of relationships (Boon, 1994).

The level of trust that develops between friends depends on a number of factors. First, our individual histories influence our capacity to trust others. Recalling the discussion of attachment styles in Chapter 2, you'll remember that early interactions with caregivers shape our beliefs about others. For those of us who got consistently loving and nurturing care, trusting others is not especially difficult. On the other hand, some children do not receive that kind of care. For them, caregivers were sometimes available and nurturing and at other times caregivers were absent or not nurturing. If caring is either absent or inconsistent, the capacity to trust others withers. Researchers think the tendency to trust or not to trust is relatively enduring unless later experiences change the early lessons about relationships (Bartholomew, 1993).

STUDENT VOICES

JAMES: *It's tough for me to really trust anybody, even my closest friends or my girlfriend. It's not that they aren't trustworthy. The problem's in me. I just have trouble putting full faith in anyone. When my parents had*

© Zigy Kaluzny/Tony Stone Images, Inc.

me, Dad was on the bottle, and Mom was thinking about divorce. He got in Alcoholics Anonymous and they stayed together, but I wonder if what was happening between them meant they weren't there for me. Maybe I learned from the start that I couldn't count on others.

Family scripts also influence how much and how quickly we trust others. Some of us were taught that people are good and we should count on them, whereas others learned that people are untrustworthy and that we shouldn't ever turn our back on anyone. Families also influence the importance we attach to friends. Did your parents have many friends? Did you see them enjoying being with their friends? Were their friends often in your home? Or did you seldom see your parents spending time with friends and were there few occasions when any of their friends were in your home? How many friends your parents had and how much they seemed to value them may have taught you an early lesson about the importance of friendship in our lives. Basic scripts from families, although not irrevocable, often affect the ease and extent of our ability to trust and our interest in maintaining good friendships.

Willingness to take risks also influences trust in relationships. There is considerable risk in trusting a friend with our secrets, fears, and flaws. The friend could always use the information against us or share our most private disclosures with others (Boon, 1994). We can never *know* for sure what friends will do with private information, but we trust them not to use it to exploit or expose us. In this sense, trust is a leap into the unknown. To emphasize the risk in trusting, it has been said that "trust begins where knowledge ends" (Lewis & Weigert, 1985, p. 462). The risk involved may explain why we trust only selected people.

Support

Communication scholars Brant Burleson and Wendy Samter (1994) report that support is a basic expectation of friendship. We expect friends to support us in times of personal stress. Once individuals leave home for college, friends often become the primary people to whom they turn for help and comfort (Adelman, Parks, & Albrecht, 1987).

There are many ways to show support. What is common among the various types of support is the relationship message "I care about you." Often we support friends by listening to their problems. The more mindfully we listen, the more support we provide. How we respond also shows support. For example, it's supportive to offer to help a friend with a problem or to talk through options. Another way we support friends is by letting them know they're not alone. When we say "I've felt that way too" or "I've had the same problem," we signal that we understand their feelings. Having the grace to accept friends when they err or hurt us is also a way to show support. To comfort friends in difficult times, we can validate their worth and help them place problems in a larger perspective that includes positive outlooks (Burleson, 1984).

Another important form of support is being available. Sometimes we can't do or say much to ease a friend's unhappiness. Breaking up with a partner, losing a parent, or being rejected by a graduate program are not matters we can change by our words or deeds. However, we can offer ourselves. We show we care by standing by friends so that at least they have company in their sadness. In one study, young adults said the essence of real friendship was "being there for each other" (Secklin, 1991). It is a great comfort to know someone is there for us no matter what.

JOSÉ: *Last year my father died back in Mexico, and I wasn't with him when he died. I felt terrible. My friend Alex spent a lot of time with me after my father died. Alex didn't do anything special, and we didn't even really talk much about my father or how I felt. But he was there for me, and that meant everything. I knew he cared even though he never said that.*

Women and men tend to differ somewhat in how they support friends. Because feminine socialization emphasizes personal communication, women generally provide more verbal emotional support than men (Aries, 1987; Becker, 1987; Duck & Wright, 1993). They are likely to talk in detail about feelings, dimensions of emotional issues, and fears that accompany distress. By talking in depth about emotional troubles, women help one another identify and ventilate feelings. In addition, intimate talk weaves friends closely together. This exemplifies closeness through dialogue.

RICH: *Girls and guys help each other out in different ways. If I don't want to think about some problem, I want to be with a guy friend. He'll take my mind off the hassle. If I'm with a girl, she'll want to talk about the problem and wallow in it, and that just makes it worse sometimes. But when I really need to talk or get something off my chest, I need a girl friend. Guys don't talk about personal stuff.*

SALLY FORTH © 1995. Reprinted with special permission of King Features Syndicate.

Men tend to rely less than women on emotional talk to support friends. Instead, they often engage in "covert intimacy," a term Swain (1989) coined to describe the indirect ways men support one another. Instead of an intense hug, which women might use to support a hurting friend, men are more likely to clasp a shoulder or playfully punch an arm. Instead of engaging in direct and sustained emotional talk, men tend to communicate support more instrumentally. This could mean giving advice on how to solve a problem or offering assistance, such as a loan or transportation. Finally, men are more likely than women to support friends by coming up with diversions (Cancian, 1987; Tavris, 1992). If you can't make a problem any better, at least you can take a friend's mind off it. "Let's go throw some darts" and "Let's check out the new movie" are offers to support a friend by providing diversions. These ways of supporting others are consistent with the masculine mode of closeness.

S T U D E N T   VOICES

BELLINO: *A year ago, a friend of mine from back home called me up to ask for a loan. I said, "sure," and asked what was up. He told me his hours had been cut back and he couldn't buy groceries for his family. I knew the problem was more than paying for groceries. I figured he also couldn't pay for lights and rent and everything else. So I talked with several of his friends in our church and we took up a collection to help him. Then I took it over and left it at his house without any note and without saying anything. He didn't have to ask for help and I didn't have to say anything. What I and the others in our congregation did was to do what was needed to help him.*

Ethnicity also influences orientations toward friendship. In a study of Japanese and American friendships Dean Barnlund (1989) found both similarities and differences. Both ethnic groups preferred friends who were similar to them in age and ethnic heritage, and both groups agreed on many of the qualities that describe friends. Commonly valued qualities in friends included understanding, respect, trust, and sincerity. Yet Japanese and U.S. citizens differed in the priority they assigned the qualities. Japanese respondents said togetherness, trust, and warmth were the most important qualities in friendship, whereas Americans listed understanding, respect, and sincerity as the top qualities. The differences in rankings reflect distinctions between Japanese and American culture. Interpersonal harmony and collective orientation are central values in Japan, and these are reflected in the qualities Japanese consider most important in friends. U.S. culture emphasizes individuality, candor, and respect—the very qualities Americans most prize in friends.

A more recent study by Mary Jane Collier (1996) identified some different priorities for friendships among four ethnic groups. European Americans place great emphasis on sincerity and freedom to express ideas. This emphasis reflects the Western priority on individuality. Consistent with traditional Asian cultural values, Asian Americans especially value courtesy, restraint, and respect for fam-

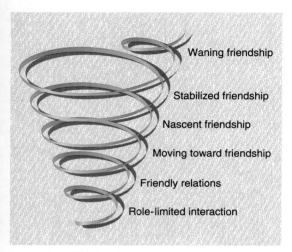

FIGURE 10.1
The Developmental Course of Friendship

ilies in their friends. Among African Americans, problem solving and respect for ethnic heritage were primary criteria in selecting friends. Relationship support and expression of feelings are priorities among Latinos and Latinas, values that reflect the premium placed on emotions in Hispanic cultures.

Although friendships reflect the influence of personal experience, gender, and ethnic heritage, there is also much common ground in what people expect and value in friendships. We expect friends to invest in friendship and to provide intimacy, acceptance, trust, and support. As a result of gender, race, ethnicity, economic class, age, and sexual orientation, we may differ in how we experience and express friendship. However, it seems that these five common expectations transcend differences among us. Yet, it's not enough for friends to have these feelings; they must also communicate them. Skills in verbal and nonverbal communication, listening, building climate, and managing conflict contribute to effective expression of friendship.

The Development and Rules of Friendship

The ways friendship grows and operates are not random. Although we're usually not aware of patterns, friendships tend to follow rules in how they develop and function.

The Developmental Course of Friendship

Most friendships develop over time in fairly patterned ways. Although intense bonds are sometimes formed quickly in unusual circumstances such as crises, the majority of friends work out their relationship in a series of stages. Bill Rawlins (1981), an interpersonal communication researcher who focuses on communication between friends, developed a six-stage model of how friendships develop (Figure 10.1).

Role-Limited Interaction   Friendships begin with an encounter in two individuals' social circle. We might meet a new person at work, through membership on an athletic team, in a club, or by chance in an airport, store, or class. The initial meeting is the first stage of interaction and, possibly, friendship. During this stage, we tend to rely on standard social rules and roles. We are polite, and we are less than fully open and disclosive, because we aren't ready to reveal our private selves. In early meetings, people don't have enough personal knowledge of each other to engage in dual perspective. Instead, they rely on more general scripts and stereotypes. Also, early interactions are often awkward and laced with uncertainty, because individuals haven't worked out their own patterns for relating to each other.

© Bob Daemmrich/Tony Stone Images, Inc.

Friendly Relations   The second stage of friendship is friendly relations, in which individuals check out the other to see whether common ground and interests exist. Jean tries to start a conversation with Paula by commenting on the teacher in a class they share. If Paula responds with her impressions of the teacher, she conveys the relationship-level message that she's interested in interacting. A businessperson may joke or engage in small talk to see if an associate wants to move beyond the acquaintance level of relating. Although friendly exchanges are not dramatic, they are useful. Through them, we explore the potential for a more personal relationship with another person.

Moving Toward Friendship   During the third stage of interaction, we start making serious moves to create a friendship. Until this stage, we stick pretty closely to social rules and norms, and we interact in contexts where we naturally meet. Moving toward friendship involves stepping beyond social roles. We might make a small self-disclosure or comment that we're angry about something to signal we'd like to personalize the relationship. We also move toward friendship when we meet outside of contexts that naturally occur. Emily might ask her associate Sam if he wants to stop at a bar for a drink before leaving for the day. Ben might ask his classmate Drew if he wants to get together to study. Sometimes we involve others to lessen the potential awkwardness of being with someone we don't yet know well. For instance, Amy might invite Stuart to a party where others will be present. As we interact more personally with others, we begin to talk about feelings, values, interests, and attitudes. This personal knowledge forms the initial foundation of friendship.

Nascent Friendship   If individuals continue to interact and to like what they discover in each other, they begin to think of themselves as friends or as becoming friends. This is the stage of nascent, or embryonic, friendship. At this point, social rules and standards become less important, and friends begin to work out their own private rules for regulating interaction. When my friend Nancy and I were in this stage, we agreed to reserve Sunday brunch for each other every week. This was a private rule we generated to accommodate our schedules and preferences. Some friends settle into patterns of getting together for specific things (watching games, shopping, racquetball, going to movies) and don't ever expand those boundaries. Other friends share a wider range of times and activities. Although friends are working out rules for their relationship during the nascent stage, often they aren't aware of the rules until later. The milestones of this stage are that individuals begin to think of themselves as friends and to work out their own patterns for interaction. "Maintaining Friendships" on the next page discusses how much time we invest in various types of friendships.

Maintaining Friendships

Do we spend more time with casual friends or best friends? The answer might surprise you. A recent study indicates that frequent interaction is more important for casual friendships than for close or best friendships. When casual friends don't see each other, they aren't sure the friendship still exists.

Lack of interaction doesn't appear to threaten relationships between best friends. Close and best friendships depend more on assurances of affection, though these need not be frequent. The best explanation is that close and best friends feel more secure in their connection than do casual friends. Because they assume they're continuing parts of each other's life, best friends don't need regular interaction.

SOURCE: Rose, S., & Serafica, F. (1986). Keeping and ending casual, close and best friendships. *Journal of Social and Personal Relationships*, 3, 275–288.

Stabilized Friendship   When friends feel established in each other's life, the friendship is stabilized. A key benchmark of this stage is the assumption of continuity. Whereas in earlier stages individuals didn't count on getting together unless they made a specific plan, stabilized friends assume they'll continue to see each other. We no longer have to ask if a friend wants to get together again. We take future encounters for granted because we consider the relationship ongoing.

Another criterion of this stage is trust, which stabilizes the friendship. Throughout earlier stages of interaction, individuals make limited disclosures to build and test trust. A close friendship is unlikely to stabilize until there is a mutually high level of trust. Once friends have earned each other's trust, many of the barriers to fully interpersonal communication disintegrate. It now feels safe to share intimate information and to reveal vulnerabilities that we normally conceal from others. As we communicate more openly, our friendships become more honest and personal. We remove social masks we wear with most people and enter into I–Thou relationships by engaging friends in their unique individuality. Stabilized friendships may continue indefinitely, in some cases lasting a lifetime.

STUDENT VOICES

MARLENE: *Martha and I go way, way back—all the way to childhood when we lived in the same housing complex. As kids we made mudpies and ran a lemonade stand together. In high school, we double-dated and planned our lives together. Then we both got married and stayed in touch, even when Martha moved away. We still sent each other pictures of our children, and we called a lot. When my last child entered college, I decided it was time for me to do that too, so I enrolled in college. Before I did that, though, I had to talk to Martha and get her perspective on whether I was nuts to go to college in my thirties. She thought it was a great idea, and she's thinking about that for herself now. For nearly forty years we've shared everything in our lives.*

Waning Friendship   As we have seen, a common expectation of friendship is investment. When one or both individuals stop investing in a friendship, it is likely to wane. Sometimes friends drift apart because each is pulled in different directions by career and family demands. In other cases, friendships deteriorate because they've run their natural course and become boring. A third reason friendships end is violations of trust or other rules friends establish for themselves. Saying "I don't have time for you now" may violate friends' tacit agreement to always make room for each other. Criticizing a friend or not sharing confidences may also breach unspoken rules between friends.

CARY: *Janet and I had been friends since our first year at school. We told each other everything and trusted each other totally. When I told her that Brad had cheated on me, I knew she would not tell anyone else. She knew I felt bad about it, plus Brad and I got back together so I didn't want anyone to know about that incident. One day I was talking with another girl and she asked me how I'd been able to trust Brad again after he cheated on me. I hadn't told her about that! I knew she was friends with Janet, so I figured that's how she knew. To me that was the ultimate betrayal. I'm still on friendly terms with Janet, but she's not a close friend, and I don't tell her anything private.*

When friendships deteriorate or suffer serious violations, communication changes in predictable ways. Defensiveness and uncertainty rise, causing individuals to be more guarded, less spontaneous, and less disclosive than they were in the stage of stabilized friendship. Communication may also become more controlling and strategic as waning friends try to protect themselves from further exposure and hurt. Yet the clearest indication that a friendship is fading may be reductions in the quantity and quality of communication. As former friends drift apart or experience hurt from each other, they are likely to interact less often and to talk about less personal and consequential topics.

Even when serious violations occur between friends, relationships can sometimes be repaired. Sometimes friends hurt us when they are under serious stress. If we attribute something we don't like to factors beyond their control, we may be willing to forgive them and continue the friendship. We may also be more willing to stay with a friend who has hurt us unintentionally than one who deliberately harmed us. For a friendship that has waned to be revived, however, requires both friends to be committed to rebuilding trust and intimacy. They must be willing to work through their feelings in open, constructive discussion.

Rules of Friendship

Friendships generally follow **relationship rules** that specify what is expected and what is not allowed. Most of the time, we're not consciously aware of relationship rules, even though we may be following them. Typically, relationship rules are unspoken understandings that regulate how people interact. For instance, most friends have a tacit understanding that they can be a little late, but they won't keep each other waiting long. A delay of 5 minutes is within the rules, but a 40-minute delay is a violation. Most friends have an unspoken understanding that private information they share is to be kept confidential.

Many rules concern what friends want and expect of each other, such as

© Tom & Dee Ann McCarthy/The Stock Market

support, time, and acceptance. Equally important are "shalt not" rules that define what won't be tolerated. For example, most Westerners would consider it a betrayal if a friend slept with their romantic partner. Similarly, we might share the rule that Cary discussed in her commentary on page 327 that friends don't tell others private information we share with them. Most of our shalt nots for friendship are inverted forms of the rules for sustaining good friendships. Although friends may never explicitly discuss their rules, the rules matter, as we discover when one is violated!

JUANITA: *Celia and I had been friends for three years before we decided to share an apartment. After a while I noticed that my best pair of earrings was missing, and then a gold necklace my father gave me disappeared. Money I was sure I had in my wallet was gone a couple of times. I thought this was strange, but it never occurred to me that Celia would steal from me. Then one day I needed one of Celia's purses that went with my outfit. She wasn't there, but since we borrowed each other's clothes all the time, I didn't think anything about getting it from her closet. When I opened the purse, I saw my earrings and necklace. I never felt so betrayed in all my life. I asked her to move out that day.*

Rules regulate both trivial and important aspects of interaction. Not interrupting may be a rule, but breaking it probably won't destroy a good friendship. On the other hand, stealing money, jewelry, or romantic partners may be the death knell of a friendship.

Some of our friendship rules reflect the unique personalities of people who are friends. Two people who enjoy backpacking may center their friendship around camping trips and day hikes. Thus, each person would expect the other to be available for outings and to enjoy them. Friends who are avid readers may spend much of their time together discussing books, and each may expect the other to share books. Yet many, if not most, of our friendship rules reflect broader influences than individual personalities. In addition to private rules that friends develop to reflect their individual styles and preferences, Westerners have a number of common rules about what friendship is—and is not, as discussed in "The Rules of Friendship."

The typical pattern through which friendships develop and the rules that guide them explain how friendships form and operate. In the next section, we consider some of the pressures and complications that sometimes jeopardize even very close and satisfying friendships.

Pressures on Friendships

Like all human relationships, friendships experience pressures that range from mild to severe. To understand the strains friends face, we'll consider internal tensions and external constraints that tug at friendships.

Internal Tensions

Friendships, like all personal connections, are vulnerable to tensions inherent in being close. **Internal tensions** are relationship stresses that grow out of individuals and their interaction. We'll consider three of these.

Relational Dialectics   In earlier chapters, we discussed relational dialectics, which are opposing human needs that create tension and propel change in close relationships. The three dialectics are tension between connection and autonomy, openness and privacy, and novelty and familiarity. These three dialectics punctuate friendship, prompting us to adjust continuously to natural yet contradictory needs.

Dialectics may strain friendships when individuals differ in their needs. For instance, there could be tension if Joe is bored and needing novelty, but his friend Andy is overstimulated and seeking calming routines. Similarly, if Andy has just broken up with a woman, he may seek greater closeness with Joe right at the time that Joe has a strong need to feel independent of others. When needs collide, friends should talk. It's important to be upfront about what you need and to be sensitive to what your friend needs. Doing this simultaneously honors yourself, your friend, and the relationship. The goal is for friends to express themselves honestly and to engage in dual perspective and sensitive listening within a supportive communication climate. When this occurs, friends can usually work out ways to meet each person's needs or at least to understand that differing needs don't reflect unequal commitment to the friendship.

STUDENT VOICES

LANA: *My girlfriends and I are so often in different places that it's hard to take care of each other. If one of my friends isn't seeing anyone special, she wants more time with me and wants to do things together. If I'm*

Japanese Friendships

The Japanese distinguish between two types of friendships. *Tsukiai* are friendships based on social obligation. These usually involve neighbors or work associates and tend to have limited lifespans. Friendships based on affection and common interests usually last a lifetime: Personal friendship is serious business. The number of personal friends is very small and stable, in contrast to friendship patterns in the United States. Friendships between women and men are rare in Japan. Prior to marriage, only 20 percent of Japanese say they have close friends of the opposite sex.

SOURCES: Atsumi, R. (1980). Patterns of personal relationships. *Social Analysis, 5,* 63–78; Mochizuki, T. (1981). Changing patterns of mate selection. *Journal of Comparative Family Studies, 12,* 318–328.

in a relationship with a guy, her needs feel demanding. But when I've just broken up, I really need my friends to fill time and talk with. So I try to remember how I feel and use that to help me accept it when my friends need my time.

Lana highlights the importance of dual perspective in dealing with tensions caused by relational dialectics. She draws on her own experience of breakups to understand her friends' perspective when they've broken up. This motivates Lana to make time to be with her friends. If she communicates her understanding and acceptance, her friends will feel she supports and cares about them.

Relational dialectics are natural and constructive forces in friendship. They keep us aware of multiple, sometimes clashing needs. In addition, because we find tension uncomfortable, dialectics motivate us to fine-tune friendships continuously. The strains dialectics spark can be managed by revising friendships and by accepting dialectical tensions as normal, ongoing relationship processes.

Diverse Communication Styles   Friendships may also be strained when friends misinterpret each other's communication. The potential for misunderstanding mushrooms as our society becomes increasingly diverse, making it more likely that some of our friends will have cultural backgrounds different from our own. Because how we communicate reflects the understandings and rules of our culture, misinterpretations are likely between friends from different cultures (Wood, 1995a). For instance, in many Asian societies, individuals are socialized to be unassuming and modest, whereas the United States encourages assertion and celebrating ourselves. Thus, a native Japanese might perceive a friend from Milwaukee as arrogant for saying "Let's go out to celebrate my acceptance to law school." A Thai woman might not get the support she wants from a friend from Brooklyn because she was taught not to assert her needs and the Brooklyn friend was taught that people should speak up for themselves. "Japanese Friendships" explores some of the cultural differences in friendship.

Misunderstandings also arise from differences among social groups in the United States. Aaron, who is White, might feel hurt if Markus, an African American friend, turns down an invitation to a concert in order to go home to care for an ailing aunt. Aaron might interpret this as a rejection by Markus, because he perceives that Markus is using the aunt as an excuse to avoid going out with him. Aaron would interpret Markus differently if he realized that, as a rule, African Americans are more communal than European Americans, so taking care of extended family members is a priority (Gaines, 1995). Ellen may feel that her friend Jed isn't being supportive when instead of empathizing with her problems, he offers advice or suggests they go out to take her mind off her troubles. Yet, he *is* showing support according to masculine rules of communication. Jed, on the other hand, may feel that Ellen is intruding on his autonomy when she pushes him to talk about his feelings. According to feminine rules of communication, however, Ellen *is* showing interest and concern.

Differences themselves aren't usually the cause of problems in friendship. Instead, how we interpret and judge others' communication is the root of tension and hurt. What Jed and Ellen did wasn't the source of their frustrations. Jed interpreted Ellen according to his communication rules, not hers, and she interpreted Jed according to her communication rules, not his. Notice that the misunderstandings result from our interpretations of others' behaviors, not the behaviors themselves. This reminds us of the need to distinguish between fact and inference.

Sexual Attraction   Sexual attraction can also cause difficulty between friends. Friendships between heterosexual men and women, or gay men, or lesbians often include sexual tensions. Because Western culture so strongly emphasizes gender and sex, it's difficult not to perceive people in sexual terms (Johnson, Stockdale, & Saal, 1991; O'Meara, 1989). Even if there is no sexual activity between friends, sexual undertones may ripple beneath the surface of their friendships.

S T U D E N T   VOICES

SHASHA: *It is so hard to be just friends with guys. When I try to be friends with a guy, he'll hit on me at some point. I tell guys if friendship is all I'm interested in and they agree, but they hit on me anyway. It's happened so much that by now I feel on guard with guys even before they start anything.*

Sexual attraction or invitations can be a problem between friends who have agreed not to have a sexual relationship. Tension over sexual attraction or interest can be present in friendships between heterosexual women and men (West, Anderson, & Duck, 1996) as well as in friendships between lesbians and between gay men (Nardi & Sherrod, 1994). Trust may be damaged if someone we consider a friend makes a pass. Further, once a friend transgresses the agreed-on boundaries of the friendship, it's hard to know how to act with each other or to feel completely comfortable.

Relational dialectics, misinterpretations of different communication styles, and sexual attraction are sources of internal tension in many friendships. Usually straightforward communication, although not always easy, is the best way to deal with these problems and to restore ease. Guidelines for effective communication that we've discussed in other chapters apply here. For example, it's important to be clear when stating your own needs and preferences. Also, it's wise to rely on I-language so that you communicate what you feel and want without assuming what your friend wants and feels. Sensitive listening and supportive communication are also helpful in keeping a friendship intact while partners address sexual tensions.

© Kathy Tarantola/The Picture Cube

External Constraints

In addition to internal tensions, friendships may encounter pressures from outside sources. Three of these are competing demands, changes, and geographic distance.

Competing Demands   Friendships exist within larger social systems that affect how they function (Allan, 1994). Because our lives are complex, we continuously struggle to balance competing demands for our time and energy. Because friendships are voluntary and not governed by formal rules, they can be neglected more easily than careers or marriages. Our work and our romantic relationships tend to be woven into our everyday lives, ensuring they will get daily attention. Time with friends, however, isn't reserved in what we must do each day. We have to make room in our lives, plan meetings, and set aside time to interact. When all that we *must* do overwhelms us, we may not get to what we *want* to do.

We may also neglect friends because of other relationships. When a new romance is taking off, we may be totally immersed in it. The excitement of getting to know a new person can absorb all of our time and thoughts. Friends may also be neglected when other important relationships in our lives are in crisis. If one of our parents is ill or another friend is having trouble, we may need all of our energy to cope with the acute situation. When we are wrapped up in other relationships in happy or anxious ways, we have little of ourselves left to give to friends. To avoid hurting friends, we should let them know when we need a leave of absence from the friendship to deal with immediate priorities. If we don't explain our inattention to friends, they may feel hurt or rejected (Wood, 1995c).

Personal Changes   Our friendships change as our lives do. Although a few friendships are lifelong, most persist for shorter periods. If you think about your experiences, you'll realize that many of your friends changed as you made major transitions in your life (Allan, 1994). The people you spent time with and counted as friends shifted when you started high school, entered college, or moved to a new town. They'll change again when you leave college, move for career or family reasons, and perhaps have children. Because one base of friendship is common interests, established friends may not be able to share new interests we develop.

S T U D E N T   VOICES

RUTH: *Sandi and I had been friends for years when I had my first baby. Gradually, we saw less of each other and couldn't find much to talk about when we did get together. She was still doing the singles scene, and I was totally absorbed in mothering. I got to know other mothers in the neighborhood, and soon I thought of them as my friends. What's funny is that last year Sandi had a baby, and it was so good to get together and talk. We reconnected with each other.*

Even if our interests don't change or our friends' interests change with ours, friendships often wither because we don't have time to take care of them (Duck, Rutt, Hurst, & Strejc, 1991). If we or members of our family have serious health problems, friendships may be neglected. Similarly, the early stages of a career require enormous amounts of energy and time. There may not be enough time or energy left to maintain friendships, even ones that matter to us. Each new context we enter realigns our friendship circles.

Lee West, Jennifer Anderson, and Steve Duck (1996), who study communication in personal relationships, point out that friendships also vary throughout a person's life. Some of these variations are discussed in "Friendships Across the Lifespan." In grammar school and high school, peer friendships are very important to most of us. During the twenties, many people are starting careers and families, and they have less time and energy to devote to friends. Later in life it seems that friends reclaim importance as people once again have more time to develop and invest in friendships.

We're most likely to become friends with people we see regularly, so where we live and work influences our choice of friends (Wellman, 1985). Similarly, unemployment alters friendships because it isolates people from their usual social networks (Allen, Waton, Purcell, & Wood, 1986). Social class affects friendships because it shapes our interests and tastes in everything from music to lifestyle. In addition, class constrains where people live and work, as well as how much money they have for socializing with friends (O'Connor, 1992). Gay and lesbian communities allow friendships to crystallize around shared interests, concerns, and political goals. Similarly, communi-

COMMUNICATION NOTES

Friendships Across the Lifespan

The nature and dynamics of friendships vary during the course of life. Most children begin forming friendships around age two when they start learning how to communicate with others. These early friendships involve limited interaction. Toddlers primarily play side by side, and each is focused more on his or her activity than on the other person.

Until age nine most children see friendships as one-way streets—something that can be helpful or convenient for them. Friends are people who assist them, not people with whom they have give-and-take relationships. People who don't help them or who cease being helpful are no longer friends. "Fair weather friends" describes friendships for children until the age of twelve.

During adolescence friendship assumes great importance for most people. Having friends is very important, and belonging to friendship cliques is a measure of self-worth. Adolescent males tend to define their friends as groups of people, usually other boys. Girls, on the other hand, tend to name only one or two peers as close friends. Thus, boys tend to have more people they call friends, and girls tend to develop more intense and personal friendships with fewer people.

Sharing personal information and activities are primary criteria for friendships among young adults, who are the age group most likely to form and maintain friendships with people of the other sex.

Friendships are more difficult to sustain if people marry, have children, and get established in careers. Many adults find it difficult to find time and energy for friends in addition to being with family and doing their jobs. Friends may also cause tension between romantic partners if they are perceived as threats to the primary relationship. Despite these complications, most adults consider friendships important in their lives.

Developing new friendships is not common among the elderly. Instead, older people tend to value long-time friends with whom they can relive events that are part of their shared lives. Many friendships among older people are ones formed between couples or between whole families when each family had young children.

SOURCES: Blieszner, R., & Adams, R. (1992). *Adult friendship*. Newbury Park, CA: Sage; Dickens, W. J., & Perlman D. (1981). Friendship over the life-cycle. In S. Duck & R. Gilmour (Eds.), *Personal relationships, 2: Developing personal relationships*. London: Academic; West, L., Anderson, J., & Duck, S. (1996). Crossing the barriers to friendship between men and women. In J. J. Wood (Ed.), *Gendered relationships*. Mountain View, CA: Mayfield.

Friendship in a Mobile Society

In 1992, the U.S. Census Bureau reported that 41.4 million people in the United States moved in the previous year. Although many of those who moved stayed within the same state, 14 million citizens moved to new states. Of course, the impact of moves on relationships is significant. Each move affects everyone in the mover's social network who is left behind.

ties for older citizens and kindergarten for younger ones are contexts in which friendships form on the basis of similarities in life stage and interests. Our friends change over the course of life as we and our interests continuously evolve.

Geographic Distance   Who are your closest friends? How often do you see them? What will happen when you locate in different parts of the country? Most friendships face the challenge of distance, and many won't survive it. Currently, as many as 90 percent of North Americans have at least one long-distance friendship (Rohlfing, 1995). In our highly mobile society, friendships are continuously in flux (see "Friendship in a Mobile Society").

Whether distance ends friendship depends on several factors. Perhaps the most obvious influence is how much individuals care about continuing to be friends. The greater the commitment, the more likely a friendship will persist despite separation. Geographic distance is the reason the majority of high school friendships dissolve when individuals begin college (Rose, 1984). Yet, the likelihood of sustaining a long-distance friendship also depends on other factors, such as socioeconomic class and gender.

Because socioeconomic class profoundly affects who we are and how we live, it's not surprising that it influences the prospect that long-distance friendships will endure. The reason is simple: money. Friendships that survive distance involve frequent phone calls and letters and visits every so often. It takes money to finance trips and long-distance calls. Thus, friends with greater economic resources are better able to maintain their relationships than are friends with less discretionary income (Willmott, 1987). Thus, people in middle and upper socioeconomic classes have a greater chance of bridging distance with friends. A second way in which socioeconomic class affects the endurance of long-distance friendships is flexibility in managing work and family. Middle- and upper-class individuals usually have generous vacations and flexibility in work schedules, so they can make time to travel. Working-class citizens tend to have less personal control over when they work and how much vacation time they get. Income also affects our ability to pay for babysitters who may make it possible for a parent to visit a friend for a weekend.

APPLY THE IDEA
Maintaining Friendship at a Distance

Do you have a long-distance friendship? If so, which of the following strategies do you use to maintain it?

- Call at least once a week.
- Call at least once a month.
- Communicate by electronic mail at least weekly.

- Call once or twice a year.
- Write letters.
- Visit weekly.
- Visit monthly.
- Visit occasionally.
- Have conversations in your head with the friend.

Now identify three ways you might strengthen the closeness between you and your friend.

Gender also affects the endurance of long-distance friendships. There appear to be two reasons why women are more likely than men to sustain ties with friends who live at a distance. First, the sexes differ in how much they value same-sex friendships and how much they give to and get from them. Compared to women, men place less value on their same-sex relationships and invest less in them (Duck & Wright, 1993). This is especially true of married men who often name their wives as their best friends (Rubin, 1985). Women are also more willing than men to adjust schedules and priorities to make time for friends (Rubin, 1985), and they are more willing to tolerate less than ideal circumstances for being with friends. For example, mothers who sustain long-distance friendships report that when they visit, they are seldom alone, because their children need attention and care. Even though these mothers say they miss the intimacy of uninterrupted conversations, they value each other enough to sustain friendships under the terms that are possible (Rohlfing, 1995). Women also report getting more out of their friendships with women than men report getting out of their friendships with men (Duck & Wright, 1993). For women more than men, friendships are a primary and important thread woven through their lives.

STUDENT VOICES

CASS: *My parents are so different from each other in their approaches to friendship. When I was growing up, Dad was on a career roll, so we were always moving to better neighborhoods or new towns. Each time we moved, he'd make a whole new set of friends. Even if his old friends lived nearby, he would want to be with the people he called his new peers. Mom is 180 degrees different. She still talks with her best friend in the town where I was born. She has stayed close to all of her good friends, and they don't change with the season like Dad's do. Once I asked him if he missed his old friends, and he said that friends were people you share common interests with so they change as your job does. That doesn't make sense to me.*

Another reason women and men differ in how likely they are to maintain long-distance friendships is that the sexes have different views of what they regard as the nucleus of closeness. As we've seen previously, shared interests and emotional involvement are the crux of closeness for many women. Both of these are achieved primarily through communication, especially personal talk (Aries, 1987; Becker, 1987). The focus of men's friendships tends to be activities, which are difficult to share across distance (Swain, 1989; Wood & Inman, 1993). Women can and do sustain ties with important friends by talking on the phone and writing. Men, on the other hand, are more likely to replace friends who have moved away with others who can share activities they enjoy (Rohlfing, 1995). Lillian Rubin's (1985) studies led her to say that women tend to develop **friends of the heart,** who remain close regardless of distance and circumstances. Rubin also noted that many men have **friends of the road,** who change as they move along the road of life and develop new interests and find themselves in new situations. It is easier to replace a friend who was a tennis partner than one with whom we shared intimate feelings and details of our life.

Like all relationships, friendships confront both inside and outside pressures and challenges. Internal tensions in friendship involve relational dialectics, diverse communication styles, and sexual attraction. External challenges to friendship include competing demands, personal changes, and distance. How we respond to these pressures and how they affect our friendships depend on many factors, including personal qualities, commitment to friends, socioeconomic class, age, and gender.

Guidelines for Communication Between Friends

To conclude this chapter, we'll consider guidelines for communicating effectively with friends. Before discussing specific guidelines, however, we should realize that the principles for healthy communication with friends echo the basic principles of good interpersonal communication that we've discussed in preceding chapters. You should be aware that your self-concept and your perceptions influence how you interpret interaction with friends. It's also important to create a confirming climate by being open, spontaneous, empathic, equal, and nonevaluative. In addition, you should keep in mind what you have learned about using verbal and nonverbal communication effectively, including when you discuss emotions. Finally, managing conflict constructively is important in friendships, as in all relationships. In addition to these general principles, we can identify four specific guidelines for satisfying communication between friends.

Engage in Dual Perspective

As in all interpersonal relationships, dual perspective is important in friendship. To be a good friend we must understand and accept our friends' perspectives, thoughts, and feelings. As we've noted before, accepting another person's perspective is not the same as agreeing with it. The point is to understand what friends feel and think and to accept that as their reality. Dual perspective helps us to understand others on *their* terms, not ours.

To exercise dual perspective, we distinguish between our judgments and perceptions, on the one hand, and what friends say and do, on the other. It's important to remember the abstraction ladder we discussed in Chapter 3. When we feel hurt or offended by something a friend says, we should keep in mind that our perceptions and inferences do not equal their behavior. A friend acts, we perceive the action selectively, we then interpret and evaluate what happened, and finally we assign meaning to it and make inferences from what we've labeled. Notice how far from the original act we move in the process of trying to make sense of it. There's lots of room for slippage as we ascend the abstraction ladder. For example, when Shereen tells her friend Kyle that she's upset and needs support, she shouldn't assume he's uninterested if he suggests they go out for the evening. As we have learned, men often support friends by trying to divert them from problems.

Two communication principles help us avoid misinterpreting our friends. First, it's useful to ask questions to find out what others mean. Shereen might ask Kyle, "Why would you want to go out when I said I needed support?" This would allow Kyle to explain that he was trying to support her in his own way: by coming up with an activity to divert Shereen from her problems. Consequently, Shereen could grasp his meaning and interpret what he did in that light. Second, we should explain, or translate, our own feelings and needs so that Kyle understands what would feel supportive to her. Shereen could say, "What would help me most right now is to have a sympathetic ear. Could we just stay in and talk about the problem?" If we make our needs clear, we're more likely to get the kind of support we value.

APPLY THE IDEA
Communicating Needs Clearly

Below are three scenarios that describe interactions in which a friend does not initially give the desired response. For each one, write out what you could say to clarify what is wanted.

1. You just found out that your car needs two new tires and alignment, and you don't have any extra cash. Worrying about money is the last thing you want to do now, with everything else on your mind. You see a friend and tell him what's happened. He says, "Sit down, let's talk about it." You don't want to talk—you want to get your mind off the problem.

You say _____

2. You are unhappy because your boyfriend/girlfriend is transferring to a school 600 miles away. You feel that you'll miss him/her and you're also worried that the relationship might not survive distance. A friend calls and you mention your concerns. In response, she says, "You can handle this. Just make sure that the two of you have e-mail accounts, and you'll be fine." Although you'd like to believe this, it seems like empty reassurance to you. You'd rather have some help sorting through your feelings.

You say _____

© Lori Adamski Peek/Tony Stone Images, Inc.

C O N T I N U E D

3. A friend tells you that she is really worried about the job market. As she talks you hear several things: worry about making a living, uncertainty about where she will be living, and doubts about self-worth. You say to your friend, "Sounds as if you are feeling pretty over-whelmed by all of this. Maybe it would help if we took one piece of the problem at a time." Your friend lets out a frustrated sigh and replies, "I don't want to analyze every bit and piece!" You're not sure what it is that your friend wants and how to help her.

You say _____

_____

Communicate Honestly

A few years ago, I confronted an ethical choice when my close friend Gayle asked me for advice. Several months earlier she had agreed to give the key-note speech at a professional conference, and now she had an opportunity to travel to Italy with her partner at the time of the conference. She wanted to accompany her partner to Italy but wondered if it was ethical to renege on her agreement to give the keynote address. Following principles we've discussed in this book, I first asked a number of questions to find out how Gayle felt and what her perspective was. It became clear she really wanted me to tell her it was okay to retract her agreement to give the speech. Because I love Gayle, I wanted to support her preference and to encourage her to do what she wanted. Yet, I didn't think it would be right for her to go back on her word, and I didn't think Gayle would respect herself in the long run if she abandoned a commitment. Also, I knew that I wouldn't respect myself if I wasn't honest with Gail. Ethically I was committed both to being honest and to supporting my friend.

I took a deep breath and told her three things: First, I said that her personal integrity was the issue and that she shouldn't withdraw her acceptance. Second, I told her I would support her and love her whatever she decided to do. And, third, I suggested there might be more than two options. At first she was quiet, clearly disappointed that I hadn't enthusiastically endorsed her dream. As we talked, we came up with the idea of her making the keynote speech and then joining her partner who would already be in Italy. Even with this plan, Gayle was dejected when she left, and I felt I'd let her down by not supporting her dream. Later that night she called to thank me for being the only friend who was really honest with her. After we'd talked, she'd realized it went against her own values to renege on her word, and nobody else had reminded her of that. Every other friend had told her to go to Italy and enjoy the trip.

Honesty is one of the most important gifts friends can give each other. Even when honesty is less than pleasant or not what we think we want to hear, we count on it from friends. In fact, people believe that honest feedback is what sets real friends apart from others (Burleson & Samter, 1994). Sometimes it's difficult to be honest with friends, as it was for me with Gayle. Yet, if we can't count on our friends for honest feedback, then where can we turn for truthfulness?

Many people make the mistake of confusing support with saying only nice things that others want to hear. Yet, this is not the essence of support. The key is caring enough about a person to look out for her or his welfare. Parents discipline children and set limits because they care about their children's long-term welfare. Colleagues who want to help each other give honest, often critical, feedback on work so that others can improve. Romantic partners who are committed tell each other when they perceive problems or when the other isn't being his or her best self. We can be supportive and loving while being honest, but to be less than honest is to betray trust placed in us. Honesty is part of what it means to care genuinely about another. Although it may be easier to tell friends what they want to hear or only nice things, genuine friendship includes honest feedback and candid talk.

STUDENT VOICES

MILANDO: *I can count on one hand (with three fingers left over!) the people who will really shoot straight with me. Most of my friends tell me what I want to hear. Yeah, that's kind of nice in the moment, but it doesn't wear well over the long haul. If I just want reinforcement for what I'm already feeling or doing, then why would I even talk to anyone else? Real friends tell you straight-up what's what.*

Grow from Differences

A third principle for forming rich friendships is to be open to diversity in people. As we learned in Chapter 4, Western culture encourages polarized thinking. We have been socialized to think in either-or terms: Either she's like me or not; either he acts like I do or he's wrong; either they support me as I want to be supported or they're not real friends. The problem with this either-or thinking is that it sharply limits interpersonal growth, as noted in "Experiencing the World's Abundance."

Egocentric mind-sets and either-or thinking limit our horizons. We can't learn and grow if we reject what and who is different simply because they're different. Most of us tend to choose friends who are like us. We feel more immediately comfortable with friends who share our values, attitudes, backgrounds, and communication rules. But if we restrict our friends to people like us, we miss out on the fascinating variety of people and relationships that are possible. It does take more time and effort to understand and become comfortable with individuals who differ from us, but the dividends of doing so can be exceptional. Forming friendships with diverse people facilitates both your growth as an individual and the richness of your interpersonal world.

Don't Sweat the Small Stuff

Samuel Johnson once remarked that most friendships die not because of major violations and problems but because of small slights and irritations that slowly destroy closeness. Johnson's point is well taken. Certainly, we are going to be irritated by a number of qualities and habits of others. If you are a punctual person, you might be annoyed by a friend who is chronically late. If you don't like prolonged telephone conversations, you may be irritated by a friend who likes to talk for hours on the phone. Feeling annoyance is normal in all relationships. What we do with that feeling, however, can make the difference between sustaining a friendship and suffocating it.

One insight into how to let go of small irritations comes from what we've learned about perception. Knowing that perceptions are subjective, you might remind yourself not to fixate on aspects of a friend that you dislike or find bothersome. There's a big difference between acknowledging irritations and letting them preoccupy us. Is the lateness really more significant than all that you value in your friend? Do your friend's good qualities compensate for the long phone conversations that you dread? You can exercise some control over your perceptions and the weight you attach to them.

S T U D E N T **VOICES**

BERNADETTE: *I grew up with a single mother, but our home was always full. She had so many friends and somebody was visiting all the time. I used to tell her that I didn't like Mrs. Jones's language or Mrs. Perry's political attitudes or the way Mr. Davis slurped his coffee. One day when I was telling her what was wrong with one of her friends, my mother said, "Keep going like that, girl, and you won't ever have any friends. If you want to have friends, don't sweat the small stuff. Just keep your eye on what's good about them."*

A second suggestion is to follow the guideline we discussed in Chapter 8: Accept and confirm others. All of us want to be accepted and valued despite any flaws we have. You want that from your friends. And they want acceptance from you. Acceptance doesn't mean you like or approve of everything in a friend. It does mean you accept the friend and don't try to change her or him to suit your personal preferences.

Summary

Friends are important in our lives. In this chapter, we learned how friendships form and how they function and change over time. We began by considering common expectations for friends, including investment, intimacy, acceptance, and support. Into our discussion of these common themes we wove insights about differences among us. We discovered there are some differences in how women and men create and express intimacy, invest in friendships, and show support. We also saw that gay and lesbian friendships largely parallel heterosexual ones in style and importance.

Friendships are ordered by developmental stages and rules. Friendships evolve gradually, moving from role-governed interactions to stable friendship and, sometimes, to waning friendship. Both social rules and private rules generated by friends provide regularity and predictability to interaction so that friends know what to expect from one another.

Like all relationships, friendships encounter challenges and tensions that stem from the relationship itself and from causes beyond it. Internal tensions of friendship include managing relational dialectics and misunderstandings and dealing with sexual attraction. External pressures on friendship are competing demands, changing personal needs and interests of friends, and geographic distance. Principles of interpersonal communication covered throughout this book suggest how we can manage these pressures, as well as the day-to-day dynamics of close friendships. In addition, communication among friends is especially enhanced by engaging in dual perspective, being honest, being open to diversity and the growth it can prompt in us, and not sweating the small stuff.

Concepts

- friends of the heart
- friends of the road
- internal tensions
- relationship rules

Thought & Discussion

1. Think about a friendship you have with a person of your sex and a friendship you have with a person of the other sex. To what extent does each friendship conform to the gender patterns described in this chapter?

2. Review the rules of friendship presented in this chapter. Do these rules show up in your friendships? Are there other rules that you would add based on your personal experiences with friendship?

3. Do you have any long-distance friends? How far away are they? How often do you see them in person? How do you manage to maintain the friendship across the distance?

4. Use your *InfoTrac College Edition* to read the table of contents for the last year's issues of *Sex Roles*. Read studies that focus on differences and similarities in how women and men engage in close relationships. Are the findings from articles you read consistent with what you've learned in this chapter?

5. Write out typical topics of talk for each stage in the evolution of friendships. How do topics change as friendships wax and wane?

6. Think about someone who is a very close or best friend. Describe the investments that you and your friend have made in the relationship. Describe how you built and communicate trust, acceptance, and closeness. Are the dynamics of your friendship consistent with those identified by researchers as discussed in this chapter?

Committed

Romantic

Relationships

Personal ads are a phenomenon of our era. From small towns to bustling cities, newspapers have column after column of ads written by people who are looking for someone to love. We want to build a life with someone and travel with that special person through the years ahead. Yet many of us are disappointed, sometimes more than once, in love relationships. Some romances that end were probably mismatches from the start. Others, however, deteriorate because partners don't know how to maintain healthy, confirming intimacy over the years. In the pages that follow, we'll discuss some of the choices you can make to increase the chances that your love relationships will endure.

PERSONALS

SBF, age 22, seeking responsible 22–30 year old S/DBM who enjoys dancing, quiet conversations, walks on beaches, and independent women. Friendship is necessary, romance possible. Send letter to Box 1234.

Successful, professional DWM looking for petite, blonde 18–25 yo who enjoys biking, travel, movies, and sailing. Should be 5'2" to 5'4", 100–105 pounds, blue eyes preferred. Send letter and photo to Box 3121.

Mature, but not old: Fifty-something widow looking for companion to share movies, travel, and time together. Send letter to Box 2131.

In this chapter, we will explore communication dynamics in committed romantic relationships. We'll begin by defining committed romantic relationships and the different styles of loving that individuals bring to romance. Next we discuss how romantic relationships evolve over time and how partners create a private culture for their intimacy. Third, we'll examine communication patterns in marriage. In the fourth section of this chapter, we consider challenges that complicate and sometimes dissolve romantic bonds. Finally, we'll identify guidelines for effective communication in committed romance.

Committed Romantic Relationships

Committed romantic relationships are voluntary relationships between unique individuals that the partners assume will be primary and continuing parts of their lives. Unlike many relationships, enduring romantic ones are voluntary, at least in Western culture. We don't pick our relatives, neighbors, or work associates. Our romantic intimates, however, are people we choose.

Committed romantic relationships also exist between unique individuals—ones who cannot be replaced. In many of our relationships, others are not irreplaceable. If a colleague at work leaves, you can get another colleague and work will go on. If your racquetball buddy moves out of town, you can find a new partner and the games will continue. Thus, most of our social relationships are I–You connections. Committed romantic relationships, in contrast, are I–Thou bonds—ones in which we invest heavily of ourselves and ones in which each person knows the other as a completely distinct individual.

Committed romantic relationships are distinct from other close relationships in two ways. First, they involve romantic and sexual feelings in addition to the sort of love we feel for friends and family. Another distinctive quality of roman-

© Rashid/Monkmeyer Press Photo

tic relationships is that they are considered primary and permanent in our society. We expect to move away from friends and family, but we assume we'll be permanently connected to a romantic partner. Current divorce rates indicate that roughly half of those who marry will separate. Even so, we think of romantic commitment (though not every romantic relationship) as permanent, and this makes romantic commitments unique.

Cultural Shaping of Romantic Ties

Views of romantic relationships vary across cultures. In some countries, marriages are arranged by families, and spouses may get to know each other only after the wedding ceremony. In other cultures, some polygamy is practiced, although typically only men have multiple mates (Werner, Altman, Brown, & Ginat, 1993). In Western societies, marriage is an autonomous choice of two individuals who live relatively independently of families. In many other societies, however, marriage joins two families, and couples are intricately connected to both families.

S T U D E N T   VOICES

MANSOORA: *I find it very odd that Americans marry only each other and not whole families. In South Africa, people marry into families. The parents must approve of the choice or marriage does not happen. After marriage, the wife moves in with the husband's family. To me this is stronger than a marriage of only two people.*

Even within a single country, views of committed romantic relationships vary over time. Whereas traditional marriage once was the only socially recognized form of romantic commitment, today we have a smorgasbord of relationship forms. Commuter marriages are increasingly common (Rohlfing, 1995), as are cohabiting arrangements (Cunningham & Antill, 1995). In the 1990s, the Census Bureau invented a formal category for cohabiting couples: POSSLQ, which is an acronym for persons of the opposite sex sharing living quarters. Approximately 25 percent of people in the United States who are nineteen or older are cohabiting or have cohabited at some time in their lives (Cunningham & Antill, 1995). The popularity of cohabitation is also rising in other countries, including Australia, Canada, and France.

Every society recognizes and gives privileges to approved relationships and withholds legitimacy from those of which it disapproves. Currently, the United States approves of marriage between heterosexual men and women, and there is increasing toleration of cohabiting heterosexuals. Social acceptance of divorce, remarriage, and single-parent families has also increased. "Divorce and

Disobedience" examines the growing acceptance of divorce in China. The traditional Western ideal of the family consisted of a male breadwinner, a female homemaker, and 2.4 children (I've often wondered about that .4 child!). That solitary ideal has given way to multiple family forms. We have dual-earner couples with children, child-free marriages, single-parent families, and couples in which men are homemakers and women are the primary or sole wage earners. A collage of romantic relationships makes up the contemporary scene.

Despite some changes in social attitudes, commitments between gays and lesbians are not yet widely accepted. The cultural bias against homosexual relationships is enforced by denying gays and lesbians privileges that heterosexual couples enjoy. In 1994, for instance, all fifty states still denied legal status to homosexual relationships. Thus, gays and lesbians can't file joint tax returns, have next-of-kin visiting privileges, insure each other as family, or will each other tax-free property. In addition, homosexual couples often face discrimination when they wish to rent or buy property or raise children (Issacson, 1989; Weston, 1991).

STUDENT VOICES

PEGGY: *I get so burned up about how society treats gay and lesbian couples. My mom and Adrienne have lived together since Mom and Daddy divorced when I was two. We've always been a family. We eat together, work out problems together, vacation together, make decisions together—everything a heterosexual family does. But my mom and Adrienne aren't accepted as a legitimate couple. We've had to move several times because they were "queers," which is what a neighbor called them. Mom's insurance company won't cover Adrienne, so they have to pay for two policies. It goes on and on. I'll tell you, though, I don't know many heterosexual couples as close or stable as Adrienne and Mom.*

Dimensions of Romantic Relationships

For years, researchers have struggled to define what romantic commitment is. As a result of their work, we now believe that romantic love consists of three dimensions: intimacy, commitment, and passion. Although we can think about these dimensions separately, actually they overlap and interact in the overall system of romantic relationships (Acker & Davis, 1992; Hendrick & Hendrick, 1989). One scholar (Sternberg, 1986) who has studied enduring romantic relationships arranges these three dimensions to form a triangle, representing the different facets of love (Figure 11.1).

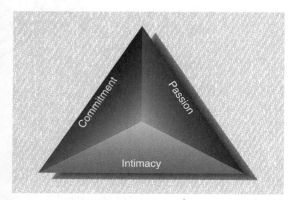

FIGURE 11.1
The Triangle of Love

Passion   For most of us, passion is what first springs to mind when we think about romance. **Passion** is intensely positive feelings and desires for another person. Passion is not equivalent to sexual or sensual emotions, although these are types of passion. In addition to erotic feelings, passion may involve intense emotional, spiritual, and intellectual attraction. The sparks and emotional high of being in love stem from passion. It's why we feel butterflies in the stomach and fall head over heels.

As much fun as passion is, it isn't the primary foundation for enduring romance. In fact, research consistently shows that passion is less central to how we think about love than intimacy and commitment. This makes sense when we realize that passion can seldom be sustained for a lifetime. Like other intense feelings, it ebbs and flows. Because passion comes and goes and is largely beyond our will, it isn't a strong basis for long-term relationships. In other words, passion may set romance apart from other relationships, but it isn't what holds romance together. To build a lasting relationship, we need something more durable.

Commitment   The something else needed is commitment, the second dimension of romantic relationships. Commitment is an intention to remain with a relationship. As we noted earlier, commitment is not the same thing as love. Love is a feeling based on rewards we get from being involved with a person. Commitment, in contrast, is a decision based on investments we put into a relationship (Lund, 1985). We choose to entwine our life and future with another person's.

S T U D E N T   VOICES

THERESA: *I'm sick of guys who say they love me but run if I try to talk about the future. They're allergic to the C-word. If you truly love someone, how can you not be committed?*

In an important study of American values, Robert Bellah and his colleagues (1985) found that most Westerners want both passion and commitment in long-term romantic relationships. We desire the euphoria of passion, but we know that it won't weather rough times or ensure compatibility and comfort on a day-in, day-out basis. We also want commitment as a stable foundation for a life together. Commitment is a determination to stay together *in spite of* trouble, disappointments, sporadic restlessness, and lulls in passion. Commitment involves responsibility, not just feeling (Beck, 1988). The responsibilities of commitment are to make a relationship a priority and to invest continuously in it.

S T U D E N T   VOICES

WADE: *I've been married for fifteen years, and we would have split a dozen times if love was all that held us together. A marriage simply can't survive on love alone. You can't count on feeling in love or passionate all the*

time. Lucy and I have gone through spells where we were bored with each other or where we wanted to walk away from our problems. We didn't because we made a promise to stay together "for better or for worse." Believe me, a marriage has both.

© David Young Wolff/Tony Stone Images, Inc.

Passion happens without effort—sometimes despite our efforts! Commitment is an act of will. Passion is a feeling; commitment is a choice. Passion may fade in the face of disappointments and troubles; commitment remains steadfast. Passion has to do with the present moment; commitment is tied to the future. Without commitment, romantic relationships are subject to the whims of transient feelings and circumstances. This is fine for the short term, but it can't sustain romance over the long haul.

APPLY THE IDEA
Measuring Love and Commitment

Think of a current or past romance to answer these questions:

1. Do you think your relationship will be permanent?
2. Do you feel you can confide in your partner about virtually anything?
3. Are you attracted to other potential partners or to a single lifestyle?
4. Would you be miserable if you couldn't be with your partner?
5. Would you find it personally difficult to end your relationship?
6. If you felt lonely, would your first thought be to seek your partner?
7. Do you feel obligated to continue this relationship?
8. Would you forgive your partner for virtually anything?
9. In your opinion, do you think your partner intends to continue this relationship?
10. Is one of your primary concerns your partner's welfare?

Commitment is measured by odd-numbered items; love is measured by even-numbered items. Based on Lund, M. (1985). The development of investment and commitment scales for predicting continuity of personal relationships. *Journal of Social and Personal Relationships*, 2, 15.

Intimacy   The third dimension of romantic relationships is intimacy. **Intimacy** includes feelings of closeness, connection, and tenderness. Unlike passion and commitment, which are distinct dimensions of romance, intimacy seems to underlie both passion and commitment (Acker & Davis, 1992). Intimacy is related to passion because both dimensions involve feelings. The link between intimacy and commitment is connectedness, which joins partners not only in the present but through the past and into the future.

Intimacy is abiding affection and warm feelings for another person. It is why partners are comfortable with each other and enjoy being together even when fireworks aren't exploding. When asked to evaluate various features of love, people consistently rate companionate features such as getting along and friendship

The Prototype of Love

Westerners appear to have a fairly specific prototype of what love is. Research repeatedly reveals that we regard feeling valued by and comfortable with another as more important than passion. Love is typified by feelings such as closeness, caring, and friendship, and by commitment, as defined by features such as trust and respect. Intimacy and commitment eclipse passion in importance. Even when people are asked what's most important for "being in love," companionate features have priority.

Do women and men differ in how important they consider the dimensions of love? Although women and men don't differ significantly in what they consider typical of love in general, they do diverge in their personal ideals for love. For both sexes, passion is less salient than companionate features. However, features linked to intimacy and commitment are even more prominent in women's personal ideals of love than in men's. The only feature that men rate higher than women is fantasy. No differences have been found among heterosexuals, gays, and lesbians.

SOURCES: Button, C. M., & Collier, D. R. (1991, June). *A comparison of people's concepts of love and romantic love.* Paper presented at the Canadian Psychological Association Conference, Calgary, Alberta; Fehr, B. (1993). How do I love thee: Let me consult my prototype. In S. W. Duck (Ed.), *Understanding relationship processes, 1: Individuals in relationships* (pp. 87–122). Newbury Park, CA: Sage; Luby, V., & Aron, A. (1990, July). *A prototype structuring of love, like, and being in-love.* Paper presented at the Fifth International Conference on Personal Relationships, Oxford, England. Rousar, E. E., III, & Aron, A. (1990, July). *Valuing, altruism, and the concept of love.* Paper presented at the Fifth International Conference on Personal Relationships, Oxford, England.

as most important. Although passionate feelings also matter, they are less central to perceptions of love than caring, honesty, respect, friendship, and trust (Fehr, 1993; Luby & Aron, 1990).

Romantic relationships are complex combinations of passion, commitment, and intimacy, and these dimensions interact. "The Prototype of Love" further explores this issue. To add to our understanding of romance, let's now consider the different styles of loving that individuals have.

Styles of Loving

- Does real love grow out of long friendship?
- Should you love someone whose background is similar to yours?
- Would you rather suffer yourself than have someone you love suffer?
- Is love at first sight possible?
- Is the real fun of love getting someone to fall for you rather than becoming seriously involved?

If you were to survey everyone in your class, you'd discover different answers to the above questions. For every person who thinks love grows out of friendship, someone else believes love at first sight is possible. For each of us who considers love the most important focus of life, another person views love as a game.

Although we accept varied tastes in everything from clothes to lifestyle, we seem less open-minded about diversity in love. Whatever we have experienced as love is what we consider "real love." Anything else we discount as "just infatuation," "a sexual fling," or "being a doormat." Yet, it appears people differ in how they love (Lee, 1973, 1988).

Just as there are three primary colors, there are three primary styles of loving. In addition, just as purple is created by blending the primary colors of blue and red, secondary love styles are made by blending primary ones. Secondary styles are as vibrant as primary

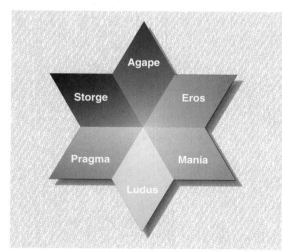

FIGURE 11.2
The Colors of Love

ones, just as purple is as lovely as red or blue. Figure 11.2 illustrates the colors of love.

© Michael Kevin Daly/The Stock Market

Primary Styles of Love   The three primary styles of love are eros, storge, and ludus. **Eros** is a powerful, passionate style of love that blazes to life suddenly and dramatically. It is an intense kind of love that may include sexual, spiritual, intellectual, or emotional attraction. Erotic love is the most intuitive and spontaneous of all styles, and it is also the fastest moving. Erotic lovers are likely to self-disclose early in a relationship, be very sentimental, and fall in love hard and fast. Although folk wisdom claims women are more romantic than men, research indicates that men are more likely than women to be erotic lovers (Hendrick & Hendrick, 1996).

S T U D E N T   VOICES

ROSA: *When I fall for someone, I fall all the way—like, I mean total and all that. I can't love halfway, and I can't go gradually, though my mother is always warning me to slow down. That's just not how I love. It's fast and furious for me.*

Storge (pronounced "store-gay") is a comfortable, even-keeled kind of love based on friendship. Storgic love tends to grow gradually and to be peaceful and stable. In most cases, it grows out of common interests, values, and life goals (Lasswell & Lobsenz, 1980). Storgic relationships don't have the great highs of erotic love, but neither do they have the fiery conflict and anger that erotic people often experience. Steadiness is storge's standard mood.

S T U D E N T   VOICES

STEPHEN: *Lisa and I have been together for fifteen years now, and it's been easy and steady between us from the start. I don't remember even falling in love way back when. Maybe I never did fall in love with Lisa. I just gradually grew into loving her and feeling we belonged to each other.*

The final primary style of love is **ludus,** which is playful love. Ludic lovers see love as a game. It's a lighthearted adventure full of challenges, puzzles, and fun, and love is not to be taken seriously. For ludics, commitment is poison. Instead, they like to play the field and enjoy falling in love; they don't seek commitment. Many people go through ludic periods but are not true ludics. After ending a long-term relationship, it's natural and healthy to avoid serious involvement for a while. Dating casually and steering clear of heavy entanglement may be wise and fun. Ludic loving may also suit people who enjoy romance but aren't ready to settle down. Research indicates that more men than women have ludic inclinations when it comes to love (Hendrick & Hendrick, 1996).

VIJAY: *I'm not ready to settle down, and I may not ever be. I really like dating and seeing if I can get a girl to fall for me, but I'm not out for anything permanent. To me, the fun is in the chase. Once somebody falls for me, I kind of lose interest. It's just not challenging anymore.*

Secondary Styles of Love   There are three secondary styles of love: pragma, mania, and agape. **Pragma,** as the name suggests, is pragmatic or practical love. Pragma blends the conscious strategies of ludus with the stable, secure love of storge. Pragmatic lovers have clear criteria for partners such as religious affiliation, career, and family background. Although many people dismiss pragma as coldly practical and not really love, this is a mistake. Pragmatic lovers aren't necessarily unfeeling or unloving at all. For them, though, practical considerations are the foundation of enduring commitments, so these must be satisfied before they let themselves fall in love. Pragmatic considerations also guide arranged marriages in which families match children for economic and social reasons.

RANCHANA: *I have to think carefully about who to marry. I must go to graduate school, and I must support my family with what I earn when I finish. I cannot marry someone who is poor, who will not help me get through school, or who won't support my family. For me, these are very basic matters.*

Mania derives its name from the Greek term *theia mania,* which means "madness from the gods" (Lee, 1973). Manic lovers have the passion of eros, but they play by ludic rules with results that can be disturbing to them and those they love. Typically unsure that others really love them, manics may devise tests and games to evaluate a partner's commitment. They may also think obsessively about a relationship and be unable to think about anyone or anything else. In addition, manic lovers often experience emotional extremes, ranging from euphoric ecstasy to bottomless despair.

PAT: *I never feel sure of myself when I'm in love. I always wonder when it will end, when my boyfriend will walk away, when he will lose interest. Sometimes I play games to see how interested a guy is, but then I get all upset if* *the game doesn't work out right. Then I just wallow in my insecurities, and they get worse the more I think about them.*

The final style of love is **agape,** which is a blend of storge and eros. The term *agape* comes from Saint Paul's admonition that we should love others without expectation of personal gain or return. Agapic lovers feel the intense passion of eros and the constancy of storge. Generous and selfless, agapic lovers will put a loved one's happiness ahead of their own without any expectation of reciprocity. For them, loving and giving to another is its own reward. Many of my students comment that agapic love sounds more possible for saints than for mere mortals. Research bears out this insight, because the original studies of love styles found no individuals who were purely agapic. However, many people have agapic tendencies in their style of loving.

"It turns out there was a computer error—we weren't made for each other after all."

© 1994 by Sidney Harris. The Wall Street Journal.

STUDENT VOICES

KEENAN: *My mother is agapic. She has moved more times than I can count because my father needed to relocate to advance. She agreed to the house he wanted and went on the vacations he wanted, even when she had other ideas. There's nothing she wouldn't do for him. I used to think she was a patsy, but I've come to see her way of loving as very strong.*

In thinking about styles of love, you should keep several points in mind. First, most of us have a combination of styles (Hendrick, Hendrick, Foote, & Slapion-Foote, 1984). So you might be primarily storgic with strong agapic inclinations or mainly erotic with an undertone of ludic mischief. Second, your style of love is not necessarily permanent. Recent studies indicate we learn how to love (Maugh, 1994), so our style of loving may change as we have more experiences in loving. Third, remember that your love style is part of an overall interpersonal system, so it is affected by all other aspects of your relationship (Hendrick & Hendrick, 1996). Your partner's style of love may influence your own. If you are primarily erotic and in love with a strong ludic, it's possible manic tendencies will be evoked. Finally, we should realize that individual styles of love are not good or bad in an absolute sense; what matters is how partners' styles fit together. An erotic partner's intensity might overwhelm a calm storgic; an agapic person might be exploited by a true ludic; the extremes of mania would clash with the serene steadiness of storge.

Although passion is important in romantic relationships, intimacy and commitment are necessary to sustain them for the long haul. We've also discussed

© Chuck Savage/The Stock Market

different styles of loving, which are one influence on how individuals experience and express romantic intimacy. To add to the knowledge we've gained, we'll now consider how committed romantic relationships develop and function.

The Organization of Romantic Relationships

Like friendships, romantic relationships tend to follow a developmental course. Initially, scholars thought relationships move through stages as a result of objective activities such as self-disclosing. More recently, however, we have realized that romance progresses based on how we perceive interaction, not on interaction itself (Honeycutt, 1993). For example, if Terry discloses personal information to Janet, then the relationship will escalate if Janet and Terry interpret self-disclosure as a move toward greater intimacy. If Janet doesn't perceive Terry's disclosure as personal, she's unlikely to feel he has made a move toward greater closeness. It is the meaning they assign to self-disclosing, not the actual act of self-disclosing, that determines how they perceive their level of intimacy.

As we learned in Chapter 3, perceiving is an active process in which we notice, organize, and interpret what goes on around us. We use cognitive schematas and information from past experiences to decide what things mean. The meanings we assign to romance, however, are not entirely individualistic. They also reflect broad cultural beliefs that we internalize as we are socialized. Because members of a society share many views, there are strong consistencies in how we perceive what happens in romantic relationships. Research shows that Western college students agree on the script for first dates (Pryor & Merluzzi, 1985). They also share ideas about how men and women should act. The majority of college students think men should initiate and plan dates and make decisions about most activities, but women control sexual activity (Rose & Frieze, 1989). In other cultures, different rules prevail. For example, in India, marriages are often arranged by parents; love is understood to be something couples develop after they wed. In Nepal, ritualistic dancing and celebrations are an important part of courtship. Although views of romantic relationships vary among cultures, every culture has shared understandings of what love is and how love develops.

Research on the evolution of romantic relationships has focused on Western society, so we know little about the developmental course of romance in other cultures. The research tells us that Westerners perceive romantic relationships as evolving through three broad phases: growth, navigation, and deterioration. Within these three broad categories, we distinguish a number of more specific stages (Figure 11.3).

Growth Stages

In moving toward romantic commitment, researchers have identified six stages of interaction that mark progressive intimacy. Usually, although not always, these stages occur in sequence.

The first stage is individuals who aren't interacting. We are aware of ourselves as individuals with particular needs, goals, love styles, and qualities that affect what we look for in relationships. Our choices of people with whom to start romance may also be influenced by aspects of ourselves of which we are unaware—for example, attachment styles and the hidden area of the Johari window.

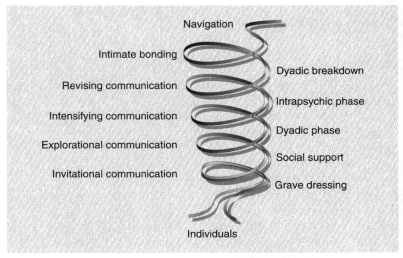

FIGURE 11.3
Developmental Stages in Romantic Relationships

S T U D E N T

EDNA: *It's funny how things change as we age. When I was first dating in my teens, the topics for small talk early in the relationship were your major, career plans, and background. Now I'm forty-seven, divorced, and dating again, and the opening topics tend to be about career achievements, past marriages, and finances.*

The second growth stage is **invitational communication** in which individuals signal they are interested in interacting and respond to invitations from others. "Want to dance?" "Where are you from?" "I love this kind of music," "Hi, my name's Shelby" are examples of bids for interaction. Invitational communication usually follows a conventional script for initial interaction. The meaning of invitational communication is found on the relationship level, not the content level. "I love this kind of music" literally means a person likes the music. On the relationship level of meaning, however, the message is "I'm available and interested. Are you?"

APPLY THE IDEA
Relationship Meanings of Invitations

Go to a place where people are likely to meet for the first time. Observe how individuals extend and respond to invitations for interaction. What are the content meanings of invitations and responses? What do you perceive as the relationship meaning of invitations and responses?

Of all the people we meet, we are attracted to only a few. The three greatest influences on initial attraction are self-concept, proximity, and similarity. How

COMMUNICATION NOTES

Bases of Romantic Attraction

Gay men tend to desire very specific physical characteristics, including an extremely attractive face, a slim and well-conditioned body, and good grooming. In addition, they want partners who are self-sufficient and have prestigious careers that yield good incomes.

Straight men also state that physical attractiveness is very important to them in romantic partners. They report looking for women who are slim and beautiful. Intelligence, status, and personality matter less than physical beauty.

Lesbians generally stress emotional and personal qualities in partners and care little about physical appearance or dress. Although some lesbians admire a "butch" look, others prefer traditional feminine beauty. Lesbians value economic independence in partners, though less so than gays.

Straight women emphasize personal qualities in romantic partners. Warmth, honesty, kindness, and personal integrity are among the qualities straight women consider important. They also value ambition and status in partners.

SOURCES: Based on Huston, M., & Schwartz, P. (1995). Relationships of lesbians and gay men. In J. T. Wood & S. W. Duck (Eds.), *Understanding relationship processes, 6: Off the beaten track: Understudied relationships* (pp. 89–121). Thousand Oaks, CA: Sage; Sprecher, S. (1989). The importance to males and females of physical attractiveness, earning potential, and expressiveness in initial attraction. *Sex Roles, 21,* 591–607.

we see ourselves affects the people we consider candidates for romance. Heterosexuals, lesbians, bisexuals, and gays seek romance with others who share their sexual orientation. "Bases of Romantic Attaction" summarizes research on heterosexual, gay, and lesbian attraction. Social class also influences whom we notice and consider appropriate for us. The myth that the United States is color-blind and classless is disproved by the fact that most people pair with others of their race and social class. Even with all of the attention to diversity in our era, research indicates that people still seek others who are similar to them (see "The Matching Game"). In fact, social prestige influences dating patterns now more than in the 1950s (Whitbeck & Hoyt, 1994). Most college students seek to date people who share their social and class backgrounds.

In addition to personal identity, proximity and similarity influence initial attraction. We can interact only with people we meet, so where we live, work, and socialize affects the possibilities for relationships. Nearness to others, however, doesn't necessarily increase liking. **Environmental spoiling** describes situations in which proximity breeds ill will. This happens when we're forced to be around others whose values, lifestyles, or behaviors conflict with our own. For the most part, we seek romantic partners who are like us. "Birds of a feather" seems more true than "Opposites attract." In general, we are attracted to people whose values, attitudes, and lifestyles are similar to ours. Similarity of personality is also linked to long-term marital happiness (Caspi & Harbener, 1990).

Explorational communication is the third stage in the escalation of romance, and it involves exchanging information to explore the possibilities for a relationship. We use communication to announce our identities and to learn about others. In this stage, individuals fish for common interests and grounds for interaction: Are you from the South? Do you like jazz? What kind of family did you come from? Have you been following the political debates? As we continue to interact with others, both breadth and depth of information increase. Because we perceive self-disclosure as a sign of trust, it tends to escalate intimacy (Berger & Bell, 1988). At this early stage of interaction, reciprocity of disclosure is expected so that one person isn't more vulnerable than the other (Duck, 1992; Miell & Duck, 1986).

If early interaction increases attraction, then individuals may dramatically escalate the relationship. During the fourth growth stage, **intensifying communication,** the partners increase the depth of their relationship by increasing personal knowledge; this allows the couple to begin creating a private culture. My students nicknamed this stage euphoria to emphasize the intensity and happiness it embodies. During this stage, partners spend more and more time together, and they rely less on external structures such as movies or parties. Instead, they immerse themselves in the budding relationship and may feel they can't be together enough. Further disclosures are exchanged, personal biographies are filled in, and partners increasingly learn how each other feels and thinks. As personal knowledge expands, dual perspective is possible. "The Chemistry of Love" on page 356 explores the biological basis of attraction between people.

STUDENT VOICES

SUSAN: *I fell in love this year after being alone for eight years after my husband died. Sometimes I think I'm crazy because I'll miss Ben at night after spending the whole day with him. We call each other several times a day just to say hello. I feel as giddy as a teenager.*

Also characteristic of the intensifying stage are idealizing and personalized communication. Idealizing involves seeing a relationship and a partner as more wonderful, exciting, and perfect than he or she really is (Hendrick & Hendrick, 1988). During euphoria, partners often exaggerate each other's virtues, downplay or fail to perceive vices, and overlook problems in the relationship. It is also during euphoria that partners begin to develop relationship vocabularies made up of nicknames and private codes. Most relationship vocabularies include terms that symbolize important experiences partners have shared. Sometimes I say "namaste" to Robbie. This is a Nepali greeting that means "I honor the spirit that is in you and the oneness of us all." Saying "namaste" reminds us of the month we spent trekking in the mountains of Nepal. Relationship vocabularies both reflect and fuel intimacy.

APPLY THE IDEA

Intimate Talk

Do you and your partner have a private language in your relationship?

- Do you have special nicknames for each other that others don't have and use?
- Do you have special words that you made up to describe experiences, activities, and feelings?
- Do you have codes that allow you and your partner to send messages in public that other people don't understand?

The Chemistry of Love

People often talk about the chemistry they have with certain others. Recent research suggests there may be a factual, biological basis to the idea that there is chemistry between people. Consider:

The *cuddle chemical* is oxytocin, which is stimulated by either physical or emotional cues. Oxytocin is released when babies nurse, making mothers nuzzle and cuddle them. Oxytocin also pours out during sexual arousal and lovemaking, making lovers want to caress and cuddle one another.

The *infatuation chemical* is phenylethylamine (PEA). Like amphetamines, PEA makes our bodies tremble when we're attracted to someone and makes us feel euphoric, happy, and energetic when we're in love.

The *attachment chemical* is really a group of morphine-like opiates that calm us and create feelings of relaxed comfort. This allows couples to form more peaceful, steady relationships than the speedlike PEA does. Opiates of the mind promote abiding commitment.

SOURCE: Ackerman, D. (1994). *A natural history of love.* New York: Random House.

CONTINUED

- How does your special relationship language reflect your relationship? How does it affect the bond?

Revising communication, although not part of escalation in all romantic relationships, is important. During this stage, partners come down out of the clouds to look at their relationship more realistically. Problems and dissatisfactions are recognized as partners evaluate the relationship's potential to survive. With the rush of euphoria over, partners consider whether this relationship is one they want for the long run. If it is, they work through obstacles to long-term viability. Many couples that fall in love and move through the intensifying stage choose not to stay together. It is entirely possible to love a person with whom we don't want to share our life or to decide that it's better to stay together without formalizing the relationship. Some older couples make this choice, because marrying can decrease their Social Security benefits.

STUDENT VOICES

THELMA: *Breaking up with Ted was the hardest thing I ever did. I really loved him, and he loved me, but I just couldn't see myself living with a Christian. My whole heritage is Jewish—it's who I am. I celebrate Hanukkah, not Christmas. Seder, Passover, and Yom Kippur are very important to me. Those aren't part of Ted's heritage, and he wouldn't convert. I loved him, but we couldn't have made a life together.*

The final growth stage is commitment, which is a decision to stay with a relationship permanently. This decision transforms a romantic relationship from one based on past and present experiences and feelings into one with a future. Prior to making a commitment, partners don't view the relationship as continuing forever. With commitment, the relationship becomes a given, around which they arrange other aspects of their lives.

Navigating

Navigating is a long-term process. Ideally, a relationship stabilizes in navigating once a commitment has been made. Navigating is the ongoing process of staying committed and living a life together, despite ups and downs and pleasant and unpleasant surprises. Although we hope to stabilize in navigating, the stage itself is full of movement. Couples continuously adjust, work through new problems, revisit old ones, and accommodate to changes in their individual and relational lives. During navigation partners also continuously experience tension from relational dialectics, which are never resolved once and for all. As partners respond to dialectical tensions, they revise and refine the nature of the relationship itself.

In relationships that do endure, ongoing navigation helps partners avoid dangerous shoals and keep their intimacy on a good course. To use an automotive analogy, navigating involves both preventive maintenance and periodic repairs (Canary & Stafford, 1994). The goals of navigating are to keep intimacy satisfying and healthy and to remedy any serious problems that arise. To understand the navigating stage, we'll discuss relational culture, placemaking, and everyday interaction.

© Sotographs/Gamma-Liaison

The nucleus of intimacy is **relational culture,** which is a private world of rules, understandings, meanings, and patterns of acting and interpreting that partners create for their relationship (Wood, 1982, 1995c). Relational culture includes how a couple manages relational dialectics. Jan and Byron may negotiate a lot of autonomy and little togetherness, whereas Louise and Teresa emphasize connectedness and minimize autonomy. Bobby and Cassandra are very open and expressive, whereas Mike and Zelda preserve more individual privacy in their marriage. There are not right and wrong ways to manage dialectics, because individuals and couples differ in what they need. What is most important is for couples to agree on how to deal with tensions between autonomy and connection, openness and privacy, and novelty and routine (Fitzpatrick & Best, 1979; Wood, 1995c).

Relational culture includes rules that partners work out. Couples develop constitutive rules, usually unspoken, about how to show anger, love, sexual interest, and so forth. They also develop routines for contact. Robbie and I catch up while we're fixing dinner each day. Other couples reserve weekends for staying in touch. Couples also develop rules for commemorating special times such as birthdays and holidays.

Romantic couples develop rituals to structure interaction. Carol Bruess and Judy Pearson (1997) identified seven rituals that are common among married couples. The couples they studied had established rituals for couple time, celebrations and play, daily routines and tasks, expressing intimacy, communicating, dealing with habits and mannerisms, and spiritual engagement. The rules and rituals that partners develop and follow provide a predictable rhythm for intimate interaction.

Placemaking is the process of creating a personal environment that is comfortable and that reflects the values, experiences, and tastes of a couple (Werner et al., 1993). In our home, Robbie and I have symbols of our travels: Tibetan carpets, a batik from Thailand, ancient masks from Nepal, and a wood carving from Mexico. We also have photographs of friends and family members who

COMMUNICATION NOTES

Absence Makes the Words Grow Fonder

Couples who have long-distance or commuter relationships face many challenges. Yet what long-distance partners say is most difficult is the loss of daily routines and conversation about everyday matters. What they miss most is sharing trivial details of their lives and small talk.

SOURCE: Gerstel, N., & Gross, H. (1985). *Commuter marriage*. New York: Guilford.

matter to us. Our CDs include much jazz, lots of Mozart, and a number of crossover artists, and we have built-in bookshelves, all overloaded, in most rooms of our home. The books, photos, music, and travel souvenirs make the house into a home that reflects who we are and what we've done together.

An especially important dimension of relational culture is everyday interaction. Partners weave the basic fabric of their relationship in day-to-day conversations that realize their togetherness. "Absence Makes the Words Grow Fonder" explores the importance of everyday interaction for couples. Most conversations between intimates aren't dramatic or noteworthy; actually, the majority of interaction is fairly routine and mundane. Yet everyday talk is more important than major celebrations and big crises in creating and sustaining intimacy (Duck, 1994b; Spencer, 1994). Ordinary talk between partners nourishes their interpersonal climate by continuously recognizing and affirming each other. Later in this chapter, we'll look more closely at the structure and dynamics of marriage, the most popular form of committed romantic relationship.

Deterioration Stages

Steve Duck, a scholar of communication in personal relationships, proposed a five-phase model of relational decline. **Dyadic breakdown** is the first phase of relational decay, and it involves degeneration of established patterns, understandings, and routines that make up a relational culture. Partners may stop talking after dinner, no longer bother to call when they are running late, and in other ways neglect the little things that tie them together. As the fabric of intimacy weakens, dissatisfaction intensifies.

There are general gender differences in the causes of dyadic breakdown. For women, unhappiness with a relationship most often arises when communication declines in quality, quantity, or both. Men are more likely to be dissatisfied by specific behaviors. For instance, men report being dissatisfied when their partners don't greet them at the door and make special meals (Riessman, 1990). For many men, dissatisfaction also arises if they have domestic responsibilities, which they feel aren't a man's job (Gottman & Carrère, 1994). Many women regard a relationship as breaking down if "We don't really communicate with each other anymore," whereas men tend to be dissatisfied if "We don't do fun things together anymore." Another gender difference is in who notices problems in a relationship. As a rule, women are more likely than men to perceive declines in intimacy. Because women are socialized to take care of relationships, they are more likely than men to notice tensions and early symptoms of problems (Cancian, 1989; Tavris, 1992).

The **intrapsychic phase** involves brooding about problems in the relationship and dissatisfactions with a partner (Duck, 1992). Women's brooding about languishing relationships tends to focus on perceived declines in closeness and

V. Clement/Jerrican/Photo Researchers, Inc.

intimate communication, whereas men's reflections more often center on lapses in joint activities and acts of consideration between partners. It's easy for the intrapsychic phase to become a self-fulfilling prophecy: As gloomy thoughts snowball and awareness of positive features of the relationship ebb, partners may actually bring about the failure of their relationship. During the intrapsychic phase, partners may begin to think about alternatives to the relationship.

The **dyadic phase** is the third stage in relational decline, and it doesn't always occur (Duck, 1992). As we saw in Chapter 9, women are more likely to respond to conflict by initiating discussion of problems, and men often deny problems or exit rather than talk about them. Communication scholars report that many people avoid talking about problems, refuse to return calls from partners, and in other ways evade confronting difficulties (Baxter, 1984; Metts, Cupach, & Bejlovec, 1989). Although this is understandable, because it is painful to talk about the decline of intimacy, avoiding problems does nothing to resolve them and may, in fact, make them worse. In formal relationships such as marriage, partners must negotiate matters such as division of property and child custody, but they may choose to talk through lawyers rather than directly to each other. What happens in the negotiation phase depends on how committed partners are, whether they perceive attractive alternatives to the relationship, and whether they have the communication skills to work through problems constructively.

If partners lack commitment or the communication skills needed to resuscitate intimacy, they enter the **social phase** of disintegration, which involves figuring out how to tell outsiders they are parting. Either separately or in collaboration, partners decide how to explain their breakup to friends, children, inlaws, and social acquaintances. When partners don't cooperatively craft a joint explanation for breaking up, friends may take sides, gossip, and disparage one or the other partner as the "bad guy"(La Gaipa, 1982).

Social support is a phase in which partners look to friends and family for support during the breakup. Others can provide support by being available and by listening mindfully. Partners may give self-serving accounts of the breakup in order to save face and secure sympathy and support from others. Thus, Beth may portray Janine as at fault and herself as the innocent party in a breakup. During this phase, partners often criticize their exes and expect friends to take their side (Duck, 1992). Although self-serving explanations of breakups are common, they aren't necessarily constructive. It's a good idea to monitor communication during this period so that we don't say things we'll later regret.

S T U D E N T   VOICES

SAMANTHA: *I really hate it when couples in our social circle divorce. It never fails that we lose one of the two of them as a friend, because each of them wants us to take sides. They each blame the other and expect us to* *help them do that, and you can't do it for both spouses. One of them won't be a friend anymore.*

Grave dressing is the final phase in relational decline, and it involves burying the relationship and accepting its end. Like individuals, relationships deserve a proper burial (Duck, 1992). During grave dressing, we work to make sense of the relationship—what it meant, why it failed, and how it affected us. Usually, individuals need to mourn intimacy that has died. Even if we initiate a breakup, we are sad about the failure to realize what seemed possible at one time. Grave dressing completes the process of relational dissolution by putting the relationship to rest so that partners can get on with their individual lives.

The stages we have discussed describe how most people perceive the course of romance. However, not all couples follow the standard pattern. Some partners skip one or more stages in the typical sequences of escalation or deterioration, and many of us cycle more than once through certain stages. For example, a couple might soar through euphoria, work out some tough issues in revising, then go through euphoria a second time. It's also normal for long-term partners to depart navigation periodically to experience both euphoric seasons and intervals of dyadic breakdown. Further, because relationships are embedded in larger systems, it's likely that romantic intimacy follows different developmental paths in other cultures.

Now that we understand how romantic relationships evolve, we're ready to consider what happens when people decide they want to stay together forever. That is the focus of the next section of this chapter.

Long-Term Commitments

What happens when romantic relationships are satisfying and when partners want to stay together? One option is marriage, but that isn't the only possibility and it isn't one that is available to everyone. We'll discuss cohabitation and gay and lesbian commitments as alternatives to marriage. Then we'll focus on marriage, which seems the preferred choice, particularly in the United States.

Nonmarital Commitments

For both personal reasons and social constraints, many people who love each other do not choose to marry. Some would marry if laws allowed them to; others reject the idea of marriage, either totally or at particular times in their lives.

Cohabitation   A substantial number of couples cohabit, and they do so for varying reasons. Some people view cohabitation as a temporary stage in which they are trying out marriage. In the United States and Canada, cohabitation is increasingly accepted, especially among people under thirty. Cohabitation is also growing in popularity in other countries. One-third of students from India, a traditional society, who attend U.S. universities reported wanting to live with someone before marrying (Davis & Singh, 1989).

Although many people think of cohabitation as a way to try out marriage, that may not be an accurate assumption. Psychologists John Cunningham and John Antill (1995) caution that cohabitation doesn't really serve as a trial marriage. In fact, cohabiting before marrying reduces the likelihood that marriage will endure (Bumpass & Sweet, 1989). One reason for this finding may be that marriage involves a firm commitment, and cohabitation is a more contingent, tentative connection, one that can be abandoned with far less difficulty than marriage.

Not all couples who live together see cohabitation as leading to marriage. For many people cohabitation is a preferred alternative, not a precursor, to marriage. For these couples, marriage is not a goal. Some care enough about each other to want to live together, but they aren't willing to make the total commitment that marriage entails. Researchers have found that a significant number of people who are cohabiting expect to marry later but do not think they will marry the person they are currently living with (Cunningham & Antill, 1995; Landale & Fennelly, 1992). For these individuals, cohabitation is an ideal that allows them to have greater intimacy than dating but less than marriage.

STUDENT VOICES

DIMITRI: *I'm crazy about Bridgette, but I'm not ready for marriage now— not even ready to think about that! There's a lot I want to do for myself and on my own before I think about settling down permanently and having a family. But I do love Bridgette and I want to be with her now and in more than a casual way.*

Other cohabiting couples perceive their relationship as a permanent commitment, but they dislike the institution of marriage. For them, cohabitation is a way to define their commitment in ways that don't reflect the roles and expectations associated with marriage.

STUDENT VOICES

AUDREY: *What I feel for Don isn't a matter of what's on a piece of paper or what could be said before a preacher. We don't need those formalities to know we love each other and want to spend our lives with each other. Both of us prefer to know we stay together because we love each other, not because of some legal contract.*

Lesbian and Gay Commitments   Marriage is not an option for everyone—at least not in many countries. Sweden and several other countries recognize same-sex unions as marriages with all of the rights associated with heterosexual marriage. In the United States and many other countries, however, same-sex

© James Wilson/Woodfin Camp & Associates, Inc.

relationships are not recognized as marriages and often not acknowledged as legal unions. Yet unwillingness to recognize the legitimacy of same-sex relationships appears to be waning. Increasingly, many localities in the United States are recognizing gay and lesbian commitments as legitimate relationships. Some members of the clergy perform ceremonies to unite same-sex couples, and many states have passed civil rights laws to ensure that same-sex partners have rights such as including each other on insurance policies.

Current estimates are that at least 10 percent of adults in the United States are gay or lesbian (Sher, 1996; Wood, 1998). Like heterosexuals, many gays and lesbians seek long-term committed relationships. Contrary to the stereotypes of gays and lesbians as flitting from one relationship to another, a majority of gays and lesbians build relationships that are as stable and enduring as those of heterosexuals. In a study of 560 gay couples, the average length of the relationship was seven years, and fully 76 percent of the men said they were committed for life ("National Survey Results," 1991). Similarly, a survey of lesbian couples found that the average length of the relationship was 5 years and 18% of them had been together for at least 11 years ("National Survey Results," 1991).

S T U D E N T   VOICES

JAY: *There may never be a time when Joe and I can "marry" in the technical sense, but we've been married in spirit for fifteen years. From the first time we got together, both of us knew the other was the one—the one for life. What we feel for each other is no different than what a man and a woman who are in love feel. We take care of each other when we're sick. We help each other out financially. We support each other emotionally. We work through problems together. We dream about the future and growing old together. If that's not a marriage, I don't know what is.*

Marriage

Cohabitation and committed same-sex relationships are two alternatives to marriage. Although increasing numbers of people select one of these relationship forms, marriage remains the most popular and most preferred form for enduring romantic commitments in the United States. We'll now look at who marries, how people get to marriage, and how marriages operate.

Who Marries?   In the United States the answer seems to be that nearly everyone marries. During their lifetimes, over 96 percent of men and 94 percent of women marry at least once (Sher, 1996). And all but 4 percent of college students say they expect to marry (Rubinson & De Rubertis, 1991).

Yet not everyone who marries stays married. According to the National Center for Health Statistics (1993), on average 2 percent of married couples divorce each year. Over the course of a lifetime, an individual's chance of getting divorced is roughly 50 percent (Notarius, 1996; Sher, 1996). And nearly a fourth of those who divorce will do so in the first seven years of marriage (Cherlin, 1992).

But not everyone who divorces will stay unmarried. Many people marry two, three, and even more times in an ongoing search for lasting intimacy. In fact, most people who divorce want to remarry, and the majority do. The high rates of remarriage testify to Americans' strong belief in marriage.

"And the prince and princess lived happily ever after, but not with each other."

From The Wall Street Journal, Nov. 6, 1996. Reprinted by permission of Cartoon Features Syndicate.

Paths to Marriage   Although most people in the United States marry, they take a variety of paths to get to the altar. One group of researchers (Cate, Huston, & Nesselroade, 1986) conducted separate interviews with 100 newly married spouses. They asked spouses to describe what happened from the time they first met the person they would marry and the marriage itself. The spouses reported four distinct pathways to marriage.

The first path featured a gradual progression toward commitment with a number of ups and downs and some conflict along the way. The second path involved a rapid escalation toward marriage with no downturns or serious conflict. The third path involved a medium-length courtship and progressive intimacy, followed by a hesitation and rethinking of the relationship, and then marriage and strong commitment. Finally, some couples engaged in a prolonged pattern in which the courtship period was extended and had many ups and downs and substantial conflict.

The different pathways toward marriage may reflect partners' love styles. For example, two people with strong eros love styles would probably follow the second pathway, which involves rapid escalation of intimacy. Two storgic people might be more likely to build their relationship more gradually, perhaps following the first or fourth pathway. Reflect on your love style and ask whether it seems consistent with your approach to intimacy.

The way we move toward marriage is also influenced by the forces that drive relationships. Catherine Surra (1987) asked newlyweds to explain what factors during their courtship were turning points in their eventual decision to marry. She found that some couples were more affected by forces external to their relationships. For instance, being surrounded by friends who are married or are planning marriages and having parents who support or oppose the relationship are external influences on the likelihood of marrying.

S T U D E N T

P HAEDRA: *It's funny how Craig and I decided to get married. We had been seeing each other for about eight months during our senior year. My three best friends were all planning weddings in the summer following*

Marital Types

1. *Vital Marriage.* In this relationship spouses are very close emotionally, and they want to be together physically as much as possible. For spouses in vital marriages, the relationship is their primary source of satisfaction and joy.

2. *Total Marriage.* This relationship is similar to the vital marriage except that partners are not so continuously together. Each has separate interests and sources of satisfaction, yet they look forward to being with each other and schedule their lives to maximize time together.

3. *Passive-Congenial Marriage.* In these relationships partners are polite, and they interact, but they typically deal with superficial matters. This has been the norm for partners since they married. For partners, activities and interests outside of the relationship are primary sources of pleasure and satisfaction.

4. *Devitalized Marriages.* Partners in these relationships don't dislike each other, but they are bored with each other and the relationship. Whereas the marriage was vital and a source of much satisfaction earlier, it now is lifeless and characterized by apathy.

5. *Conflict-Habituated Marriage.* In these relationships partners are incompatible. They remain tied to each other for reasons ranging from inertia to practical considerations (for example, children, finances). The primary dynamic between partners is conflict.

SOURCE: Cuber,. J. F., & Harroff, P. B. (1965). *Sex and the significant Americans.* Baltimore: Penguin.

graduation and so were a couple of the guys in Craig's crowd. One night we were talking about our friends marriages and he said, "Maybe we should set a date ourselves." Of course, I'd thought about marrying him but not really seriously. But then I thought that maybe it was a good idea. I mean the time seemed right since we'd both be graduating and starting to work. I love him. It's not like timing was the only reason we married, but I kind of think we wouldn't have gotten married if it had been our junior year.

Other couples emphasized internal factors when explaining why they decided to marry. Increases in love, trust, and comfort with each other are internal reasons for escalating commitment (Surra, Arizzi, & Asmussen, 1988).

Marital Types Think about the married couples that you know. Do some seem closer than others? Do some seem more traditional than others? Do some of the couples seem bored or even unhappy with each other? Probably you know couples that fit each of these descriptions. Thus, you won't be surprised to learn that researchers have identified several distinct kinds of marriages. We'll consider two ways of classifying marriage.

Over thirty years ago, a team of researchers interviewed 211 spouses (Cuber & Harroff, 1965). From their interviews the investigators were able to distinguish five distinct types of marriage. These are described in "Marital Types." The couples studied didn't necessarily stay fixed in one type of marriage. For instance, some couples began in a total marriage but later reported their marriages had gradually deteriorated into a conflict-habituated relationship in which arguments were the primary form of interaction.

Another way of classifying marriages is advanced by communication scholar Mary Ann Fitzpatrick (1988). On the basis of studying 700 marital couples, Fitzpatrick identified three distinct views of marriage held by spouses: traditional, independent, and separate. The 20 percent of couples who fit into the traditional category were highly interdependent and emotionally expressive with each other. Traditionals also share conventional views of marriage and family life, and they engage in conflict regularly. Independents made up 22 percent of the couples in Fitzpatrick's study. Independents hold less conventional views of marriage and family life. Compared to traditionals, independents are less interdependent, more emotionally expressive, and more prone to engage in conflict. The third approach toward marriage is separates, who comprised 17 percent of the couples Fitzpatrick studied. As the term implies, separates are highly autonomous. Partners give each other plenty of room, and they share less emotionally than the other two types. Separates also try to avoid conflict, perhaps because it often involves emotional expressiveness.

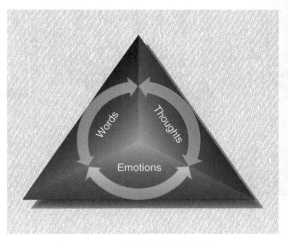

FIGURE 11.4
The Circle of Words, Thoughts, and Emotions

In Fitzpatrick's research, 60 percent of couples fit into one of these three types of marriage. But 40 percent did not. In these mixed marriages, the husband and wife subscribe to different perspectives on marriage. The most common form of mixed marriage is the separate-traditional couple. In the couples that Fitzpatrick studied, it was typically the wife who held a traditional view of marriage and wanted high interdependence and emotional closeness. Generally, husbands in mixed marriages subscribe to a separate ideology and identity. They want a high degree of autonomy, and some feel emotionally divorced from the marriage. Surprisingly, the highest levels of marital satisfaction are experienced by traditional and separate-traditional couples.

Dynamics of Marital Satisfaction   The two ways of classifying marriages give us a broad understanding of how marriages work. Yet, recognizing marital types doesn't offer us much insight into the actual functioning of marriages. What are the dynamics in marriage that affect satisfaction and endurance? According to Clifford Notarius (1996), there are three key elements, as shown in Figure 11.4, that influence satisfaction with marriage: words, thoughts, and emotions.

By words, Notarius means the process of communication between spouses. How partners talk and behave toward each other keenly affects each person. Communication influences spouses' self-esteem as well as their feelings about the relationship. Happy couples tend to communicate more support, agreement, understanding, and interest in each other than do less happy couples. In contrast, dissatisfied and unhappy marital partners engage in frequent criticism, negative statements, mindreading, and egocentric communication in which they don't rely on dual perspective (Gottman & Carrère, 1994; Notarius, 1996).

Marriage counselors Aaron Beck (1988) and Howard Markman (1990) consistently cite one form of communication that is strongly linked to dissatisfaction in marriage: Reciprocal negativity seems to fuel dissatisfaction and conflict. Couples who engage in reciprocal negativity tend to respond to negative comments with negative messages. In turn, this leads to another spiral of negative exchange and another and so on. Among satisfied couples, partners generally resist the temptation to respond to negativity with reciprocal negativity. As a result, distinct interpersonal climates are created and sustained in marriages. The differences in the communication between satisfied and dissatisfied spouses echo material we discussed regarding climate and conflict in Chapters 8 and 9.

By thoughts, Notarius means how partners think about each other and the marriage; these thoughts shape our emotions and words. From Chapter 3 you'll recall our discussion of attributional patterns, particularly the different ways that

© Randy Ury/The Stock Market

we explain what others do. Researchers (Fincham, Bradbury, & Scott, 1990) report that in satisfying marriages, partners tend to attribute nice things the other says and does to stable, internal qualities that are within individual control. For example, a wife might think, "My husband brought flowers because he is a good person who wants to let me know he loves me." On the other hand, in satisfying marriages partners tend to attribute negative actions and communication to unstable, external factors that are beyond individual control. If a husband didn't bring the cleaning home, his wife might explain it by telling herself, "He forgot because he is so overwhelmed at work right now. This isn't like him; generally he's a thoughtful person."

In less satisfying marriages, partners tend to attribute negative things the other says and does to stable, enduring qualities that are within personal control. For example, a wife might think, "My husband didn't pick up the cleaning because he is a thoughtless, selfish person who doesn't want to do anything to help me." Partners in unhappy marriages also tend to attribute positive thoughts and actions to unstable, external factors or to circumstances beyond personal control. To explain why her husband brought home flowers, a wife might think, "The florist must have had a sale, and he was in a good mood."

A third key to marital satisfaction is emotions, which we discussed in detail in Chapter 7. As we saw in that chapter, emotions are affected by words and thoughts. How we feel is affected by what we say to others and what we communicate to ourselves through self-talk. For example, the attributions that we make for our partners' behaviors affect how we feel about those behaviors. If a wife defines her husband's gift of flowers as evidence of his thoughtfulness and caring, she will feel closer and more loving toward him than if she defines the flowers as something he bought on a whim because they were on sale.

Words, thoughts, and emotions are a circle—each affects the other. What we feel affects how we communicate and how we think about ourselves, others, and our relationships. What we think about others, ourselves, and relationships influences how we feel and communicate. How we communicate shapes how we and our partners think and feel about relationships, ourselves, and each other.

The Family Life Cycle

Just as friendships and romance typically follow relatively generalizable developmental patterns, so do many marriages. According to researchers who have studied families over time (Olson & McCubbin, 1983), there are seven stages in the life cycles of most families that include children.

Although the stages that these researchers identify provide a useful general description of many families, the stages don't apply to all families. For example, they might not apply to the developmental paths of all cohabiting, gay, and lesbian couples. Also, not all of the stages apply to all heterosexual marriages. For example, couples who do not have children would not engage in stages 2, 3, 4, and 5. They might go through other stages in their life cycles, but raising and launching children would not be phases in their relationship. These stages are shown in Figure 11.5.

Stage 1: Establishing a Family   During this phase, a couple settles into marriage and works out expectations, interaction patterns, and daily routines for their shared life. Partners get accustomed to being married and to having social and legal recognition of their union.

Stage 2: Enlarging a Family   One of the major changes in family life is the addition of children. The transition to parenthood typically brings joy, problems, and new constraints for the couple. It also introduces new roles. A woman becomes not only a wife but also a mother. A man becomes not only a husband but a father. Further, one or more children decrease the amount of couple time and alter the focus of couple's communication. For most parents, children are a primary focus of conversation: How are they doing? Which of us is taking them to the doctor? The zoo? School? How do we deal with behavior problems? How do we save money for their college education?

Stage 1	**Establishing a family**—young married couple without children.
Stage 2	**Enlarging a family**—families with infants and/or preschoolers.
Stage 3	**Developing a family**— families with children in elementary or high school.
Stage 4	**Encouraging independence**—families with adolescents who are developing their own interests, activities, and social circles.
Stage 5	**Launching children**—families who are launching children into the world.
Stage 6	**Post-launching of children**—couples after all children have left home and the couple is once again the primary unit.
Stage 7	**Retirement**—couples when full-time work is no longer a part of life.

FIGURE 11.5
The Typical Life Cycle in Families with Children

S T U D E N T   VOICES

S TAN: *Just about everything in our lives changed when Dina was born. We had to sell our little two-door sports car because we couldn't use Dina's car seat in it. We used to enjoy a glass of wine before dinner, but now one of us fixes the dinner while the other feeds and bathes Dina. We used to sometimes decide on the spur of the moment to drive to the beach for a day trip, but now we either have to plan ahead and hire a babysitter or pack everything Dina will need from diapers to food to toys. There's no room for spontaneity anymore. We're both so tired from ragged sleep because Dina wakes up several times each night. When we go to bed, neither of us is interested in sex—sleep is far more appealing.*

Stan's reflection on becoming a parent is not atypical. Mari Clements and Howard Markman (1996) note that a baby is both a bundle of joy and a home-wrecker! A great deal of research shows that marital satisfaction declines after the birth of a child or children (Belsky & Rovine, 1990; Clements & Markman, 1996; Cowan, Cowan, Heming, & Miller, 1991). For many years researchers assumed the decline was due to the presence of children and the demands they make. Yet, that may not be true.

© Jose L. Pelaez/The Stock Market

A longitudinal project headed by Howard Markman (Markman, Clements, & Wright, 1991) recruited 135 couples who were planning marriage and has followed those couples on an annual basis since 1980. Markman and his colleagues have found that marital satisfaction declines after children arrive. However, they also found that marital satisfaction declines after the first few years for couples who do not have children. In other words, after the first few married years, most couples experience a dip in marital satisfaction *regardless of whether they have children*. Thus, the second stage in family life may be a time of adjusting expectations and feeling some dissatisfaction about declines in romanticism.

Stage 3: Developing a Family   Parents with young children invest a great deal of time and energy in raising the children. Children must be taught everything from potty training to manners, and parents are the primary teachers. During preschool years, most parents also devote themselves to instilling values in their children. This phase in the lives of families with children is one of establishing foundations for the children's personalities, esteem, and lives.

Stage 4: Encouraging Independence   As children enter adolescence, they seek greater autonomy so that they can establish their own identities—ones distinct from those of their parents. They don't want to spend a great deal of time with their parents. Instead, they have their own interests and want to pursue those with their peers. Usually this stage involves substantial tension between parents and children. Parents may not approve of some of their children's interests, activities, and friends. Children may feel parents are being overly protective or intruding on their privacy and independence.

Stage 5: Launching Children   This is a time of vital change for most families. Children leave home to go to college, marry, or live on their own. Parents, who for eighteen or more years have centered their lives around children, now find themselves a couple again. Research (Anderson, Russell, and Schumm, 1983) indicates that this period, often called the empty nest, is typically the time of lowest satisfaction between spouses. This is probably because husbands and wives have forgotten how to engage each other outside of their roles as parents. Many partners find they have to relearn how to be together with just each other and how to enjoy activities that don't involve their children.

S T U D E N T VOICES

GRETCHEN: *When our last child left home for college, Brant and I realized how little we had in common as a couple. We'd centered our lives around the three children and family activities. Without any of them in the home anymore, it was like Brant and I didn't know what to do with each other. At*

*first it was really awkward. If we weren't Christians, maybe we would
have divorced, but both of us feel marriage is forever. That meant we
had to rediscover each other. We went to a weekend workshop sponsored by our church. It was called "Rediscovering Love in Your
Marriage." That workshop got us started in finding our way back to
each other.*

© Norbert Schafer/The Stock Market

Stage 6: Post-Launching of Children   Following the departure of
children from the home, spouses have to redefine their marriage.
The partners have more time for each other, but that may be a blessing or a curse. For some couples, this is a time of renewed love—
almost a second honeymoon—as they enjoy the leisure of being able
to focus on their pair relationship and the freedom of not having to
plan around children's schedules. For other couples, the absence of
children makes obvious the distance between them and dissatisfaction grows.
Some couples divorce after the only or last child leaves home. Children can be
the glue that holds couples together.

Stage 7: Retirement   Retirement brings about further changes in family life and
functioning. Like other changes, those ushered in by retirement can be positive
or negative. For many people, retirement is a time when they can do what they
want instead of spending much of their time earning a living. Fran Dickson
(1995) reports that people who are happy in long-lasting marriages tend to find
pleasure in each other's presence and to enjoy the luxury of having more time
to be together. For other couples, retirement may evoke feelings of boredom
and unproductivity. People whose identity is strongly tied to their work may feel
unanchored when they retire. Naturally this discontent ripples through the
marital dyad.

   The retirement years are also ones in which the family may grow again—this
time through the addition of grandchildren. According to Mary Mares (1995),
half of African Americans are grandparents by the time they are thirty-two, and
a majority of Whites are grandparents in their fifties. Grandchildren can be
welcome new members of the family who provide interest and an additional
focus for grandparents' lives.

   Now that we understand communication dynamics in marriage and family
life, we are ready to consider some of the challenges to sustaining intimacy over
time.

Challenges to Sustaining Romantic Relationships

Enduring romantic relationships face a number of difficulties. Many of the
challenges are natural, even inevitable, in all forms of intimacy. All couples
have to deal continuously with the tensions of relational dialectics, gendered

The Second Shift

In 80 percent of dual-worker families, men work one job and women work two—the second shift begins when they come home. Not only do women do more domestic work than men, but they do work that is less satisfying and more stressful. Women tend to do the day-in, day-out jobs such as cooking, shopping, and helping children with homework. Men more often do domestic work that they can schedule to suit themselves. Mowing the lawn can be scheduled flexibly, whereas fixing meals must be done on a tight timetable. Men also are more likely to take care of occasional and fun child-care activities, such as visiting the zoo, whereas women manage the daily grind of bathing, dressing, and feeding children.

As a rule, women assume **psychological responsibility**, which involves remembering, planning, and coordinating domestic activities. Parents may alternate who takes children to the doctor, but it is usually the mother who remembers when checkups are needed, makes appointments, and reminds the father to take the child. Birthday cards and gifts are signed by both partners, but women typically assume the psychological responsibility for remembering when birthdays are and for buying cards and gifts.

SOURCE: Based on Hochschild, A., with Machung, A. (1989). *The second shift.* New York: Viking Press.

© Michael Newman/Photo Edit

dynamics, and conflicts that are sometimes severe. In addition to the generic problems of relationships, romantic partners may encounter four special complications.

Ensuring Equity

Perceived equity is very important in committed romantic relationships. **Equity** means fairness, based on the perception that both partners invest relatively equally in a relationship and benefit similarly from their investments. We all want to feel that our partners are as committed as we are and that we gain equally from being together. Although few partners demand moment-to-moment equality, most of us want our relationships to be equitable over time. Inequity tends to breed unhappiness, which lessens satisfaction and commitment and sometimes prompts affairs (Walster, Traupmann, & Walster, 1978).

Equity has multiple dimensions. We may evaluate the fairness of financial, emotional, physical, and other contributions to a relationship. One area that strongly affects relationship quality is perceived equity in housework and child care, as discussed in "The Second Shift." Inequitable division of domestic obligations fuels dissatisfaction and resentment, both of which harm intimacy (Gottman & Carrère, 1994). Marital stability is more closely linked to perceptions of equitable divisions of child care and housework than to income or sex life (Fowers, 1991; Suitor, 1991). Beginning with the Industrial Revolution, men were assigned responsibility for earning income and women for caring for children and a home. A gendered division of labor no longer makes sense, because more than 83 percent of marriages today include two wage earners (Wilkie, 1991). Unfortunately, divisions of family and home responsibilities have not changed in response to changing employment patterns. Even when both partners in heterosexual relationships work outside the home, the vast majority of child care and homemaking is done by women (Nussbaum, 1992; Okin, 1989). In only 20 percent of dual-worker families do men assume equal domestic responsibilities (Hochschild with Machung, 1989). Although many men with partners who work outside the home do contribute, they do less than a fair share. Since the 1950s, the amount of housework and child care that husbands do has risen a scant 10 percent—from 20 to 30 percent (Pleck, 1987).

CORA MAY: *I said, "Either things are going to change around here or I'm leaving." He didn't believe me, but I stood my ground. For twenty years I had done all of the housework, the cooking, and the child care, while he did none of these. Walter just went to his job each day and came back home for me to wait on him. Well, I went to my job each day too. I worked hard, and I was tired when I got home. You'd think he could figure that out, wouldn't you? It got really bad when I started taking night courses. I need to study at night, not fix meals and do laundry, so I asked him to help out. You'd think he'd been stung by a bee. He said no, so I just quit fixing his meals and left his laundry when I washed my clothes. Finally, he got with the program.*

How are domestic responsibilities managed when both partners are the same sex? Lesbian couples create more egalitarian relationships than either heterosexuals or gays. More than any other type of couple, lesbians are likely to share decision making and domestic work (Huston & Schwartz, 1995). Consequently, lesbians are least likely to perceive inequity in contributions to home life (Kurdek, 1993). Gay men, like their heterosexual brothers, use the power derived from income to authorize inequitable contributions to domestic life. In gay couples, the man who makes more money has and uses more power, both in making decisions that affect the relationship and in avoiding housework (Huston & Schwartz, 1995). This suggests that power is the basis of gendered divisions of labor and that men, more than women, seek the privileges of power, including evasion of domestic work.

The perception of inequity damages romantic relationships. It creates resentment and anger and erodes love. As resentment eclipses positive feelings, dissatisfaction mushrooms. In addition, there are health consequences. Women who work a second shift are stressed, starved for sleep, and susceptible to illness because they are continuously doing double duty (Hochschild with Machung, 1989). Successful long-term relationships in our era require more equitable divisions of home responsibilities than have been traditional.

SALLY FORTH © 1992. Reprinted with special permission of King Features Syndicate.

Danny said he didn't want to do it if we had to use condoms. I said goodnight. He drove around the block, came back and said, okay.

— Carrie J.

CARRIE J. KNOWS HOW TO GET A MAN TO WEAR A CONDOM. USING A LATEX CONDOM EVERY TIME IS THE BEST WAY TO PROTECT YOURSELF FROM HIV, THE VIRUS THAT CAUSES AIDS. FOR ADVICE ON TALKING TO YOUR PARTNER, CALL **1-800-235-2331.** TTY **617-437-1672.**

AIDS ACTION

Illustration by Jean-Philippe Delhomme/Based on a campaign created by Mullen Advertising for the AIDS Action Committee of Massachusetts, Inc.

Negotiating Safer Sex

In the HIV/AIDS era, sexual activities pose serious, even deadly, threats to romantic relationships. In 1994 the World Health Organization announced the shocking statistic that 17 million people were HIV positive, and 3 million people around the world were infected with HIV ("Three Million," 1994). Following that report, vigorous research campaigns were funded, and the results are cause for hope. As I was writing this chapter in September 1997, a report from CDC (Centers for Disease Control) stated that AIDS was no longer the number-one killer of people between the ages of twenty-five and forty-four. Between 1995 and 1996 alone the number of AIDS-related deaths dropped a dramatic 26 percent. Even so, AIDS remains deadly. It is now the second leading cause of death for people between the ages of twenty-five and forty-four ("Annual Report," 1997).

Despite vigorous public education campaigns, many individuals still don't practice safer sex, which includes abstaining, restricting sexual activity to a single partner who has been tested for HIV, and/or using latex condoms (Reel & Thompson, 1994). In a nationwide survey, only 48 percent of men and 32 percent of women reported using condoms (Clements, 1994). Not practicing safer sex puts both partners at grave risk for early death.

Why don't people who know about HIV/AIDS consistently follow safer sex techniques? Communication scholars have discovered two primary reasons. First, many individuals find it more embarrassing to talk about sex than to engage in it. They find it awkward to ask direct questions of partners ("Have you been tested for HIV?" "Are you having sex with anyone else?") or to make direct requests of partners ("I want you to wear a condom," "I would like for you to be tested for HIV before we have sex"). Naturally, it's difficult to talk explicitly about sex and the dangers of HIV/AIDS. However, it is far more difficult to live with HIV or the knowledge you infected a lover.

A second reason people sometimes fail to practice safer sex is that their rational thought and control are debilitated by drugs, alcohol, or both. In a series of studies of college students' sexual activities, communication researchers Sheryl Bowen and Paula Michal-Johnson (1995) found that safer sex precautions are often neglected when individuals drink heavily. The National Council on Alcoholism and Drug Dependence reports that sexually active teens are less likely to use condoms after drinking ("What Teens Say," 1994). Alcohol and other drugs loosen inhibitions, including appropriate concerns about personal safety. "Reasons Good Enough to Die For?" examines why people do not practice safer sex.

Discussing and practicing safer sex may be embarrassing, but there is no other sensible option. Principles of effective interpersonal communication we've discussed help ease the discomfort of negotiating safer sex. I-language that owns your feelings is especially important. It is more constructive to say "I feel unsafe having unprotected sex" than to say "Without a condom, you could give me HIV." A positive interpersonal climate is fostered by relational language, such as "we," "us," and "our relationship," to talk about sex (Reel & Thompson, 1994). Individuals who care about themselves and their partners are honest about their sexual histories and careful in their sex practices.

COMMUNICATION NOTES

Reasons Good Enough to Die For?

When students and members of singles organizations were asked about their sexual activities, these were the top five reasons they reported for not practicing safer sex:

1. I knew my partner. We'd discussed our past sexual experiences.
2. I use another form of birth control.
3. A condom wasn't available at the time.
4. Things happened too fast.
5. I didn't feel I was at risk.

SOURCE: Reel, B. W., & Thompson, T. L. (1994). A test of the effectiveness of strategies for talking about AIDS and condom use. *Journal of Applied Communication Research, 22,* 127–141.

Avoiding Violence and Abuse

Although we like to think of romantic relationships as loving, many are not. Violence and abuse are unfortunately common between romantic partners, and they cut across lines of class, race, and ethnicity (French, 1992; West, 1995). Violence is high not only in heterosexual marriage but also in heterosexual cohabitation. In fact, cohabiting couples have the highest incidence of violence of all couples (Cunningham & Antill, 1995; White & Bondurant, 1996). Cohabiting women suffer one and one-half to two times more physical abuse than married women, perhaps because their partners are less committed than husbands (Ellis, 1989).

The majority of detected violence and abuse in intimacy seems to be committed by men against women. Currently in the United States, a woman is beaten every 12 seconds by a husband or intimate, and four women a day are beaten to death (Brock-Utne, 1989). In a single year, at least 2 million women are battered by current or former partners (Orange County Health Department, 1997). Established patterns of abuse lead to the estimate that one in five women in the United States will be physically abused by a male partner during her lifetime (Orange County Health Department, 1997). Rape and date rape are escalating, especially when individuals have been drinking ("What Teens Say," 1994). Verbal and emotional abuse cause deep and lasting scars (Vachss, 1994). And dysfunctional relationships, often called toxic connections, seem to be rising (Wright & Wright, 1995).

Mental health counselors who specialize in violence have come to the conclusion that relationships in which men abuse women are not rare but exemplify in extreme form the traditional power dynamics that structure relationships between women and men (Goldner, Penn, Sheinberg, & Walker, 1990). Men are taught to use power to assert themselves and to compete with others, whereas women are socialized to defer and preserve relationships. When

© Thelma Shumsky/The Image Works

these internalized patterns combine in heterosexual relationships, a foundation exists for men to abuse women and for women to tolerate it, rather than be disloyal (West, 1995). This may explain why national surveys reveal that an alarming 25 percent of women and 30 percent of men regard violence as a normal part of relationships (Gelles, 1987; Jones, 1994).

KATRINA: *It's hard for me to believe now, but I was in an abusive relationship, and it took me a long time to get out of it. The first time Ray hit me, I was so surprised I didn't know what to do, so I didn't do anything. The next time, I told him to stop or I'd leave. He said how sorry he was and promised never to hit me again, and then he was real sweet for a long time. I felt like he really did love me, and I felt I should stand by him. And then it happened again. I went to talk to my minister, and he told me my Christian duty was to honor the marriage vows I made before God, so I went back again. Each time Ray beat up on me, he'd follow it with being romantic and sweet, so I'd get sucked back in. I didn't finally leave him until he threw me down some stairs and dislocated my shoulder.*

Violence seldom stops without intervention. Instead it follows a predictable cycle, just as Katrina described: Tension mounts in the abuser, the abuser explodes by being violent, the abuser then is remorseful and loving, the victim feels loved and that the relationship is working, and then tension mounts up and the cycle begins again (see Figure 11.6 on page 375).

Being loyal in the face of abuse, a response to conflict that we discussed in Chapter 9, is inappropriate because it doesn't protect a victim's safety. Relationships that are violent and abusive are unhealthy for everyone involved. They obviously jeopardize the comfort, health, and sometimes the survival of victims of violence. Less obvious is the damage experienced by abusers. Using physical force against others is a sign of weakness—an admission that a person can't exercise power in intellectual or emotional ways and must resort to the crudest and least imaginative methods of influence. Further, abusers can destroy relationships that they need and want.

APPLY THE IDEA
Resisting Violence

No one should tolerate violence, especially from a person who claims to love her or him. If you are being abused, seek counseling to discover and think through your options. If you suspect someone you care about is being abused, be a real friend and talk with the person. Too often signs of abuse are ignored because we find it awkward to talk about violence between intimates. However, standing by and doing nothing is a kind of abuse in itself. If you are abusing someone you care about, get professional help.

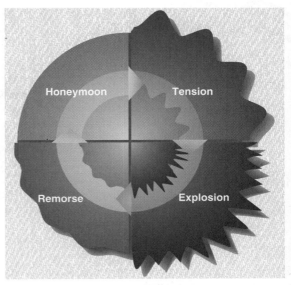

FIGURE 11.6
The Cycle of Abuse

Surviving Distance

In Chapter 10, we discussed the challenges distance poses for friendship. Geographic separation can be even more difficult for romantic couples because Western culture teaches us to expect to live with our partners. The assumption of living together permanently, however, isn't universal. Some Asians and Hispanics come to the United States alone and work several years before bringing spouses and children to join them. In Nepal, many Tamong men who live in the southern hill country move to the city of Kathmandu for six months of each year, and they serve as guides, cooks, and porters for treks into the Himalayas. Westerners facing long-distance relationships might take heart from the fact that couples in other cultures manage to stay together despite long periods of living apart.

Many of us will be involved in long-distance romantic relationships because they are increasingly common (U.S. Bureau of the Census, 1992). Fully 70 percent of college students are or have been in long-distance romances (Rohlfing, 1995). The number of long-distance romantic relationships will increase further as more partners pursue independent careers and as extended travel becomes part of more people's jobs. Many couples who share the same home will still be apart a great deal of the time. Last year, my partner Robbie was on the road more than 120 days, and I was gone from our home for nearly 100!

Researchers have identified three problems, or tensions, commonly experienced in long-distance relationships. Perhaps the greatest problem is the lack of daily sharing of small events and unrealistic expectations about time together. Not being able to share small talk and daily routines is a major loss. As we have seen, sharing the ordinary comings and goings of days helps partners keep their lives woven together. The routine conversations of romantic partners form and continuously reform the basic fabric of their relationship. Everyday talk is how couples connect in countless little moments that shape the overall climate of the relationship.

The lack of routine contact leads to the second problem faced by couples who live apart: unrealistic expectations for time together. Based on twenty-five years of studying marriages, psychologist and marriage counselor John Gottman (1997) reports that the mundane, ordinary moments couples share are what build love and establish a positive emotional climate between people. Because partners have so little time together, they often believe every moment must be perfect. They feel that there should be no harsh words or conflict and that they should be happily focused on each other for all the time they have together.

COMMUNICATION NOTES

Difficulties in Long-Distance Romance

Partners involved in long-distance romantic relationships in the United States report the following challenges:

1. It takes money to maintain long-distance relationships.
2. It's hard for partners to negotiate comfortable rules for each partner's in-town relationships.
3. Partners are hyperconscious about the limited time they do have together. Expectations for good sharing and no rough spots can be unrealistic.
4. It's hard to assess relationships when you aren't with your partner.
5. You miss many nonverbal cues in phone calls.
6. You can't share daily news about your lives.

SOURCES: Gross, H. E. (1980). Couples who live apart: Time/place disjunctions and their consequence. *Symbolic Interaction, 3,* 69–82; Rohlfing, M. (1995). Doesn't anybody stay in one place anymore? An exploration of the understudied phenomenon of long-distance relationships. In J. T. Wood & S. W. Duck (Eds.), *Understanding relationship processes, 6: Off the beaten track: Understudied relationships,* (pp. 173–196). Thousand Oaks, CA: Sage.

Yet, this is an unrealistic expectation. Conflict and needs for autonomy are natural and inevitable in all romantic relationships. They may be even more likely in reunions of long-distance couples, because partners are used to living alone and have established independent rhythms that may not mesh well.

A third common problem in long-distance relationships is unequal effort that the two partners invest in maintaining the connection. According to Vicki Helgeson (1994), one of the major reasons that long-distance couples break up is that one partner is doing most of the work to sustain contact and to take care of the relationship. The inequity in investment creates resentment in the person who is assuming the majority of the work to keep the relationship alive. "Difficulties in Long-Distance Romance" explores the challenges of these relationships.

STUDENT VOICES

MARIA: *When Miguel found a good job in another state, he moved, and both of us thought our relationship would survive. We had talked about marrying when I finished school, so we were pretty serious. At first we did okay, even though it was hard. I would write every day and he wrote me once or twice each week. One of us called the other every week. Then his letters got less frequent. Then it seemed I was always the one who called him. I told him he was acting like he wasn't committed anymore, but he said he was just busy. I think that was true, but it didn't matter after a while. The upshot is that he was too busy for us, and I couldn't keep the relationship going on my own.*

The good news is that these problems don't necessarily sabotage long-distance romance. Most researchers report that partners can maintain satisfying commitments despite geographic separation (Rohlfing, 1995). In fact, there are some noteworthy advantages of long-distance relationships. James Reske and Laura Stafford (1990) report that the very everydayness that geographically separated partners miss is a boon to romance. Because couples aren't together continuously, they tend to be more loving when they are together and to feel more passionately about each other. Also, partners who live apart are able to focus on their individual projects and ambitions without the distraction of a constant companion.

The strategies devised by college students (see "Coping with Geographic Separation") are sound guidelines for sustaining intimacy across distance.

Notice that these strategies reflect many of the communication principles we've discussed in this and previous chapters. Because partners don't have the comfort of everyday interaction, it is especially important to build climates that are trusting, open, and honest in long-distance relationships. It's also critical that couples who live apart focus on what is positive and good about the relationship and even the separation. One important advantage of living apart is that each partner can concentrate more fully on work, school, or other priorities (Gross, 1980). This may allow partners to advance in their careers so that when they are reunited they have secure jobs and better than average resources.

Romantic relationships experience many of the pressures that beset all personal relationships. Three problems that pose special difficulty for romantic partners are achieving equity, negotiating safer sex, and managing the strains of separation. Commitment, flexibility, and effective interpersonal communication help partners meet the challenges of keeping romance healthy and satisfying over the long term.

Guidelines for Communication Between Romantic Partners

Enduring romantic relationships are important sources of personal growth and happiness. Keeping love and commitment alive for a lifetime is one of the greatest challenges we all face. To meet the challenge of sustaining intimacy over the long term, practice the interpersonal communication skills we've discussed throughout this book: Build supportive climates, listen mindfully, engage in dual perspective, express your feelings clearly, and deal constructively with conflicts. In addition, three specific guidelines apply to intimate communication.

COMMUNICATION NOTES

Coping with Geographic Separation

College students report nine coping strategies they use to sustain intimacy across long distances.

1. Recognize that long-distance relationships are common; you're not alone.
2. Create more social support systems (friends) while separated from a romantic partner.
3. Communicate creatively—send video- and audiotapes.
4. Before separating, work out ground rules for going out with friends, phoning, visiting, and writing.
5. Use time together "wisely" to be affectionate and to have fun together. Being serious all the time isn't constructive.
6. Maintain honesty. Especially when partners live apart, they need to be straight with each other.
7. Build an open, supportive communication climate so that you can talk about issues and feelings.
8. Maintain trust by abiding by ground rules that were agreed on, phoning when you say you will, and keeping lines of communication open.
9. Focus on the positive aspects of separation.

SOURCE: Westefield, J. S., & Liddell, D. (1982). Coping with long-distance relationships. *Journal of College Student Personnel, 23,* 550–551.

© Peter L. Chapman

Show Respect and Consideration

For romantic intimacy to remain healthy and satisfying, partners need to demonstrate continuously that they value and respect each other. As obvious as this guideline seems, many couples don't follow it. Sometimes we treat strangers with more respect and kindness than we offer romantic partners. It's easy to take for granted a person who is a continuing part of our life and to be less loving, respectful, and considerate than we should be.

JACKSON: *One of the things I love most about Meleika is the way she starts each day. Before getting out of bed, she reaches over and kisses my cheek. Then she gets up and showers while I sneak a little more shut-eye. When I get up, the first thing she always says is "morning love." That is such a great way to start each day. Even after five years of marriage she starts each day by letting me know I matter.*

Consideration and respect don't magically infuse relationships just because we know about interpersonal communication skills, such as those we've discussed in this book. For a respectful, confirming climate to exist, partners must *practice* effective interpersonal communication in the relationship. We should be as mindful of good communication when we enter a dialogue with established romantic partners as when we talk with casual acquaintances.

Romantic partners should be respectful of each other, particularly when discussing problems and complaints. Disagreement is natural and often constructive, but how we disagree with a partner is critical. Studies of marriages reveal differences between how satisfied and dissatisfied spouses talk about complaints and problems. Satisfied couples assert grievances and express anger and disagreement. Dissatisfied couples, however, communicate criticism, contempt, and sometimes disgust (Gottman & Carrère, 1994). It would be appropriate for Mary to tell Simon, "I feel angry when you smoke in the house because the smell bothers me." However, it would be personally disrespectful for Mary to say, "Smoking is a filthy, repulsive habit. Every time you light a cigarette you look revolting." The first statement is a civil complaint about a behavior; the second statement is a vicious attack on Simon's personal worth.

Both our relationships and our self-respect are at stake in how we act toward intimate partners. As we learned in Chapter 1, communication is irreversible. Harsh words and personal insults cannot be taken back once we've said them. Neither can we retract sneers, scowls, and other nonverbal behaviors that express contempt. Because we cannot undo communication or its impact, we need to be mindful of what we say and how we say it.

Don't Sweat the Small Stuff

If this guideline sounds familiar, it should. We first discussed it in Chapter 10 as a guideline for maintaining healthy friendships. The guideline also pertains to romantic relationships. If we want them to last, we have to be willing to overlook many minor irritations and frustrations. When two people live together continuously, it is natural for each person's habits and qualities to annoy the other sometimes. We all have quirks and mannerisms that may irritate others—the toothpaste cap left off the tube, the clinking of a coffee spoon, watching football every Sunday.

© Frank Siteman/The Picture Cube, Inc.

To avoid negative fixation on irritations, we can take responsibility for our perceptions and how we respond to them. My partner Robbie is hopelessly forgetful, and that isn't going to change. If I focus on that (all of the things he forgets to do, the errands he forgets to run), I make myself unhappy with him and our marriage. Notice that I am owning responsibility for how I choose to focus my perceptions and how I act in response. A better choice if I want to have a good marriage is for me to remind myself of the many qualities I love in him and to put his forgetfulness in perspective.

Monitoring attributions can also help us avoid sweating the small stuff. I felt very differently about Robbie's forgetfulness once I defined it as something beyond his control, rather than as something he could overcome if he chose. We can also monitor the self-serving attribution that may lead us to overestimate our good qualities and behaviors and underestimate those of our partner. For example, when I used to get angry at Robbie for being forgetful, I conveniently overlooked my own failings and his grace in accepting them. I am not as punctual as Robbie is, so he's often ready and waiting for me. Yet he seldom shows irritation at my tardiness. Realizing that he accepts qualities in me he doesn't like makes it easier for me to return the favor.

Make Daily Choices That Enhance Intimacy

Perhaps the most important guideline for sustaining romantic relationships is to be aware that they are creative projects that reflect the choices partners make. Relationships are not things we enter but processes we create and continuously refine. Realizing that we are choice makers enables us to take responsibility for our choices and how they chart the course of intimacy.

The romantic relationships we create reflect a series of personal choices. Although we are not always aware that we are making choices, we continuously choose who we will be and what kind of relationships we will fashion. Intimate partners choose to sustain closeness or let it wither, to build climates that are open or closed and defensive, to rely on constructive or destructive communication to deal with conflict, to fulfill or betray trust, and to enhance or diminish each other's self-concept.

Too often we focus on large choices such as whether to commit, how to manage a serious conflict, or how to celebrate an anniversary. As important as major choices are, they don't make up the basic fabric of a relationship (Wood, 1995c). Instead, undramatic, day-to-day choices sculpt the quality of intimacy. Do you listen mindfully to a partner when you are tired? Do you continue to invest in intimacy after the initial euphoria has waned? Do you care enough about a relationship to work through crises and conflicts? Do you neglect your partner when you've had a rough day? Do you exert the effort to use dual perspective so that you can understand your partner on her or his terms? Seemingly small choices like these shape the quality of intimacy and the individuals in it. Although they appear small and insignificant, our ordinary, daily choices weave the basic fabric of our romantic relationships. By being aware of the impact of our "small" choices, we can make ones that continuously enhance the quality of intimacy.

CHAPTER
Summary

In this chapter, we focused on the dynamics of romantic relationships. We have seen that they are complex blends of intimacy, commitment, and passion. Although passion may be the most dramatic dimension of romantic relationships, it is not necessarily the most important for long-term stability and happiness. Commitment, or the intention to stay together, and intimacy, or feelings of warmth and connection, are also critical for love that lasts. Love, however, comes in many forms, and we considered six distinct styles of loving and how they might combine in romantic relationships.

The typical developmental course of romance begins with an escalation phase in which communication concentrates on gaining personal knowledge and building a private culture for the relationship. If individuals decide to stay together permanently, they commit to a future of intimacy. At that point they enter the extended phase of navigating in which they continuously adjust to small and large changes in their individual and joint lives. If a romantic bond falters, partners follow a path of deterioration, moving from dissatisfaction to negotiation to grave dressing in which they lay the relationship to rest.

For couples who stay together, there are alternatives to marriage. Lesbians and gays who make enduring commitments in the United States do so without legal recognition of their relationship. A substantial number of heterosexuals choose cohabitation, either as a short-term option or as the lasting form for their relationship. For the majority of heterosexuals, marriage remains the preferred form of relationship. In this chapter we saw that marriages operate in different ways with different effects on marital stability and partners' satisfaction, individuality, and closeness.

In addition to the normal challenges that all relationships face, romantic bonds experience unique pressures and problems. Among these are achieving equity between partners, negotiating safer sex, responding to violence and abuse, and managing love at a distance. These and other difficulties are best handled by practicing good interpersonal communication, showing respect for partners, and recognizing the impact of so-called small choices on the quality of a relationship. Following these guidelines, as well as others identified in previous chapters, should enhance your ability to create satisfying romantic relationships that can stand the test of time.

KEY
Concepts

- agape
- committed romantic relationships
- dyadic breakdown

- dyadic phase
- environmental spoiling
- equity

- eros
- explorational communication
- grave dressing

- intensifying communication
- intimacy
- intrapsychic phase
- invitational communication
- ludus
- mania
- navigating
- passion
- placemaking
- pragma
- psychological responsibility
- relational culture
- revising communication
- social phase
- social support
- storge

FOR FURTHER Thought & Discussion

1. Use your *InfoTrac College Edition* to look up current information on marriages and divorces in the United States. Access the most recent year of *Information Please Almanac.* Can you find statistics on how many people married in the most recent year for which there is a report? What was the average age of women and men who married? How many marriages were first, second, or third marriages? How many divorces were reported in the most recent year for which information is available? Is there information on the average length of marriages that end in divorce?

2. If you have a current romantic partner, can you identify her or his love style? How does it fit with your own love style? Does understanding love styles give you any new insights into dynamics in your relationship?

3. Have you been or are you currently involved in a long-distance relationship? If so, have you experienced one or more of the three special problems of long-distance relationships discussed in this chapter? Did you or do you follow the suggestions for maintaining contact that were presented in this chapter?

4. Have you experienced relationships in which love or commitment, but not both, were present? Describe relationships in which there was love but not commitment. Describe relationships in which there was commitment, but not love. What can you conclude about the impact of each?

5. Think about the paths to marriage discussed in this chapter. Can you apply this material to your own current or past relationships? If you have been in event-driven relationships, how would you describe them? How would you describe relationship-driven relationships?

6. This chapter discussed some gender differences in romantic relationships. Do the differences identified by researchers apply to your own relationships? How do you see gender operating in your romantic relationships?

7. Within your romantic relationships, have you and partners shared equally in any household tasks? How were divisions of labor worked out between you?

Although *Interpersonal Communication: Everyday Encounters* is drawing to a close, the conversation we've launched in these pages will continue. Interpersonal communication will be central to your life in the years ahead. As I reflect on what we've discussed since the introduction, I perceive three threads that weave through the entire book.

Communication Creates and Reflects Identity

Communication is both an important source of personal identity and a primary means by which we express who we are. Our sense of personal identity grows directly out of interpersonal communication. We enter the world without any clear sense of self, and we look to others to tell us who we are. Parents, grandparents, siblings, and others who are significant in the first years of our life provide us with reflected appraisals that express how they see us and our value. Family members also shape our attachment styles and the scripts we follow in dealing with conflict, expressing emotions, and engaging in other forms of interpersonal communication. As we venture beyond the confines of family, we continue to learn from others and to see ourselves through the eyes of others. Peers, teachers, friends, and romantic partners communicate their views of us, and those become part of how we see ourselves and how we define our paths of personal growth. They also provide us with additional scripts and perspectives that we may rely on in our interpersonal communication.

Identity not only grows out of interpersonal communication but also is expressed in communication. How we communicate expresses who we are. Verbally and nonverbally, we announce that we are dominant or deferential, outgoing or introverted, caring or indifferent, emotionally expressive or reserved, egotistical or interested in others, assertive or passive, accepting or judgmental, and so forth.

Interpersonal Communication Is Central to Relationships

Communication is the heart of personal relationships. The health and endurance of personal relationships depend in large measure on our ability to communicate effectively. For relationships to be satisfying, we need to know how to express our feelings, needs, and ideas in ways that others can under-

stand. We also need to know how to
listen sensitively and responsively to people
in our lives so that they feel safe being open
and honest with us. Interpersonal communication skills also allow us to create climates
that are supportive and affirming so that our
relationships are healthy. Communication is
the basis of meaning in human relationships,
and it is the primary way we build, refine, sustain, and transform close connections with others.

© C. J. Allen/Stock, Boston

Interpersonal Communication Takes Place in a Diverse World

A third theme of this book is that social diversity shapes and is reflected in communication. We've seen that our social standpoints affect how we communicate
and how we interpret the communication of others. What is normal or desirable in one social group may be offensive or odd in other communities. Once
we understand that standpoints shape communication, we are able to see that
there are no absolutely right or wrong styles of communicating. Our ways of
communicating, then, reflect not just our individual identities but also standpoints that are shaped by the social groups to which we belong.

Diverse cultures and the communication styles they cultivate offer rich
opportunities to learn about others and ourselves. The more we interact with
people whose backgrounds, beliefs, and communication styles differ from our
own, the more we will grow as individuals and as members of a common world.

What you've studied about interpersonal communication should give you
insight into how each of these themes applies in your current life. Let's now
consider how they pertain to our personal and collective future.

The Road Ahead

Interpersonal communication will be as much a part of your everyday life in
the future as it is today, although it may assume different forms and functions
in the years ahead. The skills and perspectives we've discussed in this book will
serve you well in meeting the challenges that will accompany changes in yourself, relationships, and society.

In the coming years, your interpersonal relationships will change both in
anticipated and surprising ways. Some of the friends you have today will still be
close in years to come, whereas others will fade away and new people will
assume importance in your life. Some romances of the moment will flourish
and endure, and others will wither. New people will come into your life, and
familiar ones will leave. Each person who enters or exits your life will affect
your personal identity.

There will also be changes and surprises in *how* people go about the process of forming and sustaining relationships. The trend toward long-distance romances and friendships will grow as more individuals who care about each other find they cannot live and work in the same location. Technology will also alter how we communicate with friends and romantic partners. Increasingly, we will rely on electronic forms of communication to sustain important personal relationships. Currently, I use e-mail to stay in daily contact with a man who has been my friend for twenty years, and I am looking forward to meeting in person a woman with whom I've become friendly through electronic communication. Many of my students rely on e-mail to communicate daily with parents and siblings. In the future, friends, romantic partners, and family members will make increasing use of the Internet to stay in touch.

Finally, interpersonal communication and relationships will evolve in response to changes in the larger society. Medical advances will stretch the average lifespan further, so that a promise to stay together "'til death do us part" will involve a greater time commitment than it does today. Longer lives will also increase the number of older people in society and the opportunities for them to be part of our friendships and families. Relationship forms that are not recognized or approved today may be accepted in the future. Interaction with an increasing diversity of people will change our perspective on what relationships are and how to sustain them. In addition, the horizons diversity fosters will broaden the options we recognize for creating our own relationships.

Neither you nor I can foresee what lies ahead for us and for our world. However, we can predict with assurance that there will be changes in us, others, and cultural life. Whatever changes we experience, we can be sure that interpersonal communication will continue to be central to our happiness and effectiveness.

In *Interpersonal Communication: Everyday Encounters* and the course it accompanies, you have learned a good deal about interpersonal communication. I hope that the understandings you've gained and the skills you've acquired will be valuable to you in the years ahead. If you commit to practicing and continuously enlarging the principles and skills introduced in this book, then you are on the threshold of a lifelong journey that will enrich you and your relationships with others. I wish all of that and more for you.

Julia T. Wood

A

abstract   Removed from concrete reality. Symbols are abstract because they are inferences and generalizations abstracted from a total reality.

agape   A secondary style of loving that is selfless and based on giving to others, not receiving rewards or returns from them. Agape is a blend of eros and storge.

ambiguous   Unclear meaning. Symbols are ambiguous because their meanings vary from person to person, context to context, and so forth.

ambushing   Listening carefully for the purpose of attacking a speaker.

anxious/resistant attachment style   This style tends to develop when a caregiver behaves inconsistently toward a child—sometimes being loving and other times being rejecting or neglectful.

arbitrary   Random or unnecessary. Symbols are arbitrary because there is no necessary reason for any particular symbol to stand for a particular referent.

artifacts   Personal objects we use to announce our identities and personalize our environments.

assertion   Clearly and nonjudgmentally stating what we feel, need, or want. Assertion is not synonymous with aggression because aggression involves putting our needs ahead of, and sometimes at the cost of, others' needs.

attachment styles   Patterns of parenting that teach children who they are, who others are, and how to approach relationships.

attributions   Causal accounts that explain why things happen and why people act as they do.

B

bracketing   Noting an important issue that comes up in the course of discussing other matters and that needs to be discussed at a later time. Bracketing allows partners to stay

effectively focused on a specific issue at one time but to agree to deal with other issues later.

C

chronemics   A type of nonverbal communication concerned with how we perceive and use time to define identities and interaction.

cognitive complexity   Determined by the number of constructs used, how abstract they are, and how elaborately they interact to create perceptions.

cognitive labeling view of emotions   Theory that claims what we feel is shaped by how we label physiological responses.

commitment   A decision to remain with a relationship. Commitment is one of three dimensions of enduring romantic relationships, and it has more impact on relationship continuity than does love alone. It is also an advanced stage in the process of escalation in romantic relationships.

committed romantic relationships   Voluntary connections we presume will be primary and continuing parts of our lives. Committed romantic relationships include three dimensions: intimacy, passion, and commitment.

communication rules   Shared understandings of what communication means and what behaviors are appropriate in various situations.

conflict   Exists when individuals who depend on each other express different views, interests, or goals and perceive their differences as incompatible or as opposed by the other.

constitutive rules   Communication rules that define what communication means by specifying how certain communicative acts are to be counted.

constructivism   Theory that states that we organize and interpret experience by applying cognitive structures called schemata.

content level of meaning   Refers to

the content or denotative information in communication. Content-level meanings are literal.

contracting   Building a solution through negotiation and acceptance of parts of proposals for resolution. Contracting is usually present in the later stages of constructive conflict.

counterfeit emotional language   Communication that seems to express feelings but doesn't actually describe what a person is feeling.

culture   Beliefs, understandings, practices, and ways of interpreting experience that are shared by a number of people.

D

deep acting   Management of inner feelings.

defensive listening   Perceiving personal attacks, criticisms, or hostile undertones in communication when none are intended.

direct definition   Communication that explicitly tells us who we are by specifically labeling us and reacting to our behaviors. Direct definition usually occurs first in families and also in interaction with peers and others.

dismissive attachment style   Promoted by caregivers who are disinterested, rejecting, or abusive toward children. Unlike people who develop fearful attachment styles, those with a dismissive style do not accept the caregiver's view of them as unlovable. Instead, they dismiss others as unworthy and thus do not seek close relationships.

downers   People who communicate negatively about us and reflect negative appraisals of our self-worth.

dual perspective   The ability to understand both your own and another's perspective, beliefs, thoughts, and feelings.

dyadic breakdown   The first stage of relational decay. Dyadic breakdown involves degeneration of established patterns, understandings, and routines that make up a relational culture and that sustain intimacy on a day-to-day basis.

dyadic phase Stage of relational deterioration that involves discussing problems and negotiation.

ego boundaries Define where an individual stops and the rest of the world begins.

emotional intelligence The ability to recognize which feelings are appropriate in which situations and the skill to communicate those feelings effectively.

emotions Processes that are shaped by physiology, perceptions, social experience, and language.

emotion work Effort invested to make ourselves feel what our culture defines as appropriate and to not feel what our culture defines as inappropriate in particular situations.

empathy Ability to feel with another person—to feel what she or he feels in a situation.

environmental spoiling Process by which proximity breeds ill will.

equity Fairness, based on the perception that both partners invest relatively equally in a relationship and benefit similarly from their investments. Perceived equity is a primary influence on satisfaction with relationships.

eros A powerful, passionate style of love that blazes to life suddenly and dramatically. Eros is one of the three primary styles of loving.

ethics Branch of philosophy that deals with moral principles and codes of conduct. Interpersonal communication involves ethical issues.

ethnocentrism The assumption that our culture and its norms are the only right ones. Ethnocentric communication reflects certainty, which tends to create defensive communication climates.

exit response One of four ways of responding to conflict. The exit response is to leave conflict either psychologically (by tuning out disagreement) or physically (by walking away or even leaving the relation-

ship). The exit response is active and generally destructive.

explorational communication The third stage in relational escalation, which involves exchanges of information to check out the possibilities of a relationship.

fearful attachment style Cultivated when the caregiver in the first bond communicates in consistently negative, rejecting, or even abusive ways to a child.

feedback Responses to messages. Feedback may be verbal, nonverbal, or both; it may be intentional or unintentional.

feeling rules Culturally based guidelines that tell us what we have a right to feel or are expected to feel in specific situations.

framing rules Culturally based guidelines that define the emotional meaning of situations and events.

friends of the heart Friends who remain close, regardless of distance and changes in individuals' lives.

friends of the road Friends who are temporary and with whom intimacy is not sustained when one of the friends moves or changes occur.

fundamental attribution error Overestimating the internal causes of others' behavior and underestimating the external causes.

games Interactions in which the real conflicts are hidden or denied and a counterfeit excuse is created for arguing or put-downs.

grace Granting forgiveness or putting aside personal needs when it is not required or expected. Grace reflects generosity of spirit.

grave dressing The final phase in relational decline, it involves burying the relationship and putting it to rest.

haptics The sense of touch and what it means. Haptics is one form of nonverbal communication.

hate speech Language that radically dehumanizes others.

hearing A physiological activity that

occurs when sound waves hit our eardrums. Unlike listening, hearing is a passive process.

identity scripts Guides to action based on rules for living and identity. Initially communicated in families, scripts define our roles, how we are to play them, and basic elements in the plot of our lives.

I–It communication Impersonal communication in which individuals are treated as objects or instruments for our purposes.

I-language Language that takes personal responsibility for feelings by using words that own the feelings and do not project the responsibility for feelings onto others.

implicit personality theory Assumptions about which qualities fit together in human personalities. Implicit personality theories are often unconscious.

indexing Technique to remind us that evaluations are not static, not unchanging. Indexing links evaluations to specific times and/or circumstances.

intensifying communication Stage in the escalation of romantic relationships that increases the depth of a relationship by increasing personal knowledge and allowing a couple to begin creating a private culture. Also called euphoria.

interactive models Models that represent communication as a process in which listeners are involved in sending messages back to speakers through feedback.

interactive view of emotions Claims that social rules and understandings shape what people feel and how they do or don't express feelings.

internal tensions Relationship stresses that grow out of individuals and their interaction.

interpersonal climate The overall feeling, or emotional mood, of a relationship.

interpersonal communication A selective, systemic, ongoing process in which unique individuals interact to reflect and build personal knowledge and to create meanings.

interpersonal communication competence   Communication that is interpersonally effective and appropriate. Competence includes abilities to monitor oneself, engage in dual perspective, enact a range of communication skills, and adapt communication appropriately.

interpretation   The subjective process of evaluating and explaining perceptions.

intimacy   Includes feelings of closeness, connection, and tenderness between lovers. Intimacy is one of three dimensions of committed romantic relationships.

intrapsychic phase   The second phase in disintegration of romantic relationships, this involves brooding about problems in the relationship and dissatisfactions with a partner.

investment   Something put into a relationship that cannot be recovered should the relationship end. Investment, more than rewards and love, increases commitment.

invitational communication   The second stage in the escalation phase of romantic relationships. In this stage, individuals signal they are interested in interacting and respond to invitations from others.

irrational beliefs   Debilitating ways of evaluating our emotions and ourselves. Irrational beliefs hinder our ability to manage and express emotions effectively.

I–Thou communication   Fully interpersonal communication in which individuals acknowledge and deal with each other as unique individuals who meet fully in dialogue.

I–You communication   Interaction that is midway between impersonal and interpersonal communication. In I–You relationships, communicators acknowledge each other as human beings but do not know and act toward each other as unique individuals in their totalities.

K

kinesics   Body position and body motions, including those of the face.

kitchensinking   Unproductive form of conflict communication in which everything except the kitchen sink is thrown into the argument.

L

letting go   To free ourselves of anger, blame, and judgments about another and what she or he did. Letting go of these feelings is part of showing grace.

linear models   Models that represent communication as a one-way process that flows in one direction—from sender to receiver. Linear models do not capture the dynamism of communication or the active participation of all communicators.

listening   A complex process that consists of being mindful; hearing; selecting and organizing information; interpreting communication; responding; and remembering.

listening for information   One of three goals of listening. Listening for information focuses on gaining and evaluating ideas, facts, opinions, reasons, and so forth.

listening for pleasure   One of three goals of listening. Listening for pleasure is motivated by a desire to enjoy rather than to gain information or support others.

listening to support others   One of three goals of listening. Listening to support others focuses more on the relationship level of meaning than on the content level of meaning. It aims to understand and respond to others' feelings, thoughts, and perceptions in ways that affirm them.

literal listening   Listening only to the content level of meaning and ignoring the relationship level of meaning.

loaded language   An extreme form of evaluative language that relies on words that strongly slant perceptions and, thus, meanings.

lose–lose   An orientation toward conflict in which it is assumed that nobody can win and everyone loses from engaging in conflict.

loyalty response   One of four ways of responding to conflict. The loyalty response consists of silent allegiance to a relationship and a person when conflict exists. Loyalty is passive and tends to be constructive.

ludus   One of three primary styles of love. Ludus is playful love in which the goal is not commitment but to have fun at love as a game or a series of challenges and maneuvers.

M

mania   One of three secondary styles of loving made up of eros and ludus. Mania is passionate, sometimes obsessive love that includes emotional extremes.

metacommunication   Communication about communication. When excessive, as in unproductive conflict interaction, metacommunication becomes self-absorbing and diverts partners from the issues causing conflict.

mindfulness   A concept from Zen Buddhism that refers to being fully present in the moment. Being mindful is the first step of listening and the foundation for all others.

mindreading   Assuming we understand what another person thinks or how another person perceives something.

minimal encouragers   Communication that gently invites another person to elaborate by expressing interest in hearing more.

models   Representations of what something is and how it works.

monitoring   The capacity to observe and regulate your own communication.

monopolizing   Continuously focusing communication on ourselves instead of on the person who is talking.

N

navigating   After relationships have escalated to commitment, partners navigate continuously, adjusting and reworking interaction to keep a relationship satisfying and healthy. Ideally, this stage lasts a lifetime.

neglect response   One of four ways of responding to conflict. The neglect response is to deny or minimize problems. The neglect response is passive and tends to be destructive.

noise   Anything that distorts communication so that it is more difficult for individuals to understand each other.

nonverbal communication   All forms of communication other than words themselves. Nonverbal communication includes inflection and other vocal qualities as well as several other behaviors.

orgasmic view of emotions   Theory that external phenomena cause physiological changes that lead us to experience emotions. Also called James-Lange view of emotions.

paraphrasing   A method of clarifying another's meaning by reflecting our interpretations of his or her communication back to him or her.

particular others   One source of social perspectives that individuals use to define themselves and guide how they think, act, and feel. The perspectives of particular others are the viewpoints of specific individuals who are significant to the self.

passion   Intensely positive feelings and desires for another person. Passion is based on rewards from involvement and is not equivalent to commitment. It is one of three dimensions of enduring romantic relationships.

passive aggression   Attacking while denying doing so. Passive aggression is a means of covertly expressing conflict, anger, or both.

perception   An active process of selecting, organizing, and interpreting people, objects, events, situations, and activities.

perceptual view of emotions   Theory that claims subjective perceptions shape what external phenomena mean and what emotions we associate with external phenomena. Also called appraisal theory.

personal constructs   Bipolar mental yardsticks that allow us to measure people and situations along specific dimensions of judgment.

person-centeredness   Ability to perceive individuals as unique and to differentiate them from social roles and generalizations based on membership in social groups.

perspective of the generalized other   The collection of rules, roles, and attitudes endorsed by the whole social community in which we live.

placemaking   Process of creating a physical environment that is comfortable and that reflects the values, experiences, and tastes of individuals.

Physical environment is part of relational culture, which is the nucleus of intimacy.

pragma   A secondary style of loving that is pragmatic or practical in nature. Pragma is a blend of storge and ludus.

process   An ongoing, continuous, dynamic flow that has no clear-cut beginnings or endings and that is always evolving and changing. Interpersonal communication is a process.

prototypes   Knowledge structures that define the clearest or most representative examples of some category.

proxemics   A type of nonverbal communication that includes space and how we use it.

pseudolistening   Pretending to listen.

psychological responsibility   Responsibility to remember, plan, and coordinate domestic work and child care. In general, women assume psychological responsibility for child care and housework, even if both partners share in the actual tasks.

punctuation   Defining the beginning and ending of interaction or interaction episodes.

rational-emotive approach to feelings   Approach that emphasizes using rational thinking to challenge and change debilitating emotions that undermine self-concept and self-esteem.

reflected appraisal   Process of seeing and thinking about ourselves in terms of the appraisals of us that others reflect.

regulative rules   Communication rules that regulate interaction by specifying when, how, where, and with whom to talk about certain things.

relational culture   A private world of rules, understandings, and patterns of acting and interpreting that partners create to give meaning to their relationship. Relational culture is the nucleus of intimacy.

relational dialectics   Opposing forces, or tensions, that are normal parts of all relationships. The three relational

dialectics are autonomy/intimacy, novelty/routine, and openness/closedness.

relationship level of meaning   Refers to what communication expresses about the relationship between communicators. Three dimensions of relationship-level meanings are liking or disliking, responsiveness, and power (control).

relationship rules   Guidelines that friends or romantic partners have for their relationships. Usually relationship rules are not explicit, but tacit, understandings.

remembering   The process of recalling what you have heard. This is the sixth part of listening.

responding   Symbolizing your interest in what is being said with observable feedback to speakers during the process of interaction. This is the fifth of six elements in listening.

revising communication   A stage in the escalation of romantic relationships that many, but not all, couples experience. Revising involves evaluating a relationship and working out any obstacles or problems before committing for the long term.

scripts   One of four cognitive schemata. Scripts define expected or appropriate sequences of action in particular settings.

secure attachment style   The most common and most positive attachment style. This style develops when the caregiver responds in a consistently attentive and loving way to a child.

selective listening   Focusing on only selected parts of communication. We listen selectively when we screen out parts of a message that don't interest us or with which we disagree, and also when we rivet attention on parts of communication that do interest us or with which we agree.

self   A multidimensional process that involves forming and acting from social perspectives that arise and evolve in communication with others and ourselves.

self-disclosure   Revealing personal information about ourselves that others are unlikely to discover in other ways.

self-fulfilling prophecy   Acting in ways that bring about expectations or judgments of ourselves.

self-sabotage   Self-talk that communicates we are no good, we can't do something, we can't change, and so forth. Self-sabotaging communication undermines belief in ourselves and motivation to change and grow.

self-serving bias   Tendency to attribute our positive actions and successes to stable, global, internal influences that we control, and to attribute negative actions and failures to unstable, specific, external influences beyond our control.

self-talk   Ways that we communicate with ourselves that affect how we feel and act. Self-talk is intrapersonal communication.

social comparison   Involves comparing ourselves with others to form judgments of our own talents, abilities, qualities, and so forth.

social phase   Part of relational disintegration in which partners figure out how to inform outsiders that the relationship is ending.

social support   Phase of relational decline in which partners look to friends and family for support during the trauma of breaking up.

speech community   Group of people who share norms, regulative rules, and constitutive rules for communicating and interpreting the communication of others.

standpoint theory   Claims that a culture includes a number of social groups that offer particular material,

symbolic, and social conditions that distinctively shape the perceptions, identities, and opportunities of members of those groups.

static evaluation   Assessments that suggest something is unchanging. "Bob is impatient" is a static evaluation.

stereotypes   Predictive generalizations about people and situations.

storge   A comfortable, friendly kind of love, often likened to friendship. It is one of three primary styles of loving.

surface acting   Controlling outward expression in inner feelings.

symbols   Abstract, arbitrary, and ambiguous representations of other phenomena, including feelings, events, ideas, relationships, situations, and individuals.

systemic   A quality of interpersonal communication that means it takes place within multiple systems that influence what is communicated and what meanings are constructed. Examples of systems affecting communication are physical context, culture, personal histories, and previous interactions between people.

T

totalizing   Responding to a person as if one aspect of him or her is the total of who he or she is.

transactional models   Models that represent communication as a dynamic process that changes over time and in which participants assume multiple roles.

trust   Entails two factors: (1) belief in another's reliability (he or she will do what is promised); (2) emotional

reliance on another to care about and protect our welfare. Trust is believing that private information about us is safe with another person because she or he cares for us and will look out for our welfare.

U

uppers   People who communicate positively about us and who reflect positive appraisals of our self-worth.

V

voice response   One of four responses to conflict. The voice response involves communicating about differences, tensions, and disagreements. Voice responses are active and can be constructive for individuals and relationships.

vultures   An extreme form of downers. They not only communicate negative images of us but actually attack our self-concepts.

W

win–lose   An orientation toward conflict that assumes one person wins at the expense of another person whenever conflict arises.

win–win   An orientation toward conflict that assumes everyone can win, or benefit, from engaging in conflict and that it is possible to generate resolutions that satisfy everyone.

Y

you-language   Language that projects responsibility for feelings or actions onto other people. You-language is not recommended for interpersonal communication.

Acitelli, L. (1988). When spouses talk to each other about their relationship. *Journal of Social and Personal Relationships, 5,* 185–199.

Acitelli, L. (1993). You, me, and us: Perspectives on relationship awareness. In S. W. Duck (Ed.), *Understanding relationship processes, 1: Individuals in relationships* (pp. 144–174). Newbury Park, CA: Sage.

Acker, M., & Davis, M. H. (1992). Intimacy, passion and commitment in adult romantic relationships: A test of the triangular theory of love. *Journal of Social and Personal Relationships, 9,* 21–51.

Ackerman, D. (1994). *A natural history of love.* New York: Random House.

Adelman, M. B., Parks, M. R., & Albrecht, T. L. (1987). Supporting friends in need. In T. L. Albrecht, M. B. Adelman, & Associates (Eds.), *Communicating social support* (pp. 105–125). Beverly Hills, CA: Sage.

Adler, R., & Towne, N. (1993). *Looking out/looking in* (7th ed.). Fort Worth, TX: Harcourt Brace Jovanovich.

Ainsworth, M. D. S., Blehar, M. C., Waters, E., & Wall, S. (1978). *Patterns of attachment: A psychological study of the strange situation.* Hillsdale, NJ: Erlbaum.

Alexander, E. R., III. (1979). The reduction of cognitive conflict: Effects of various types of communication. *Journal of Conflict Resolution, 23,* 120–138.

Allan, G. (1994). Social structure and relationships. In S. W. Duck (Ed.), *Understanding relationship processes, 3: Social context and relationships* (pp. 1–25). Newbury Park, CA: Sage.

Allen, S., Waton, A., Purcell, K., & Wood, S. (1986). *The experience of unemployment.* Basingstoke: Macmillan.

American games, Japanese rules. (1988). Frontline documentary.

National Public Television. Cited in Ferrante, J. (1992). *Sociology: A global perspective* (p. 102). Belmont, CA: Wadsworth.

Anders, G. (1997, September 4). Doctors learn to bridge cultural gaps. *Wall Street Journal,* pp. B1, B4.

Andersen, M. L., & Collins, P. H. (Eds.). (1992). *Race, class, and gender: An anthology.* Belmont, CA: Wadsworth.

Anderson, S., Russell, C., & Schumm, W. (1983). Perceived marital quality and family life cycle categories: A further analysis. *Journal of Marriage and the Family, 45,* 127–139.

Annual report on Americans' health "a wealth of good news." (1997, September 12). *Raleigh News and Observer,* p. 8A.

Argyle, M., & Henderson, M. (1985). The rules of relationships. In S. W. Duck & D. Perlman (Eds.), *Understanding personal relationships: An interdisciplinary approach* (pp. 63–84). Beverly Hills, CA: Sage.

Aries, E. (1987). Gender and communication. In P. Shaver (Ed.), *Sex and gender* (pp. 149–176). Newbury Park, CA: Sage.

Arnett, R. C. (1986). The inevitable conflict and confronting in dialogue. In J. Stewart (Ed.), *Bridges, not walls* (4th ed., pp. 272–279). New York: Random House.

Atsumi, R. (1980). Patterns of personal relationships. *Social Analysis, 5,* 63–78.

AXIS Center for Public Awareness of People with Disabilities, 4550 Indianola Avenue, Columbus OH 43214.

Bach, G. R., & Wyden, P. (1973). *The intimate enemy: How to fight fair in love and marriage.* New York: Avon.

Bachen, C., & Illouz, E. (1996). Imagining romance: Young people's cultural models of romance and love. *Critical Studies of Mass Communication, 13,* 279–308.

Barker, L., Edwards, R., Gaines, C., Gladney, K., & Holley, F. (1981). An investigation of proportional time spent in various communication activities by college students. *Journal of Applied Communication Research, 8,* 101–109.

Barnlund, D. (1989). *Communication styles of Japanese and Americans: Images and reality.* Belmont, CA: Wadsworth.

Bartholomew, K. (1993). From childhood to adult relationships: Attachment theory and research. In S. W. Duck (Ed.), *Understanding relationship processes, 2: Learning about relationships* (pp. 30–62). Newbury Park, CA: Sage.

Bartholomew K., & Horowitz, L. M. (1991). Attachment styles among young adults: A test of a four-category model. *Journal of Personality and Social Psychology, 61,* 226–244.

Bass, A. (1993, December 5). Behavior that can wreck a marriage. *Raleigh News and Observer,* p. 8E.

Bates, E. (1994, fall). Beyond black and white. *Southern Exposure,* pp. 11–15.

Bateson, M. C. (1990). *Composing a life.* New York: Penguin/Plume.

Baxter, L. A. (1984). Trajectories of relationship disengagement. *Journal of Social and Personal Relationships, 7,* 141–178.

Baxter, L. A. (1985). Accomplishing relational disengagement. In S. Duck & D. Perlman (Eds.), *Understanding personal relationships: An interdisciplinary approach* (pp. 243–265). Beverly Hills, CA: Sage.

Baxter, L. A. (1987). Self-disclosure and relationship disengagement. In V. Derlega & J. H. Berg (Eds.), *Self-disclosure: Theory, research, and therapy* (pp. 155–174). New York: Plenum.

Baxter, L. A. (1988). A dialectical perspective on communication strategies in relationship development. In S. W. Duck, D. F. Hay, S. E.

Hobfoll, W. Iches, & B. Montgomery (Eds.), *Handbook of personal relationships* (pp. 257–273). London: Wiley.

Baxter, L. A. (1990). Dialectical contradictions in relational development. *Journal of Social and Personal Relationships, 7,* 69–88.

Baxter, L. A. (1993). The social side of personal relationships: A dialectical perspective. In S. Duck (Ed.), *Understanding relationship processes, 3: Social context and relationships* (pp. 139–165). Newbury Park, CA: Sage.

Baxter, L. A., & Simon, E. P. (1993). Relationship maintenance strategies and dialectical contradictions in personal relationships. *Journal of Social and Personal Relationships, 10,* 225–242.

Be civil. (1994, July 5). *Wall Street Journal,* p. A1.

Beck, A. (1988). *Love is never enough.* New York: Harper & Row.

Becker, C. S. (1987). Friendship between women: A phenomenological study of best friends. *Journal of Phenomenological Psychology, 18,* 59–72.

Begley, S. (1997, spring/summer special issue). How to build a baby's brain. *Newsweek,* pp. 27–30.

Bellah, R., Madsen, R., Sullivan, W., Swindler, A., & Tipton, S. (1985). *Habits of the heart: Individualism and commitment in American life.* Berkeley, CA: University of California Press.

Bellamy, L. (1996, December 18). Kwanzaa cultivates cultural and culinary connections. *Raleigh News and Observer,* pp. 1F, 9F.

Belsky, J., & Rovine, M. (1990). Patterns of marital change across the transition to parenthood: Pregnancy to three years postpartum. *Journal of Marriage and the Family, 52,* 5–19.

Belsky, J., & Pensky, E. (1988). Developmental history, personality, and family relationships: Toward an emergent family system. In R. A. Hinde & J. Stevenson-Hinde (Eds.), *Relationships within families: Mutual influences* (pp. 193–217). Oxford: Clarendon.

Benjamin, D., & Horwitz, T. (1994, July 14). German view: "You Americans work too hard—and for what?" *Wall Street Journal,* pp. B1, B6.

Berg, J. H. (1987). Responsiveness and self-disclosure. In V. J. Derlega & J. H. Berg (Eds.), *Self-disclosure: Theory, research, and therapy.* New York: Plenum.

Berger, C. R., & Bell, R. A. (1988). Plans and the initiation of social relationships. *Human Communication Research, 15,* 217–235.

Bergner, R. M., & Bergner, L. L. (1990). Sexual misunderstanding: A descriptive and pragmatic formulation. *Psychotherapy, 27,* 464–467.

Berko, I. (1987, June 2). The coloring of Bird. *The New York Times,* p. D27.

Berko, R., Wolvin, A., & Wolvin, D. (1995). *Communicating: A social and career focus.* Boston: Houghton Mifflin.

Berne, E. (1964). *Games people play.* New York: Grove.

Bernstein, B. (Ed.). (1973). *Class, codes, and control* (vol. 2). London: Routledge and Kegan Paul.

Bernstein, B. (1974). *Class, codes, and control: Theoretical studies toward a sociology of language* (rev. ed.). New York: Shocken.

Best, J. (1989). *Images of issues: Typifying contemporary social problems.* New York: Aldine de Gruyter.

Birdwhistell, R. (1970). *Kinesics and context.* Philadelphia: University of Pennsylvania Press.

Blieszner, R., & Adams, R. (1992). *Adult friendship.* Newbury Park, CA: Sage.

Blumstein, P., & Schwartz, P. (1983). *American couples: Money, work, and sex.* New York: William Morrow.

Bolton, R. (1986). Listening is more than merely hearing. In J. Stewart (Ed.), *Bridges, not walls* (4th ed., pp. 159–179). New York: Random House.

Boon, S. (1994). Dispelling doubt and uncertainty: Trust in romantic relationships. In S. W. Duck (Ed.), *Understanding relationship processes, 4: Dynamics of relationships* (pp. 86–111). Thousand Oaks, CA: Sage.

Bosmajian, H. (1974). *The language of oppression.* Washington, DC: Public Affairs Papers.

Bowen, S. P., & Michal-Johnson, P. (1995). Sexuality in the AIDS era. In S. W. Duck & J. T. Wood (Eds.), *Understanding relationship processes, 5: Relationship challenges* (pp. 150–180). Thousand Oaks, CA: Sage.

Bowlby, J. (1973). *Separation: Attachment and loss* (Vol. 2). New York: Basic.

Bowlby, J. (1988). *A secure base: Parent–child attachment and healthy human development.* New York: Basic.

Boyd, R. (1996, October 9). Notion of separate races rejected. *Raleigh News and Observer,* pp. 1A, 15A.

Bozzi, V. (1986, February). Eat to the beat. *Psychology Today,* p. 16.

Bradbury, T. N., & Fincham, F. D. (1990). Attributions in marriage: Review and critique. *Psychological Bulletin, 107,* 3–33.

Braithwaite, D. (1996). "Persons first": Exploring different perspectives on the communication of persons with disabilities. In E. B. Ray (Ed.), *Communication and disenfranchisement: Social health issues and implications* (pp. 449–464). Hillsdale, NJ: Erlbaum.

Brazelton, T. B. (1997, spring/summer special issue). Building a better self-image. *Newsweek,* pp. 76–77.

Brehm, S. (1992). *Intimate relations* (2nd ed.). New York: McGraw-Hill.

Brock-Utne, B. (1989). *Feminist perspectives on peace and peace education.* New York: Pergamon.

Bruess, C., & Pearson, J. (1997). Interpersonal rituals in marriage and adult friendship. *Communication Monographs, 64,* 25–46.

Buber, M. (1957). Distance and relation. *Psychiatry, 20,* 97–104.

Buber, M. (1970). *I and thou* (Walter Kaufmann, Trans.). New York: Scribner.

Buckley, M. (1992). Focus on research: We listen a book a day; we speak a book a week: Learning from Walter Loban. *Language Arts, 69,* 622–626.

Bumpass, L. L., & Sweet, J. A. (1989). National estimates of cohabitation. *Demography, 26,* 615–625.

Burgoon, J. K., Buller, D. B., Hale, J. L., & deTurck, M. A. (1984). Relational messages associated with nonverbal behaviors. *Human Communication Research, 10,* 351–378.

Burgoon, J. K., Buller, D. B., & Woodhall, G. W. (1989). *Nonverbal communication: The unspoken dialogue.* New York: Harper & Row.

Burleson, B. R. (1984). Comforting communication. In H. E. Sypher & J. L. Applegate (Eds.), *Communication by children and adults: Social cognitive and strategic processes* (pp. 63–104). Beverly Hills, CA: Sage.

Burleson, B. R. (1987). Cognitive complexity. In J. C. McCroskey & J. A. Daly (Eds.), *Personality and interpersonal communication* (pp. 305–349). Newbury Park, CA: Sage.

Burleson, B. R., & Samter, W. (1994). A social skills approach to relationship maintenance: How individual differences in communication skills affect the achievement of relationship functions. In D. J. Canary & L. Stafford (Eds.), *Communication and relational maintenance.* Orlando: Academic.

Business bulletin. (1996, July 18). *Wall Street Journal,* p. A1.

Butterfield, F. (1982). *China: Alive in the bitter sea.* New York: Times Books.

Button, C. M., & Collier, D. R. (1991, June). *A comparison of people's concepts of love and romantic love.* Paper presented at the Canadian Psychological Association Conference, Calgary, Alberta.

Caldera, Y. M., Huston, A. C., & O'Brien, M. (1989). Social interactions and play patterns of parents and toddlers with feminine, masculine, and neutral toys. *Child Development, 60,* 70–76.

Campbell, S. M. (1986). From either-or to both-and relationships. In J. Stewart (Ed.), *Bridges, not walls* (4th ed., pp. 262–270). New York: Random House.

Canary, D., & Stafford, L. (Eds.). (1994). *Communication and relational maintenance.* New York: Academic.

Canary, D., & Dindia, K. (eds.). (1998). *Sex differences and similarities in communication.* Mahwah, NJ: Erlbaum.

Cancian, F. (1987). *Love in America.* Cambridge, MA: Cambridge University Press.

Cancian, F. (1989). Love and the rise of capitalism. In B. Risman & P. Schwartz (Eds.), *Gender in intimate relationships* (pp. 12–25). Belmont, CA: Wadsworth.

Capella, J. N. (1991). The biological origins of automated patterns of human interaction. *Communication Theory, 1,* 4–35.

Carl, W. (1998). A sign of the times. In J. T. Wood, *But I thought you meant . . . : Misunderstandings in human communication* (pp. 195–208). Mountain View, CA: Mayfield.

Carnes, J. (1994, spring). An uncommon language. *Teaching Tolerance,* pp. 56–63.

Caspi, A., & Harbener, E. S. (1990). Continuity and change: Assortive marriage and the consistency of personality in adulthood. *Journal of Personality and Social Psychology, 58,* 250–258.

Cassirer, E. (1944). *An essay on man.* New Haven, CT: Yale University Press.

Cate, R. M., Huston, T. L., and Nesselroade, J. R. (1986). Premarital relationships: Toward the identification of alternative pathways to marriage. *Journal of Social and Clinical Psychology, 4,* 3–22.

Cathcart, D., & Cathcart, R. (1997). The group: A Japanese context. In L. Samovar & R. Porter (Eds.), *Intercultural communication: A reader* (8th ed., pp. 329–339). Belmont, CA: Wadsworth.

Cherlin, A. (1992). *Marriage, divorce, remarriage.* Cambridge, MA: Harvard University Press.

Chodorow, N. (1989). *Feminism and psychoanalytic theory.* New Haven, CT: Yale University Press.

Christensen, A., & Heavey, C. (1990). Gender and social structure in the demand/withdraw pattern in marital conflict. *Journal of Personality and Social Psychology, 59,* 73–81.

Cissna, K. N. L., & Sieburg, E. (1986). Patterns of interactional confirmation and disconfirmation. In J. Stewart (Ed.), *Bridges, not walls* (4th ed., pp. 230–239). New York: Random House.

Civickly, J. M., Pace, R. W., & Krause, R. M. (1977). Interviewer and client behaviors in supportive and defensive interviews. In B. D. Ruben (Ed.), *Communication yearbook, 1* (pp. 347–362). New Brunswick, NJ: Transaction.

Clements, M. (1994, August 7). Sex in America today. *Parade,* pp. 4–6.

Clements, M., & Markman, H. (1996). The transition to parenthood: Is having children hazardous to marriage? In N. Vanzetti & S. Duck (Eds.), *A lifetime of relationships* (pp. 290–310). Pacific Grove, CA: Brooks/Cole.

Cloven, D. H., & Roloff, M. E. (1991). Sense-making activities and interpersonal conflict: Communicative cures for the mulling blues. *Western Journal of Speech Communication, 55,* 134–158.

Coates, J., & Cameron, D. (1989). *Women in their speech communities: New perspectives on language and sex.* London: Longman.

Collier, M. J. (1996). Communication competence problematics in ethnic friendships. *Communication Monographs, 63,* 314–336.

Condry, S. M., Condry, J. C., & Pogatshnik, L. W. (1983). Sex differences: A study of the ear of the beholder. *Sex Roles, 9,* 697–704.

Conover, T. (1987). *Coyotes: A journey through the secret world of America's illegal aliens.* New York: Vintage.

Cooley, C. H. (1912). *Human nature and the social order.* New York: Scribner.

Cooley, C. H. (1961). The social self. In T. Parsons, E. Shils, K. D. Naegele, & J. R. Pitts (Eds.), *Theories of society* (pp. 822–828). New York: Free Press.

Copeland, L., & Griggs, L. (1985). *Going international.* New York: Random House.

Cosby, P. (1973). Self-disclosure: A literature review. *Psychological Bulletin, 79*, 73–91.

Cowan, C., Cowan, P., Heming, G., & Miller, N. (1991). Becoming a family: Marriage, parenting, and child development. In P. A. Cowan & M. Hetherington (Eds.), *Family transitions* (pp. 79–109). Hillsdale, NJ: Erlbaum.

Cox, R. (1995). President of the National Sierra Club, 1994–1996. Personal communication.

Cozart, E. (1996, November 1997). Feng Shui. *Raleigh News and Observer*, p. D1.

Crockett, W. (1965). Cognitive complexity and impression formation. In B. A. Maher (Ed.), *Progress in experimental personality research, 2*. New York: Academic.

Cronen, V., Pearce, W. B., & Snavely, L. (1979). A theory of rule-structure and types of episodes and a study of perceived enmeshment in undesired repetitive patterns ("URPs"). In D. Nimmo (Ed.), *Communication yearbook, 3*. New Brunswick, NJ: Transaction.

Crossen, C. (1997, July 10). Blah, blah, blah. *Wall Street Journal*, p. 1A, 6A.

Cuber, J. F., & Harroff, P. B. (1965). *Sex and the significant Americans*. Baltimore: Penguin.

Cunningham, J. A., Strassberg, D. S., & Haan, B. (1986). Effects of intimacy and sex-role congruency on self-disclosure. *Journal of Social and Clinical Psychology, 4*, 393–401.

Cunningham, J. D., & Antill, J. K. (1995). Current trends in nonmarital cohabitation: The great POSSLQ hunt continues. In J. T. Wood & S. W. Duck (Eds.), *Understanding relationship processes, 6: Off the beaten track: Understudied relationships* (pp. 148–172). Thousand Oaks, CA: Sage.

Cupach, W. R., & Comstock, J. (1990). Satisfaction with sexual communication in marriage: Links to sexual satisfaction and dyadic adjustment. *Journal of Social and Personal Relationships, 7*, 179–182.

Cutrona, C. E. (1982). Transitions to college: Loneliness and the process of social adjustment. In L. A. Peplau & D. Perlman (Eds.), *Loneliness: A sourcebook of current theory, research, and therapy* (pp. 291–309). New York: Wiley Interscience.

Cyberscope, (1996, December 23). *Newsweek*, p. 10.

Davis, K. (1940). Extreme isolation of a child. *American Journal of Sociology, 45*, 554–565.

Davis K. (1947). A final note on a case of extreme isolation. *American Journal of Sociology, 52*, 432–437.

Davis, V. T., & Singh, R. (1989). Attitudes of university students from India toward marriage and family life. *International Journal of Sociology of the Family, 19*, 43–57.

de Becker, G. (1997). *The gift of fear: Survival signals that protect us from violence*. New York: Little Brown.

DeFrancisco, V. (1991). The sounds of silence: How men silence women in marital relations. *Discourse and Society, 2*, 413–423.

Delia, J., Clark, R. A., & Switzer, D. (1974). Cognitive complexity and impression formation in informal social interaction. *Speech Monographs, 41*, 299–308.

Derlega, V. J., & Berg, J. H. (1987). *Self-disclosure: Research, theory, and therapy*. New York: Plenum.

Dewar, H. (1997, May 11). Threads of a new nation. *Raleigh News and Observer*, pp. 23A–24A.

Dews, B., & Law, C. (Eds.). (1995). *This fine place so far from home: Voices of academics from the working class*. Philadelphia: Temple University Press.

Dickens, W. J., & Perlman, D. (1981). Friendship over the life-cycle. In S. Duck & R. Gilmour (Eds.), *Personal relationships, 2: Developing personal relationships*. London: Academic.

Dickson, F. (1995). The best is yet to be: Research on long-lasting marriages. In J. T. Wood & S. Duck (Eds.), *Understanding relationship processes, 6: Understudied relationships* (pp. 22–50). Thousand Oaks, CA: Sage.

Dimmitt, B. (1997, July). Chelsey's missing smile, *Reader's Digest*, 87–93.

Dindia, K. (1994). A multiphasic view of relationship maintenance strategies. In D. Canary & L. Stafford (Eds.), *Communication and relational maintenance* (pp. 91–112). New York: Academic.

Dindia, K., & Fitzpatrick, M. A. (1985). Marital communication: Three approaches compared. In S. Duck & D. Perlman (Eds.), *Understanding personal relationships: An interdisciplinary approach* (pp. 137–157). Newbury Park, CA: Sage.

Dixson M., & Duck, S. W. (1993). Understanding relationship processes: Uncovering the human search for meaning. In S. W. Duck (Ed.), *Understanding relationship processes, 1: Individuals in relationships* (pp. 175–206). Newbury Park, CA: Sage.

Dolan, R. E., & Worden, R. L. (Eds.). (1992). *Japan: A country study*. Washington, DC: Library of Congress.

Duck, S. W. (1985). Social and personal relationships. In M. L. Knapp & G. R. Miller (Eds.), *Handbook of interpersonal communication* (pp. 655–686). Beverly Hills, CA: Sage.

Duck, S. W. (1990). Relationships as unfinished business: Out of the frying pan and into the 1990s. *Journal of Social and Personal Relationships, 7*, 5–24.

Duck, S. W. (1992). *Human relationships* (2nd ed.). Newbury Park, CA: Sage.

Duck, S. W. (1994a). *Meaningful relationships*. Thousand Oaks, CA: Sage.

Duck, S. W. (1994b). Steady as (s)he goes: Relational maintenance as a shared meaning system. In D. Canary & L. Stafford (Eds.), *Communication and relational maintenance* (pp. 45–60). New York: Academic.

Duck, S. W., Pond, K., & Leatham, G. (1994). Loneliness and the evaluation of relational events. *Journal of Social and Personal Relationships, 11*, 253–276.

Duck, S. W., Rutt, D. J., Hurst, M. H., & Strejc, H. (1991). Some evident truths about conversation in everyday relationships: All communications are not created equal. *Human Communication Research, 18*, 228–267.

Duck, S. W., & Wright, P. H. (1993). Reexamining gender differences in same-gender friendships: A close look at two kinds of data. *Sex Roles, 28,* 709–727.

Eadie, W. F. (1982). Defensive communication revisited: A critical examination of Gibb's theory. *Southern Speech Communication Journal, 47,* 163–177.

Eaves, M., & Leathers, D. (1991). Context as communication: McDonalds vs. Burger King. *Journal of Applied Communication, 19,* 263–289.

Eckman, P., Friesen, W., & Ellsworth, P. (1971). *Emotion in the human face: Guidelines for research and an integration of findings.* Elmsford, NY: Pergamon.

Egan, G. (1973). Listening as empathic support. In J. Stewart (Ed.), *Bridges, not walls.* Reading, MA: Addison-Wesley.

Eichenbaum, L., & Orbach, S. (1987). *Between women: Love, envy, and competition in women's friendships.* New York: Viking.

Ekman, P. & Davidson, R. (Eds.) (1994). *The nature of emotions: Fundamental questions.* New York: Oxford University Press.

Ellis, A. (1962). *Reason and emotion in psychotherapy.* New York: Lyle Stuart.

Ellis A., & Harper, R. (1975). *A new guide to rational living.* Englewood Cliffs, NJ: Prentice-Hall.

Ellis, D. (1989). Male abuse of a marriage or cohabiting female partner. *Violence and Victims, 4,* 235–255.

Ernst, F., Jr. (1973). *Who's listening? A handbook of the transactional analysis of the listening function.* Vallejo, CA: Addresso'set.

Estes, W. K. (1989). Learning theory. In A. Lessold & R. Glaser (Eds.), *Foundations for a psychology of education.* Hillsdale, NJ: Erlbaum.

Faludi, S. (1991). *Backlash: The undeclared war against American women.* New York: Crown.

Fantini, A. E. (1991). Bilingualism: Exploring language and culture. In L. Malave & G. Duquette (Eds.), *Language, culture, and cognition: A collection of studies on first and second language acquisition* (pp.

110–119). Bristol, PA: Multilingual Matters, Ltd.

Fehr, B. (1993). How do I love thee: Let me consult my prototype. In S. W. Duck (Ed.), *Understanding relationship processes, 1: Individuals in relationships* (pp. 87–122). Newbury Park, CA: Sage.

Fehr, B., & Russell, J. A. (1991). Concept of love viewed from a prototype perspective. *Journal of Personality and Social Psychology, 60,* 425–438.

Ferrante, J. (1992). *Sociology: A global perspective.* Belmont, CA: Wadsworth.

Ferrante, J. (1995). *Sociology: A global perspective* (2nd ed.). Belmont, CA: Wadsworth.

Fincham, F. D., & Bradbury, T. N. (1987). The impact of attributions in marriage: A longitudinal analysis. *Journal of Personality and Social Psychology, 53,* 510–517.

Fincham, F. D., Bradbury, T. N., & Scott, C. K. (1990). Cognition in marriage. In F. D. Fincham & T. N. Bradbury (Eds.), *The psychology of marriage: Basic issues and applications* (pp. 118–119). New York: Guilford.

Finkelstein, J. (1980). Considerations for a sociology of emotions. *Studies in Symbolic Interaction, 3,* 111–121.

Fisher, B. A. (1987). *Interpersonal communication: The pragmatics of human relationships.* New York: Random House.

Fisher, J. D., & Byrne, D. (1975). Too close for comfort: Sex differences in response to invasions of personal space. *Journal of Personal and Social Psychology, 32,* 15–21.

Fitzpatrick, M. A. (1988). *Between husbands and wives: Communication in marriage.* Newbury Park, CA: Sage.

Fitzpatrick, M. A., & Best, P. (1979). Dyadic adjustment in relational types: Consensus, cohesion, affectional expression and satisfaction in enduring relationships. *Communication Monographs, 46,* 167–178.

Fletcher, G. J., & Fincham, F. D. (1991). Attribution in close relationships. In G. J. Fletcher & F. D. Fincham (Eds.), *Cognition in close relationships* (pp. 7–35). Hillsdale, NJ: Erlbaum.

Fletcher, G. J., Fincham, F. D., Cramer, L., & Heron, N. (1987). The role of attributions in the development of dating relationships. *Journal of Personality and Social Psychology, 51,* 875–884.

Floyd, K., & Parks, M. (1995). Manifesting closeness in the interactions of peers: A look at siblings and friends. *Communication Reports, 8,* 69–76.

Fowers, B. J. (1991). His and her marriage: A multivariate study of gender and marital satisfaction. *Sex Roles, 24,* 209–221.

Fox-Genovese, E. (1991). *Feminism without illusions.* Chapel Hill: University of North Carolina Press.

French, M. (1992). *The war against women.* New York: Summit.

Fridlund, A. J. (1994). *Human facial expression.* San Diego: Academic.

Frijda, N. H. (1986). *The emotions.* Cambridge, England: Cambridge University Press.

Gaines, S., Jr. (1995). Relationships among members of cultural minorities. In J. T. Wood & S. W. Duck (Eds.), *Understanding relationship processes, 6: Off the beaten track: Understudied relationships* (pp. 51–88). Thousand Oaks, CA: Sage.

Gans, H. (1995). *The war against the poor: The underclass and antipoverty policy.* New York: Basic.

Garner, T. (1994). Oral rhetorical practice in African American culture. In A. González, M. Houston, & V. Chen (Eds.), *Our voices: Essays in culture, ethnicity, and communication* (pp. 81–91). Los Angeles: Roxbury.

Gelles, R. (1987). *Family violence* (2nd ed.). Newbury Park, CA: Sage.

George L. (1995, December 26). Holiday's traditions are being formed. *Raleigh News and Observer,* pp. C1, C3.

Gerstel, N., & Gross, H. (1985). *Commuter marriage.* New York: Guilford.

Gibb, J. (1961). Defensive communication. *Journal of Communication, 11,* 141–148.

Gibb, J. R. (1964). Climate for trust formation. In L. Bradford, J. Gibb, & K. Benne (Eds.), *T-group theory and laboratory method* (pp. 279–309). New York: Wiley.

Gibb, J. R. (1970). Sensitivity training as a medium for personal growth and improved interpersonal relationships. *Interpersonal Development, 1,* 6–31.

Gibbs, J. T. (1992). Young black males in America: Endangered, embittered, and embattled. In M. L. Andersen & P. H. Collins (Eds.), *Race, class, and gender: An anthology* (pp. 267–276). Belmont, CA: Wadsworth.

Goldner, V., Penn, P., Sheinberg, M., & Walker, G. (1990). Love and violence: Gender paradoxes in volatile attachments. *Family Process, 19,* 343–364.

Goleman, D. (1995a). *Emotional intelligence.* New York: Bantam.

Goleman, D. (1995b, November–December). What's your emotional intelligence? *Utne Reader,* pp. 74–76.

Good-looking lawyers make more money, says a study by economists. (1996, January 4). *Wall Street Journal,* p. A1.

Gottman, J. (1979). *Marital interaction: Experimental investigations.* New York: Academic.

Gottman, J. (1993). The roles of conflict engagement, escalation or avoidance in marital interaction: A longitudinal view of five types of couples. *Journal of Consulting and Clinical Psychology, 61,* 6–15.

Gottman, J. (1997, May). Findings from 25 years of studying marriage. Paper presented at the Conference of the Coalition of Marriage, Family and Couples Education, Arlington, VA.

Gottman, J., & Carrère, S. (1994). Why can't men and women get along? Developmental roots and marital inequities. In D. J. Canary & L. Stafford (Eds.), *Communication and relational maintenance* (pp. 203–229). New York: Academic.

Gottman, J., Markman, H. J., & Notarius, C. (1977). The topography of marital conflict: A sequential analysis of verbal and nonverbal behavior. *Journal of Marriage and the Family, 39,* 461–477.

Gottman, J., Notarius, C., Gonso, J., & Markman, H. J. (1976a). A *couple's guide to communication.* Champaign, IL: Research Press.

Gottman, J., Notarius, C., Markman, H., Banks, S., Yoppi, B., & Rubin, M. E. (1976b). Behavior exchange theory and marital decision making. *Journal of Experimental Social Psychology, 34,* 14–23.

Greenberg, S. (1997, spring/summer special issue). The loving ties that bind. *Newsweek,* pp. 68–72.

Gross, H. E. (1980). Couples who live apart: Time/place disjunctions and their consequence. *Symbolic Interaction, 3,* 69–82.

Hakuta, K. (1986). *Mirror of language: The debate on bilingualism.* New York: Basic.

Hall, E. (1976). *Beyond culture.* New York: Doubleday.

Hall, E. T. (1966). *The hidden dimension.* New York: Anchor.

Hall, E. T. (1968). Proxemics. *Current Anthropology, 9,* 83–108.

Hall, J. A. (1978). Gender effects in decoding nonverbal cues. *Psychological Bulletin, 85,* 845–857.

Hall, J. A. (1987). On explaining gender differences: The case of nonverbal communication. In P. Shaver & C. Hendricks (Eds.), *Sex and gender* (pp. 177–200). Newbury Park, CA: Sage.

Hamachek, D. (1992). *Encounters with the self* (3rd ed.). Fort Worth: Harcourt Brace Jovanovich.

Hansen, J. E., & Schuldt, W. J. (1984). Marital self-disclosure and marital satisfaction. *Journal of Marriage and the Family, 46,* 923–926.

Haraway, D. (1988). Situated knowledges: The science question in feminism and the privilege of partial perspective. *Signs, 14,* 575–599.

Harding, S. (1991). *Whose science? Whose knowledge? Thinking from women's lives.* Ithaca, NY: Cornell University Press.

Harris, M., Walters, L., & Waschall, S. (1991). Gender and ethnic differences in obesity-related behaviors and attitudes in a college sample. *Journal of Applied Social Psychology, 21,* 1545–1566.

Harris, T. J. (1969). *I'm OK, you're OK.* New York: Harper & Row.

Hayakawa, S. I. (1962). *The use and misuse of language.* New York: Fawcett.

Hayakawa, S. I. (1964). *Language in thought and action* (2nd ed.). New York: Harcourt, Brace & World.

Hecht, M. L., Marston, P. J., & Larkey, L. K. (1994). Love ways and relationship quality in heterosexual relationships. *Journal of Social and Personal Relationships, 11,* 25–44.

Hegel, G. W. F. (1807). *Phenomenology of mind* (J. B. Baillie, Trans.). Germany: Wurzburg & Bamburg.

Heider, F. (1958). *The psychology of interpersonal relations.* New York: Wiley.

Helgeson, V. (1994). Long-distance romantic relationships: Sex differences in adjustment and breakup. *Personal and Social Psychology Bulletin, 20,* 254–266.

Hendrick, C., & Hendrick, S. (1988). Lovers wear rose colored glasses. *Journal of Social and Personal Relationships, 5,* 161–184.

Hendrick, C., & Hendrick, S. (1989). Research on love: Does it measure up? *Journal of Personality and Social Psychology, 56,* 784–794.

Hendrick, C., & Hendrick, S. (1996). Gender and the experience of heterosexual love. In J. T. Wood (Ed.), *Gendered relationships.* Mountain View, CA: Mayfield.

Hendrick, C., Hendrick, S., Foote, F. H., & Slapion-Foote, M. J. (1984). Do men and women love differently? *Journal of Social and Personal Relationships, 2,* 177–196.

Henley, N. M. (1977). *Body politics: Power, sex and nonverbal communication.* Englewood Cliffs, NJ: Prentice-Hall.

Higginbotham, E. (1992). We were never on a pedestal: Women of color continue to struggle with poverty, racism, and sexism. In M. L. Andersen & P. H. Collins (Eds.), *Race, class, and gender: An anthology* (pp. 183–190). Belmont, CA: Wadsworth.

Hochschild, A. (1979). Emotion work, feeling rules, and social structure. *American Journal of Sociology, 85,* 551–575.

Hochschild, A. (1983). *The managed heart.* Berkeley: University of California Press.

Hochschild, A. (1990). Ideology and emotion management: A perspective and path for future research. In T. Kemper (Ed.), *Research agendas in the sociology of emotions* (pp. 117–142). New York: State University of New York Press.

Hochschild, A., with Machung, A. (1989). *The second shift*. New York: Viking.

Hojat, M. (1982). Loneliness as a function of selected personality variables. *Journal of Clinical Psychology, 38*, 136–141.

Honeycutt, J. M. (1993). Memory structures for the rise and fall of personal relationships. In S. W. Duck (Ed.), *Understanding relationship processes, 1: Individuals in relationships* (pp. 30–59). Newbury Park, CA: Sage.

Honeycutt, J. M., Woods, B., & Fontenot, K. (1993). The endorsement of communication conflict rules as a function of engagement, marriage and marital ideology. *Journal of Social and Personal Relationships, 10*, 285–304.

Houston, M. (1994). When black women talk with white women: Why dialogues are difficult. In A. González, M. Houston, & V. Chen (Eds.), *Our voices: Essays in culture, ethnicity, and communication* (pp. 133–139). Los Angeles: Roxbury.

Houston, M., & Wood, J. T. (1996). Difficult dialogues, expanded horizons: Communicating across race and class. In J. T. Wood (Ed.), *Gendered relationships* (pp. 39–56). Mountain View, CA: Mayfield.

Howard, J. W., & Dawes, R. M. (1976). Linear prediction of marital happiness. *Personality and Social Psychology Bulletin, 2*, 478–480.

Huston, M., & Schwartz, P. (1995). Relationships of lesbians and gay men. In J. T. Wood & S. W. Duck (Eds.), *Understanding relationship processes, 6: Off the beaten track: Understudied relationships* (pp. 89–121). Thousand Oaks, CA: Sage.

Huston, T. L., McHale, S. M., & Crouter, A. C. (1985). When the honeymoon is over: Changes in the marriage relationship over the first year. In R. Gilmour & S. Duck (Eds.), *The emerging field of per-* *sonal relationships* (pp. 109–132). Hillsdale, NJ: Erlbaum.

ILA (1995, April). An ILA definition of listening. *ILA Listening Post, 53* p. 4.

Issacson, W. (1989, November 20). Should gays have marriage rights? *Time,* pp. 101–102.

It doesn't add up. (1997, May 19). *Newsweek,* n. p.

Izard, C. E. (1991). *The psychology of emotions*. New York: Plenum.

James, K. (1989). When twos are really threes: The triangular dance in couple conflict. *Australian and New Zealand Journal of Family Therapy, 10*, 179–186.

James, W. (1890). *Principles of psychology,* 2 vols. New York: Henry Holt Company.

James, W., & Lange, C. B. (1922). *The emotions*. Baltimore: Williams and Wilkins.

Johnson, C. B., Stockdale, M. S., & Saal, F. E. (1991). Persistence of men's misperceptions of friendly cues across a variety of interpersonal encounters. *Psychology of Women Quarterly, 15*, 463–465.

Johnson, F. L. (1989). Women's culture and communication: An analytic perspective. In C. M. Lont & S. A. Friedley (Eds.), *Beyond the boundaries: Sex and gender diversity in communication* (pp. 301–316). Fairfax, VA: George Mason University Press.

Jones, A. (1994). *Next time she'll be dead: Battering and how to stop it.* Boston: Beacon.

Jones, E., & Gallois, C. (1989). Spouses' impressions of rules for communication in public and private marital conflicts. *Journal of Marriage and the Family, 51,* 957–967.

Jones, G. P., & Dembo, M. H. (1989). Age and sex role differences in intimate friendships during childhood and adolescence. *Merrill-Palmer Quarterly of Behavior and Development, 35*, 445–462.

Jones, W. H., & Moore, T. L. (1989). Loneliness and social support. In M. Hojat & R. Crandall (Eds.), *Loneliness: Theory, research, and applications* (pp. 145–156). Newbury Park, CA: Sage.

Kaye, L. W., & Applegate, J. S. (1990). Men as elder caregivers: A response to changing families. *American Journal of Orthopsychiatry, 60,* 86–95.

Keeley, M. P., & Hart, A. J. (1994). Nonverbal behavior in dyadic interaction. In S. W. Duck (Ed.), *Understanding relationship processes, 4: Dynamics of relationships* (pp. 135–162). Thousand Oaks, CA: Sage.

Kelley, H. H. (1967). Attribution theory in social psychology. In D. Levine (Ed.), *Nebraska symposium on motivation* (vol. 15, pp. 192–238). Lincoln: University of Nebraska Press.

Kelly, C., Huston, T. L., & Cate, R. M. (1985). Premarital relationship correlates of the erosion of satisfaction in marriage. *Journal of Social and Personal Relationships, 2,* 167–178.

Kelly, G. A. (1955). *The psychology of personal constructs*. New York: Norton.

Kemper, T. (1987). How many emotions are there? Wedding the social and autonomic components. *American Journal of Sociology, 93,* 263–289.

Keyes, R. (1992, February 22). Do you have the time? *Parade,* pp. 22–25.

Kilpatrick, J. (1996, June 1). An odd word or two—but don't dis the dictionary. *Raleigh News and Observer,* p. 15A.

Knapp, M. L. (1972). *Nonverbal communication in human interaction.* New York: Holt, Rinehart & Winston.

Kohlberg, L. (1958). *The development of modes of thinking and moral choice in the years 10 to 16.* Unpublished doctoral dissertation, University of Chicago.

Korzybski, A. (1958). *Science and sanity* (4th ed.). Lakeville, CT: International Non-Aristotelian Library Publishing Company.

Kovecses, Z. (1990). *Emotion concepts.* New York: Springer-Verlag.

Kozol, J. (1995). *Amazing grace: The lives of children and the conscience of a nation.* New York: Crown.

Kurdek, L. A. (1993). The allocation of household labor in gay, lesbian, and heterosexual married couples. *Journal of Social Issues, 49,* 127–139.

Labor letter. (1994, July 16). *Wall Street Journal*, p. A1.

Labov, W. (1972). *Sociolinguistic patterns*. Philadelphia: University of Pennsylvania Press.

La Gaipa, J. J. (1982). Rituals of disengagement. In S. W. Duck (Ed.), *Personal relationships, 4: Dissolving personal relationships*. London: Academic.

Laing, R. D. (1961). *The self and others*. New York: Pantheon.

Lakoff, G., & Johnson, M. (1980). *Metaphors we live by*. Chicago: University of Chicago Press.

Landale, N., & Fennelly, K. (1992). Informal unions among mainland Puerto Ricans: Cohabitation or an alternative to legal marriage? *Journal of Marriage and the Family, 54*, 269–280.

Langer, S. (1953). *Feeling and form: A theory of art*. New York: Scribner.

Langer, S. (1979). *Philosophy in a new key: A study in the symbolism of reason, rite, and art* (3rd ed.). Cambridge, MA: Harvard University Press.

Langston, D. (1992). Tired of playing monopoly? In M. L. Andersen & P. H. Collins (Eds.), *Race, class, and gender: An anthology* (pp. 110–119). Belmont, CA: Wadsworth.

Lasswell, M., & Lobsenz, N. M. (1980). *Styles of loving*. New York: Doubleday.

Laswell, H. (1948). The structure and function of communication in society. In L. Bryson (Ed.), *The communication of ideas*. New York: Harper & Row.

Leathers, D. G. (1976). *Nonverbal communication systems*. Boston: Allyn & Bacon.

Leathers, D. G. (1986). *Successful nonverbal communication: Principles and applications*. New York: Macmillan.

Lee, J. A. (1973). *The colours of love: An exploration of the ways of loving*. Don Mills, Ontario, Canada: New Press.

Lee, J. A. (1988). Love-styles. In R. J. Sternberg & M. L. Barnes (Eds.), *The psychology of love* (pp. 38–67). New Haven, CT: Yale University Press.

Lee, W. S. (1994). On not missing the boat: A processual method for intercultural understanding of idioms and lifeworld. *Journal of Applied Communication Research, 22*, 141–161.

Leland, J., & Beals, G. (1997, May 5). In living color. *Newsweek*, pp. 58–60.

LePoire, B. A., Burgoon, J. K., & Parrott, R. (1992). Status and privacy restoring communication in the workplace. *Journal of Applied Communication Research, 4*, 419–436.

Lewis, J. D., & Weigert, A. J. (1985). Social atomism, holism and trust. *Sociological Quarterly, 26*, 455–471.

Liang, S. (1997, summer). Mix: A multiethnic women's dialogue. *Hues*, pp. 22–23, 56.

Little girl has smile surgery. (1995, December 16). *Raleigh News and Observer*, p. 14A.

Lofland, L. (1985). The social shaping of emotion: The case of grief. *Symbolic Interaction, 8*, 171–190.

Lorde, A. (1992). Age, race, class, and sex: Women redefining difference. In M. L. Andersen & P. H. Collins (Eds.), *Race, class, and gender: An anthology* (pp. 495–502). Belmont, CA: Wadsworth.

Luby, V., & Aron, A. (1990, July). *A prototype structuring of love, like, and being in-love*. Paper presented at the Fifth International Conference on Personal Relationships, Oxford, England.

Lund, M. (1985). The development of investment and commitment scales for predicting continuity of personal relationships. *Journal of Social and Personal Relationships, 2*, 3–23.

Lytton, H., & Romney, D. M. (1991). Parents' differential socialization of boys and girls: A meta-analysis. *Psychological Bulletin, 109*, 267–296.

Mahany, B. (1997, August 7). A hands-on study of language. *Raleigh News and Observer*, pp. 1E, 3E.

Main, M. (1981). Avoidance in the service of attachment. In K. Immelmann, G. Barlow, L. Petrenovich, & M. Main (Eds.), *Behavioral development: The Beilfield interdisciplinary project*.

New York: Cambridge University Press.

Major, B., Schmidlin, A. M., & Williams, L. (1990). Gender patterns in social touch: The impact of setting and age. In C. Mayo & N. M. Henley (Eds.), *Gender and nonverbal behavior* (pp. 3–37). New York: Springer-Verlag.

Malandro, L. A., & Barker, L. L. (1983). *Nonverbal communication*. Reading, MA: Addison-Wesley.

Maltz, D. N., & Borker, R. (1982). A cultural approach to male–female miscommunication. In J. J. Gumpertz (Ed.), *Language and social identity* (pp. 196–216). Cambridge, England: Cambridge University Press.

Manning, A. (1996, March 6). Signing catches on as a foreign language. *USA Today*, p. 4D.

Mares, M. (1995). The aging family. In M. Fitzpatrick & A. Vangelisti (Eds.), *Explaining family interactions*. Thousand Oaks, CA: Sage.

Markman, H. (1990). *Advances in understanding marital distress*. Unpublished manuscript. University of Denver.

Markman, H., Clements, M., & Wright, R. (1991, April). Why father's pre-birth negativity and a first-born daughter predict marital problems: Results from a ten-year investigation. Paper presented at a symposium at the biennial meeting of the Society for Research in Child Development, Seattle.

Markman, H. J. (1981). Prediction of marital distress: A 5-year follow-up. *Journal of Consulting and Clinical Psychology, 49*, 760–762.

Maslow, A. H. (1968). *Toward a psychology of being*. New York: Van Nostrand Reinhold.

Masters, W. H., & Johnson, V. E. (1979). *Homosexuality in perspective*. Boston: Little, Brown.

Maugh, T., II. (1994, November 26). Romantics seem to be bred, not born. *Raleigh News and Observer*, pp. 1A, 4A.

Mazur, E. (1989). Predicting gender differences in same-sex friendships from affiliation motive and value. *Psychology of Women Quarterly, 13*, 277–291.

McCormick, J., & Begley, S. (1996, December 9). How to raise a tiger. *Newsweek*, pp. 52–59.

McDowell, D. (1989, July 17). He's got to have his way. *Time*, pp. 92–94.

McGurl, M. (1990, June 3). That's history, not black history. *The New York Times Book Review*, p. 13.

McNeill, D. (1992). *Hand and mind: What gestures reveal about thought*. Chicago: University of Chicago Press.

Mead, G. H. (1934). *Mind, self, and society*. Chicago: University of Chicago Press.

Mehrabian, A. (1981). *Silent messages: Implicit communication of emotion and attitudes* (2nd ed.). Belmont, CA: Wadsworth.

Metts, S., Cupach, W. R., & Bejlovec, R. A. (1989). "I love you too much to ever start liking you": Redefining romantic relationships. *Journal of Social and Personal Relationships, 6*, 259–274.

Miell, D. E., & Duck, S. W. (1986). Strategies in developing friendship. In V. J. Derlega & B. A. Winstead (Eds.), *Friendship and social interaction* (pp. 129–143). New York: Springer-Verlag.

Miller, G. R., & Parks, M. R. (1982). Communication in dissolving relationships. In S. W. Duck (Ed.), *Personal relationships, 4: Dissolving personal relationships* (pp. 127–154). London: Academic.

Miller, J. B. (1993). Learning from early relationship experience. In S. W. Duck (Ed.), *Understanding relationship processes, 2: Learning about relationships* (pp. 1–29). Newbury Park, CA: Sage.

Mochizuki, T. (1981). Changing patterns of mate selection. *Journal of Comparative Family Studies, 12*, 318–328.

Monkerud, D. (1990, October). Blurring the lines. Androgyny on trial. *Omni*, pp. 81–86.

Monsour, M. (1992). Meanings of intimacy in cross- and same-sex friendships. *Journal of Social and Personal Relationships, 9*, 277–295.

Montgomery, B. M. (1988). Quality communication in personal relationships. In S. W. Duck (Ed.),

Handbook of personal relationships (pp. 343–366). New York: Wiley.

Morris, D. (1997, March–April). The civility wars: Is poverty more vulgar than profanity? *Utne Reader*, pp. 15–16.

Mosley-Howard, S., & Evans, C. (1997). Relationships in the African American family. Paper presented at the 1997 Conference of the International Network on Personal Relationships, Oxford, Ohio.

Mulac, A., Wiemann, J. M., Widenmann, S. J., & Gibson, T. W. (1988). Male/female language differences and effects in same-sex and mixed-sex dyads: The gender-linked language effect. *Communication Monographs, 55*, 315–335.

Nardi, P. M., & Sherrod, D. (1994). Friendship in the lives of gay men and lesbians. *Journal of Social and Personal Relationships, 11*, 185–199.

Narem, T. R. (1980). Try a little TLC. *Science, 80*, 15.

National Center for Health Statistics, (1993). Births, marriages, divorces, and deaths for 1992. *Monthly vital statistics report 41* (no. 12). (DHHS Publication No. PHS 83–1120). Hyattsville, MD: Public Health Service.

National survey results of gay couples in long-lasting relationships. (1990). *Partners: Newsletter for Gay and Lesbian Couples*, pp. 1–16.

Newman, P. (1964, February). "Wild man" behavior in New Guinea Highlands community. *American Anthropologist, 66*, 1–19.

New York public library desk reference (pp. 189–191). (1989). New York: Simon & Schuster/Songstone Press.

Noller, P. (1986). Sex differences in nonverbal communication: Advantage lost or supremacy regained? *Australian Journal of Psychology, 38*, 23–32.

Noller, P. (1987). Nonverbal communication in marriage. In D. Perlman & S. Duck (Eds.), *Intimate relationships: Development, dynamics, and deterioration* (pp. 149–176). Newbury Park, CA: Sage.

Notarius, C. I. (1996). Marriage: Will I be happy or will I be sad? In N. Vanzetti & S. Duck (Eds.), *A life-*

time of relationships (pp. 265–289). Pacific Grove, CA: Brooks/Cole.

Nussbaum, J. E. (1992, October 18). Justice for women! *New York Review of Books*, pp. 43–48.

Nyquist, M. (1992, fall). Learning to listen. *Ward Rounds* (pp. 11–15). Evanston, IL: Northwestern University Medical School.

O'Connor, P. (1992). *Friendships between women*. London: Harvester Wheatsheaf.

Okin, S. M. (1989). *Gender, justice, and the family*. New York: Basic.

Olien, M. (1978). *The human myth*. New York: Harper & Row.

Olson, D., & McCubbin, H. (1983). *Families: What makes them work?* Thousand Oaks, CA: Sage.

O'Meara, J. D. (1989). Cross-sex friendship: Four basic challenges of an ignored relationship. *Sex Roles, 21*, 525–543.

O'Neill, M. (1997, January 12). Asian folk art of feng shui hits home with Americans. *Raleigh News and Observer*, p. 6E.

Orange County Health Department (1997, September 5). Informational material provided at the Community Solutions to Family Violence Conference, Chapel Hill, NC.

Osborne, A. (1996, summer). The paradox of effort and grace. *Inner Directions*, pp. 4–6.

Park M. (1979). *Communication styles in two different cultures: Korean and American*. Seoul: Han Shin.

Patterson, M. L. (1992). A functional approach to nonverbal exchange. In R. S. Feldman & B. Rime (Eds.), *Fundamentals of nonverbal behavior* (pp. 458–495). New York: Cambridge University Press.

Patton, B. R., & Ritter, K. (1976). *Living together . . . female/male communication*. Columbus, OH: Merrill.

Pearce, W. B., Cronen, V. E., & Conklin, F. (1979). On what to look at when analyzing communication: A hierarchical model of actors' meanings. *Communication, 4*, 195–220.

Pearson, J. C. (1985). *Gender and communication*. Dubuque, IA: Brown.

Pennebaker, J. W. (1997). *Opening up: The healing power of expressing emotions* (rev. ed.). New York: Guilford.

Perry, J., the Rev. (1996, summer). Applying meditation to everyday life. *Inner Directions*, pp. 21–23, 26.

Petersen, A. (1996, December 20). One person's "geometric pattern" can be another's sacred saying. *Wall Street Journal*, p. B1.

Petersen, W. (1997). *Ethnicity counts.* New York: Transaction.

Petronio, S. (1991). Communication boundary management: A theoretical model of managing disclosure of private information between married couples. *Communication Theory, 1,* 311–335.

Pettigrew, T. F. (1967). Social evaluation theory: Consequences and applications. In D. Levine (Ed.), *Nebraska symposium on motivation* (pp. 241–311). Lincoln: University of Nebraska Press.

Phillips, G. M., & Wood, J. T. (1983). *Communication and human relationships.* New York:Macmillan.

Piaget, J. (1932/1965). *The moral judgment of the child.* New York: Free Press.

Pierson, J. (1995, November 20). If sun shines in, workers work better, buyers buy more. *Wall Street Journal* pp. B1, B8.

Planalp, S. (1997, September). Personal correspondence.

Pleck, J. H. (1987). American fathering in historical perspective. In M. S. Kimmel (Ed.), *Changing men: New directions in research on men and masculinity* (pp. 83–97). Englewood Cliffs, NJ: Prentice-Hall.

Politically correct monikers are labeled incorrect. (1995, November 7). *Wall Street Journal*, p. A1.

Pomerleau, A., Bolduc, D., Malcuit, G., & Cossette, L. (1990). Pink or blue: Environmental stereotypes in the first two years of life. *Sex Roles, 22,* 359–367.

Popenoe, D. (1996). *Life without father.* New York: Free Press.

Proctor, R. (1991). *An exploratory analysis of responses to owned messages in interpersonal communication.* Doctoral dissertation, Bowling Green University, Bowling Green, Ohio.

Pryor, J. B., & Merluzzi, T. V. (1985). The role of expertise in processing social interaction scripts. *Journal of Experimental Social Psychology, 21,* 362–379.

Public pillow talk. (1987, October). *Psychology Today*, p. 18.

Raphael, M. (1997, May 13). It's true: Drivers move slowly if you want their space. *Raleigh News and Observer*, p. 1A.

Raspberry, W. (1994, July 5). Major gains in minorities' grades at Tech. *Raleigh News and Observer*, p. 9A.

Rawlins, W. K. (1981). *Friendship as a communicative achievement: A theory and an interpretive analysis of verbal reports.* Doctoral dissertation, Temple University, Philadelphia.

Rawlins, W. K. (1994). Being there and growing apart: Sustaining friendships during adulthood. In D. Canary & L. Stafford (Eds.), *Communication and relational maintenance* (pp. 275–294). New York: Academic.

Reel, B. W., & Thompson, T. L. (1994). A test of the effectiveness of strategies for talking about AIDS and condom use. *Journal of Applied Communication Research, 22,* 127–141.

Reis, H. T., Senchak, M., & Solomon, B. (1985). Sex differences in the intimacy of social interaction: Further examination of potential explanations. *Journal of Personality and Social Psychology, 48,* 1204–1217.

Reisenzaum, R. (1983). The Schachter theory of emotion: Two decades later. *Psychological Bulletin, 94,* 239–264.

Reske, J., & Stafford, L. (1990). Idealization and communication in long-distance premarital relationships. *Family Relations, 39,* 274–290.

Ribeau, S. A., Baldwin, J. R., & Hecht, M. L. (1994). An African-American communication perspective. In L. Samovar & R. Porter (Eds.), *Intercultural communication: A reader* (7th ed., pp. 140–147). Belmont, CA: Wadsworth.

Riessman, C. (1990). *Divorce talk: Women and men make sense of personal relationships.* New Brunswick, NJ: Rutgers University Press.

Rohlfing, M. (1995). Doesn't anybody stay in one place anymore? An exploration of the understudied phenomenon of long-distance relationships. In J. T. Wood & S. W. Duck (Eds.), *Understanding relationship processes, 6: Off the beaten track: Understudied relationships* (pp. 173–196). Thousand Oaks, CA: Sage.

Root, M. P. P. (1990). Disordered eating habits in women of color. *Sex Roles, 22,* 525–536.

Rose, S., & Frieze, I. H. (1989). Young singles' scripts for a first date. *Gender and Society, 3,* 258–268.

Rose, S., & Serafica, F. (1986). Keeping and ending casual, close and best friendships. *Journal of Social and Personal Relationships, 3,* 275–288.

Rose, S. M. (1984). How friendships end: Patterns among young adults. *Journal of Social and Personal Relationships, 1,* 267–277.

Rosenberg, M. (1979). *Conceiving the self.* New York: Basic.

Rousar, E. E., III, & Aron, A. (1990, July). *Valuing, altruism, and the concept of love.* Paper presented at the Fifth International Conference on Personal Relationships, Oxford, England.

Rowland, D. (1985). *Japanese Business Etiquette.* New York: Warner.

Ruberman, T. R. (1992, January 22–29). Psychosocial influences on mortality of patients with coronary heart disease. *Journal of the American Medical Association, 267,* 559–560.

Rubin, L. (1985). *Just friends: The role of friendship in our lives.* New York: Harper & Row.

Rubinson, L., & De Rubertis, L. (1991). Trends in sexual attitudes and behaviors of a college population over a 15 year period. *Journal of Sex Education and Therapy, 17,* 32–42.

Ruddick, S. (1989). *Maternal thinking: Towards a politics of peace.* Boston: Beacon.

Rusbult, C. (1987). Responses to dissatisfaction in close relationships: The exit–voice–loyalty–neglect model. In D. Perlman & S. W. Duck (Eds.), *Intimate relationships: Development, dynamics, and deterioration* (pp. 109–238). London: Sage.

Rusbult, C. E., Johnson, D. J., & Morrow, G. D. (1986). Impact of couple patterns of problem solving on distress and nondistress in dating relationships. *Journal of Personality and Social Psychology, 50*, 744–753.

Rusbult, C. E., & Zembrodt, I. M. (1983). Responses to dissatisfaction in romantic involvement: A multidimensional scaling analysis. *Journal of Experimental Social Psychology, 19*, 274–293.

Rusbult, C. E., Zembrodt, I. M., & Iwaniszek, J. (1986). The impact of gender and sex-role orientation on responses to dissatisfaction in close relationships. *Sex Roles, 15*, 1–20.

Rusk, T., & Rusk, N. (1988). *Mind traps: Change your mind, change your life.* Los Angeles: Price, Stern, Sloan.

Saarni, C. (1990). Emotional competence: How emotions and relationships become integrated. In R. A. Thompson (Ed.), *Socioemotional development: Nebraska symposium on motivation* (pp. 115–182). Lincoln: University of Nebraska Press.

Sallinen-Kuparinen, A. (1992). Teacher communicator style. *Communication Education, 41*, 153–166.

Samover, L., & Porter, R. (1995). *Intercultural communication: A reader* (7th ed.). Belmont, CA: Wadsworth.

Samovar, L., & Porter, R. (Eds.). (1994). *Intercultural communication: A reader.* Belmont, CA: Wadsworth.

Scarf, M. (1987). *Intimate partners.* New York: Random House.

Schachter, S. (1964). The interaction of cognitive and physiological determinants of emotion states (pp. 138–173). In P. Leiderman & D. Shapiro (eds.), *Psychobiological approaches to social behavior.* Stanford, CA: Stanford University Press.

Schachter, S., & Singer, J. (1962). Cognitive, social, and physiological determinants of emotional state. *Psychological Review, 69*, 379–399.

Schiminoff, S. B. (1980). *Communication rules: Theory and research.* Newbury Park, CA: Sage.

Schmanoff, S. (1985). Expressing emotions in words: Verbal patterns of interactions. *Journal of Communication, 35*, 16–31.

Schmanoff, S. (1987). Types of emotional disclosures and request compliance between spouses. *Communication Monographs, 54*, 85–100.

Schmitt, R. (1997, September 11). Judges try curbing lawyers' body language antics. *Wall Street Journal*, pp. B1, B7.

Schneider, D. (1997). Implicit personality theory: A review. *Psychological Bulletin, 27*, 294–309.

Schramm, W. (1955). *The process and effects of mass communication.* Urbana: University of Illinois Press.

Sebeok, T. A., & Rosenthal, R. (Eds.). (1981). *The Clever Hans phenomenon: Communication with horses, whales, apes and people.* New York: New York Academy of Sciences.

Secklin, P. (1991, November). *Being there: A qualitative study of young adults' descriptions of friendship.* Paper presented at the Speech Communication Association Convention, Atlanta.

Secord, P. F., Bevan, W., & Katz, B. (1956). The Negro stereotype and perceptual accentuation. *Journal of Abnormal and Social Psychology, 54*, 78–83.

Seligman, M. E. P. (1990). *Learned optimism: How to change your mind and your life.* New York: Simon & Schuster/Pocket Books.

Shannon, C, & Weaver, W. (1949). *The mathematical theory of communication.* Urbana: University of Illinois Press.

Shattuck, T. R. (1980). *The forbidden experiment: The story of the wild boy of Aveyron.* New York: Farrar, Straus & Giroux.

Shaver, P., Schwartz, J., Kirson, D., & O'Connor, C. (1987). Further explorations of a prototype approach. *Journal of Personality and Social Psychology, 52*, 1061–1086.

Shaver, P., Wu, S., & Schwartz, J. (1992). Cross-cultural similarities and differences in emotion and its representation: A prototype approach. In M. S. Clark (Ed.), *Emotion* (pp. 175–212). Newbury Park, CA: Sage.

Sher, T. G. (1996). Courtship and marriage: Choosing a primary partner. In N. Vanzetti & S. Duck (Eds.), *A lifetime of relationships* (pp. 243–264). Pacific Grove, CA: Brooks/Cole.

Sherrod, D. (1989). The influence of gender on same-sex friendships. In C. Hendrick (Ed.), *Close relationships* (pp. 164–186). Newbury Park, CA: Sage.

Shott, S. (1979). Emotion and social life: A symbolic interactionist analysis. *American Journal of Sociology, 84*, 1317–1334.

Shotter, J. (1993). *Conversational realities: The construction of life through language.* Newbury Park, CA: Sage.

Simon, S. B. (1977). *Vulture: A modern allegory on the art of putting oneself down.* Niles, IL: Argus Communications.

Smitherman, G. (1994). *Black talk: Words and phrases from the hood to the amen corner.* Boston: Houghton Mifflin.

Snell, W. E., Jr., Hawkins, R. C., II, & Belk, S. S. (1988). Stereotypes about male sexuality and the use of social influence strategies in intimate relationships. *Journal of Clinical and Social Psychology, 7*, 42–48.

Spain, D. (1992). *Gendered spaces.* Chapel Hill: University of North Carolina Press.

Spear, W. (1995). *Feng shui made easy: Designing your life with the ancient art of placement.* New York: HarperCollins.

Spencer, T. (1994). Transforming relationships through ordinary talk. In S. W. Duck (Ed.), *Understanding relationship processes, 4: Dynamics of relationships* (pp. 58–85). Thousand Oaks, CA: Sage.

Spitz, R. (1965). *The first year of life.* New York: International Universities Press.

Spitzack, C. (1990). *Confessing excess.* Albany: State University of New York Press.

Spitzack, C. (1993). The spectacle of anorexia nervosa. *Text and Performance Quarterly, 13*, 1–21.

Sprecher, S. (1989). The importance to males and females of physical attractiveness, earning potential, and expressiveness in initial attraction. *Sex Roles, 21*, 591–607.

Stacey, J. (1996). *In the name of the father: Rethinking family values in a postmodern age.* Boston: Beacon.

Stearns, C., & Stearns, P. (1986). *Anger: The struggle for emotional control in*

America's history. Chicago: University of Chicago Press.

Stephenson, S. J., & D'Angelo, G. (1973). *The effects of evaluative/empathic listening and self-esteem on defensive reactions in dyads*. Paper presented to the International Communication Association. Montreal, Quebec, Canada.

Sternberg, R. J. (1986). A triangular theory of love. *Psychological Review, 93,* 119–135.

Stewart, J. (1986). *Bridges, not walls* (4th ed.). New York: Random House.

Stewart, L. P., Stewart, A. D., Friedley, S. A., & Cooper, P. J. (1990). *Communication between the sexes: Sex differences and sex role stereotypes* (2nd ed.). Scottsdale, AZ: Gorsuch Scarisbrick.

Stone, R. (1992). The feminization of poverty among the elderly. In M. L. Andersen & P. H. Collins (Eds.), *Race, class, and gender: An anthology* (pp. 201–214). Belmont, CA: Wadsworth.

Strege, J. (1997). *Tiger: A biography of Tiger Woods*. New York: Bantam Doubleday.

Suitor, J. J. (1991). Marital quality and satisfaction with the division of household labor across the family life cycle. *Journal of Marriage and the Family, 53,* 221–230.

Surra, C. (1987). Mate selection as social transition. In D. Perlman & S. Duck (Eds.), *Intimate relationships: Development, dynamics and deterioration* (pp. 88–120). Newbury Park, CA: Sage.

Surra, C., Arizzi, P., & Asmussen, L. (1988). The association between reasons for commitment and the development and outcome of marital relationships. *Journal of Social and Personal Relationships, 5,* 47–64.

Swain, S. (1989). Covert intimacy: Closeness in men's friendships. In B. Risman & P. Schwartz (Ed.), *Gender and intimate relationships* (pp. 71–86). Belmont, CA: Wadsworth.

Sypher, B. (1984). Seeing ourselves as others see us. *Communication Research, 11,* 97–115.

Tannen, D. (1990). *You just don't understand: Women and men in conversation*. New York: William Morrow.

Tavris, C. (1989). *Anger: The misunderstood emotion*. New York: Simon & Schuster.

Tavris, C. (1992). *The mismeasure of woman*. New York: Simon & Schuster.

Templin, N. (1994, October 17). Wanted: Six bedrooms, seven baths for empty nesters. *Wall Street Journal*, pp. B1, B7.

Thomas, V. G. (1989). Body-image satisfaction among black women. *Journal of Social Psychology, 129,* 107–112.

Three million around the world contracted AIDS in last year. (1994, August 9). *Raleigh News and Observer*, p. 5A.

Ting-Toomey, S. (1991). Intimacy expressions in three cultures: France, Japan, and the United States. *International Journal of Intercultural Relations, 15,* 29–46.

Toffler, A. (1970). *Future shock*. New York: William Morrow.

Toffler, A. (1980). *The third wave*. New York: William Morrow.

Tolhuizen, J. H. (1989). Communication strategies for intensifying dating relationships: Identification, use, and structure. *Journal of Social and Personal Relationships, 6,* 413–434.

Townsend, P. (1962). Quoted on p. 146 in A. Fontana, *The last frontier: The social meaning of growing old*. Beverly Hills, CA: Sage.

Trainor, B. (1996, May 20). Commit suicide over a medal? An ex-general gives his view. *The New York Times*, p. A8.

Treichler, P. A., & Kramarae, C. (1983). Women's talk in the ivory tower. *Communication Quarterly, 31,* 118–132.

Trotter, R. J. (1975, October 25). The truth, the whole truth, and nothing but . . . *Science News, 108,* 269.

Ueland, B. (1992, November/December). Tell me more: On the fine art of listening. *Utne Reader*, pp. 104–109.

U.S. Bureau of the Census. (1992). *Current population reports, geographical mobility* (pp. 20–463). Washington, DC: U.S. Government Printing Office.

U. S. Bureau of the Census. (1994). *Current population reports, geographic mobility*. Washington, DC: U.S. Government Printing Office.

Vachss, A. (1994, August 28). You carry the cure in your own heart. *Parade*, pp. 4–6.

Vangelisti, A. (1993). Couples' communication problems: The counselor's perspective. *Journal of Applied Communication Research, 22,* 106–126.

Vanyperen, N. W., & Buunk, B. P. (1991). Equity theory and exchange and communal orientation from a cross-national perspective. *Journal of Social Psychology, 131,* 5–20.

Varkonyi, C. (1996, June 22). Color code. *Raleigh News and Observer*, pp. 1–2E.

Villarosa, L. (1994, January). Dangerous eating. *Essence*, pp. 19–21, 87.

Walker, M. B., & Trimboli, A. (1989). Communicating affect: The role of verbal and nonverbal content. *Journal of Language and Social Psychology, 8,* 229–248.

Walster, E., Traupmann, J., & Walster, G. W. (1978). Equity and extramarital sexuality. *Archives of Sexual Behavior, 7,* 127–141.

Watzlawick, P., Beavin, J., & Jackson, D. D. (1967). *Pragmatics of human communication*. New York: Norton.

Weaver, C. (1972). *Human listening: Processes and behavior*. Indianapolis: Bobbs-Merrill.

Weber, S. N. (1994). The need to be: The socio-cultural significance of black language. In L. Samovar & R. Porter (Eds.), *Intercultural communication: A reader* (7th ed., pp. 221–226). Belmont, CA: Wadsworth.

Weiner, N. (1997). *The human use of human beings*. New York: Avon.

Weiss, S. E. (1987). The changing logic of a former minor power. In H. Binnendijk (Ed.), *National negotiating styles* (pp. 44–74). Washington DC: U.S. Department of State.

Wellman, B. (1985). Domestic work, paid work, and net work. In S. W. Duck & D. Perlman (Eds.), *Understanding personal relationships*. Beverly Hills, CA: Sage.

Wells, W., & Siegel, B. (1961). Stereotyped somatypes. *Psychological Reports, 8,* 77–78.

Werner, C., Altman, I., & Oxley, D. (1985). Temporal aspects of homes: A transactional perspective. In I. Altman & C. M. Werner (Eds.), *Home environments: Vol. 8. Human behavior and environment: Advances in theory and research* (pp. 1–32). Beverly Hills, CA: Sage.

Werner, C. M., Altman, I., Brown, B. B., & Ginat, J. (1993). Celebrations in personal relationships: A transactional/dialectical perspective. In S. W. Duck (Ed.), *Understanding relational processes, 3: Social context and relationships* (pp. 109–138). Newbury Park, CA: Sage.

Werner, C. M., & Haggard, I. M. (1985). Temporal qualities of interpersonal relationships. In G. R. Miller & M. L. Knapp (Eds.), *Handbook of interpersonal communication* (pp. 59–99). Beverly Hills, CA: Sage.

West, J. (1995). Understanding how the dynamics of ideology influence violence between intimates. In S. W. Duck & J. T. Wood (Eds.), *Understanding relationship processes, 5: Confronting relationship challenges* (pp. 129–149). Thousand Oaks, CA: Sage.

West, L., Anderson, J., & Duck, S. (1996). Crossing the barriers to friendship between men and women. In J. T. Wood (Ed.), *Gendered relationships*. Mountain View, CA: Mayfield.

Westefield, J. S., & Liddell, D. (1982). Coping with long-distance relationships. *Journal of College Student Personnel, 23*, 550–551.

Weston, K. (1991). *Families we choose: Lesbian, gays, kinship.* New York: Columbia University Press.

Wexner, L. B. (1954). The degree to which colors (hues) are associated with mood-tones. *Journal of Applied Psychology, 38*, 432–435.

Whan, K. (1997, August 10). UNC study observes link between health, loving support. *The Chapel Hill Herald*, p. 7.

What teens say about drinking. (1994, August 7). *Parade*, p. 9.

Whitbeck, L. B., & Hoyt, D. R. (1994). Social prestige and assortive mating: A comparison of students from 1956 and 1988. *Journal of Social and Personal Relationships, 11*, 137–145.

White, B. (1989). Gender differences in marital communication patterns. *Family Process, 28*, 89–106.

White, J., & Bondurant, B. (1996). Gendered violence in intimate relationships. In J. T. Wood (Ed.), *Gendered relationships*. Mountain View, CA: Mayfield.

Whorf, B. (1956). *Language, thought, and reality.* New York: MIT Press/Wiley.

Wiemann, J. M., & Harrison, R. P. (Eds). (1983). *Nonverbal interaction.* Beverly Hills, CA: Sage.

Wilkie, J. R. (1991). The decline in men's labor force participation and income and the changing structure of family economic support. *Journal of Marriage and the Family, 53*, 111–122.

Williams, D. G. (1985). Gender, masculinity–femininity, and emotional intimacy in same-sex friendship. *Sex Roles, 12*, 587–600.

Willmott, P. (1987). *Friendship networks and social support.* London: Policy Studies Institute.

Wilson, J. A. R., Robick, M. C., & Michael, W. B. (1974). *Psychological foundations of learning and teaching* (2nd ed.). New York: McGraw-Hill.

Winzeler, R. (1990). Amok: Historical, psychological, and cultural perspectives. In W. J. Karim (Ed.), *Emotions of culture: A Malay perspective* (pp. 97–122). Oxford, England: Oxford University Press.

Wolf, N. (1991). *The beauty myth.* New York: William Morrow.

Woo, E. (1995, December 18). Stereotypes may psych out students. *Raleigh News and Observer*, pp. 1A, 10A.

Wood, J. T. (1982). Communication and relational culture: Bases for the study of human relationships. *Communication Quarterly, 30*, 75–84.

Wood, J. T. (1986). Different voices in relationship crises: An extension of Gilligan's theory. *American Behavioral Scientist, 29*, 273–301.

Wood, J. T. (1992a). *Spinning the symbolic web.* Norwood, NJ: Ablex.

Wood, J. T. (1992b). Telling our stories: narratives as a basis for theorizing sexual harassment. *Journal of Applied Communication Research, 4*, 349–363.

Wood, J. T. (1993). Engendered relations: Interaction, caring, power, and responsibility in intimacy. In S. W. Duck (Ed.), *Understanding relationship processes, 3: Social context and relationships* (pp. 26–54). Newbury Park, CA: Sage.

Wood, J. T. (1994a). Engendered identities: Shaping voice and mind through gender. In D. Vocate (Ed.), *Intrapersonal communication: Different voices, different minds* (pp. 145–167). Hillsdale, NJ: Erlbaum.

Wood, J. T. (1994b). Gender and relationship crises: Contrasting reasons, responses, and relational orientations. In J. Ringer (Ed.), *Queer words, queer images: The construction of homosexuality* (pp. 238–265). New York: New York University Press.

Wood, J. T. (1994c). Gender, communication, and culture. In L. Samovar & R. Porter (Eds.), *Intercultural communication: A reader* (7th ed., pp. 155–164). Belmont, CA: Wadsworth.

Wood, J. T. (1994d). *Gendered lives: Communication, gender, and culture.* Belmont, CA: Wadsworth.

Wood, J. T. (1994e). *Who cares? Women, care, and culture.* Carbondale: University of Southern Illinois Press.

Wood, J. T. (1995a). Diversity in dialogue: Communication between friends. In J. Makau & R. Arnett (Eds.), *Ethics of communication in an age of diversity.* Urbana: University of Illinois Press.

Wood, J. T. (1995b). Feminist scholarship and research on relationships. *Journal of Social and Personal Relationships, 12*, 103–120.

Wood, J. T. (1995c). *Relational communication.* Belmont, CA: Wadsworth.

Wood, J. T. (Ed.). (1996). *Gendered relationships.* Mountain View, CA: Mayfield.

Wood, J. T. (1997). Clarifying the issues. *Personal Relationships, 4*, 221–228.

Wood, J. T. (1998). *But I thought you meant . . . : Misunderstandings in human communication.* Mountain View, CA: Mayfield.

Wood, J. T., Dendy, L., Dordek, E., Germany, M., & Varallo, S. (1994). Dialectic of difference: A thematic analysis of intimates' meanings for differences. In K. Carter & M. Presnell (Eds.), *Interpretive approaches to interpersonal communication* (pp. 115–136). New York: State University of New York Press.

Wood, J. T., & Inman, C. C. (1993). In a different mode: Masculine styles of communicating closeness. *Journal of Applied Communication Research, 21,* 279–295.

Wren, C. S. (1990, October 16). A South Africa color bar falls quietly. *The New York Times,* pp. Y1, Y10.

Wright, P. H., & Scanlon, M. B. (1991). Gender role orientations and friendship: Some attenuation but gender differences still abound. *Sex Roles, 24,* 551–566.

Wright, P. H., & Wright, K. (1995). Codependency: Personality syndrome or relationship process? In S. Duck & J. T. Wood (Eds.), *Understanding relationship processes, 5: Confronting relationship challenges* (pp. 109–128). Thousand Oaks, CA: Sage.

WuDunn, S. (1991, April 17). Romance, a novel idea, rocks marriages in China. *The New York Times,* pp. B1, B12.

Yerby, J., Buerkel-Rothfuss, N., & Bochner, A. (1990). *Understanding family communication.* Scottsdale, AZ: Gorsuch Scarisbrick.

Zorn, T. (1995). Bosses and buddies: Constructing and performing simultaneously hierarchical and close friendship relationships. In J. T. Wood & S. W. Duck (Eds.), *Understanding relationship processes, 6: Off the beaten track: Understudied relationships* (pp. 122–147). Thousand Oaks, CA: Sage.

INDEX

Boldface page numbers indicate definitions of terms.

A

Abstraction ladder, 108–109, 337
Abstract language, 115–116, 128
  levels of, 141–142
Abuse, 50, 373–375
Acceptance of others, 4, 11
Accuracy, 141–143
Active listening, 208
Acknowledgment, 256, 259
African Americans, 4, 16, 49–50, 91,
    108, 111, 120, 124, 126, 128,
    135–136, 163, 324, 330
Agape, 351
Age, 69, 92–93
Aggression, 268–269
AIDS, 124, 372
Ambiguity, 114–115. *See also* Symbols
Ambushing, 197–198
Anger, 213, 217, 218, 220, 231, 232, 235,
    241
Anxious resistant attachment style, **53**
Appraisal theory, 220. *See also*
    Perceptual view of emotions
Artifacts, **162**–164
  and gender, 164
  and racial identity,
    163
  and relationship meanings, 163
Asian, 83, 86, 117, 124, 140, 149, 224,
    323–324, 330
Asian Americans, 4, 5, 16, 323–324
Assertion, **268**–269
  during conflict, 303
Attachment styles, **52**–53, 320
  anxious/resistant, **53**
  dismissive, **52**–53
  fearful, **52**
  secure, **52**
Attributional errors, 88–90
  fundamental attribution error, **89**–90
  self-serving bias, 88–89
Attributional patterns and relationship
    satisfaction, 90, 365–366, 379
Attributions, 87–88, 90, 365–366, 379
Autonomy/connection dialectic, 252,
    329

B

Black, 108, 111, 124–126
Black talk, 136
Bracketing, **303**, 307
Braggadocio, 120
Buber, Martin, 18–19, 256

C

Carolyn, 3, 26, 97, 162, 213
Certainty, 261–262
Chinese, 250, 269, 295, 345
Chronemics, **169**–170, 306–307
Clarity, 141–143
Class, 62–64, 333, 334
Climate. *See* Communication climate
Cognitive complexity, **98**–99
Cognitive labeling view of emotions,
    221–222
Cohabitation, 344, 360–361, 366
Closeness in dialogue, 134, 251, 315–316,
    322
Closeness in doing, 134, 251, 316–317,
    323
Commitment, **248**–249, 346–347,
    370
Committed romantic relationships:
  challenges to, 369–377
  dimensions of, 346–348
  guidelines for communication in,
    377–380
  intimacy, **347**–348
  love, 248
  organization of, 352–360
  passion, 248, **346**
  respect, 378
Communication:
  competence, **38**–43
  and culture, 116–119, 138, 149,
    155–157, 169–170
  development of self, 47–77
  distinguished from interpersonal
    communication, 17
  of emotions, 229–234, 237–242
  field of, 2–3
  and identity, 382
  irreversible, 32, 238
  to satisfy needs, 10–16
Communication climate, **245**–275, 304,
    326
Communication continuum, 17–20
Communication rules, **119**–120, 121
  constitutive rules, **120**–121
  regulative rules, **120**
Communication system, 24–26
Commuter marriage, 344
Confirmation/disconfirmation in rela-
    tionships, 255, 256–268
  acknowledgment, 256, 259
  during conflict, 299, 300–302, 306
  endorsement, 257–258, 259
  in friendships, 336
  levels of, 257, 259
  recognition, 256, 259
Conflict, **279**, 277–311, 336, 376, 377
  communication patterns during,
    298–302
  constructive, 302–305, 306
  covert, 282–284
  and cultural background, 294–296
  and gender, 99, 296–297
  management, 287–291
  natural in relationships, 281–282
  overt, 282–284
  and personal growth, 285–286
  principles of, 280–287
  responses to, 291–294
    exit, **292**
    loyalty, **293**
    neglect, **292**–293
    voice, **293**–294
  and sexual orientation, 297–298
  social influences on, 294–298
  unproductive, 299–302
  views of, 287–290
    lose–lose, **287**–288
    win–lose, **288**–289, 304
    win–win, **289**–290, 307–308, 311
Constitutive rules. *See*
    Communication rules
Constructive communication, 237–239,
    302–306
Constructivism, 83–87
  personal constructs, 84–85
  prototypes, **83**–84
  scripts, 86–87, 281
  stereotypes, 87–88, 128
Content meaning, 29. *See also*
    Meanings
Contextual qualifications, 175–176
Contracting, **304**
Control, 263–264

Counterfeit emotional language, **235**–236
Counterproposals, **301,** 304
Cross-complaining, 300, 304
Cultural values, 67–68, 93–95, 116–119, 138, 149
   and conflict, 294–296
   and emotions, 223–227
   and nonverbal communication, 155–157
   and time, 169–170
Culture, 93–97
   and approaches to conflict, 294–296
   and communication, 67–68, 93–95, 116–119, 138, 149, 223–227
   and nonverbal communication, 155–157
   and romantic relationships, 344–345

D

Deaf, 118, 132
Deep acting, **225**–226
Defensive climate, 260–266
Defensive listening, **196**–197, 277, 302–303
Defensiveness, 238, 260–266
Defensive/supportive climates, 260–266
   certainty/provisionalism, 261–262
   control/problem orientation, 263–264
   evaluation/description, 260–261
   neutrality/empathy, 264–265
   strategy/spontaneity, 262–263
   superiority/equality, 265–266
Demand-withdraw pattern, 122
Description, 260–261
Development:
   of family, 368
   of friendship, 324–327
   of romantic relationships, 352–360
Direct definition, 49–51. *See also* Identity scripts
Disabled. *See* Persons with disabilities
Disconfirmation, 139–140, 299, 300–302
Diverse listening styles, 191–193
Diversity, 4–6, 15–16
   and communication, 4–6, 15–16, 117, 383, 330–331
   and culture, 67–68, 116–119, 138, 149, 155–157, 169–170, 294–296
   and listening style, 191–193
   in relationships, 272
   as route to personal growth, 4–5, 137–138, 339–340
Divorce, 344
Dogmatism, 301
Downers, **75**–76

Dual perspective, **41**–42, 137–138, 248, 302, 304, 330, 336–337, 377
Dyadic breakdown, 358. *See also* Relational decline
Dyadic phase, 359. *See also* Relational decline

E

Eating disorders, 161
Ego boundaries, 58
Egocentrism, 41, 301, 339
Empathy, **99**–100, 264–265
Emotional abuse, 50
Emotional competence, 214
Emotional intelligence, **214**–217
   measurement of, 218
Emotions, **218,** 217–228, 366
   and communication, 213–243
   and cultural values, 156
   expression, modes of, 237–238
   guidelines for effective communication of, 237–242
   identifying, 237
   ineffective expression of, 234–236
   obstacles to effective communication of, 229–234
   perceptual influences on, 219–220
   physiological influences on, 219
   social influences on, 222–228
   views of, 219–228
Emotion work, **226**–227
Encouraging independence, 368
Endorsement, 257–258, 259
Enlarging a family, 367–368
Environmental factors, **165**–167
Environmental racism, 169
Environmental spoiling, **354**
Equality, 265–266
Equity, 370–371
Eros, 349
Establishing a family, 367
Ethics of interpersonal communication, 28–29, **32,** 43, 338
   and conflict, 286, 311
   and emotions, 243
   and friendship, 323–324
   and listening, 209
   and nonverbal communication, 177
Ethnocentrism, 261
Exit response to conflict, **292**
Explorational communication, 354
Euphoria, 354–355
European Americans, 323
   as norm, 4, 61, 67
Evaluation, 260–261
Eye contact, 159, 181

F

Facts, 104–105
Family life cycle, 366–369
Fathers, 58
Feedback, **21,** 300
Feeling rules, 223, 235
Feminine communication rules, 133
Feminine speech community, 133–135, 315–316, 322–323
Femininity, 57, 67–69
Feng Shui, 166–167
Framing rules, **223**–225
Freedom of nonverbal speech, 159
Friendly relations, 325
Friendship, 313–341
   acceptance, 318–319, 340
   closeness through dialogue, 134, 315–316, 322
   closeness through doing, 134, 316–317, 323
   development of, 324–327
   emotional closeness, 315–318
   external constraints, 332–336
   honesty, 338–339
   internal tensions, 329
   investment in, 314–315
   across the lifespan, 333
   rules of, 327–328, 329
   support, 321–322
   trust, 320–321, 326
Friends of the heart, 336
Friends of the road, 336
Fundamental attribution error, **89**–90, 106–107

G

Games, **283**–284
Gay, 69, 82, 114, 126, 132, 297–298, 319–320, 333, 361–362, 366, 371
Gender, 62, 68, 95–97, 132–135
   and communication styles, 132–135
   and conflict, 99, 297–298
   and expression of emotions, 231
   and feeling rules, 231–232
   and friendship, 335–336
   and interruptions, 195
   and listening, 192
   and power, 154
   and relational deterioration, 358
   and self disclosure, 250–251, 315–317, 322–323
Gender speech communities, 132–135
   rules of, 133
Gendered standpoints, 96
Generalities, speaking in, 234
Generalized other, 60–66

Goals for improving self-concept, 72–74
Grace, **309**–310
Graffiti, 127, 145
Grave dressing, 360

H

Haptics, **160**
Hate speech, **127**, 145
Hearing, **180**, 182
  distinguished from listening, 180
Heterosexuality, 4, 5, 67, 344–345
Hispanic, 6, 16, 108, 295
HIV, 372–373
Homosexuality, 4, 62–63, 66–67, 82, 126, 319, 345
Honesty, 258, 338–339

I

I, 130–131, 239
Idealizing, 355
Identity, 382
Identity scripts, 51
I–It communication, 18
I-language, 138–139, 331
  and communicating emotions, 235
  and nonverbal communication, 175
I–ME dialogues, 131
Impersonal communication, 17–18
Implicit personality theory, **100**–101
Improving verbal communication:
  acccuracy and clarity, 141–143
  engaging in dual perspective, 41–42, 137–138, 336–337
  owning feelings and thoughts, 138–139, 235, 238–239
  respecting others, 139–140
Independents, 364–365
Indexing, **143**–144
Individualism, 67, 94, 224
Ineffective listening, 179–180, 187–193, 302–303
Inferences, 104–105
Intensifying communication, 354–355
Interactive models of interpersonal communication, 21–23
Interactive view of emotions, **223**–227
Interdependence, 279–280
Internal dialogues, 47–48
Interpersonal communication, **24**
  guidelines for, 38–43
  models of, 20–24
  principles of, 31–38
  process, 26–27
  rule-guided, 119–121, 148–149
  selective, 24
  systemic, 24–26, 301
  unique, 26, 343

Interpersonal communication competence, **38**–43
  dual perspective, **41**–42, 302, 304
  ethical commitment, 43, 286
  monitoring, **42**–43
  person-centered communication, 40–41
Interpretation, 87–91. *See also* Perception
  tentativeness of, 174–176
Interruptions, 300, 303
Intimacy, **347**–348
  through dialogue, 134, 252, 315–316, 322
  through doing, 134, 251, 316–317, 323
Intrapsychic phase, 358–359
Investment, **247**–248, 347–348, 376
Invitational communication, 353
Irrational beliefs, **240**–242
Irreversiblity of communication, 32, 238, 378
Isolation, 12–13, 172
I–Thou communication, 19, 40, 99, 343
I–You communication, 18–19, 343

J

James-Lange view of emotions, 219
Japanese communication style, 4, 117, 135, 288, 295, 323, 329
Judgment, suspension of, 202–203

K

Kinesics, **157**–160
Kitchensinking, 300, 303
Korean, 83, 269
Kwanzaa, 117, 165

L

Labels, 107–109, 124–127
  monitoring, 107–109
  and perception, 124
  and relationships, 125
  and totalizing, 125
Ladder of abstraction, 108–109, 337
Language, 113–134
  and accuracy, 141–143
  and clarity, 141–143
  and class, 63
  concrete, 141–142
  I-language, 138–139, 175, 235
  qualified, 142–143
  tentative, 104
  you–language, 138–139, 175, 235
Latinas, 5
Launching children, 368–369
Lesbians, 69, 82, 126, 128, 132, 297–298, 319–320, 333, 361–362, 366, 371
Letting go, **309**

Liking, 153–154
Linear model of interpersonal communication, 20–21
Listening, **180**, 179–209
  active, 208
  aids to recall, 200–201
  and conflict, 302–303
  distinguished from hearing, 180
  extent of, 179–180
  external obstacles to, 188–189
    message complexity, 188–189
    message overload, 188
    noise, 189
  goals of, 199–206
    for information, 199–201
    for pleasure, 199
    to support others, 202–206
  guidelines for, 206–208
  internal obstacles to, 189–193
    lack of effort, 191
    not recognizing diverse listening styles, 191–193
    prejudgment, 190–191
    preoccupation, 190
  process of, 180–187
    being mindful, **181**–182, 300
    interpreting, 185–186
    physically receiving messages, 182–183
    remembering, 187
    responding, **186**–187
    selecting and organizing material, 183–184
  types of nonlistening, 193–199
    ambushing, **197**–198
    defensive, **196**–197
    literal, **198**
    monopolizing, **194**–195
    pseudolistening, **193**–194
    selective listening, **196**
Literal listening, **198**
Loaded language, **126**–127
Long-distance friendships, 334–335, 341, 384
Long-distance romantic relationships, 375–377, 384
Lose–lose orientation to conflict, **287**–288
Love, 248–249, 347–348
Loyalty response to conflict, **293**
Ludus, 349–350

M

Mainstream, 5
Mania, 350
Marriage, 362–366
  dynamics of satisfaction, 365–366
  paths to, 363–364

stability of, 370
types of, 364–365
Masculine communication rules, 133
Masculine speech community, 133–135,
    316–317, 322–323
Masculinity, 67–69
Maslow's hierarchy of needs, 10–16, 319
ME, 130–131, 239, 241
Mead, George Herbert, 57–66
Meanings, 29–31, 32–36
    and attributions, 88
    content level, 29
    relationship level, 29–31, 308
    subjective, 119
Mediterranean cultures, 294–295
Message complexity, 188–189
Message overload, 188
Metacommunication, 33–36
    during conflict, 301
    and gender, 36
Mindfulness, 181–182, 200, 202, 206,
    300
Mindreading, 103, 300
Minimal encouragers, 204
Minorities, 145
Mnemonics, 201
Monitoring, 42–43, 107–109, 121, 131
    of nonverbal communication,
    173–174
    self-talk, 239–240
Monopolizing, 194–195
Mothers, 58
Moving toward friendship, 325

N

Nascent friendship, 325
Native Americans, 86, 108, 117, 132, 172
Navigation, 356–358
Needs, 10–16
    belonging, 11–13
    Maslow's hierarchy of, 10–14
    participating in a diverse world,
    15–16
    physical, 10–11
    safety, 11
    self-actualization, 14–15
    self-esteem, 13–14
Neglect response to conflict, 292–293
Neutrality, 264–265
Neutralization, 254
Noise, 20, 25, 189
Nonlistening, 193–199
Nonmarital commitments, 360–362
Nonverbal communication, 31, 34, 145,
    144–177
    artifacts, 162–164
    chronemics, 156, 169–170, 306–307
    continuous, 150

culture-bound, 149
differences from verbal, 149–150
environmental factors, 165–167
haptics, 160
improvement of, 173–176
kinesics, 157–160
multichanneled, 150
paralanguage, 170–172
physical appearance, 160–162
principles of, 150–157
proxemics and personal space,
    167–169
rule guided, 148–149
silence, 172–173
similarities to verbal, 148–149
symbolic, 148
touch. See Haptics
types of, 157–173
Novelty/predictability dialectic,
    252–253, 329

O

Openness/closedness dialectic, 253–254,
    329
Organismic view of emotions, 219
Organization, 83–87. See also
    Perception
Owning thoughts and feelings, 138–139,
    235, 238–239, 278

P

Paralanguage, 170–172
Paraphrasing, 203–204, 242
Particular others, 59–60
Passion, 346
Passive aggression, 382
Perception, 80–81, 80–111
    checking, 104
    improvement of, 101–108
    influences on, 91–101
        age, 92–93
        cognitive abilities, 98–100
        culture, 82–83, 93–95
        expectations, 82, 83
        needs, 82
        physiology, 91–92
        self, 100–101
        social roles, 97–98
    ladder of abstraction, 108–109
    process of, 81–91
        interpretation, 87–91
        organization, 83–87
        selection, 80
    subjectivity of, 101–102
Perceptual view of emotions, 220–221
Personal constructs, 84–85
Personal qualifications, 174–175

Personal relationships, elements of
    acceptance, 318–320
    comfort with relational dialectics,
    251–255
    commitment, 248–249
    emotional closeness, 315–318
    investment, 247–248, 314–315
    support, 321–325
    trust, 249–251, 320–321
Personal space. See Proxemics
Person-centered communication,
    40–41
Person-centeredness, 40–41, 99
Persons with disabilities, 69, 118, 126,
    258
Perspective of the generalized other,
    60–66
Physical appearance, 167–169
Placemaking, 347–358
POSSLQ, 344
Post launching of children, 369
Pragma, 350
Prejudgment, 190–191
Preoccupation, 190
Problem-orientation, 263–264
Process, 23, 26–27, 57–59
    of communication, 26–27
    of listening, 180–187
    of perception, 80–91
    of relationships,
    of self, 57–59, 74
Prototypes, 83–84
    of love, 348
Provisionalism, 261–262
Proxemics, 167–169
Proximity, 353–354
Pseudolistening, 193–194
Psychological responsibility, 370
Punctuation, 122–123
    demand-withdraw pattern, 122
    punctuating interaction, 122–123

Q

Qualified language, 142–143

R

Race, 61–62, 69
    and artifacts, 163
    and listening style, 192
Rational-emotive approach to feelings,
    240–242
Reappropriation, 127
Recall, aids to, 200–201
Reciprocity, 250
Recognition, 256, 259
Reflected appraisal, 60
Reframing, 255
Regulation of interaction, 151–152

Regulative rules, **120**. *See*
    Communication rules
Relational culture, **357**
Relational decline, 358–360
  dyadic breakdown, 358
  dyadic phase, 359
  grave dressing, 360
  intrapsychic phase, 358–359
  social phase, 359
  social support, 359–360
Relational dialectics, **252**–255, 266–267,
    329–330, 357
  autonomy/connection, 252
  novelty/predictability, 252–253
  openness/closedness, 253–254
  responses to, 254–255
Relational escalation, 353–356
  explorational communication, 354
  intensifying communication, 354–355
  invitational communication, 353
  revising communication, 356
Relational stability, 370
Relationship meaning, 29–31, 152–156,
    308
  liking/affection, 30, 153–154
  in nonverbal communication,
    152–156
  power/control, 30, 167, 154–156
  responsiveness, 30, 152–153
Relationship rules, 327–328, 329
Religion, 17, 95
Remarriage, 344, 345, 363
Remembering, 187
Responding, 186–187
  to conflict, 291–294
  to criticsm, 272–274
  to others' emotional communica-
    tion, 242
  to relational dialectics, 254–255
Responsibility, 249
Responsive listening, 187, 299, 306
Retirement, 369
Revising communication, 356
Rewards, 346
Rituals, 357
Robbie, 3, 163, 280, 355, 357, 375, 379
Role-limited interaction, 324–325
Romantic attraction, 354
Romantic relationships, **343**–381
  challenges to, 369–377
  development of, 352–360
  dimensions of, 345–348
  guidelines for, 377–380
  script for, 89, 352
Rule-guided, 119–122, 148–149
  and nonverbal communication,
    148–149
Rules, 327–328

Safer sex, negotiation of, 372–373
Scripts, 86–87, 321
  for conflict, 281
  for romance, 89, 352
Second shift, 370
Selection, 81–83, 254
Selective listening, **196**, 299
Self, 47–78
  and family, 49–54
    attachment styles, **51**–**52**, 51–54
    direct definition, 49–51
    identity scripts, 51
  multidimensional, 57
  and peers, 54–57
    reflected appraisal, **54**, 60
    social comparison, **55**
  and perception, 100–101
  as process, 57–59
  social perspectives, influence of,
    60–66
    gender, 62
    generalized other, **60**–66
    particular others, **59**–60
    race, 61–62
    sexual orientation, 62–63
    socioeconomic class, 63–64
  and society, 56–57
Self-actualization, 14
Self-concept, 47–77
  improving, 70–77
  and knowledge of self, 271
Self-disclosure, **249**–251, 278, 318, 321
  appropriateness of, 270–271
  benefits of, 271
  and gender, 250, 251
  risks of, 271
Self-esteem, 13
Self-fulfilling prophecy, 48–49
Self-reflection, 130–132
Self-sabotage, **76**
Self-serving bias, **88**–89, 105–106
Separates, 364–365
Separation, 254
Sexual attraction, 331
Sexual identity, 66
Sexual orientation, 62–63, 67, 69, 82,
    297–298
Signing, 180, 182
Silence, 172–173
Social comparison, **55**
Social diversity. *See* Diversity
Socialization, 60–66
  and fathers, 58
  and gender, 296–297
  and mothers, 58
Social order:
  and feeling rules, 224–226

Social perspectives, 66–70
  changeable, 70
  constructed, 66–67
  variable, 66–68
Social phase, 359
Social roles, 233
Social support, 359–360
Socioeconomic class. *See* Class
Speech communities, **132**–136, 192
Spontaneity, 262–263
Stabilized friendship, 326
Standpoint, **95**–97
Static evaluation, **143**–144
Stereotypes, **85**–86, 128
Storge, 349
Strategy, 262–263
Styles of love, 348–351, 363
Stylin', 163–164
Superiority, 265–266
Support:
  in listening, 202–206, 304
Supportive climate, 260–266, 302–305,
    377
Surface acting, **226**
Symbols, **113**–116, 123–131
  abstract, **115**–116
  ambiguous, **114**–115
  arbitrary, **113**–114
  and nonverbal communication, 148
Symbolic abilities, 123–132
  definition, 124–126
  evaluation, 126–128
  hypothetical thought, 129
  organization, 128
  self-reflection, 130–131
System, 24–26, 305–306
Systemic, 24–26, 301

Technology, 384
Tentative language, 104
Tentativeness, 174–176
Territoriality, 155, 162–163
Time. *See* Chronemics
Timing, 306–307
Totalizing, **125**, 128. *See also*
    Stereotypes; Symbolic abilities
Touch, 156. *See also* Haptics
Traditionals, 364
Transactional model of interpersonal
    communication, 23–24
Trust, 249–251, 320–321, 326

Unproductive communication,
    299–302
Uppers, 75

V

Verbal communication, 113–145
    constitutive rules, **120**–121
    and culture, 116–119
    differences from nonverbal commu-
        nication, 149–150
    improvement of, 137–144
    principles of, 116–123
    regulative rules, 120
    rule guided, 119–121
    similarities to nonverbal communi-
        cation, 148–149

Violence, 373–375
Voice response to conflict, **293**–294
Vultures, **76**

 W

Waning friendship, 326–327
Whiteness, 5, 61, 67, 330
Whorf-Sapir view of language, 118

Win–lose orientation to conflict,
    288–289, 304
Win–win orientation to conflict,
    289–290, 307–308, 311

 Y

Yom Kippur, 117
You-language, 138–139, 175–176, 235